SRA Imagine It!

Unit 5 • What's the Weather?

Level 1

Program Authors

Carl Bereiter
Andrew Biemiller
Joe Campione
Iva Carruthers
Doug Fuchs
Lynn Fuchs
Steve Graham
Karen Harris
Jan Hirshberg
Anne McKeough
Peter Pannell
Marsha Roit
Marlene Scardamalia
Marcy Stein
Gerald H. Treadway Jr.
Michael Pressley

EXAMINATION COPY

McGraw Hill SRA

Columbus, OH

Acknowledgments

Grateful acknowledgment is given to the following publishers and copyright owners for permissions granted to reprint selections from their publications. All possible care has been taken to trace ownership and secure permission for each selection included. In case of any errors or omissions, the Publisher will be pleased to make suitable acknowledgments in future editions.

READ ALOUD
I CALL IT SKY by Will C. Howell, illustrated by John Ward. © 1999 by Will C. Howell. Published by arrangement with Walker & Co.

BIG BOOK
From WHEN A STORM COMES UP by Allan Fowler, copyright © 1995 by Children's Press. All rights reserved. Reprinted by permission of Children's Press an imprint of Scholastic Library Publishing, Inc.

LISTEN TO THE RAIN by Bill Martin Jr. and John Archambault, illustrated by James Endicott. Text copyright © 1988 by Bill Martin Jr. and John Archambault. Illustrations copyright © 1988 by James Endicott. Reprinted by permission of Henry Holt and Company, LLC.

ON THE SAME DAY IN MARCH by Marilyn Singer, illustrated by Frane Lessac. Copyright © 2000 by Marilyn Singer. Used by permission of HarperCollins Publishing.

SRAonline.com

SRA

Printed in the United States of America.

Send all inquiries to this address:
SRA/McGraw-Hill
4400 Easton Commons
Columbus, OH 43219-6188

ISBN: 978-0-07-609493-6
MHID: 0-07-609493-6

1 2 3 4 5 6 7 8 9 WEB 15 14 13 12 11 10 09 08 07

The McGraw-Hill Companies

National Advisory Board

Patricia Appell
Instructional Interventionist
Annapolis, MD

Christine P. Collins
Former Assistant Superintendent for Instruction and Curriculum
Weymouth, MA

Betsy Degen
Curriculum Director
Shawnee Mission, KS

Bryan Ertsgaard
Teacher
Dayton, OH

James T. Garvin
Assistant Principal
Charlotte, NC

Patsy M. Hall
Title I Professional Development Coordinator
Indianapolis, IN

Michelle L. King
Reading Enhancement Coach
Indianapolis, IN

Deb Owen
Assistant Superintendent for Curriculum and Instruction
Effingham, IL

Patricia Schmella
Curriculum Director
Toppenish, WA

JoAnn Schweda
Teacher
Worley, ID

Sylvia Teahan
Teacher
Medford Lakes, NJ

Joseph Turner
Assistant Principal
Indianapolis, IN

Sue Wennerberg
Teacher
Oak Park, IL

Contributing Author

Michael Milone
Assessment Specialist
Placitas, NM

Literature Consultant

Dr. Laura Apol
Professor, Michigan State University
East Lansing, MI

Program Reviewers

Noemi Arteaga-Gonzales
Teacher
San Antonio, TX

Susan Beede
Consulting Teacher
Nampa, ID

Lisa Beringer
Teacher
Bonita Springs, FL

Paula Bleakley
Teacher
Leesburg, FL

Lisa Bohanan
Instructional Specialist
Pflugerville, TX

Judi Braxton
Reading Coach
Marianna, FL

Benjamin Broadwater
Teacher
Fort Worth, TX

Jodie Broussard
Reading Coach
Pensacola, FL

Jennifer Brown-Mendoza
Reading First Coach
Hominy, OK

Kristine Cain
Teacher
Pensacola, FL

Kellie Campbell
Teacher
Cocoa, FL

Caroline Carithers
Reading Resource Teacher
Pensacola, FL

Jenny Cronan
Literacy Coach
Pittsburg, CA

Margo DiBasio
Reading Specialist
Chelsea, MA

Jennie Eddy
Title I Literacy Coach
Moore, OK

Bryan Ertsgaard
Teacher
Dayton, OH

Tami Ethridge
Instructional Coach
Lancaster, SC

Pamela C. Fendrick
Reading Coach
Tallahassee, FL

Melanie Flores
Teacher
Austin, TX

Tim Francisco
Teacher
Colorado Springs, CO

Kari Franklin
Reading Coach
Pensacola, FL

Rosa Elia Garcia
Reading Specialist
San Antonio, TX

Ashley Garrett
Teacher
Austin, TX

James T. Garvin
Assistant Principal
Charlotte, NC

Dr. Marsha R. Glover
Elementary Reading and Language Arts Developer
Tallahassee, FL

Elaine M. Grohol
Elementary Instructional Specialist
Kissimmee, FL

Patricia Ingles
Teacher
Laguna Niguel, CA

Sarah Jordan
Literacy Specialist
Longview, WA

Cindy Kearney
Teacher
Tulsa, OK

Kim Kempa
Teacher
Santa Ana, CA

Kathy Kindelan
Reading Specialist
Winter Haven, FL

Michelle L. King
Reading Enhancement Coach
Indianapolis, IN

Linda Ann Kosinski
Reading First Coordinator
La Quinta, CA

Sheryl Kurtin
Elementary Specialist, Curriculum and Instruction
Sarasota, FL

Teresa Lopez
Supervisor, Academic Achievement and Accountability
Bakersfield, CA

Jan Maglione
Teacher
Upton, MA

Barbara Maspero
Teacher
San Antonio, TX

Chaitra S. McGrew
Teacher
Austin, TX

Kathy McGuire
Instructional Coach
Roseburg, OR

Becky McPherson
Literacy Coach
Cuthbert, GA

Sheila Menning
Teacher
Largo, FL

Tamarah Michalek
Teacher
Roseburg, OR

Michele Mower
Director of Professional Development
Fontana, CA

Pamela W. Patterson
Instructional Specialist
East Point, GA

Susan Patterson
Reading Coach
Charlotte, NC

Angela Pilcher
Teacher
Stockton, CA

Dr. Jan Rauth
Educational Consultant
Longview, WA

Carlotta Ruiz
Reading Coach
Elk Grove, CA

Dr. Lynda Samons
Curriculum Director
Magnet Cove, AR

Jake Schweikhard
Teacher
Tulsa, OK

Nancy Snyder
Reading Coach
Spring Hill, FL

Dyan Wagner
District Reading Specialist and Intervention Coordinator
Milwaukee, WI

Darlene Watson
Instructional Lead Teacher
Valdosta, GA

Linda Webb
LA Program Specialist
Stockton, CA

Sue Wennerberg
Teacher
Oak Park, IL

Gayle Wilson
Preprimary Department Head
Jacksonville, FL

Linda Wiltz
Instructional Support Teacher
Orlando, FL

Meet the Imagine It! Authors

Carl Bereiter, Ph.D.

A professor emeritus and special advisor on learning technology at the Ontario Institute for Studies in Education, University of Toronto, Dr. Bereiter also invented Computer Supported Intentional Learning Environments, the first networked system for collaborative learning, with Dr. Marlene Scardamalia.

Andrew Biemiller, Ph.D.

A coordinator of elementary teacher education programs at the University of Toronto for thirty-six years, Dr. Biemiller's research on vocabulary development and instruction has had a significant effect on the shape of vocabulary instruction for elementary education in the twenty-first century.

Joe Campione, Ph.D.

A leading researcher on cognitive development, individual differences, assessment, and the design of innovative learning environments, Dr. Campione is a professor emeritus in the School of Education at University of California, Berkeley.

Iva Carruthers, Ph.D.

Equipped with both hands-on and academic experience, Dr. Carruthers serves as a consultant and lecturer in educational technology and matters of multicultural inclusion.

Doug Fuchs Ph.D.

Dr. Fuchs, the Nicholas Hobbs Professor of Special Education and Human Development at Vanderbilt University, has conducted programmatic research on response-to-intervention as a method for preventing and identifying children with learning disabilities and on reading instructional methods for improving outcomes for students with learning disabilities.

Lynn Fuchs, Ph.D.

A co-director of the Kennedy Center Reading clinic at Vanderbilt University, Dr. Fuchs also conducted research on assessment methods for enhancing instructional planning and instructional methods for improving reading and math outcomes for students with learning disabilities.

Steve Graham, Ph.D.

A professor of literacy at Vanderbilt University, Dr. Graham's research focuses on identifying the factors that contribute to writing development and writing difficulties.

Karen Harris, Ph.D.

The Currey-Ingram Professor of Special Education and Literacy at Vanderbilt University, Dr. Harris's research focuses on theoretical and intervention issues in the development of academic and self-regulation strategies among students who are at risk.

Jan Hirshberg, Ed.D.

Focusing on how children learn to read and write and the logistics of teaching reading and writing in the early grades, Dr. Hirshberg works as a language arts resource coordinator and consultant in Alexandria, Virginia.

Anne McKeough, Ph.D.

A professor in the Division of Applied Psychology at the University of Calgary, Dr. McKeough teaches graduate courses in cognitive development and educational assessment, as well as teacher preparation courses to undergraduates.

Peter Pannell, MA
Principal of Longfellow Elementary School in Pasadena, California, Mr. Pannell has worked to develop the literacy of countless students. To help accomplish this goal, he wrote and implemented a writing project that allowed his students to make great strides in their writing performance.

Marsha Roit, Ed.D.
The Director of Professional Development for SRA/McGraw-Hill, Dr. Roit spends considerable time in classrooms developing reading curricula and working with teachers and administrators in effective instructional practices.

Marlene Scardamalia, Ph.D.
Dr. Scardamalia is the Presidents' Chair in Education and Knowledge Technologies at the University of Toronto and is also the Director of the Institute for Knowledge Innovation and Technology. She received the 2006 World Award of Education from the World Cultural Council for outstanding work in education.

Marcy Stein, Ph.D.
Professor and founding faculty member of the education program at the University of Washington, Tacoma, Dr. Stein teaches At-Risk and Special Education graduate and teacher certification programs.

Gerald H. Treadway Jr, Ph.D.
Chair of the Literacy Education Program and professor of education at San Diego State University, Dr. Treadway teaches classes on reading methods, English Language Learner methods, balanced reading programs, assessment, and reading comprehension. He is also a consultant for the California Reading and Literature Project.

In memoriam

Michael Pressley, Ph.D.
1951–2006
Dr. Pressley was a tireless supporter of education. He championed the rights of all children to a quality education, made seminal contributions in research and practice, and nurtured the development of a host of beginning teachers, young scholars, and editors. While his work and spirit lives on in those he influenced and inspired, there is no substitute for the real thing. We will all miss his wisdom and friendship every day.

Unit 5

Table of Contents

What's the Weather?

First Reader

Lessons 11–15

Additional Reading

You may wish to provide the following titles to students for additional theme-related reading.

What Makes the Weather by Janet Palazzo

What Is the Sun? by Reeve Lindbergh

Rain by Marion Dane Bauer

Bringing the Rain to Kapiti Plain by Verna Aardema

Windsongs and Rainbows by Burton Albert

The Cloud Book by Tomie dePaola

January Rides the Wind: A Book of Months by Charlotte F. Otten

Feel the Wind by Arthur Dorros

Splish! Splash! A Book about Rain by Joseph Sherman

Note: You should preview any trade books and videos for appropriateness in your classroom before recommending them to students.

Unit 5

OVERVIEW

What's the Weather?

Everybody talks about weather. Why? Because weather plays an important part in our daily lives. Weather helps us decide what to wear to school, but it also determines whether farmers will have good crops. Weather is always changing and always interesting.

Theme Connection

Fine Art

Ask students to describe the weather in the photograph on these pages. Ask them what season it appears to be.

Ansel Adams. *Snow Covered Apple Tree in Front of Half Dome, Yosemite National Park, California.* 1930. © Ansel Adams Publishing Rights Trust.

BIG Idea

What is weather?

Unit 5

Launching the Theme

Setting Up the Theme

No matter where they live, students have many weather-related experiences. They have experienced changes in daily weather and changes across seasons. This unit will build on what students already know about weather and help them understand more about what weather is, how it works, and how we measure it.

To interest students about What's the Weather?, try one of the following ideas:

- Ask students to make sounds like the wind, thunder, and rain.
- Play the Unit 5 ***eBackground Builders*** video.

Inquiry Over the next three weeks, students will conduct a unit investigation by observing and measuring the weather.

Concept/Question Board

To learn more about the theme What's the Weather?, display a **Concept/Question Board** in your classroom. This will be a place where you and students post concepts and questions about weather. The **Concept/Question Board** can be displayed on a wall or a dry-erase board. The following materials will encourage students to post their ideas and questions on the Board: Weather cut-out shapes, construction paper, markers, and magazines.

Start the **Concept/Question Board** for students by

- displaying weather maps from newspapers.
- displaying photographs or illustrations of weather instruments.

Each week students will gain a better understanding of weather as they progress through the unit inquiry.

After discussing the Big Idea question "What is weather?" discuss with students the following questions. You can use these questions as a starting point for inquiry.

- What is the weather typically like at this time of year?
- What different kinds of weather are there?

BIG Idea

What is weather?

Read the Big Idea question to students. Then have them tell what they know about the weather.

Using the Inquiry Planner

Students will research the theme What's the Weather? using the steps below.

	Steps	Models
Week 1	Generate ideas and questions for the **Concept/Question Board.**	*What is weather?* *What different kinds of weather are there?* *How does the weather change over the seasons?*
	Decide on a problem or question to research and make a conjecture.	*How can weather be measured? Special instruments can be used to measure weather.*
Week 2	Collect information, and confirm or revise conjectures and questions.	*Thermometers measure the temperature, and wind socks can measure the speed and direction of wind. A rain gauge can show how much rain has fallen.*
Week 3	Prepare a presentation.	*I will create a book about measuring weather to share my information.*

Unit 5

About the Authors and Illustrators

Allan Fowler

Author of *When a Storm Comes Up*

Writing nonfiction books for young readers is **Allan Fowler's** specialty. He likes to explain how things work and why things happen. Do you know why the moon seems to change shape or how magnets work? You can read books by Fowler to find out. His fact-filled books cover lots of topics, mostly in science. Fowler lives in Chicago and likes to travel when he has the chance.

Bill Martin Jr.

An author of *Listen to the Rain*

Bill Martin Jr. was a teacher, a school principal, a textbook editor, and a storyteller. Martin learned to love storytelling from his grandmother and his fifth-grade teacher, who read to the class every day. He was fascinated by the sounds and rhythm of language. Martin said his writing process began with talking. When he wrote a story, he talked it through many times to see if he was saying what he meant. Martin wrote more than three hundred books for children.

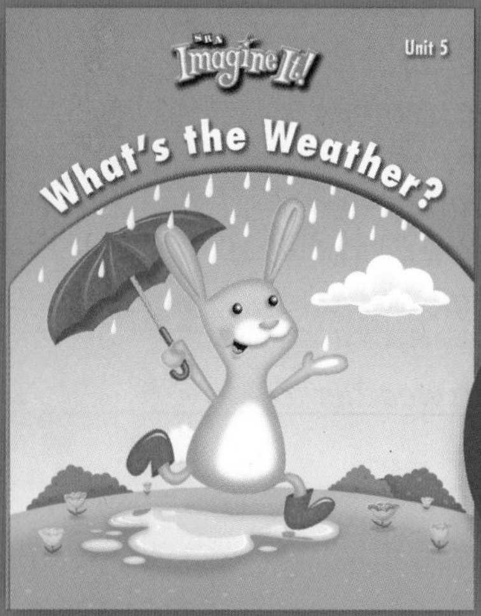

Big Book

John Archambault

An author of *Listen to the Rain*

John Archambault is a poet, journalist, and storyteller who worked with Bill Martin Jr. for more than ten years. Martin and Archambault teamed up to write many award-winning books.

Marilyn Singer

An author of *On the Same Day in March: A Tour of the World's Weather*

Marilyn Singer loves animals! She enjoys writing about animal behavior and the natural world. For several years Singer was a high school English teacher in New York City. One day when she was sitting in the Brooklyn Botanic Garden, she wrote a story featuring talking insect characters she'd made up when she was eight years old. Since then, Singer has published more than sixty books for young readers. Singer lives in New York, where a day in March might be cold and windy or warm and sunny.

Frané Lessac

Illustrator of *On the Same Day in March: A Tour of the World's Weather*

Born in New Jersey, **Frané Lessac** loves to travel. She enjoys sharing her art based on her worldwide journeys. Lessac is the illustrator of more than twenty books for children.

Unit Skills

★ Phonemic Awareness ★ Phonics ★ Fluency ★ Vocabulary ★ Comprehension

Week 1

Preparing to Read

Phonics ★
- ✓ /ē/ Spelled *e, e_e, ee, ea*

Fluency ★
- ***Decodables*** 68–70
- High-Frequency Words *(or, two, be, green, take)*

Reading and Responding

Comprehension ★

Strategies
- Making Connections
- Asking Questions
- Clarifying
- Visualizing

Skills
- ✓ Main Idea and Details

✓ **Selection Vocabulary** ★

Inquiry

Language Arts

Writing
Lists

Penmanship
The Letters *u* and *m*

Listening/Speaking/Viewing
Listening: Fact or Opinion?

Grammar
✓ Capitalization

Week 2

Preparing to Read

Phonics ★
- ✓ /ē/ Spelled *_y, _ie_*
- ✓ /s/ Spelled *cy*

Fluency ★
- ***Decodables*** 71–74
- High-Frequency Words *(every, could, boy, some, going, here)*

Reading and Responding

Comprehension ★

Strategies
- Clarifying
- Visualizing
- Asking Questions
- Making Connections
- Summarizing
- Predicting

Skills
- Compare and Contrast
- Main Idea and Details
- ✓ Cause and Effect

✓ **Selection Vocabulary** ★

Inquiry

Language Arts

Writing
Writing News Stories

Penmanship
The Letters *v* and *w*

Listening/Speaking/Viewing
Speaking: Informal and Formal Language

Grammar
✓ Capitalization and Punctuation

Week 3

Preparing to Read

Phonics ★
- ✓ /ā/ Spelled *ai_, _ay*
- ✓ /ī/ Spelled *_igh, _y,* and *_ie*

Fluency ★
- ***Decodables*** 75–78
- High-Frequency Words *(day, way, sleep, don't, my, too, came, me, right)*

Reading and Responding

Comprehension ★

Strategies
- Asking Questions
- Making Connections
- Clarifying

Skills
- Main Idea and Details
- ✓ Sequence
- Cause and Effect

✓ **Selection Vocabulary** ★

Inquiry

Language Arts

Writing
Writing Instructions

Penmanship
The Letters *k* and *z*

Listening/Speaking/Viewing
Speaking: Clear Speech

Grammar
✓ Plural Nouns

Key: ★ = five components of Reading ✓ = Formal Assessment

Unit 5

Assessment Plan for Making AYP

AYP is an ongoing cycle.

1 Screen

Administer the initial Benchmark Assessment as a screener to target students who are at risk for failing end of year measures.

Diagnose students' strengths and weaknesses, and differentiate instruction according to their abilities.

2 Diagnose and Differentiate

Diagnosing, differentiating instruction, and monitoring progress is an ongoing cycle.

3 Monitor Progress

Monitor progress weekly, monthly, or any time as needed with both formal and informal assessments.

4 Measure Outcomes

Administer summative Assessments such as Lesson, Benchmark, or state assessments to measure student outcomes.

1 Screen

For students entering class after the school year has begun, administer the initial ***Benchmark Assessment*** to target students at risk for reading failure.

2 Diagnose and Differentiate

RtI

Use the results from the ***Lesson Assessments, Benchmark Assessments,*** and informal observation measures to diagnose students' strengths and weaknesses and to differentiate instructions individually and in small groups.

	Approaching Level	On Level	English Learner	Above Level
Leveled Practice	• ***Reteach 1*** • ***Workshop Kit*** - Activities - Games • ***Curriculum Connections***	• ***Skills Practice 1*** • ***Workshop Kit*** - Activities - Games • ***Intervention Guide*** • ***Curriculum Connections***	• ***English Learner Support Activities*** • ***Workshop Kit*** - Activities - Games	• ***Challenge Activities 1*** • ***Workshop Kit*** - Activities - Games
Technology	• ***eSkills & eGames*** • ***eDecodables***	• ***eSkills & eGames*** • ***eDecodables***	• ***eSkills & eGames*** • ***eDecodables***	• ***eSkills & eGames*** • ***eDecodables***

3 Monitor Progress

Between ***Benchmark Assessments,*** use the following to monitor student progress. Regroup students daily or as needed, based on these formative assessment results.

Monitor Progress

Formal Assessment

- Writing Rubrics
- ***Lesson Assessments***
- ***eAssess***
- Comprehension Observation Log
- ***Skills Practice***

4 Measure Outcomes

Assess student understanding and mastery of skills by using the ***Lesson Assessments*** or ***Benchmark Assessments.***

Unit 5

Resources to Monitor Progress

	Week 1
Skills Practice 1	Phonics, pp. 177–178, 181–184, 187–190 Writing, pp. 179–180 Grammar, Usage, and Mechanics, pp. 185–186
Decodables	***Decodable*** 68: *A Zebra* ***Decodable*** 69: *Summer Heat* ***Decodable*** 70: *Green River*
Lesson Assessment Book 1	Lessons 1–5, pp. 57–60

Technology e-Suite

	Week 1
e Skills	
e Decodables	***Decodable*** 68: *A Zebra* ***Decodable*** 69: *Summer Heat* ***Decodable*** 70: *Green River*
e Games	
e Fluency	
e Assess	***Lesson Assessment Book 1,*** Unit 5, Lessons 1–5

Key: ✓ = Formal Assessment

Week 2

Phonics, pp. 191–192, 195–198, 201–204
Writing, pp. 193–194
Grammar, Usage, and Mechanics, pp. 199–200

Decodable 71: *A Party for Puppies*
Decodable 72: *A Fancy Jacket*
Decodable 73: *Skating*
Decodable 74: *Marcy & Sally*

Lessons 6–10, pp. 61–64

Unit 5 Phonics
Unit 5 Vocabulary
Unit 5 Writing

Decodable 71: *A Party for Puppies*
Decodable 72: *A Fancy Jacket*
Decodable 73: *Skating*
Decodable 74: *Marcy & Sally*

Skill: Initial sound/spellings

Lesson Assessment Book 1, Unit 5, Lessons 6–10

Week 3

Phonics, pp. 205–206, 209–212, 215–218
Writing, pp. 207–208
Grammar, Usage, and Mechanics, pp. 213–214

Decodable 75: *The Gray Rainy Day*
Decodable 76: *The Opossum at Night*
Decodable 77: *Why, Bly?*
Decodable 78: *Wait for Me*

Lessons 11–15, pp. 65–70

Unit 5 Phonics
Unit 5 Vocabulary
Unit 5 Writing

Decodable 75: *The Gray Rainy Day*
Decodable 76: *The Opossum at Night*
Decodable 77: *Why, Bly?*
Decodable 78: *Wait for Me*

Skill: Long-vowel sound/spellings

Lesson Assessment Book 1, Unit 5, Lessons 11–15

Lesson 1-5 Overview

Lesson Planner

Preparing to Read

MATERIALS

- ✦Routines 1–4, 6–11
- ✦***Sound/Spelling Cards*** 5, 28
- ✦***Skills Practice 1,*** pp. 177–178, 181–184, 187–190
- ✦***Decodables*** 68–70

Day 1

Daily Warm-Ups, p. T24

Introduce the Sound/Spelling

/ē/ Spelled *e* and *e_e,* p. T25

Phonemic Awareness Listening for /ē/, p. T25

✓ **Phonics**

- Blending, pp. T26–T27
- Developing Oral Language, p. T27
- Guided Practice, p. T28
- Dictation, p. T29

✓ **Fluency/Reading a Decodable**

Decodable 68, pp. T30–T31

Day 2

Daily Warm-Ups, p. T40

✓ **Phonics**

- Review /ē/ Spelled *e* and *e_e,* pp. T41–T42
- Developing Oral Language, p. T42
- Guided Practice, p. T43
- Dictation: Word Building Game, p. T43

Reading and Responding

MATERIALS

- ✦***Read Aloud Collection:*** *I Call It Sky*
- ✦Routines 12, 13
- ✦***Home Connection,*** pp. 33–36
- ✦***What's the Weather? Big Book,*** pp. 4–31, 60
- ✦***Reading Transparency*** 20
- ✦Writer's Notebooks

Day 1

Read Aloud Collection: *I Call It Sky,* pp. T32–T34

✓ **Discussing the Read Aloud,** p. T35

Preview the Unit

- Browsing, p. T36
- Set Goals, p. T36

Concept/Question Board, p. T37

Day 2

Build Background, p. T44

Preview and Prepare, p. T45

✓ **Building Vocabulary,** p. T46

Reading the Selection, p. T47

Reading Recommendations, p. T47

What's the Weather? Big Book, pp. 4–27 (1st READ)

Comprehension Strategies, pp. T48–T59

✓ **Discussing the Selection,** p. T60

Vocabulary Review, p. T61

Print and Book Awareness Ellipses, p. T61

Language Arts

MATERIALS

- ✦Routines 14–16
- ✦***Transparencies*** 17, 36, 37
- ✦***Alphabet Letter Cards***
- ✦***Language Arts Big Book,*** pp. 39–40, 183
- ✦***Skills Practice 1,*** pp. 179–180, 185–186
- ✦***What's the Weather? Big Book***
- ✦***Lesson Assessment Book 1,*** pp. 57–60
- ✦Writer's Notebooks
- ✦Portfolios

Day 1

Writing Lists Prewriting, pp. T38–T39

Penmanship Alphabet Practice: The Letters *u* and *m,* p. T39

Day 2

Writing Lists Prewriting, p. T62

Penmanship Alphabet Practice: The Letters *u* and *m,* p. T63

Grammar, Usage, and Mechanics Capitalization, pp. T64–T65

Monitor Progress

✓ = **Formal Assessment**

Day 1

- ✓ **Phonics, p. T28**
- ✓ **Fluency, p. T30**
- ✓ **Comprehension, p. T35**

Day 2

- ✓ **Phonics, p. T43**
- ✓ **Vocabulary, p. T46**
- ✓ **Comprehension, p. T60**

Phonemic Awareness ★ Phonics ★ Fluency ★ Vocabulary ★ Comprehension

Day 3

Daily Warm-Ups, p. T66

Introduce the Sound/Spelling

/ē/ Spelled *ee* and *ea*, p. T67

Phonics

- Blending, pp. T68–T69
- Developing Oral Language, p. T69
- Guided Practice, p. T70
- Dictation, p. T71

Fluency/Reading a Decodable

Decodable 69, pp. T72–T73

Reading Recommendations, p. T74

Vocabulary Review, p. T75

What's the Weather? Big Book, pp. 4–27

2nd READ

Comprehension Skills Main Idea and Details, pp. T76–T87

Reading with a Writer's Eye Text-Illustration Relationship, pp. T76–T87

Fine Art, p. T88

Science Connection Hot Air Rising, p. T89

Writing Lists Drafting, pp. T90–T91

Grammar, Usage, and Mechanics Review Capitalization, pp. T92–T93

Blending, p. T70
Vocabulary, p. T75
Main Idea and Details, p. T75
Writing, p. T91
Grammar, p. T93

Day 4

Daily Warm-Ups, p. T94

Phonics

- Review /ē/ Spelled *ee* and *ea*, pp. T95–T96
- Developing Oral Language, p. T96
- Guided Practice, p. T97
- Dictation: Word Building Game, p. T97

Build Background, p. T98

Preview and Prepare, p. T99

Building Vocabulary, p. T100

Reading the Poem, p. T101

Reading Recommendations, p. T101

What's the Weather? Big Book, pp. 28–31

Comprehension Strategies

- Visualizing, p. T102
- Clarifying, p. T103

Elements of Poetry, p. T104

Discussing the Poem, p. T104

Vocabulary Review, p. T105

Writing Lists Revising, p. T106

Listening/Speaking/Viewing Listening: Fact or Opinion?, p. T107

Phonics, p. T97
Vocabulary, p. T100
Comprehension, p. T104

Day 5 Review

Daily Warm-Ups, p. T108

Phonics

- Review /ē/ Spelled *e, e_e, ee,* and *ea,* pp. T109–T110
- Developing Oral Language, p. T110
- Guided Practice, p. T111
- Dictation, p. T111

Fluency/Reading a Decodable

Decodable 70, pp. T112–T113

Inquiry Process Generate Ideas and Questions, p. T114

Concept/Question Board, p. T115

Writing Lists Editing and Publishing, pp. T116–T117

Penmanship Alphabet Practice: Review Letters *u* and *m,* p. T118

Grammar, Usage, and Mechanics Review Capitalization, p. T119

Phonics, p. T111
Inquiry, p. T115
Penmanship, p. T119
***Lesson Assessment Book 1,* pp. 57–60**

Lessons 1-5 Overview

Student Resources

Big Books

Focus Question What kinds of storms are there?
When a Storm Comes Up
by Allan Fowler
It feels good to be out in the sunshine on a warm day.
5

What's the Weather? Big Book, pp. 4–5

Focus Question What does a rainstorm sound like?
Listen to the Rain
by Bill Martin Jr. and John Archambault
illustrated by James Endicott
Listen to the rain,
the whisper of the rain,
the slow soft sprinkle,
the drip-drop tinkle,
the first wet whisper of the rain.
28
Listen to the rain,
the singing of the rain,
the tiptoe pitter-patter,
the splish and splash and splatter,
the steady sound,
the singing of the rain.
29

What's the Weather? Big Book, pp. 28–29

A Zebra
by Ethan Cruz
illustrated by Rusty Fletcher

Decodables 68–70

Curriculum Connections

Card 1

Wind, O Wind!

Wind is moving air.

It can blow from the north or the south.

It can blow from the east or the west.

In science... we learn that a wind vane tells ...rection the wind blows.

...o the letter N for North.

...y from the North.

Science
Grade 1 • Unit 1
Back to School

Card 22

Iceland's People and Animals

Iceland is a country that is an island. It is in the northern Atlantic Ocean. It is not too hot or too cold. Many people who live there fish for food.

Some animals live on Iceland too. Puffins are black-and-white seabirds that live on the island. They have colorful beaks. They build nests in the rocks.

Social Studies
Grade 1 • Unit 2
Where Animals Live

...gs, Four Legs

...he farm
...will see
...eir nests
...o under trees.
...e two legs,
...o have four.
...ose look.
...e any more?

How many legs do 2 owls have altogether?

How many legs do 3 sheep have altogether?

Math
Grade 1 • Unit 2
Where Animals Live

Card 29

Pedro's Dream Animals

Pedro Linares was very sick. He had a scary dream. He saw animals in the clouds. The animals were not real. They had scales and tentacles.

Then Pedro woke up. He made the animals from his dream. His family made more. Today these animals are famous around the world.

Art
Grade 1 • Unit 2
Where Animals Live

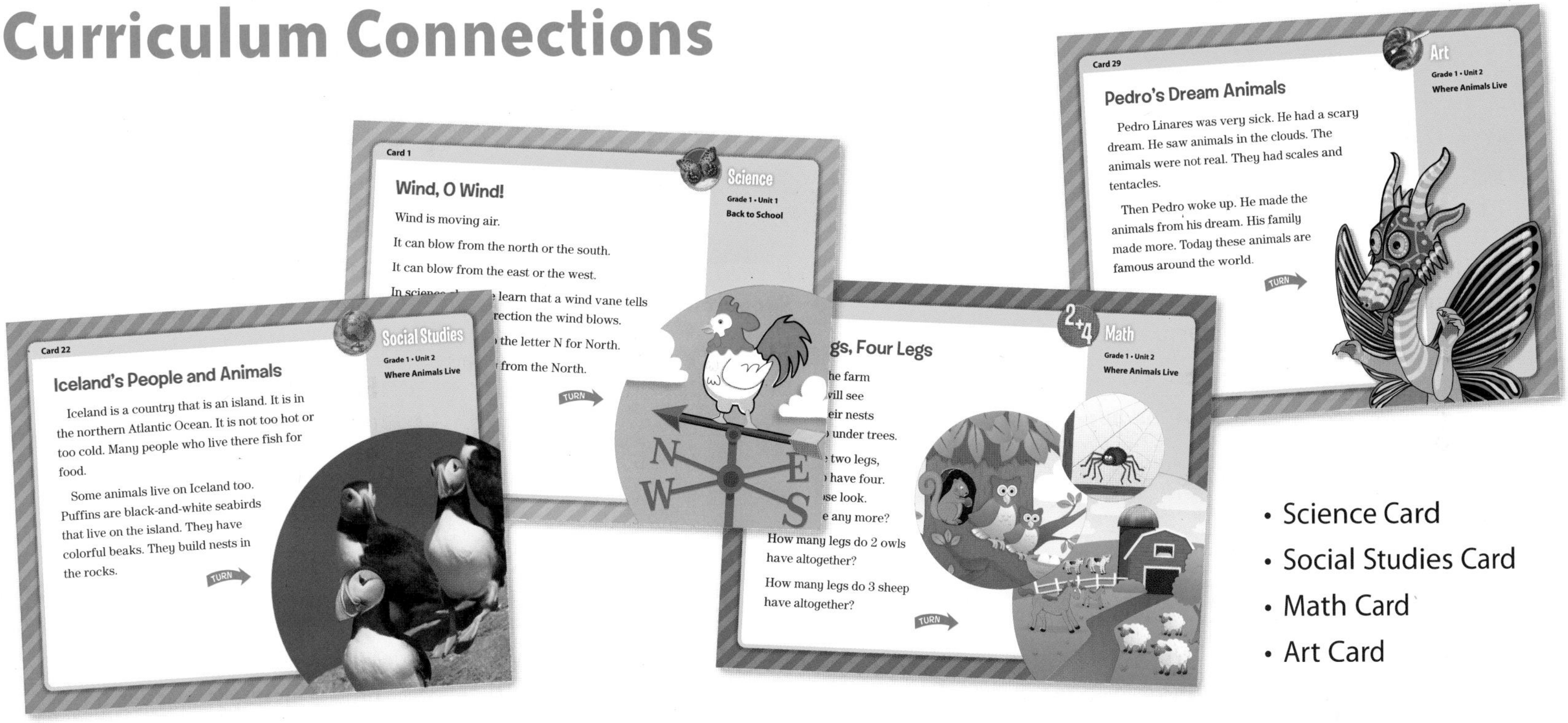

- Science Card
- Social Studies Card
- Math Card
- Art Card

Additional Skills Practice

Approaching Level	On Level	English Learner	Above Level
Reteach 1	**Skills Practice 1**	**English Learner Support Activities**	**Challenge Activities 1**
• /ē/ Spelled *e, e_e*, pp. 137–138	• /ē/ Spelled *e, e_e*, pp. 177–178, 181–182	Unit 5, Lessons 1–5	• /ē/ Spelled *e, e_e*, p. 69
• Capitalization, pp. 139–140	• Writing a List, pp. 179–180		• Capitalization, p. 70
• /ē/ Spelled *ee, ea*, pp. 141–142	• /ē/ Spelled *ee, ea*, pp. 183–184, 187–188		• /ē/ Spelled *ee, ea*, p. 71
• Phonics Review, pp. 143–144	• Capitalization, pp. 185–186		• Phonics Review, p. 72
	• Phonics Review, pp. 189–190

Lesson 1-5 Overview

Differentiating Instruction for Workshop

AYP

Day 1

	Approaching Level	On Level	English Learner	Above Level
Preparing to Read				
	Phonics: Before the lesson, preteach the words in the blending lines, or after the lesson, repeat the blending lines using vowel-first blending or sound-by-sound blending. **Fluency:** Have students reread ***Decodable*** 68 with you.	**Phonics:** Have students extend the sentences in blending and write them on paper. **Fluency:** Have students reread ***Decodable*** 68 with partners.	**Phonics:** See ***English Learner Support Guide*** Unit 5 Lesson 1. **Fluency:** Have students reread ***Decodable*** 68 with partners.	**Phonics:** Have students write three sentences using words from the blending lines. **Fluency:** Have students reread ***Decodable*** 68 with partners.
Reading and Responding				
	Vocabulary: Use the ***SRA Imagine It! Photo Library CD,*** objects, stick drawings, and pantomime to preteach the vocabulary words for *I Call It Sky*. **Comprehension:** Read *I Call It Sky* to students before you read it to the class, and discuss the main idea of the selection with them.	**Vocabulary:** Have students draw a picture for each of the vocabulary words and write a sentence about their pictures. **Comprehension:** Have students write a summary of *I Call It Sky*.	**Vocabulary:** Use the ***SRA Imagine It! Photo Library CD*** pictures or objects to help students understand the vocabulary in *I Call It Sky*. **Comprehension:** Read *I Call It Sky* to students before reading it to the class to help them understand the main points of the selection.	**Vocabulary:** Have students draw a picture for each of the vocabulary words and write a sentence about their pictures. **Comprehension:** Have students write a summary of *I Call It Sky*.
Language Arts				
	Penmanship: Have students practice tracing the letters *u* and *m* using the ***Lowercase Sandpaper Letters*** in the ***Workshop Kit.***	**Penmanship:** Have students practice writing the letters *u* and *m* on the ***Write-On Boards.***	**Writing:** See ***English Learner Support Guide*** Unit 5 Lesson 1. **Penmanship:** Have students practice writing the letters *u* and *m* on the ***Write-On Boards.***	**Penmanship:** Have students write words they see in the classroom with the letters *u* and *m*.

Day 2

	Approaching Level	On Level	English Learner	Above Level
Preparing to Read	**Phonics:** Have students complete ***Reteach 1*** pages 137–138 to practice /ē/ spelled *e* and *e_e*. **Fluency:** Have students reread ***Decodable*** 68 with you and find words in the story with /ē/ spelled *e* and *e_e*.	**Phonics:** Have students write three sentences using words from the blending lines. **Fluency:** Have students reread ***Decodable*** 68 with partners.	**Phonics:** See ***English Learner Support Guide*** Unit 5 Lesson 2. **Fluency:** Have students reread ***Decodable*** 68 with partners.	**Phonics:** Have students complete ***Challenge Activities 1*** page 69 for a challenge with the /ē/ sound spelled *e* and *e_e*. **Fluency:** Have students reread ***Decodable*** 68 with partners.
Reading and Responding	**Vocabulary:** Use the ***SRA Imagine It! Photo Library CD,*** objects, stick drawings, and pantomime to help students visualize the vocabulary words. **Comprehension:** Read "When a Storm Comes Up" to students before reading it to the entire class. Review the comprehension strategies.	**Vocabulary:** Have students create flash cards with the vocabulary words on one side and their definitions or pictures on the other side. **Comprehension:** Have students write a sentence in their Writer's Notebooks about "When a Storm Comes Up."	**Vocabulary:** See ***English Learner Support Guide*** Unit 5 Lesson 2. **Comprehension:** See ***English Learner Support Guide*** Unit 5 Lesson 2. .	**Vocabulary:** Pair students with others who need help, and have them use words in sentences to show their meanings. **Comprehension:** Have students write a sentence in their Writer's Notebooks about "When a Storm Comes Up."
Language Arts	**Grammar, Usage, and Mechanics:** Help students look in their ***Little Big Books*** to find words that begin with capital letters.	**Grammar, Usage, and Mechanics:** Have students look in their ***Little Big Books*** to find words that begin with capital letters.	**Writing:** See ***English Learner Support Guide*** Unit 5 Lesson 2. **Grammar, Usage, and Mechanics:** See ***English Learner Support Guide*** Unit 5 Lesson 2.	**Grammar, Usage, and Mechanics:** Have students look in their ***Little Big Books*** to find words that begin with capital letters.

Lesson 1-5 Overview

Differentiating Instruction for Workshop

AYP

Day 3

	Approaching Level	On Level	English Learner	Above Level
Preparing to Read	**Phonics:** Before the lesson, preteach the words in the blending lines, or after the lesson, repeat the blending lines using vowel-first blending or sound-by-sound blending. **Fluency:** Have students reread ***Decodable*** 69 with you.	**Phonics:** Have students extend the sentences in blending and write them on paper. **Fluency:** Have students reread ***Decodable*** 69 with partners.	**Phonics:** See ***English Learner Support Guide*** Unit 5 Lesson 3. **Fluency:** Have students reread ***Decodable*** 69 with partners.	**Phonics:** Have students choose three words from the blending lines and write clues for each one to share with partners. **Fluency:** Have students reread ***Decodable*** 69 with partners.
Reading and Responding	**Vocabulary:** Help students draw and label pictures to show the meaning of each vocabulary word. **Comprehension:** Help students identify the details in "When a Storm Comes Up."	**Vocabulary:** Have students illustrate the vocabulary words and write a sentence about each illustration. **Comprehension:** Have students identify the main idea and details of a selection from a previous unit.	**Vocabulary:** Review the vocabulary words with students, and have them use the words in oral sentences. **Comprehension:** See ***English Learner Support Guide*** Unit 5 Lesson 3.	**Vocabulary:** Have students use the vocabulary words to tell a story. **Comprehension:** Have students listen to or read a new selection applying the skill main idea and details as they read.
Language Arts	**Writing:** Review with students the purpose of lists and how to write them. Help them improve their lists. **Grammar, Usage, and Mechanics:** Have students complete ***Reteach 1*** pages 139–140 for practice with plural nouns.	**Writing:** Provide students with pictures from magazines that show weather-related activities, and have them make lists based on what they see. **Grammar, Usage, and Mechanics:** Have students play the Singular and Plural Nouns card game in the ***Workshop Kit.***	**Writing:** Help students work on their drafts. See ***English Learner Support Guide*** Unit 5 Lesson 3. **Grammar, Usage, and Mechanics:** See ***English Learner Support Guide*** Unit 5 Lesson 3.	**Writing:** Have students draw pictures of weather-related activities, and have them make a list of what they included in their pictures. **Grammar, Usage, and Mechanics:** Have students complete ***Challenge Activities 1*** page 70 for a challenge with plural nouns.

Day 4

	Approaching Level	On Level	English Learner	Above Level
Preparing to Read				
	Phonics: Have students complete ***Reteach 1*** pages 141–142 to practice /ē/ spelled *ee* and *ea*.	**Phonics:** Have students find words in the ***What's the Weather? Big Book*** that contain /ē/ spelled *ee* and *ea*.	**Phonics:** See ***English Learner Support Guide*** Unit 5 Lesson 4.	**Phonics:** Have students complete ***Challenge Activities 1*** page 71 for a challenge with the /ē/ sound spelled *ee* and *ea*.
Reading and Responding				
	Vocabulary: Use the ***SRA Imagine It! Photo Library CD*** pictures, objects, stick drawings, and pantomime to help students visualize the words. **Comprehension:** Provide additional modeling of the visualizing strategy using a previously read selection.	**Vocabulary:** Have students create flash cards with the words and definitions. **Comprehension:** Have students select one of the vocabulary words from "Listen to the Rain" and illustrate a scene around that word.	**Vocabulary:** See ***English Learner Support Guide*** Unit 5 Lesson 4. **Comprehension:** See ***English Learner Support Guide*** Unit 5 Lesson 4.	**Vocabulary:** Pair students with others who need practice, and have them use the words in sentences to show their meanings. **Comprehension:** Have students write about something they visualized as they listened to the poem.
Language Arts				
	Writing: Help students with their writing. **Listening/Speaking/ Viewing:** Review with students the difference between fact and opinion. Use examples from the lesson or your own examples.	**Writing:** Have students share their lists with partners. **Listening/Speaking/ Viewing:** Have students write an example of a fact and an opinion and share their examples with partners.	**Writing:** See ***English Learner Support Guide*** Unit 5 Lesson 4. **Listening/Speaking/ Viewing:** Review the Fact and Opinion lesson with students.	**Writing:** Have students share their lists with partners. **Listening/Speaking/ Viewing:** Have students write an example of a fact and an opinion and share their examples with partners.

Lesson 1-5 Overview

Differentiating Instruction for Workshop

AYP

Day 5

Approaching Level	On Level	English Learner	Above Level
Preparing to Read			
Phonics: Have students complete ***Reteach 1*** pages 143–144 to practice /ē/ spelled *e*, *e_e*, *ee*, and *ea*. **High-Frequency Words:** Review the high-frequency words students have learned this week. Then have students find these words in their ***Little Big Books.*** **Fluency:** Have students read ***Decodable*** 70 with you.	**Phonics:** Have students play the Puzzle Word Game using words from the ***Decodables.*** See the Level Appendix for directions. **High-Frequency Words:** Have partners use the ***High-Frequency Flash Cards*** to practice the words they have learned this week. **Fluency:** Have students reread ***Decodable*** 70 with partners.	**Phonics:** See ***English Learner Support Guide*** Unit 5 Lesson 5. **High-Frequency Words:** Have partners use the ***High-Frequency Word Flash Cards*** to practice the words they have learned this week. **Fluency:** Have students reread ***Decodable*** 70 with partners.	**Phonics:** Have students complete ***Challenge Activities 1*** page 72 for a challenge with the /ē/ sound spelled *e*, *e_e*, *ee*, and *ea*. **High-Frequency Words:** Have students write sentences using the high-frequency words they have learned this week. **Fluency:** Have students reread ***Decodable*** 70 with partners.
Reading and Responding			
Inquiry: Model some ideas and questions to help students.	**Inquiry:** Have students start thinking about the questions they want to choose.	**Inquiry:** Have students start thinking about the questions they want to choose.	**Inquiry:** Have students help others who are having trouble forming ideas and questions.
Language Arts			
Penmanship: Have students use the ***Alphabet Letter Cards*** to practice tracing the models for *u* and *m*.	**Penmanship:** Have students practice writing words from "When a Storm Comes Up" or "Listen to the Rain" that have lowercase *u* or *m*.	**Grammar, Usage, and Mechanics:** See ***English Learner Support Guide*** Unit 5 Lesson 5. **Penmanship:** Have students practice writing words from "When a Storm Comes Up" or "Listen to the Rain" that have lowercase *u* or *m*.	**Penmanship:** Give students pages from newspapers and magazines, and have them look for and copy words that have lowercase *u* or *m*.

Resources for

Differentiating Instruction RtI

English Learner

English Learner Support Guide, Unit 5, Lessons 1–5

English Learner Support Activities, Unit 5, Lessons 1–5

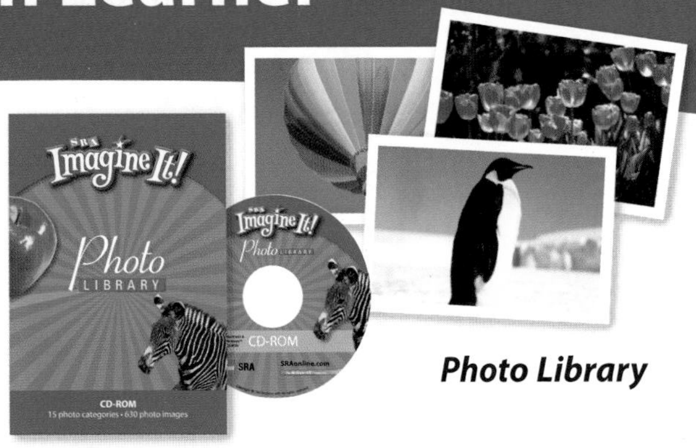

Photo Library

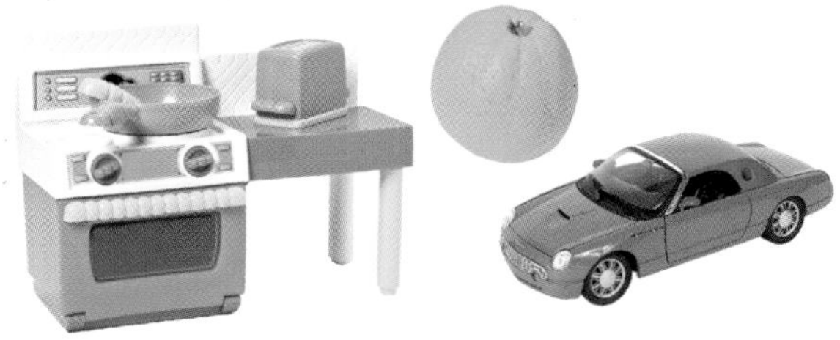

English Learner Realia Kit

Approaching Level

Intervention

Intervention Guide, Unit 5, Lessons 1–5

Intervention Workbook, Unit 5, Lessons 1–5

Workshop Kits

Technology

- ***eBig Books***
- ***eSkills & eGames***
- ***eDecodables***
- ***eAssess***

Listening Library CD, Unit 5

Lessons 1-5 Overview

Lesson Assessment

Monitor Progress to Differentiate Instruction

Use these summative assessments along with your informal observations to assess student mastery.

UNIT 5 What's the Weather? • Lessons 1–5

Name ______ Date ______ Score ______

Letters and Sounds

Teacher: I will say a word. I want you to fill in the bubble under the answer that shows how to spell that word.

Teacher: The word is *heat.* Fill in the bubble under the word *heat.*

1.	heut	heat	hoat

Teacher: The word is *deal.* Fill in the bubble under the word *deal.*

2.	dule	dale	deal

Teacher: The word is *here.* Fill in the bubble under the word *here.*

3.	hure	here	har

Teacher: The word is *feet.* Fill in the bubble under the word *feet.*

4.	feet	fite	faet

Teacher: The word is *east.* Fill in the bubble under the word *east.*

5.	east	iste	aste

Lesson Assessment Book 1 • What's the Weather? UNIT 5 • Lessons 1–5 57

Lesson Assessment Book 1, p. 57

UNIT 5 What's the Weather? • Lessons 1–5 *(continued)*

Name ______ Date ______ Score ______

High-Frequency Words

Teacher: Listen carefully to what I say. Fill in the bubble under the answer you think is correct.

Teacher: Fill in the bubble under the word *or . . . or.*

1.	or	ur	er

Teacher: Fill in the bubble under the word *two . . . two.*

2.	twi	tou	two

Teacher: Fill in the bubble under the word *be . . . be.*

3.	bi	be	ba

Teacher: Fill in the bubble under the word *green . . . green.*

4.	green	grien	geren

Teacher: Fill in the bubble under the word *take . . . take.*

5.	tike	tayk	take

58 UNIT 5 • Lessons 1–5 What's the Weather? • Lesson Assessment Book 1

Lesson Assessment Book 1, p. 58

UNIT 5 What's the Weather? • Lessons 1–5 *(continued)*

Name ______ Date ______ Score ______

Main Idea and Details

Teacher: Listen to what I say and the question. Fill in the bubble under the answer you think is correct.

Teacher: There are different kinds of farms. Many have cows and horses. Others have corn and wheat. Some have only trees and are called orchards. What is this story mostly about? The answers are *farms, cows, trees.*

1.	farms	cows	trees

Teacher: Wendy's house is near a lake. Which of these is near Wendy's house? The answers are *river, ocean, lake.*

2.	river	ocean	lake

Teacher: The children liked to look at clouds in the sky. What did the children like to look at in the sky? The answers are *stars, clouds, birds.*

3.	stars	clouds	birds

Teacher: The book was on the floor in the kitchen. What was the book on? The answers are *table, floor, chair.*

4.	table	floor	chair

Teacher: It was a cold day, but it was not rainy or snowy. What kind of day was it? The answers are *cold, rainy, snowy.*

5.	cold	rainy	snowy

Lesson Assessment Book 1 • What's the Weather? UNIT 5 • Lessons 1–5 59

Lesson Assessment Book 1, p. 59

UNIT 5 What's the Weather? • Lessons 1–5 *(continued)*

Name ______ Date ______ Score ______

Special Text

Teacher: Listen carefully to what I say. Fill in the bubble under the answer you think is correct.

Teacher: Fill in the bubble under a *date . . .* a *date.*

1.	July 4	Karen	Dallas

Teacher: Fill in the bubble under a *number . . .* a *number.*

2.	j	B	9

Teacher: Fill in the bubble under a *time . . .* a *time.*

3.	100	3:30	big

Teacher: Fill in the bubble under the *number word . . .* the *number word.* The answers are *five, pick, moon.*

4.	five	pick	moon

Teacher: Fill in the bubble under the *time words . . .* the *time words.* The answers are *Betty's room, he isn't, one o'clock.*

5.	Betty's room	he isn't	one o'clock

60 UNIT 5 • Lessons 1–5 What's the Weather? • Lesson Assessment Book 1

Lesson Assessment Book 1, p. 60

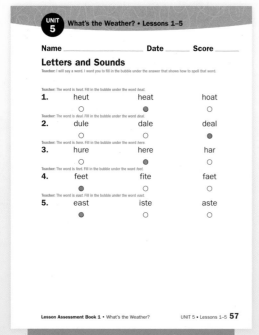

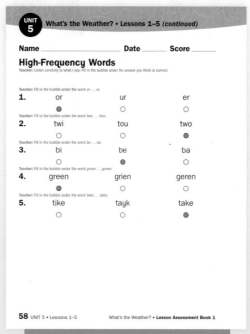

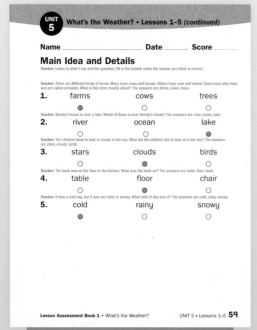

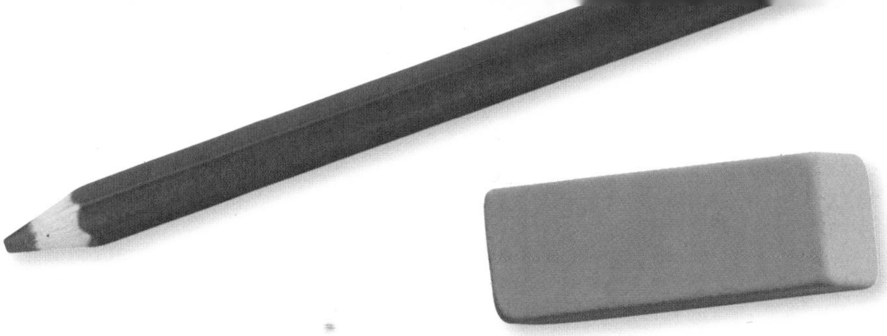

Formal Assessment

Lesson Assessment Book 1

Comprehension Observation Log

Student ______ Date ______

Unit ______ Lesson ______ Selection Title ______

General Comprehension
Concepts discussed: ______

Behavior Within a Group
Articulates, expresses ideas: ______

Joins discussions: ______

Collaborates (such as *works well with other students, works alone*): ______

Role in Group
Role (such as *leader, summarizer, questioner, critic, observer, non-participant*): ______

Flexibility (changes roles when necessary): ______

Use of Reading Strategies
Uses strategies when needed (either those taught or student's choice of strategy)/Describes strategies used: ______

Changes strategies when appropriate: ______

Changes Since Last Observation

92 Comprehension Observation Log • **Lesson Assessment Book 1**

Lesson Assessment Book 1, p. 92

The Comprehension Observation Log, found in the ***Lesson Assessment Annotated Teacher's Edition,*** is a vehicle for recording anecdotal information about individual student performance on an ongoing basis. Information such as students' strengths and weaknesses can be recorded at any time the occasion warrants. It is recommended that you maintain a folder for each student where you can store the logs for purposes of comparison and analysis as the school year progresses. You will gradually build up a comprehensive file that reveals which students are progressing smoothly and which students need additional help.

Preparing to Read

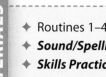

OBJECTIVES

Students will

- blend, spell, and read words that contain /ē/ spelled *e* and *e_e*.
- build fluency by reading ***Decodable*** 68.

MATERIALS

- Routines 1–4, 6–7, 9–11
- ***Sound/Spelling Cards*** 5, 28
- ***Skills Practice 1,*** pp. 177–178
- ***Decodable*** 68, *A Zebra*

Teacher Tip

MATERIALS You will need to prepare five index cards for the Developing Oral Language activity. Put a star on one of the cards. Number the remaining cards 1, 2, 3, and 4. Place the cards in a box or bag.

Differentiating Instruction — English Learners

IF . . . students are native speakers of Spanish, **THEN . . .** keep in mind that Spanish does not use comparative endings. Instead, Spanish uses the words *más* (more) or *menos* (less.) Example: *Tú eres más alto que yo.* (You are taller—or *more tall*—than I.)

Daily Warm-Ups

Copy the Morning Message on the board or on chart paper. Have students complete the sentence and answer the question. Read the message aloud, and discuss it with students. **Possible Answers** *fall; Today it is cloudy.*

MORNING MESSAGE

Good morning! Today we will read a selection about the weather in different seasons of the year. Our season is ______________. What is the weather like today?

Daily Language Review

This activity reviews comparative adjectives. Write the following sentence on the board, or generate a similar one with your students, and have students make the proper correction: An ant is small than a cat. *An ant is smaller than a cat.*

What Am I? Game

To review long-vowel sounds and spellings, have students play What Am I? As students respond to the questions, write their answers on the board. Have them identify the long-vowel sound/spelling in each word.

I am a spring month that begins with the /ā/ sound. What am I? *April, /ā/ spelled* a

I am a shape with three sides. I have the /ī/ sound. What am I? *triangle, /ī/ spelled* i

I am the opposite of *shut*. I begin with the /ō/ sound. What am I? *open, /ō/ spelled* o

Introduce the Sound/Spelling

ROUTINE 1

/ē/ Spelled *e* and *e_e*

- Display ***Sound/Spelling Card*** 28—Long E. Follow Routine 1, introducing sounds and spellings, calling attention to the picture of the letters on the card as a reminder that the spellings on this card say /ē/.
- Point to ***Sound/Spelling Card*** 5—Hen, and have students say the /e/ sound. Contrast /e/ and /ē/ by teaching students the following rhyme and having them say it several times:

  E's my name.
  Two sounds for me:
  Short *e* in *hen,*
  Long *e* in *he*.

- Point to the *e* and *e_e* spellings on the Long E card, and explain that these are two ways to spell /ē/. Tell students that when they come to a word with a single *e*, they may have to try both the /e/ sound and the /ē/ sound to see which is correct. Remind students that the letter *e* at the end of a word can make the vowel before it long and that a vowel by itself can be long. Point out the spellings with an *e* at the end on the other long-vowel cards to help students see the pattern—*a_e, i_e, o_e,* and *u_e.*

Phonemic Awareness

Listening for /ē/

Read aloud the following words, and have students signal thumbs-up and say the sound if they hear /ē/.

book	bake	**between**	**evening**
scene	**seed**	settle	sudden
we	maple	**trapeze**	kingdom

Sound/Spelling Card 28

Teacher Tips

CONTRASTING /e/ AND /ē/ Write the rhyme on chart paper, and display it in the classroom for future reference.

SOUNDS AND SPELLINGS Use tape or a self-sticking note to cover the other /ē/ spellings until they are introduced in later lessons in this unit. You may want to tell students that only a few words have the /ē/ spelling *e_e*. This is in contrast to /ā/ spelled *a_e,* /ī/ spelled *i_e,* /ō/ spelled *o_e,* and /ū/ spelled *u_e*.

PHONEME SEGMENTATION For segmentation practice, choose words from the Phonemic Awareness activity for students to say sound by sound. /b/ /ā/ /k/.

Differentiating Instruction: English Learners

IF . . . students are native speakers of Spanish or certain other languages, **THEN . . .** they may associate the letter name *e* with the letter *i,* because in their native languages *i* represents a sound similar to English /ē/. These students will need extra practice associating the letter *e* with its English name and with the /ē/ sound.

Teacher Tips

BLENDING In Lines 1 and 2, refer to Routine 2 for the sound-by-sound blending technique because this is the first time students are exposed to these spellings. If students are ready, refer to Routine 4 for the whole-word procedure for the remaining words on the lines.

SYLLABICATION To help students blend the words and build fluency, demonstrate syllabication using the decodable multisyllable words on the word lines.

re • gal	e • ven	e • lect
e • lev • en	com • plete	

SCHWA Because the final *e* in *even* and *eleven* has the schwa sound, you may want to indicate this by putting a dot over the appropriate letter in each word.

Differentiating Instruction English Learners

IF . . . students are native speakers of Spanish or of certain other languages, **THEN . . .** they may associate the letter name *a* with the letter *e*, because in their native languages *e* represents a sound similar to English /ā/.

Phonics

ROUTINE 2 ROUTINE 3 ROUTINE 4 ROUTINE 10 ROUTINE 11

Blending

Use Routine 2, sound-by-sound blending, Routine 3, whole-word blending, and Routine 4, blending sentences, to blend the words and sentences. Use Routine 10, closed syllables, and Routine 11, open syllables, to have students blend the multisyllable words.

Line 1	be	we	she	he
Line 2	these	theme	regal	even
Line 3	here	complete	elect	eleven
Line 4	Eve	Steve	Pete	pet

Sentence 1	Is she related to Beth or Gene?
Sentence 2	Steve is sick with a fever and a cold.

Line 1 **/ē/ spelled *e***

Point out that each word contains the /ē/ sound spelled *e*.

Line 2 **/ē/ spelled *e* and *e_e***

Blend the words by breaking them into syllables. Remind students that the vowel sound in an open syllable is usually long.

Some students may not be familiar with the word *regal*. Say the word in a sentence such as *In her new blue velvet dress and silver shoes, the girl looked as regal as a princess.*

Line 3 **/ē/ spelled *e* and *e_e***

If students are not familiar with the word *complete,* use it in a sentence such as *When you complete your homework, you may play outside.*

Line 4 **/ē/ spelled *e_e* and /e/ spelled *e***

Ask students why *Eve, Steve,* and *Pete* begin with capital letters. *They are names of people.* Ask how the word *pet* is different from the other words on the line and why. Pet *has the /e/ sound, and the other words have the /ē/ sound.*

Sentences 1–2

Before blending the sentences, write the word *or* on the board. Tell students they will see this word many times in their reading. Although they have learned /or/ spelled *or*, they should begin to read the word automatically. Have students read the word and use it in sentences. Then write *or* on an index card, and add it to the High-Frequency Word Bank. Have students reread the sentences several times to build fluency.

Developing Oral Language

To review the words, you will need a box or bag and the five index cards you prepared for this activity. Have students take turns choosing a line, drawing a card, and reading the word that corresponds to the number on the card. If a student draws the star card, he or she can choose any word to read or can choose a line and read all the words on it.

Guided Practice

Help students complete ***Skills Practice 1*** pages 177–178 for practice with /ē/ spelled *e* and *e_e* and for dictation. Review the sound/spellings at the top of page 177. Then have students read and write the words and sentences at the bottom of the page. Help students complete the sentences on page 178. Students can use the bottom of the page for dictation.

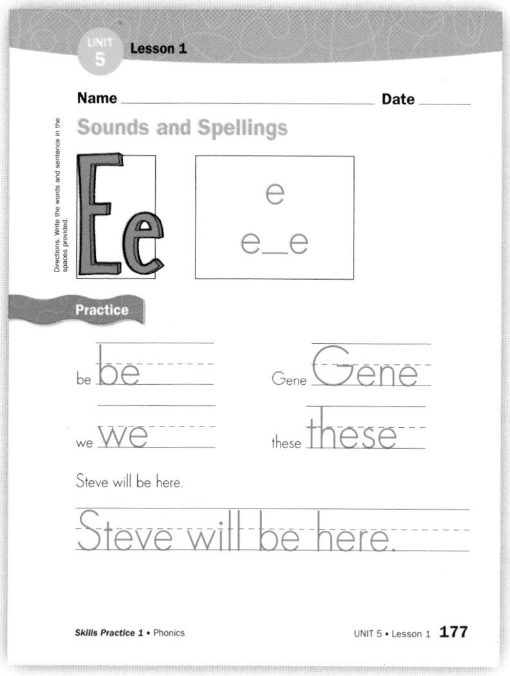
UNIT 5 Lesson 1

Name ______ Date ______

Sounds and Spellings

Directions: Write the words and sentence in the spaces provided.

Ee

e
e_e

Practice

be be   Gene Gene

we we   these these

Steve will be here.

Steve will be here.

Skills Practice 1 • Phonics   UNIT 5 • Lesson 1 177

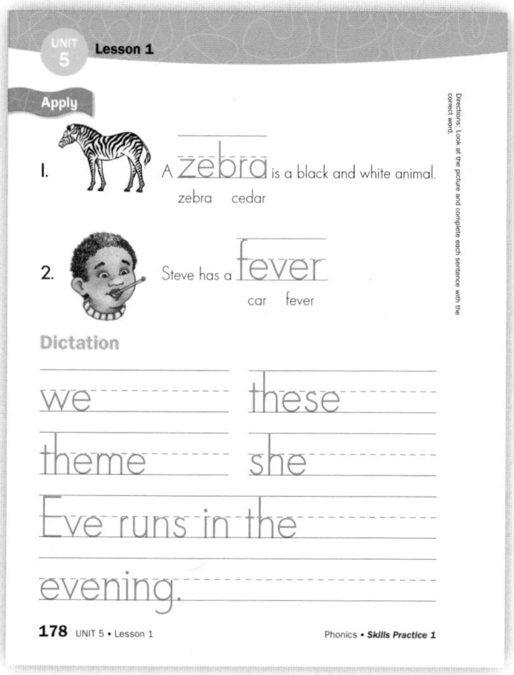
UNIT 5 Lesson 1

Apply

Directions: Look at the picture and complete each sentence with the correct word.

1. A zebra is a black and white animal.
zebra cedar

2. Steve has a fever
car fever

Dictation

we these
theme she
Eve runs in the
evening.

178 UNIT 5 • Lesson 1   Phonics • *Skills Practice 1*

Skills Practice 1, pp. 177–178

Monitor Progress

to Differentiate Instruction
Formal Assessment

DICTATION As students spell words, notice who refers to the ***Sound/Spelling Cards*** and spells the words correctly.

APPROACHING LEVEL

IF . . .	THEN . . .
IF . . . students need additional practice with /ē/ spelled *e* and *e_e*,	**THEN . . .** during Workshop, dictate words for them to spell using the ***Write-On Board*** and magnetic letters.

ON LEVEL

IF . . .	THEN . . .
IF . . . students are on level with /ē/ spelled *e* and *e_e*,	**THEN . . .** pair them, and have them play a game from ***eSkills.***

ABOVE LEVEL

IF . . .	THEN . . .
IF . . . students need a challenge with /ē/ spelled *e* and *e_e*,	**THEN . . .** make two lists, each with three words that contain only the target sound/spellings. Pair students, and tell them to take turns dictating words from their list for their partners to spell.

Dictation

ROUTINE 6 ROUTINE 7

Use Routine 6, whole-word dictation, and Routine 7, sentence dictation, with the words and sentence below. If students are unsure which /ē/ spelling to use, tell them. Be sure to help students proofread the words after completing each line.

Line 1	we	these
Line 2	theme	she
Sentence	Eve runs <u>in</u> <u>the</u> evening.	

Teacher Tips

HIGH-FREQUENCY WORDS The word *in* is a decodable high-frequency word. Encourage students to write it without sounding it out. If they have difficulty, tell them they can spell the word sound by sound.

PHONEME SEGMENTATION Say words with long-vowel sounds, and have students identify all the sounds in the word. For example, for *wheel*, students would respond /hw/ /ē/ /l/. Have them segment other words such as *these, Gene, maybe,* and *Steve*.

WORD CHART Create a word chart on which students can list words that contain /ē/ spelled *e* and *e_e*. Encourage them to look for words with these sound/spellings to add to the chart.

Fluency/Reading a Decodable Book

ROUTINE 9

Core Decodable 68: *A Zebra*

Phonics Focus: /ē/ Spelled *e* and *e_e*

High-Frequency Words

Review the high-frequency word *or* that students learned in blending, by writing it on the board, spelling it, and having students say the word. Have a volunteer use the word in a sentence. Review other high-frequency words by pointing to them in the High-Frequency Word Bank and having students read them.

Reading the Decodable

- Follow Routine 9, reading a ***Decodable,*** as you read the story with students.
- Have students read the title, browse the story, and discuss what they think the story will be about.
- The first time through, have students read a page silently. Then have one student read it aloud. Repeat this procedure for each page.
- Reread the story at least twice, calling on various students to read. Then have the entire class do a choral reading of the story.

Responding

- After reading, be sure to talk about the story and answer any questions students have. Ask students to identify any difficult words in the book.

by Ethan Cruz
illustrated by Rusty Fletcher
We made a recent visit to a ranch.

These horses have a big secret.
A zebra runs with them.
4
But which is the zebra?
These horses will not tell.
5

Teacher Tip

SOUND/SPELLING CARDS Remind students to refer to the ***Sound/Spelling Cards*** if they are unsure of a sound/spelling.

Monitor Progress to Differentiate Instruction

Formal Assessment

As students read ***Decodable*** 68, note those who are having trouble with the /ē/ sound/spellings or other sound/spellings.

APPROACHING LEVEL	**IF . . .** students are having difficulty decoding the words or answering the questions,	**THEN . . .** during Workshop, review ***Sound/Spelling Card*** 28—Long E and any other ***Sound/Spelling Cards*** students need to review. Then reread ***Decodable*** 68 with them, and ask them the questions again.
ON LEVEL	**IF . . .** students are on level,	**THEN . . .** have them quiz one another during Workshop using the ***High-Frequency Flash Cards.***
ABOVE LEVEL	**IF . . .** students are ready for a challenge,	**THEN . . .** encourage them to browse and read classroom library books.

We looked and looked all over.
But we did not even get a hint.

6

So has the zebra left?
Or is he just well hidden?

7

For the time being, we cannot tell.
Can you spot a zebra?

8

Teacher Tip

GRAMMAR Have students find the plural noun (add *s*) in the story. *horses*

✦ Have students retell the story.

✦ As students answer the following questions, make sure they focus on the words in the story rather than getting the answers by listening or from the pictures. Have students answer by pointing to and reading aloud the answers in the text:

- **Where do they visit?** *a ranch*
- **What do these horses have?** *a big secret*
- **What runs with these horses?** *a zebra*

Building Fluency

Have students build fluency by rereading ***Core Decodable*** 68 twice with a partner. The first time through, one partner should read the odd-numbered pages and the other partner the even-numbered pages. The second time through, they should switch pages. For additional practice with /ē/ spelled *e* and *e_e,* have students read ***Practice Decodable*** 57, *Picnic Weather*. Have students record their readings on their Personal Title sheets, noting the title of each book, the date, and any difficult words they encountered.

Core Decodable 68

A Zebra

High-Frequency Word Introduced in Core Decodable 68

or

Previously Introduced High-Frequency Words

a	girl	just	then
after	go	like	there
all	got	little	they
am	had	look	this
an	has	make	to
and	have	of	up
as	he	on	walk
ask	help	out	was
at	her	over	we
big	him	red	well
but	his	ride	went
call	I	said	were
can	if	see	what
did	in	she	when
do	is	six	will
down	it	that	with
for	its	the	yes
get	jump	them	you

Sound/Spelling Correspondences in Core Decodables

1. Pre-decodable
2. Pre-decodable
3. Pre-decodable
4. Pre-decodable
5. Pre-decodable
6. /s/ spelled *s*, /m/ spelled *m*, /a/ spelled *a*
7. /t/ spelled *t, tt*
8. Review
9. /d/ spelled *d*
10. /n/ spelled *n*
11. /i/ spelled *i*
12. /h/ spelled *h_*
13. Review
14. /p/ spelled *p*
15. /l/ spelled *l, ll*
16. /o/ spelled *o*
17. /b/ spelled *b*
18. Review
19. /k/ spelled *c*
20. /aw/ spelled *al*
21. /k/ spelled *k*, ■*ck*
22. /r/ spelled *r*
23. /f/ spelled *f, ff*
24. /s/ spelled *ss*
25. Review
26. /g/ spelled *g*
27. /j/ spelled *j*, ■*dge*
28. /u/ spelled *u*
29. /z/ spelled *z, zz*
30. /z/ spelled *_s*
31. Review
32. /ks/ spelled ■*x*
33. /e/ spelled *e*
34. -ed ending: /ed/, /d/
35. -ed ending: /t/
36. /e/ spelled *_ea_*
37. Review
38. /sh/ spelled *sh*
39. /th/ spelled *th*
40. /ch/ spelled *ch*, ■*tch*
41. /or/ spelled *or, ore*
42. Review
43. /ar/ spelled *ar*
44. /m/ spelled *_mb*
45. /w/ spelled *w_*
46. /hw/ spelled *wh_*
47. /er/ spelled *er, ir*
48. /er/ spelled *ur*
49. Review
50. Schwa
51. Review schwa
52. /ng/ spelled ■*ng*
53. /nk/ spelled ■*nk*
54. /kw/ spelled *qu_*
55. Review
56. /y/ spelled *y_*
57. /v/ spelled *v*
58. Syllable -le
59. /ā/ spelled *a* and *a_e*
60. Review
61. /ī/ spelled *i* and *i_e*
62. /s/ spelled *ce, ci_*
63. /j/ spelled *ge, gi_*
64. Review
65. /ō/ spelled *o* and *o_e*
66. /ū/ spelled *u* and *u_e*
67. Review
68. /ē/ spelled *e* and *e_e*

Decodable 68, inside back cover

Reading and Responding

OBJECTIVES

Students will
- activate prior knowledge about weather.
- learn weather-related vocabulary words.
- listen to and discuss *I Call It Sky.*
- browse and make predictions about unit selections.
- set reading goals for the unit.
- be introduced to the What's the Weather? **Concept/Question Board.**

MATERIALS
- ***Read Aloud Collection:*** *I Call It Sky*
- Routine 12
- ***Home Connection,*** pp. 33–34
- Writer's Notebooks

Teacher Tips

ACTIVATE PRIOR KNOWLEDGE Use this discussion to become aware of any misconceptions students might have about weather, wind, or the effects of weather changes. This is important because research shows that to make sense of the world, young students often develop their own theories about how nature "works." As you talk with students about weather, be alert for information in the selections that can help students rethink and revise their theories to make them more accurate.

SEASONS If you are in a region that does not experience distinct changes in weather across seasons, talk with students about the four seasons and the different kinds of weather most often associated with each one. In addition, discuss any changes in weather that they do experience in the different seasons, such as more rain or hot dry days.

Vocabulary Tip

Before reading aloud *I Call It Sky*, introduce these vocabulary words to students. Say each word and its definition. Then use the word in a sentence.

breeze a gentle movement of the air

clouds Plural of **cloud:** a group of small drops of water or bits of ice that float high in the air

sky the air above Earth

Read Aloud

Activate Prior Knowledge

Ask students the following questions to activate their knowledge of weather:

- *What is weather?* **Possible Answer** *Weather is rain and snow.*
- *What is air?* **Possible Answer** *Air is what we breathe. Air is the open space above Earth and all around us.*
- *What is wind? moving air*
- *What are the names of the four seasons? spring, summer, fall/autumn, winter*
- *What types of weather are typically associated with each season?* **Possible Answers** *Spring weather is warm and sometimes rainy. Summer is hot. Fall weather is colder than summer. Winter is the coldest season of all. In some places, winter weather brings snow.*

I Call It Sky by Will C. Howell

Children celebrate weather across the seasons. As they run through spring breezes, fly kites on warm summer days, disappear into a fall fog, and taste snowflakes in winter, the children show how weather works and how it affects our lives.

Fluency

When you read *I Call It Sky*, have students listen carefully and attentively as you model appropriate reading rate, expression, and intonation.

ROUTINE 12

Reading Recommendations

Read aloud *I Call It Sky* following Routine 12, reading the selection. The Teacher Tips throughout the selection contain comprehension instruction. Use these and your own prompts to help students better comprehend the selection. Help students understand that the story has *several* children talking about various kinds of weather. Encourage students to listen for the description of air by each child.

Focus Questions What kinds of weather are there? What kind of weather do you enjoy?

I Call It Sky

by Will C. Howell

Every morning, when sunlight jumps through my window, I burst out the door. I am surrounded by air. It nips at my nose and tosses my hair. It is inside me when I breathe, and it is outside me everywhere.

In the summer, the warm air is quiet. It does not move much.

But sometimes the warm air wakes up and glides by my face just enough to kiss my cheek. I call it a breeze.

In the fall, the air grows wet and heavy. It huddles close to the ground. I cannot see through it. I call this fog.

Sometimes wet air gathers in big black bunches of clouds. When the clouds get too heavy, they squeeze out rain.

In the winter, clouds freeze and shiver, and they toss down the snow instead.

In the spring, I feel the air dash and dart around me. It rages through the trees and sweeps the ground. I call it wind.

I know all about air. It is the place where birds soar. It teases the grass . . . and makes me warm or cold.

I know about the quiet summer air because I can see the still flowers resting on green picket stems.

I know about a summer breeze because I can hear it stirring the leaves nesting in the branches. I like to listen to the secrets it whispers to me.

I Call It Sky

Teacher Tips

BEFORE READING Encourage students to make predictions based on the title of *I Call It Sky*.

DURING READING Describe what you visualize after reading one of the descriptive lines in the selection.

Technology

LISTENING LIBRARY Have students listen to this selection again during Workshop. Listening to the text once it is familiar will help them better understand the concepts.

Read Aloud

I know about fog in the fall because I can step into it and feel its wetness hide me. I like to disappear into the fog and pretend that I am invisible.

I know about rain because I can feel its drops tickle my eyelashes and trickle over the tip of my nose. I like to stand under my umbrella and watch the raindrops splash at my feet.

I know about the snow because I can stick out my tongue and taste it. I like to run after snowflakes, which flutter down like a million white butterflies, and catch them.

I know about the wind in the spring because it carries the smells of the new grass and fresh flowers and leads me into the fields where they grow. I like to run with my kite and play tug-of-war with the wind.

Every night, when the stars begin to pop into their places, I am surrounded by air. It slips under my clothes and trails me into the house. It fills up my room and sits on the edge of my bed.

Even when I cannot see it or catch it in my hands or taste it or smell it or feel it on my face, I still know the air is there. It welcomes the sun in the morning and frames the stars at night. I call it sky.

Teacher Tips

DURING READING Prompt students to make connections with the children's activities in the selection, such as flying a kite or smelling fresh flowers.

AFTER READING Model asking questions at the end of this selection, such as What have we learned about air? or How do we know air is all around us? You may want to record the questions and post them on the **Concept/Question Board.**

Discussing the Read Aloud

- After reading *I Call It Sky,* review with students the four seasons. Then ask students the following questions to check their comprehension of the story:
  - *What did you learn about air and wind in this story?* **Possible Answer** *I learned that air is inside me and outside all around me.*
  - *In the story, how did the air differ in each season?* *The air was warm and friendly in summer. The air was wet and heavy and foggy in fall. The air was cold in winter. In spring, the air dashed and darted around.*
  - *What are our five senses? sight, smell, hearing, taste, and touch*
  - *Think about summer. What can you smell in the summer?* **Possible Answer** *I smell food grilling.*
  - *Think about fall. What do you taste?* **Possible Answer** *I taste my grandpa's sweet potatoes.* *What do you see?* **Possible Answer** *I see leaves changing colors.*
  - *Think about winter. What do you feel?* **Possible Answer** *I feel cold.*
  - *Think about spring. What do you hear?* **Possible Answer** *I hear lots of birds chirping.*
  - *How are the seasons in the story like our seasons? How are they different?* **Possible Answer** *The seasons in the story are exactly like our seasons.*
- Review the Focus Questions with students: "What kinds of weather are there?" **Possible Answer** *There are more kinds of weather than the Read Aloud talked about.* "What kinds of weather do you enjoy?" **Possible Answer** *I love summer because I can play at the pool with my friends.*
- Review with students the vocabulary introduced in *I Call It Sky*. Have students role-play the word *breeze* by gently waving their arms. For the word *clouds,* have students describe clouds they have seen. Help students understand the idea of sky by having them identify things they have seen in the sky, such as birds, planes, and hot-air balloons.

Concept/Question Board

Have students post on the Board illustrations of the seasons described in the story. Encourage students to write sentences to go with their illustrations.

Monitor Progress
to Differentiate Instruction
Formal Assessment

COMPREHENSION During the discussion of *I Call It Sky,* note which students are easily and accurately answering questions and those who cannot answer questions.

APPROACHING LEVEL

IF . . . students are unable to answer the comprehension questions, **THEN . . .** during Workshop, reread *I Call It Sky*. Help students identify information in the selection that can help them answer the questions.

ON LEVEL

IF . . . students answered most of the questions correctly, **THEN . . .** during Workshop, have them choose one of the seasons from the story and illustrate it.

ABOVE LEVEL

IF . . . students can easily and accurately answer the comprehension questions, **THEN . . .** during Workshop, have them write one or two sentences about one of the seasons.

BIG Idea

After reading *I Call It Sky,* read the Big Idea question. Discuss with students how the selection helps answer this question.

Teacher Tips

BROWSING The purpose of browsing is to help students think about what will be read and to build a sense of anticipation for the reading. When students browse fiction selections, have them browse only the first few pages so they do not figure out the story ending.

SETTING GOALS Students who set their own goals for reading will read with a greater sense of engagement, and they tend to notice more than students whose goals are set for them.

WORD BANK Begin a What's the Weather? Word Bank. To set up the What's the Weather? Word Bank, you may want to have students group words by the type of weather or the season to which they relate. Include *I Call It Sky* selection, expanding, and concept vocabulary words for the unit. Have students suggest other theme-related words to add to the Word Bank.

Writer's Notebook

Students will use the inquiry section of their Writer's Notebooks to record daily observations of the weather. Have students create a two-column What's the Weather? chart in the inquiry section. They can use the first column for the date and the second column for their weather observations.

Preview the Unit

Browsing

✦ Have students examine and share their thoughts about the illustrations on the covers of the ***What's the Weather? Big Book*** and the ***First Reader.***

✦ Have students browse the selections in this unit. Remind them that good readers often browse a book before reading it so they can get an idea of what the book is about.

✦ After browsing, ask students to make predictions concerning what the selections might be about and what they might learn from the selections.

Set Goals

✦ Explain to students that in this unit, they will work toward the following goals:

- To understand weather concepts, including what causes different kinds of weather, how weather is measured, and how it affects people's lives
- To identify and understand the parts of a book, including glossaries
- To identify sentences, sentence boundaries, and paragraphs in print
- To identify and understand the purpose of different end punctuation marks, quotation marks, and ellipses
- To understand and apply rules for capitalization and comma usage

✦ Tell students that as part of their unit Inquiry, they will keep weather records in their Writer's Notebooks. Explain that throughout the unit, they will use their notebooks to write their weather observations each day and record information from their investigations.

Concept/Question Board

- Remind students that the **Concept/Question Board** will help them explore the unit theme What's the Weather? To start the **Concept/Question Board,** have students talk about different kinds of weather they have experienced. Say several weather-related words such as *rainy, sunny, snowy, windy,* and *cloudy.* Call on students to use the words in sentences to tell what they might see, hear, and feel on a day with such weather and how the weather affects what they do on that day. Write the sentences on index cards, and post them on the Concept portion of the **Concept/Question Board.** Tell students they can add other sentences to the Board throughout the unit.
- Use chart paper to prepare a What's the Weather? chart to hang on or near the Board and on which students can record the weather each day.
- Brainstorm additional things that would be appropriate to post on the What's the Weather? **Concept/Question Board,** such as
  - newspaper or magazine pictures that show different kinds of weather.
  - photographs of themselves under umbrellas in the rain, in the snow building snowmen, in the sun at the beach, or in any other weather-related setting.
  - weather maps from newspapers or magazines.
  - brochures or fact sheets about weather forecasting or about how to prepare for different kinds of serious weather.
  - questions about weather and how it works.
- Remind students to do the following throughout the unit:
  - Post questions, comments, articles, illustrations, and objects related to the unit theme What's the Weather?
  - Write answers or notes on someone else's question(s).
  - Read and listen to stories about weather at home. Share these stories with the class, and post the title and author's name on the Board.
  - Watch the weather segments of local television newscasts, and report to the class about the predicted weather and the accuracy of the prediction.
- Remind students to put their names or initials on anything they post.

Teacher Tips

THEME CONNECTION If possible, bring in a kite. Make arrangements with the school in advance for a time and a safe place to fly the kite with students.

LITERATURE Have students select age and ability appropriate fiction and nonfiction materials to read based on interest and teacher recommendations. By encouraging students to read daily, they will begin building a core base of knowledge about the unit theme.

Concept/Question Board

As you start this unit, decorate the board with plastic decals or construction paper cutouts of weather icons such as the sun, lightning, white clouds, gray clouds with rain, snow, puffs of wind, and fog.

From Your Teacher **Home Connection**

Give each student a copy of ***Home Connection*** page 33. This same information is also available in Spanish on ***Home Connection*** page 34. Have students complete the activity provided at home.

OBJECTIVES

Students will
- ✦ learn what a list is and how to write one.
- ✦ use pictures to generate ideas for writing.
- ✦ form the letters *u* and *m* correctly.
- ✦ control the size and spacing of letters.

MATERIALS

- ✦ Routine 14
- ✦ ***Transparencies*** 36, 37
- ✦ ***Language Arts Big Book,*** pp. 39–40
- ✦ ***What's the Weather? Big Book,*** p. 60
- ✦ ***Alphabet Letter Cards***

Traits of Good Writing

Ideas Writers use pictures to help generate ideas for their work.

Differentiating Instruction English Learners

IF . . . students are familiar with another writing system, **THEN . . .** they may not know that English is normally written from left to right, and the format of a list may be confusing to them. Some languages are written and read vertically or from right to left. Make sure English Learners understand the difference between the format of a list and the format of a paragraph. Provide practice in tracking print as needed.

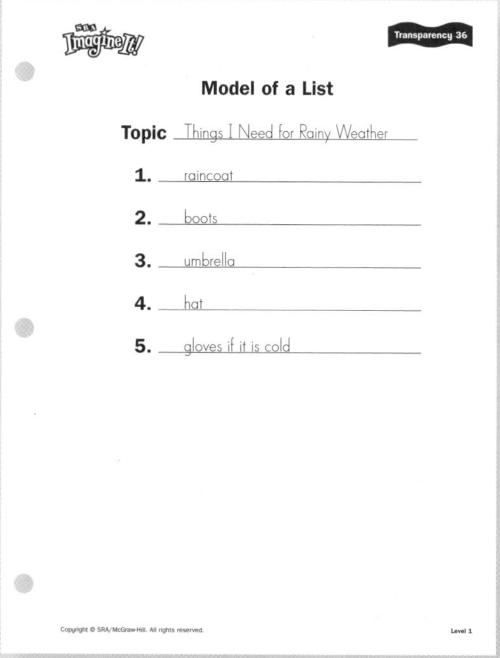

SRA Imagine It! Transparency 36

Model of a List

Topic Things I Need for Rainy Weather

1. raincoat
2. boots
3. umbrella
4. hat
5. gloves if it is cold

 Level 1

Transparency 36

Writing Lists

ROUTINE 14

Prewriting

Teach—Using Pictures

- ✦ Use the example on ***Transparency*** 36 to introduce lists as a form of personal writing. Explain that a list is a group of words that belong together. A writer can use a list in various ways:
  - To get ideas
  - To remember the things they need
  - To help them remember things to do
- ✦ Refer to ***Language Arts Big Book*** pages 39–40 for other examples of lists.
- ✦ Next, display the fine arts photograph by Ansel Adams on ***What's the Weather? Big Book*** page 60. Tell students that the tree featured is an apple tree in Yosemite National Park in California. Have students recall how they described the photograph earlier. Explain that pictures such as this one can help them get ideas for their writing.

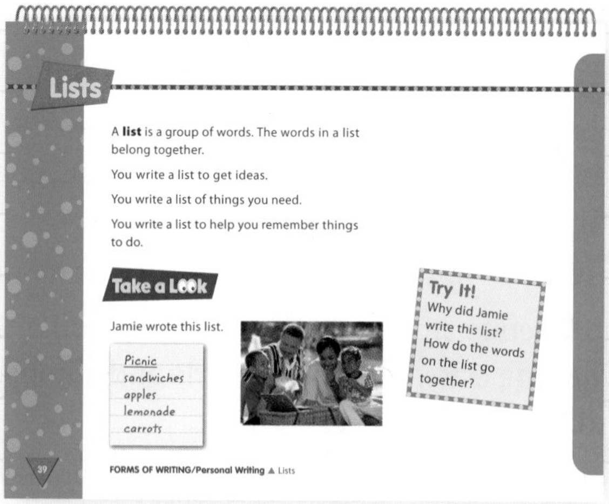

Language Arts Big Book, p. 39

Writing Lists, cont.

Teacher Modeling: Use the photograph as you model how to use lists to generate ideas for writing. Write your list on the board as you say *This picture shows snow, so it must be cold. I'm going to write a story about visiting Yosemite National Park in winter. First, I'll need the right clothes for going outside when it's cold, so I'll make a list of things to wear. I'll need a coat, a scarf, gloves, and boots.*

Guided Practice

- Remind students that using pictures to think of ideas is an important writing strategy. Explain that they can use pictures as inspiration when adding details to their writing as well.
- Have students use the Ansel Adams photograph to brainstorm ideas for a winter-themed list. Provide students with assistance in applying the strategy until they can do it on their own. If necessary, suggest the following topics: *Things they might see in the park in winter; Things they might do in the park in winter; Things they might take along on a visit to the park in winter.*
- Circulate, and help students focus on one main topic for their lists. Then encourage them to add at least three details to the items on their lists. Allow those who struggle to work with a partner if necessary.

Teacher Tip

PENMANSHIP For practice writing *u*, use a model that shows the strokes in different colors.

Penmanship

Alphabet Practice: The Letters *u* and *m*

Teach

Model how to form lowercase *u* and *m* by writing the letters on ***Transparency*** 37. Describe each stroke of the handwriting models as you trace them. Point out similarities in how these two letters are written—both letters have straight lines and curves.

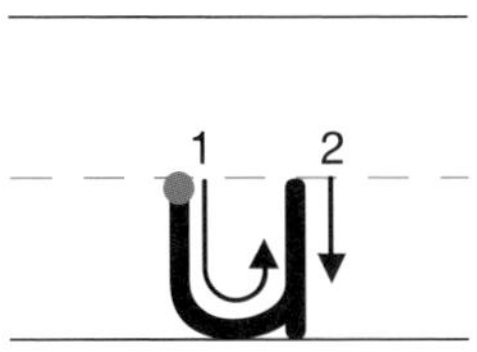

Starting point, straight down, curving around right and up, straight up, straight back down: small *u*

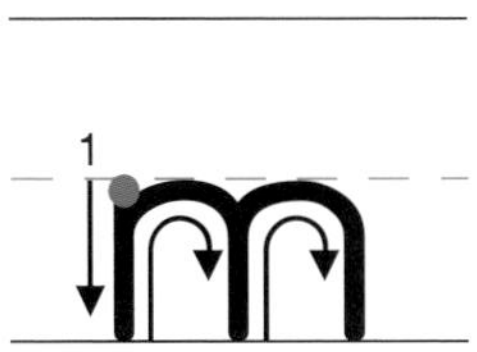

Starting point, straight down, back up, around right, straight down, back up, around right, straight down: small *m*

Guided Practice

Help students use their index fingers to trace the letters *u* and *m* on the ***Alphabet Letter Cards*** as they say each letter name.

Apply

For letter-formation practice, provide students with handwriting paper. Have them write the letters *u* and *m* four times within the lines as they say the letter names. Have students proofread their line by circling any incorrect letters and making them better by rewriting them. Then have them underline their best *u* and *m*.

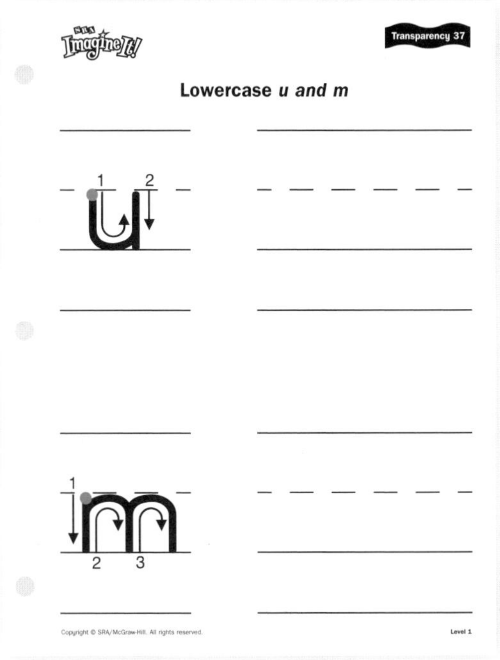

Transparency 37

Preparing to Read

OBJECTIVES

Students will

- blend, spell, and read words that contain /ē/ spelled *e* and *e_e*.
- write words with /ē/ spelled *e* and *e_e*.

MATERIALS

- Routines 3–4, 8, 10–11
- ***Sound/Spelling Card*** 28
- ***Skills Practice 1,*** pp. 181–182

Teacher Tip

ALPHABETIZING Have students practice alphabetizing. Choose a few words from the High-Frequency Word Bank that each begin with a different letter. Have students put these words in alphabetical order.

Daily Warm-Ups

Copy the Morning Message on the board or on chart paper. Have students answer the question. Read the message aloud, and discuss it with students. **Possible Answers** *loud, strong, scary*

MORNING MESSAGE

Good morning! Weather is not always nice. Sometimes we have a storm. Today we will read a selection about storms. What words describe storms?

Daily Language Review

To review comparative adjectives, write the following sentence on the board, or generate a similar one with students. Then have them say the correct form of comparative: This shirt is the small in the store. *This shirt is the smallest in the store.*

Sound/Spelling Game

Name a ***Sound/Spelling Card,*** such as the Jump card, and have students say the sound and spellings the card represents. Call on a student to say and spell a word that contains the sound/spelling. Continue with two or three other cards, such as the Vacuum, Bird, and Yaks cards or use cards that have given the class difficulty. **Possible Answers** *jog, page, giant*

Phonics

ROUTINE 3 ROUTINE 4 ROUTINE 10 ROUTINE 11

Review: /ē / Spelled *e* and *e_e*

Blending

Point to the *e* and *e_e* spellings on ***Sound/Spelling Card*** 28—Long E, and remind students that these are two ways to spell /ē/. Use Routine 3, whole-word blending, and Routine 4, blending sentences, to blend the words and sentences. Use Routine 10, closed syllables, and Routine 11, open syllables, to have students blend the multisyllable words.

Line 1	begin	began	equal	decide
Line 2	delete	trapeze	secret	**before**
Line 3	compete	stampede	Japanese	athlete
Line 4	recite	female	decode	return

Sentence 1	Pete likes <u>to</u> swing <u>on</u> <u>the</u> trapeze.
Sentence 2	<u>A</u> cute kitten hid behind <u>the</u> shrub.

Lines 1–2 **/ē/ spelled *e* and *e_e***

Have students identify the spelling for /ē/ in each word. */ē/ spelled* e

The word *before* is also in the selection "When a Storm Comes Up." Tell students it means "some time ago," and use it in a sentence such as *I brush my teeth before I go to bed at night.*

Line 3 **/ē/ spelled *e_e***

If students are not familiar with the word *stampede*, use it in a sentence such as *The frightened herd of zebras galloped together in a stampede across the plains.*

Line 4 **/ē/ spelled *e***

After blending these words, ask students what three of these words have in common. *Recite, female,* and *decode have the /ē/ sound spelled* e, *as well as another long-vowel sound spelled vowel consonant* e.

Sentences 1–2

Have students read the sentences several times to build fluency.

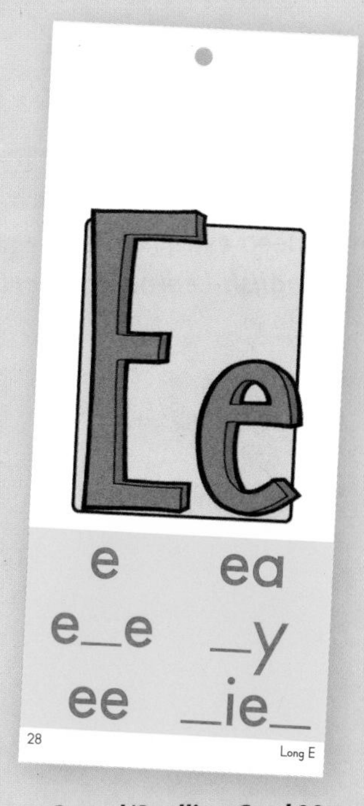

Sound/Spelling Card 28

Teacher Tips

CONTRASTING /e/ AND /ē/ Refer students to the rhyme introduced in Lesson 1, and have them repeat it with you.

SCHWA Because the *o* in *compete* has the schwa sound, you may want to indicate this by putting a dot over the *o* in that word.

SYLLABICATION To help students blend the words and build fluency, use the syllabication below of the multisyllable words on the word lines.

be • gin	be • gan	e • qual
de • cide	de • lete	tra • peze
se • cret	be • fore	com • pete
stam • pede	Ja • pa • nese	ath • lete
re • cite	fe • male	de • code
re • turn		

Developing Oral Language

For each question below, call on a student to read the word on the word lines and to use it in a sentence.

- What do we call someone who plays sports? *athlete*
- Which word means "to say or read something aloud"? *recite*
- What is a short bar an acrobat swings on? *trapeze*
- What is another name for a girl or woman? *female*
- What is the opposite of *after?* *before*

Differentiating Instruction **English Learner**

IF . . . students need extra help with phonics,
THEN . . . use ***English-Learner Support Guide*** Unit 5.

Guided Practice

Help students complete ***Skills Practice 1*** pages 181–182 to review /ē/ spelled *e* and *e_e*. Have students complete the sentences on page 181. Then have students chorally read the complete sentences. Have students complete the puzzle on page 182 by choosing the /ē/ words that correctly answer the clues.

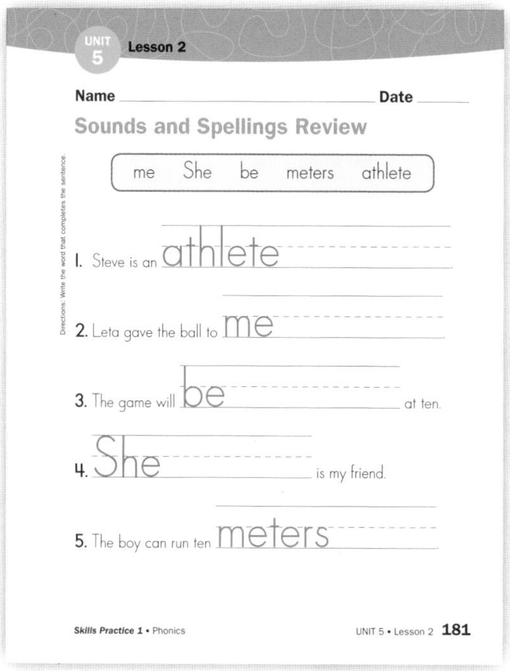
UNIT 5 Lesson 2

Name ______ Date ______

Sounds and Spellings Review

Directions: Write the word that completes the sentence.

me She be meters athlete

1. Steve is an athlete
2. Leta gave the ball to me
3. The game will be at ten.
4. She is my friend.
5. The boy can run ten meters

Skills Practice 1 • Phonics UNIT 5 • Lesson 2 181

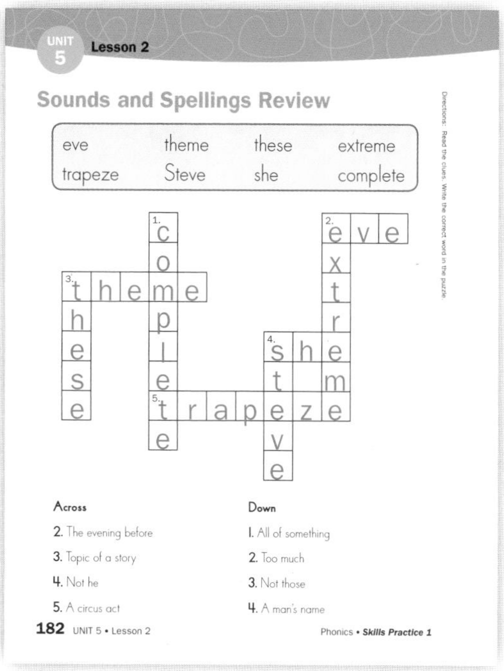
UNIT 5 Lesson 2

Sounds and Spellings Review

Directions: Read the clues. Write the correct word in the puzzle.

eve theme these extreme trapeze Steve she complete

Across
2. The evening before
3. Topic of a story
4. Not he
5. A circus act

Down
1. All of something
2. Too much
3. Not those
4. A man's name

182 UNIT 5 • Lesson 2 Phonics • Skills Practice 1

Skills Practice 1, pp. 181–182

Dictation: Word Building Game

ROUTINE 8

Use Routine 8, word building, to have students spell the following words in the Word Building game using paper and pencil.

hen
he
be
we
wet
pet
Pete

Teacher Tip

WORD BUILDING GAME Be sure to have students proofread and correct their spelling before dictating the next word. Remind them to circle any words they think could be better and to write these words again above or beside the original word.

Monitor Progress

to Differentiate Instruction
Formal Assessment

DICTATION Observe students during dictation to identify those who may need additional help. Work with them during Workshop.

APPROACHING LEVEL

IF . . . students need additional practice with /ē/ spelled *e* and *e_e*, **THEN . . .** help them complete ***Reteach 1*** pages 137–138.

ON LEVEL

IF . . . students can blend and segment words with /ē/ spelled *e* and *e_e*, **THEN . . .** have them play the Long-Vowel board game in the ***Workshop Kit.***

ABOVE LEVEL

IF . . . students need a challenge with /ē/ spelled *e* and *e_e*, **THEN . . .** have them complete ***Challenge Activities 1*** page 69.

Reading and Responding

OBJECTIVES

Students will

- activate prior knowledge about storms.
- set purposes for reading.
- learn selection vocabulary words.
- understand a table of contents.
- use the comprehension strategies Asking Questions, Making Connections, and Clarifying.
- identify and understand the use of ellipses.

MATERIALS

- ***What's the Weather? Big Book,*** pp. 4–27
- Routines 12, 13
- Writer's Notebooks

Teacher Tip

ACTIVATE PRIOR KNOWLEDGE Use this discussion to become aware of any misconceptions or misunderstandings students might have about what causes storms. Be alert for information in the selection that can help students rethink and revise their theories to make them more accurate.

From Your Teacher Home Connection

Give each student a copy of ***Home Connection*** page 35. This same information is also available in Spanish on ***Home Connection*** page 36. After students have listened to each selection, encourage them to discuss it with their families and complete the activity provided.

Build Background

ROUTINE 12

Activate Prior Knowledge

Ask students the following questions to determine their prior knowledge of weather and storms:

- *What can happen when wind is strong?* **Possible Answer** *When wind is strong, it can blow things down.*
- *What is rain?* **Possible Answer** *Rain is water falling from the sky.*
- *What can happen when it rains a lot?* **Possible Answer** *Lots of rain can cause floods. Too much rain can wash things away.*
- *What happens when it does not rain enough?* **Possible Answers** *The grass and flowers do not grow. The grass and flowers might wilt or turn brown.*
- *What is thunder?* **Possible Answer** *Thunder is a loud noise that sometimes happens during a storm.*
- *What is lightning?* **Possible Answer** *Lightning is a flash of light in the sky.*
- *What is snow?* **Possible Answer** *Snow is frozen water that falls from the sky.*
- *What can happen when a lot of snow falls?* **Possible Answers** *When a lot of snow falls, schools close, and cars and buses can't go anywhere. The electricity goes off, and we can't go outside.*

Background Information

- Explain to students that water is necessary for plants to grow. Water goes into the ground and up through the roots of plants.
- Tell students that water can come in liquid form such as rain and in solid form such as snow. The form of water depends on the weather.
- Explain to students that weather changes from day to day. Weather also changes during the year. These changes during the year are called seasons.
- Review the words *thunderstorm, lightning,* and *dangerous* from the selection. Understanding these words will help students build a background for the reading of the selection.
  - **thunderstorm** a rainstorm that has thunder and lightning
  - **lightning** a flash of light in the sky that sometimes occurs during a thunderstorm
  - **dangerous** likely to cause something bad to happen

Preview and Prepare

ROUTINE 12

Browse

✦ Follow Routine 12, reading the selection, to prepare students for the selection. Have students turn to the Table of Contents in ***What's the Weather? Big Book.*** Have volunteers point to the title "When a Storm Comes Up," the author's name, and the beginning page number as you read them aloud.

✦ Have a volunteer turn to ***Big Book*** page 4. Tell students to browse the first few pages of the selection to look for difficult or unfamiliar words and for clues to what the selection is about. **Possible Answers** *difficult words: heavier, rolling; clues: sunshine, rain, and snow* Define and explain these words to students. Have students provide examples of something that is heavy. Then have them tell something else that is heavier. Demonstrate *rolling* by rolling a ball across the floor.

✦ Using the information they gained from browsing the selection, including the title and the illustration, have students make predictions as to what the selection is about.

Set Purposes

✦ Review with students some of the purposes for reading that they have learned, such as for enjoyment or to learn new information about weather.

✦ Ask students what the purposes for reading this selection might be. Write them on the board. Some suggestions are the following:

- To find out about different kinds of storms
- To learn the effects of storms

✦ After reading the selection, have students return to these purposes.

Fluency

Read aloud "When a Storm Comes Up." Have students listen carefully and follow along as you model appropriate reading rate, expression, and intonation. Read the descriptions of weather with expression. This will help students better understand the differences in the types of weather.

Teacher Tips

GLOSSARY The words *weather* (page 6), *pouring* (page 10), *flashes* (page 12), *column* (page 22), *whirl* (page 22), *government* (page 24), and *weather service* (page 24) appear in the Glossary. As students browse and identify interesting words or phrases, you may want to use the opportunity to model glossary use for students. Turn to the Glossary, find each word, and read each entry.

HIGH-FREQUENCY WORDS As students browse, you may want to have them look for the high-frequency words they know. The following high-frequency words appear in the selection: *it, to, on, a, out, in, but, the, can't, all, you, or, is, little, and, if, when, its, see, of, can, get, go, after, have, they, that, this, walk, make, big, over, down, up, has, them, for, just, an.*

SETTING GOALS Students who set their own goals for reading will read with a greater sense of engagement, and they tend to notice more than students whose goals are set for them.

BEGINNING DICTIONARY As students browse the selection, have them look up any unfamiliar words in a beginning dictionary.

BIG Idea

What is weather?

Before reading the selection, reread the Big Idea question. Tell students to keep this question in mind as they listen to the selection.

Selection Vocabulary

flashes Plural of **flash:** a sudden streak of lightning (page 12)

shelter to cover or protect (page 24)

funnel a cone-shaped form (page 22)

Teacher Tips

SEMANTIC MAP Begin a semantic map by using chart paper or a transparency. Have students identify the theme, and write it at the center of the map. Add the selection vocabulary words and any common words they can think of that relate to the unit theme.

DIGITAL TOOLS Have students look for definitions of selection vocabulary or difficult words from the text using an online dictionary.

Building Vocabulary

ROUTINE 13

- Use Routine 13, selection vocabulary, to introduce the vocabulary words to students. Write the words on the board or on a transparency.
  - Have volunteers point to the plural spelling of *flashes* and tell the rule. *For words that end with* sh, *add* es. Have volunteers use the word to describe lightning. **Possible Answer** *I have seen lightning flashes in the sky.*
  - Briefly review the sound/spelling in *funnel*. Have students point to the *el* spelling for /l/. Have volunteers tell what a funnel is. **Possible Answer** *A funnel is like the shape of an ice-cream cone.*
  - Have students name different kinds of structures that can be used to take *shelter,* such as a house or a tent. **Possible Answer** *den, apartment, doghouse, barn*
- Explain to students that some words have multiple meanings. The words *funnel, flashes,* and *shelter* can be nouns or verbs. Give an example of the verb form of the words, and have students tell the difference between the word meanings. Tell students to listen and look for these words as they hear the selection. Have students identify the appropriate meaning of the word in context and whether the word is used as a noun or a verb in the sentence.

Monitor Progress to Differentiate Instruction

Formal Assessment

VOCABULARY During the Building Vocabulary exercises, notice which students seem to understand the words and their meanings and which students seem confused.

APPROACHING LEVEL	**IF . . .** students are struggling with words and their definitions,	**THEN . . .** use the ***SRA Imagine It! Photo Library CD*** objects, stick drawings, and pantomime to help them visualize the words.
ON LEVEL	**IF . . .** students would benefit from additional practice with the vocabulary words,	**THEN . . .** have them make flash cards with words and their definitions.
ABOVE LEVEL	**IF . . .** students need a challenge,	**THEN . . .** pair them with students who need help, and have them use the words in sentences to show their meanings.

Reading the Selection

Genre Informational Writing

Tell students that "When a Storm Comes Up" is an example of informational writing. It was written to explain and provide facts about different kinds of storms. Informational writing includes one or more of the following elements:

- It contains facts that can be checked in other sources such as in encyclopedias and newspapers or on the Internet.
- It is about real people, animals, places, and events.
- It often includes maps, diagrams, charts, tables, photographs, and other illustrations to help readers understand.
- It can answer many of our questions about a topic.

Comprehension Strategies

During the first reading of "When a Storm Comes Up," model and prompt the use of the following comprehension strategies:

- Asking Questions
- Making Connections
- Clarifying

Focus Question

Read and discuss the Focus Question on page 4. Encourage students to think about the Focus Question as you read "When a Storm Comes Up."

Reading Recommendations

ROUTINE 12

You will read this selection over a two-day period following Routine 12, reading the selection.

Day 2 Read the entire selection, modeling and prompting the use of the comprehension strategies.

Day 3 Reread the entire selection, focusing on the comprehension skills and the Reading with a Writer's Eye element.

Teacher Tip

MODELING STRATEGIES Reading aloud to students provides them with opportunities to hear how good readers apply the comprehension strategies they are learning. Read with expression and enthusiasm, and model how you use the strategies to get information from and better understand the selection. Encourage students to apply these strategies during their reading.

Phonics

1st READ

Words in the selection containing sound/spellings from recent phonics lessons appear in boxes like this throughout the selection. At the end of the first reading, students should be prompted to identify the sound/spellings of these words.

Focus Question What kinds of storms are there?

When a Storm Comes Up

by Allan Fowler

4

It feels good to be out in the sunshine on a warm day. ❶

5

What's the Weather? Big Book, pp. 4–5

Phonics

/ē/ spelled *e:* be (page 5)

1st READ

Comprehension Strategies

❶ **Making Connections** Teacher Prompt: *It does feel good to be out in the sunshine on a warm day. The sun doesn't just warm me outside, it brightens the way I feel inside too. It makes me want to work in my garden or take a walk in the park. What does the warm sunshine make you want to do?* **Possible Student Response** *The warm sunshine makes me want to go outside and play in the park.*

But the weather can't be nice all the time.

6

In fact, you should be glad it sometimes rains. 2
7

What's the Weather? Big Book, pp. 6–7

❷ **Asking Questions** Teacher Modeling: *I'm not glad when the rain spoils my plans to work in the garden, so I wonder why the text says we should be glad it sometimes rains. Let's continue reading to see whether we can answer our questions.*

Comprehension Check

Why do you think we should be glad when it rains? **Possible Answer** *We need rain to make things grow and for drinking water.*

Phonics

/ē/ spelled *e:* be (pages 6, 7)

Teacher Tip

GLOSSARY The word *weather* on page 6 can be found in the Glossary.

Nothing could grow without rain—no fruits or vegetables, no trees or grass or flowers. 3
A light rain is called a drizzle.
A little heavier rain is a shower.
8
9

What's the Weather? Big Book, pp. 8–9

Phonics

/ō/ spelled *o:* no (page 8)

Teacher Tip

RECREATIONAL READING Because it is important to read daily to your students, choose a book from the Additional Reading listed in the Unit Overview, and find a time during the day to read the book aloud to your students.

1st READ

Comprehension Strategies

3 Answering Questions Teacher Modeling: *This page answers my question. It tells us that we need rain sometimes so that vegetables, fruits, trees, grass, and flowers will grow. We use all these things in our lives. We eat fruits and vegetables. We climb trees or use them for houses. And we run and play on grass. Without rain, we wouldn't have these things. The author is right, we should be glad sometimes when it rains!*

Comprehension Check

What happens to plants when there is not enough rain? **Possible Answers** *Plants can't grow. They dry up or die.*

And if it's really pouring? That's a rainstorm. 4

10

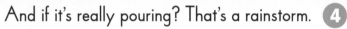

When the sky becomes very dark,
a thunderstorm could be on its way.

11

What's the Weather? Big Book, pp. 10–11

4 Clarifying Teacher Prompt: *I want to clarify the difference in the kinds of rain mentioned in the text—*drizzle, shower, *and* rainstorm. *The text says that a drizzle is a light rain and that a shower is a heavier rain. A rainstorm has the most rain of all. But a shower also means rain that falls for a short period of time. So the difference is how hard and how long it's raining. Is there anything you don't understand? Think of a question that might help you better understand what you are learning.* **Possible Student Responses** *Why does the sky become dark before a thunderstorm? I know thunderstorms don't just come at night. The picture looks like the sky is really full of clouds. Maybe that is why the sky gets dark.*

Phonics

/ē/ spelled *e:* becomes, be (page 11)

Teacher Tips

GLOSSARY The word *pouring* on page 10 can be found in the Glossary.

TYPES OF RAIN Explain to students that a rain shower is a short period of rain that can be light to very heavy. Rain showers can start and stop suddenly. Drizzle is light rain that may last for a short period of time or all day. Rainstorms have heavy rain and can also be short or long.

Even before the heavy rain reaches you, you might see flashes of lightning and hear deep, rolling thunder. 5

Lightning can be dangerous, so you'd better get indoors!

12 13

What's the Weather? Big Book, pp. 12–13

Phonics and Fluency

/ē/ spelled *e:* before (page 12); be (page 13)
/ē/ spelled *e_e:* Even (page 12)
/ō/ spelled *o:* rolling (page 12); so (page 13)

Differentiating Instruction **English Learner**

IF . . . students have difficulty with the differences in the meanings of *drizzle, shower, rainstorm,* and *thunderstorm,* **THEN . . .** during Workshop, reread these pages, and use the photographs to show the differences in the amount of rain falling in each kind of weather.

1st READ

Comprehension Strategies

5 Making Connections Teacher Modeling: *I've seen thunderstorms before, and I've noticed that before the rain gets to where I am, I see some flashes of lightning and hear far-off thunder. Have you seen lightning? What did you see and hear?* **Possible Answers** *I saw bright flashes of light streaks in the sky. The lightning was far away. After I saw lightning, I heard loud thunder a few seconds later.*

Comprehension Check

What is one sign that a thunderstorm might be on the way? **Possible Answers** *A storm might be on the way when the sky becomes dark. A storm might be on the way when you see lightning and hear thunder.*

Does it snow a lot where you live?
After a snowstorm, it's fun to go sledding . . .

14

or to build a snowman . . .
or to have a snowball fight. 6

15

What's the Weather? Big Book, pp. 14–15

6 Making Connections Teacher Prompt: *I haven't been sledding, but the children in the picture on page 14 make it look like fun. I have built snowmen, and that was a lot of fun! What does this remind you of doing?* **Possible Student Response** *I went sledding with my older brother once. The first time it was scary, but then it was fun.*

Teacher Tips

GLOSSARY The word *flashes* on page 12 can be found in the Glossary.

EFFECTIVE COMMUNICATION Remind students to speak clearly and use describing words when they make connections and share their personal experiences.

Phonics

/ō/ spelled *o:* go (page 14)

But it's not fun for the people who must shovel paths in the snow so they can leave their houses . . .

16

or who must dig their cars out of the snow.
A storm that brings this much snow is called a blizzard. 7

17

What's the Weather? Big Book, pp. 16–17

Concept/Question Board

Have students help you keep a list of the names of different kinds of weather and storms. Add the list to the **Concept/Question Board.** Encourage students to use these terms as they talk about weather. You may also want to have students bring in pictures of different kinds of weather to post on the Board.

Phonics

/ō/ spelled *o:* so (page 16)

1st READ

Comprehension Strategies

7 Clarifying Teacher Prompt: *The text says that a storm that brings enough snow to make people shovel paths and dig out their cars is called a blizzard. Can someone check the photographs to see just how much snow a blizzard can bring?* **Possible Student Response** *From the way the snow is piled on the car and the house in those pictures, I can see that a blizzard can bring a lot of snow. Do you understand the selection? Do you have any questions? They may help you better understand the selection.* **Possible Student Response** *I don't understand why the text says that snow is no fun. I love to play in the snow. When we reread and look at the picture, we can see that there is a lot of snow. Shoveling that much snow has to be hard work and could wear you out!*

Some storms bring sleet, a mixture of rain and snow.

You have to walk very carefully, because sleet can make the sidewalks icy and slippery.

18

In a hailstorm, raindrops freeze into ice before they reach the ground. Hail can be as big as this.

But don't worry, hailstones are almost always much smaller. 8

19

What's the Weather? Big Book, pp. 18–19

8 **Clarifying** Teacher Prompt: *The text has given us a great deal of information about snowstorms and ice storms. Let's stop and clarify to make sure that we understand the text. Can someone tell us the difference between a blizzard, sleet, and hail?* **Possible Student Response** *A storm with lots of snow is a blizzard. A mixture of snow and rain or ice and rain is called sleet. Hail is made of raindrops that freeze before they reach the ground. Do you have any questions? Clarifying may help you better understand the selection.* **Possible Student Response** *I didn't understand why the guy in the picture is using an umbrella when there is snow on the ground, but then I remembered that sleet is a mixture of snow and rain.*

Comprehension Check

How is a blizzard different from a thunderstorm? **Possible Answer** *A blizzard brings lots of snow, and a thunderstorm brings lots of rain.*

Writer's Notebook

Have students write the words *blizzard, sleet,* and *hail* and their definitions in their Writer's Notebooks. Then have students draw a picture and write a sentence correctly using one of the words.

Phonics

/ē/ spelled *e:* because (page 18); be (page 19)

Among the worst kinds of storms are hurricanes and tornados. A hurricane forms over the ocean. 9

When it reaches land, the winds may be so strong that they blow trees down . . .

20

the rains so heavy that they cause floods . . .

the waves so high that they wash houses and sand beaches into the sea.

21

What's the Weather? Big Book, pp. 20–21

Phonics

/ē/ spelled *e:* be (page 20)

/ō/ spelled *o:* tornadoes, over, ocean (page 20); so (pages 20, 21)

Teacher Tip

GLOSSARY The words *column* and *whirl* on page 22 can be found in the Glossary.

1st READ

Comprehension Strategies

9 **Clarifying** Teacher Modeling: *The text says hurricanes are among the worst kinds of storms. I don't understand what makes them so bad. I'll keep reading and see whether the photographs on these pages can help me understand. I see trees bending in the wind and lots of water and waves being blown over houses at a beach, so I think hurricanes are bad storms. They have strong winds and heavy rain, and they cause high waves that wash things away.*

Comprehension Check

So far, you have read about some storms with rain and some with snow. What do you think causes some storms to have rain while others have snow or ice? **Possible Answer** *The temperature; if it's warm, storms have rain. If it's cold, storms have snow and ice.*

A tornado forms over land. The winds whirl around in a tall, funnel-shaped column. 10
22

Cars, roofs, even entire houses can be sucked up off the ground by a tornado.

23

What's the Weather? Big Book, pp. 22–23

10 Asking Questions Teacher Prompt: *The text says that tornadoes whirl around in a tall, funnel-shaped column. I wonder what causes tornadoes to form like that. Does this text make you think of any questions?* **Possible Student Responses** *I wonder how big tornadoes are. I wonder how fast tornadoes move. Let's read on to see whether we can find answers.*

Phonics

/ē/ spelled *e_e:* even (page 23)

/ō/ spelled *o:* over (page 22); tornado (pages 22, 23)

Teacher Tip

HURRICANES AND TORNADOES These storms can be frightening to children, especially to those who have lived through them or seen their damage. Take note of any students who seem uncomfortable or upset by these pages, and talk to them privately during Workshop.

The government has a weather service that works to learn when a hurricane or tornado is forming and which way it is going. 11

The weather service tries to warn the people who live along the storm's path in time for them to leave the area or take shelter.

24

In this way, many lives are saved. But nothing can stop a tornado or a hurricane from causing damage to property and to the land.

25

What's the Weather? Big Book, pp. 24–25

Phonics

/ē/ spelled *e:* area (page 24)

/ō/ spelled *o:* going (page 24); tornado (pages 24, 25)

Teacher Tip

GLOSSARY The terms *government* and *weather service* on page 24 can be found in the Glossary.

1st READ

Comprehension Strategies

11 **Answering Questions** Teacher Prompt: *The text doesn't tell me what causes tornadoes to form, but now we know the government has a service that detects and observes when hurricanes or tornadoes are forming and where they might go. Maybe this service can also tell me how tornadoes form. I'll see whether I can find a Web site for more information. Did the text answer your questions? If so, share the information from the selection that answered your question.* **Possible Student Response** *I wondered how big tornadoes are. The text didn't answer my question yet. Maybe I can find my answer on a Web site too.*

So next time it's raining a little too hard for you to go out and play . . .

26

be thankful that it's just an ordinary storm. 12
27

What's the Weather? Big Book, pp. 26–27

12 Making Connections Teacher Prompt: *The next time it rains, I'll make a connection to this selection and be thankful the rain is ordinary and not a storm. Can you make a connection to the information in the selection?* **Possible Student Response** *I'll be glad for the rain because it helps things grow.*

Comprehension Check

What kind of damage can a hurricane do? **Possible Answer** *It can flood cities, wash away houses, and blow down trees.*

What kind of damage can a tornado do? **Possible Answer** *It can suck cars and houses off the ground.*

Phonics

/ō/ spelled *o:* so, go (page 26)

/ē/ spelled *e:* be (page 27)

Writer's Notebook

Have students draw a picture and write a sentence about "When a Storm Comes Up" in their Writer's Notebooks. Remind them of the different kinds of storms they read about, and brainstorm some things they might want to say about the selection. Encourage students to use the high-frequency words and selection vocabulary words in their sentences.

Monitor Progress

to Differentiate Instruction
Formal Assessment

During the discussion of the selection, note which students offer thoughtful responses and which students seem confused.

APPROACHING LEVEL

IF . . . students had difficulty understanding "When a Storm Comes Up,"	**THEN . . .** have them listen to the selection on the ***Listening Library CD*** during Workshop and summarize as they listen.

ON LEVEL

IF . . . students understood "When a Storm Comes Up,"	**THEN . . .** have them write one sentence about the selection, including the main idea and details.

ABOVE LEVEL

IF . . . students need a challenge,	**THEN . . .** have them write about their favorite parts of a storm from the selection.

Discussing the Selection

✦ As students discuss the selection, have them effectively apply listening and speaking strategies including taking turns, staying on topic, and facing the speaker. Ask students the following questions to check their comprehension of "When a Storm Comes Up":

- *Why can't the weather be sunny all the time? If we didn't have rain sometimes, then plants wouldn't grow.*
- *What does the government weather service do? It detects where storms are forming and which way they are going, and it warns people to take shelter or get out of the way.*
- *Why should you be thankful for an "ordinary" rainstorm? Ordinary rainstorms probably won't damage anything.*

✦ Also, have students return to the Focus Question on page 4. Read the question aloud, and have students answer and discuss the question. Encourage students to return to the text when answering their questions.

Discussing Strategy Use

Talk about comprehension strategies you modeled as you read the selection. Have students think about how they used strategies to help them better understand the selection.

- How did you clarify words or confusing passages? **Possible Answer** *I thought about other words in the sentence.*
- How did you make connections with information in the text? **Possible Answer** *I thought about how my dad watches weather forecasts to help me know what clothes to wear.*
- How did you use information in the text to answer questions? **Possible Answer** *When I had questions, I listened for information that would answer my questions.*

Purposes for Reading

Review the purposes set for reading "When a Storm Comes Up." Have students tell whether they met their purposes for reading. Have them identify information from the text that talks about the purposes:

- To find out about different kinds of storms
- To learn what causes storms

Vocabulary Review

- Review the selection vocabulary words with students by pointing to the words on the board or by displaying the transparency you made. Then call on students to use one of the words to answer the following questions:
  - Which word describes the shape of a tornado? *funnel*
  - Which word describes lightning? *flashes*
  - Which word means "to cover or protect?"*shelter*
- Next have students make lists of examples for each vocabulary word. For example, items having a funnel shape include an ice-cream cone, a megaphone, and a funnel for a car. Listing examples will help students relate the vocabulary to prior knowledge.

Print and Book Awareness

Print and Book Awareness

Punctuation: Ellipsis

- Review the use of the ellipsis with students. Ask a volunteer to explain when and why authors use these three dots. *An ellipsis is used to tell the reader to pause or that a sentence is going to be completed on another page and to build interest in the selection.*
- Say the following, pausing briefly for the ellipsis: *The rain poured down, and the lightning flashed, and then all of a sudden . . . the sun came out and the rain went away!* Point out that by pausing, you created some interest in what might happen next. Explain that authors often do the same when they write. Write the sentence on the board, using the ellipsis.
- Review pages in "When a Storm Comes Up" that contain an ellipsis and how the author uses it to build interest in the information in the text.

BIG Idea

What is weather?

After reading the selection, read the Big Idea question. Discuss with students how the selection helps answer this question.

Selection Vocabulary

flashes (page 12)
funnel (page 22)
shelter (page 24)

Teacher Tips

WORD BANK Have students tell you where to add the selection vocabulary words on the What's the Weather? Word Bank.

HIGH-FREQUENCY WORDS To help students review the high-frequency words they have learned, say some of the words aloud, and have students point to each one in the selection. Remind them to look at the High-Frequency Word Bank for help.

Phonics

Have students practice identifying sound/spellings from recent lessons. Turn to a page in the selection, and say a sound/spelling that appears on that page. Then have students point to the word with that sound/spelling. Remind them to look at ***Sound/Spelling Cards*** for help.

Language Arts

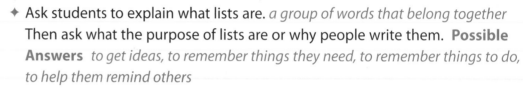

OBJECTIVES

Students will

- continue learning about writing lists.
- use pictures to generate ideas for writing.
- form the letters *u* and *m* correctly.
- control the size and spacing of letters.
- understand that the names of people and the pronoun *I* begin with capital letters.

MATERIALS

- ***What's the Weather? Big Book,*** pp. 4, 19
- ***Transparency*** 37
- ***Language Arts Big Book,*** p. 183
- Writer's Notebooks
- Portfolios

Traits of Good Writing

Ideas Writers use pictures to help generate ideas and details to add to their work.

Writing Lists

Prewriting

Teach—Using Pictures

- Ask students to explain what lists are. *a group of words that belong together* Then ask what the purpose of lists are or why people write them. **Possible Answers** *to get ideas, to remember things they need, to remember things to do, to help them remind others*
- Open the ***What's the Weather? Big Book*** to page 4 in "When a Storm Comes Up," and point to the picture of the lightning flash near a house. Remind students that pictures such as this one can help them get ideas for their writing.
- Model how to use a picture to help make a list of writing ideas by saying *This picture shows a thunderstorm. I think I'll write about what I might see, hear, and feel if I were in that house during the thunderstorm.* On the board, write the following:

Things I'd See	
dark clouds	lightning flashes
lots of rain	trees swaying in the wind

Guided Practice

Have students help you make lists of things you might hear or feel during a storm. **Possible Answers** *Hear: thunder, leaves blowing, rain against the window; Feel: wind, rain, the house shaking*

Penmanship

Alphabet Practice: The Letters *u* and *m*

Teach

- Review how to form lowercase *u* and *m* by writing the letters on the board as you describe the process. See the Level Appendix for penmanship models.
- If students need additional support, display the letter models on ***Transparency*** 37. Ask students how these two letters are similar. *Both have straight lines and curves.*

Guided Practice

- Have students follow your model to write each letter twice within the lines as they say the letter names. Tell them to underline their best *u* and *m*.
- Write the following words on the board: *must, jump, much, bump*. Read the words, and have students write them on handwriting paper to practice letter formation.
- Have students proofread their line by circling any incorrect words and making them better by rewriting them above or next to the original words. Then have them underline their best words.
- Look for additional opportunities during writing activities and in other subject areas to provide handwriting practice and to encourage and praise students when they form the letters *u* and *m* correctly.

Teacher Tip

CAPITAL LETTERS Although students are reviewing the formation of lowercase letters, tell them that as they write they should check the ***Sound/Spelling Cards*** to see how to form the capitals of *u* and *m*.

Differentiating Instruction English Learners

IF . . . students are native speakers of Spanish, Tagalog (Filipino), or certain other languages, **THEN . . .** they may need extra practice saying /u/ and associating it with the letter *u*. These languages lack the /u/ sound found in English.

Teacher Tip

WRITING LINK As students work on the writing activities in this unit, tell them to think about the capitalization rules they have learned for proper nouns and the pronoun *I*.

Differentiating Instruction **English Learners**

IF . . . students need extra help with capitalization, **THEN . . .** see ***English Learner Support Guide*** Unit 5 Lesson 2 to help them understand capitalizing proper nouns and the pronoun *I*.

Grammar, Usage, and Mechanics

Capitalization: Names of People and Pronoun *I*

Teach

- Display ***What's the Weather? Big Book*** page 19. Read the first three sentences, and then quickly review the rule for capitalizing the first word in a sentence.
- Then ask students to generate some names of people they know and write their responses on the board. Use their examples to explain that these are proper nouns and we capitalize them when writing.
- Write the following sets of words on the board, and ask students whether they notice anything similar about the nouns:

girl	Sarah Miller	boy	Jeff Potter
sister	Alex	brother	Mike
doctor	Dr. Wilson	dad	Mr. Chavez
mom	Mrs. Chavez	teacher	Ms. Abrams

- Point to *girl* and *Sarah,* and explain that *girl* is a common noun, but *Sarah* is a proper noun because it is the girl's name. Point to the capital *S* in *Sarah* and the *M* in *M*iller. Explain that the first and last names of a person always start with capital letters. Repeat the procedure for *boy* and *Jeff Potter, sister* and *Alex,* and *brother* and *Mike*.
- Next point to *doctor* and *Dr. Wilson,* and explain that *doctor* is a common noun. It can mean any doctor, but *Dr. Wilson* is the name of one specific doctor. *Dr.* and *Wilson* are proper nouns, so both start with a capital letter. Point to *D* and *W,* and ask students to name each letter. *capital D and capital W* Repeat the procedure for the other names.

Capitalization, cont.

- Finally, write the following sentence on the board: *I sat outside because I love the sun.* Have a volunteer circle each underlined *I*. Tell students that the pronoun *I* is another special name for a person that is always capitalized.
- Refer to ***Language Arts Big Book*** page 183 for more information and examples of these capitalization rules.

Guided Practice

Write the following sentences on the board, and then read them aloud as you point to each word. Have students tell which words require capital letters and why.

- Where do bonnie and her brother live? *Bonnie; name of one girl*
- When i called marty, mrs. daniels said he was doing homework. *The pronoun* I *is always a capital letter;* Marty *is the name of one boy;* Mrs. Daniels *is the name of a person.*

Apply

- Have students suggest sentences about three people in the class that use proper nouns or the pronoun *I*. Write their responses on the board, but leave out the correct capitalization; for example, *suzy, matt, and i went to dan's house.*
- Then have students copy the sentences from the board and edit them for correct capitalization in their Writer's Notebooks. **Possible Answer** *Suzy, Matt, and I went to Dan's house.*
- If time permits, have students search their Portfolios for sentences that use proper nouns and the pronoun *I*. Have them correct a few sentences using their new capitalization skills and then share their favorite sentence with a partner.

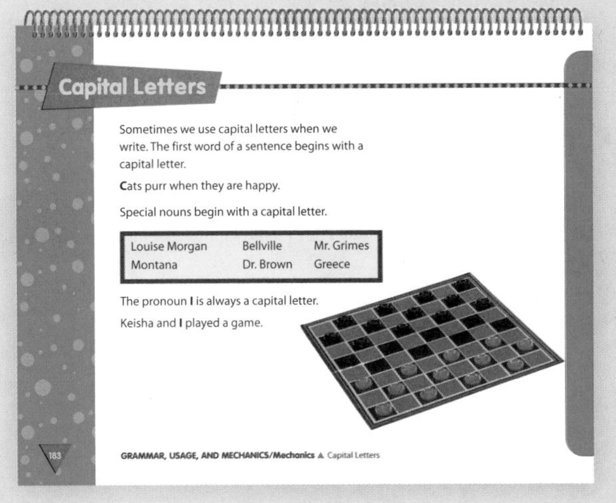
Capital Letters

Sometimes we use capital letters when we write. The first word of a sentence begins with a capital letter.

Cats purr when they are happy.

Special nouns begin with a capital letter.

Louise Morgan	Bellville	Mr. Grimes
Montana	Dr. Brown	Greece

The pronoun **I** is always a capital letter.

Keisha and **I** played a game.

183

GRAMMAR, USAGE, AND MECHANICS/Mechanics ▲ Capital Letters

Language Arts Big Book**,** p. 183

Preparing to Read

OBJECTIVES

Students will

- blend, spell, and read words that contain /ē/ spelled *ee* and *ea*.
- build fluency by reading ***Decodable*** 69.

MATERIALS

- Routines 1–4, 6–7, 9–11
- ***Sound/Spelling Card*** 28
- ***Skills Practice 1,*** pp. 183–184
- ***Decodable*** 69–*Summer Heat*

Daily Warm-Ups

Copy the Morning Message on the board or on chart paper. Have students answer the question. Read the message aloud, and discuss it with students. **Possible Answer** *One kind of storm is a tornado.*

MORNING MESSAGE

Good morning! Today we will reread the selection about storms. Storms happen when there is too much wind, rain, snow, or ice. What kind of storms can you name?

Daily Language Review

To review capitalization, write the following sentence on the board, or generate a similar one with students, and have them make corrections: i went to the store with kate. *I went to the store with Kate.*

Find a Word

- Write words with long-vowel spellings on the board. Name a long-vowel sound, and have a student go to the board and touch any word that contains the sound.
- Give a signal for the class to read the word. Then have a student identify and circle the spelling of the long vowel. Continue until all the words have been read. Words to use include the following:

like	safe	unit	me
open	cube	vote	complete

Introduce the Sound/Spelling

ROUTINE 1

/ē/ Spelled *ee* and *ea*

- Tell students that they are going to learn two more spellings for the /ē/ sound. Point to ***Sound/Spelling Card*** 28—Long E, and review the spellings *e* and *e_e.*
- Use Routine 1, introducing sounds and spellings, to introduce *ee* and *ea.* Point to the spellings *ee* and *ea* on the ***Sound/Spelling Card,*** and have students say the /ē/ sound. Explain that the *ea* and *ee* spellings can be found at the beginning, middle, or end of a word.
- Point to the *ea* spelling. Remind students that this spelling can also represent the /e/ sound, Card 5—Hen, as in *head, bread,* and *feather.*
- Have students use their index fingers to write the *ee* and *ea* spellings in the air, on their palms, or on the surface in front of them as they say the sound. Do this several times.
- Have students think of words with the /ē/ sound. Write the students' suggestions on the board.
- Review Card 28—Long E and the four spellings the students have learned—*e, e_e, ee,* and *ea.*

Sound/Spelling Card 28

Teacher Tips

SOUND/SPELLINGS You may want to remind students that there are not many words with /ē/ spelled *e_e.*

PHONEME SEGMENTATION Give students a word, and have them identify all the sounds in the word. For example, for *smile,* students would respond with /s/ /m/ /ī/ /l/. Have them segment other words, such as *silent, reason, feel,* and so on.

Teacher Tips

BLENDING In Lines 1 and 2, refer to Routine 2 for the sound-by-sound blending technique because this is the first time students are exposed to these spellings. If students are ready, refer to Routine 3 for the whole-word procedure for the remaining words on the lines.

SYLLABICATION To help students blend the words and build fluency, use the syllabication below of the multisyllable words on the word lines.

ea • gle   pea • nut   be • neath

Differentiating Instruction — English Learners

IF . . . students are native speakers of Spanish or certain other languages, **THEN . . .** they may pronounce the vowel sound in *dread* and *thread* like the /ā/ sound, and they may have difficulty hearing the contrast between the /e/ and /ā/ sounds. Use the following word pairs to help them master this contrast: *gate/get, late/let, mane/men, raid/red, sale/sell.*

Phonics

ROUTINE 2 ROUTINE 3 ROUTINE 4 ROUTINE 10 ROUTINE 11

Blending

Use Routine 2, sound-by-sound blending, Routine 3, whole-word blending, and Routine 4, blending sentences, to blend the words and sentences. Use Routine 10, closed syllables, and Routine 11, open syllables, to have students blend the multisyllable words.

Line 1	meet	meat	see	sea
Line 2	clean	neat	tree	three
Line 3	eat	leaf	sleep	streets
Line 4	bead	bread	treat	thread

Sentence 1	Dean, did you use two clean sheets to make the bed?
Sentence 2	Did you feel the cold breeze at the beach?

Line 1 **/ē/ spelled *ee* and *ea***

After students blend the words, point to and say *see* and *sea*, and ask them whether they hear a difference in how the words sound. *no* Remind students that some words that sound the same have different spellings and different meanings. Remind them that these words are called *homophones*. Point to the word *see*, and ask a student to say the word in a sentence. Do the same for *sea*. Repeat the procedure for *meet* and *meat*. Tell students to pay attention when they read and write to make sure they understand the meanings of homophones.

Lines 2–3 **/ē/ spelled *ee* and *ea***

Have students locate the /ē/ spelling in each word. Remind them that these spellings can occur at the beginning, middle, or end of a word.

Line 4 **/ē/ spelled *ea* and /e/ spelled *ea***

After blending these words, ask students to identify those that have the /e/ sound. *bread, thread*

Sentences 1–2

Before blending the sentences, write the word *two* on the board. Tell students they will see this word many times when they read, but the spellings do not make the sounds we expect. Read the word, repeat it, and have students repeat it. Then spell *two* together. Tell students this word refers to the number two. Ask volunteers to use the word *two* in sentences. Then write *two* on an index card, and add it to the High-Frequency Word Bank.

Developing Oral Language

To review the words, have students find and erase the following words:

- a word that rhymes with *deep* *sleep*
- a word that means "a large body of water" *sea*
- the number before *four* *three*
- the opposite of *messy* *neat*

Teacher Tip

LONG e CHART Ask students to add to the chart more words that have /ē/ spelled *ea* or *ee.*

Monitor Progress

to Differentiate Instruction

Formal Assessment

BLENDING Observe students to identify those who may need additional help. Work with them during Workshop.

APPROACHING LEVEL

IF . . . students are having difficulty with whole-word blending,	**THEN . . .** drop back to sound-by-sound blending.

ON LEVEL

IF . . . students are on level with blending,	**THEN . . .** make two lists of three words that contain the target spellings. Pair students, and tell them to take turns dictating words from their lists for their partner to spell.

ABOVE LEVEL

IF . . . students are ready for a challenge,	**THEN . . .** have them choose three of the words from the blending lines and write a sentence for each word.

Guided Practice

Help students complete ***Skills Practice 1*** pages 183–184 for practice with the /ē/ sound spelled *ee* and *ea* and for dictation. Review the sound/spellings at the top of page 183 together. Then have students read and write the words and sentence. Have the class chorally read the complete sentences. Students can use the bottom of page 184 for dictation.

UNIT 5 Lesson 3

Name Date

Directions: Write the words and sentence in the spaces provided.

Sounds and Spellings

Ee

ee
ea

Practice

peek peek clean clean

Can you teach me to read?

Can you teach me to read?

Skills Practice 1 • Phonics UNIT 5 • Lesson 3 183

UNIT 5 Lesson 3

Apply

Directions: Look at the picture. Then unscramble the words and write a complete sentence.

leaps. seal A

A seal leaps.

Dictation

lean dream
seed free
Lee eats a peach each week.

184 UNIT 5 • Lesson 3 Phonics • Skills Practice 1

Skills Practice 1, pp. 183–184

Dictation

ROUTINE 6 ROUTINE 7

Use Routine 6, whole-word dictation, and Routine 7, sentence dictation, with the following words and sentence. Be sure to have students proofread the words as they finish each line.

Line 1	lean	dream
Line 2	seed	free
Sentence	Lee eats a peach each week.	

Differentiating Instruction English Learners

IF . . . students have difficulty recording unknown dictated words, **THEN . . .** first write each word on the board and read its correct pronunciation.

Fluency/Reading a Decodable Book

ROUTINE 9

Core Decodable 69: *Summer Heat*

Phonics Focus: /ē/ Spelled *ee* and *ea*

High-Frequency Words

Review the high-frequency word *two* that students learned in Blending by writing it on the board, spelling the word, and having students say the word. Have a volunteer use the word in a sentence. Review other high-frequency words by pointing to them in the High-Frequency Word Bank and having students read them.

Reading the Decodable

- Follow Routine 9, reading a ***Decodable,*** as you read the story with students.
- Have students read the title, browse the story, and discuss what they think the story will be about.
- The first time through, have students read a page silently. Then have one student read it aloud. Repeat this procedure for each page.
- Reread the story at least twice, calling on various students to read. Then have the entire class do a choral reading of the story.

Responding

- After reading, be sure to talk about the story and answer any questions students have. Ask students to identify any difficult words in the book.
- Have students retell the story.

Teacher Tip

SOUND/SPELLING CARDS Remind students to refer to the ***Sound/Spelling Cards*** if they are unsure of a sound/spelling.

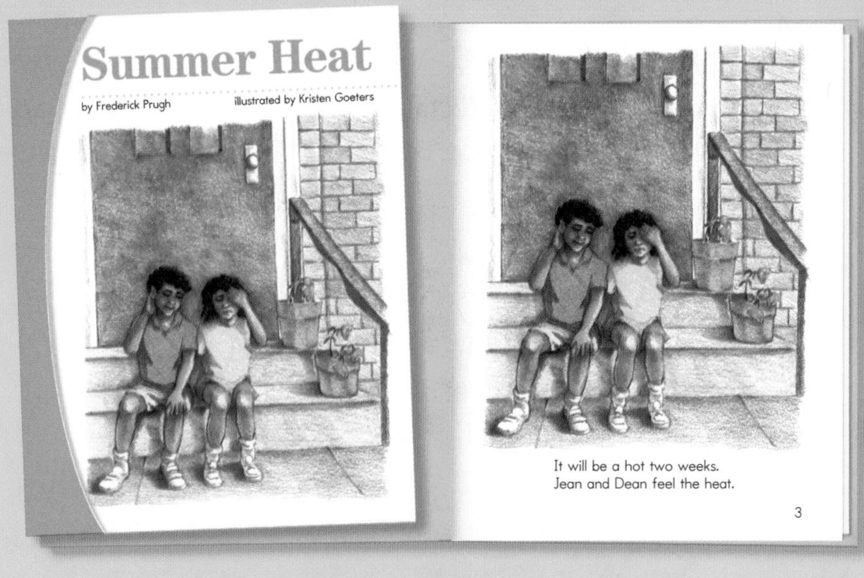
Summer Heat
by Frederick Prugh
illustrated by Kristen Goeters
It will be a hot two weeks.
Jean and Dean feel the heat.
3

"Time for the beach you two?" asks Mom.
"Yes!" yell Jean and Dean.
4
Cars fill the streets.
They drive east to the beach.
5

Jean and Dean reach the beach.
The two kids see and smell the sea.

6

Jean sticks her two feet in the sea.
Dean feels the sea breeze.

7

"Mom, the beach is neat," Jean calls.
"I agree," adds Dean.

8

Teacher Tip

GRAMMAR Have students find the plural nouns (add *s*) in the story.
weeks, streets, kids

✦ As students answer the following questions, make sure they focus on the words in the story rather than getting the answers by listening or from the pictures. Have students answer by pointing to and reading aloud the answers in the text:

- **Where do Jean and Dean go?** *to the beach*
- **What does Jean stick into the sea?** *her two feet*
- **What does Jean tell Mom?** *The beach is neat.*

Building Fluency

Have students build fluency by rereading ***Core Decodable*** 69 twice with a partner. The first time through, one partner should read the odd-numbered pages and the other partner the even-numbered pages. The second time through, they should switch pages. For additional practice with /ē/ spelled *ee* and *ea,* have students read ***Practice Decodable*** 58, *East or West*. Have students record their readings on their Personal Title sheets, noting the title of each book, the date, and any difficult words they encounter.

Core Decodable 69
Summer Heat

High-Frequency Word Introduced in Core Decodable 69

two

Previously Introduced High-Frequency Words

a	girl	just	them	you
after	go	like	then	
all	got	little	there	
am	had	look	they	
an	has	make	this	
and	have	of	to	
as	he	on	up	
ask	help	or	walk	
at	her	out	was	
big	him	over	we	
but	his	red	well	
call	I	ride	went	
can	if	said	were	
did	in	see	what	
do	is	she	when	
down	it	six	will	
for	its	that	with	
get	jump	the	yes	

Sound/Spelling Correspondences in Core Decodables

1. Pre-decodable
2. Pre-decodable
3. Pre-decodable
4. Pre-decodable
5. Pre-decodable
6. /s/ spelled *s*, /m/ spelled *m*, /a/ spelled *a*
7. /t/ spelled *t, tt*
8. Review
9. /d/ spelled *d*
10. /n/ spelled *n*
11. /i/ spelled *i*
12. /h/ spelled *h_*
13. Review
14. /p/ spelled *p*
15. /l/ spelled *l, ll*
16. /o/ spelled *o*
17. /b/ spelled *b*
18. Review
19. /k/ spelled *c*
20. /aw/ spelled *al*
21. /k/ spelled *k*, ■*ck*
22. /r/ spelled *r*
23. /f/ spelled *f, ff*
24. /s/ spelled *ss*
25. Review
26. /g/ spelled *g*
27. /j/ spelled *j*, ■*dge*
28. /u/ spelled *u*
29. /z/ spelled *z, zz*
30. /z/ spelled *_s*
31. Review
32. /ks/ spelled ■*x*
33. /e/ spelled *e*
34. -ed ending: /ed/, /d/
35. -ed ending: /t/
36. /e/ spelled *_ea_*
37. Review
38. /sh/ spelled *sh*
39. /th/ spelled *th*
40. /ch/ spelled *ch*, ■*tch*
41. /or/ spelled *or, ore*
42. Review
43. /ar/ spelled *ar*
44. /m/ spelled *_mb*
45. /w/ spelled *w_*
46. /hw/ spelled *wh_*
47. /er/ spelled *er, ir*
48. /er/ spelled *ur*
49. Review
50. Schwa
51. Review schwa
52. /ng/ spelled ■*ng*
53. /nk/ spelled ■*nk*
54. /kw/ spelled *qu_*
55. Review
56. /y/ spelled *y_*
57. /v/ spelled *v*
58. Syllable -le
59. /ā/ spelled *a* and *a_e*
60. Review
61. /ī/ spelled *i* and *i_e*
62. /s/ spelled *ce, ci_*
63. /j/ spelled *ge, gi_*
64. Review
65. /ō/ spelled *o* and *o_e*
66. /ū/ spelled *u* and *u_e*
67. Review
68. /ē/ spelled *e* and *e_e*
69. /ē/ spelled *ee* and *ea*

Decodable Book 69, inside back cover

OBJECTIVES

Students will

- review vocabulary by listening to and discussing the selection.
- apply the comprehension skill Main Idea and Details.
- discuss "When a Storm Comes Up."
- appreciate and talk about fine art.
- understand the science of a tornado.

MATERIALS

- ***What's the Weather? Big Book,*** pp. 4–27, 60
- Routine 12
- ***Transparency*** 20
- Writer's Notebooks

Teacher Tips

THEME CONNECTIONS Remind students that as you read, they should think about how the selection relates to the unit theme What's the Weather? and how it might help them generate ideas for Inquiry.

MATERIALS For the Science Connection experiment, you will need a large black trash bag and two feet of yarn or string.

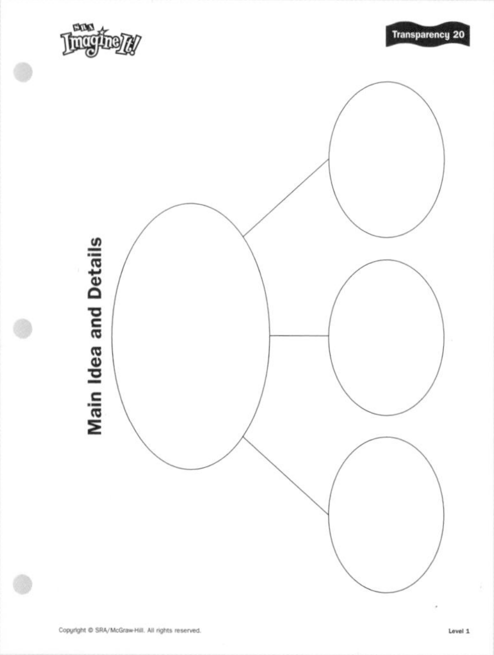

Transparency 20

Reading Recommendations

ROUTINE 12

Retelling

- Use Routine 12, reading the selection, to reread "When a Storm Comes Up." Before rereading the selection, have students use the pictures in the ***What's the Weather? Big Book*** to help them retell specific details heard in the selection. Prompt them as needed to ensure they recall each type of rain and storm mentioned in the selection. Remind students to use effective communication when they retell the facts of the selection. Have them use appropriate volume and describing words, and remind them to speak clearly.
- As students retell the selection, record the facts on chart paper or on the board. After the retelling, use the chart to review the selection.

2nd READ

Comprehension Skills

As you reread "When a Storm Comes Up," apply the comprehension skill Main Idea and Details. Use ***Transparency*** 20 to record the main ideas and details you and the students identify. You will be recording multiple main ideas and details. You may want to make multiple copies of the transparency so you can keep the information for each of the spreads as you read. Prepare the transparency in advance by labeling the large box Main Ideas and each small box Details.

2nd READ

Reading with a Writer's Eye

In this rereading of "When a Storm Comes Up," you will also discuss with students how the author uses photographs to add to or help explain the information in the text. Students will learn and talk about how illustrations or photographs help readers better understand a selection.

Review Vocabulary

- Have students use each selection vocabulary word in an oral sentence. You may want to use the following sentence starters:
  - There were many flashes from cameras when _____.
  - I used a funnel to pour _____ into _____.
  - We took shelter because _____.
- Help them expand their sentences by asking *who, what, where, when, why,* and *how* questions.
- You will introduce seven expanding vocabulary words to students as the selection is reread. These words are identified in boxes where they appear in the selection. As you come to each word in the selection, read to students the word, the definition, and the sample sentence. Understanding these words will help students better comprehend the selection.
- You may want to group students for further vocabulary review. Assign one vocabulary word to each group of students. Then have students think of as many words as possible that describe their group's vocabulary word. Then have them tell why or how each word relates to the vocabulary word. You may want to use the following example: *The word is* snow. *Words that describe snow: cold, wet, white, pretty, made up of flakes. The color of snow is white, and it feels cold and wet. I think snow is pretty. I see snow fall from the sky in tiny flakes.*

Monitor Progress to Differentiate Instruction

Formal Assessment

Observe students as they create sentences using selection vocabulary. Notice which students use vocabulary appropriately in their sentences and which students seem confused about the proper use of the word(s).

APPROACHING LEVEL

IF . . . students need additional practice with the vocabulary words, THEN . . . help them draw and label pictures to show the meaning of each word.

ON LEVEL

IF . . . students have difficulty with one of the vocabulary words, THEN . . . pair them, and have them play one of the games in ***eSkills.***

ABOVE LEVEL

IF . . . students need a challenge, THEN . . . have them use the vocabulary words to tell a story.

Selection Vocabulary

flashes (page 12)
funnel (page 22)
shelter (page 24)

Teacher Tip

HIGH-FREQUENCY WORDS Before rereading the selection, remind students of the high-frequency words for this selection. The following high-frequency words appear in the selection: *it, to, on, a, out, in, but, the, can't, all, you, or, is, little, and, if, when, its, see, of, can, get, go, after, have, they, that, this, walk, make, big, over, down, up, has, them, for, just, an.*

Monitor Progress to Differentiate Instruction

Formal Assessment

MAIN IDEA AND DETAILS As students identify main ideas and details, note who is participating and understanding the comprehension skill.

APPROACHING LEVEL

IF . . . students need additional practice with the comprehension skill Main Idea and Details, THEN . . . have them practice identifying main idea and details with you during Workshop.

ON LEVEL

IF . . . students are able to apply the comprehension skill, THEN . . . have them identify main ideas and details of a selection from a previous unit.

ABOVE LEVEL

IF . . . students need a challenge, THEN . . . have them listen to or read a new selection, applying the skill as they read.

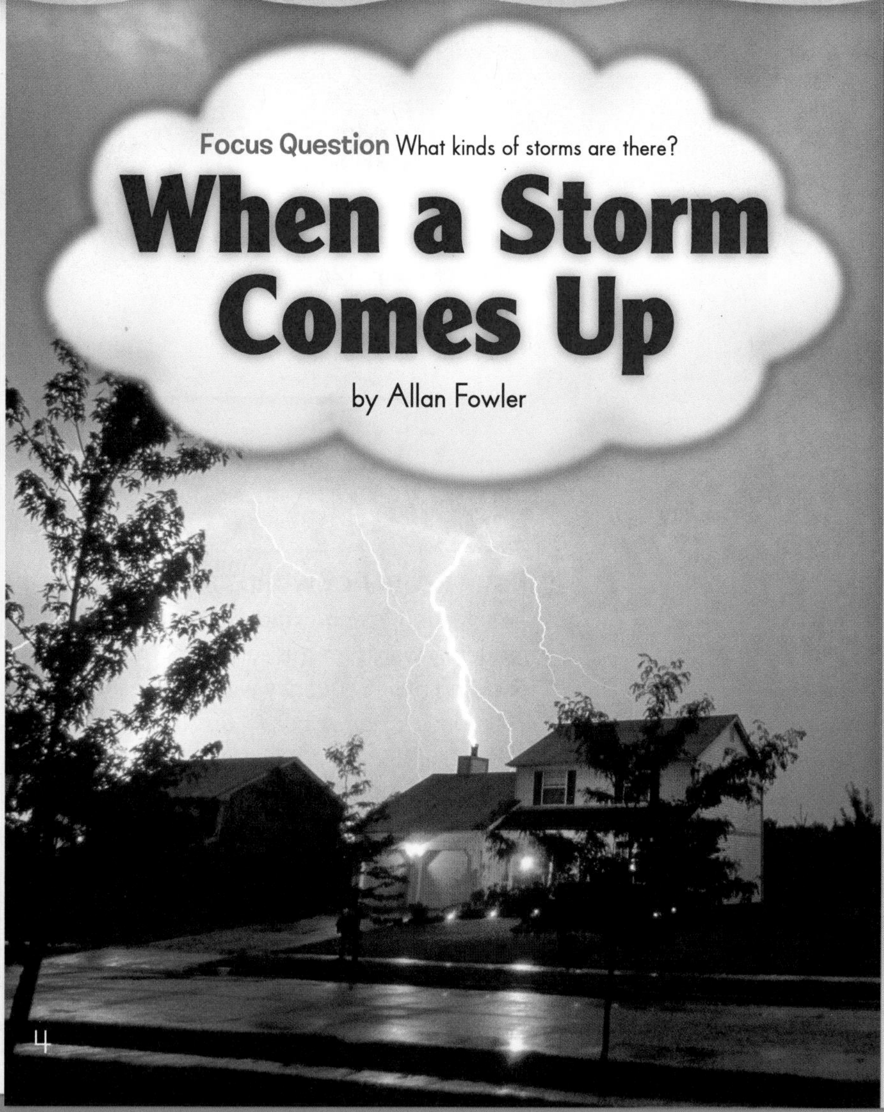
Focus Question What kinds of storms are there?
When a Storm Comes Up
by Allan Fowler
4

It feels good to be out in the sunshine on a warm day.

5

What's the Weather? Big Book, pp. 4–5

Teacher Tips

SENTENCE BOUNDARIES Remind students about the focus of recent Print and Book Awareness lessons—sentence boundaries. Have students identify the beginning and end of the sentence. Then have them identify the type of sentence.

LISTEN ATTENTIVELY Tell students that they will discuss important information from the selection during this second reading. Remind students to listen attentively so they can participate in discussion using details from the text.

2nd READ

Comprehension Skills

Main Idea and Details

After reading these pages, remind students that readers better understand what they are reading if they can identify the main ideas in the selection as well as the details that add to or support each of those ideas. Point to the photograph and reread the sentence on page 5. Tell students that the picture supports the author's main idea that being in the sunshine on a warm day feels good. Ask students to find details in the picture or text that support this main idea. Have them tell you where to record their responses on the transparency. Leave room to record information throughout the reading. **Possible Answers** *The children are jumping in the sand; they have happy expressions.*

But the weather can't be nice all the time.

6

In fact, you should be glad it sometimes rains.
7

What's the Weather? Big Book, pp. 6–7

Reading with a Writer's Eye

2nd READ

Text-Illustration Relationship

- Tell students that "When a Storm Comes Up" is an example of informational writing. The author, Allan Fowler, wants his readers to have information about different kinds of storms. To help readers understand information, Fowler uses photographs to show each kind of storm. The photos help explain or add to what is stated in the text.
- Ask students to look at the photograph on page 7. *The text says you should be glad when it sometimes rains. How does the author use a photograph to show this idea?* *The child is happy in the rain.*

Teacher Tip

PLURAL NOUNS You may want to remind students about the focus of recent grammar lessons—plural nouns. Encourage students to identify the plural noun and the plural spelling on these pages.

Nothing could grow without rain—no fruits or vegetables, no trees or grass or flowers.
8
A light rain is called a drizzle.
A little heavier rain is a shower.
9

What's the Weather? Big Book, pp. 8–9

Teacher Tip

FLUENCY Although students are not expected to read "When a Storm Comes Up," your reading will serve as a good model of fluent reading.

2nd READ

Comprehension Skills

Main Idea and Details

- After reading page 8, ask students to identify the main idea and the details that support this idea. *Main idea: Rain helps things grow. Without rain, nothing would grow. Details: Fruits, vegetables, trees, grass, and flowers wouldn't grow without rain.*

- After reading pages 9 and 10, ask students to identify the main idea and the details that support this idea. *Main idea: Rain comes in many different ways. Details: Sometimes rain is a drizzle, a shower, or a rainstorm.*

- Have students tell you where on the transparency to record each response.

And if it's really pouring? That's a rainstorm.
10

When the sky becomes very dark,
a thunderstorm could be on its way.
11

What's the Weather? Big Book, pp. 10–11

Reading with a Writer's Eye

2nd READ

Text-Illustration Relationship

- Ask students to look at the photographs on page 9. Remind them that the text says a drizzle is a light rain, and a shower is a heavier rain. Ask how the author uses photographs to show the difference between a drizzle and a shower. *The child in the photograph of a drizzle is standing in the light rain; the children in the shower are huddling under an umbrella.*
- Ask students to look at the photograph on page 10. Remind them that the text says a rainstorm happens when it is pouring. Ask how the author uses the photograph and text to show the rainstorm. **Possible Answers** *The people are running. The umbrella doesn't look like it is working well. The hair looks like it is wet and flying around.*

Teacher Tip

PHOTOGRAPHS It may be helpful to have students describe what they see in these photographs. Discussing what they see can help them better understand the text-photograph relationship.

Even before the heavy rain reaches you, you might see flashes of lightning and hear deep, rolling thunder.

12

Lightning can be dangerous, so you'd better get indoors!

13

What's the Weather? Big Book, pp. 12–13

Teacher Tip

PLURAL NOUNS You may want to remind students about the focus of recent grammar lessons—plural nouns. Encourage students to identify the plural nouns and the plural spelling on these pages.

2nd READ

Comprehension Skills

Main Idea and Details

- After reading pages 11 and 12, explain the main idea of this text: Certain signals tell us when a thunderstorm is on the way. Ask students to identify those signals and the details that support this idea. *The sky becomes dark; you might see lightning and hear thunder.*
- Have students look at the photograph on page 13 as you reread the text. Ask students to identify the main idea of the text. *Lightning can be dangerous.*
- After reading pages 14 and 15, ask students to identify the main idea of the text. *Snow can be fun after a snowstorm.*
- Have students tell you where on the transparency to record each response.

Does it snow a lot where you live?
After a snowstorm, it's fun to go sledding . . .

14

or to build a snowman . . .
or to have a snowball fight.

15

What's the Weather? Big Book, pp. 14–15

Reading with a Writer's Eye

2nd READ

Text-Illustration Relationship

- Ask students to look at the photograph on page 13. Ask how the author uses a photograph to support the idea that lightning can be dangerous. *It shows lightning flashing behind a house.*
- Ask students to look at the photographs on pages 14 and 15. Ask how the author uses the photographs and text to support the idea that it can be fun after a snowstorm. **Possible Answer** *All the people are smiling. They look like they are having fun.*

Teacher Tips

WEATHER DRILLS Use the reading of this selection as an opportunity to review with students any severe weather drills that are in place at your school.

PRINT AND BOOK AWARENESS Point to the ellipsis on page 14. Explain that authors sometimes use these three dots to show that the reader should pause or that a sentence is continued on another page. Explain that doing this can add interest to the reading. Reread the sentence, pausing at the ellipsis before continuing the sentence on page 15. Pause again for the ellipsis on that page, and then read to the end of the sentence.

But it's not fun for the people who must shovel paths in the snow so they can leave their houses . . .

16

or who must dig their cars out of the snow. A storm that brings this much snow is called a blizzard.

17

What's the Weather? Big Book, pp. 16–17

Teacher Tip

PUNCTUATION Have students find the ellipsis on page 16. Help students recall that these three dots tell the reader to pause or that a sentence is continued on another page. Reread the sentence, pausing at the ellipsis before continuing the sentence on page 17.

2nd READ

Comprehension Skills

Main Idea and Details

✦ After reading pages 16 through 19, ask students the following:

- *What is the main idea of the text? Sometimes storms are dangerous and not fun.*
- *What details support this idea? People have to shovel a path from their houses. They have to dig out their cars from the snow. Sleet makes sidewalks slippery. Some hail can be big.*

✦ Have students tell you where on the transparency to record each response.

Some storms bring sleet, a mixture of rain and snow.

You have to walk very carefully, because sleet can make the sidewalks icy and slippery.

18

In a hailstorm, raindrops freeze into ice before they reach the ground. Hail can be as big as this.

But don't worry, hailstones are almost always much smaller.

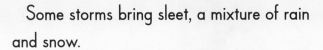

19

What's the Weather? Big Book, pp. 18–19

Reading with a Writer's Eye

2nd READ

Text-Illustration Relationship

- Ask students to look at the photographs on pages 16 and 17. Ask how the author uses photographs to support the idea that it is not always fun after a snowstorm. **Possible Answer** *The people look cold, and the ones who are shoveling a path and digging out a car look like they are working hard.*
- Point to the photographs on pages 18 and 19. Ask how the author uses photographs to support the idea that sleet and hail can be dangerous. **Possible Answer** *The man with the umbrella is walking carefully so he won't fall. Two different pictures show sizes of hail.*

Teacher Tip

SENTENCE BOUNDARIES Remind students about the focus of recent Print and Book Awareness lessons—sentence boundaries. Have students identify the beginning and end of the sentence. Then have them identify the type of sentence.

Day 3 Reading and Responding

Among the worst kinds of storms are hurricanes and tornados. A hurricane forms over the ocean.

When it reaches land, the winds may be so strong that they blow trees down . . .

20

the rains so heavy that they cause floods . . .

the waves so high that they wash houses and sand beaches into the sea.

21

What's the Weather? Big Book, pp. 20–21

Teacher Tips

PRINT AND BOOK AWARENESS Have students find the ellipsis on page 20. Remind students that ellipses tell the reader to pause or that a sentence is continued on another page. Reread the sentence, pausing at the ellipsis before continuing the sentence on page 21.

PLURAL NOUNS You may want to remind students about the focus of recent grammar lessons—plural nouns. Encourage students to identify the plural nouns and the plural spelling on these pages.

2nd READ

Comprehension Skills

Main Idea and Details

- Ask students to identify the main ideas of the text on pages 20 through 23. *Hurricanes and tornadoes are among the worst kinds of storms. Hurricanes form over water and can cause a lot of damage.*
- Ask students what details support the idea that hurricanes are bad storms. *Hurricanes cause flooded streets and high waves that wash away beaches.*
- Have students tell you where on the transparency to record each response.

A tornado forms over land. The winds whirl around in a tall, funnel-shaped column.

22

Cars, roofs, even entire houses can be sucked up off the ground by a tornado.

23

What's the Weather? Big Book, pp. 22–23

Reading with a Writer's Eye

2nd READ

Text-Illustration Relationship

Point to the photographs on pages 20 and 21. Ask how the photographs support the idea that hurricanes are bad storms. **Possible Answers** *The cars are stuck in high water. The waves are huge. The winds look strong because they are blowing the trees sideways.*

Expanding Vocabulary

whirl to spin quickly in a circle (page 22)
I like to *whirl* around when I dance.

column a cylinder-shaped structure (page 22)
The *column* looks like a juice can.

entire all or completely (page 23)
Because she was hungry, she ate the *entire* meal.

sucked Past tense of **suck:** to draw in (page 2)
He *sucked* the juice through the straw.

The government has a weather service that works to learn when a hurricane or tornado is forming and which way it is going.

The weather service tries to warn the people who live along the storm's path in time for them to leave the area or take shelter.

24

In this way, many lives are saved. But nothing can stop a tornado or a hurricane from causing damage to property and to the land.

25

What's the Weather? Big Book, pp. 24–25

Expanding Vocabulary

government the group of people in charge of the country (page 24)

The *government* has made new rules about voting.

forming taking shape (page 24)

The students are *forming* a circle.

property something that is owned (page 25)

My mom's *property* includes a barn and a house.

2nd READ

Comprehension Skills

Main Idea and Details

- After reading page 24, ask students to identify the main idea. *The government's weather service helps people learn about storms.*
- Have them recall details from the text that support this idea. *The weather service monitors conditions to learn when a storm is forming and which way it is going. It warns people so they have time to find shelter or to get out of the way of a storm.*
- Have students tell you where on the transparency to record each response.

So next time it's raining a little too hard for you to go out and play . . .

26

be thankful that it's just an ordinary storm.
27

What's the Weather? Big Book, pp. 26–27

2nd READ

Reading with a Writer's Eye

Text-Illustration Relationship

Point to the photograph on page 25. Read the sign, "National Hurricane Center." Ask students how the author uses photographs and text together to tell about the weather. **Possible Answer** *It shows how someone at the weather center works to learn about storms.*

Checking Comprehension

Ask students the following questions to check their comprehension of "When a Storm Comes Up":

- *How are hurricanes and tornadoes alike? They have strong winds and cause damage.*
- *How are hurricanes and tornadoes different? Hurricanes form over water, and tornadoes form over land.*

Teacher Tip

PRINT AND BOOK AWARENESS Have students find the ellipsis on page 26. Encourage them to state the purpose of these three dots.

Technology

LISTENING LIBRARY Have students listen to the selection again on the ***Listening Library CD.***

Audio CD

Teacher Tip

WORD BANK Encourage students to use words from the What's the Weather? Word Bank when discussing the fine art in this unit.

Fine Art

- Display ***What's the Weather? Big Book*** page 60. Have students focus attention on *Beach Scene* by William James Glackens. Tell students they can explore the unit theme What's the Weather? through images such as this one as well as through reading. Have them talk about the painting, mentioning anything they see in it that interests or puzzles them. Have students share their thoughts and opinions about this piece of fine art, including whether they like it or not and why. Ask them how the art makes them feel.

What's the Weather?, p. 60

- Share with students any information about the artist and the painting that you choose. For example, you might tell them that Glackens was an American artist who lived from 1870 to 1938 and liked to paint scenes that involved people doing ordinary things.

- Ask students the following questions to help them understand the fine art connection to weather:
  - *What is the setting for the painting?* *a beach*
  - *What different things are people doing?* *wading in water, walking on the beach, sitting under an umbrella*
  - *What is the weather like?* *sunny and warm*
  - *What season do you think it is?* *summer*
  - *How does the painting fit with the What's the Weather? theme?* **Possible Answers** *The painting takes place on a beach, where it is warm. The painting shows warm weather.*

Science Connection

Hot Air Rising

- Discuss with students the effect of the sun on Earth. Have them talk about how it feels when the sun shines on them. **Possible Answers** *It feels hot. It makes my skin warm.* Tell students that in this experiment, they will learn two very important things about weather. First, they will learn that the sun heats things on Earth. The heated things on Earth and the sun work together to heat the air. Second, they will learn that hot air rises.
- To begin your experiment, in an air-conditioned room or a cool area, open and then gather air in a black trash bag. With the bag fully inflated, tie the end in a tight knot to seal in the air. Next, tie a length of yarn or string tightly above the knot. Tie the trash bag to a sunny spot outside. The string or yarn should be long enough to allow the bag to rest on the ground, but it must be long enough to allow the balloon to rise into the air.
- Now tell students that their experiment may take several hours. Continue checking the trash bag as the day progresses. Ideally, the trash bag will be heated by the sun, causing the air inside the bag to heat up and expand. The hot air inside the bag weighs less than the cooler air outside the bag, which causes the bag to float into the air.

Teacher Tips

WEATHER PERMITTING For this experiment, the weather should be sunny with little to no wind. If it is sunny but too windy, placing the trash bag in a sunny location inside is also an option.

LITERATURE Have students select age- and ability-appropriate fiction and nonfiction materials to read based on interest and teacher recommendations. By encouraging students to read daily, they will begin building a core base of knowledge about the unit theme.

Concept/Question Board

Have students illustrate and label multiple stages of the experiment such as gathering cold air, connecting the bag of cold air to a pole outside, and the sun heating the bag of air and making the bag rise. Tell them to post their illustrations on the Board.

OBJECTIVES

Students will

- prepare a draft of a list.
- use pictures to generate writing ideas.
- review that the names of people and the pronoun *I* begin with capital letters.
- learn that names of special places and special things also begin with capital letters.

MATERIALS

- ***What's the Weather? Big Book,*** p. 14
- ***Skills Practice 1,*** pp. 179, 185–186

Differentiating Instruction English Learners

IF . . . students are unfamiliar with snow and related activities, **THEN . . .** use pictures or actions to show the meanings of the activities that students name. As you model making a snowman, ask a proficient English speaker to draw pictures that show what you are saying.

Teacher Tip

WARM CLIMATES If students have never experienced snow because of the climate in your area, they may have difficulty relating to this activity. Some students may adapt well to the unfamiliar, but if you think your students will struggle, have them make lists using a warm-weather topic instead. For example, they could list ways to decorate a sand castle.

Writing Lists

Drafting

Teach

- Open the ***What's the Weather? Big Book*** to the photograph on page 14 of children on a sled. Remind students that pictures such as this one can help them get ideas for their writing.
- Model making a list as you say *The children in this picture are playing in the snow. I'd like to make a list of things you can do outside in the snow.* Ask students to look at the photograph to help them think of ideas for some winter activities. Then write their answers in a list on the board. **Possible Answers** *build a snowman, ski, ice-skate* If no one mentions building a snowman, add it to the list yourself.

Guided Practice

- Next, start a new list on building a snowman that students will finish as a draft. **Teacher Modeling:** *Now I'll make a list on how we could build a snowman. First, we would make big snowballs.* (write: make big snowballs) *Then, we would put one snowball on top of the other.* (write: put one snowball on the other) *Then, we would shape the snowballs to look like a real person.* (write: shape snowman) *Finally, we would decorate the snowman.* (write: decorate snowman)
- Conclude by modeling how to decide on and write a title for the list, such as "Building a Snowman." Discuss the list with students, and ask them to suggest more things they might do to make a snowman. Keep the list on the board for the Lesson 4 writing activity.

Writing Lists, cont.

Apply

- Have students fill out the audience and purpose sections on ***Skills Practice 1*** page 179. Then have them use the space at the bottom of page 179 to organize a draft of their lists for building a snowman. Tell them to copy the title from the board and then to use any items from your list that they choose. They can also add their own items. Explain that this is just a draft, which they will revise and complete later.
- As students draft their lists, tell them to think about what they learned during the Reading with a Writer's Eye activity earlier in the day. Remind them that an author uses illustrations to add to or help explain the information in the text so that readers better understand the selection. Tell them that they may want to start brainstorming an illustration that would describe the subject of their list.

Monitor Progress to Differentiate Instruction

Formal Assessment

LISTS As students draft their lists, note their progress.

APPROACHING LEVEL

IF . . . students need additional practice with making lists, **THEN . . .** help them make simple lists such as the names of the seasons or kinds of weather.

ON LEVEL

IF . . . students complete the activity without difficulty, **THEN . . .** give them pictures from magazines that show weather-related activities, such as children raking leaves or planting a garden, and help them make lists based on what they see.

ABOVE LEVEL

IF . . . students need a challenge with making lists, **THEN . . .** have them draw pictures of weather-related activities, such as sledding or playing in the park, and help them make a list of what they included in their pictures.

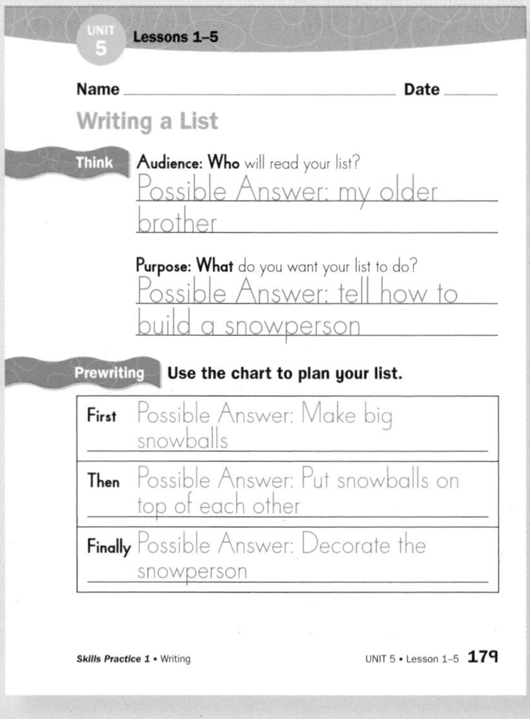
UNIT 5 Lessons 1–5

Name ______ Date ______

Writing a List

Think

Audience: Who will read your list?
Possible Answer: my older brother

Purpose: What do you want your list to do?
Possible Answer: tell how to build a snowperson

Prewriting Use the chart to plan your list.

First	Possible Answer: Make big snowballs
Then	Possible Answer: Put snowballs on top of each other
Finally	Possible Answer: Decorate the snowperson

Skills Practice 1 • Writing UNIT 5 • Lesson 1–5 179

Skills Practice 1, p. 179

Differentiating Instruction **English Learners**

IF . . . students need extra help with capitalization, **THEN . . .** see ***English Learner Support Guide*** Unit 5 Lesson 3 to help them understand capitalizing proper nouns and the pronoun *I*.

Teacher Tips

TIME MANAGEMENT If students have difficulty finishing both ***Skills Practice 1*** review pages in today's lesson, give them time to finish during Workshop, or have them take the pages home for homework.

WRITING LINK As students work on the writing activities in this unit, tell them to think about the capitalization rules they have learned for proper nouns and the pronoun *I*.

Grammar, Usage, and Mechanics

Capitalization: Special Things, Special Places

Teach

- Ask students to share some names of people in the school or in their families. Then ask them to explain what they should do to the first letter when writing these names to review capitalization. Conclude the review by asking them what they should do when writing the pronoun *I*.
- Next, ask students to think of names of special things or special places in your area such as schools, parks, or landmarks. Write their suggestions on the board, and use them to explain that the names of special things and special places should also always be capitalized when writing.
- Ask students to think of famous things or places they have heard of from around the world. Write their suggestions on the board along with the common noun that goes with each name. Examples:

landmark	Grand Canyon;	boat	Titanic;
ballpark	Wrigley Field;	bridge	Golden Gate Bridge;

- Read the pairs of words, and explain that the first word in each is a common noun, and the second word is the proper name of one such common noun. Ask students what the difference is between each set of words, and then have volunteers circle the capital letter used in each proper noun. If necessary, explain that only the name is capitalized when writing about a special place or thing.

Guided Practice

- Write the sentences below on the board, and read them aloud with the class. Have students come to the board to identify and change the letters that should be capitalized and tell why.
  - luke goes to east lake school. L *in* Luke, *it is a name;* E, L, *and* S *in* East Lake School, *it is place.*
  - sue and i visited the alamo last summer. S *in* Sue, *it is a name;* I *is a pronoun;* A *in* alamo, *it is a place.*

Apply

- Help students begin ***Skills Practice 1*** pages 185–186 to review the capitalization skills covered in Lessons 7 and 8. Do the first few practice problems as a class, and then answer any questions as they complete the pages. If necessary, review the instructions with students to help with any reading or decodability issues.
- If time permits, have students use some of the examples they have suggested today to compose three new sentences that feature correctly capitalized proper nouns. Have them share their favorite sentences with partners.
- Remind students that when drafting or revising, they should think about and use the capitalization rules they have learned so far this year. Tell them to make sure they have capitalized any proper nouns or the pronoun *I* in their snowman lists.

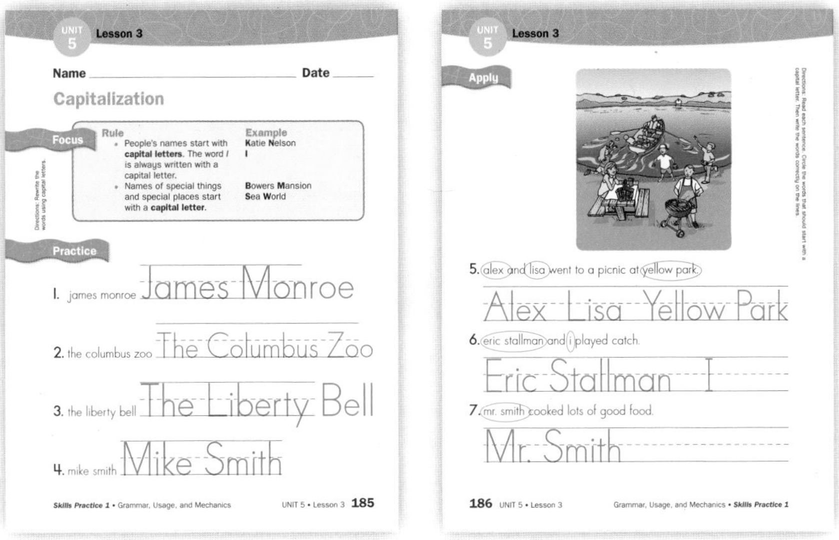
UNIT 5 Lesson 3

Name Date

Capitalization

Focus

Rule	Example
People's names start with **capital letters**. The word *I* is always written with a capital letter.	Katie Nelson I
Names of special things and special places start with a **capital letter**.	Bowers Mansion Sea World

Practice

1. james monroe James Monroe
2. the columbus zoo The Columbus Zoo
3. the liberty bell The Liberty Bell
4. mike smith Mike Smith

Skills Practice 1 • Grammar, Usage, and Mechanics UNIT 5 • Lesson 3 185

UNIT 5 Lesson 3

Apply

5. alex and lisa went to a picnic at yellow park.
Alex Lisa Yellow Park
6. eric stallman and i played catch.
Eric Stallman I
7. mr. smith cooked lots of good food.
Mr. Smith

186 UNIT 5 • Lesson 3 Grammar, Usage, and Mechanics • Skills Practice 1

Skills Practice 1, pp. 185–186

Monitor Progress

to Differentiate Instruction

Formal Assessment

CAPITALIZATION As students practice identifying proper nouns, note who can find these nouns easily and remember to capitalize the first letter.

APPROACHING LEVEL

IF . . . students need additional practice with capitalization skills,	**THEN . . .** have them complete ***Reteach 1*** pages 139–140.
IF . . . students have difficulty with the concept after working on the ***Reteach 1*** pages,	**THEN . . .** complete ***Intervention Guide*** Unit 5 Lesson 3 or play the Capitalization game from the ***Workshop Kit*** with them during Workshop.

ON LEVEL

IF . . . students understand the concept but need practice,	**THEN . . .** have them play the Capitalization game from the ***Workshop Kit,*** or compose three sentences using proper nouns.

ABOVE LEVEL

IF . . . students need to challenge their capitalization skills,	**THEN . . .** have them complete ***Challenge Activities 1*** page 70.

OBJECTIVES

Students will
- blend, spell, and read words that contain /ē/ spelled *ee* and *ea*.
- identify compound words.

MATERIALS
- Routines 3–4, 8, 10–11
- ***Sound/Spelling Card*** 28
- ***Skills Practice 1,*** pp. 187–188

Teacher Tip

MORNING MESSAGE If it is raining now, have students describe what they hear.

Differentiating Instruction English Learners

IF . . . students have difficulty pronouncing the letter *r,* **THEN . . .** keep in mind that the English /r/ differs from the sound represented by *r* in most other languages, so pronunciation of this sound is difficult for many English Learners. Give students ample opportunities to listen to English speakers pronouncing words with *r* and to practice echoing their classmates.

Daily Warm-Ups

Copy the Morning Message on the board or on chart paper. Have students answer the questions. Read the message aloud, and discuss it with students. **Possible Answer** *I have listened to the rain. It sounded like gentle drops from a sink.*

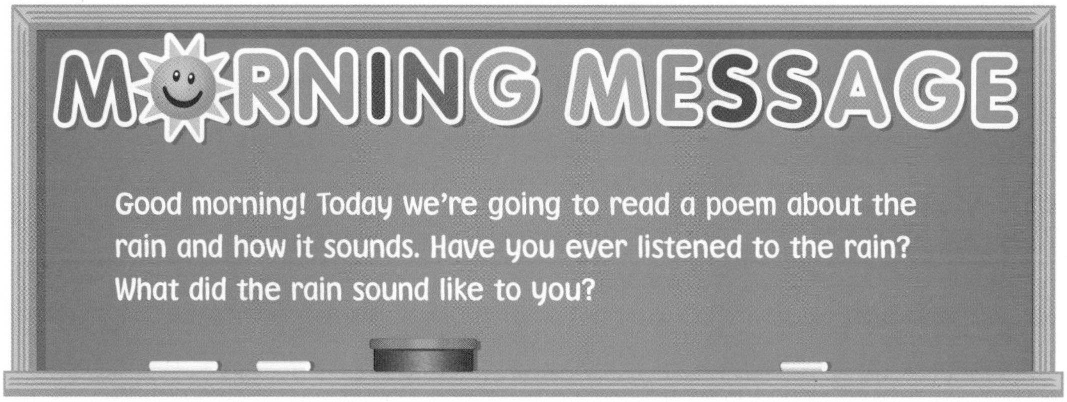
MORNING MESSAGE
Good morning! Today we're going to read a poem about the rain and how it sounds. Have you ever listened to the rain? What did the rain sound like to you?

Daily Language Review

To review capitalization, write the following sentence on the board, or generate a similar one with students, and have students make corrections: alex and i will help mrs. smith rake leaves. *Alex and I will help Mrs. Smith rake leaves.*

Quick Change Game

Tell students that they will change one word to another by changing spellings. Write the word *strap* on the board, and have students tell you what new word to write.

- Write *strap* without the *s*. *trap*
- Change the *p* in *trap* to *y*. *tray*
- Drop the *t* in *tray*. *ray*
- Change the *r* in *ray* to *p*. *pay*
- Add *l* after *p* in *pay*. *play*

Phonics

ROUTINE 3 ROUTINE 4 ROUTINE 10 ROUTINE 11

Review: /ē/ Spelled *ee* and *ea*

Blending

- Point to ***Sound/Spelling Card*** 28—Long E to review the sound and the *ee* and *ea* spellings. Point to the *ee* and *ea* spellings on the card, and remind students that these are two ways to spell /ē/. Remind students that these spellings can be found at the beginning, middle, or end of a word.
- Use Routine 3, whole-word blending, and Routine 4, blending sentences, to blend the words and sentences. Use Routine 10, closed syllables, and Routine 11, open syllables, to have students blend the multisyllable words.

Line 1	seam	steam	heel	wheel
Line 2	week	weak	beat	beet
Line 3	teach	teeth	be	bee
Line 4	weekend	nineteen	teammate	seashore

Sentence 1	The seal eats two fish.
Sentence 2	Eve will make green beans or rice.

Lines 1–2 **/ē/ spelled *ea* and *ee***

- Have students give the meaning of each word on Line 1. Have them notice that adding a letter changes a word and its meaning.
- Remind students that some words are homophones—they sound the same but have different spellings and different meanings. Point to *week*, and ask a student to use the word in a sentence. Do the same for *weak*. Repeat the procedure for *beat* and *beet*. Tell students to pay attention when they read and write to make sure they understand the meanings of homophones.

Sound/Spelling Card 28

Teacher Tips

THE *ea* SPELLING FOR /e/ AND /ē/ Remind students that the *ea* spelling can also represent the /e/ sound, as in *head, bread,* and *weather*. Explain that most often, however, this spelling represents the /ē/ sound.

SYLLABICATION To help students blend the words and build fluency, use the syllabication below of the multisyllable words on the word lines.

week • end	nine • teen
team • mate	sea • shore

Preparing to Read

Line 3 **/ē/ spelled *ea, e,* and *ee***

Have students identify the /ē/ spelling in each word. *teach, teeth, be, bee* Tell students that the word *teach* means "to help someone learn about something." Use *teach* in a sentence, such as *I teach my dog tricks.*

Line 4 **/ē/ spelled *ee* and *ea;* /e/ spelled *ea* and *e***

Ask students to identify the two words in each compound word on this line.

Sentences 1–2

Before blending the sentences, quickly review the high-frequency words *the, two, will, make,* and *or* by pointing to them in the High-Frequency Word Bank. Have students reread the sentences several times to build fluency.

Developing Oral Language

To review the words, play the I'm Thinking of a Word game. Use the following clues as you say, I'm thinking of a word . . .

- *that is a vegetable.* beet
- *that is an insect.* bee
- *that is a part of the body.* heel
- *that is a place to go on vacation.* seashore

Guided Practice

Help students complete ***Skills Practice 1*** pages 187–188 to review /ē/ spelled *ee* and *ea*. Have students complete the sentences on page 187. Have students read the sentences on page 188. Then have them write the sentence that correctly describes the picture.

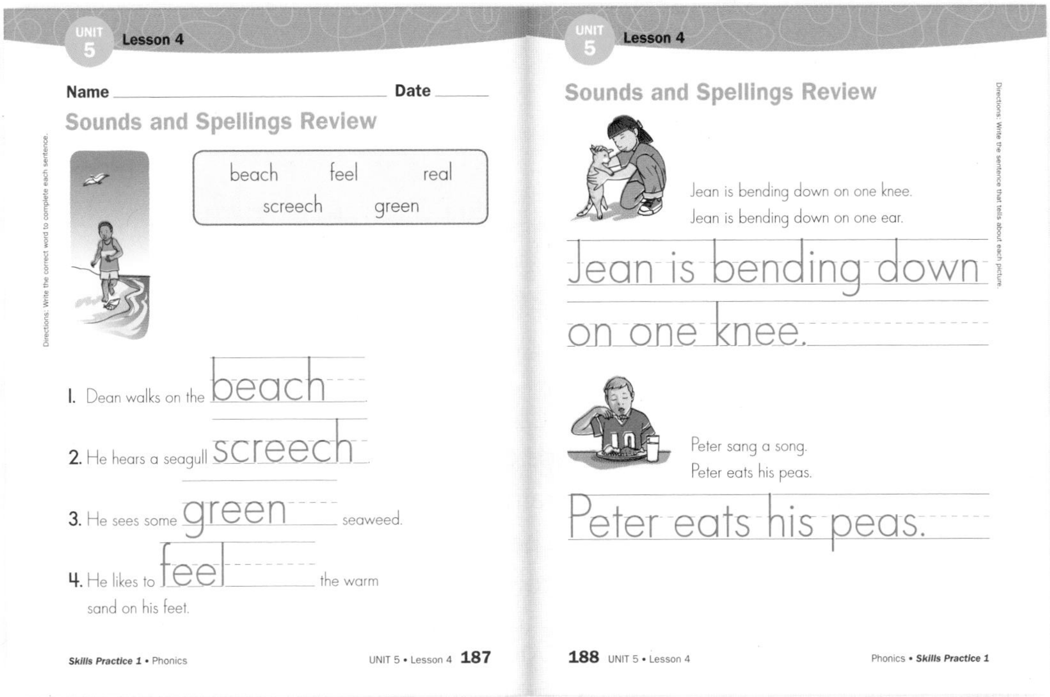
UNIT 5 Lesson 4

Name ________________ Date ______

Sounds and Spellings Review

Directions: Write the correct word to complete each sentence.

beach feel real
screech green

1. Dean walks on the beach
2. He hears a seagull screech
3. He sees some green seaweed.
4. He likes to feel the warm sand on his feet.

Skills Practice 1 • Phonics UNIT 5 • Lesson 4 **187**

UNIT 5 Lesson 4

Sounds and Spellings Review

Directions: Write the sentence that tells about each picture.

Jean is bending down on one knee.
Jean is bending down on one ear.

Jean is bending down on one knee.

Peter sang a song.
Peter eats his peas.

Peter eats his peas.

188 UNIT 5 • Lesson 4 Phonics • *Skills Practice 1*

Skills Practice 1, pp. 187–188

ROUTINE 8

Dictation: Word Building Game

Use Routine 8, word building, to have students spell the following words in the Word Building game. Provide a sentence for words that are homophones. Suggestions are provided.

see *(I see the pretty flowers.)*

seem *(It doesn't seem to be crowded at the park.)*

seed

deed

deal

meal

meat *(The cafeteria served meat and vegetables.)*

meet *(I can't wait to meet my new classmate.)*

sheet

she

Teacher Tip

WORD BUILDING GAME Have students proofread their words before you dictate the next word. Remind them to circle any words they think could be better and to write these words correctly above or beside the original word. Remind students that they can ask for help if they are unsure of which spelling to use.

Monitor Progress

to Differentiate Instruction
Formal Assessment

DICTATION As students spell words, notice who uses the ***Sound/Spelling Cards*** and spells the words correctly. Note students who are asking for help with the /ē/ spellings.

APPROACHING LEVEL

IF . . . students need additional practice with /ē/ spelled *ee* and *ea*, **THEN . . .** help them complete ***Reteach*** pages 141–142.

ON LEVEL

IF . . . students can blend and spell words with /ē/ spelled *ee* and *ea*, **THEN . . .** have them find words in the ***What's the Weather? Little Big Book*** that contain the /ē/ sound spelled *ee* and *ea*.

ABOVE LEVEL

IF . . . students need a challenge with /ē/ spelled *ee* and *ea*, **THEN . . .** have them complete ***Challenge Activities 1*** page 71.

OBJECTIVES

Students will

- use the Table of Contents to locate the first page of "Listen to the Rain."
- develop vocabulary about rain.
- listen to and discuss the poem.
- use the comprehension strategy Visualizing.
- identify use of vivid language.

MATERIALS

- ***What's the Weather? Big Book,*** pp. 28–31
- Routines 12, 13

Focus Question What does a rainstorm sound like?
Listen to the Rain
by Bill Martin Jr. and John Archambault
illustrated by James Endicott
Listen to the rain,
the whisper of the rain,
the slow soft sprinkle,
the drip-drop tinkle,
the first wet whisper of the rain.
28

What's the Weather? Big Book, p. 28

Poetry

Build Background

ROUTINE 12

Activate Prior Knowledge

- Remind students of the different kinds of rain they read about in "When a Storm Comes Up": drizzle, shower, rainstorm, and thunderstorm. Ask volunteers to describe the difference between a drizzle and a shower and between a rainstorm and a thunderstorm.
- If you like to use music in your classroom, consider playing a recording of nature sounds that include sounds of rain during this lesson. Continue to play this recording, when appropriate, throughout the day.

Background Information

- Tell students that the genre of "Listen to the Rain" is poetry. Remind students that poetry often includes rhyme and rhythm and that sentences are divided into parts.

Preview and Prepare

ROUTINE 12

Browse

- Follow Routine 12, reading the selection, to prepare students for the reading of the poem. Begin by having students turn to the Table of Contents page in the ***What's the Weather? Big Book.*** Have volunteers point to the poem's title, the poet's name, the illustrator's name, and the beginning page number of "Listen to the Rain" as you read them aloud.
- Turn to page 28, and have students identify the title and the author of the poem. Read aloud the name of the illustrator. Then have students browse the poem. Ask students to identify unfamiliar, difficult, or interesting words, or point out words that students may find confusing, such as *pitter-patter* and *hurly-burly.* Tell students a *pitter-patter* is a light sound or beat. Explain to students that *hurly-burly* is loud and noisy sound.

Set Purposes

- Have students identify a purpose for reading a poem. *for enjoyment, to hear entertaining words that describe rain, to think differently about rain* Remind them that poets often use many vivid words to make it easier for readers to make pictures in their minds of what happens in the poem. This makes reading the poem more enjoyable.
- After reading the selection, have students return to these purposes.

Fluency

Have students listen carefully and follow along as you model appropriate reading rate. Reading the poem with the appropriate reading rate will draw attention to the rhythm of the poem. Be sure to read the descriptions of the rain with expression. This will help students enjoy the sounds described in the poem.

BIG Idea

What is weather?

Before reading the poem, reread the Big Idea question. Tell students to keep this question in mind as they listen to the selection.

Teacher Tips

GLOSSARY The words *sprinkle* (page 28) and *pouring* (page 30) appear in the Glossary. As students browse and identify interesting words or phrases, you may want to use the opportunity to model glossary use for students. Turn to the Glossary, find each word, and read each entry.

HIGH-FREQUENCY WORDS As students browse, you may want to have them look for the high-frequency words they know. The following high-frequency words appear in the selection: *to, the, of, and, all, a.*

SETTING GOALS Students who set their own goals for reading selections will listen with a greater sense of engagement, and they tend to notice more than students whose goals are set for them.

Selection Vocabulary

sprinkle a light rain (page 28)

Teacher Tips

SEMANTIC MAP Continue to have students build upon the semantic map. Have them add selection vocabulary words and words they have learned throughout the unit.

DIGITAL TOOLS Have students look for definitions of selection vocabulary or difficult words from the text using an online dictionary.

Building Vocabulary

ROUTINE 13

- Use Routine 13, selection vocabulary, to introduce the selection vocabulary word to students. Write the word on the board or on a transparency. Explain to students that the word *sprinkle* can describe rain. A *sprinkle* is a light rain.
- Next, have students explain the types of activities they would do or would not do in a sprinkle. Make sure they use the word *sprinkle* in their sentences. Help them expand their sentences asking *who, what, when, where,* and *why* questions.
- Introduce one expanding vocabulary word to students during the second reading of the selection. Read the word, the definition, and the sample sentence. Understanding this word will help students better comprehend the selection.

Monitor Progress to Differentiate Instruction

Formal Assessment

VOCABULARY During the Building Vocabulary exercises, notice which students provide examples that use the accurate meaning of the vocabulary word and which students seem confused about the proper use of the word.

APPROACHING LEVEL

IF . . . students are struggling with the vocabulary words and their definitions,	**THEN . . .** use the ***SRA Imagine It! Photo Library CD,*** objects, stick drawings, and pantomime to help them visualize the words.

ON LEVEL

IF . . . students would benefit from additional practice with the vocabulary words,	**THEN . . .** have them make flash cards with words and definitions.

ABOVE LEVEL

IF . . . students need a challenge,	**THEN . . .** pair them with others who need help, and have them use the words in sentences to show their meanings.

Reading the Poem

Genre Poetry

✦ Have students identify the genre of "Listen to the Rain." *poetry* If necessary, remind them of the elements of poetry, including rhythm, repetition, sentences broken into parts, and rhyming words.

✦ As you read aloud "Listen to the Rain" in this lesson, model fluent reading by varying your intonation, reading rate, and expression to capture the meanings of words used to describe different kinds of rain.

1st READ

Comprehension Strategies

Model and prompt the use of the following comprehension strategies:

- Visualizing
- Clarifying

2nd READ

Elements of Poetry

Reread "Listen to the Rain." Introduce the element of poetry Language Use. Explain to students that writers and poets often use words that can shape the ideas, feelings, and actions of readers and listeners. The way the author uses these words helps the reader understand what the writer is trying to describe or say.

Focus Question

Before reading the poem, read the Focus Question on page 28 to students. Remind them to keep this question in mind as they listen to the poem.

Reading Recommendations

ROUTINE 12

Day 4 Read the entire poem twice today following Routine 12, reading the selection. The first time, model and prompt the use of the comprehension strategies. The second time, focus on the element of poetry Language Use.

Phonics

Words in the selection containing sound/spellings from recent phonics lessons appear in boxes like this throughout the selection. At the end of the first reading, students should be prompted to identify the sound/spellings of these words.

Teacher Tip

CHALLENGING CONCEPTS Poems can be conceptually challenging text. Have students listen to the poem several times and help them better understand the ideas in the poem.

Concept/Question Board

Have students recall the words they used in the Morning Message to describe rain. Write the words in a list, and have students think of a title. Post the list on the **Concept/Question Board.** After you read the poem, have students add any new words they learned. Encourage students to use these words when they are talking or writing about rain.

Focus Question What does a rainstorm sound like?

Listen to the Rain ①

by Bill Martin Jr. and John Archambault
illustrated by James Endicott

Listen to the rain,
the whisper of the rain,
the slow soft sprinkle,
the drip-drop tinkle,
the first wet whisper of the rain. ②

28

Listen to the rain,
the singing of the rain,
the tiptoe pitter-patter,
the splish and splash and splatter,
the steady sound,
the singing of the rain.

29

What's the Weather? Big Book, pp. 28–29

Teacher Tip

GLOSSARY The words *sprinkle* (page 28) and *pouring* (page 30) appear in the What's the Weather? Glossary.

1st READ

Comprehension Strategies

① Visualizing Teacher Modeling: *I like to get a picture in my mind as I read. It helps me better understand what is happening. As you listen to this poem, try to picture in your mind what is happening.*

② Visualizing Teacher Prompt: *As I read the first page, I picture in my mind walking in the rain. The rain is falling softly on me. It is light, like a feather. Does anyone visualize anything different?* **Possible Student Response** *I visualize an animal with tiny drops of rain falling on its face.* *Remember to continue to visualize as I read the rest of the poem.*

Listen to the rain,
the roaring pouring rain,
the hurly-burly
topsy-turvy ❸
lashing gnashing teeth of rain,
the lightning-flashing
thunder-crashing
sounding pounding roaring rain,
leaving all outdoors a muddle,
a mishy mushy muddy puddle.

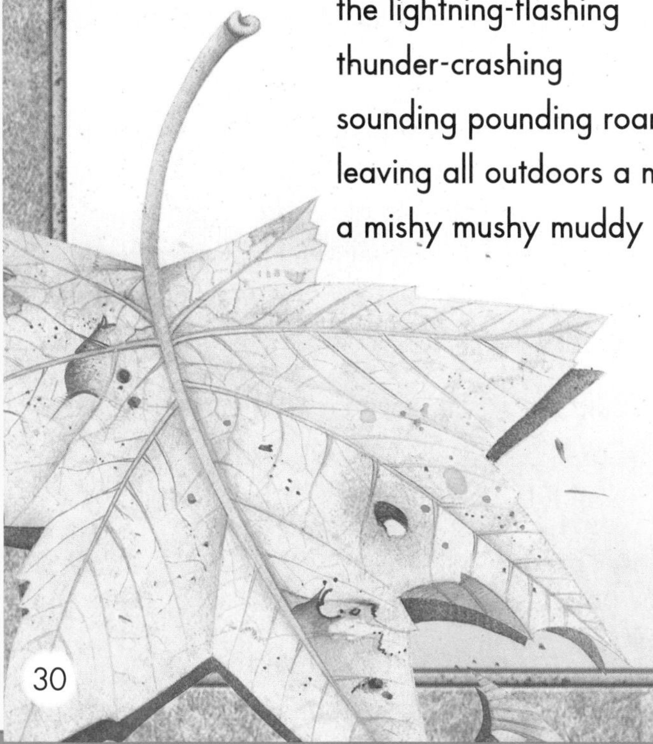

30

Listen to the quietude, ❹
the silence and the solitude
of after-rain,
the dripping, dripping, dropping,
the slowly, slowly stopping
the fresh
wet
silent
after-time
of rain.

31

What's the Weather? Big Book, pp. 30–31

❸ **Clarifying** Teacher Modeling: *I'm not sure what* topsy-turvy *means. Let's clarify that word. We know that pouring rain falls hard and fast. And sometimes it's very windy, and that can make the rain move in all directions. I think* topsy-turvy *means "moving in all directions." We can look it up in a dictionary to make sure we're correct.*

❹ **Clarifying** Teacher Modeling: *I don't recognize the word* quietude, *but I do recognize the word* quiet *at the beginning of the word. It means "silent, or making no noise." The word* quietude *must mean something close to that. Sometimes it helps to look at the parts of a word that we don't know.*

Phonics

/ē/ spelled *ee:* teeth (page 30)
/ē/ spelled *ea:* leaving (page 30)

Expanding Vocabulary

pouring flowing or heavy (page 30)
We were very wet from the *pouring* rain.

Monitor Progress

to Differentiate Instruction
Formal Assessment

VISUALIZING Observe students' use of the Visualizing strategy. Note which students are able to describe in detail their mental pictures and which students struggle to think of images or thoughts to share.

APPROACHING LEVEL

IF . . . students need additional help with Visualizing,	**THEN . . .** provide additional modeling of the strategy, using a previously read selection.

ON LEVEL

IF . . . students are comfortable with Visualizing,	**THEN . . .** have them select one of the vocabulary words from the poem and illustrate a scene around that word.

ABOVE LEVEL

IF . . . students need a challenge with Visualizing,	**THEN . . .** have them write about the scene that they visualized during the poem.

Technology

LISTENING LIBRARY During Workshop, have students listen to the ***Listening Library CD*** for a proficient model of oral reading.

Audio CD

Elements of Poetry

Language Use

- Tell students that in the poem "Listen to the Rain," the author uses many different kinds of words to talk about and describe rain. The use of these words can help give the reader new ideas and feelings. Tell students that each page of the poem talks about a different kind of rain.
- Have students listen as you say words from the poem that describe each kind of rain. Then have them repeat two or three of the words several times with the same expression you used. For example, say the words from page 28 of the poem that describe the beginning of rain. *Whisper, slow soft sprinkle, drip-drop tinkle* Then have students slowly and softly whisper the word *whisper* several times. Repeat this process for each type of rain.
- Remind students of the way you said the words as you read the poem. Have them follow your model to say "slow soft sprinkle," "roaring pouring rain," "tiptoe pitter-patter," and "dripping, dripping, dropping."
- Help students further understand the importance of language use by the author. Prompt them to describe how they felt and what they saw as they listened to the words about each kind of rain.
- This poem contains many examples of alliteration. Alliteration is the repetition of the same sound at the beginning of several words in a phrase or a sentence, such as Peter picked a peck of pickled peppers. Help students recognize the alliteration on each page by asking them to identify the repeating sounds after you reread the page. Ask the question *What sound do you keep hearing at the beginning of words?*
- Tell students that repeating the same sounds in a poem can make it fun to read. It can also add to the rhythm of the poem.

Discussing the Poem

- Have students do the follow activities to check their comprehension of "Listen to the Rain":
  - Ask students to share their thoughts and reactions to the poem as well as any questions they have. Encourage them to ask and answer for themselves questions such as the following: What did I find interesting in the poem? What is the poem about? Why would someone else want to read it?

- Ask students to use their senses to describe different kinds of rain. What would each kind look like? **Possible Answers** *like someone whispering softly; like an angry, wet, furry dog growling and shaking water; like a wet towel dripping water on the floor* How would it feel to walk in a drizzle? **Possible Answer** *like playing in a water sprinkler* A rainstorm? **Possible Answers** *wet and soggy; scary*

✦ Talk about comprehension strategies you modeled as you read the poem. Have students think about how they used strategies to help them better understand the selection.

- *How did visualizing help you better understand the ideas in the poem "Listen to the Rain"? What did you visualize?* **Possible Answer** *Visualizing helped me get excited about the poem because I felt like I was in the rain that the poem talks about. I visualized being in the rain during the summer and playing in the puddles.*
- *How did you clarify words or confusing passages?* **Possible Answer** *I clarified things that confused me by asking questions and listening to the poem again.*

✦ Also have students return to the Focus Question on page 28 of the selection. Read the question aloud, and have students answer and discuss the question. Encourage students to return to the text when answering the question.

Purposes for Reading

Review the purposes set for reading "Listen to the Rain." Have students tell whether they met their purposes for reading. Have them identify information from the text that talks about the purpose:

- For enjoyment
- To hear entertaining words that describe rain
- To think differently about rain

Vocabulary Review

Review the selection vocabulary word with students by pointing to the word on the board or by displaying the transparency you made. Then call on students to use the word in a sentence. If students need help, use the following sentence starter:

A sprinkle of ___________ *fell on* ___________.

Teacher Tips

WORD BANK Have students add the selection vocabulary word as well as any other weather-related words to the What's the Weather? Word Bank.

HIGH-FREQUENCY WORDS To help students review the high-frequency words they have learned, say some of the words aloud, and have students point to each one in the selection. Remind them to look at the High-Frequency Word Bank for help.

BIG Idea

What is weather?

After reading the poem, read the Big Idea question. Discuss with students how the poem helps answer this question.

Phonics

Have students practice identifying sound/spellings from recent lessons. Turn to a page in the selection, and say a sound/spelling that appears on that page. Then have students point to the word with that sound/spelling. Remind them to look at ***Sound/Spelling Cards*** for help.

Selection Vocabulary

sprinkle (page 28)

Day 4 **Language Arts**

OBJECTIVES

Students will
- revise a written list by adding detail.
- listen carefully to distinguish fact from opinion.
- discuss facts and opinions on weather.

MATERIALS

- Routine 15
- ***Skills Practice 1,*** p. 180
- ***Transparency*** 17

Teacher Tip

ART Bring in three white foam balls or three paper plates, some construction paper, and glue. Assemble the balls or plates into the shape of a snowman. Then let each student draw or cut out a decoration and glue his or her piece onto the "class snowman."

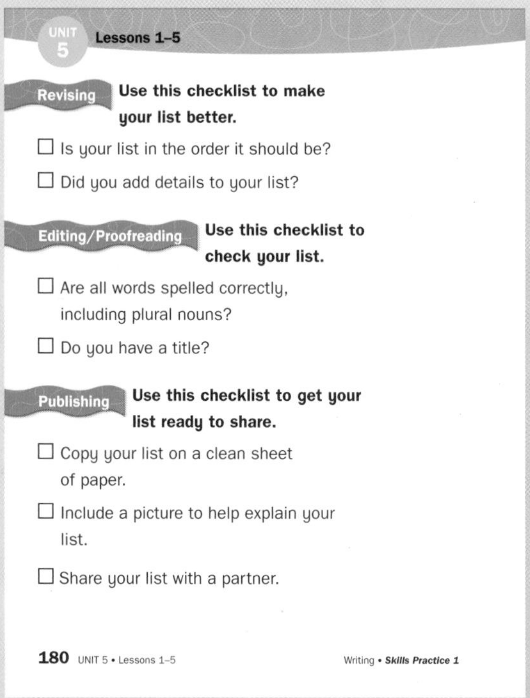
UNIT 5 Lessons 1–5

Revising **Use this checklist to make your list better.**

- ☐ Is your list in the order it should be?
- ☐ Did you add details to your list?

Editing/Proofreading **Use this checklist to check your list.**

- ☐ Are all words spelled correctly, including plural nouns?
- ☐ Do you have a title?

Publishing **Use this checklist to get your list ready to share.**

- ☐ Copy your list on a clean sheet of paper.
- ☐ Include a picture to help explain your list.
- ☐ Share your list with a partner.

180 UNIT 5 • Lessons 1–5 Writing • *Skills Practice 1*

Skills Practice 1, p. 180

Writing Lists

Revising

Teach—Adding Details

- Review your draft "Building a Snowman" list with students. Explain that you will read your draft to see whether you need to change any words or add information.
- **Teacher Modeling** *I think my list will be more useful if I name the exact things I need to build a snowman, so I'm going to say exactly what I need to decorate it.* Point to the fourth line of the list as you say *I'm going to change this line from* decorate snowman *to* decorate with a carrot for a nose, with a hat, with a scarf, and with rocks for eyes.

Use a caret as you make corrections to your list. Remind students that they learned about using carets to add details and text when revising during last week's activity. Explain that your added details give your list more information and make it interesting to read. Encourage students to do the same with their lists.

Guided Practice

- Have students follow your model to revise their draft lists. Tell them to use the revising checklist on ***Skills Practice 1*** page 180 to check their work. Review the points of the checklist as needed to make sure students understand each part.
- Circulate to help them with spelling, capitalization, and punctuation. Have students work together to add details to their lists. Remind them that specific details will support the ideas in their lists, and make their writing more interesting. Encourage them to add at least three specific details. Remind students to make sure that any proper nouns or the pronoun *I* are spelled correctly in their writing.

Listening/Speaking/Viewing

Listening: Fact or Opinion?

Teach

- Ask students to recall what genre of writing is used in "When a Storm Comes Up." *informational writing* Help them briefly review some elements of informational writing. **Possible Answers** *It contains facts that can be checked; it is about real people, animals, events, and things.*

- Tell students that although poetry such as "Listen to the Rain" sometimes can provide facts, poets most often use poems to express their personal feelings, ideas, and opinions about something. Explain that opinions can change from person to person but facts do not.

- Read the following statements, and explain why each one is a fact or an opinion.
  - Hurricanes form over water. *Fact; We know from books and weather people that hurricanes form over water.*
  - Raindrops look pretty as they fall from the sky. *Opinion; Some people think rain is pretty, but someone who wanted to play outside might not enjoy the sight of rain at all.*

Guided Practice

Say the following, and ask students to decide which statement is a fact and which is an opinion and why:

- Rain is needed for plants to grow. *fact*
- Rain sings and laughs. *opinion*
- Thunderstorms are angry. *opinion*
- Thunderstorms usually have heavy rain and lightning. *fact*
- A drizzle is a light rain. *fact*
- A sprinkle is a wet whisper of rain. *opinion*

Apply

Tell students to think about the selections they have read so far in Unit 5 and come up with facts and opinions about weather. Use ***Transparency*** 17 to write some of their examples under the headings Fact and Opinion.

Teacher Tip

GUIDED PRACTICE If students have difficulty distinguishing between fact and opinion, explain that a fact is supported by scientific evidence or personal experience. An opinion contains personal ideas and feelings, so you might disagree with someone else's opinion.

Differentiating Instruction: English Learners

IF . . . students have difficulty distinguishing between facts and opinions, **THEN . . .** introduce or review the words *feelings, ideas,* and *beliefs.* Explain how each of the opinions in the Guided Practice activity expresses one person's feelings or ideas.

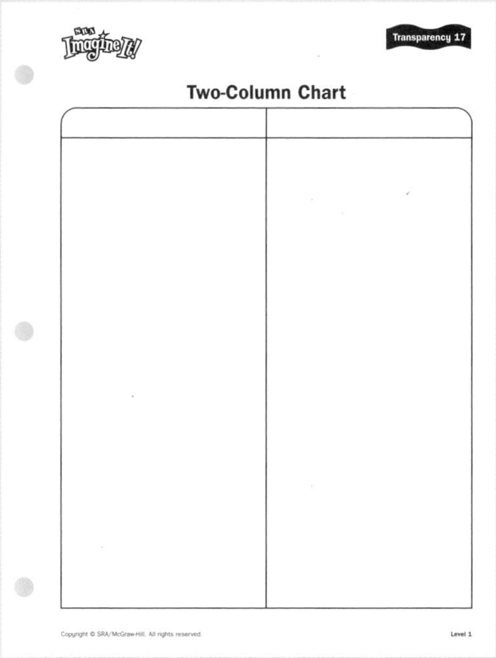

Transparency 17

Preparing to Read

OBJECTIVES

Students will

- blend, spell, and read words with /ē/ spelled *e, e_e, ee,* and *ea.*
- build fluency by reading ***Decodable*** 70.

MATERIALS

- Routines 3–4, 6–7, 9
- ***Sound/Spelling Card*** 28
- ***Skills Practice 1,*** pp. 189–190
- ***Decodable*** 70, *Green River*

Teacher Tip

DAILY WARM-UPS If students do not understand the words used in the Daily Warm-Up activities, use the ***SRA Imagine It! Photo Library CD,*** objects, stick drawings, or pantomime to help them visualize the words.

Differentiating Instruction **English Learners**

IF . . . students would benefit from extra practice with antonyms, **THEN . . .** point out the antonym pairs in the Morning Message *(wet/dry, hot/cold, light/heavy.)* Then challenge students to name antonyms for other simple words, such as *big (small), up (down),* and *in (out.)*

Daily Warm-Ups

Copy the Morning Message on the board or on chart paper. Have students answer the question. Read the message aloud, and discuss it with students. **Possible Answer** *The weather service keeps track of the weather.*

MORNING MESSAGE

Good morning! We know weather can be wet or dry and hot or cold. Rain can be light or heavy. Wind can be a breeze or a tornado. How do we know how wet, hot, or windy the weather is?

Daily Language Review

To review capitalization, write the following sentence on the board, or generate a similar one with students, and have students make corrections: mr green can fix the shelf. *Mr. Green can fix the shelf.*

Which Doesn't Belong? Game

Write the words *tip, tap,* and *pit* on the board. Blend and read the words, and ask students which word does not belong and why. Accept any response that students can explain. **Possible Answers** pit *because it doesn't begin with* t; tap *because it doesn't have the same letters as* tip *and* pit Continue with one or more of these word sets: *lake, bake, bike; hope, hip, hop; peas, please, peg.*

Phonics

ROUTINE 3 ROUTINE 4

Review: /ē/ Spelled *e, e_e, ee,* and *ea*

Blending

- Display ***Sound/Spelling Card*** 28—Long E to review the sound and the *e, e_e, ee,* and *ea* spellings. Point to the *e* and *e_e* spellings on the card, and remind students that these are two ways to spell /ē/. Remind students that these spellings can be found at the beginning, middle, or end of a word.
- Use Routine 3, whole-word blending, and Routine 4, blending sentences, to blend the words and sentences.

Line 1	we	weep	free	feel
Line 2	sweet	green	sheep	deep
Line 3	lean	heap	meet	meat
Line 4	feast	least	bread	thread

Sentence 1	Please take the bread with peach jam.
Sentence 2	We will be cheering for the green team.

Line 1 **/ē/ spelled *e* and *e_e***

Have volunteers come to the board and underline the spelling for /ē/ in each word. *we, weep, free, feel*

Lines 2–3 **/ē/ spelled *ea* and *ee***

After reading the words, have students identify the /ē/ spellings in each word. Tell students that *sweet* can mean "kind," and use the word in a sentence such as *The sweet girl gave her sister a hug.* Say the words *meet* and *meat,* and ask students to define each word. Then have a volunteer use each word in a sentence.

Sound/Spelling Card 28

Differentiating Instruction **English Learners**

IF . . . students are unable to identify the correct words, **THEN . . .** for oral practice and vocabulary building, ask them to repeat the words their classmates say.

Line 4 **/ē/ spelled *ea* and /e/ spelled *ea***

Ask students to point out the difference between the *ea* words on this line. *The ea spellings in* feast *and* least *make the /ē/ sound, and the ea spelling in* bread *and* thread *makes the /e/ sound.*

Sentences 1–2

Before blending the sentences, write the high-frequency words *be, green,* and *take* on the board. Tell students they will see these words many times in their reading. Although they will have learned all the sound/spellings in these words, they should begin to read these words automatically. Have students read these words and use them in sentences. Then write *be, green,* and *take* on index cards, and add them to the High-Frequency Word Bank.

Developing Oral Language

To review the words, write the following words on the board, have students read each one, and ask students to find and read words on the lines that rhyme with and have the same spelling for /ē/ as the words below:

- seep *sheep, deep*
- beast *feast, least*
- bean *lean*
- leap *heap*
- she *we*

Guided Practice

Help students complete ***Skills Practice 1*** pages 189–190 for practice with /ē/ spelled *e, e_e, ee,* and *ea*. Have students write the correct word under each picture on page 189. Have students complete the sentences on page 190. Students can use the bottom of the page for dictation.

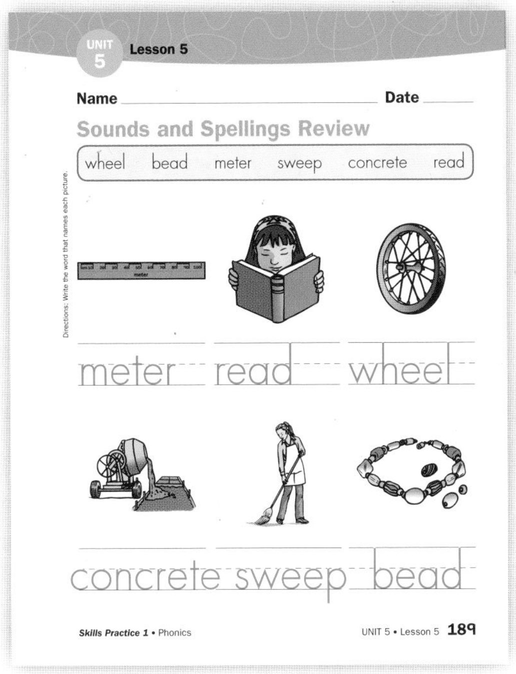
UNIT 5 Lesson 5

Name ______ Date ______

Sounds and Spellings Review

wheel bead meter sweep concrete read

Directions: Write the word that names each picture.

meter read wheel

concrete sweep bead

Skills Practice 1 • Phonics UNIT 5 • Lesson 5 189

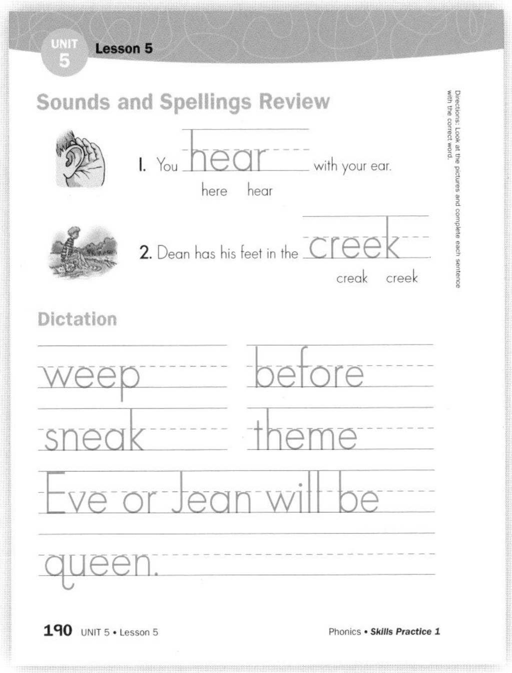
UNIT 5 Lesson 5

Sounds and Spellings Review

1. You hear with your ear.
here hear

2. Dean has his feet in the creek.
creak creek

Directions: Look at the pictures and complete each sentence with the correct word.

Dictation

weep before

sneak theme

Eve or Jean will be queen.

190 UNIT 5 • Lesson 5 Phonics • Skills Practice 1

Skills Practice 1, pp. 189–190

Dictation

ROUTINE 6 ROUTINE 7

Use Routine 6, whole-word dictation, and Routine 7, sentence dictation, with the following words and sentence. Be sure to have students proofread the words after completing each line.

Line 1	delete	before
Line 2	sneak	weep
Sentence	Eve <u>or</u> Jean <u>will</u> <u>be</u> <u>the</u> queen.	

Teacher Tips

HIGH-FREQUENCY WORDS The words *or, will,* and *be* are decodable high-frequency words. Encourage students to write them without sounding them out. If they have difficulty, tell them they can spell the words sound by sound.

DICTATION Remind students that they may ask which spelling to use for /ē/.

Monitor Progress

to Differentiate Instruction
Formal Assessment

DICTATION As students spell words, notice who uses the ***Sound/Spelling Cards*** and spells the words correctly. Note students who are asking for help with the /ē/ spellings.

APPROACHING LEVEL

IF . . . students need additional practice with /ē/, **THEN . . .** have them complete ***Reteach 1*** pages 143–144.

ON LEVEL

IF . . . students can blend and spell words with /ē/, **THEN . . .** pair them, and have them play a game from ***eSkills & eGames.***

ABOVE LEVEL

IF . . . students need a challenge with /ē/, **THEN . . .** have them complete ***Challenge Activities 1*** page 72.

Fluency/Reading a Decodable Book

ROUTINE 9

Core Decodable 70: Green River

Phonics Focus: Review /ē/ Spelled *e*, *e_e*, *ee*, and *ea*

High-Frequency Words

Review the high-frequency words *be*, *green*, and *take* that students learned in blending. Point to them in the High-Frequency Word Bank, or write them on the board, spell the words, and have students say the words. Have a volunteer use the words in sentences. Review other high-frequency words by pointing to them in the High-Frequency Word Bank and having students read them.

Reading the Decodable

- Follow Routine 9, reading a ***Decodable,*** as you read the story with students.
- Have students read the title, browse the story, and discuss what they think the story will be about.
- The first time through, have students read a page silently. Then have one student read it aloud. Repeat this procedure for each page.
- Reread the story at least twice, calling on various students to read. Then have the entire class do a choral reading of the story.

Responding

- After reading, be sure to talk about the story and answer any questions students have. Ask students to identify any difficult words in the book.

Teacher Tip

SOUND/SPELLING CARDS Remind students to refer to the ***Sound/Spelling Cards*** if they are unsure of a sound/spelling.

Green River
by Joaquin Garcia
illustrated by Lyle Miller

These kids will take a trip.
It will be down Green River.
3

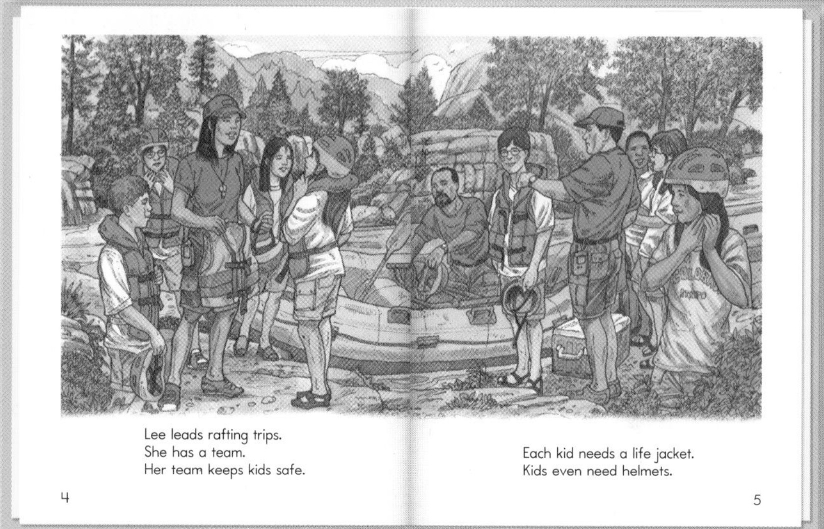
Lee leads rafting trips.
She has a team.
Her team keeps kids safe.
4
Each kid needs a life jacket.
Kids even need helmets.
5

The kids and team have three rafts.
The kids sit on raft seats.
6
At first, the trip is not fast.
Kids see fish in the clean river.
7

Kids paddle past big rocks and green trees.
The sun shines on Green River.
8
Lee looks up.
She spots an eagle.
The kids see it.
9

Then the river is between steep cliffs.
The rafts go faster.

10

The kids paddle hard and deep.
The river splashes faces.

11

The rafts leap up and down.
Kids smile. Kids scream.

12

The rafts go faster.
Green River has little, white bubbles.

13

Rocks seem to pop up!
The rafts speed past them.

14

At last, the river is not so fast.
Each kid takes a deep breath.

15

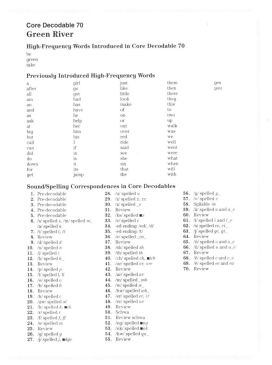

The trip is over.
But it was so exciting!

16

✦ Have students retell the story.

✦ As students answer the following questions, make sure they focus on the words in the story rather than getting the answers by listening or from the pictures. Have students answer by pointing to and reading aloud the answers in the text:

- **Who leads rafting trips?** *Lee*
- **What do the children see in the clean river?** *fish*
- **What does Lee spot in the sky?** *an eagle*
- **What is the river between?** *steep cliffs*

Building Fluency

Have students build fluency by rereading ***Core Decodable*** 70 twice with a partner. The first time through, one partner should read the odd-numbered pages and the other partner the even-numbered pages. The second time through, they should switch pages. For additional practice with the /ē/ sound/spellings, have students reread one or more of the following books: ***Core Decodables*** 68–69 or ***Practice Decodables*** 57–58. Have students record their readings on their Personal Title sheets, noting the title of each book they read, the date, and any difficult words they encountered.

Core Decodable 70
Green River

High-Frequency Words Introduced in Core Decodable 70

be
green
take

Previously Introduced High-Frequency Words

a	girl	just	them	yes
after	go	like	then	you
all	got	little	there	
am	had	look	they	
an	has	make	this	
and	have	of	to	
as	he	on	two	
ask	help	or	up	
at	her	out	walk	
big	him	over	was	
but	his	red	we	
call	I	ride	well	
can	if	said	went	
did	in	see	were	
do	is	she	what	
down	it	six	when	
for	its	that	will	
get	jump	the	with	

Sound/Spelling Correspondences in Core Decodables

1. Pre-decodable
2. Pre-decodable
3. Pre-decodable
4. Pre-decodable
5. Pre-decodable
6. /s/ spelled *s*, /m/ spelled *m*, /a/ spelled *a*
7. /t/ spelled *t, tt*
8. Review
9. /d/ spelled *d*
10. /n/ spelled *n*
11. /i/ spelled *i*
12. /h/ spelled *h_*
13. Review
14. /p/ spelled *p*
15. /l/ spelled *l, ll*
16. /o/ spelled *o*
17. /b/ spelled *b*
18. Review
19. /k/ spelled *c*
20. /aw/ spelled *al*
21. /k/ spelled *k,* ■*ck*
22. /r/ spelled *r*
23. /f/ spelled *f, ff*
24. /s/ spelled *ss*
25. Review
26. /g/ spelled *g*
27. /j/ spelled *j,* ■*dge*
28. /u/ spelled *u*
29. /z/ spelled *z, zz*
30. /z/ spelled *_s*
31. Review
32. /ks/ spelled ■*x*
33. /e/ spelled *e*
34. -ed ending: /ed/, /d/
35. -ed ending: /t/
36. /e/ spelled *_ea_*
37. Review
38. /sh/ spelled *sh*
39. /th/ spelled *th*
40. /ch/ spelled *ch,* ■*tch*
41. /or/ spelled *or, ore*
42. Review
43. /ar/ spelled *ar*
44. /m/ spelled *_mb*
45. /w/ spelled *w_*
46. /hw/ spelled *wh_*
47. /er/ spelled *er, ir*
48. /er/ spelled *ur*
49. Review
50. Schwa
51. Review schwa
52. /ng/ spelled ■*ng*
53. /nk/ spelled ■*nk*
54. /kw/ spelled *qu_*
55. Review
56. /y/ spelled *y_*
57. /v/ spelled *v*
58. Syllable -le
59. /ā/ spelled *a* and *a_e*
60. Review
61. /ī/ spelled *i* and *i_e*
62. /s/ spelled *ce, ci_*
63. /j/ spelled *ge, gi_*
64. Review
65. /ō/ spelled *o* and *o_e*
66. /ū/ spelled *u* and *u_e*
67. Review
68. /ē/ spelled *e* and *e_e*
69. /ē/ spelled *ee* and *ea*
70. Review

Decodable 70, inside back cover

Reading and Responding

OBJECTIVES

Students will
- generate ideas and questions about weather.
- decide on a question.
- make a conjecture.

MATERIALS
- Writer's Notebooks
- ***What's the Weather? Big Book***

Inquiry Planner

Week 1
- Generate ideas and questions for the **Concept/Question Board.**
- Decide on a problem or question to research and make a conjecture.

Week 2
- Collect information, and confirm or revise the conjectures and questions.

Week 3
- Prepare a presentation.

Teacher Tips

NONPRINT MEDIA Have students use nonprint media such as the ***eBackground Builders*** video to discuss how nonprint media affect their thoughts and feelings about the theme.

DIGITAL RESEARCH Provide students with a list of specific Web sites that can be used to gather information and generate ideas for their Inquiry investigations.

INQUIRY TIPS By this time in the year, you might want to encourage students to make multiple conjectures about one class question and to work in small groups to investigate those conjectures. Provide as much structure and guidance as students need.

Inquiry Process

Generate Ideas and Questions

Whole-Group Time

Whole Group

- Talk about the two selections you have read this week: "When a Storm Comes Up" and "Listen to the Rain." Discuss the storms and the different sounds of rain. Have students tell their own stories about weather. Remind students of the questions modeled in Getting Started.
  - What causes weather to change?
  - What causes rain and snow?
  - How can you tell how hot or cold it is outside?
- Ask students what the selections make them wonder about. Help students turn their "wondering" statements into questions. Record their questions on chart paper, and add them to the **Concept/Question Board.** Explain that as they read more about weather, they will find more information to use to answer these questions. This will help them do their research on weather.
- Discuss the questions with students, and have them as a group choose three or four questions to investigate as a class. Remind students what conjectures are—educated guesses—by modeling some examples. Then have them choose one of the questions and make their own conjectures. Move around the room to check students' progress and help them record their conjectures on sticky notes. Have students post their conjectures beside their selected questions on the **Concept/Question Board.**
- Display the weather chart. Discuss with students the current weather conditions. Have students share their observations and record them on the chart. Remind them that as they learn more about weather, more precise information will be added to the chart.
- Have students use the information on the chart to write their first weather observation in their Writer's Notebooks. Encourage them to illustrate their observations, using the appropriate weather symbols they have learned.

Small-Group Time

Small Group

- If you prefer to have students work in groups for Inquiry, help them set up their groups based on which question they want to make a conjecture about, and review the Small-Group Time rules.
- Meet with each group to discuss their question and conjecture and to make sure students know what they are to do.
- Help each group record its conjecture, and have students post the conjectures on the **Concept/Question Board.**
- Remind students that they can use references such as nonfiction books, beginning dictionaries, and the Internet to help formulate their questions and conjectures.

Concept Vocabulary

The first concept vocabulary word in the What's the Weather? unit is *temperature.* Write the word on an index card, and post it in your room. Read the word for students, and have them practice saying it. Talk to the students about the words meaning and what it has to do with the weather. Next use the word in a sentence. Continue to have students build upon the semantic map. Have them add word's from the selection and words they have learned while doing their Inquiry research. Remind students that you will refer to these words during the day, and ask them to use the words as well. Have students tell you where to add the concept vocabulary word on the What's the Weather? Word Bank.

Concept/Question Board

During Small-Group Time, have students post questions, pictures, and articles about measuring weather. Possibilities include

- articles from magazines or newspapers about scientists using instruments to measure storms.
- downloaded pictures from the Internet of different kinds of measurement instruments. You may need to make suggestions about tools students should look for.
- words found in newspaper stories about storms or changing weather.

Teacher Tips

REFERENCE BOOKS Have students use simple reference materials, such as nonfiction books and beginning dictionaries, to find information about weather. Some titles include the following:

Seasons: Everyday Science by Peter Riley

Feel the Wind by Arthur Dorros

Monitor Progress

to Differentiate Instruction

Formal Assessment

GENERATE IDEAS AND QUESTIONS Note how quickly students are putting their ideas and questions together.

APPROACHING LEVEL

IF . . . students are having difficulty generating ideas and questions,	**THEN . . .** model some ideas and questions that may help their thinking process. You may need to help students limit their options as they generate ideas and questions.

ON LEVEL

IF . . . students are generating ideas and questions,	**THEN . . .** have them start thinking about the questions they may want to use to form conjectures.

ABOVE LEVEL

IF . . . students need a challenge,	**THEN . . .** have them help students who are still having trouble forming ideas and questions.

OBJECTIVES

Students will

- edit, illustrate, and share their written lists.
- form the letters *u* and *m* correctly.
- control the size and spacing of letters.
- review that the names of people, special places, special things, and the pronoun *I* begin with capital letters.

MATERIALS

- Routines 15, 16
- ***Skills Practice 1,*** p. 180
- Portfolios
- ***Lesson Assessment Book 1,*** pp. 57–60

Teacher Tip

PLAN AHEAD Set up an area in the classroom where students can easily share their lists and snowman art.

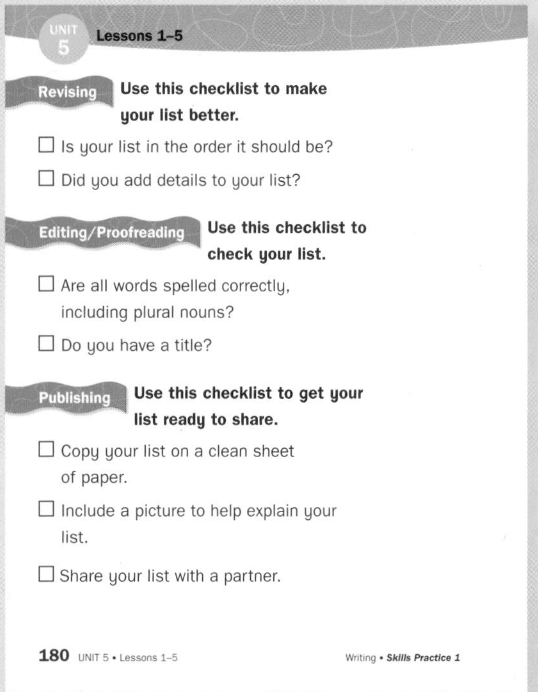
UNIT 5 Lessons 1–5

Revising **Use this checklist to make your list better.**

- ☐ Is your list in the order it should be?
- ☐ Did you add details to your list?

Editing/Proofreading **Use this checklist to check your list.**

- ☐ Are all words spelled correctly, including plural nouns?
- ☐ Do you have a title?

Publishing **Use this checklist to get your list ready to share.**

- ☐ Copy your list on a clean sheet of paper.
- ☐ Include a picture to help explain your list.
- ☐ Share your list with a partner.

180 UNIT 5 • Lessons 1–5 Writing • *Skills Practice 1*

Skills Practice 1, p. 180

Writing Lists

ROUTINE 15 ROUTINE 16

Editing and Publishing

Teach

- Tell students they should always look over their work for mistakes before they turn it in. Explain that errors can make their lists confusing to a reader.
- Use your revised snowman list from Lesson 4 to model how to check for spelling, punctuation, and capitalization errors. Work through the editing checklist on ***Skills Practice 1*** page 180 as a class.
- Remind students to check that any proper nouns or the pronoun *I* are spelled correctly.

Guided Practice

- Remind students that adding details can make their lists more informative and interesting. If necessary, suggest they add details about the items they would use to decorate their snowman. If time permits, explain that they could even make a brand-new list of decorations they could use to combine with their original. Point out that lists have many uses in planning and organizing their writing.
- Encourage students to use a caret to add text as they make their final edits. Tell them to proofread their work for mistakes one last time and to make any corrections before creating their final lists.
- Have students complete the publishing checklist on ***Skills Practice 1*** page 180. Read through the instruction with students to make sure they understand each part of the checklist.

Apply

- Encourage students to think of creative ways to share their writing. **Possible Answers** *Create an illustration for each step; take or find a photo of a decorated snowman and attach it to their list; bring in some of the items they would use to decorate a snowman and pass them around as they read their lists.*
- If time permits, have students practice their list presentations with partners. Then invite volunteers to share their lists with the class. Encourage them to describe in detail how they would decorate their snowman.
- Have students share any illustrations they have created for their lists. Remind them that in the Reading with a Writer's Eye activities this week they learned that authors use illustrations to add to or help explain the information in the text so that readers better understand the selection. Ask each speaker to explain how he or she used an illustration to add to his or her list.
- After each student reads his or her snowman list, have volunteers tell what they liked about the speaker's ideas. Allow time for students to ask questions and offer helpful suggestions.
- Congratulate students on writing such good lists. Display their writing on a bulletin board, or have them add it to their Portfolios.

Teacher Tip

LISTENING Before students read their lists to the class, remind them of their attentive listening skills, including sitting quietly, making eye contact, and facing the speaker.

Differentiating Instruction English Learners

IF . . . students need extra help with writing lists, **THEN . . .** see ***English Learner Support Guide*** Unit 5 Lessons 1–5.

Differentiating Instruction

English Learners

IF . . . students have difficulty with handwriting, **THEN . . .** keep in mind that some students may be more familiar with other writing systems than they are with the Roman alphabet. Be alert for students who need extra help with handwriting.

Teacher Tip

LETTER SIZE Check students' writing for letters that are written too small or too large. Remind them that letters within words should be uniform in size.

Penmanship

Alphabet Practice: The Letters *u* and *m*

Guided Practice

Review how to form lowercase *u* and *m,* and then distribute handwriting paper. Have students write each letter twice within the lines as they say its name. Tell them to proofread their letters and underline their best *u* and *m*.

Apply

To monitor students' handwriting fluency, write the following sentence on the board: *Tim and Gus jumped in the mud.* Read it to students, and tell them to copy the sentence onto their paper as quickly as they can without making any mistakes. After two or three minutes, have them proofread their sentence by circling any incorrect words and making them better by rewriting them above or next to the original words. Then have students underline their best *u* and *m*.

Monitor Progress to Differentiate Instruction

Formal Assessment

PENMANSHIP Check students' handwriting to make sure the letters *u* and *m* are formed correctly and have the proper spacing.

APPROACHING LEVEL

IF . . . students need additional practice,	THEN . . . have them use the ***Alphabet Letter Cards*** to practice tracing the model during Workshop.
IF . . . students have difficulty with letter formation,	THEN . . . give them paper copies of ***Transparency*** 37 to trace the models for *u* and *m*. Then have students practice writing each letter twice.

ON LEVEL

IF . . . students form the letters *u* and *m* correctly,	THEN . . . give them a list of words to copy from the selection that contains the letters *u* and *m*.

ABOVE LEVEL

IF . . . students are ready for a challenge,	THEN . . . give them pages of text from newspapers or magazines, and have them look for and copy words that contain *u* or *m*.

Grammar, Usage, and Mechanics

Review: Capitalization of Proper Nouns and Pronoun *I*

Guided Practice

✦ Briefly review the capitalization skills learned in this week's lessons by asking students to suggest sentences that use proper nouns or the pronoun *I*. Write their suggestions on the board, ignoring any capitalization. Then have students write each sentence and edit the nouns for capitalization. Examples:

- mark and tracie go to frost day school. *Mark and Tracie go to Frost Day School.*
- lisa and i visited the sears tower. *Lisa and I visited the Sears Tower.*
- i saw the liberty bell with my class. *I saw the Liberty Bell with my class.*

✦ Circulate to help students read the example sentences and identify the proper nouns as necessary.

Apply

Tell students to reread one of the compositions in their Portfolios and look for places they should capitalize a proper noun or the pronoun *I*. Have them select three sentences to edit and rewrite using their capitalization skills. Then have them share their favorite sentence with a partner.

Teacher Tips

PLAN AHEAD Display ***Language Arts Big Book*** page 183 as a reference if you think students will struggle with today's review of proper noun capitalization.

MECHANICS Tell students to remember the rules for capitalizing proper nouns and the pronoun *I* as they write in their What's the Weather? Notebooks and ***Skills Practice 1.*** Tell them to work with partners to check each other's capitalization as they work on their Inquiry investigations.

Differentiating Instruction: English Learners

IF . . . students have difficulty remembering to capitalize *I* or ask why *I* is capitalized, **THEN . . .** explain that capitalization rules vary among languages, and review that the word *I* is always capitalized in English.

Monitor Progress ✓ Formal Assessment

Use ***Lesson Assessment Book 1*** pages 57–60 to assess students' understanding of the skills taught in Lessons 1–5.

Lesson 6-10 Overview

Lesson Planner

	Day 1	Day 2
Preparing to Read MATERIALS ✦Routines 1–11 ✦***Alphabet Flash Cards*** ✦***Sound/Spelling Cards*** 19, 25, 28 ✦***Skills Practice 1,*** pp. 191–192, 195–198, 201–204 ✦***Decodables*** 71–74	**Daily Warm-Ups,** p. T132 **Introduce the Sound/Spelling** /ē/ Spelled _*y* and _*ie*_, p. T133 ✓ **Phonics** • Blending, pp. T134–T135 • Developing Oral Language, p. T135 • Guided Practice, p. T136 • Dictation: Word Building Game, p. T137 **Fluency/Reading a Decodable** ***Decodable*** 71, pp. T138–T139	**Daily Warm-Ups,** p. T162 ✓ **Phonics** • Review /ē/ Spelled _*y* and _*ie*_, pp. T163–T164 • Developing Oral Language, p. T164 • Guided Practice, p. T165 • Dictation, p. T165
Reading and Responding MATERIALS ✦***What's the Weather? Big Book,*** pp. 32–60 ✦Routines 12, 13 ✦***Transparencies*** 1, 14 ✦***Home Connection*** pp. 37–38 ✦***First Reader,*** pp. 5–15 ✦Writer's Notebooks	**Build Background,** p. T140 **Preview and Prepare,** p. T141 ✓ **Building Vocabulary,** p. T142 **Reading the Selection,** p. T143 **Reading Recommendations,** p. T143 ***What's the Weather? Big Book,*** pp. 32–59 (1st READ) ✓ **Comprehension Strategies** • Clarifying, pp. T144, T148, T151–T155, T157 • Visualizing, pp. T145–146, T150, T156 **Discussing the Selection,** p. T158 ✓ **Vocabulary Review,** p. T159	**Reading Recommendations,** p. T166 **Vocabulary Review,** p. T167 ***What's the Weather? Big Book,*** pp. 32–59 (2nd READ) ✓ **Comprehension Skills** Compare and Contrast, pp. T168–T181 **Reading with a Writer's Eye** Patterned Repetition, pp. T168–T177 **Checking Comprehension,** p. T181 **Fine Art,** p. T182 **Science Connection** Tornado in a Bottle, p. T183
Language Arts MATERIALS ✦Routines 14–16 ✦***Transparencies*** 30, 30c, 38–39 ✦***Alphabet Letter Cards*** ✦***Skills Practice 1,*** pp. 193–194, 199–200 ✦***Language Arts Big Book,*** pp. 22–23, 184, 186 ✦***First Reader,*** pp. 14–15 ✦***Lesson Assessment Book*** 1, pp. 61–64 ✦Portfolios	**Writing News Stories** Prewriting, pp. T160–T161 **Penmanship** Alphabet Practice: The Letters *v* and *w*, p. T161	**Writing News Stories** Prewriting, pp. T184–T185 **Penmanship** Alphabet Practice: The Letters *v* and *w*, p. T186 **Grammar, Usage, and Mechanics** Capitalization, p. T187
Monitor Progress ✓ = **Formal Assessment**	✓ **Phonics, p. T136** ✓ **Vocabulary, pp. T142, T159** ✓ **Comprehension, p. T144**	✓ **Phonics, p. T165** ✓ **Comprehension, p. T167** ✓ **Penmanship, p. T186**

★ Phonemic Awareness ★ Phonics ★ Fluency ★ Vocabulary ★ Comprehension

Day 3

Daily Warm-Ups, p. T188

Introduce the Sound/Spelling
/s/ Spelled *cy,* p. T189

Phonemic Awareness Listening for /s/, p. T189

✓ **Phonics**
- Blending, pp. T190–T191
- Developing Oral Language, p. T191
- Guided Practice, p. T192
- Dictation: Word Building Game, p. T193

✓ **Fluency/Reading a Decodable**
Decodable 72, pp. T194–T195

Build Background, p. T196
Preview and Prepare, p. T197
✓ **Building Vocabulary,** p. T198
Reading the Selection, p. T199
First Reader, pp. 5–9
Comprehension Strategies, pp. T200, T202
✓ **Comprehension Skills,** pp. T201, T203
Reading with a Writer's Eye, p. T203
Discussing the Selection, p. T204
Vocabulary Review, p. T205
Build Print and Book Awareness, p. T205

Writing News Stories Drafting, pp. T206–T207
✓ **Grammar, Usage, and Mechanics** Capitalization, pp. T208–T209

✓ **Phonics, pp. T191, T192**
✓ **Fluency, p. T194**
✓ **Vocabulary, p. T198**
✓ **Comprehension, p. T203**
✓ **Grammar, p. T209**

Day 4

Daily Warm-Ups, p. T210

✓ **Phonics**
- Review /s/ Spelled *s, ce, ci_, cy,* pp. T211–T212
- Developing Oral Language, p. T212
- Guided Practice, p. T213
- Dictation, p. T213

Fluency/Reading a Decodable
Decodable 73, pp. T214–T215

Build Background, p. T216
Preview and Prepare, p. T217
Building Vocabulary, p. T218
Reading the Selection, p. T219
First Reader, pp. 10–15
✓ **Comprehension,** pp. T220–T223
Reading with a Writer's Eye, pp. T221, T223
Discussing the Selection, p. T224
Vocabulary Review, p. T225
Build Print and Book Awareness, p. T225
Fine Art, p. T226
Science Connection, p. T227

Writing News Stories Revising, pp. T228–T229
Listening/Speaking/Viewing Language: Informal and Formal Language, p. T229

✓ **Phonics, pp. T213, T218**
✓ **Comprehension, p. T223**

Day 5 Review

Daily Warm-Ups, p. T230

✓ **Phonics**
- Review /ē/ Spelled _*y* and _*ie*_ and /s/ Spelled *cy,* pp. T231–T232
- Developing Oral Language, p. T232
- Guided Practice, p. T233
- Dictation: Word Building Game, p. T233

Fluency/Reading a Decodable
Decodable 74, pp. T234–T235

✓ **Inquiry Process** Collect Information and Confirm or Revise Conjectures and Questions, p. T236
Concept/Question Board, p. T237

Writing News Stories Editing and Publishing, pp. T238–T239
Penmanship Alphabet Practice: The Letters *v* and *w,* p. T240
✓ **Grammar, Usage, and Mechanics** Review Capitalization, p. T241

✓ **Phonics, p. T233**
✓ **Inquiry, p. T237**
✓ ***Lesson Assessment Book 1,* pp. 61–64**

Lessons 6-10 Overview

Student Resources

Big Book

What's the Weather? Big Book, pp. 32–33

First Reader

Focus Questions What are clouds made of?
How does water change?
Clouds, Rain, Snow, and Ice
All clouds are made of small
drops of water called droplets.
5

First Reader, pp. 4–5

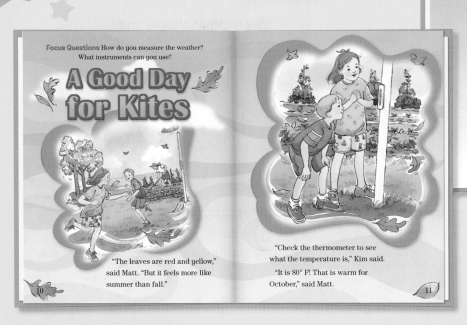

Focus Questions How do you measure the weather?
What instruments can you use?
A Good Day for Kites
"The leaves are red and yellow," said Matt. "But it feels more like summer than fall."
10
"Check the thermometer to see what the temperature is," Kim said.
"It is 80° F! That is warm for October," said Matt.
11

First Reader, pp. 10–11

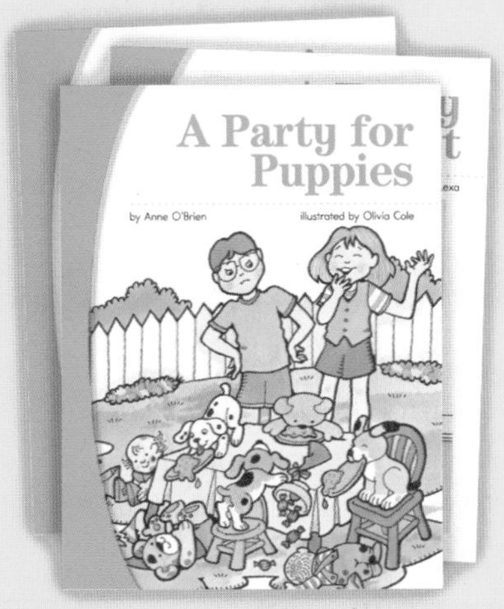
A Party for Puppies
by Anne O'Brien
illustrated by Olivia Cole

Decodables 71–74

Curriculum Connections

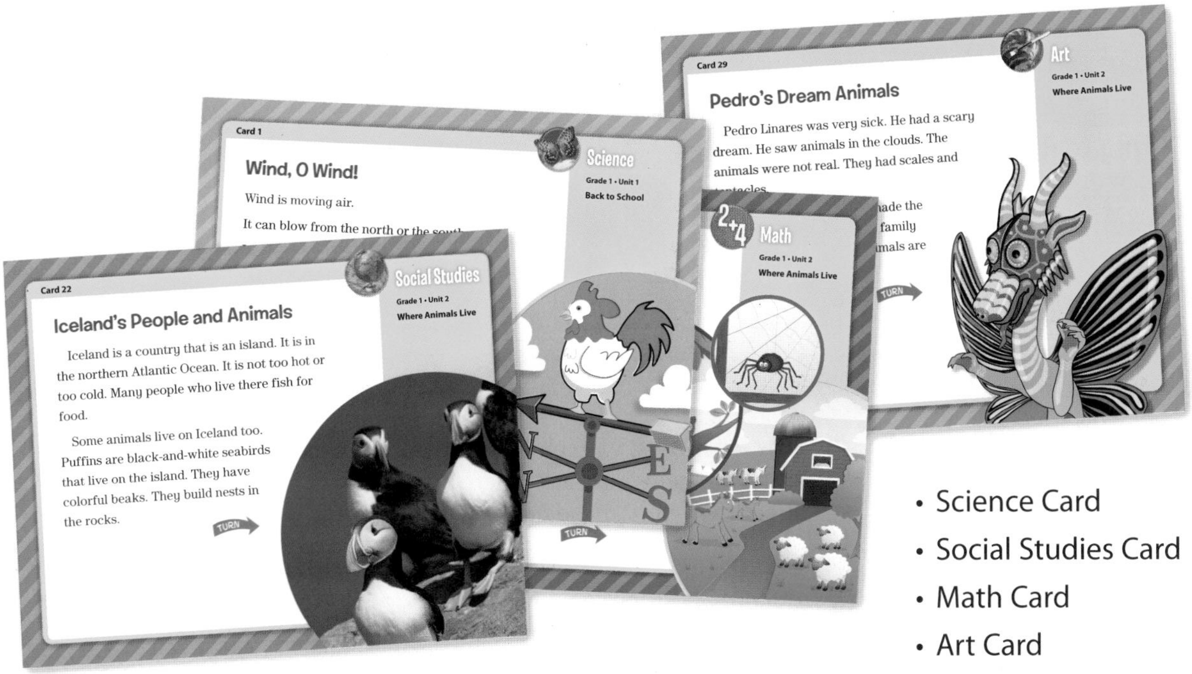
Card 29
Art
Grade 1 • Unit 2
Where Animals Live
Pedro's Dream Animals
Pedro Linares was very sick. He had a scary dream. He saw animals in the clouds. The animals were not real. They had scales and
Card 1
Science
Grade 1 • Unit 1
Back to School
Wind, O Wind!
Wind is moving air.
Math
Grade 1 • Unit 2
Where Animals Live
Card 22
Social Studies
Grade 1 • Unit 2
Where Animals Live
Iceland's People and Animals
Iceland is a country that is an island. It is in the northern Atlantic Ocean. It is not too hot or too cold. Many people who live there fish for food.
Some animals live on Iceland too. Puffins are black-and-white seabirds that live on the island. They have colorful beaks. They build nests in the rocks.
TURN

- Science Card
- Social Studies Card
- Math Card
- Art Card

Additional Skills Practice

Approaching Level

Reteach 1

- /ī/ Spelled _y, _ie_, pp. 145–146
- Capitalization, pp. 147–148
- /s/ Spelled *cy*, pp. 149–150
- Phonics Review, pp. 151–152

On Level

Skills Practice 1

- /ī/ Spelled _y, _ie_, pp. 191–192, 195–196
- Writing a News Story, pp. 193–194
- /s/ Spelled *cy*, pp. 197–198, 201–202
- Capitalization, pp. 199–200
- Phonics Review, pp. 203–204

English Learner

English Learner Support Activities

Unit 5, Lessons 6–10

Above Level

Challenge Activities 1

- /ī/ Spelled _y, _ie_, p. 73
- Capitalization, p. 74
- /s/ Spelled *cy*, p. 75
- Phonics Review, p. 76

Lesson 6-10 Overview

Differentiating Instruction
for Workshop

AYP

Day 1

	Approaching Level	On Level	English Learner	Above Level
Preparing to Read	**Phonics:** Repeat the dictation lesson with students.	**Phonics:** Pair students, and have them play a game in the ***Workshop Kit.***	**Phonics:** See ***English Learner Support Guide*** Unit 5 Lesson 6.	**Phonics:** Pair students, and have them play a game in the ***Workshop Kit.***
Reading and Responding	**Vocabulary:** Use the ***SRA Imagine It! Photo Library CD*** to help students understand the vocabulary words. Help them draw and label pictures that demonstrate the meaning of each word. **Comprehension:** Reread "On the Same Day in March" with students and share your visualizations with them.	**Vocabulary:** Pair students, and have them quiz each other about the words' meanings. **Comprehension:** Have students illustrate something they visualized as they listened to "On the Same Day in March."	**Vocabulary:** See ***English Learner Support Guide*** Unit 5 Lesson 6. **Comprehension:** See ***English Learner Support Guide*** Unit 5 Lesson 6.	**Vocabulary:** Have students create flash cards of the vocabulary words by writing a word on one side and its definition on the other. **Comprehension:** Have students illustrate something they visualized as they listened to "On the Same Day in March." Then have them write the words from the text that helped them make those visualizations.
Language Arts	**Penmanship:** Have students practice tracing the letters *v* and *w* using the ***Lowercase Sandpaper Letters*** in the ***Workshop Kit.***	**Penmanship:** Have students practice writing the letters *v* and *w* on the ***Write-On Boards.***	**Writing:** See ***English Learner Support Guide*** Unit 5 Lesson 6. **Penmanship:** Have students practice writing the letters *v* and *w* on the ***Write-On Boards.***	**Penmanship:** Have students write words they see in the classroom with the letters *v* and *w*.

Day 2

	Approaching Level	On Level	English Learner	Above Level
Preparing to Read	**Phonics:** Have students complete ***Reteach 1*** pages 145–146 to practice /ē/ spelled _*y*.	**Phonics:** Have students extend the sentences in blending and write them on paper.	**Phonics:** See ***English Learner Support Guide*** Unit 5 Lesson 7.	**Phonics:** Have students complete ***Challenge Activities 1*** page 73.
Reading and Responding	**Comprehension:** Have students compare familiar things such as school supplies or animals.	**Comprehension:** Have students choose two places from "On the Same Day in March" and compare and contrast them.	**Comprehension:** See ***English Learner Support Guide*** Unit 5 Lesson 7.	**Comprehension:** Have students compare and contrast a place from "On the Same Day in March" with the city or town they live in.
Language Arts	**Penmanship:** Have students use the ***Lowercase Sandpaper Letters*** in the ***Workshop Kit*** to practice tracing the letters *v* and *w*.	**Penmanship:** Have partners or small groups use the ***Write-On Boards*** to take turns writing rows of the letters *v* and *w*.	**Writing:** See ***English Learner Support Guide*** Unit 5 Lesson 7. **Grammar, Usage, and Mechanics :** See ***English Learner Support Guide*** Unit 5 Lesson 7.	**Penmanship:** Have students look for and copy words that contain *v* or *w* in the ***What's the Weather? Little Big Book.***

Lesson 6-10 Overview

Differentiating Instruction
for Workshop

AYP

Day 3

	Approaching Level	On Level	English Learner	Above Level
Preparing to Read				
	Phonics: Review the words in the blending lines with students. **Fluency:** Review ***Sound/Spelling Card*** 19 and any other ***Sound/Spelling Cards*** students need to review. Then have students look through ***Decodable*** 72 and find words with /s/ spelled *cy.*	**Phonics:** Have students look for and copy words that contain /s/ spelled *cy* in previously read selections. **Fluency:** Have students quiz one another using the ***High-Frequency Flash Cards.***	**Phonics:** See ***English Learner Support Guide*** Unit 5 Lesson 8. **Fluency:** Have students reread a ***Decodable*** to build fluency.	**Phonics:** Give students pages of text from newspapers or magazines, and have them find words with /s/ spelled *cy.* **Fluency:** Have students reread ***Decodable*** 72 into a recorder and then listen to themselves read.
Reading and Responding				
	Vocabulary: Use the ***SRA Imagine It! Photo Library CD*** to help students understand the words in "Clouds, Rain, Snow, and Ice." **Comprehension:** Have students categorize ***Sound/Spelling Cards*** into groups of animals and machines.	**Vocabulary:** Pair students, and have them use theme-related words to tell each other stories about weather. **Comprehension:** Have students play the Classify and Categorize card game in the ***Workshop Kit.***	**Vocabulary:** Use pictures and props to show the meanings of the words in "Clouds, Rain, Snow, and Ice." See ***English Learner Support Guide*** Unit 5 Lesson 8. **Comprehension:** Introduce words such as *group, kind, type,* and *sort.* Emphasize that to sort or categorize is to group things that have something in common. See ***English Learner Support Guide*** Unit 5 Lesson 8.	**Vocabulary:** Pair students, and have them use theme-related words to write stories about weather. **Comprehension:** Have students play the Classify and Categorize card game in the ***Workshop Kit.***
Language Arts				
	Writing: Help students draft their news stories. **Grammar, Usage, and Mechanics:** Have students complete ***Reteach 1*** pages 147–148 for practice with capital letters.	**Writing:** Have students begin illustrating their news stories. **Grammar, Usage, and Mechanics:** Have students play a game in the ***Workshop Kit.***	**Writing:** Have students continue drafting their news stories. See ***English Learner Support Guide*** Unit 5 Lesson 8. **Grammar, Usage, and Mechanics:** See ***English Learner Support Guide*** Unit 5 Lesson 8.	**Writing:** Have students begin illustrating their news stories. **Grammar, Usage, and Mechanics:** Have students complete ***Challenge Activities 1*** page 74 for a challenge with capital letters.

Day 4

	Approaching Level	On Level	English Learner	Above Level
Preparing to Read				
	Phonics: Have students complete ***Reteach 1*** pages 149–150 to practice /s/ spelled *ce, ci_*, and *cy*.	**Phonics:** Have students extend the sentences in the blending lines.	**Phonics:** Review the dictation words with students by writing them on the board and reading their correct pronunciations. See ***English Learner Support Guide*** Unit 5 Lesson 9.	**Phonics:** Have students complete ***Challenge Activities 1*** page 75 for a challenge with the /s/ sound spelled *ce, ci_*, and *cy*.
Reading and Responding				
	Comprehension: Provide additional modeling of the strategy Predicting using a previously read selection.	**Comprehension:** Preview a weather-related library book, and predict what the book is about.	**Comprehension:** Read "A Good Day for Kites" to students before the class reads it. Discuss vocabulary related to the skill Cause and Effect, such as *because, since, therefore, as a result*, and *so*. See ***English Learner Support Guide*** Unit 5 Lesson 9.	**Comprehension:** Have students help on level students with their predictions. Have them confirm or adjust their predictions by reading the book.
Language Arts				
	Writing: Have students practice reading their stories to you like reporters.	**Writing:** Have students practice reading their stories to one another like reporters.	**Writing:** Have students practice reading their stories to you like reporters. See ***English Learner Support Guide*** Unit 5 Lesson 9.	**Writing:** Have students practice reading their stories to one another like reporters.

Lesson 6–10 Overview

Differentiating Instruction for Workshop

AYP

Day 5

	Approaching Level	On Level	English Learner	Above Level
Preparing to Read				
	Phonics: Have students complete ***Reteach 1*** pages 151–152 to practice /ē/ spelled *_ie_* and *_y* and /s/ spelled *cy.*	**Phonics:** Have students play a game in the ***Workshop Kit.***	**Phonics:** See ***English Learner Support Guide*** Unit 5 Lesson 10.	**Phonics:** Have students complete ***Challenge Activities 1*** page 76 for a challenge with the /ē/ sound spelled *_ie_* and *_y* and /s/ spelled *cy.*
Reading and Responding				
	Inquiry: Review a list of resources or tools students can use for research. Help students find appropriate tools.	**Inquiry:** Help students find additional sources, including digital tools, that can be used to find information for their investigations.	**Inquiry:** Help students find additional sources, including digital tools, that can be used to find information for their investigations.	**Inquiry:** Have students begin preparing their presentations.
Language Arts				
	Writing: Make a video of students as they report their news stories. Play the videos to the class during the writing lesson. As students are waiting, have them finish their illustrations.	**Writing:** Make a video of students as they report their news stories. Play the videos to the class during the writing lesson. As students are waiting, have them finish their illustrations.	**Writing:** Make a video of students as they report their news stories. Play the videos to the class during the writing lesson. As students are waiting, have them finish their illustrations. See ***English Learner Support Guide*** Unit 5 Lesson 9. **Grammar, Usage, and Mechanics:** See ***English Learner Support Guide*** Unit 5 Lesson 10.	**Writing:** Make a video of students as they report their news stories. Play the videos to the class during the writing lesson. As students are waiting, have them finish their illustrations.

Resources for

Differentiating Instruction

English Learner

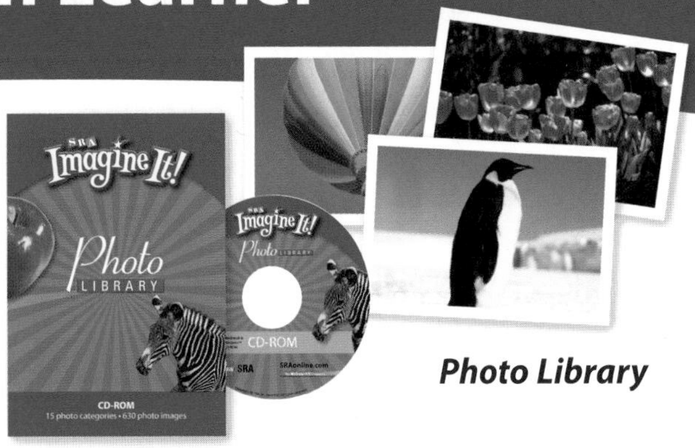

Photo Library

English Learner Realia Kit

Approaching Level

Intervention

Intervention Guide, Unit 5, Lessons 6–10

Intervention Workbook, Unit 5, Lessons 6–10

Workshop Kits

Technology

- ***eBig Books***
- ***eSkills & eGames***
- ***eDecodables***
- ***eAssess***

Listening Library, Unit 5

Lessons 6-10 Overview

Lesson Assessment

Monitor Progress to Differentiate Instruction

Use these summative assessments along with your informal observations to assess student mastery.

UNIT 5 What's the Weather? • Lessons 6–10

Name ______________ Date ______ Score ______

Letters and Sounds

Teacher: This activity is about letter sounds. I will say a letter sound. I want you to fill in the bubble under the word that ends with that sound.

Teacher: Which word ends with the sound /ng/ . . . /ng/?

1.	hard	luck	sing
	○	○	●

Teacher: Which word ends with the sound /v/ . . . /v/?

2.	fish	five	fit
	○	●	○

Teacher: Which word ends with the sound /nk/ . . . /nk/?

3.	bank	list	math
	●	○	○

Teacher: Which word ends with the sound /ē/ . . . /ē/?

4.	party	ride	made
	●	○	○

Teacher: Which word ends with the sound /j/ . . . /j/?

5.	stamp	third	ledge
	○	○	●

Lesson Assessment Book 1 • What's the Weather? UNIT 5 • Lessons 6–10 61

Lesson Assessment Book 1, p. 61

UNIT 5 What's the Weather? • Lessons 6–10 *(continued)*

Name ______________ Date ______ Score ______

High-Frequency Words

Teacher: Listen carefully to what I say. Fill in the bubble under the answer you think is correct.

Teacher: Fill in the bubble under the word *every . . . every.*

1.	evere	everi	every
	○	○	●

Teacher: Fill in the bubble under the word *could . . . could.*

2.	culde	could	couwd
	○	●	○

Teacher: Fill in the bubble under the word *boy . . . boy.*

3.	boy	boye	boi
	●	○	○

Teacher: Fill in the bubble under the word *some . . . some.*

4.	sume	some	somm
	○	●	○

Teacher: Fill in the bubble under the word *going . . . going.*

5.	goind	goeng	going
	○	○	●

62 UNIT 5 • Lessons 6–10 What's the Weather? • Lesson Assessment Book 1

Lesson Assessment Book 1, p. 62

UNIT 5 What's the Weather? • Lessons 6–10 *(continued)*

Name ______________ Date ______ Score ______

Cause and Effect

Teacher: Listen carefully to what I say. Fill in the bubble under the answer you think is correct.

Teacher: Sheri was late, so she hurried to the bus. She forgot her backpack. She also forgot her lunch. Which answer tells why Sheri had to hurry to the bus? The answers are *backpack, late, lunch.*

1.	backpack	late	lunch
	○	●	○

Teacher: The rabbit was sitting in a field eating some grass. It heard a noise and ran to its hole. Which answer tells what the rabbit did when it heard the noise? The answers are *sit, eat, run.*

2.	sit	eat	run
	○	○	●

Teacher: The cat jumped up on the table. It knocked a dish to the ground. The dog ran into the living room. Ben dashed to the kitchen to see what happened. Which answer tells who knocked a dish to the ground? The answers are *cat, dog, Ben.*

3.	cat	dog	Ben
	●	○	○

Teacher: Leaves got in the drain. When it rained, the water had no place to go. It flooded the house and ruined the rugs. Which answer tells what blocked the drain? The answers are *leaves, rain, rugs.*

4.	leaves	rain	rugs
	●	○	○

Teacher: Linda shoveled snow with her parents. They cleared the sidewalk so no one would slip. They walked to a restaurant for lunch when they were finished. Later that day, Linda's back felt sore. Which answer tells what made Linda's back sore? The answers are *slipping, shoveling, walking.*

5.	slipping	shoveling	walking
	○	●	○

Lesson Assessment Book 1 • What's the Weather? UNIT 5 • Lessons 6–10 63

Lesson Assessment Book 1, p. 63

UNIT 5 What's the Weather? • Lessons 6–10 *(continued)*

Name ______________ Date ______ Score ______

Grammar, Usage, and Mechanics

Teacher: Listen carefully to what I say. Fill in the bubble under the answer you think is correct.

Teacher: Fill in the bubble under the adjective, the word that describes. The answers are *big, run, hat.*

1.	big	run	hat
	●	○	○

Teacher: Fill in the bubble under the adjective that compares. The answers are *red, sit, taller.*

2.	red	sit	taller
	○	○	●

Teacher: Fill in the bubble under the word that is plural, or more than one thing. The answers are *hat, pens, lamp.*

3.	hat	pens	lamp
	○	●	○

Teacher: Fill in the bubble under the word that is plural, or more than one thing. The answers are *babies, sister, friend.*

4.	babies	sister	friend
	●	○	○

Teacher: Fill in the bubble under the word that should always begin with a capital letter. The answers are *Me, Us, I.*

5.	Me	Us	I
	○	○	●

64 UNIT 5 • Lessons 6–10 What's the Weather? • Lesson Assessment Book 1

Lesson Assessment Book 1, p. 64

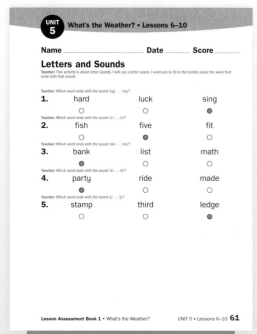

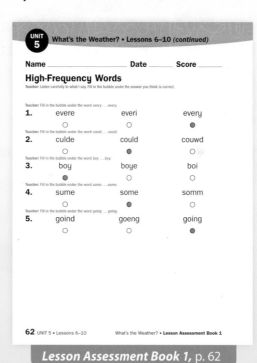

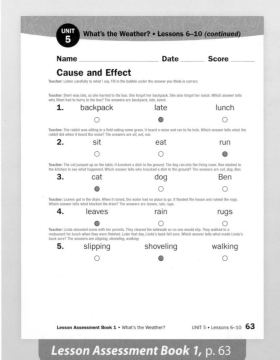

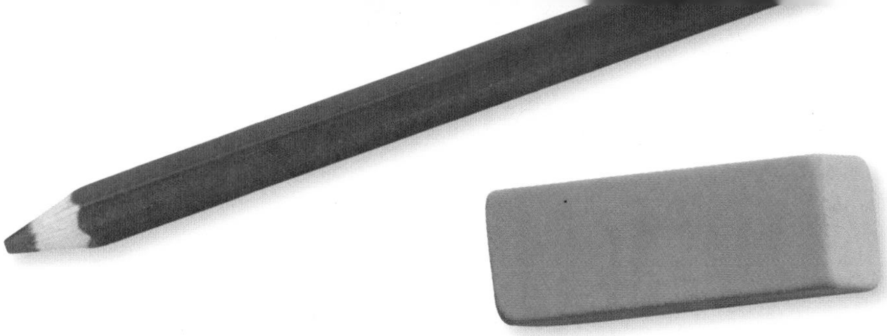

Lesson Assessment Book 1

Comprehension Observation Log

Student ______ Date ______

Unit ______ Lesson ______ Selection Title ______

General Comprehension
Concepts discussed: ______

Behavior Within a Group
Articulates, expresses ideas: ______

Joins discussions: ______

Collaborates (such as *works well with other students, works alone*): ______

Role in Group
Role (such as *leader, summarizer, questioner, critic, observer, non-participant*): ______

Flexibility (changes roles when necessary): ______

Use of Reading Strategies
Uses strategies when needed (either those taught or student's choice of strategy)/Describes strategies used: ______

Changes strategies when appropriate: ______

Changes Since Last Observation

92 Comprehension Observation Log • **Lesson Assessment Book 1**

Lesson Assessment Book 1, p. 92

Formal Assessment

The Comprehension Observation Log, found in the ***Lesson Assessment Annotated Teacher's Edition,*** is a vehicle for recording anecdotal information about individual student performance on an ongoing basis. Information such as students' strengths and weaknesses can be recorded at any time the occasion warrants. It is recommended that you maintain a folder for each student where you can store the logs for purposes of comparison and analysis as the school year progresses. You will gradually build up a comprehensive file that reveals which students are progressing smoothly and which students need additional help.

Preparing to Read

OBJECTIVES

Students will

- blend, spell, and read words that contain /ē/ spelled _y and _ie_.
- build fluency by reading ***Decodable*** 71.

MATERIALS

- Routines 1–4, 8–9
- ***Alphabet Flash Cards***
- ***Sound/Spelling Cards*** 25, 28
- ***Skills Practice 1,*** pp. 191–192
- ***Decodable*** 71, *A Party for Puppies*

Teacher Tip

WORD CHART Ask students to add more words that have /ē/ spelled _y or _ie_ to the word chart.

Daily Warm-Ups

Copy the Morning Message on the board or on chart paper. Have students answer the question. Read the message aloud, and discuss it with students. **Possible Answer** *Today it is cool and breezy.*

MORNING MESSAGE

Good morning! The weather is not the same everywhere. We are going to read about what the weather is like on the same day in other parts of the world. What is our weather today?

Daily Language Review

To review capitalization, write the following sentence on the board, or generate a similar one with students, and have students make corrections: marcus and tom will ride the bus. *Marcus and Tom will ride the bus.*

Before and After Game

Have students sit in a circle. Shuffle the ***Alphabet Flash Cards,*** and go around the circle, showing a different card to each student. Each student should name the letter shown and tell which letter follows it in the alphabet. Vary the game by having students name the letter that comes before the one shown or the letters that come before and after.

Introduce the Sound/Spelling

ROUTINE 1

/ē/ Spelled _y and _ie_

- Point to ***Sound/Spelling Card*** 25—Yaks, and have students review the sound for *y*_. Explain that this is the sound for the letter *y* when it is at the beginning of words such as *yes* and *yet.* Remind students that the blank following the letter tells them where the sound comes in a word. Ask whether *y* has a consonant or vowel sound and how the card can help them know this. *Consonant: The* y *is black, which means it is a consonant; vowels are red.*

- Point to ***Sound/Spelling Card*** 28—Long E, and review the previously-learned spellings. Use Routine 1, introducing sounds and spellings, to introduce /ē/ spelled _*y* and _*ie*_. Point to the _*y* spelling, and ask why it is red. *It serves as a vowel on this card.* Explain that *y* is the only letter that can be a vowel or consonant depending upon its placement in a word. Ask what the blank means. *The* y *comes at the end of a syllable or word.*

- On the board, write the words *happy, lazy,* and *story.* Blend and say each word with students. Point out that the /ē/ sound spelled _*y* appears at the end of words with two or more syllables. Many words of two or more syllables that end with an /ē/ sound have this _*y* spelling, such as funny and empty.

- Point to the _*ie*_ spelling on ***Sound/Spelling Card*** 28. Say that this is one more spelling for the /ē/ sound. Have students explain the meaning of the blanks. *This spelling does not usually come at the beginning or end of a word. The spelling has a consonant before and after.*

- Explain that the _*y* and _*ie*_ often are related to each other. Remind them of the rule they have learned for changing *y* to *i* and adding *es* to form plurals of some nouns that end in *y* and usually are preceded by a consonant. Write the word *buddy* on the board, and ask students to blend and read it. Then have them tell you how to spell its plural form. Write *buddies,* and have them blend and say it.

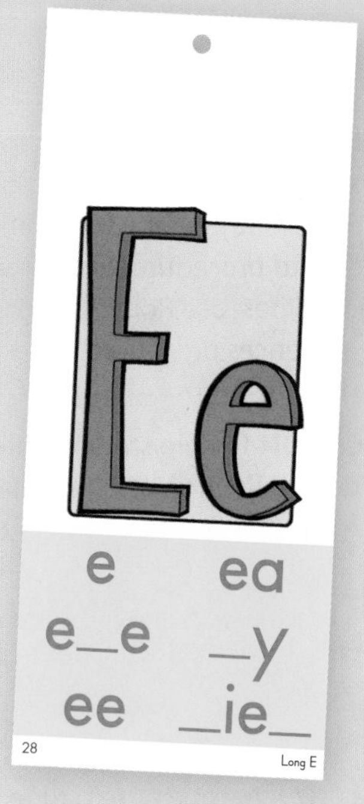

Sound/Spelling Card 28

Teacher Tips

STUDENT NAMES If any students have names that end with /ē/ spelled _*y*, invite them to write their names on the board. Have them point to the _*y* and say the sound. If any students have names that end with _*y* but have the /ī/ sound, such as *Ty* or *Guy,* briefly explain that this is another vowel sound for *y* that they will learn later. Have them say the two long-vowel sounds to hear the difference.

SPELLING PATTERN Review the following rhyme:

For more than one,
no need to guess.
Change *y* to *i* and add *es.*

Teacher Tips

BLENDING For Lines 1 and 2, refer to Routine 2 for the sound-by-sound blending procedure. If students are ready, refer to Routine 3 for the whole-word procedure for the remaining words on the lines. Use Routine 4 for the blending sentences procedure.

SYLLABICATION To help students blend the words and build fluency, use the syllabication below of the multisyllable words on the word lines.

ba • by	ba • bies	la • dy	la • dies
sha • dy	ti • ny	po • ny	spee • dy
heav • y	stead • y	read • y	leaf • y

VOCABULARY If necessary, tell students that *yield* means "to give in."

Differentiating Instruction: English Learners

IF . . . students are native speakers of Spanish or certain other languages, **THEN . . .** they may associate the letter name *e* and the /ē/ sound with the letter *i*, because in their native languages *i* represents a sound similar to English /ē/. These students will need extra practice associating the letter *e* with its English name and with the /ē/ sound.

Phonics

ROUTINE 2 ROUTINE 3 ROUTINE 4 ROUTINE 10 ROUTINE 11

Blending

Use Routine 2, sound-by-sound blending, Routine 3, whole-word blending, and Routine 4, blending sentences, to have students blend the words and sentences. Use Routine 10, closed syllables, and Routine 11, open syllables, to have students blend the multisyllable words.

Line 1	field	yield	thief	brief
Line 2	baby	babies	lady	ladies
Line 3	shady	tiny	pony	speedy
Line 4	heavy	steady	ready	leafy

Sentence 1: The lazy little puppy sleeps every morning.

Sentence 2: Did you see the tiny bunnies run across the street?

Line 1 /ē/ spelled _*ie*_

Be sure to write the _*ie*_ spelling as a unit as the students blend the words. Have them notice the consonants before and after the spelling.

Line 2 /ē/ spelled _*y* and _*ie*_

Ask students where they hear the /ē/ sound in each word. Explain that a final *y* in a word with more than one syllable is usually pronounced /ē/.

Line 3 /ē/ spelled _*y*

After blending these words, ask what the spellings have in common. *Each word has the /ē/ spelled* y, *and each also has another long-vowel sound.* The word *tiny* is also in the selection "On the Same Day in March." Tell students it means "very small," and use it in a sentence such as *The baby is tiny.*

Line 4 **/ē/ spelled _y and /e/ spelled *ea***

Ask students which word has two spellings for /ē/. *leafy*

Sentences 1–2

Write the word *every* on the board. Tell students that this is a word they will see many times in their reading and that the spellings do not make the sounds we expect. Read the word, repeat it, and have students read it. Then spell *every* together. Tell students that *every* means "each one." Invite volunteers to use the word in sentences. Write the word on an index card, and add it to the High-Frequency Word Bank.

Developing Oral Language

To review the words, call on students to find the following words on the word lines:

- Words with two spellings for /ē/ *speedy, leafy*
- Nouns that end with _*y* *baby, lady, pony*
- A word that is the opposite of *huge* *tiny*
- A word that means the same as *short* *brief*

Monitor Progress

to Differentiate Instruction
Formal Assessment

DICTATION As students spell words, notice who refers to the ***Sound/Spelling Cards*** and spells the words correctly.

APPROACHING LEVEL

IF . . . students need additional practice with dictation, **THEN . . .** review the words during Workshop.

ON LEVEL

IF . . . students are on level with dictation, **THEN . . .** pair them, and have them play a game from ***eSkills.***

ABOVE LEVEL

IF . . . students need a challenge with dictation, **THEN . . .** have them use one of the activities in the ***Workshop Kit.***

Guided Practice

Have students complete ***Skills Practice 1*** pages 191–192 to review /ē/ spelled *_y* and *_ie_*. Review the sound/spellings at the top of page 191. Have students write the words and sentences. Have students complete the sentences on page 192. Then have students chorally read the complete sentences.

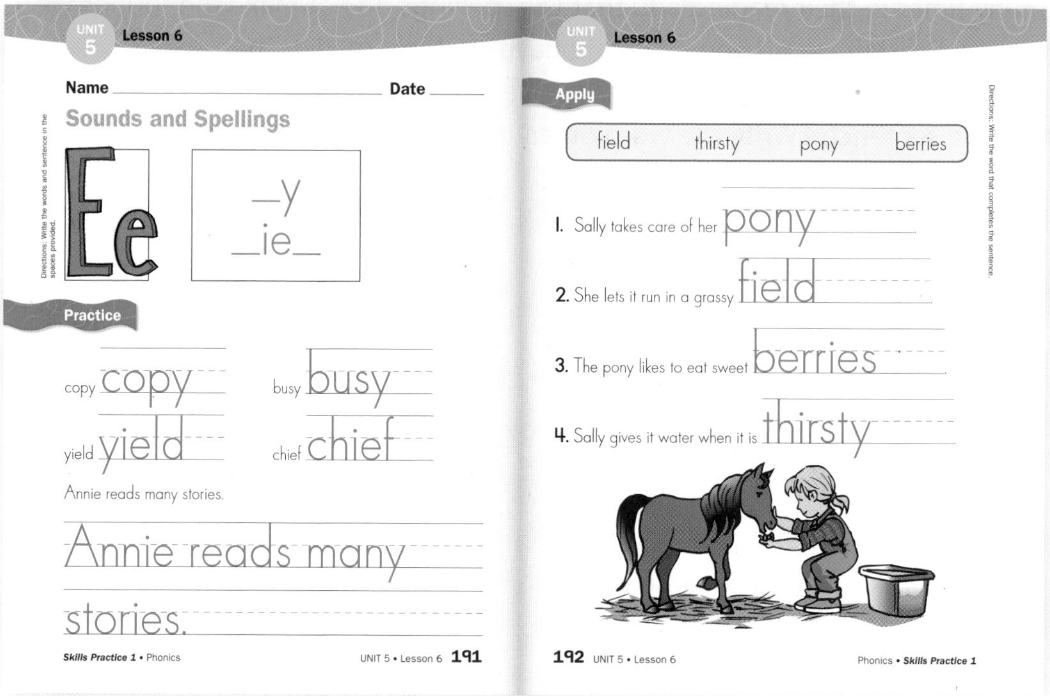
UNIT 5 Lesson 6

Name ______ Date ______

Directions: Write the words and sentence in the spaces provided.

Sounds and Spellings

Ee

_y
_ie_

Practice

copy copy busy busy
yield yield chief chief

Annie reads many stories.

Annie reads many stories.

Skills Practice 1 • Phonics UNIT 5 • Lesson 6 191

UNIT 5 Lesson 6

Apply

Directions: Write the word that completes the sentence.

field thirsty pony berries

1. Sally takes care of her pony
2. She lets it run in a grassy field
3. The pony likes to eat sweet berries
4. Sally gives it water when it is thirsty

192 UNIT 5 • Lesson 6 Phonics • Skills Practice 1

Skills Practice 1, pp. 191–192

ROUTINE 8

Dictation: Word Building Game

Use Routine 8, word building, to have students spell words in the Word Building game. Have students proofread the words after completing each one. Remind them to circle any words or parts of words that could be written better and to write the whole word correctly above or beside the original word. Have students use pencil and paper for the following words:

brief

chief

leaf

leafy

lazy

hazy

Teacher Tips

LONG-VOWEL SPELLINGS Do not be concerned if the students have not yet mastered all the long-vowel spellings that have been introduced. Encourage them to ask which spelling to use. The students will have many more opportunities to write words with long vowels and will gain confidence with the spellings through practice.

DICTATION As an extension, have students choose a word to use in a sentence.

Fluency/Reading a Decodable Book

ROUTINE 9

Core Decodable 71: *A Party for Puppies*

Phonics Focus: Review /ē/ Spelled _y and _*ie*_

High-Frequency Words

Review the high-frequency word *every* that students learned in Blending. Point to it in the High-Frequency Word Bank, or write it on the board, spell the word, and have students say the word. Have a volunteer use it in a sentence. Review other high-frequency words by pointing to them in the High-Frequency Word Bank and having students read them.

Reading the Decodable

- Follow Routine 9, reading a ***Decodable,*** as you read the story with students.
- Have students read the title, browse the story, and discuss what they think the story will be about.
- The first time through, have students read a page silently. Then have one student read it aloud. Repeat this procedure for each page.
- Reread the story at least twice, calling on various students to read. Then have the entire class do a choral reading of the story.

Responding

- After reading, be sure to talk about the story and answer any questions the students have. Ask students to identify any difficult words in the book.
- Have students retell the story.

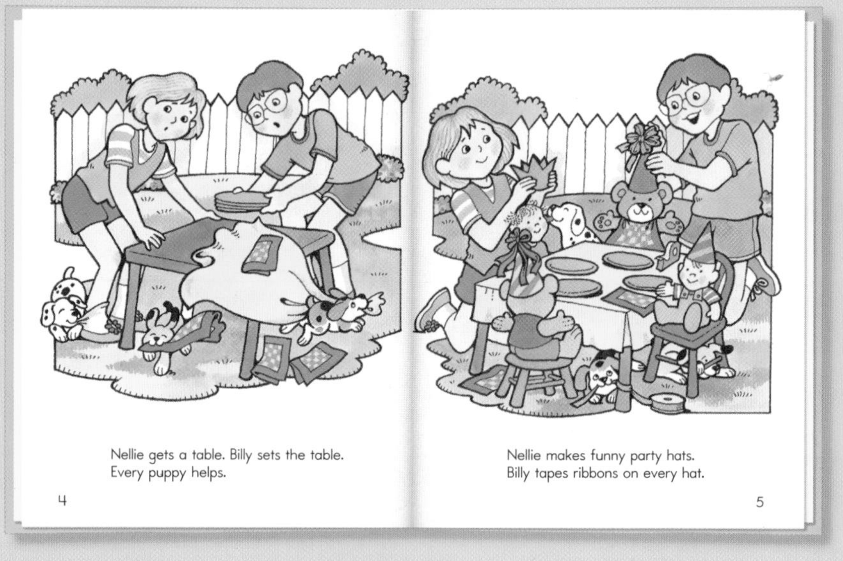

Nellie gets a table. Billy sets the table.
Every puppy helps.
4
Nellie makes funny party hats.
Billy tapes ribbons on every hat.
5

Teacher Tip

SOUND/SPELLING CARDS Remind students to refer to the ***Sound/Spelling Cards*** if they are unsure of a sound/spelling.

Nellie has garden treats.
Billy places a treat on every plate.
Every puppy helps.

6

Nellie gets more yummy treats.
"No more help, please!" yells Nellie.

7

The party is over. Happy puppies help clean up.
"Thanks for the help," Billy mutters.

8

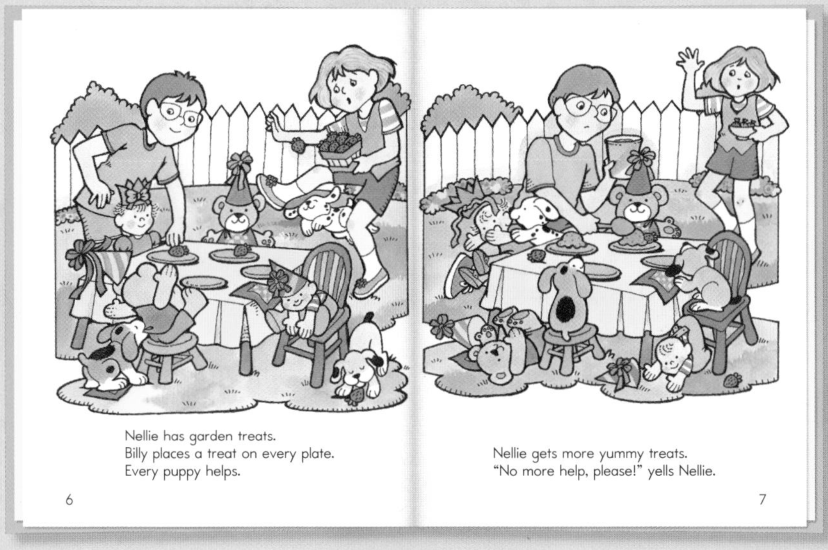

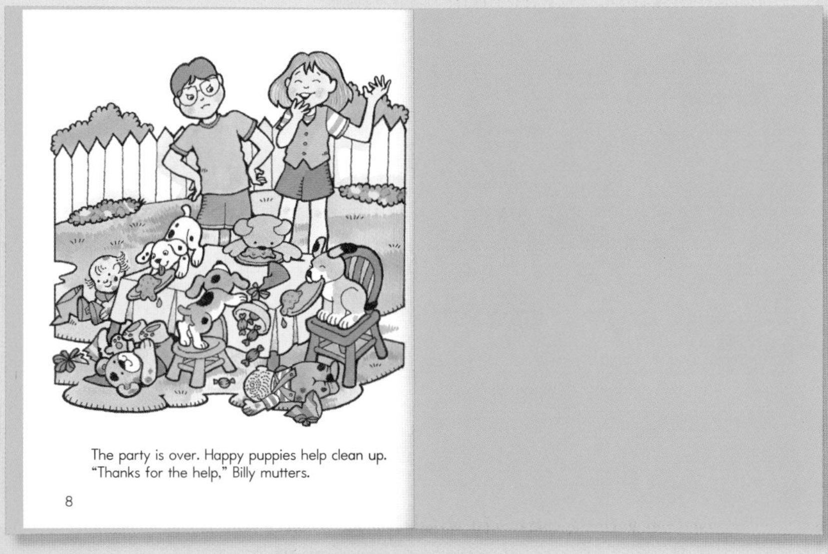

✦ As students answer the following questions, make sure they focus on the words in the story rather than getting the answers by listening or from the pictures. Have students answer by pointing to and reading aloud the answers in the text:

- **Whom do Nellie and Billy invite to their parties?**
 Nellie's babies and teddies

- **What does Nellie make?** *funny party hats*

- **Who helps clean up?** *funny puppies*

Building Fluency

Have students build fluency by rereading **Core Decodable** 71 twice with a partner. The first time through, one partner should read the odd-numbered pages and the other partner the even-numbered pages. The second time through, they should switch pages. For additional practice with /ē/ spelled _y and _ie_, have students read **Practice Decodable** 59, *Hot or Cold*. Have students record their readings on their Personal Title sheets, noting the title of each book, the date, and any difficult words they encountered.

Core Decodable 71
A Party for Puppies

High-Frequency Word Introduced in Core Decodable 71
every

Previously Introduced High-Frequency Words

a	get	its	take	when
after	girl	jump	that	will
all	go	just	the	with
am	got	like	them	yes
an	green	little	then	you
and	had	look	there	
as	has	make	they	
ask	have	of	this	
at	he	on	to	
be	help	or	two	
big	her	out	up	
but	him	over	walk	
call	his	red	was	
can	I	ride	we	
did	if	said	well	
do	in	see	went	
down	is	she	were	
for	it	six	what	

Sound/Spelling Correspondences in Core Decodables

1. Pre-decodable	30. /z/ spelled _s	60. Review	
2. Pre-decodable	31. Review	61. /ī/ spelled i and i_e	
3. Pre-decodable	32. /ks/ spelled ■x	62. /s/ spelled ce, ci_	
4. Pre-decodable	33. /e/ spelled e	63. /j/ spelled ge, gi_	
5. Pre-decodable	34. -ed ending /ed/, /d/	64. Review	
6. /s/ spelled s, /m/ spelled m, /a/ spelled a	35. -ed ending /t/	65. /ō/ spelled o and o_e	
	36. /e/ spelled _ea_	66. /ū/ spelled u and u_e	
7. /t/ spelled t, tt	37. Review	67. Review	
8. Review	38. /sh/ spelled sh	68. /ē/ spelled e and e_e	
9. /d/ spelled d	39. /th/ spelled th	69. /ē/ spelled ee and ea	
10. /n/ spelled n	40. /ch/ spelled ch, ■tch	70. Review	
11. /i/ spelled i	41. /or/ spelled or, ore	71. /ē/ spelled _y, _ie_	
12. /h/ spelled h_	42. Review		
13. Review	43. /ar/ spelled ar		
14. /p/ spelled p	44. /m/ spelled _mb		
15. /l/ spelled l, ll	45. /w/ spelled w_		
16. /o/ spelled o	46. /hw/ spelled wh_		
17. /b/ spelled b	47. /er/ spelled er, ir		
18. Review	48. /er/ spelled ur		
19. /k/ spelled c	49. Review		
20. /aw/ spelled al	50. Schwa		
21. /k/ spelled k, ■ck	51. Review schwa		
22. /r/ spelled r	52. /ng/ spelled ■ng		
23. /f/ spelled f, ff	53. /nk/ spelled ■nk		
24. /s/ spelled ss	54. /kw/ spelled qu_		
25. Review	55. Review		
26. /g/ spelled g	56. /y/ spelled y_		
27. /j/ spelled j, ■dge	57. /v/ spelled v		
28. /u/ spelled u	58. Syllable -le		
29. /z/ spelled z, zz	59. /ā/ spelled a and a_e		

Decodable 71, inside back cover

Reading and Responding

OBJECTIVES

Students will
- activate prior knowledge about weather.
- understand a table of contents.
- set and check purposes for reading.
- preview vocabulary words.
- use the comprehension strategies Visualizing, Asking Questions, and Clarifying.
- learn about glossaries.

MATERIALS
- ***What's the Weather? Big Book,*** pp. 32–59
- Routines 12, 13
- Writer's Notebooks
- ***Home Connection,*** pp. 37–38

Teacher Tips

MATERIALS You will need a globe throughout this lesson. Place the globe so all students can see it clearly. Before the lesson, use different-colored stickers to mark the locations of the places mentioned in the selection.

ACTIVATE PRIOR KNOWLEDGE Use this discussion to become aware of any misconceptions or misunderstandings students may have about weather. For example, some students might think spring comes at the same time each year throughout the world. Be alert for information in the selection that can help students rethink their ideas, and replace them with more accurate ones.

Differentiating Instruction **English Learners**

IF . . . students are unfamiliar with North American seasons, **THEN . . .** use pictures and a calendar to introduce them. You may wish to encourage English Learners to describe seasons in their native countries. For example, students from Asia may describe monsoon and dry seasons.

Build Background

Activate Prior Knowledge

Ask students the following questions to determine their prior knowledge of kinds of weather and different places around the world.

- *What are the four seasons? spring, summer, winter, fall/autumn*
- *The month of March is in which season? spring*
- *What kind of weather do we usually have in March?* **Possible Answers** *rainy; windy and stormy; warm; sometimes sunny and sometimes cloudy*
- *Have you ever lived in or visited a place that had different kinds of weather in March? What was that weather like?* **Possible Answer** *I was born in Haiti. It can be really hot in March.*

Background Information

- Before reading, show students a globe. Point to and name the equator. Demonstrate that this imaginary line runs all around the middle of Earth. Use a sticker to mark your location in the United States. Tell students that our country is north, or above the line, of the equator. Say that this northern half of Earth is called the northern hemisphere. Point to South America, and say that it is south, or below the line, of the equator in the part of Earth called the southern hemisphere. Use different-colored stickers to mark and name the North Pole and the South Pole.
- It may be helpful to let students know that the seasons are different in the southern hemisphere versus the northern hemisphere. Explain briefly that when the sun is shining on the North Pole, it is summer in the northern hemisphere and winter in the southern hemisphere. For example, the seasons in the Arctic and in Antarctica are opposite from each other. When it gets warmer in the Arctic, it gets colder in Antarctica. When spring is coming to the Arctic, fall is coming to Antarctica.

Preview and Prepare

ROUTINE 12

Browse

- Follow Routine 12, reading the selection, to prepare students for the reading. Begin by having students locate the Table of Contents in ***What's the Weather? Big Book.*** Have volunteers point to the title, the author's name, the illustrator's name, and the beginning page number of "On the Same Day in March" as you read them aloud.
- Have a volunteer turn to page 32. Have students compare the title to that on the Table of Contents page to make sure they have the correct selection. Read aloud the name of the illustrator.
- Have students browse the first few pages of the selection to look for difficult or unfamiliar words and for clues to what the selection is about. Students may point to words such as *stalking, boulevards, swallows, dazzles,* or *crouched.* Help students by showing pictures, reading definitions from a glossary, or role-playing the meaning of the word or words.
- Using the information they gained from browsing the selection, including the title and the illustrations, have students make predictions as to what the selection is about.

Set Purposes

- Ask students what the purposes for reading this selection might be. Write them on the board. Some suggestions include the following:
  - To find out how the weather is different in different places of the world
  - To learn what causes the weather to be different in different places
- After reading the selection, have students return to these purposes.

Fluency

As you read "On the Same Day in March," have students listen carefully and follow along as you model appropriate reading rate, expression, and intonation. The appropriate rate and intonation will help point out the patterned repetition in this selection. With appropriate fluency, students will more easily recognize the repeated text and be able to focus on the differences in the weather.

Teacher Tips

GLOSSARY The words *Canada* (page 34), *patch* (page 35), *markets* (page 36), *huddled* (page 37), *Texas Panhandle* (page 39), *twister* (page 39), *fog* (page 40), *Louisiana* (page 41), *swamp* (page 41), *China* (page 42), *kites* (page 43), *pearls* (page 45), *sparkles* (page 48), *weather* (page 53), *Australia* (page 54), *crouched* (page 55), *shore* (page 55), *autumn* (page 56), and *flock* (page 56) appear in the Glossary. As students browse and identify interesting words or phrases, you may want to use the opportunity to model glossary use for students. Turn to the Glossary, find each word, and read each entry.

HIGH-FREQUENCY WORDS As students browse, you may want to have them look for the high-frequency words they know. The following are some of the high-frequency words that appear in the selection: *a, of, the, on, in, as, ride, to, just, when, you, can't, that, like, and, can, but, is.*

CHALLENGING CONCEPTS This selection can be conceptually challenging text for students. Have students listen to the selection for the main ideas. Have them listen to the selection several times and help them better understand the ideas in the text.

From Your Teacher Home Connection

Give each student a copy of ***Home Connection*** page 37. This same information is also available in Spanish on ***Home Connection*** page 38. After students have listened to each selection, encourage them to discuss it with their families and complete the activity provided.

BIG Idea

What is weather?

Before reading the selection, reread the Big Idea question. Tell students to keep this question in mind as they listen to the selection.

Selection Vocabulary

weather the condition of the air at a specific time or place (page 32)

sparkles to glitter; to shine (page 48)

Teacher Tips

SEMANTIC MAP Continue to have students build upon the semantic map. Have them add words from the selection and words they have learned throughout the unit.

DIGITAL TOOLS Have students look for definitions of selection vocabulary or difficult words from the text using an online dictionary.

Research in Action

One teacher who participates in Inquiry research helped students use the Internet to check the weather around the world in several places the children chose. Students recorded the weather on a weather chart. The teacher reported that this activity was highly motivating and that it had the added benefits of addressing the Social Studies curriculum. *(Anne McKeough)*

Building Vocabulary

ROUTINE 13

- Use Routine 13, selection vocabulary, to introduce the vocabulary words to students. Write the words on the board or on a transparency.
- Have students identify different types of weather. **Possible Answers** *clear; sunny; rainy; snowy*
- Ask volunteers to name things that sparkle. **Possible Answers** *stars; diamonds; water when the sun shines on it*
- Tell students to listen and look for these words as you read the selection.

Monitor Progress to Differentiate Instruction

Formal Assessment

VOCABULARY During the Building Vocabulary exercise, note which students are initiating responses and which students seem to be waiting for cues from other students.

APPROACHING LEVEL

IF . . . students would benefit from additional work with the vocabulary words,

THEN . . . use the ***SRA Imagine It! Photo Library CD*** to help students understand the words.

ON LEVEL

IF . . . students are on level,

THEN . . . pair them, and have them quiz each other about the words' meanings.

ABOVE LEVEL

IF . . . students need a challenge,

THEN . . . have them play a game from the ***Workshop Kit.***

Reading the Selection

Genre Informational Writing

Tell students that "On the Same Day in March" is an example of informational writing. It was written to explain and provide facts about different kinds of weather. Informational writing includes one or more of the following elements:

- It contains facts that can be checked in other sources such as in encyclopedias and newspapers or on the Internet.
- It is about real people, animals, places, and events.
- It often includes maps, diagrams, charts, tables, photographs, and other illustrations to help readers understand.

Comprehension Strategies

During the first reading of "On the Same Day in March," model and prompt the use of the following comprehension strategies:

- Visualizing
- Asking Questions
- Clarifying

1st READ

Focus Question

Read and discuss the Focus Question at the top of page 32. Encourage students to think about the Focus Question as you read "On the Same Day in March."

Reading Recommendations

ROUTINE 12

You will read this selection over a two-day period following Routine 12, reading the selection.

Day 1 Read the entire selection, modeling and prompting the use of the comprehension strategies.

Day 2 Reread the entire selection, focusing on the comprehension skills and the Reading with a Writer's Eye element.

Monitor Progress
to Differentiate Instruction
Formal Assessment

VISUALIZING While prompting students for responses to the Visualizing strategy, note which students are initiating responses and which students seem to be waiting for cues from other students.

APPROACHING LEVEL

IF . . . students have difficulty with Visualizing,	**THEN . . .** during Workshop, reread these pages with students, and share your mental pictures with them. Then ask which words in the text helped them make those pictures.

ON LEVEL

IF . . . students are comfortable with Visualizing,	**THEN . . .** during Workshop, have them illustrate something they visualized from the selection.

ABOVE LEVEL

IF . . . students need a challenge with Visualizing,	**THEN . . .** during Workshop, have them illustrate something they visualized from the selection. Then have them write the words from the text that helped them make those pictures.

Phonics

Words in the selection containing sound/spellings from recent phonics lessons appear in boxes like this throughout the selection. At the end of the first reading, students should be prompted to identify the sound/spellings of these words.

Reading and Responding

Focus Question How is the weather different around the world?

On the Same Day in March

A Tour of the World's Weather

by Marilyn Singer
illustrated by Frané Lessac

32

In the **Arctic**
Polar bears ride on floes of ice,
stalking seals, wishing fish,
as the six-month sun begins to rise
slowly in the Arctic skies. ❶
On the same day in March . . .

33

What's the Weather? Big Book, pp. 32–33

Phonics

/ē/ spelled _y: slowly (page 33)

Differentiating Instruction **English Learner**

IF . . . English learners are having difficulty clarifying, **THEN . . .** refer to the ***English-Learner Support Guide*** Unit 5 Lesson 6.

1st READ

Comprehension Strategies

❶ **Clarifying** Teacher Modeling: *I wonder what "a six-month sun" is. The text begins "In the Arctic," and I've read that the Arctic has sun for only six months of the year. So because this is a day in March, I guess that's when the Arctic sun first starts to appear. I can find more details about when the sun begins to appear in the Arctic by using an encyclopedia or the Internet.*

in **Alberta, Canada**

Just when you can't even remember spring,
that wild chinook blows in like a dragon,
and quicker than you can say Medicine Hat,

34

the biggest snow fort ever
is nothing but a dragon-shaped patch
in somebody's backyard. 2

On the same day in March . . .

35

What's the Weather? Big Book, pp. 34–35

2 Visualizing Teacher Modeling: *The author has created a wonderful "word picture" here. She makes the chinook wind, which is a strong, warm wind, into a dragon that breathes on the snow fort and melts it into a dragon-shaped patch. Can you make a mental picture of the wind as a dragon? Remember that dragons are make-believe creatures that breathe fire and roar. Can you see the patch of melted snow?*

Comprehension Check

What is the weather like in the Arctic and in Alberta, Canada, on the same day in March? **Possible Answer** *The weather is starting to warm up. The ice is starting to break up in the Arctic, and the strong, warm chinook winds are melting the snow in Alberta.*

Phonics

/ē/ spelled _*y*: somebody's (page 35)

Teacher Tips

PRONUNCIATION chinook (shi no͝ok′)

GLOSSARY The terms *weather* (page 32), *Canada* (page 34), and *patch* (page 35) can be found in the Glossary.

LISTEN ATTENTIVELY Remind students to listen attentively so they can participate in discussion using details from the text.

in **Paris, France**
The sun slips out, still winter pale. ❸
But all over the city,
at bus stops and markets,
on small streets and grand boulevards,
people hurrying to work or school,

36

people, huddled in their coats and scarves,
sitting at the outdoor cafés and sipping
chocolat—
all of them turn up their faces
to enjoy the sun's shy smile.

On the same day in March . . .

37

What's the Weather? Big Book, pp. 36–37

Teacher Tip

PRONUNCIATION chocolat (shō kō law')

Phonics

/ē/ spelled *_y:* city, hurrying (page 36)

1st READ

Comprehension Strategies

❸ **Visualizing** Teacher Prompt: *The text says that on this March day in Paris, the sun is still "winter pale." That makes me picture a sun that is just barely shining. It's a pale yellow rather than the bright orange it will be in summer. How do you visualize a pale sun?* **Possible Student Response** *I see an old yellow shirt that's been washed too many times.*

in New York City
It's too gray to play outside today.
The parents sigh, the little kids complain.
But the basketball players stay in the
school yard, arguing what's worse—
snow or sleet or freezing rain.

On the same day in March . . .

38

in the **Texas Panhandle**
They said it was just a tiny twister—
not big enough to spin a horse
or hoist a cow.
But it did suck up a bucket of water
and give Grandma's dirty old truck
the first wash it's had in weeks. 4

On the same day in March . . .

39

What's the Weather? Big Book, pp. 38–39

4 **Asking Questions** Teacher Prompt: *The text says that on this day in Texas in March, there was a "twister." What kind of weather is that? A twister is described as "not big enough to spin a horse," but it did "suck up a bucket of water," and that makes me think a twister is kind of like a tornado. What do you think?* **Possible Student Response** *In "When a Storm Comes Up," we learned that a tornado is one of the worst kinds of storms. If a twister is like a tornado, it is a gentle kind of tornado.*

Comprehension Check

On the same day in March, how is the weather in New York City different from the weather in the Texas Panhandle? In New York City, it's gray and cold. It may be snowing or sleeting. In Texas, it's very windy—there is a small tornado.

Phonics

/ē/ spelled _*y:* city (page 38); tiny, dirty (page 39)

Teacher Tip

GLOSSARY The terms *markets* (page 36), *huddled* (page 37), *Texas Panhandle* (page 39), and *twister* (page 39) can be found in the Glossary.

in the Nile Valley
Fog threads through the temples. 5

40

in a **Louisiana bayou**
Fog settles on the swamp.
On the same day in March . . .

41

What's the Weather? Big Book, pp. 40–41

Phonics

/ē/ spelled _*y*: Valley (page 40)

Teacher Tips

GLOSSARY The terms *fog* (page 40), *Louisiana* (page 41), *swamp* (page 41), *China* (page 42), and *kites* (page 43) can be found in the Glossary.

FLUENCY Although students are not expected to read "On the Same Day in March," your reading will serve as a good model of fluent reading.

1st READ

Comprehension Strategies

5 Clarifying Teacher Modeling: *The text says the fog "threads through the temples." I'm not sure what that means. Let's clarify the meaning of the word* threads. *We know that a piece of thread can go in and around a needle. If I look at the picture on page 40, I can see that the fog looks like it goes in front of and behind the columns. I think* threads *means that the fog goes through the openings of the columns. Look it up in a dictionary to make sure we are correct.*

in **Xian, China**
In the park
the old men and small children guess:
What will the wind carry today? 6

42

Clouds of blue-winged swallows,
dust that hurts their eyes,
rain from up the mountain,
kites shaped like butterflies? 7
On the same day in March . . .

43

What's the Weather? Big Book, pp. 42–43

6 Asking Questions Teacher Modeling: *The text is about a March day in China. I can tell the weather is windy, but I'm not sure I understand the line "What will the wind carry today?" What does carry mean? I'll read on to see whether I can find some information to answer my question.*

7 Answering Questions Teacher Modeling: *Oh, yes, now I see. What the wind might "carry" is what it might blow from one place to another. That might be something nice, like birds or kites, or it might be dust that gets in the eyes.*

Comprehension Check

On the same day in March, how is the weather in the Nile Valley like the weather in Louisiana? It's foggy in both places.

Teacher Tip

PRONUNCIATION Xian (shēahn)

Phonics

/ē/ spelled _y: carry (page 42)

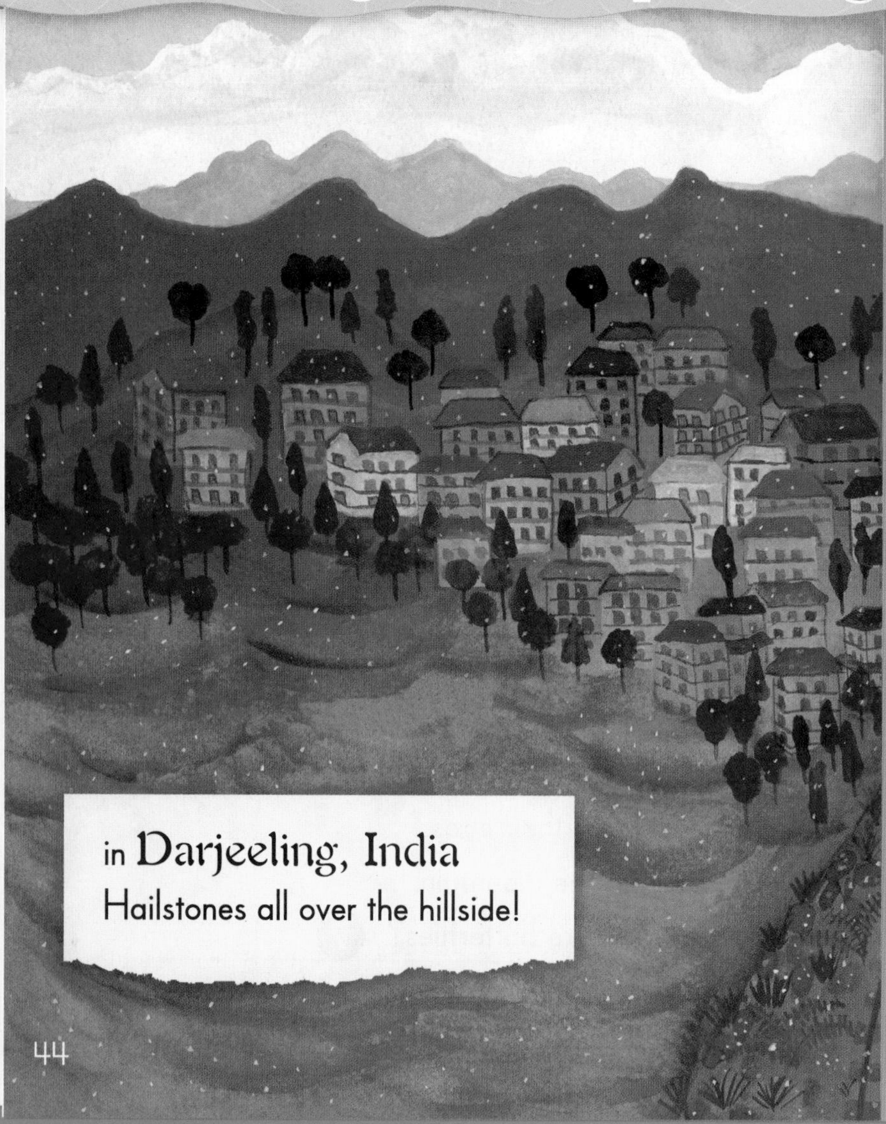
in Darjeeling, India
Hailstones all over the hillside!
44

No one is happy
except little sister,
who thinks the moon has broken and scattered
its necklace of pearls. 8

On the same day in March . . .

45

What's the Weather? Big Book, pp. 44–45

Phonics

/ē/ spelled _y: happy (page 45)

Teacher Tips

PRONUNCIATION Darjeeling (där jē´ ling)

GLOSSARY The word *pearls* (page 45) can be found in the Glossary.

1st READ

Comprehension Strategies

8 Visualizing Teacher Prompt: *Hailstones are shiny, and when they hit the ground they sometimes bounce a little, just like pearls or beads bounce and scatter all over the place when a necklace breaks. I picture the moon as a girl looking surprised or sad as her necklace accidentally breaks, and the pearls scatter and bounce all over the ground. What do you picture?* **Possible Student Response** *I picture the moon as a girl who is mad about something, so she breaks her necklace and scatters the pearls.*

in **Central Thailand**
It's too hot to plant rice.
It's too hot to pick rice. 9
RICE
But it's not too hot to spell R I C E
on the blackboard in the school.
On the same day in March . . .
46
47

What's the Weather? Big Book, pp. 46–47

9 Clarifying Teacher Prompt: *The text says it is "too hot to plant rice" and "too hot to pick rice." I try not to do hard work when it is really hot outside. Working hard in the heat can make you sick. I know the text says it is hot outside. Planting and picking rice must be hard work. Have you ever been working outside when it was really hot?* **Possible Student Response** *I was playing outside when it was hot, and my mom made me come inside to cool down and to drink water.*

Comprehension Check

Why can't people in Thailand plant rice? The weather is too hot.

Teacher Tip

FOCUS It may be difficult for young children to remain focused for long periods of time. Allow students to reenact the events from these pages so they can move around while remaining connected to the selection.

Differentiating Instruction

English Learners

IF . . . students have difficulty participating in the discussion, **THEN . . .** ask questions that can be answered by nodding, saying *yes* or *no,* or using a short phrase. Examples: *Are the seasons different in the northern and southern hemispheres? yes When it is spring in the northern hemisphere, what season is it in the southern hemisphere? fall*

Reading and Responding

in Dakar, Senegal
Sunlight sparkles on the market. 10
48
in Barbados
Sunlight dazzles on the sand.
On the same day in March . . .
49

What's the Weather? Big Book, pp. 48–49

Teacher Tips

PRONUNCIATION Dakar, Senegal (də • kär′ sen • i • gôl′)

Barbados (bär • bā′ • dōs)

GLOSSARY The word *sparkles* (page 48) can be found in the Glossary.

1st READ

Comprehension Strategies

⑩ **Clarifying** Teacher Prompt: *The text says the sunlight sparkles on the market. When I think of the word* sparkles, *I think of colorful jewels shining in the light. I know that jewels can come in many colors such as red, green, yellow, and blue. I think the author is trying to tell us that the clothing, fruits, and vegetables at the market are colorful. What do you think? How did you clarify the text?* **Possible Student Response** *I think you are right. I see many different colors of clothing and many colors of things to buy.*

Comprehension Check

Look at the pictures. What is happening on a sunny March day in the Senegal market? The people are selling and buying food.

What is happening on a sunny March day in Barbados? Some people are playing a game on the beach, and other people are playing in the water.

in **Northern Kenya**
The rains come,
and all in one day,
they leave the gift of a river.
Everyone, hurry!

50

Come drink! Come play!
Before the sun shines
and, all in one day,
takes the river away. 11

On the same day in March . . .

51

What's the Weather? Big Book, pp. 50–51

11 **Clarifying** Teacher Modeling: *I'm not sure what is happening on this page. I think I'll reread the last page to see whether that helps me figure it out. Let's see. The rains come and bring water the people need and enjoy. The rain does not last for long. When the rains stop, the sun will dry up everything, and then the river will go away. Do you have any questions or do you need something clarified?* **Possible Student Response** *Who is they? The text says "they leave the gift of a river." Let's reread to see whether we can figure this out.*

Comprehension Check

What is happening in Kenya on this day in March? Everyone is happy to play in water that will be gone quickly.

Phonics

/ē/ spelled _*y:* everyone, hurry (page 50)

Differentiating Instruction **English Learner**

IF . . . students are unable to answer the comprehension questions, **THEN . . .** during Workshop, reread "On the Same Day in March." Help students identify information in the selection that can help them answer the questions.

in the Amazon Basin, Brazil
Grandpapa is always late.
The rain is always on time,
arriving at three o'clock yesterday,
three o'clock tomorrow,
three o'clock today.

52

"Only the weather wears a watch,"
Grandpapa likes to say,
whenever he or the rain makes everyone wait. 12

On the same day in March . . .

53

What's the Weather? Big Book, pp. 52–53

Phonics

/ē/ spelled _y: Only, everyone (page 53)

Teacher Tip

GLOSSARY The terms *Australia* (page 54) and *crouched* (page 55) can be found in the Glossary.

1st READ

Comprehension Strategies

12 Clarifying Teacher Modeling: *I'm not sure what is happening on this page. I think I'll reread the last page to see whether that helps me figure it out. Let's see. The text says that the rain is always on time, arriving at 3 o'clock each day. So when Grandpapa says that "only the weather wears a watch," I understand that it must rain at around the same time every day during this season.*

Comprehension Check

What does the text tell you about the rain in the Amazon Basin of Brazil on a day in March? It comes at about the same time every day.

in **Darwin, Australia**
Board up the windows!
Bring in the boat!

54

Better to be like crocodiles crouched
on the shore than to be out sailing the sea
when the willy-willies come to call. 13
On the same day in March . . .

55

What's the Weather? Big Book, pp. 54–55

13 **Clarifying** Teacher Prompt: *I've never heard the term* willy-willies *before. From the text, I know that it is windy in Australia on this day in March, so I think* willy-willies *is the name for a kind of strong wind, maybe like a twister or tornado. I can check that by going to the Internet. Do you understand what I've read? Do you have any questions?* **Possible Student Response** *I'm confused. What does* board up the windows *mean? If we look at the illustration, we can see boards across the windows, and the trees look like they are being pushed over by the wind. Sometimes, winds can be so strong they break windows. These boards will help protect the windows.*

Comprehension Check

How are chinooks and twisters alike? *Both are strong winds.*

Phonics

/ē/ spelled _ie_: willy-willies (page 55)

Teacher Tip

CLARIFYING Be sure students understand the selection. Tell them to ask clarifying questions when they do not understand ideas in the text.

in **Patagonia, Argentina**
Over the wide, dry plain
autumn shears the clouds like a flock of sheep. 14

56

"Catch the wool," Mama teases her
youngest son.
He doesn't understand why these white puffs
vanish wet and cold
in his fat warm hands.

On the same day in March . . .

57

What's the Weather? Big Book, pp. 56–57

Teacher Tips

GLOSSARY The terms *autumn* (page 56), *flock* (page 56), and *shore* (page 59) can be found in the Glossary.

MATERIALS Keep the globe nearby as you discuss the selection. Use it to help students find the locations of different places from the selection.

1st READ

Comprehension Strategies

14 **Visualizing** Teacher Prompt: *For fun, sometimes I look at clouds. I try to visualize different animals or things from the shapes of the clouds. I can visualize the fuzzy, fluffy sheep in the clouds in these pictures. What kinds of things do you visualize when you look at clouds?* **Possible Student Response** *I visualize a rabbit with a big white tail.*

Comprehension Check

What is the boy really catching? The boy is really catching snow.

58

in **Antarctica**

Penguins scramble on the shore,
seeking mates, missing fish,
as the six-month sun begins to slice
down below the Antarctic ice. 15

All on the same day in March!

59

What's the Weather? Big Book, pp. 58–59

15 **Clarifying** Teacher Prompt: *Here's another mention of the "six-month sun," which is how long the Arctic has sun. But this page isn't about the Arctic; it's about Antarctica. Are the Arctic and Antarctica the same thing? I'll look at the globe. No, the Arctic is here—there's the North Pole. And Antarctica is here—there's the South Pole. Do you understand what I've read? Do you have any questions?* **Possible Student Response** *I'm confused about the word* slicing. *What does* slice down below the Antarctic ice *mean? If we look at the illustration, we can see that only half of the sun is visible. It looks like the sun is cutting right through the ice.*

Vocabulary Tip

Have students identify the meaning of the word *weather* and use it in a sentence.

Then have students tell meaning of the word *sparkle*. Then have them list things that sparkle from page 48 in their ***Big Book*** and things that sparkle in the world.

Differentiating Instruction English Learners

IF . . . students need help understanding vocabulary, **THEN . . .** use pictures to show meanings.

Writer's Notebook

Have students choose two places they read about and draw pictures in their Writer's Notebooks to compare and contrast the weather in those places on the same day in March. Brainstorm some possible pairs of places, such as the Texas Panhandle and Darwin, Australia. Help them write sentences telling how the weather in their illustrations is the same or different.

Phonics

Have students practice identifying sound/spellings from recent lessons. Turn to a page in the selection, and say a sound/spelling that appears on that page. Then have students point to the word with that sound/spelling. Remind them to look at ***Sound/Spelling Cards*** for help.

BIG Idea

What is weather?

After reading the selection, read the Big Idea question. Discuss with students how the selection helps answer this question.

Concept/Question Board

Have students help you make a list of different kinds of weather conditions in the selection that they might want to find out more about, including chinooks, twisters, and willy-willies. Add the list to the **Concept/Question Board,** and encourage students to find and post additional information and pictures about each one.

Discussing the Selection

✦ Ask students the following to check their comprehension of the selection:

- *What did we learn about weather in various parts of the world?* **Possible Answers** *Some places have rainy weather, like Kenya and the Amazon Basin in Brazil. Some parts of the world have very cold weather, like the Arctic, Antarctica, and Alberta, Canada. Many places around the world have weather that is different from where we live.*
- *How is the weather where we live the same or different from the weather we read about?* **Possible Answer** *Sometimes, our weather is rainy like in the Amazon basin in Brazil, and other times it is warm like in Barbados.*
- *What do you think was the most interesting weather we read about?* **Possible Answer** *When the rains come in Northern Kenya, then they stop and the river dries up.*
- *How do the seasons differ in the northern and southern hemispheres? The seasons are reversed; when it is spring in the northern hemisphere, it is fall in the southern hemisphere.*

✦ Have students return to the Focus Question on page 32 of the selection. Select a student to read the question aloud, and have students answer and discuss the questions. Encourage students to return to the text when answering their questions.

✦ Have students identify any words they found confusing or difficult in the selection, such as *except* and *crouched*. Have students use a beginning dictionary to look up the meanings of the words.

Discussing Strategy Use

Have students talk about how strategies were used to help them better understand the selection.

- How did you clarify words or confusing passages?
- How did visualizing help you get more from the selection?
- How did you use information in the text to answer questions?

Purposes for Reading

Review the purposes set for reading "On the Same Day in March." Have students tell whether they met their purposes for reading. Have them identify information from the text that talks about the purposes they set:

- To find out how the weather is different in different places of the world
- To learn what causes the weather to be different in different places

Vocabulary Review

- On the board or on a transparency, write the following incomplete sentences. Have students review the selection vocabulary words by saying the word that completes the sentence. Write the word in the blank.

  The sunlight ________ on the jewelry. *sparkles*

  The ________ yesterday was rainy, but today it is sunny. *weather*

- Next have students relate the words to prior knowledge by telling about weather they have experienced and about something they have seen that sparkles.

Print and Book Awareness

Print and Book Awareness

Review Glossary and Punctuation: Ellipses

- Before reviewing ellipses, review the purpose of a glossary by having students locate the Glossary in their ***Big Books*** and then having them tell what a glossary is. *A glossary is the part of a book that contains some words from the selections in the book and the word meanings. The words in a glossary appear in alphabetical order.*
- Review the use of ellipses with students. Ask a volunteer to explain when and why authors use these three dots. *to tell the reader to pause to build interest or that a sentence is going to be completed on another page*
- Say the following, pausing briefly for the ellipsis: *At that very moment across town . . . a boy was fixing his bike.* Point out that by pausing, you created some interest in what might happen next. Remind them that authors often do the same when they want readers to pay close attention to what is happening. Write the sentence on the board, using the ellipsis. Have students read it with you, pausing for the ellipsis.
- Review pages in "On the Same Day in March" that contain an ellipsis and how the author uses ellipses to build interest.

Teacher Tips

WORD BANK Have students add the selection vocabulary words as well as any new weather-related words they have read or talked about to the What's the Weather? Word Bank.

HIGH-FREQUENCY WORDS To help students review the high-frequency words they have learned, say some of the words aloud, and have students point to each one in the selection. Remind them to look at the High-Frequency Word Bank for help.

Selection Vocabulary

weather (page 32)
sparkles (page 48)

Monitor Progress

to Differentiate Instruction
Formal Assessment

Observe students as they create sentences using selection vocabulary. Notice which students use vocabulary appropriately in their sentences and which students seem confused about the proper use of the word(s).

APPROACHING LEVEL

IF . . . students need additional practice with vocabulary words,	**THEN . . .** help them draw and label pictures to show the meaning of each word.

ON LEVEL

IF . . . students are comfortable with vocabulary words,	**THEN . . .** pair them, and have them play ***eSkills*** games.

ABOVE LEVEL

IF . . . students need a challenge,	**THEN . . .** have them play ***eSkills*** games.

OBJECTIVES

Students will
- learn about features of a newspaper.
- make notes to write a weather news story.
- form the letters *v* and *w* correctly.
- control the size and spacing of letters.

MATERIALS
- Routine 14
- ***Transparencies*** 38, 39
- ***Alphabet Letter Cards***

Writing News Stories

ROUTINE 14

Prewriting

Teach—Making Notes

- Show students a newspaper, and explain what newspapers are. *daily or weekly publications with stories that tell about things that are happening in the community and around the world* Point to individual stories on the front page of the newspaper. Explain that each story gives readers new information about a person, an event, or a thing.
- Point to and read the weather forecast. Then explain that this is the weather that scientists predict will happen. Show the U.S. weather map, and have students notice how the weather is different in various parts of the country.
- Read students a news story from your local paper about the weather. If one is not available, use the sample news story on ***Transparency*** 38. Explain that newspapers often contain stories about the weather because it is so important in our lives.
- Tell students that starting today, they are going to be weather reporters. They will make notes that will help them write a news story about the weather.

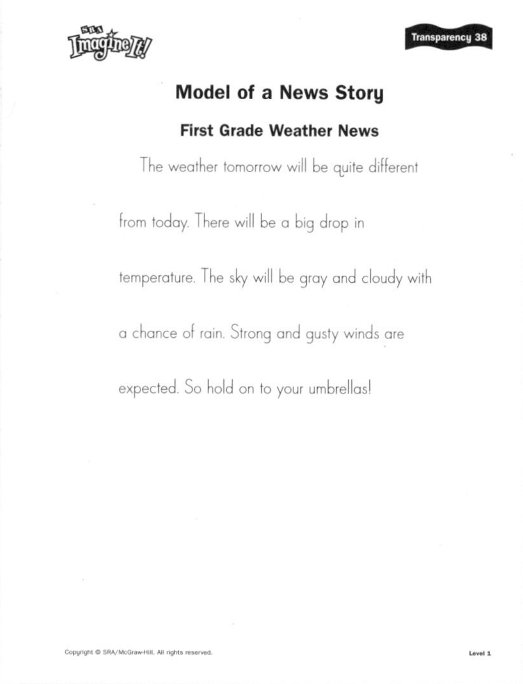
Transparency 38

Model of a News Story

First Grade Weather News

The weather tomorrow will be quite different from today. There will be a big drop in temperature. The sky will be gray and cloudy with a chance of rain. Strong and gusty winds are expected. So hold on to your umbrellas!

 Level 1

Transparency 38

Teacher Tip

PLAN AHEAD Have available a newspaper that contains a weather forecast and a U.S. weather map. Also select a newspaper story about the weather. It might be about storm damage from wind, rain, or snow; problems caused by the lack of or too much rain; people enjoying the first warm day of spring; or weather forecasts for the coming week.

Differentiating Instruction: English Learners

IF . . . students need extra help with writing news stories, **THEN . . .** see ***English Learner Support Guide*** Unit 5 Lessons 6–10 to help them understand how to organize their ideas and information.

Writing News Stories, cont.

Teacher Modeling: Model how to make notes for writing a weather news story. Say *I think I will write a news story about the weather today. First, I'll need to go outside and make notes about what I see.* Then, describe the weather you observe in your area. An example could be *Today is cloudy, and we have some rain, so I'll write* cloudy *and* rainy. *It's also warm, so I'll add* warm *to the notes. We haven't had any bad storms for a while, so I'll make a note of that too. What other notes do you think I should make to get ready to write a news story about the weather?*

- Explain to students why taking notes is an important strategy for collecting and organizing information before beginning to write. Make sure they understand why the strategy is important, when to apply it, and how to use it.

Guided Practice

Have students help you generate ideas for additional notes about the weather on the board or on chart paper. For example, ask whether the wind is blowing. If so, how strong is it? Is the rain a drizzle, a shower, or a thunderstorm? Are the clouds dark or white? Is the weather warmer or cooler than it was last week?

Assessment

You will use the Writing Rubrics found in the Level Appendix to evaluate students' news stories. You may use any of the rubrics for Genre, Writing Process, and Writing Traits. Share with students what you will be looking for when assessing their news stories.

Traits of Good Writing

Ideas The writer uses short phrases or single words to take notes before writing.

Penmanship

Alphabet Practice: The Letters *v* and *w*

Teach

Model how to form lowercase *v* and *w* by writing the letters on ***Transparency*** 39. Describe each stroke on the handwriting models as you trace them. Point out similarities in how these two letters are written—both letters have straight lines.

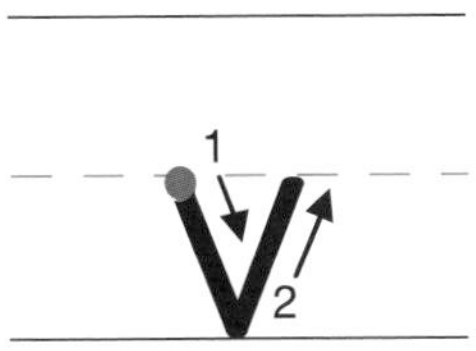

Starting point, slanting down right, slanting up right: small *v*

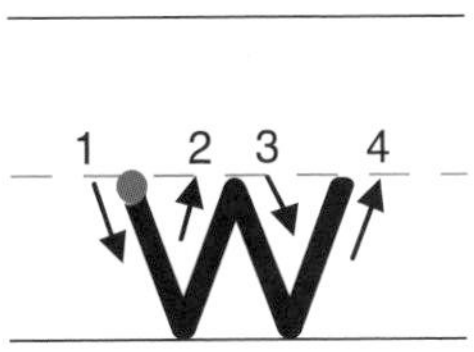

Starting point, slanting down right, slanting up right, slanting down right, slanting up right: small *w*

Guided Practice

Help students use their index fingers to trace the letters *v* and *w* on the ***Alphabet Letter Cards*** as they say each letter name.

Apply

- For letter-formation practice, provide students with handwriting paper. Have them write the letters *v* and *w* four times within the lines as they say the letter names.
- Have students proofread their line by circling any incorrect letters and making them better by rewriting them. Then have them underline their best *v* and *w*.

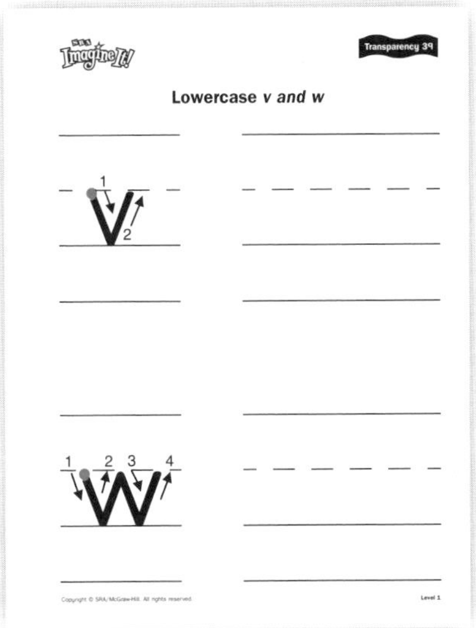

Transparency 39

Preparing to Read

OBJECTIVES

Students will

- blend, spell, and read words that contain /ē/ spelled _y and _ie_.
- identify compound words.

MATERIALS

- Routines 3–7, 10–11
- ***Sound/Spelling Card*** 28
- ***Skills Practice 1,*** pp. 195–196

Teacher Tip

SOUND/SPELLING CARD REVIEW Review the ***Sound/Spelling Cards*** throughout the day. Review when you are waiting in line to go somewhere, waiting for dismissal, and so on.

Daily Warm-Ups

Copy the Morning Message on the board or on chart paper. Have students answer the question. Read the message aloud, and discuss it with students. **Possible Answer** *On the same day, it can be rainy in one place and sunny in another place.*

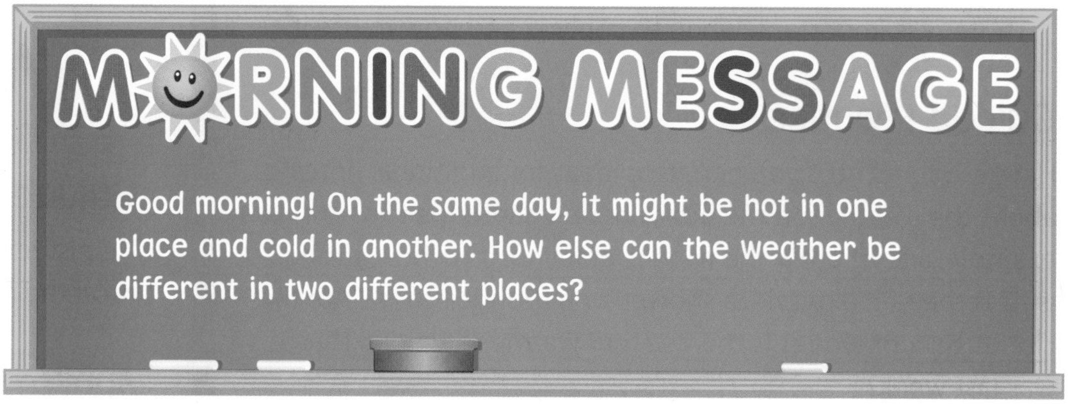
MORNING MESSAGE
Good morning! On the same day, it might be hot in one place and cold in another. How else can the weather be different in two different places?

Daily Language Review

To review capitalization, write the following sentence on the board, or generate a similar one with students, and have students make corrections: grace and I went to the grand canyon last summer. *Grace and I went to the Grand Canyon last summer.*

Sound/Spelling Review

Name a ***Sound/Spelling Card,*** and have a student say the sound the card represents and a word that contains the sound. Have the class tell where in the word the sound appears—beginning, middle, or end.

Phonics

ROUTINE 3 ROUTINE 4 ROUTINE 10 ROUTINE 11

Review: /ē/ Spelled _y and _ie_

Blending

Point to ***Sound/Spelling Card*** 28—Long E, and review the /ē/ spellings. Pay special attention to the _y and _ie_ spellings.

Use Routine 3, whole-word blending, and Routine 4, blending sentences, to have students blend the words and sentences. Use Routine 10, closed syllables, and Routine 11, open syllables, to have students blend the multisyllable words.

Line 1	happy	sleepy	party	city
Line 2	relief	chief	shield	achieve
Line 3	bunnies	ponies	jellies	pennies
Line 4	cornfield	copycat	babysitter	ladybug

Sentence 1	They ran in the muddy field.
Sentence 2	The three ponies were tiny.

Line 1 **/ē/ spelled _y**

Have students identify the spelling for /ē/. _y Have them say the words syllable by syllable. The words *happy* and *city* are also in the selection "On the Same Day in March." Explain the meaning of each word and have students use each word in a sentence.

Line 2 **/ē/ spelled _ie_**

Have students identify the spelling for /ē/. _ie_

Sound/Spelling Card 28

Teacher Tips

SYLLABICATION To help students blend the words and build fluency, use the syllabication below of the multisyllable words on the word lines.

hap • py	sleep • y
par • ty	cit • y
re • lief	a • chieve
bun • nies	po • nies
jel • lies	pen • nies
corn • field	cop • y • cat
ba • by • sit • ter	la • dy • bug

SCHWA Because the *a* in *achieve* has the schwa sound, you may want to indicate this by putting a dot over the *a* in *achieve*.

Differentiating Instruction **English Learners**

IF . . . students are native speakers of Vietnamese, Hmong, or Cantonese,
THEN . . . they may need extra practice blending multisyllabic words. In these languages, all words are monosyllabic.

Line 3 **/ē/ spelled _*ie*_**

Ask students what the words have in common. *They are plural nouns.* Have them identify the singular form of each word. *bunny, pony, jelly, penny* Ask what sound/spelling the singular forms end with. */ē/ spelled _y*

Line 4 **/ē/ spelled _*ie*_ and _*y***

Ask students what the words have in common. *They are compound words.* Ask students to identify the two words in each compound word in this line.

Sentences 1–2

Review the high-frequency words before writing the sentences. Have students reread the sentences to promote fluency.

Developing Oral Language

Have a student choose and read a word, and use the word in a sentence. Call on other students to extend the sentence by asking *where, what, when,* and *which* questions. Then have another student erase the word. **Possible Answer** *The bunnies were eating carrots. (Where?) The bunnies were eating carrots in the garden.*

Guided Practice

Have students complete ***Skills Practice 1*** pages 195–196 for practice with the /ē/ sound spelled _y and _ie_ and for dictation. Have students unscramble the letters to write words on page 195. Have students write the word that matches each picture on page 196. Students can use the bottom of the page for dictation.

UNIT 5 Lesson 7

Name ________ Date ______

Sounds and Spellings Review

Directions: Unscramble the letters and write the word that names the picture.

a p h y p — happy
s n p i e o — ponies
e l i a d s — ladies
t c y i — city
y n u b n — bunny
e r s b i e r — berries

Skills Practice 1 • Phonics UNIT 5 • Lesson 7 195

UNIT 5 Lesson 7

Sounds and Spellings Review

Directions: Write the word that goes with each picture.

cherries thirty babies

babies thirty cherries

Dictation

baby babies
lady ladies
Molly studies history.

196 UNIT 5 • Lesson 7 Phonics • *Skills Practice 1*

Skills Practice 1, pp. 195–196

Dictation

ROUTINE 5 ROUTINE 6 ROUTINE 7

Use dictation Routine 5, sounds-in-sequence, Routine 6, whole-word dictation, and Routine 7, sentence dictation, with the following:

Line 1	baby	babies
Line 2	lady	ladies
Sentence	Molly studies history.	

Teacher Tip

Remind students to refer to the ***Sound/Spelling Cards.*** Encourage them to ask which spelling to use.

Monitor Progress

to Differentiate Instruction
Formal Assessment

DICTATION As students spell words, notice who uses the ***Sound/Spelling Cards*** and spells the words correctly. Note students who are asking for help with the long-vowel spellings.

APPROACHING LEVEL

IF . . . students need additional practice with phonics and dictation, THEN . . . have them complete ***Reteach 1*** pages 145–146.

ON LEVEL

IF . . . students are on level with phonics and dictation, THEN . . . pair them, and have them play a game from ***eSkills.***

ABOVE LEVEL

IF . . . students need a challenge with phonics and dictation, THEN . . . have them complete ***Challenge Activities 1*** page 73.

OBJECTIVES

Students will

- review vocabulary.
- apply the comprehension skill Compare and Contrast.
- identify capitalization of *I* and names of people.
- talk about and appreciate fine art.

MATERIALS

- ***What's the Weather? Big Book,*** pp. 32–61
- Routine 12
- ***Transparency*** 1
- Writer's Notebooks

Teacher Tips

MATERIALS Place a globe or world map so all students can see it clearly. Make sure the location of each place mentioned in the selection is marked with a sticker. You may also want to keep a chart of the various types of weather that occur in "On the Same Day in March."

WEATHER PERMITTING For this experiment, the weather should be sunny with little to no wind. If it is sunny but too windy, placing the trash bag in a sunny location inside is also an option.

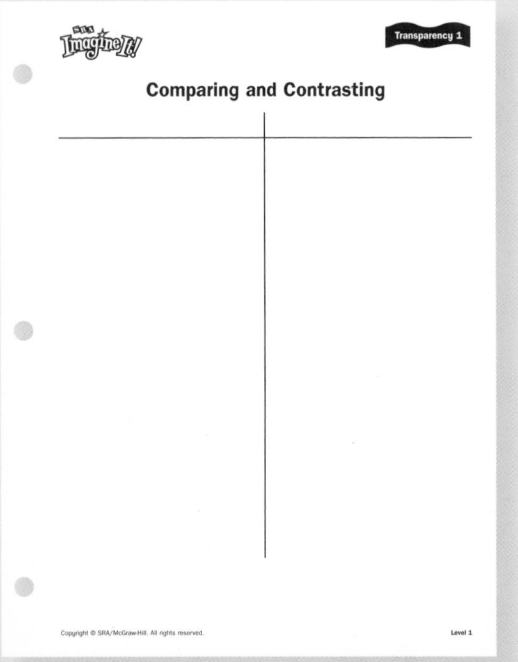

Imagine It! Transparency 1

Comparing and Contrasting

Level 1

Transparency 1

Reading Recommendations

ROUTINE 12

Retelling

- Before rereading "On the Same Day in March," have students follow along as you read the place names in the ***What's the Weather? Big Book.*** Have them use the names and pictures to retell specific details of information heard in the selection. Prompt them as needed to ensure that they recall correctly the weather conditions for each place named. Be sure students are speaking clearly and using appropriate volume as they retell the facts of the selection.
- Remind students that they will need to listen attentively during the rereading of the selection so they can participate in discussions and respond to questions.

2nd READ

Comprehension Skills

- As you reread "On the Same Day in March," work with students to apply the comprehension skill Compare and Contrast. Use ***Transparency*** 1 to record comparisons and contrasts that you and students make as you reread the selection.
- Students should understand how to use the Compare and Contrast transparency at this point in the year. Be sure to have students tell you where on the transparency to record their responses.

2nd READ

Reading with a Writer's Eye

In this rereading of "On the Same Day in March," discuss with students how the author organizes information using patterned repetition to make the selection more interesting and to help readers better understand it.

Vocabulary Review

Have students use each selection vocabulary word in an oral sentence. Help them expand their sentences by asking *who, what, where, when, why,* and *how* questions.

Introduce six expanding vocabulary words to students as the selection is reread. These words and definitions will help students better comprehend the selection.

Teacher Tip

BEGINNING DICTIONARY Before students hear the selection for a second time, have them look up any unfamiliar words in a beginning dictionary. Then have them read the entry.

Concept/Question Board

Have students use the selection vocabulary words and high-frequency words to write sentences about the weather to add to the **Concept/ Question Board.**

Differentiating Instruction: English Learners

IF . . . students need help contributing to the **Concept/Question Board, THEN . . .** encourage them to craft their postings in their native languages. Help them to also include vocabulary or short phrases in English with their posts.

Selection Vocabulary

sparkles (page 48)
weather (page 32)

Monitor Progress to Differentiate Instruction

Formal Assessment

COMPARE AND CONTRAST As students compare and contrast, note who is participating and understanding the comprehension skill.

APPROACHING LEVEL	**IF . . .** students are having difficulty comparing and contrasting things in the text,	**THEN . . .** have them compare simple things they are familiar with such as school supplies.
ON LEVEL	**IF . . .** students could use more practice with comparing or contrasting,	**THEN . . .** have them choose two places from the selection and compare and contrast the two places.
ABOVE LEVEL	**IF . . .** students are able to apply the skill with ease,	**THEN . . .** have them compare and contrast a place from the selection with the city you live in.

Day 2

Reading and Responding

Focus Question How is the weather different around the world?

On the Same Day in March

A Tour of the World's Weather

by Marilyn Singer

illustrated by Frané Lessac

32

In the **Arctic**
Polar bears ride on floes of ice,
stalking seals, wishing fish,
as the six-month sun begins to rise
slowly in the Arctic skies.
On the same day in March . . .

33

What's the Weather? Big Book, pp. 32–33

Teacher Tip

GEOGRAPHY As you read each place name in the selection, point to it on the globe.

Differentiating Instruction English Learners

IF . . . students have difficulty understanding the concept of comparing and contrasting or stating comparisons and contrasts, **THEN . . .** use pictures or demonstrations to teach basic vocabulary for comparing and contrasting, including *and, both, same, but,* and *different.*

2nd READ

Comprehension Skills

Compare and Contrast

Before reading these pages, remind students that readers can better understand what they are reading if they can find ways in which the settings, events, people, and things are similar and ways in which they are different.

- As students compare and contrast, have them tell you where on ***Transparency*** 1 to record each response. Leave room to add information throughout the reading.
- Ask students how a drizzle is similar to a thunderstorm and how they are different from each other. *Both are kinds of rain. A drizzle is a light rain, and a thunderstorm is a heavy rain; a thunderstorm has thunder and lightning, and a drizzle doesn't.*
- After reading pages 32–35, ask students to use the text and pictures to tell how the weather in the Arctic is similar to and different from the weather in Alberta, Canada, on the same day in March. **Possible Answers** *Similarities: The weather is cold in both places, and both places have snow and ice. Differences: The six-month sun comes to the Arctic, but Alberta, Canada, doesn't have a six-month sun.*

in **Alberta, Canada**
Just when you can't even remember spring,
that wild chinook blows in like a dragon,
and quicker than you can say Medicine Hat,

34

the biggest snow fort ever
is nothing but a dragon-shaped patch
in somebody's backyard.

On the same day in March . . .

35

What's the Weather? Big Book, pp. 34–35

Reading with a Writer's Eye

2nd READ

Text Structure: Patterned Repetition

Remind students that "On the Same Day in March" is an example of informational writing. Tell students that authors can organize informational writing to make it easier for readers to understand and to make a specific point. One way to organize the writing is by using a group of words repeatedly throughout a selection. These words can give readers a clue about the main idea. The patterned text also helps readers compare and contrast information in the selection. In this selection, the main idea is that on the same day, the weather is different in different places. Tell students to watch for text that is repeated in this selection.

- Ask students what group of words is repeated on pages 33 and 35? *On the same day in March . . .*

Expanding Vocabulary

Introduce six expanding vocabulary words to students as the selection is reread.

patch a small plot (page 35)

We made our garden on a small *patch* of land.

Teacher Tip

DIGITAL TOOLS Have students use an online dictionary to determine the meaning of any words they do not understand in this selection.

in **Paris, France**
The sun slips out, still winter pale.
But all over the city,
at bus stops and markets,
on small streets and grand boulevards,
people hurrying to work or school,

36

people, huddled in their coats and scarves,
sitting at the outdoor cafés and sipping
chocolat—
all of them turn up their faces
to enjoy the sun's shy smile.

On the same day in March . . .

37

What's the Weather? Big Book, pp. 36–37

Teacher Tip

PRINT AND BOOK AWARENESS Point to the ellipsis on page 37. Remind students that authors sometimes use these three dots to show that the reader should pause.

Expanding Vocabulary

pale light in color (page 36)

In spring, people like to wear *pale* colors like pink.

huddled Past tense of **huddle:** to crowd together (page 37)

The animals *huddled* together to stay warm.

2nd READ

Comprehension Skills

Compare and Contrast

- As students compare and contrast, have them tell you where on the transparency to record each response. After reading pages 36 and 37, ask students to use the text and pictures to compare and contrast the people in the two illustrations and what they tell about the weather.
- After reading pages 38 and 39, ask students to compare the weather in New York and the Texas Panhandle. **Possible Answers** *It is March in both areas. In New York, it is gray and cold. The Texas Panhandle has a tiny twister.*

in New York City
It's too gray to play outside today.
The parents sigh, the little kids complain.
But the basketball players stay in the
school yard, arguing what's worse—
snow or sleet or freezing rain.

On the same day in March . . .

38

in the **Texas Panhandle**
They said it was just a tiny twister—
not big enough to spin a horse
or hoist a cow.
But it did suck up a bucket of water
and give Grandma's dirty old truck
the first wash it's had in weeks.

On the same day in March . . .

39

What's the Weather? Big Book, pp. 38–39

Reading with a Writer's Eye

2nd READ

Text Structure: Patterned Repetition

Tell students that patterned repetition is a group of words used repeatedly throughout a selection. Remind students that authors use repetition to make it easier for readers to understand the text and to know what to expect in a selection.

- Which group of words is repeated on pages 37, 38, and 39? *On the same day in March . . .*
- What does the author want you to do when you read these words? *pause and think about the main idea and get ready to compare the weather in different places*

Teacher Tips

PRINT AND BOOK AWARENESS You may want to have students point to the ellipsis on page 38. Have students explain the purpose of an ellipsis.

GLOSSARY Point out the word *twister.* Tell students that they can find the meaning of this word in the Glossary. Have them find the word *twister* in the Glossary. Then read the sample sentence. Have them look at the illustration that accompanies the Glossary text.

Day 2 Reading and Responding

in the Nile Valley
Fog threads through the temples.

40

in a **Louisiana bayou**
Fog settles on the swamp.
On the same day in March . . .

41

What's the Weather? Big Book, pp. 40–41

Teacher Tip

PRINT AND BOOK AWARENESS Have students point to the ellipsis on these pages and tell you when to pause as you read.

Expanding Vocabulary

fog thick mist; a cloud of small drops of water (page 40)

Fog is a cloud that is close to the ground.

swamp wet, spongy ground (page 41)

It is hard to walk through a *swamp*.

2nd READ

Comprehension Skills

Compare and Contrast

✦ As students compare and contrast, have them tell you where on the transparency to record each response. Leave plenty of room to record information throughout the selection.

✦ To help students compare and contrast the information on pages 40–43, ask them the following questions:

- *Which weather condition is the same in the Nile Valley of Egypt and in the Louisiana bayou? fog*
- *How is the weather in Xian, China, different from the weather in the Nile Valley? The Nile Valley has fog and Xian, China, doesn't; Xian, China, has strong wind, and the Nile Valley doesn't.*

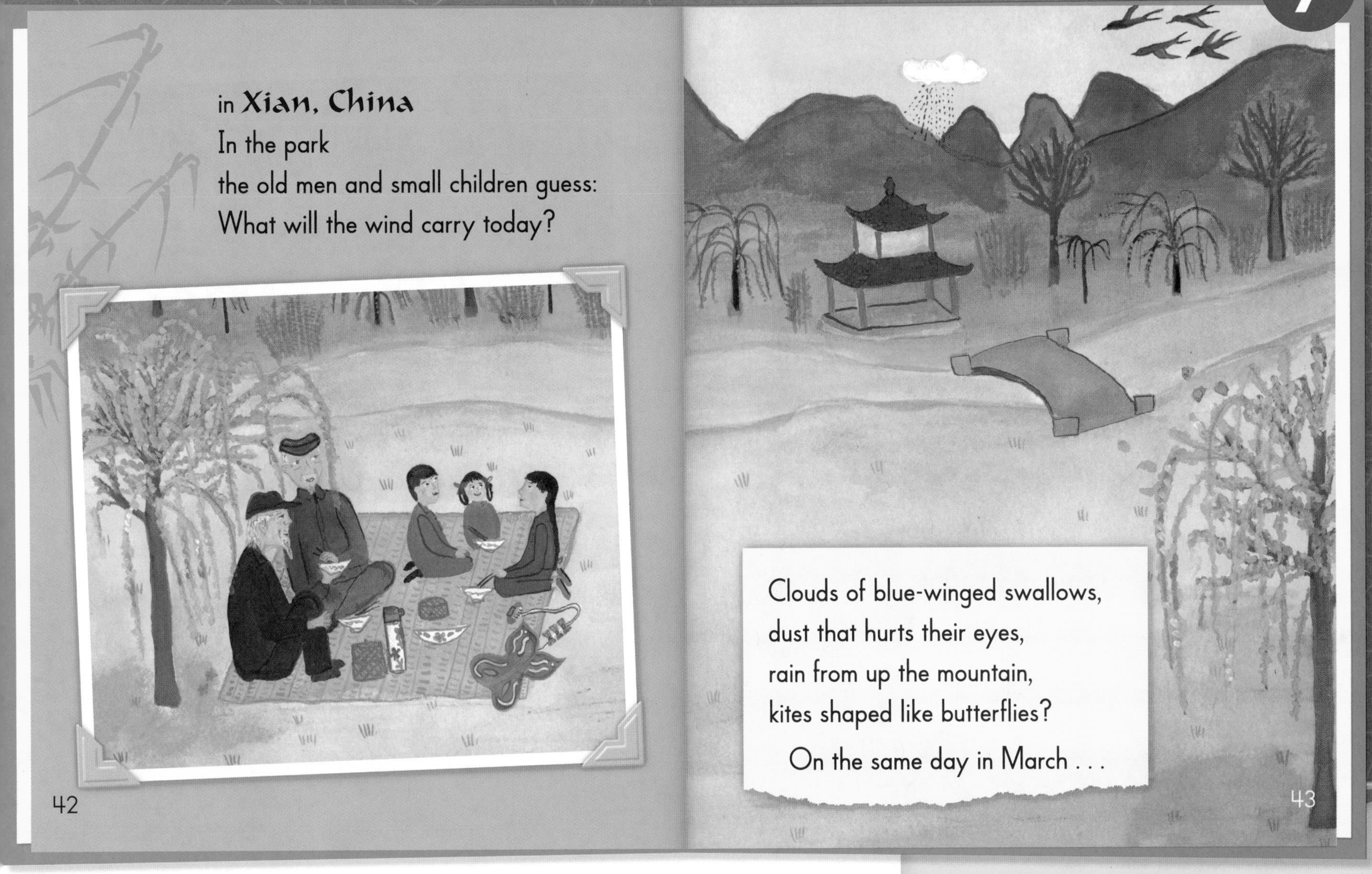
in **Xian, China**
In the park
the old men and small children guess:
What will the wind carry today?

Clouds of blue-winged swallows,
dust that hurts their eyes,
rain from up the mountain,
kites shaped like butterflies?
On the same day in March . . .

42 43

What's the Weather? Big Book, pp. 42–43

Reading with a Writer's Eye

2nd READ

Text Structure: Patterned Repetition

Have students look back at the text on pages 33–43. Have them identify the first word on each page of the selection. Help students recognize that the word *in* is the first word on most pages. Tell students that the author uses the word *in* to alert the reader that she is going to talk about a new place. Have students continue to look for this pattern of text so they will know when a new place is being described.

Teacher Tips

WRITING When you talk about the different ways authors use patterned repetition, you may want to suggest to students that they try to use patterned repetition in their writing.

CAPITALIZATION You may want to revisit this selection when students review the grammar skills in Lesson 8. "On the Same Day in March" contains several examples of capitalization of special things and places.

in Darjeeling, India
Hailstones all over the hillside!
44
No one is happy
except little sister,
who thinks the moon has broken and scattered
its necklace of pearls.
On the same day in March . . .
45

What's the Weather? Big Book, pp. 44–45

Teacher Tip

PRINT AND BOOK AWARENESS Have students find the ellipsis on page 45. Ask what these three dots show. *that the reader should pause*

2nd READ

Comprehension Skills

Compare and Contrast

- As students compare and contrast, have them tell you where on the transparency to record each response. Leave room for additional information throughout the selection.
- After reading pages 44 and 45, ask students to use the text and pictures to compare and contrast Darjeeling in India and Alberta in Canada. **Possible Answers** *Both places have hills. Darjeeling has hailstones. In Alberta, snow is melting.*
- After reading pages 46 and 47, ask students to use the text and pictures to compare and contrast this school with their own school. **Possible Answers** *In both schools, students learn how to read and write. In our school, we have walls and air conditioners. The school in the illustration doesn't have walls.*

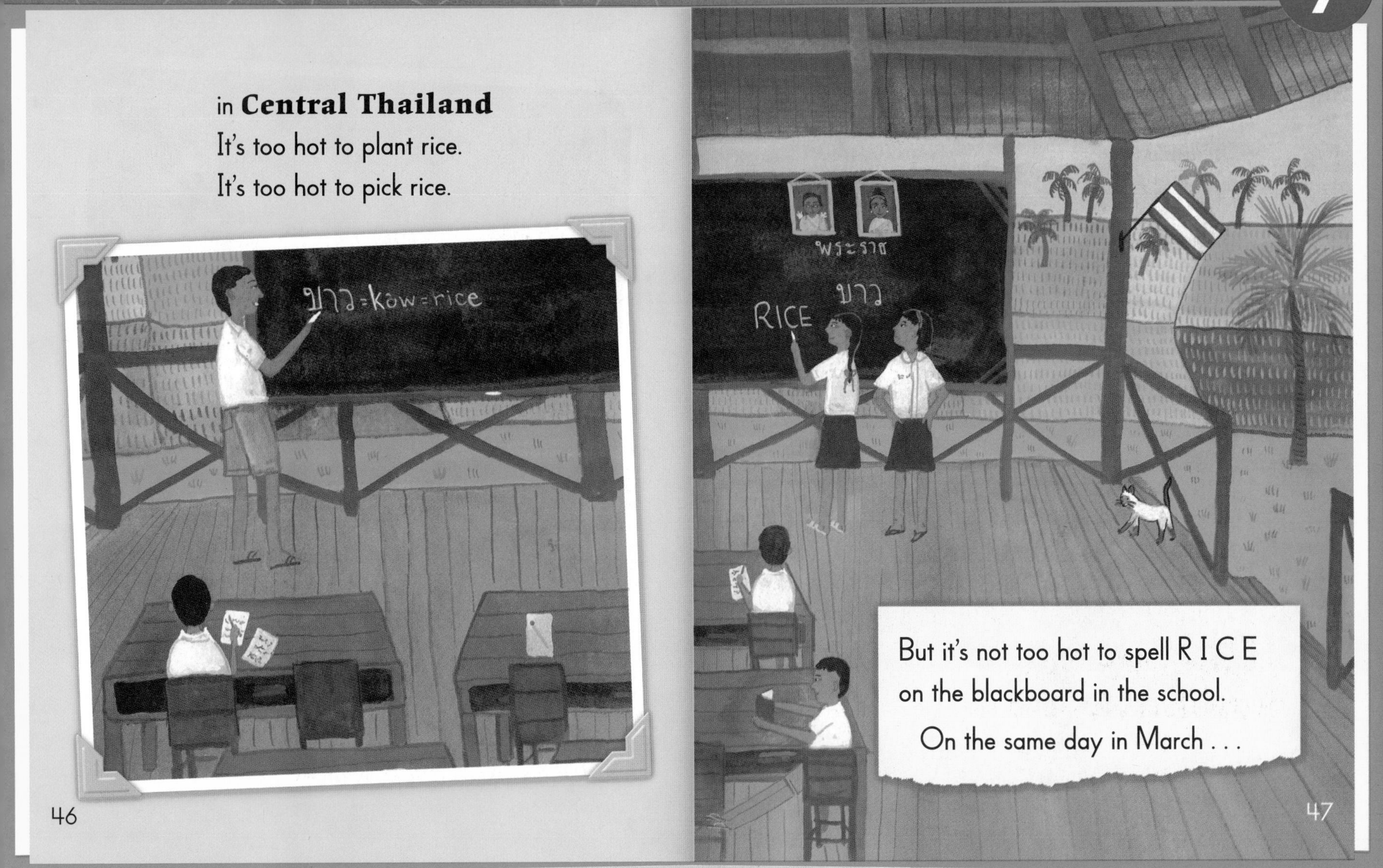
in **Central Thailand**
It's too hot to plant rice.
It's too hot to pick rice.

But it's not too hot to spell R I C E
on the blackboard in the school.
On the same day in March . . .

46 47

What's the Weather? Big Book, pp. 46–47

Reading with a Writer's Eye

2nd READ

Text Structure: Patterned Repetition

After reading pages 45–47, have students find and read the group of words "On the same day in March . . ." *pages 45 and 47* Then ask the following question:

What does the author want you to do when you see these words? The author wants us to pause, think about the weather, and get ready to compare it to the weather someplace else

Teacher Tip

STRATEGY USE Even though the second reading focuses on comprehension skills and Reading with a Writer's Eye, students should be encouraged to continue using comprehension strategies to help them better understand the selection.

in Dakar, Senegal
Sunlight sparkles on the market.
48
in Barbados
Sunlight dazzles on the sand.
On the same day in March . . .
49

What's the Weather? Big Book, pp. 48–49

Teacher Tip

GLOSSARY Point out the word *sparkles*. Tell students they can find the meaning of this word in the Glossary. Turn to the Glossary. Have them find the word *sparkles*. Then read the sample sentence. Have them look at the illustration that accompanies the Glossary text.

2nd READ

Comprehension Skills

Compare and Contrast

- As students compare and contrast, have them tell you where on the transparency to record each response. Leave room for additional information throughout the selection.
- After reading pages 48 through 51, ask students the following questions:
  - *How is the weather in Barbados the same as the weather in Dakar, Senegal?* *It is sunny and hot in both places.*
  - *How is the weather in Dakar, Senegal, different from the weather in northern Kenya?* *It is sunny and dry in Dakar, and it rains heavily in Kenya.*

in **Northern Kenya**
The rains come,
and all in one day,
they leave the gift of a river.
Everyone, hurry!
50

Come drink! Come play!
Before the sun shines
and, all in one day,
takes the river away.

On the same day in March . . .

51

What's the Weather? Big Book, pp. 50–51

Reading with a Writer's Eye

2nd READ

Text Structure: Patterned Repetition

Have students recall what the selection is about. Ask students what the author tells about each location. Help them understand that the story talks about many different places, the weather in those places, and the activities that are happening because of the weather. Tell students the author organizes the information about each place in the same way. Explain to students that this organization is another way the author uses patterned repetition in the selection.

Teacher Tip

PRINT AND BOOK AWARENESS Have students find the ellipses on pages 49 and 51 and explain their purpose.

in the Amazon Basin, Brazil
Grandpapa is always late.
The rain is always on time,
arriving at three o'clock yesterday,
three o'clock tomorrow,
three o'clock today.

52

"Only the weather wears a watch,"
Grandpapa likes to say,
whenever he or the rain makes everyone wait.

On the same day in March . . .

53

What's the Weather? Big Book, pp. 52–53

Teacher Tips

VERBS You may want to remind students about the focus of past grammar lessons—verbs. Encourage students to identify the verbs on these pages.

ADJECTIVES You may want to remind students about the focus of past grammar lessons—adjectives, or describing words. Encourage students to identify the adjectives on these pages.

2nd READ

Comprehension Skills

Compare and Contrast

- As students compare and contrast, have them tell you where on the transparency to record each response. Leave room for additional information throughout the selection.
- After reading pages 52 and 53, ask students the following:
  How is the rain in the Amazon Basin different from the rain in northern Kenya? **Possible Answer** *The rain in Kenya comes all on one day, but the rain in the Amazon Basin arrives every day at the same time.*

in Darwin, Australia
Board up the windows!
Bring in the boat!
54
Better to be like crocodiles crouched
on the shore than to be out sailing the sea
when the willy-willies come to call.
On the same day in March . . .
55

What's the Weather? Big Book, pp. 54–55

Reading with a Writer's Eye

Text Structure: Patterned Repetition

After reading these pages, have students find and read the group of words "On the same day in March . . ." *pages 53 and 55* Then ask the following question:

What does the author want you to do when you see these words? The author wants us to pause, think about the weather, and get ready to compare it to the weather someplace else

Teacher Tip

PRINT AND BOOK AWARENESS Have students find the ellipses on pages 53 and 55.

Reading and Responding

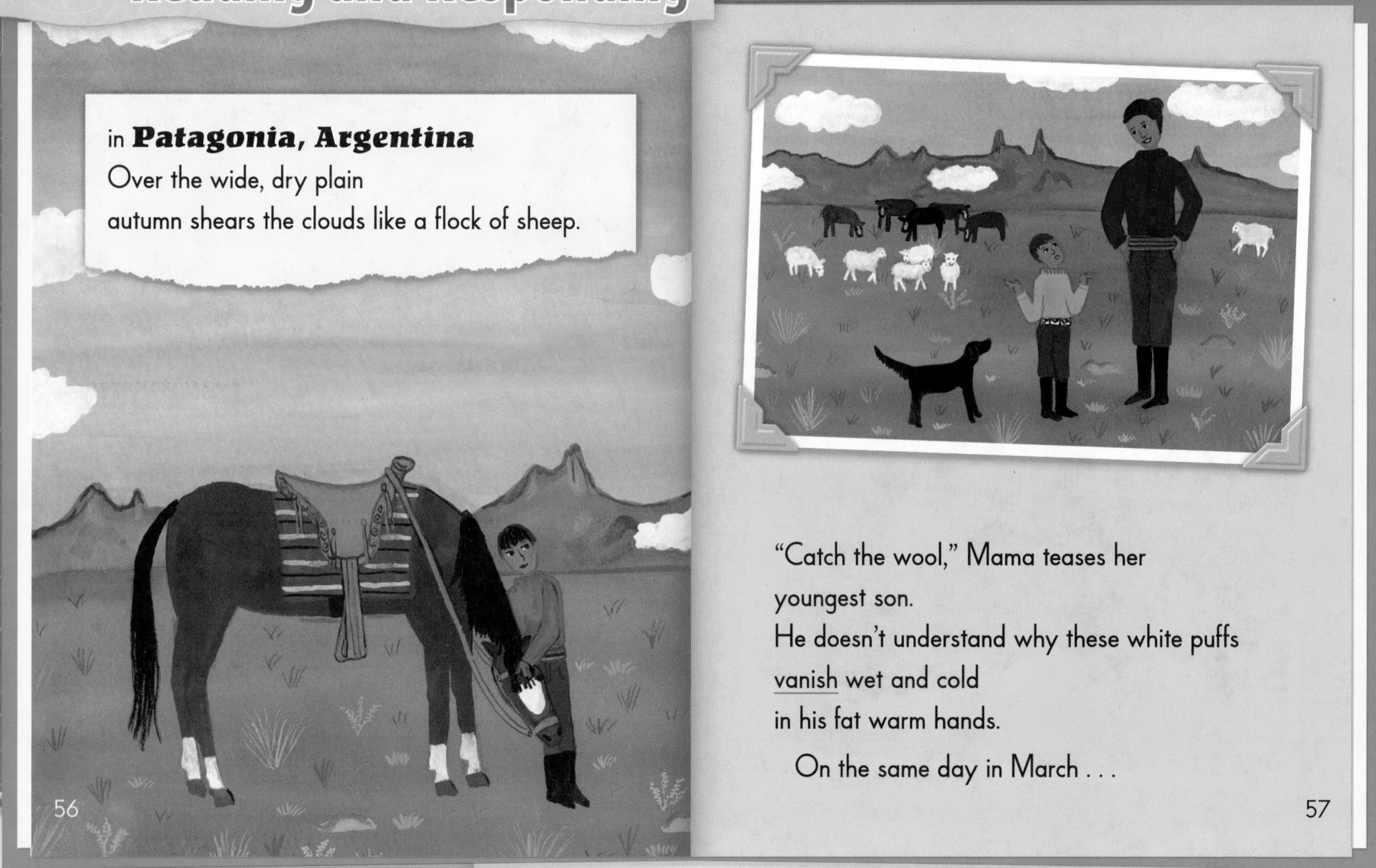

in **Patagonia, Argentina**
Over the wide, dry plain
autumn shears the clouds like a flock of sheep.

56

"Catch the wool," Mama teases her
youngest son.
He doesn't understand why these white puffs
vanish wet and cold
in his fat warm hands.

On the same day in March . . .

57

What's the Weather? Big Book, pp. 56–57

Expanding Vocabulary

vanish to disappear (page 57)

When the sun comes up, the stars seem to *vanish.*

2nd READ

Comprehension Skills

Compare and Contrast

As students compare and contrast, have them tell you where on the transparency to record each response. Leave room for additional information throughout the selection.

- After reading these pages, talk about the personification of autumn and the simile used by the author. Point out that she says autumn is like a farmer shearing sheep. Then ask the following:
  - *How is autumn cutting the tops off clouds like a farmer shearing sheep? Autumn uses wind to blow the tops off clouds; a farmer uses shears to cut the wool from sheep.*
  - *How is autumn really different from a farmer? Autumn isn't a person; it can't use shears; it doesn't really cut the tops off clouds.*
- On page 57, the author compares snow to wool. Ask how snow and wool are the same and how they are different. *They are both white and fluffy. Snow is wet and cold; wool is dry.*

58

in **Antarctica**

Penguins scramble on the shore,
seeking mates, missing fish,
as the six-month sun begins to slice
down below the Antarctic ice.
All on the same day in March!

59

What's the Weather? Big Book, pp. 58–59

Checking Comprehension

- ✦ Use the globe to point to places mentioned in the selection as you ask students the following questions to check their comprehension of the selection.
- What was the weather like in the Nile Valley of Egypt? *foggy*
- What kind of weather was Darjeeling, India, experiencing? *Hailstones were falling.*
- What kind of weather was happening in Patagonia, Argentina? *snow*
- Reread the final page of the selection. Point out the word *All* and the exclamation mark. Ask students why this page is different. *It is the end.*
- ✦ Have students compare and contrast what they have learned in "On the Same Day in March" with what they learned from "When a Storm Comes Up." **Possible Answers** *In "When a Storm Comes Up," we learned about kinds of weather in kinds of storms. In "On the Same Day in March," we learned about weather throughout the world.*

Concept/Question Board

To help students relate the text to their world, you may want to have them illustrate a scene from the selection and a scene showing the weather you are experiencing in your area. Have them list words describing the weather in each scene.

Teacher Tip

VOCABULARY Have students use selection vocabulary or theme-related vocabulary when discussing the fine art piece.

Differentiating Instruction **English Learners**

IF . . . students are native Spanish speakers, **THEN . . .** ask them to read the title of the painting aloud in Spanish and then to translate it into English. Then ask students who are from Mexico, as the artist is, to raise their hands.

Fine Art

Fine Art

What's the Weather? p. 60

- Display ***What's the Weather? Big Book*** page 60. Have students focus attention on *Detalle del sol de Fiesta de la ciudad* by Roberto Montenegro. Tell students they can explore the theme What's the Weather? through images such as this one as well as through reading. Have them talk about the painting, mentioning anything they see in it that interests or puzzles them.
- Share with students any information about the artist and the painting that you choose. For example, you might tell them that Montenegro was an artist who was born in Mexico in 1885. He sometimes painted frescoes, or large paintings on the walls of buildings.
- Ask students to describe the expression on the face of the sun and to notice how the sun is framed by the scaffolding. **Possible Answer** *The sun looks serious, as if it is her job to warm the city.*
- Have students talk about how the painting relates to weather. **Possible Answer** *It shows the sun, which plays an important part in the kind of weather we have.*

Science Connection

Tornado in a Bottle

Have a student fill one bottle two-thirds full of water. Have another student add the food coloring to the water. Place a metal washer (or twist the "tornado connector") over the top of the bottle. Turn the empty second bottle upside down, and attach it to the washer (or twist it on the connector). Fasten the two bottles together tightly with duct tape.

Turn the bottles so that the one containing water is on top. While holding the bottles firmly, whirl the top bottle rapidly. A small funnel-shaped "tornado" will form in the top bottle as the water rushes into the bottom one.

Explain that this happened because the water in the top bottle flowed into the lower one, which was full of air. The water pushed the air into the top bottle. The air formed a "hole" in the water that was rushing into the bottom bottle, which made the funnel shape.

Tell students that real tornadoes are formed when cool air rushes into hot air. Because the cool air, like water, is heavier than the hot air, it pushes down on the hot air. Sometimes the hot air can make a hole in the cool air. Then the hot air swirls up through the hole. This makes a whirling column that forms a tornado's funnel shape.

Teacher Tips

HOME You may want to make copies of the instructions for the tornado experiment. These can be sent home with students for them to try with a parent or an adult.

LITERATURE Have students select age- and ability-appropriate fiction and nonfiction materials to read, based on interest and teacher recommendations, to begin a core base of knowledge about the unit theme.

Concept/Question Board

Encourage students and their families to take photographs of the tornado experiments and bring them to class to post on the **Concept/Question Board.**

OBJECTIVES

Students will

- identify a purpose and an audience for a news story.
- form the letters *v* and *w* correctly.
- control the size and spacing of letters.
- understand that the names of days and months begin with capital letters.
- use a comma between a date and a year.

MATERIALS

- Routines 14, 15
- ***Transparencies*** 30, 30c, 39
- Writer's Notebooks
- ***Skills Practice 1,*** p. 193
- ***Language Arts Big Book,*** pp. 184, 186
- Portfolios

Teacher Tips

PLAN AHEAD You will need a newspaper, a magazine, and a book to begin today's lesson.

VOCABULARY Encourage students to consider using some of the selection vocabulary words they have learned so far in this unit when planning and writing their weather news stories.

WRITING OPTIONS As a parallel to Inquiry, students can write a news story that explains the weather conditions the class has recorded so far. Some above level students may be able to write a story on a recent weather event, such as a strong thunderstorm or snowstorm. Encourage these students to make notes on the facts of the event by answering the questions *who, what, where,* and *when.*

Writing News Stories

ROUTINE 14

Prewriting

Teach—Identifying Audience and Purpose

- Show students a newspaper, a magazine, and a book (see Teacher Tip). Have them identify the newspaper and ask them to explain what it is. *daily or weekly publication with stories that tell about things that are happening in the community and around the world.*
- Discuss with students what a news story is. *a story in a newspaper that gives new information to readers about a person, an event, or a thing* Remind them they will be writing a news story about the weather.
- Then tell students that before writers begin to write, they think about what they want to say, or the purpose for their writing. They also think about the audience or who will read it, for their writing.
- Model how to determine a purpose and the audience for a weather news story using ***Transparencies*** 30 and 30c. *I want to write a story that gives readers important information about our weather or a recent weather event. I need to be sure my story gives facts.*
- Next, ask students to suggest additional facts for your notes. Then briefly model organizing your notes for a weather news story into a web. Tell students they will work on their own webs later.

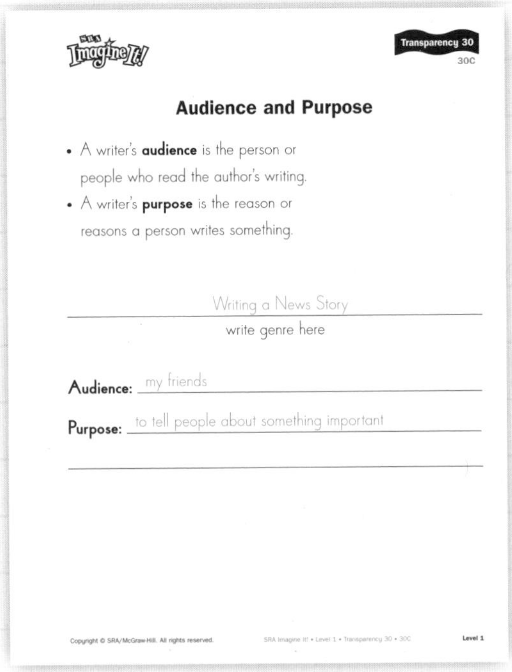

Imagine It!

Transparency 30
30C

Audience and Purpose

- A writer's **audience** is the person or people who read the author's writing.
- A writer's **purpose** is the reason or reasons a person writes something.

Writing a News Story
write genre here

Audience: my friends

Purpose: to tell people about something important

Copyright © SRA/McGraw-Hill. All rights reserved. SRA Imagine It! • Level 1 • Transparency 30 • 30C Level 1

Transparencies 30, 30c

Writing News Stories, cont.

Guided Practice

ROUTINE 15

- Have students break into small groups to discuss the audience and purpose of their weather news stories. If necessary, prompt them with questions such as *Why do people use newspapers? Who would be interested in a news story about weather? How would people use the information included in your stories?*
- Then ask them to choose a purpose and an audience for their stories. If necessary, suggest that they can write a weather news story for other students to read to learn about this week's weather, or recent weather events.
- Tell students to add to the notes you made as a class for writing a news story about the weather in their Writer's Notebooks. Circulate to help them add new ideas and details to their notes. They will use this information as they complete their plans for writing.

Apply

- Have students complete the audience and purpose sections on ***Skills Practice 1*** page 193. Then have them use their notes to organize their ideas using the web at the bottom of the page. Circulate to help with any reading, or model again how to use an organizing web.

Traits of Good Writing

Voice Writers consider their audience and purpose as they decide what information is important to include in their writing.

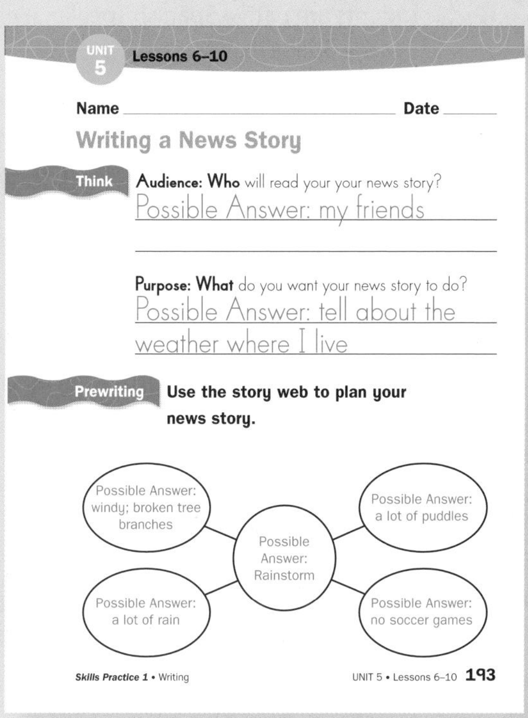
UNIT 5 Lessons 6–10

Name ____ Date ____

Writing a News Story

Think **Audience: Who** will read your your news story?
Possible Answer: my friends

Purpose: What do you want your news story to do?
Possible Answer: tell about the weather where I live

Prewriting **Use the story web to plan your news story.**

Skills Practice 1 • Writing UNIT 5 • Lessons 6–10 193

Skills Practice 1, p. 193

Technology

eSkills contains writing activities that students can use to practice organizing ideas and information.

Penmanship

Alphabet Practice: The Letters *v* and *w*

Teach

- Review how to form lowercase *v* and *w* by writing the letters on the board as you describe the process. See the Level Appendix for penmanship models.
- If students need additional modeling of the strokes for lowercase *v* and *w*, review the letter models on ***Transparency*** 39. Ask students how these two letters are similar. *Both have straight lines.*

Guided Practice

Have students follow your model to write each letter twice within the lines as they say its name. Tell them to proofread their letters and underline their better *v* and *w*.

Apply

Write the following words on the board: *wing, wave, vest.* Read the words, and have students write them on handwriting paper to practice letter formation.

- Have students proofread their line by circling any incorrect words and making them better by rewriting them above or next to the original words. Then have them underline their best words.

Teacher Tip

PENMANSHIP AND VOCABULARY Look for opportunities throughout the week for students to practice handwriting, using vocabulary words from the reading selection. This reinforces handwriting and vocabulary development in the same activity.

Differentiating Instruction English Learners

IF . . . students are native Spanish speakers who know the Spanish alphabet, **THEN . . .** they may notice that the English alphabet has one letter that does not appear in Spanish *(w)* and that it lacks *ch, ll,* and *ñ,* which are all letters in the Spanish alphabet.

Monitor Progress to Differentiate Instruction

Formal Assessment

PENMANSHIP Check students' handwriting to make sure the letters *v* and *w* are formed correctly and have the proper spacing.

APPROACHING LEVEL	**IF . . .** students have difficulty with letter formation,	**THEN . . .** have them use the ***Sandpaper Letter Cards*** from the ***Workshop Kit*** to practice tracing the model during Workshop.
	IF . . . students need additional practice forming the letters *v* and *w*,	**THEN . . .** give them paper copies of ***Transparency*** 39 to trace the model for *v* and *w*. Then have them practice writing each of the letters twice.
ON LEVEL	**IF . . .** students form the letters *v* and *w* correctly,	**THEN . . .** have partners or small groups use the ***Write-On Boards*** to take turns writing rows of each letter.
ABOVE LEVEL	**IF . . .** students are ready for a challenge,	**THEN . . .** have them look for and copy words that contain *v* or *w* in the ***What's the Weather? Little Big Book.***

Grammar, Usage, and Mechanics

Capitalization: Days of the Week and Months of the Year
Punctuation: Commas between Date and Year

Teach

- Write today's day and date on the board. For example, *Today is Tuesday, March 15, 2009.* Have volunteers circle and say the capital letters. *T; M* Then explain that like the names of people and special things and places, the names of days and months are proper nouns. Remind students that a proper noun always begins with a capital letter.
- Refer to ***Language Arts Big Book*** page 184 for examples of capitalizing the names of days of the week and months of the year.
- Briefly review all the names of the days of the week and months of the year. Then write the following names of days and months on the board: *tuesday, september, friday, june.* Have students copy the words, replacing the first letter in each with the correct capital.
- Next use today's date to explain the rule for using commas in dates. Point to the comma between the date and the year, and explain that commas go between some words and numbers in a sentence. Explain that the comma makes the date easier to read by separating the day number from the number of the year. Refer to ***Language Arts Big Book*** page 186 for other examples.

Guided Practice

- **Teacher Modeling** On the board, write the following sentence: The last saturday game was on august 10 2007.
- Ask students to tell you which words should begin with a capital letter and why. *Saturday, because it is a day of the week; August, because it is a month* Erase each letter, and replace it with a capital. As you write, have students say the name of the letter. *capital S, capital A* Then have students tell you where the comma should go in the sentence. *between 10 and 2007*

Apply

- Tell students to reread one of the pieces in their Portfolios and look for places they should capitalize a day or month or use a comma. Have them select a few sentences to edit and rewrite using their capitalization skills. Then have them share their favorite sentences with partners.

Teacher Tips

VOCABULARY As you review the days of the week and months of the year, write each word on an index card and post it on the wall. Tell students that these are sight words they should memorize to use during reading and writing.

WRITING LINK Remind students to think about and use the capitalization skills they have learned so far in this unit as they plan and draft their news stories.

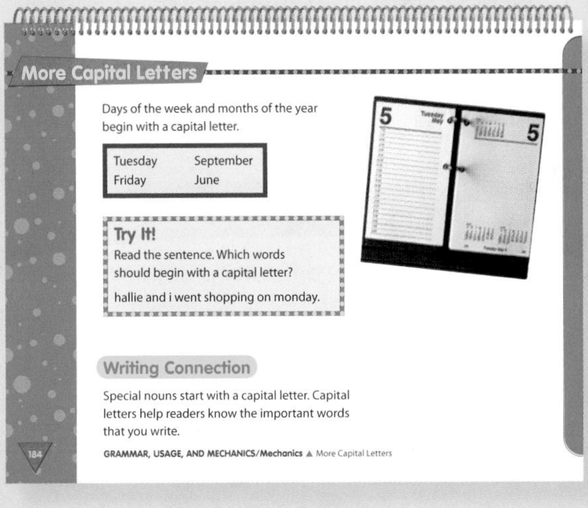

More Capital Letters

Days of the week and months of the year begin with a capital letter.

Tuesday	September
Friday	June

Try It!
Read the sentence. Which words should begin with a capital letter?
hallie and i went shopping on monday.

Writing Connection
Special nouns start with a capital letter. Capital letters help readers know the important words that you write.

184 GRAMMAR, USAGE, AND MECHANICS/Mechanics ▲ More Capital Letters

Language Arts Big Book, p. 184

OBJECTIVES

Students will

- blend, spell, and read words that contain /s/ spelled *cy*.
- build fluency by reading ***Decodable*** 72.

MATERIALS

- Routines 2–5, 10–11
- ***Sound/Spelling Card*** 19
- ***Skills Practice 1,*** pp. 197–198
- ***Decodable*** 72, *A Fancy Jacket*

Teacher Tip

WORD CHART Have students add more words that have /s/ spelled *cy* to the /s/ word chart.

Differentiating Instruction English Learners

IF . . . students have difficulty pronouncing certain sounds, **THEN . . .** provide extra practice producing those sounds in simple, one-syllable words.

Daily Warm-Ups

Copy the Morning Message on the board or on chart paper. Have students answer the question. Read the message aloud, and discuss it with students.
Possible Answer *Rain can sometimes become hail.*

MORNING MESSAGE

Good morning! Today we will read a story about clouds, rain, and snow. Some clouds bring rain. Other clouds bring snow. What do you know about rain or snow?

Daily Language Review

To review capitalization, write the following sentence on the board, or generate a similar one with students, and have students make corrections: On our trip we will see the golden gate bridge. *On our trip we will see the Golden Gate Bridge.*

Riddle Me This Game

- Display these ***Sound/Spelling Cards:*** Gopher, Robot, Lamb, Ball. Ask students to say the sound for each card as you point to it. Then tell them to determine the word the cards spell but not to say it. Have them say the word together when you say, "What's my word?" *grab* Switch the Gopher card and the Ball card, and ask students to determine and say the new word. *brag*
- Repeat this process for other words such as the following:
  - Ball, Lamb, Timer, Bird *batter*
  - Quacking ducks, Lamb, Camera *quack*
  - Lion, Long E, Dinosaur, Bird *leader*
  - Hound, Lamb, Popcorn, Long E *happy*
  - Sausages, Timer, Pig, Noodles, Jump, Long e *stingy*

Introduce the Sound/Spelling

/s/ Spelled *cy*

- Point to ***Sound/Spelling Card*** 19—Sausages, and ask students what sound the spellings *s*, *ce*, and *ci_* make. Remind them that when the letter *c* is followed by *e* or *i*, it says /s/. Say that /s/ is the soft sound for *c* and that *e* and *i* work to make the sound soft. To contrast hard and soft sounds, write these words on the board, and have students say them:

  castle center cold circle

- Tell students they will learn a new spelling for /s/ today. Point to *cy*, and explain that this is another way /s/ is spelled. Say that *y* also works to make the sound soft.

Sound/Spelling Card 19

Phonemic Awareness

Listening for /s/

Read aloud the following words, and have students signal thumbs-up when they hear /s/.

cyclone	card	carrot	**encyclopedia**
comb	curl	**tricycle**	**Lucy**
cucumber	**fancy**	**pricy**	pack
space	**ice**	**cent**	climb

Teacher Tip

PHONEME SEGMENTATION For segmentation practice, choose words from the Phonemic Awareness activity for students to say sound by sound, for example, /f/ /a/ /n/ /s/ /ē/.

Teacher Tips

BLENDING For words on Lines 1 and 2, refer to Routine 2 for the sound-by-sound blending technique. If students are ready, refer to Routine 3 for the whole-word procedure for the remaining words on the lines. Use Routine 4 for the blending sentences procedure.

SYLLABICATION To help students blend the words and build fluency, use the syllabication below of the multisyllable words on the word lines.

i • cy	spi • cy	fan • cy
Nan • cy	la • cy	Tra • cy
ci • der	cit • y	pen • cil
Mar • cy	Quin • cy	Sta • cy

/S/ SPELLED CY Many of the words that start with *cy* have an /ī/ sound. Because students have not learned /ī/ spelled _*y*, students will be exposed only to words with *cy* at the end in this lesson.

VOCABULARY If necessary, tell students that *vacancy* means "an empty space."

Phonics

ROUTINE 2 ROUTINE 3 ROUTINE 4 ROUTINE 10 ROUTINE 11

Blending

Use Routine 2, sound-by-sound blending, Routine 3, whole-word blending, and Routine 4, blending sentences, to have students blend the words and sentences. Use Routine 10, closed syllables, and Routine 11, open syllables, to have students blend the multisyllable words.

Line 1	icy	spicy	fancy	Nancy
Line 2	lace	lacy	trace	Tracy
Line 3	cent	sent	cider	city
Line 4	pencil	Marcy	Quincy	Stacy

Sentence 1 Macy wore <u>her</u> lacy dress <u>to</u> <u>the</u> dance.

Sentence 2 <u>Could</u> <u>you</u> taste <u>the</u> spicy beans?

Line 1 **/s/ spelled *cy***

Have students identify the spelling for /s/ and say where it appears in each word: beginning, middle, end. *The /s/ sound spelled cy appears at the end of each word.*

Line 2 **/s/ spelled *ce* and /s/ spelled *cy***

Have students identify the spelling for /s/ in each word.

Line 3 **/s/ spelled *ce, s,* and *ci_***

Have students identify the homophones *cent* and *sent*. Reinforce students' understanding by engaging them in creating sentences using each word. Have students identify the spelling for /s/ in each word.

Line 4 **/s/ spelled *ci_* and *cy***

Ask students why *Marcy, Quincy,* and *Stacy* are capitalized. *They are names of people.*

Sentences 1–2

Write the word *could* on the board. Read the word, repeat it, and have students read it. Then spell *could* together. Invite volunteers to use the word in sentences. Write the word on an index card, and add it to the High-Frequency Word Bank.

Developing Oral Language

To review the words, call on a student to underline the word that answers each question below and then to use the word in a sentence.

- What word could you use to describe a food that burns your mouth? *spicy*
- What word describes a fabric? *lacy*
- Which word means "a drink made from apples?" *cider*
- Which word could describe the sidewalk on a cold, snowy day? *icy*
- Which word names something you can use to write and draw? *pencil*

Monitor Progress to Differentiate Instruction

Formal Assessment

BLENDING As students spell words, notice who uses the ***Sound/Spelling Cards*** and spells the words correctly. Note students who are asking for help with the spellings.

APPROACHING LEVEL

IF . . .	THEN . . .
IF . . . students need additional practice with /s/ spelled *cy*,	**THEN . . .** work with a small group to practice this sound/spelling during Workshop using the ***Write-On Boards.***

ON LEVEL

IF . . .	THEN . . .
IF . . . students blend and read words with /s/ spelled *cy* correctly,	**THEN . . .** have partners or small groups look for and copy words that contain this sound/spelling in previously read selections during Workshop.

ABOVE LEVEL

IF . . .	THEN . . .
IF . . . students are ready for a challenge,	**THEN . . .** give them pages of text from newspapers or magazines, and have them identify and copy words that contain /s/ spelled *cy*.

Guided Practice

Have students complete ***Skills Practice 1*** pages 197–198 to review /s/ spelled *cy*. Have students write the words and sentences on page 197. Have students choose and write the correct word to complete each sentence on page 198.

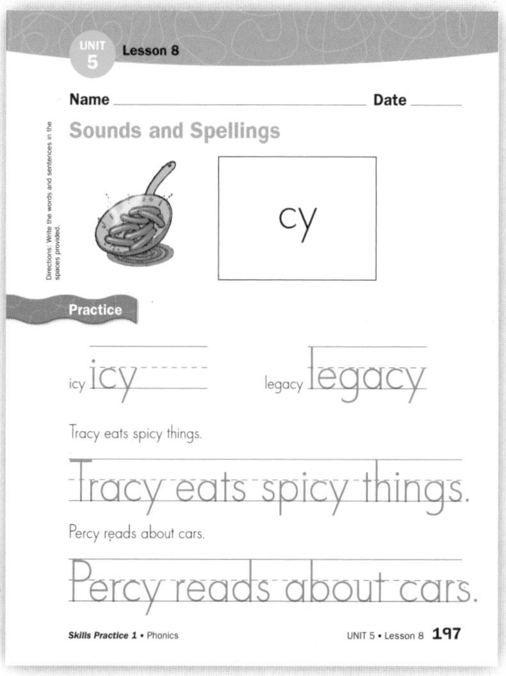
UNIT 5 Lesson 8

Name ______ Date ______

Sounds and Spellings

Directions: Write the words and sentences in the spaces provided.

cy

Practice

icy icy

legacy legacy

Tracy eats spicy things.

Tracy eats spicy things.

Percy reads about cars.

Percy reads about cars.

Skills Practice 1 • Phonics UNIT 5 • Lesson 8 197

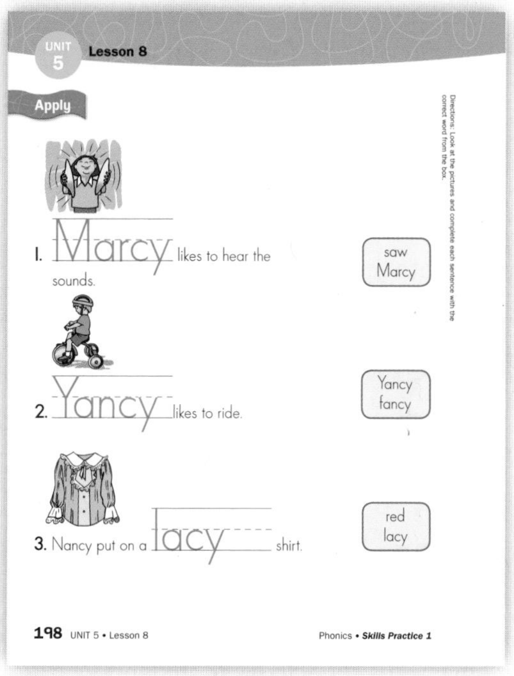
UNIT 5 Lesson 8

Apply

Directions: Look at the pictures and complete each sentence with the correct word from the box.

1. Marcy likes to hear the sounds. saw Marcy

2. Yancy likes to ride. Yancy fancy

3. Nancy put on a lacy shirt. red lacy

198 UNIT 5 • Lesson 8 Phonics • *Skills Practice 1*

Skills Practice 1, pp. 197–198

Monitor Progress

to Differentiate Instruction

Formal Assessment

DICTATION As students spell words, notice who uses the ***Sound/Spelling Cards*** and spells the words correctly. Note students who are asking for help with /s/ spelled *cy.*

APPROACHING LEVEL

IF . . . students need additional practice with dictation, **THEN . . .** preteach words with the target sounds/spellings during Workshop. Then have students use the ***Write-On Boards*** to write these words as you dictate them.

ON LEVEL

IF . . . students are on level with dictation, **THEN . . .** have them use one of the activities in the ***Workshop Kit.***

ABOVE LEVEL

IF . . . students need a challenge with dictation, **THEN . . .** make two lists of three words that contain the target spellings. Pair them, and tell them to take turns dictating words from their lists for their partners to spell.

ROUTINE 8

Dictation: Word Building Game

Use Routine 8, word building, to have students spell words in the Word Building game.

Have students proofread the words after completing each one. Remind them to circle any words or parts of words that could be better and to write the whole word correctly above or beside the original word. Have students use pencil and paper for the following words:

Jen
Jean
Jane
Jan
fan
fancy
Nancy
Darcy
Percy

Teacher Tip

CAPITALIZATION Review with students the rules for capitalizing names of people.

Fluency/Reading a Decodable Book

ROUTINE **9**

Core Decodable 72: A Fancy Jacket

Phonics Focus: /s/ Spelled cy

High-Frequency Words

Review the high-frequency word *could* that students learned in Blending. Point to it in the High-Frequency Word Bank, or write it on the board, spell the word, and have students say the word. Have a volunteer use it in a sentence. Review other high-frequency words by pointing to them in the High-Frequency Word Bank and having students read them.

Reading the Decodable

✦ Follow Routine 9, reading a **Decodable,** as you read the story with students.

✦ Have students read the title, browse the story, and discuss what they think the story will be about.

✦ The first time through, have students read a page silently. Then have one student read it aloud. Repeat this procedure for each page.

✦ Reread the story at least twice, calling on various students to read. Then have the entire class do a choral reading of the story.

Nancy's fancy jacket was thin.
She could feel the winter chill.

3

Nancy wished she could run.
But the sidewalk was icy.
She could fall.

4

Mom looked at Nancy.
She could tell Nancy was freezing.

5

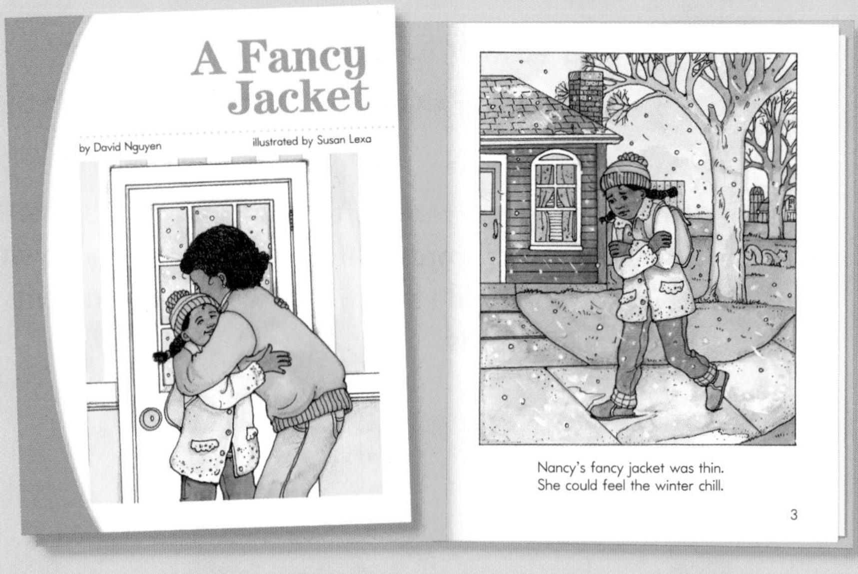

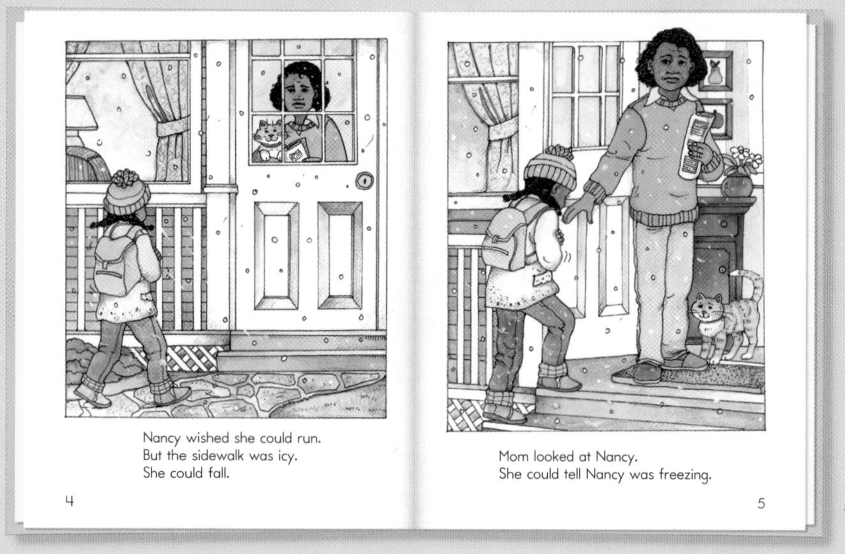

🍎 Teacher Tip

SOUND/SPELLING CARDS Remind students to refer to the *Sound/Spelling Cards* if they are unsure of a sound/spelling.

Monitor Progress to Differentiate Instruction

Formal Assessment ✓

Observe students as they read **Decodable** 72. Note any students who are having trouble with the /s/ sound spelled *cy* or other sound/spellings.

APPROACHING LEVEL	IF . . . students are having difficulty decoding the words,	THEN . . . during Workshop, review *Sound/Spelling Card* 19—Sausages and any other *Sound/Spelling Cards* students need to review. Then have students look through **Decodable** 72 and find words with the /s/ sound spelled *cy*.
ON LEVEL	IF . . . students are on level,	THEN . . . have them quiz one another during Workshop using the *High-Frequency Flash Cards.*
ABOVE LEVEL	IF . . . students are ready for a challenge,	THEN . . . encourage them to browse and read classroom library books.

Mom hugged Nancy.
"That fancy jacket is thin," Mom said.
6
Nancy's teeth chattered.
"Yes, it is lacy," said Nancy.
"It isn't for winter."
7

Mom made hot, spicy tea.
"I feel better," said Nancy.
"Hot, spicy tea is for winter."
8

Responding

- After reading, be sure to talk about the story and answer any questions students have. Ask students to identify any difficult words in the book.
- Have students retell the story.
- As students answer the following questions, make sure they focus on the words in the story rather than getting the answers by listening or from the pictures. Have students answer by pointing to and reading aloud the answers in the text:
  - **Is Nancy's fancy jacket thick or thin?** *thin*
  - **What is the sidewalk like?** *icy*
  - **What does Mom make?** *hot, spicy tea*

Building Fluency

Have students build fluency by rereading ***Core Decodable*** 72 twice with a partner. The first time through, one partner should read the odd-numbered pages and the other partner the even-numbered pages. The second time through, they should switch pages. For additional practice with /s/ spelled *cy*, have students read ***Practice Decodable*** 60, *Tracy, Stacy, Marcy, and Tommy*. Have students record their readings on their Personal Title sheets, noting the title of each book, the date, and any difficult words they encountered.

Core Decodable 72

A Fancy Jacket

High-Frequency Word Introduced in Core Decodable 72

could

Previously Introduced High-Frequency Words

a	for	it	six	what
after	get	its	take	when
all	girl	jump	that	will
am	go	just	the	with
an	got	like	them	yes
and	green	little	then	you
as	had	look	there	
ask	has	make	they	
at	have	of	this	
be	he	on	to	
big	help	or	two	
but	her	out	up	
call	him	over	walk	
can	his	red	was	
did	I	ride	we	
do	if	said	well	
down	in	see	went	
every	is	she	were	

Sound/Spelling Correspondences in Core Decodables

1. Pre-decodable
2. Pre-decodable
3. Pre-decodable
4. Pre-decodable
5. Pre-decodable
6. /s/ spelled *s*, /m/ spelled *m*, /a/ spelled *a*
7. /t/ spelled *t, tt*
8. Review
9. /d/ spelled *d*
10. /n/ spelled *n*
11. /i/ spelled *i*
12. /h/ spelled *h_*
13. Review
14. /p/ spelled *p*
15. /l/ spelled *l, ll*
16. /o/ spelled *o*
17. /b/ spelled *b*
18. Review
19. /k/ spelled *c*
20. /aw/ spelled *al*
21. /k/ spelled *k*, ■*ck*
22. /r/ spelled *r*
23. /f/ spelled *f, ff*
24. /s/ spelled *ss*
25. Review
26. /g/ spelled *g*
27. /j/ spelled *j*, ■*dge*
28. /u/ spelled *u*
29. /z/ spelled *z, zz*
30. /z/ spelled *_s*
31. Review
32. /ks/ spelled ■*x*
33. /e/ spelled *e*
34. -ed ending: /ed/, /d/
35. -ed ending: /t/
36. /e/ spelled *_ea_*
37. Review
38. /sh/ spelled *sh*
39. /th/ spelled *th*
40. /ch/ spelled *ch*, ■*tch*
41. /or/ spelled *or, ore*
42. Review
43. /ar/ spelled *ar*
44. /m/ spelled *_mb*
45. /w/ spelled *w_*
46. /hw/ spelled *wh_*
47. /er/ spelled *er, ir*
48. /er/ spelled *ur*
49. Review
50. Schwa
51. Review schwa
52. /ng/ spelled ■*ng*
53. /nk/ spelled ■*nk*
54. /kw/ spelled *qu_*
55. Review
56. /y/ spelled *y_*
57. /v/ spelled *v*
58. Syllable -le
59. /ā/ spelled *a* and *a_e*
60. Review
61. /ī/ spelled *i* and *i_e*
62. /s/ spelled *ce, ci_*
63. /j/ spelled *ge, gi_*
64. Review
65. /ō/ spelled *o* and *o_e*
66. /ū/ spelled *u* and *u_e*
67. Review
68. /ē/ spelled *e* and *e_e*
69. /ē/ spelled *ee* and *ea*
70. Review
71. /ē/ spelled *_y, _ie_*
72. /s/ spelled *cy*

Decodable 72, inside back cover

Reading and Responding

OBJECTIVES

Students will

- activate prior knowledge.
- understand and use a table of contents.
- set and check purposes for reading.
- learn vocabulary words.
- use the comprehension strategies Visualizing, Making Connections, and Summarizing.
- use the comprehension skill Classify and Categorize.

MATERIALS

- ***First Reader,*** pp. 5–9
- Routines 12, 13
- Writer's Notebooks

Teacher Tips

WORD REVIEW Review the word *precipitation* with students. Remind them that this word means "moisture that falls from the sky, including rain, snow, and ice." Have students find the word in the What's the Weather? Word Bank and say it several times.

CLOUDS The descriptions of clouds and rain are simplified in this text. Many more characteristics determine cloud type and when it rains. Be alert to more advanced student knowledge of clouds and precipitation.

Build Background

Activate Prior Knowledge

- Ask students to recall the other selections they have read in this unit to answer the following questions:
  - What is a cloud? **Possible Answer** *A cloud is a collection of small drops of water or bits of ice that float high in the sky*
  - What is rain? **Possible Answer** *Rain is water falling from the sky*
  - What is snow? **Possible Answer** *small drops of frozen water that fall from the sky*
  - What is ice? **Possible Answer** *Ice is frozen water*
- Have students describe various clouds they have seen, including shape, size, and color. If possible, have them look outside and describe the clouds in the sky.
- Have students look back in their ***What's the Weather? Big Book.*** Have them tell specific details of the different types of rain they learned about in "When a Storm Comes Up."

Background Information

- To help students prepare to read the selection, review the words *rain, snow,* and *ice*. Tell students that these are forms of water. When water gets really cold, it gets hard or it freezes. Tell them that *freeze* means "to harden because of the cold."
- Tell them the meaning of the word *wispy*. Write the word on the board, and read it aloud. Have students repeat the word. Explain that *wispy* is an adjective—it is a describing word. *Wispy* means "thin or small pieces." Read the sample sentence to help students understand the meaning of the word.

The *wispy* clouds look like thin or small pieces of cotton in the sky.

ROUTINE 12

Preview and Prepare

Browse

- Follow Routine 12, reading the selection, to prepare students to read the selection. Begin by displaying the cover of the ***First Reader.*** Point to and read aloud the title.
- Have students locate the Table of Contents, and point to the title of the selection, "Clouds, Rain, Snow, and Ice." Have students read the title along with you as you point to each word. Point to page number 5, and have a volunteer read it and tell what the number means. Turn to page 5.
- Prompt students to browse the selection by commenting on the illustrations and predicting how they might relate to the text. On page 6, for example, you might say *This page shows clouds. I know that* clouds *is part of the title, so I predict this page will be about clouds.*
- Have students browse the first few pages to look for clues to what the selection is about and for difficult and unfamiliar words. Students may identify one or more of the following words: *wispy, cirrus,* or *cumulus*. Tell students that *wispy* is like a broom without many pieces. Tell them that *cirrus* and *cumulus* are types of clouds and they will learn more about them in the story.

Set Purposes

- Have students think about the information they gained while browsing. Ask students to use this information to tell what the purposes for reading this selection might be. Write the purposes on the board. Some suggestions include the following:
    - To find out about different kinds of clouds
    - To learn why it rains or snows
- After reading the selection, have students return to these purposes.

Fluency

- Have students apply letter-sound knowledge to decode phonetically regular words quickly and accurately as they read this selection.
- With the ***First Reader*** stories, students begin the transition to reading more challenging text. Have students adjust their reading rate based on this new challenging text.
- As students read "Clouds, Rain, Snow, and Ice," have them practice accuracy and appropriate reading rate. Remind them to pause at end punctuation marks.

Teacher Tips

GLOSSARY The words *cirrus* (page 6) and *pond* (page 7) appear in the Glossary. As students browse and identify interesting words or phrases, you may want to use the opportunity to have students practice glossary use. Have them locate and turn to the Glossary, find each word, and read each entry.

HIGH-FREQUENCY WORDS Before students read this story, use the High-Frequency Word Bank to review the high-frequency words they have learned. The following are some of the high-frequency words that appear in this selection: *and, all, of, a, little, they, big, when, the, in, get, to, this, is, with.*

SETTING GOALS Students who set their own goals for reading will read with a greater sense of engagement, and they tend to notice more than students whose goals are set for them.

Differentiating Instruction: English Learners

IF . . . students need help with reading fluency,
THEN . . . have them listen as you read aloud a short section of text, and then have them read aloud the same text themselves.

BIG Idea

What is weather?

Before reading the selection, reread the Big Idea question. Tell students to keep this question in mind as they listen to the selection.

Selection Vocabulary

sleet freezing rain (page 8)

Teacher Tips

SEMANTIC MAP Continue to have students build upon the semantic map. Have them add words from the selection and words they have learned throughout the unit.

DIGITAL TOOLS Have students look for definitions of selection vocabulary or difficult words from the text using an online dictionary.

Building Vocabulary

ROUTINE 13

- Use Routine 13, selection vocabulary, to introduce the vocabulary word. Write the word on the board or on a transparency. Explain the meaning of the word and use it in a sentence.
- Have students identify the spelling for /ē/ in *sleet*. *ee* Ask a volunteer to use the word in a sentence about weather.
- Tell students to look for this word as they read the selection.
- You will introduce one expanding vocabulary word to students as the selection is reread. The word is identified in a box where it appears in the selection. When you come to the word in the selection, read to students the word, the definition, and the sample sentence. Understanding this word will help students better comprehend the selection.

Monitor Progress to Differentiate Instruction — Formal Assessment

VOCABULARY During the Building Vocabulary exercise, note which students are initiating responses and which students seem to be waiting for cues from other students.

APPROACHING LEVEL	**IF . . .** students would benefit from additional work with unit vocabulary,	**THEN . . .** use the ***SRA Imagine It! Photo Library CD*** to help them understand the word.
ON LEVEL	**IF . . .** students understand most vocabulary words,	**THEN . . .** pair them, and have them use theme-related words to tell each other stories about weather.
ABOVE LEVEL	**IF . . .** students are ready for a challenge,	**THEN . . .** pair them, and have them play one of the games in ***eSkills.***

Reading the Selection

Genre Informational Writing

Tell students that "Clouds, Rain, Snow, and Ice" is an example of informational writing. It was written to explain and provide facts about different kinds of clouds and precipitation. Then briefly review some of the elements of informational writing. For example, it contains facts that can be checked in other sources such as encyclopedias and newspapers or on the Internet.

Comprehension Strategies

As students read "Clouds, Rain, Snow, and Ice," model and prompt the use of the following comprehension strategies:

- Visualizing
- Making Connections
- Summarizing

Comprehension Skills

As students reread "Clouds, Rain, Snow, and Ice," apply the comprehension skill Classify and Categorize.

Reading with a Writer's Eye

As students reread "Clouds, Rain, Snow, and Ice," you will discuss how the author uses examples to help readers understand topics and ideas.

Focus Questions

Read and discuss the Focus Questions on page 5. Encourage students to think about the Focus Questions as they read "Clouds, Rain, Snow, and Ice."

Reading Recommendations

ROUTINE 12

Day 3 **ORALLY** Students will read the entire selection twice today. Follow Routine 12, reading the selection. The first time, model and prompt the use of the comprehension strategies. The second time, focus on the comprehension skill and Reading with a Writer's Eye elements.

Differentiating Instruction **English Learners**

IF . . . students need help understanding vocabulary, **THEN . . .** use pictures and props to show meanings.

Teacher Tips

1st READ

THEME CONNECTIONS Remind students that as they read, they should think about how the selection relates to the theme What's the Weather? and about how it might help them generate ideas for Inquiry.

1st READ

READING THE SELECTION Although students are already reading ***Decodables,*** at first they may feel challenged to read the stories in the ***First Reader.*** If you think students will struggle with reading this story, read it to them for the first reading. For the second reading of the story, have students read this story chorally. If students are not able to read it chorally, have them echo read with you on the second reading.

PARTNER READING LIST As students begin to reread selections on their own, have them keep track of what they read. They can add this information to the Partner Reading List. Tell them to write the title of each selection they read and the date they read it. If they read a selection in a group, have them write the names of the group members.

EFFECTIVE COMMUNICATION Remind students to speak clearly and use describing words when they make connections and share their personal experiences.

Phonics

Words in the selection containing sound/spellings from recent phonics lessons appear in boxes like this throughout the selection. At the end of the first read, students should be prompted to identify the sound/spellings of these words.

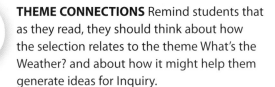

Focus Questions What are clouds made of? How does water change?

Clouds, Rain, Snow, and Ice

All clouds are made of small drops of water called droplets. ❶

5

First Reader, p. 5

Teacher Tip

GLOSSARY The words *cirrus* (page 6) and *pond* (page 7) can be found in the Glossary.

Phonics

/ō/ spelled *o:* hold (page 6)
/ā/ spelled *a:* a (page 6)
/ū/ spelled *u:* cumulus (page 6)
/ē/ spelled *ea:* really (page 7)
/ē/ spelled *ee:* free (page 7)

1st READ

Comprehension Strategies

❶ **Making Connections** Teacher Modeling: *We've read about clouds, and we know they are made of small drops of water. I've seen many different clouds, such as thick clouds and thin clouds.*

❷ **Visualizing** Teacher Prompt: *I can visualize these two kinds of clouds. The cirrus cloud is small, soft, and light. The cumulus cloud, though, is dark and big. Can you see these different kinds of clouds?* **Possible Student Responses** *I can see cumulus clouds. They're big, and they look like whales. I see cirrus clouds that look like thick feathers in the sky!*

❸ **Summarizing** Teacher Modeling: *To make sure I understand what I've read, I'm going to stop and summarize. Clouds are made of droplets of water and there are different kinds of clouds. If there are few droplets, they make cirrus clouds. If there are many droplets, they make cumulus clouds. When droplets in clouds get really big, they fall to the ground as rain.*

Small wispy clouds hold a little water. They are called cirrus clouds. Big black clouds hold a lot of water. They are called cumulus clouds. 2

6

When the droplets of water in the clouds get really big, they break free and fall to the ground. They are raindrops.

This pond is filled with water from the rain. 3

7

First Reader, pp. 6–7

Comprehension Skills

2nd READ

Classify and Categorize

- Review the comprehension skill Classify and Categorize by writing Sports, Food, and Pets on the board. Explain that these are categories. Have students identify and tell some words that fit into each category.
- Write these categories on the board or on chart paper: Clouds and Water. Reread pages 5–7, and have students listen for any words about weather they might put in the categories. **Possible Answers** *Clouds: wispy, cirrus, cumulus; Water: drops, droplets, rain, raindrops, pond*

Teacher Tip

REREAD Tell students to monitor their comprehension of the text. If they do not understand, tell them to reread the text.

Differentiating Instruction English Learners

IF . . . students have difficulty understanding the concept of categorizing or discussing categories, **THEN . . .** introduce or review words such as *group, kind, type,* and *sort.* Emphasize that to sort or categorize things is to group things that have something in common.

When it is very cold, the water falls to the ground as snow or sleet.

8

When it is very cold, the water in ponds and puddles will freeze. It turns to ice. The water is solid so you can skate on it. Have fun! ❹

9

First Reader, pp. 8–9

Phonics

/ō/ spelled *o:* cold (pages 8, 9); so (page 9)
/ē/ spelled *ee:* sleet (page 8); freeze (page 9)
/ī/ spelled *i_e:* ice (page 9)
/ā/ spelled *a_e:* skate (page 9)

1st READ

Comprehension Strategies

❹ **Summarizing** Teacher Modeling: *I'm going to summarize quickly what I've found out on the last two pages of the selection. It tells what happens when the weather is very cold. When it is cold, water from clouds falls as snow or sleet. Water on the ground, like puddles or ponds, freezes and becomes ice.*

Comprehension Check

What causes rain? When the droplets of water in clouds get really big, they break free from the clouds and fall to the ground as raindrops.

What causes the water from clouds to become snow, sleet, or ice? **Possible Answers** *When the temperatures get very cold, water from the clouds change to snow, sleet, or ice.*

Comprehension Skills

2nd READ

Classify and Categorize

Next, write the words *Solid* and *Liquid* on the board. Explain that *liquid* means "things that flow." Help them find words in the selection that fit into each category. **Possible Answers** *Solid: snow, sleet, ice, ground; Liquid: rain, water, droplets, drops*

Reading with a Writer's Eye

2nd READ

Text Structure: Using Examples

Tell students that authors help readers understand a selection by using examples to explain a topic or an idea.

- What examples does the author give for kinds of clouds? *cirrus and cumulus clouds*
- What examples does the author give of kinds of water in solid form? *snow, sleet, ice*

Monitor Progress to Differentiate Instruction

Formal Assessment

CLASSIFY AND CATEGORIZE During the second reading of the story, note how students are applying the Classify and Categorize skill.

APPROACHING LEVEL

IF . . . students have difficulty with the comprehension skill Classify and Categorize,	**THEN . . .** during Workshop, give them sets of ***Individual Sound/Spelling Cards*** that show different farm and wild animals, such as hen, pig, yak, lion, and fox, and cards that show machines, such as fan and washer. Help students identify and classify pictures for each category: Animals and Machines. Next have students classify the animal cards into Farm Animals and Wild Animals.

ON LEVEL

IF . . . students are comfortable applying the comprehension skill Classify and Categorize,	**THEN . . .** have them play a game from the ***Workshop Kit.***

ABOVE LEVEL

IF . . . students need a challenge with the comprehension skill Classify and Categorize,	**THEN . . .** have them play a game from the ***Workshop Kit.***

Expanding Vocabulary

solid firm and hard (page 9)

Ice is *solid*. Water is not.

Differentiating Instruction: English Learner

IF . . . English learners are having difficulty with the skill Classify and Categorize,
THEN . . . refer to the ***English Learner Support Guide*** Unit 5 Lesson 8.

Writer's Notebook

Have students refer to the illustrations in "Clouds, Rain, Snow, and Ice" to draw and label pictures of cirrus and cumulus clouds. Help them write sentences that tell about each type of cloud. Then have students write a complete sentence to go with their drawings. Remind them to begin each sentence with a capital letter and end with a punctuation mark.

Concept/Question Board

Have students use the Internet to find photographs of different kinds of clouds they can download, label, and post on the **Concept/Question Board.**

Differentiating Instruction **English Learners**

IF . . . students have difficulty participating in the discussion, **THEN . . .** ask questions that can be answered with a nod, a *yes* or *no*, or a short phrase. Examples: *Are all clouds made of the same thing?* yes *When water droplets in a cloud fall to the ground, what are they called?* raindrops

Phonics

Have students practice identifying sound/spellings from recent lessons. Turn to a page in the selection, and say a sound/spelling that appears on that page. Then have students point to the word with that sound/spelling. Remind them to look at ***Sound/Spelling Cards*** for help.

BIG Idea

What is weather?

After reading the story, read the Big Idea question. Discuss with students how the story helps answer this question.

Discussing the Selection

- Before discussing the selection, have students retell the story. Remind them to use effective communication when they retell the facts of the selection. Have them use appropriate volume and describing words, and remind them to speak clearly.
- As the class discusses the selection, tell students to participate courteously in the discussion. Tell students they should listen attentively and take turns.
- Ask students the following to check their comprehension of the selection.
  - *What are all clouds made of?* *Clouds are made of small drops of water called droplets, or tiny pieces of ice.*
  - *What happens when the water droplets in a cloud get big?* *They break free of the cloud and fall to the ground as raindrops.*
  - *What are some solid forms of water?* *Some solid forms of water are snow, sleet, ice.*
- Tell students that there are many kinds of clouds. Have them look back at the text and identify the names of the clouds they learned about in this selection. *cirrus and cumulus* There are many causes for the differences among types of clouds. Some of the reasons include temperature and the amount of water that is in the cloud.
- Have students return to the Focus Questions on page 5 of the story. Select a student to read the question aloud, and have students answer and discuss the questions. Encourage students to return to the text when answering their questions.
- Talk about the comprehension strategies students used as they read the selection. Have students think about how they used strategies to help them better understand the selection.
  - *How did visualizing help you better understand the ideas in the story? What did you visualize?* **Possible Answer** *Visualizing helped me see the ice in the puddles when it is cold.*
  - *How did you make connections with information in the text?* **Possible Answer** *I thought about snow that I have seen before.*
  - *How did summarizing help you understand the story?* **Possible Answer** *Summarizing helped me think about things I heard in the beginning of the story.*

Purposes for Reading

Review the purposes set for reading "Clouds, Rain, Snow, and Ice." Have students tell whether they met their purposes for reading. Have them identify information from the text that talks about the purposes.

- To find out about different kinds of clouds
- To learn why it rains or snows

Vocabulary Review

Review the selection vocabulary word with students by pointing to the word on the board or by displaying the transparency you made. Then call on students to use the word to create and share sentences about "Clouds, Rain, Snow, and Ice."

Print and Book Awareness

Print and Book Awareness

Connection between Printed and Spoken Language

- To review the connection between printed and spoken language, say the following words: *get, fall, ground, raindrops*. Have students say each word and then tell how many syllables it has. *Get, fall, and ground have one syllable; raindrops has two syllables.* Ask which word "sounds the longest" and why. *raindrops, because it has two syllables*
- Tell students to find the words *get* and *ground* in the text on page 7 of "Clouds, Rain, Snow, and Ice." Ask which word is longer in print. *ground* Remind them that words that look long in print do not always sound long when they are spoken. Say that it is important to listen for the individual sounds in a word—to try to determine how it looks and is spelled in print.

Teacher Tips

WORD BANK Have students add the selection vocabulary word and any expanding vocabulary words to the What's the Weather? Word Bank.

UNIT VOCABULARY This story has one selection vocabulary word. You may want to take this opportunity to review vocabulary from earlier in the unit that students find difficult.

HIGH-FREQUENCY WORDS To help students review the high-frequency words they have learned, say some of the words aloud, and have students point to each one in the selection. Remind them to look at the High- Frequency Word Bank for help.

Selection Vocabulary

sleet (page 8)

Technology

LISTENING LIBRARY Encourage students to listen to "Clouds, Rain, Snow, and Ice" on the ***Listening Library CD*** during Workshop for a model of fluent reading.

Audio CD

OBJECTIVES

Students will

- consider their audience and purpose for writing as they prepare a draft of a news story.
- understand that the names of days and months begin with capital letters.
- use a comma between a date and a year.

MATERIALS

- ***Skills Practice 1,*** pp. 193, 199–200
- ***Sound/Spelling Cards***
- Writer's Notebooks

Teacher Tip

DRAFTING If students need additional help drafting their weather news stories, pair them, and tell them to share their ideas. Students may work better and generate more ideas if they can talk to you or other students about an assignment during Workshop.

Differentiating Instruction English Learners

IF . . . students are unable to generate sentences for a story draft, **THEN . . .** encourage them to use words, phrases, or drawings to express their ideas. Help them shape these starting points into sentences.

Writing News Stories

Drafting

Teach—Using Audience and Purpose

- Ask students to explain what a news story is. *a story in a newspaper that gives new information to readers about a person, an event, or a thing* Remind them that they are writing a news story about the weather.
- Review with students the audience they chose and the purpose they set for their writing. **Possible Answer** *a story for other students to read so they will know what kind of weather we have observed this week.*

Guided Practice

- Use your model notes to create a sample draft on the board. Have students suggest which sections of your notes you should include in your weather news story. Tell them to use your draft as a model when they write.

Apply

- Tell students to use the notes they made in Lessons 6 and 7 to begin writing a news story about the weather. Tell them to keep their audience and purpose in mind as well as their plan from page 193 of ***Skills Practice 1.*** Encourage them to turn each idea or phrase from their plan into a sentence or two in their draft news stories.

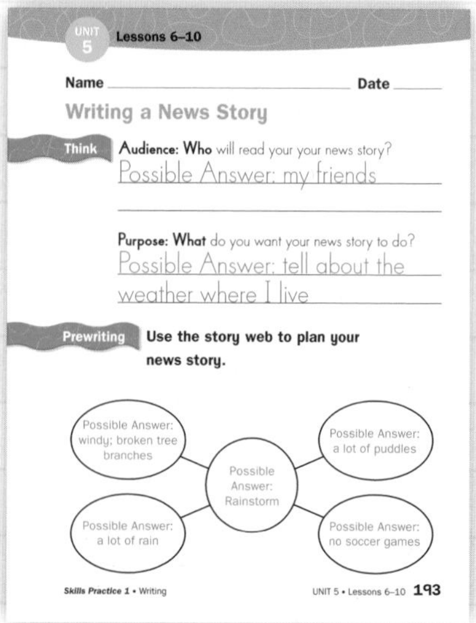

UNIT 5 Lessons 6–10

Name ______ Date ______

Writing a News Story

Think **Audience: Who** will read your your news story?
Possible Answer: my friends

Purpose: What do you want your news story to do?
Possible Answer: tell about the weather where I live

Prewriting **Use the story web to plan your news story.**

Possible Answer: Rainstorm
Possible Answer: windy; broken tree branches
Possible Answer: a lot of puddles
Possible Answer: a lot of rain
Possible Answer: no soccer games

Skills Practice 1 • Writing UNIT 5 • Lessons 6–10 193

Skills Practice 1, p. 193

Writing News Stories, cont.

- As students begin to draft their weather news stories, remind them of the Reading with a Writer's Eye activity from earlier on using examples. Explain that newspaper reporters will also use examples to help readers understand the main idea of a story. Encourage them to use examples to describe the weather conditions or event featured in their stories.
- If students have difficulty generating text, suggest that they write sentences that describe what the weather has been like, what they think it might be like for the next few days, or what kind of clothes people have been wearing in this weather.
- If students are writing about a recent weather event, remind them to answer the questions *who, what, where,* and *when* in their stories. Encourage them to place the most important information at the beginning of their news stories.
- Tell students to use the ***Sound/Spelling Cards*** and the High Frequency Word Bank to help them spell words correctly in their drafts.
- Remind them to think about the capitalization skills they have learned so far in this unit. Tell them to make sure any proper nouns or names of dates and months used in their stories are capitalized.

Research in Action

Monitor students' writing progress. Confer with them about what they are doing well and what you plan to do to help them write better. Establish how you will help them develop the necessary knowledge, skills, and strategies to improve their writing.
(Steve Graham and Karen Harris)

Differentiating Instruction

English Learners

IF . . . students need extra help with writing news stories, **THEN . . .** see ***English Learner Support Guide*** Unit 5 Lessons 6–10 to help them understand how to turn their ideas and information into sentences.

Teacher Tips

MECHANICS If students have difficulty finishing both mechanics review pages, give them more time during Workshop, or have them finish the page for homework.

WRITING LINK As students work on their weather news stories, tell them to remember the capitalization skills they have learned in this unit.

Differentiating Instruction **English Learners**

IF . . . students have difficulty with capitalization, **THEN . . .** bear in mind that capitalization rules vary among languages. Notice where students are having difficulty, and review the relevant capitalization rules with them.

Grammar, Usage, and Mechanics

Capitalization: Review Days of the Week and Months of the Year
Punctuation: Review Commas between Date and Year

Teach

- Write the following sentence on the board:

  We will go to the city on tuesday, october 8 2008.

- Ask students which words should begin with a capital letter and why. Tuesday *is the name of a day of the week;* October *is the name of a month.* Next have students tell you where the comma should go in the sentence. *between* 8 *and* 2008
- Discuss the rules for capitalizing the names of days of the week and months of the year and for using commas in dates. Remind students that the comma makes the date easier to read by separating the day number from the number of the year.

Guided Practice

Have volunteers practice writing familiar dates on the board. These could include well-known holidays, birthdays, or special family events. Remind them to think about what words should be capitalized and where commas should be placed as they work.

Capitalization and Punctuation, cont.

Apply

- Help students begin the capitalization and comma use review on ***Skills Practice 1*** pages 199–200. Work through the first few practice problems as a class, and then circulate and answer any questions as students complete the pages.
- If necessary, review the instruction with students to help with any reading or decodability issues.
- If time permits, have students use some of the dates generated during the Guided Practice section to compose new sentences in their Writer's Notebooks. Circulate to help with any reading as students practice using this capitalization skill. Then tell them to share with partners their favorite sentence featuring the name of a day and month.

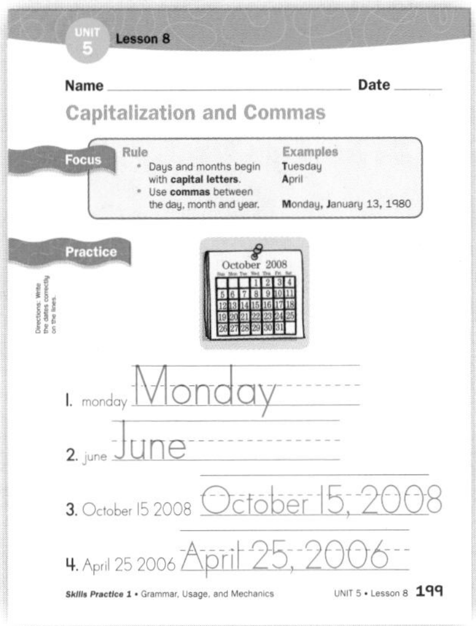
UNIT 5 Lesson 8

Name ______ Date ______

Capitalization and Commas

Focus
Rule
• Days and months begin with capital letters.
• Use commas between the day, month and year.
Examples
Tuesday
April
Monday, January 13, 1980

Practice

1. monday Monday
2. june June
3. October 15 2008 October 15, 2008
4. April 25 2006 April 25, 2006

Skills Practice 1 • Grammar, Usage, and Mechanics UNIT 5 • Lesson 8 199

Skills Practice 1, p. 199

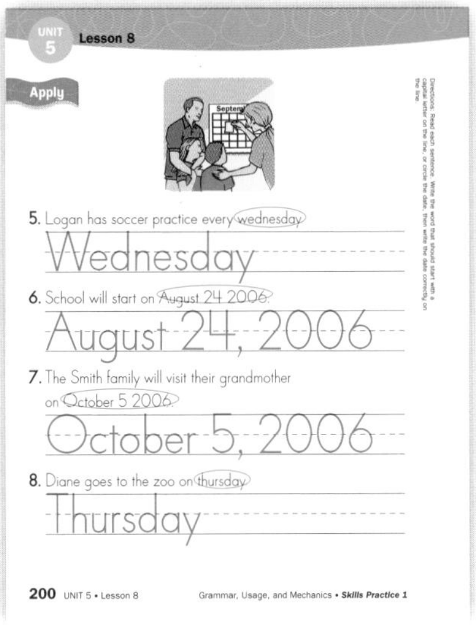
UNIT 5 Lesson 8

Apply

5. Logan has soccer practice every wednesday. Wednesday
6. School will start on August 24 2006. August 24, 2006
7. The Smith family will visit their grandmother on October 5 2006. October 5, 2006
8. Diane goes to the zoo on thursday. Thursday

200 UNIT 5 • Lesson 8 Grammar, Usage, and Mechanics • Skills Practice 1

Skills Practice 1, p. 200

Monitor Progress

to Differentiate Instruction

Formal Assessment

MECHANICS As students take notes in their What's the Weather? Notebooks, observe which students list the day and date at the top of each page, correctly capitalizing and using commas as needed.

APPROACHING LEVEL

IF . . . students need additional practice with capitalization and comma use,	**THEN . . .** have them complete ***Reteach 1*** pages 147–148.
IF . . . students have difficulty with the concept after working on the ***Reteach 1*** pages,	**THEN . . .** complete ***Intervention Guide*** Unit 5, Lesson 8 or play the Capitalization and Punctuation I game from the ***Workshop Kit*** with them during Workshop.

ON LEVEL

IF . . . students understand the concept but need practice,	**THEN . . .** have them play the Capitalization and Punctuation I game from the ***Workshop Kit.***

ABOVE LEVEL

IF . . . students are ready for a challenge with capitalization and comma use,	**THEN . . .** have them complete ***Challenge Activities 1*** page 74.

OBJECTIVES

Students will

- blend, spell, and read words that contain /s/ spelled *s, ce, ci_,* and *cy*.
- build fluency by reading ***Decodable*** 73.

MATERIALS

- Routines 3–7, 9–11
- ***Sound/Spelling Card*** 19
- ***Skills Practice 1,*** pp. 201–202
- ***Decodable*** 73, *Skating*

Teacher Tip

TIMING Remember to switch unpredictably between asking the entire group to respond and calling on individuals. This helps students attend more closely to the game.

Differentiating Instruction **English Learners**

IF . . . students have difficulty understanding when nouns are capitalized, **THEN . . .** bear in mind that capitalization rules vary among languages. Provide students with extra practice as needed.

Daily Warm-Ups

Copy the Morning Message on the board or on chart paper. Have students answer the question. Read the message aloud, and discuss it with students. **Possible Answer** *A windy day is the best day to fly a kite.*

MORNING MESSAGE
Good morning! Today we will read a story about flying kites.
What is a good day to fly a kite?

Daily Language Review

To review capitalization, write the following sentence on the board, or generate a similar one with students, and have them make corrections: In new york, we will see a ship named *sea queen*. *In New York, we will see a ship named* Sea Queen.

Consonant Riddle Game

Play the Consonant Riddle game with students. Ask them to say the word that answers each of the following:

What begins with /fr/ and rhymes with *sneeze? freeze*

What begins with /dr/ and rhymes with *five? drive*

What begins with /pl/ and rhymes with *cane? plane*

What begins with /w/ and rhymes with *sleeve? weave*

What begins with /t/ and rhymes with *went? tent*

Phonics

ROUTINE 3 ROUTINE 4 ROUTINE 10 ROUTINE 11

Review: /s/ Spelled *s, ce, ci_,* and *cy*

Blending

✦ Point to ***Sound/Spelling Card*** 19—Sausages, and review the sound and spellings for this card. Point to the *ce, ci_,* and *cy* spellings, and remind students that when the letter *c* is followed by *e, i,* or *y,* it says the soft sound, /s/.

Use Routine 3, whole-word blending, and Routine 4, blending sentences, to have students blend the words and sentences. Use Routine 10, closed syllables, and Routine 11, open syllables, to have students blend the multisyllable words.

Line 1	sent	cent	sell	cell
Line 2	brace	space	rice	twice
Line 3	city	cities	spice	spicy
Line 4	race	pace	mice	cast

Sentence 1	The boy traced his hand on the paper.
Sentence 2	Sally had braces on some of her teeth.

Line 1 **/s/ spelled *s* and *ce***

After blending, have students point out the homophones *sent* and *cent.* Have students use each word in a sentence. **Possible Answers** *I sent my grandma a letter. A penny is equal to one cent.*

Line 2 **/s/ spelled *ce***

Be sure to write the *a_e* and *i_e* spellings as a unit when writing the words. Have students identify the *vowel _ e* long-vowel spelling in each word.

Line 3 **/s/ spelled *s, ci_,* and *cy***

Have students identify the /s/ spelling in each word.

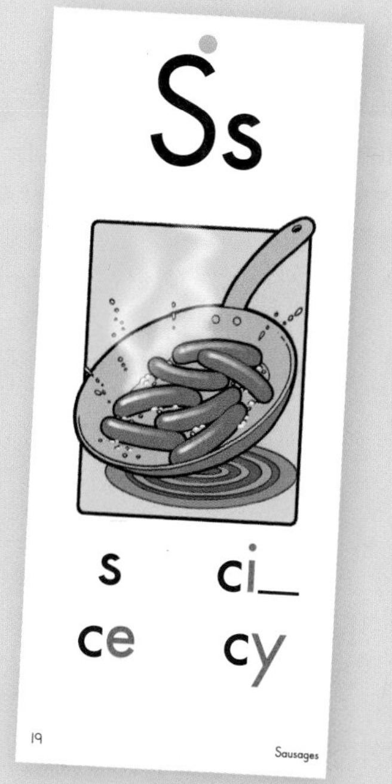

Sound/Spelling Card 19

Teacher Tips

CONTRASTING /s/ AND /k/ SPELLED *c_*
To reinforce the two sounds of *c*, have students contrast words with the /s/ and /k/ sounds spelled *c*. Some examples include *carry, cinch, cure, cement, act,* and *face.*

SYLLABICATION To help students blend the words and build fluency, use the syllabication below of the multisyllable words on the word lines.

civ • ic civ • il fan • cy

Differentiating Instruction — English Learners

IF . . . students have difficulty with consonant blends, **THEN . . .** bear in mind that some languages do not have consonant blends, and some have only a few consonants that appear in the final position. Unfamiliar final consonant sounds will be especially difficult for students to pronounce. Say slowly and distinctly the two sounds that make each final consonant blend.

Differentiating Instruction **English Learner**

IF . . . students need extra help with phonics,
THEN . . . see ***English Learner Support Guide*** Unit 5.

Line 4 **/k/ spelled *c* and /s/ spelled *ce***

Ask which words on the line have a hard *c* sound. *cost, cast* Ask which words have /s/ spelled *s*. *cast, cost*

Sentences 1–2

Write the words *boy* and *some* on the board. Read the words, repeat them, and have students read them. Then spell *boy* and *some* together. Invite volunteers to use the words in sentences. Write each word on an index card, and add the cards to the High-Frequency Word Bank.

Developing Oral Language

To review the words, call on a student to read a word and use it in a sentence to answer each riddle. Then erase the word.

- I'm a piece of money. What am I? *cent*
- I'm the opposite of *buy*. What am I? *sell*
- I add flavor to food. What am I? *spice*
- I am the opposite of *plain*. What am I? *fancy*
- I am another word for a mobile phone. What am I? *cell*

Guided Practice

Have students use ***Skills Practice 1*** pages 201–202 to review /s/ spellings. Have students complete the puzzle on page 201. Have students choose and write the correct words to complete the sentences at the top of page 202. Students can use the bottom of the page for dictation.

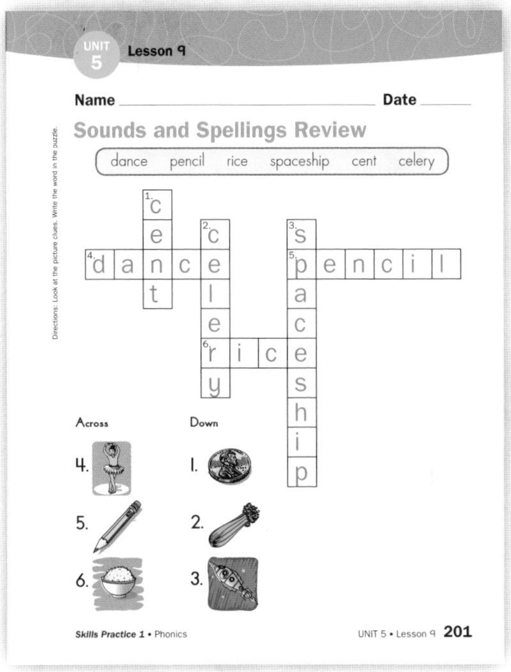
UNIT 5 Lesson 9

Name ______ Date ______

Sounds and Spellings Review

Directions: Look at the picture clues. Write the word in the puzzle.

dance pencil rice spaceship cent celery

Across: 4. dance 5. pencil 6. rice

Down: 1. cent 2. celery 3. spaceship

Skills Practice 1 • Phonics UNIT 5 • Lesson 9 201

UNIT 5 Lesson 9

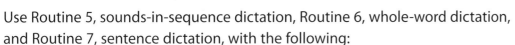

Sounds and Spellings Review

Directions: Write the correct word from the box to complete the sentence.

I saw three cats run under the chair. (city cats)

Macy's doll has a pretty face. (face seven)

Dictation

center cinder

safe nice

The police officer said Stacy saved the kitten.

202 UNIT 5 • Lesson 9 Phonics • Skills Practice 1

Skills Practice 1, pp. 201–202

Dictation

ROUTINE 5 ROUTINE 6 ROUTINE 7

Use Routine 5, sounds-in-sequence dictation, Routine 6, whole-word dictation, and Routine 7, sentence dictation, with the following:

Line 1	center	cinder
Line 2	safe	nice
Sentence	The police officer said Stacy saved the kitten.	

Teacher Tip

WORD CHART Ask students to add more words that have different spellings for /s/.

Differentiating Instruction English Learners

IF . . . students have difficulty recording unknown dictated words, **THEN . . .** write each word on the board, and read its correct pronunciation.

Monitor Progress to Differentiate Instruction
Formal Assessment

DICTATION As students practice writing their dictation words, note who seems to know the words well and who needs additional help during Workshop.

APPROACHING LEVEL

IF . . . students need additional practice with the spellings for /s/, **THEN . . .** use ***Reteach 1*** pages 149–150.

ON LEVEL

IF . . . students are on level with dictation, **THEN . . .** have them use one of the activities in the ***Workshop Kit.***

ABOVE LEVEL

IF . . . students need a challenge with dictation, **THEN . . .** use ***Challenge Activities 1*** page 75.

Fluency/Reading a Decodable Book

ROUTINE 9

Core Decodable 73: Skating

Phonics Focus: Review /s/ Sound/Spellings

High-Frequency Words

Review the high-frequency words *boy* and *some* that students learned in Blending. Point to them in the High-Frequency Word Bank, or write them on the board, spell the words, and have students say the words. Have a volunteer use the words in sentences. Review other high-frequency words by pointing to them in the High-Frequency Word Bank and having students read them.

Reading the Decodable

- Follow Routine 9, reading a ***Decodable,*** as you read the story with students.
- Have students read the title, browse the story, and discuss what they think the story will be about.
- The first time through, have students read a page silently. Then have one student read it aloud. Repeat this procedure for each page.
- Reread the story at least twice, calling on various students to read. Then have the entire class do a choral reading of the story.

Responding

- After reading, be sure to talk about the story and answer any questions students have. Ask students to identify any difficult words in the book.

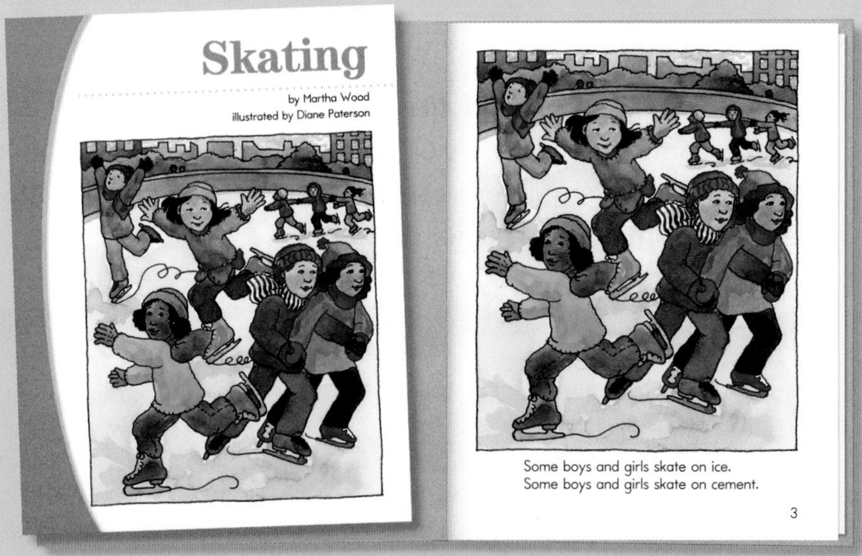

Skating
by Martha Wood
illustrated by Diane Paterson
Some boys and girls skate on ice.
Some boys and girls skate on cement.
3

This girl takes lessons at City Center.
She skates in fancy circles.
4
This boy also ice skates.
He is fast, but not fancy.
5

Teacher Tip

SOUND/SPELLING CARDS Remind students to refer to the ***Sound/Spelling Cards*** if they are unsure of a sound/spelling.

Since this boy was three, he has skated.
He skates on cement.
6
This girl races on skates.
At some places, she races on ice.
At some places, she races on cement.
7

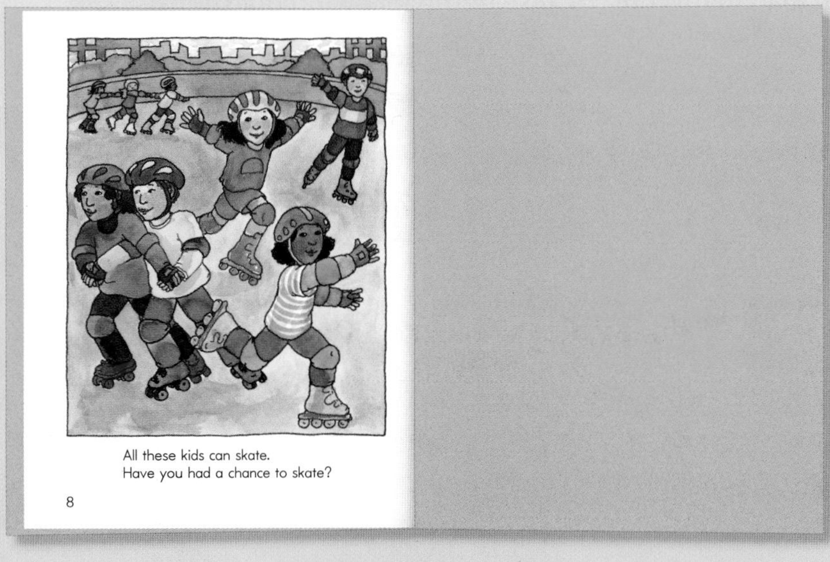

All these kids can skate.
Have you had a chance to skate?
8

- ✦ Have students retell the story.
- ✦ As students answer the following questions, make sure they focus on the words in the story rather than getting the answers by listening or from the pictures. Have students answer by pointing to and reading aloud the answers in the text:
  - **Where do boys and girls skate?** *on ice or on cement*
  - **How does the girl on page 4 skate?** *in fancy circles*
  - **Where does the boy on page 6 skate?** *on cement*

Building Fluency

Have students build fluency by rereading ***Core Decodable*** 73 twice with a partner. The first time through, one partner should read the odd-numbered pages and the other partner the even-numbered pages. The second time through, they should switch pages. For additional practice with the /s/ sound/spellings, have students read ***Practice Decodable*** 61, *Salt on Ice.* Have students record their readings on their Personal Title sheets, noting the title of each book, the date, and any difficult words they encountered.

Core Decodable 73

Skating

High-Frequency Words Introduced in Core Decodable 73

boy
some

Previously Introduced High-Frequency Words

a	every	is	she	were
after	for	it	six	what
all	get	its	take	when
am	girl	jump	that	will
an	go	just	the	with
and	got	like	them	yes
as	green	little	then	you
ask	had	look	there	
at	has	make	they	
be	have	of	this	
big	he	on	to	
but	help	or	two	
call	her	out	up	
can	him	over	walk	
could	his	red	was	
did	I	ride	we	
do	if	said	well	
down	in	see	went	

Sound/Spelling Correspondences in Core Decodables

1. Pre-decodable
2. Pre-decodable
3. Pre-decodable
4. Pre-decodable
5. Pre-decodable
6. /s/ spelled s, /m/ spelled m, /a/ spelled a
7. /t/ spelled t, tt
8. Review
9. /d/ spelled d
10. /n/ spelled n
11. /i/ spelled i
12. /h/ spelled h_
13. Review
14. /p/ spelled p
15. /l/ spelled l, ll
16. /o/ spelled o
17. /b/ spelled b
18. Review
19. /k/ spelled c
20. /aw/ spelled al
21. /k/ spelled k, ■ck
22. /r/ spelled r
23. /f/ spelled f, ff
24. /s/ spelled ss
25. Review
26. /g/ spelled g
27. /j/ spelled j, ■dge
28. /u/ spelled u
29. /z/ spelled z, zz
30. /z/ spelled _s
31. Review
32. /ks/ spelled ■x
33. /e/ spelled e
34. -ed ending: /ed/, /d/
35. -ed ending: /t/
36. /e/ spelled _ea_
37. Review
38. /sh/ spelled sh
39. /th/ spelled th
40. /ch/ spelled ch, ■tch
41. /or/ spelled or, ore
42. Review
43. /ar/ spelled ar
44. /m/ spelled _mb
45. /w/ spelled w_
46. /hw/ spelled wh_
47. /er/ spelled er, ir
48. /er/ spelled ur
49. Review
50. Schwa
51. Review schwa
52. /ng/ spelled ■ng
53. /nk/ spelled ■nk
54. /kw/ spelled qu_
55. Review
56. /y/ spelled y_
57. /v/ spelled v
58. Syllable -le
59. /ā/ spelled a and a_e
60. Review
61. /ī/ spelled i and i_e
62. /s/ spelled ce, ci_
63. /j/ spelled ge, gi_
64. Review
65. /ō/ spelled o and o_e
66. /ū/ spelled u and u_e
67. Review
68. /ē/ spelled e and e_e
69. /ē/ spelled ee and ea
70. Review
71. /ē/ spelled _y, _ie_
72. /s/ spelled cy
73. Review /s/ spellings

Decodable 73, inside back cover

Reading and Responding

OBJECTIVES

Students will

- activate prior knowledge about wind and weather.
- learn vocabulary words.
- use the comprehension strategies Making Connections and Predicting.
- use the comprehension skill Cause and Effect.
- understand the use of quotation marks.

MATERIALS

- ***First Reader,*** pp. 10–15
- Routines 12, 13
- ***What's the Weather? Big Book,*** p. 60
- ***Transparency*** 14

Teacher Tips

MATERIALS If you have a kite, show it to students as you ask the questions about kites.

HOME You may want to make copies of the instructions for the tornado experiment. These can be sent home with students for them to try with a parent or an adult.

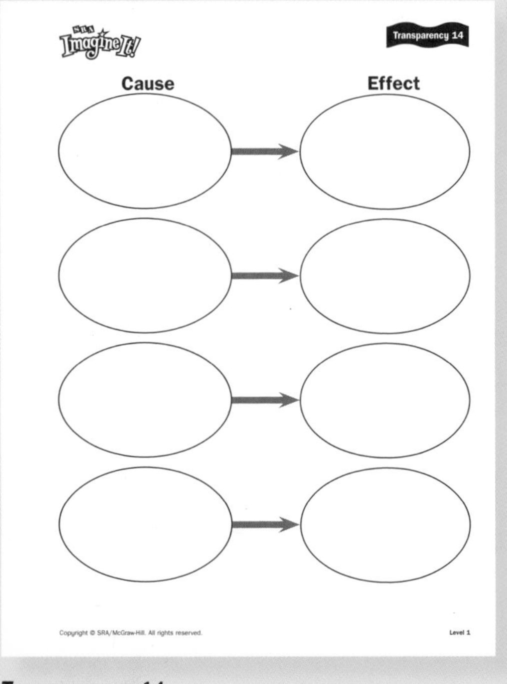

Transparency 14

Build Background

Activate Prior Knowledge

Ask students to think about what they already know and to recall the other selections they have read in this unit to answer the following questions:

- What are the four seasons? *spring, summer, fall/autumn, winter*
- In our part of the world, in what season is October? *fall/autumn*
- What makes a kite stay in the sky? **Possible Answers** *wind; air*
- What happens to a kite if the wind stops blowing? *It falls to the ground.*

Background Information

- Tell students that the genre of "A Good Day for Kites" is realistic fiction. Explain that realistic fiction has events, people, and places that seem real but are not.
- Review the ideas of cause and effect with students. This will prepare them for the concepts of wind's effect on a kite.

Preview and Prepare

ROUTINE 12

Browse

- Follow Routine 12, reading the selection, to prepare students to read the selection. Begin by displaying the cover of the ***First Reader.*** Point to and read aloud the title.
- Have students locate and turn to the Table of Contents, and point to the title of the selection "A Good Day for Kites." Have students read the title along with you as you point to each word. Point to the page number 10, and have a volunteer read it and tell what the number means. Turn to page 10.
- Demonstrate how to browse the selection by commenting on illustrations and by predicting how they might relate to the text. On page 12, for example, you might say *On this page, I see children looking at something flying in the air from a pole, but it's not a kite. I don't see any kites at all on the page. I wonder what the children are looking at. I wonder what that has to do with flying a kite.*
- Have students browse the first few pages to look for clues to what the selection is about and for difficult or unfamiliar words. For example, students may identify the degree symbol and the word *Fahrenheit*. Tell students that the small circle is the symbol for degrees, which is how we measure temperature. Then say that Fahrenheit is the name for a way to measure temperature.

Set Purposes

- Have students think about the information they gained while browsing. Ask students to use this information to tell what the purposes for reading this selection might be. Write them on the board. Some suggestions are the following:
  - To find out what makes kites stay in the sky
  - To find out how to tell where and how hard the wind is blowing
- After reading the selection, have students return to these purposes.

Fluency

- Have students apply letter-sound knowledge to decode phonetically regular words quickly and accurately as they read this selection.
- With the ***First Reader*** stories, students begin the transition to reading more challenging text. Have students adjust their reading rate based on this new challenging text.
- As students read "A Good Day for Kites," have them focus on expression and intonation. Remind them to pause at end punctuation marks.

Teacher Tips

GLOSSARY The terms *thermometer* (page 11) and *wind sock* (page 12) appear in the Glossary. As students browse and identify interesting words or phrases, you may want to use the opportunity to have students practice glossary use. Have students locate and turn to the Glossary, find the word, and read the entry.

HIGH-FREQUENCY WORDS As students browse, you may want to have them look for the high-frequency words they know. The following are some of the high-frequency words that appear in the selection: *the, red, said, but, it, like, to, see, what, is, that, for, look, at, out, a, to, go, get.*

BIG Idea

What is weather?

Before reading the selection, reread the Big Idea question. Tell students to keep this question in mind as they listen to the selection.

Differentiating Instruction: English Learner

IF . . . students would benefit from reading "A Good Day for Kites" before the class reads it, **THEN . . .** read it with them during Workshop, encouraging them to ask questions and to clarify anything they do not understand.

Selection Vocabulary

thermometer an instrument used to measure the temperature (page 11)

Teacher Tips

WORD REVIEW As students read the selections in the ***First Reader,*** they will find weather-related words they have seen and learned in previous selections in this unit, such as *wind*. When these words occur, prompt students to recall their meanings and to provide examples of the word. This will expand and deepen their understanding of the words.

SEMANTIC MAP Continue to have students build upon the semantics map. Have them add words from the selection and words they have learned throughout the unit.

DIGITAL TOOLS Have students look for definitions of selection vocabulary or difficult words from the text using an online dictionary.

Building Vocabulary

ROUTINE 13

- Use Routine 13, selection vocabulary, to introduce the vocabulary word to students. Write the word on the board or on a transparency.
  - Have students look up the word *thermometer* in a picture dictionary or in the glossary. Have students tell what they see in the illustration.
  - Have students clap out the syllables in *thermometer* as you say the word—ther • mom • e • ter. Ask a volunteer to say what he or she can find out by using a thermometer. *exactly how hot or cold it is*
  - Tell students to look for this word as they read the selection.
- You will introduce one expanding vocabulary word to students as the selection is reread. The word is identified in a box where it appears in the selection. When you come to the word in the selection, read to students the word, the definition, and the sample sentence. Understanding this word will help students better comprehend the selection.

Monitor Progress to Differentiate Instruction — Formal Assessment

DECODING As students read, notice how they are decoding words containing sound/spellings they have learned.

APPROACHING LEVEL	**IF . . .** students are having difficulty decoding previously learned sound/spellings,	**THEN . . .** review problem sound/spellings with them during Workshop.
ON LEVEL	**IF . . .** students are able to decode most previously learned sound/spellings,	**THEN . . .** remind them to use the ***Sound/Spelling Cards*** to help them.
ABOVE LEVEL	**IF . . .** students are able to decode all the words in the story,	**THEN . . .** have them practice reading the story for fluency during Workshop.

Reading the Selection

Genre Realistic Fiction

Tell students that "A Good Day for Kites" is an example of realistic fiction. It has characters that seem real and things that did not happen but *could* happen in real life. Briefly review the elements of realistic fiction.

- It has people or animals that seem real.
- It has events and places that seem real.
- It is about things that did not happen but *could* happen in real life.

Comprehension Strategies

As students read "A Good Day for Kites," model and prompt the use of the following comprehension strategies:

- Making Connections
- Predicting

Comprehension Skills

As students reread "A Good Day for Kites," apply the comprehension skill Cause and Effect.

Reading with a Writer's Eye

As students reread "A Good Day for Kites," discuss how the author uses dialogue to make the story interesting.

Focus Questions

Read and discuss the Focus Questions on page 10. Encourage students to think about the Focus Questions as they read "A Good Day for Kites."

Reading Recommendations

ROUTINE 12

Day 4 **ORALLY** Students will read the entire selection twice today. Follow Routine 12, the reading selection routine. The first time, model and prompt the use of the comprehension strategies. The second time, focus on the comprehension skills and Reading with a Writer's Eye.

Differentiating Instruction **English Learners**

IF . . . students need help understanding vocabulary, **THEN . . .** use a picture or an actual thermometer to show the meaning.

Teacher Tips

1st READ

PARTNER READING LIST Have students add information about this selection to their Partner Reading Lists. Remind them to write the title of the selection, the author's name, and the date they read it. If they also read the selection in a group, have them write the names of the group members.

2nd READ

READING THE SELECTION If students are struggling with the ***First Reader*** stories, read "A Good Day for Kites" to the class for the first reading. Focus on reading with expression and intonation. During the second reading, have students do an oral reading of the story.

2nd READ

FACT OR FICTION Although this selection is realistic fiction, it also contains some facts. This presents an excellent opportunity for students to differentiate fact from fiction. During the second reading, have students note which elements of the story are fact and which elements are fiction.

Phonics

Words in the selection containing sound/spellings from recent phonics lessons appear in boxes like this throughout the selection. At the end of the first reading, students should be prompted to identify the sound/spellings of these words.

Reading and Responding

Focus Questions How do you measure the weather? What instruments can you use?

A Good Day for Kites

"The leaves are red and yellow," said Matt. "But it feels more like summer than fall." ❶

10

"Check the thermometer to see what the temperature is," Kim said.

"It is 80° F! That is warm for October," said Matt. ❷

11

First Reader, pp. 10–11

Phonics

/s/ spelled *s:* sock, kites, Let's (page 12); set, kites, socks, sky (page 13)

Teacher Tips

GLOSSARY The words *thermometer* (page 11) and *wind sock* (page 12) appear in the Glossary at the back of the ***First Reader***.

MULTIPLE MEANINGS The word *fall* has multiple meanings. Have students use the words in the story to tell the appropriate meaning of the word *fall* as it is used here.

1st READ

Comprehension Strategies

❶ **Making Connections** Teacher Prompt: *I've seen red and yellow leaves. Have you? When and where?* **Possible Student Response** *I've seen red and yellow leaves on trees in the fall, when the leaves turn colors.*

❷ **Making Connections** Teacher Modeling: *I can understand why Matt and Kim think the weather is hot for October. Where we live, October is usually a cool month.*

❸ **Predicting** Teacher Prompt: *It takes a lot of wind to fly a kite. I predict the wind will be too strong to fly the kites. What are your predictions?* **Possible Student Response** *I predict the wind will be just right to fly the kites.*

❹ **Confirming Predictions** Teacher Prompt: *My prediction was not confirmed. The kites are flying. Was your prediction confirmed?* **Possible Student Response** *My prediction was confirmed. They were able to fly their kites.*

"It is windy, Matt. Look at the wind sock. The wind is pushing it out. Today would be a good day to fly our kites," Kim said. 3

"Let's go get them," said Matt.

12

"Ready, set, go!" Matt yelled. "Our kites look like wind socks in the sky!" 4

13

First Reader, pp. 12–13

Comprehension Skills

2nd READ

Cause and Effect

Review with students that a *cause* is why something happens and that an *effect* is what happens.

- Reread page 13. What happens on that page? *The kites fly.*
- What causes the kites to fly so high? *It is windy.*

Have students tell you where on ***Transparency*** 14 to record each response.

Reading with a Writer's Eye

2nd READ

Dialogue

Remind students that "A Good Day for Kites" is realistic fiction. Explain that when authors write realistic fiction, they make their characters seem like real people by having them talk the way real people talk. Explain that "talk written down" is called *dialogue.*

Differentiating Instruction **English Learners**

IF . . . students have difficulty identifying and discussing causes and effects, **THEN . . .** introduce or review vocabulary related to cause and effect, such as *because, since, therefore, as a result,* and *so.*

Expanding Vocabulary

wind sock a sleeve, open at both ends, that measures wind direction and speed (page 12) The *wind sock* went in the direction of the breeze.

Reading and Responding

"Our kites are going the same way as the wind," said Kim. "They look like the real wind sock!" 5

14

"What a good day for kites!" said Matt. "The temperature is warm. It is windy, and our kites are flying high!"

15

First Reader, pp. 14–15

Phonics

/s/ spelled *s:* kites, same, sock (page 14)
/s/ spelled *s:* kites (page 15)

Teacher Tips

CAPITALIZATION Remind students about the focus of the grammar lessons—capitalization of names of people. Have students point to and identify the capital letters on these pages.

SELF-CORRECT As students read, make sure they practice self-correction when they make a mistake in their reading.

1st READ

Comprehension Strategies

5 Making Connections Teacher Prompt: *Kim says her kite is going the same way as the wind. I know you have to pay attention to the way the wind blows when you're flying a kite. Once, when I was flying a kite, the wind suddenly changed directions, and my kite almost pulled me around in a circle! What connections can you make?* **Possible Student Response** *When I flew a kite, the wind was so strong it made me run.*

Comprehension Check

Why do Matt and Kim look at the thermometer and at the wind sock? to see what the temperature is and to see whether the wind is strong enough to fly their kites

Comprehension Skills

2nd READ

Cause and Effect

✦ Reread page 14. Ask the following questions, and have students tell you where on ***Transparency*** 14 to record each response. What happens to make Kim's kite look like a wind sock? *When the wind changes direction, so does the kite.*

✦ *The effect is that it is a good day for kites. What is the cause?* **Possible Answer** *The temperature is warm and it is windy. This makes it a good day for kites.*

Reading with a Writer's Eye

Dialogue

Remind students that "talk written down" is called *dialogue.*

- Have students look at page 14. Point to the opening and closing quotation marks. Ask students what they are called. *quotation marks* Ask students to explain what quotation marks show. *The words said by a character are between these sets of marks*. Have students find and say the first word of Kim's quotation and then the last word she says. our *and* wind Have students find the words *said Kim*. Explain that these words tell readers which character in a story is talking.
- Point out that in this selection, the author wants to give readers information about weather and to keep them interested in the selection. This is why the author tells a story about children flying a kite and why he lets his characters tell how they found out about the weather.

Differentiating Instruction — English Learners

IF . . . English learners are having difficulty with Cause and Effect, **THEN . . .** refer to ***English Learner Support Guide*** Unit 5 Lesson 9.

IF . . . students are not accustomed to seeing quotation marks in dialogue, **THEN . . .** make sure they understand that in English, quotation marks are used to set off a speaker's exact words. In Spanish, for example, dashes are used to set off a speaker's exact words.

Technology

LISTENING LIBRARY Encourage students to listen to "A Good Day for Kites" on the ***Listening Library CD*** during Workshop for a model of fluent reading.

Monitor Progress to Differentiate Instruction — Formal Assessment

PREDICTING As you prompt students to use the comprehension strategy, note which students are able to create predictions and which students wait for cues from you or other students.

APPROACHING LEVEL	**IF . . .** students have difficulty with the comprehension strategy Predicting,	**THEN . . .** provide additional modeling of the strategy using a previously read selection.
ON LEVEL	**IF . . .** students are able to grasp the strategy,	**THEN . . .** have them preview a weather-related library book and offer their predictions on what the book is about.
ABOVE LEVEL	**IF . . .** students need a challenge,	**THEN . . .** have them work with on-level students on their predictions on the weather-related library book, and have them confirm or adjust their predictions by reading the books.

Writer's Notebook

Have students use the illustrations in the selection as models for drawing wind socks and kites. Tell them to show the wind socks and kites when the wind is strong and when only a light breeze is blowing. Help them label their drawings. Then have students write a complete sentence to go with their drawings. Remind them to begin each sentence with a capital letter and end with a punctuation mark.

Concept/Question Board

Have students use the Internet to find photographs of real wind socks that they can download, label, and post on the **Concept/Question Board.**

Teacher Tip

HIGH-FREQUENCY WORDS To help students review the high-frequency words they have learned, say some of the words aloud, and have students point to each one in the selection. Remind them to look at the High-Frequency Word Bank for help.

Differentiating Instruction

English Learners

IF . . . students have difficulty participating in the discussion, **THEN . . .** ask questions that can be answered with a nod, a *yes* or *no,* or a short phrase. Examples: *Does wind make the kites fly?* yes *When the kites are in the sky, what are they like?* wind socks

Discussing the Selection

- Before discussing the selection, have students retell the story. Remind them to use effective communication when they retell the facts of the selection. Have them use appropriate volume and describing words, and remind them to speak clearly.
- As the class discusses the selection, tell students to participate courteously in the discussion. Tell students they should listen attentively and take turns.
- Ask students the following:
  - *What is unusual about the October weather?* It is hot. October is usually cooler than that.
  - *What makes the kites fly?* The strong wind keeps them in the sky.
  - *How are the kites in the sky like wind socks?* They are going in the same direction as the wind. When the wind changes direction, so do the kites.
- Have students return to the Focus Questions on page 10 of the story. Select a student to read each question aloud, and have students answer and discuss the questions. Encourage students to return to the text when answering their questions.
- Talk about comprehension strategies used as students read the selection. Have students think about how they used strategies to help them better understand the selection.
  - *How did predicting help you think about what would happen in the story? What did you predict?* **Possible Answer** Predicting helped me try to figure out what would happen. I predicted that Matt and Kim would fly the kites.
  - *How did you make connections with information in the text?* **Possible Answer** I thought about when I tried to fly a kite with my grandpa.

Purposes for Reading

Review the purposes set for reading "A Good Day for Kites." Have students tell whether they met their purposes for reading. Have them identify information from the text that talks about the purposes:

- To find out what makes kites stay in the sky
- To learn how to tell how hard the wind is blowing

Vocabulary Review

- Review the meaning of the word *thermometer* with students. Draw a thermometer on the board or on chart paper. Include numbers along the thermometer. Demonstrate a certain temperature by shading the thermometer up to that point. Then make statements about the weather using the following sentence frames *My thermometer shows that it is _____ degrees. It is _____ outside.* 65; cool
- Next give each student a temperature in degrees Fahrenheit, such as 32 degrees. Using your model, have them create a drawing of a thermometer showing the temperature you have given them. Then have them use the sentence frames above to make statements about the weather.

Print and Book Awareness

Print and Book Awareness

Punctuation: Quotation Marks

- Remind students that when characters in a selection say something, the words they say are put between quotation marks.
- Write the following sentence on the board. Ask students to identify the opening and closing quotation marks and then to read the exact words said by the speaker.

  "It is a very windy day," said Pete.

  If students read the words *said Pete,* tell them that these words are not part of what was said. Then identify who said it.
- Have students look through "A Good Day for Kites" for examples of dialogue. Call on volunteers to read only the words said by a character. Have them identify who said the words.
- Conclude by having each student write a sentence about the selection and place quotation marks at the beginning and the end of the sentence. Help students add commas, the word *said,* and their names to complete the sentences.

BIG Idea

What is weather?

After reading the story, read the Big Idea question. Discuss with students how the story helps answer this question.

Selection Vocabulary

thermometer (page 11)

Teacher Tips

WORD BANK Have students add the selection vocabulary word and any expanding vocabulary words to the What's the Weather? Word Bank.

UNIT VOCABULARY This story has one selection vocabulary word. You may want to take this opportunity to review vocabulary from earlier in the unit that students find difficult.

Concept/Question Board

Have students look for pictures of thermometers or wind socks in magazines and on the Internet. Have them label the pictures and post them on the **Concept/Question Board.**

Teacher Tip

VOCABULARY Encourage students to use words from the What's the Weather? Word Bank as they talk about the photograph.

Fine Art

What's the Weather? Big Book p. 60

- Display ***What's the Weather? Big Book*** page 60. Have students focus attention on the photograph *Snow Covered Apple Tree in Front of Half Dome, Yosemite National Park, California* by Ansel Adams.
- Share with students any information about the photographer that you choose. For example, you might tell them that Ansel Adams was a famous American photographer who lived from 1902 until 1984. He took many photographs of places in California.
- Remind students that they talked about this photograph at the beginning of the unit. Have them recall their responses, and then ask whether they have additional responses now that they have read a great deal about weather. Have them talk about the photograph, mentioning anything new they see and using their information about weather to add to their understanding of what the photograph shows.
- Have students share their thoughts and opinions about this piece of fine art, including whether they like it or not and why. Ask them how the art makes them feel, such as happy or sad, excited or tired, cold or warm.

Science Connection

Physical Properties of Ice, Water, and Steam

Show students the glass of water. Invite a volunteer to pour the water into the cup. Point out that the water takes the shape of the cup and that water is not hard. Discuss that these are the properties of a liquid.

Invite a volunteer to tap on the ice cube. Discuss that it is hard and cannot be poured like water. Review with students that these are the properties of a solid.

Place the cup of water in a microwave or other heat source, and heat it on high until it boils and releases steam. Be sure to use a craft stick to break up the pressure built by heating the water so the water does not pop and burn someone. Review with students that the steam does not have one shape, can move about freely, and is not a liquid or a solid. Point out that these are the properties of a gas.

Teacher Tips

SAFETY Make sure students understand the importance of safety around heat sources. Tell them never to use appliances or other heat sources without the permission and supervision of an adult.

LITERATURE Have students select age- and ability-appropriate fiction and nonfiction materials to read, based on interest and teacher recommendations, to begin a core base of knowledge about the unit theme.

OBJECTIVES

Students will

- revise and add details to their weather news stories.
- understand the differences between informal and formal language.

MATERIALS

- Routines 14, 15
- ***Language Arts Big Book,*** pp. 22–23
- ***Sound/Spelling Cards***
- ***Skills Practice 1,*** p. 194
- ***First Reader,*** pp. 14–15

Writing News Stories

Revising

ROUTINE 14

Teach—Adding Details

- Tell students that today they will revise their weather news stories. Explain that they can improve their stories by adding detail to the information and rewriting unclear sentences. Use ***Language Arts Big Book*** pages 22–23 to review information about making their writing better.
- Review your news story draft from Lesson 8 with students. Explain that you will check it to see whether you need to change any words or add information.
- **Teacher Modeling** *I'm going to read over my draft to see whether I can add any words that would make my story more interesting. I've said the weather is warm and rainy, but I haven't said how warm or how much rain. I can add details such as the temperature and that the rain is a drizzle and not a thunderstorm. Then I need to go over what I've written to check my spelling and captialization of proper nouns.*
- Remind students that as they revise, they can use the ***Sound/Spelling Cards*** and the High-Frequency Word Bank to check their spelling.
- Tell students that news stories often include information on days or dates. Encourage them to add information like this to their drafts, such as the day and date of the weather they observed or of a recent storm.

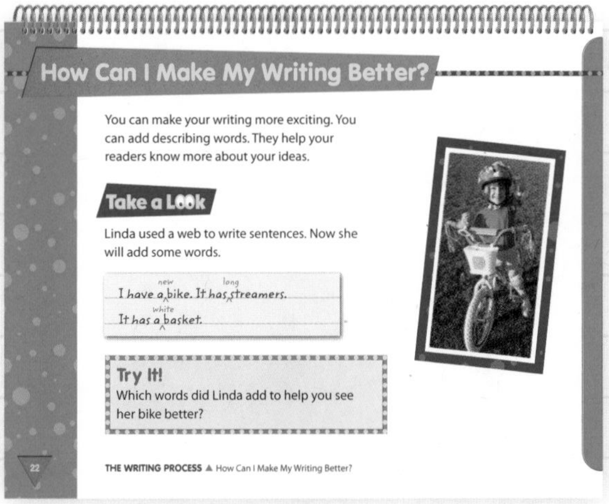

How Can I Make My Writing Better?

You can make your writing more exciting. You can add describing words. They help your readers know more about your ideas.

Take a Look

Linda used a web to write sentences. Now she will add some words.

I have a new bike. It has long streamers.
It has a white basket.

Try It!
Which words did Linda add to help you see her bike better?

22 THE WRITING PROCESS ▲ How Can I Make My Writing Better?

Language Arts Big Book, p. 22

Teacher Tips

GRAMMAR LINK Tell students that news stories often include names of people and special places. Remind them to check their stories for proper names that should be capitalized.

READING LINK As students revise their stories, remind them of the Reading with a Writer's Eye activity on dialogue from earlier. Tell them that newspaper reporters often write dialogue in their news stories to include what someone they interviewed may have said.

Traits of Good Writing

Ideas Writers add detail as they revise to make their ideas more exciting or informative.

Voice Writers think about their audience as they revise, making sure all sentences are clear and easy to read.

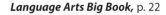

Writing News Stories, cont.

Guided Practice

ROUTINE 15

✦ Help students use your model and the information from the ***Language Arts Big Book*** to revise their news stories. Tell them to use the revising checklist on ***Skills Practice 1*** page 194 to check their work. Review the instruction as necessary to make sure students understand each part of the checklist. If students struggle, model aloud how you would use each point.

✦ Remind them that when writing an informative sentence, they should stay on topic and include details. Encourage students to make sure their informative news paragraph focuses on the topic of weather and includes at least three details in their sentences. Explain that they can add details to news stories by answering the *who, what, where, when,* and *why* questions.

✦ Circulate to help them with spelling, capitalization of proper nouns, and punctuation. Check that students add weather-related descriptive details and reread their work for clarity.

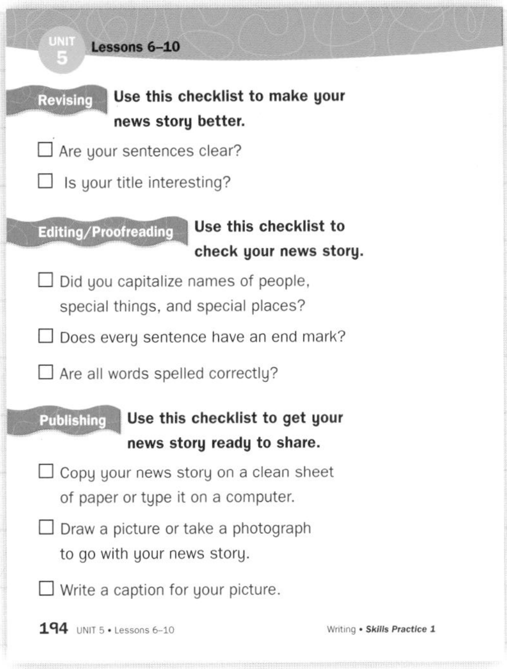
UNIT 5 Lessons 6–10

Revising **Use this checklist to make your news story better.**

☐ Are your sentences clear?

☐ Is your title interesting?

Editing/Proofreading **Use this checklist to check your news story.**

☐ Did you capitalize names of people, special things, and special places?

☐ Does every sentence have an end mark?

☐ Are all words spelled correctly?

Publishing **Use this checklist to get your news story ready to share.**

☐ Copy your news story on a clean sheet of paper or type it on a computer.

☐ Draw a picture or take a photograph to go with your news story.

☐ Write a caption for your picture.

194 UNIT 5 • Lessons 6–10 Writing • *Skills Practice 1*

Skills Practice 1, p. 194

Listening/Speaking/Viewing

Language: Informal and Formal Language

Teach

✦ Tell students that informal language is the kind of language we use when we talk to our family or friends. We are relaxed, and we may use words without worrying too much about how they sound.

✦ Formal language is the language we use when we talk to teachers in school and to grown-ups we meet outside our homes. Explain that when we are with friends, we might describe the weather by saying *Wow! I don't like the way the wind is messing up my hair today.* With a teacher, however, we might say *The wind is too strong today.*

✦ Tell students that the author of "A Good Day for Kites" used fictional characters to tell about the weather. The author wrote dialogue for the characters that made them sound like real people. This helps keep readers interested in the selection.

Guided Practice

✦ Have students look at the dialogue in "A Good Day for Kites" on pages 14–15 of the ***First Reader*** and explain why the language is more informal than formal. Point out the following language example: On page 14, Kim says her kite looks like a wind sock, but an author using more formal language might have written: "Kites move in the same direction the wind is blowing."

✦ Have pairs of students practice using formal and informal language by discussing today's selection.

Differentiating Instruction **English Learners**

IF . . . students have difficulty understanding some informal language either in the selection or in their classmates' everyday usage,
THEN . . . encourage them to share the words or expressions that cause them difficulty, and challenge proficient English speakers to explain.

Day 5 **Preparing to Read**

OBJECTIVES

Students will

- blend, spell, and read words that contain /ē/ spelled _y and _ie and /s/ spelled *cy*.
- build fluency by reading ***Decodable*** 74.

MATERIALS

- Routines 3–4, 8–11
- ***Sound/Spelling Cards*** 19, 28
- ***Skills Practice 1,*** pp. 203–204
- ***Decodable*** 74, *Marcy and Sally*

Differentiating Instruction **English Learners**

IF . . . students are native speakers of Spanish or one of the other Romance languages, **THEN . . .** they may seem confused by the capitalization of the pronoun *I*. In these languages, *I* is capitalized only when it begins a sentence.

Technology

eSkills provides Web-based practice with ***Imagine It!*** sounds and spellings. For more information about this program, visit **SRAonline.com.**

Daily Warm-Ups

Copy the Morning Message on the board or on chart paper. Have students answer the questions. Read the message aloud, and discuss it with students. **Possible Answer** *A thermometer measures the temperature. A wind sock measures the wind.*

MORNING MESSAGE

Good morning! Today we will learn how to use a thermometer. We will also read about wind socks. What can a thermometer tell us? What can a wind sock tell us?

Daily Language Review

To review capitalization, write the following sentence on the board, or generate a similar one with students. Have students make corrections: I told mr. lee i was born in tampa, florida. *I told Mr. Lee I was born in Tampa, Florida.*

Which Does Not Belong? Game

Write the words *safe, sent*, and *cut* on the board. Blend and read the words. Ask students which word does not belong and why. Accept any response that students can explain. **Possible Answers** cut, *because it does not begin with* s; safe, *because it does not end with* t. Continue with one or more of these word sets: *space, sent, cents; page, pitch, judge.*

Phonics

ROUTINE 3 ROUTINE 4 ROUTINE 10 ROUTINE 11

Review: /ē/ Spelled *y* and *_ie_* and /s/ Spelled *cy*

Blending

- Point to ***Sound/Spelling Card*** 28—Long E, and review the sound and spellings on the card. Point to the blank in *_y*, and review what it means. *The _y comes at the end of a word.* Point to the *_ie_* spelling on the ***Sound/Spelling Card.*** Have students explain the meaning of the blanks. *This sound does not usually come at the beginning or end of a word. The spelling usually has a consonant before and after.*
- Display ***Sound/Spelling Card*** 19—Sausages, and have students review the sound for this card.
- Use Routine 3, whole-word blending, and Routine 4, blending sentences, to have students blend the words and sentences. Use Routine 10, closed syllables, and Routine 11, open syllables, to have students blend the multisyllable words.

Line 1	funny	sunny	rainy	windy
Line 2	happy	puppy	fancy	bunny
Line 3	niece	piece	shield	field
Line 4	parties	copies	ponies	stories

Sentence 1 Billie is going to study after dinner.

Sentence 2 Was Jamie here to get a piece of pie?

Sound/Spelling Cards 19, 28

Teacher Tips

SYLLABICATION To help students blend the words and build fluency, use the syllabication below of the multisyllable words on the word lines.

fun • ny	sun • ny	rain • y
win • dy	hap • py	fan • cy
bun • ny	par • ties	pup • py
cop • ies	po • nies	stor • ies

PACE The morning activities should be paced quickly. Progress through them without spending too much time on each activity. The activities can be altered to fit your students' needs.

Preparing to Read

Differentiating Instruction **English Learners**

IF . . . students are unable to identify the words that match the clues, **THEN . . .** for oral practice and vocabulary building, ask them to repeat the words their classmates say.

Line 1 **/ē/ spelled _*y***

Have students identify the spelling of /ē/ for each word on the line. *_y*

Line 2 **/ē/ spelled _*y* and /s/ spelled *cy***

Ask students to give the plural spelling for *puppy* and *bunny*. Ask them to say the rule for forming the plural of nouns that end in *_y*. *puppies, bunnies; change* y *to* i *and add* es

Line 3 **/ē/ spelled _*ie*_**

Have students identify the spelling of /ē/ for each word on the line. *_ie_*

Line 4 **/ē/ spelled *ie***

Have students notice the spelling *_ie_*for /ē/. Have them notice that in these words, the spelling comes at the end of the word. Remind students that often when you change a word ending in *_y* to mean more than one, you change the *y* to *i* and add *es*.

Sentences 1–2

Write the words *going* and *here* on the board. Read the words, repeat them, and have students read them. Then spell *going* and *here* together. Invite volunteers to use the words in sentences. Write each word on an index card, and add it to the High-Frequency Word Bank. Have students read each sentence several times to build fluency.

Developing Oral Language

To review the words, call on students to find the following:

- a word with the /k/ for *c* *copies*
- a word that is the name for a family member *niece*
- a word that describes the weather *sunny, windy, rainy*
- a word that describes small horses *ponies*
- a word that is another name for a rabbit *bunny*

Guided Practice

Have students use ***Skills Practice 1*** pages 203–204 to review the _*y* and _*ie*_ spellings for /ē/ and the *cy* spelling for /s/. Have students complete the sentences on page 203. Have students choose the word that correctly identifies each picture on page 204.

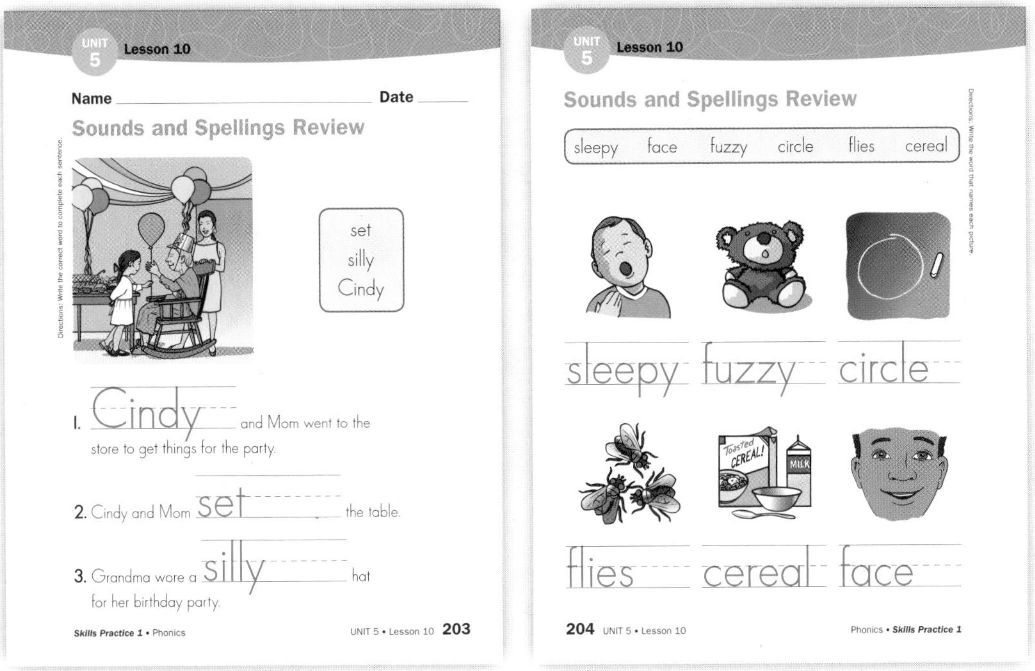

UNIT 5 Lesson 10

Name ______ Date ______

Sounds and Spellings Review

Directions: Write the correct word to complete each sentence.

set
silly
Cindy

1. Cindy and Mom went to the store to get things for the party.
2. Cindy and Mom set the table.
3. Grandma wore a silly hat for her birthday party.

Skills Practice 1 • Phonics — UNIT 5 • Lesson 10 203

UNIT 5 Lesson 10

Sounds and Spellings Review

Directions: Write the word that names each picture.

sleepy	face	fuzzy	circle	flies	cereal

sleepy fuzzy circle

flies cereal face

204 UNIT 5 • Lesson 10 — Phonics • Skills Practice 1

Skills Practice 1, pp. 203–204

Dictation: Word Building Game

ROUTINE 8

Use Routine 8, word building, to have students spell words in the Word Building game. Have students use pencil and paper for the following words:

fleece
flee
feel
field
yield
shield

Monitor Progress

to Differentiate Instruction
Formal Assessment

DICTATION As students spell words, notice who uses the ***Sound/Spelling Cards*** and spells the words correctly. Note students who are asking for help with the spellings.

APPROACHING LEVEL

IF . . . students need additional practice with dictation, **THEN . . .** have them complete ***Reteach 1*** pages 151–152.

ON LEVEL

IF . . . students are on level with dictation, **THEN . . .** have them use one of the activities in the ***Workshop Kit.***

ABOVE LEVEL

IF . . . students need a challenge with dictation, **THEN . . .** have them complete ***Challenge Activities 1*** page 76.

Fluency/Reading a Decodable Book

ROUTINE 9

Core Decodable 74: *Marcy and Sally*

Phonics Focus: Review /ē/ Spelled _y and _ie_; /s/ Spelled cy

High-Frequency Words

Review the high-frequency words *going* and *here* that students learned in Blending. Point to them in the High-Frequency Word Bank, or write them on the board, spell the words, and have students say the words. Have a volunteer use the words in sentences. Review other high-frequency words by pointing to them in the High-Frequency Word Bank and having students read them.

Reading the Decodable

- Follow Routine 9, reading a ***Decodable,*** as you read the story with students.
- Have students read the title, browse the story, and discuss what they think the story will be about.
- The first time through, have students read a page silently. Then have one student read it aloud. Repeat this procedure for each page.
- Reread the story at least twice, calling on various students to read. Then have the entire class do a choral reading of the story.

Responding

- After reading, be sure to talk about the story and answer any questions students have. Ask students to identify any difficult words in the book.
- Have students retell the story.

Teacher Tip

SOUND/SPELLING CARDS Remind students to refer to the ***Sound/Spelling Cards*** if they are unsure of a sound/spelling.

Marcy and Sally

by Howard Lee illustrated by Lorinda Cauley

Marcy's home was next to Sally's.
Sally was Marcy's best pal.

3

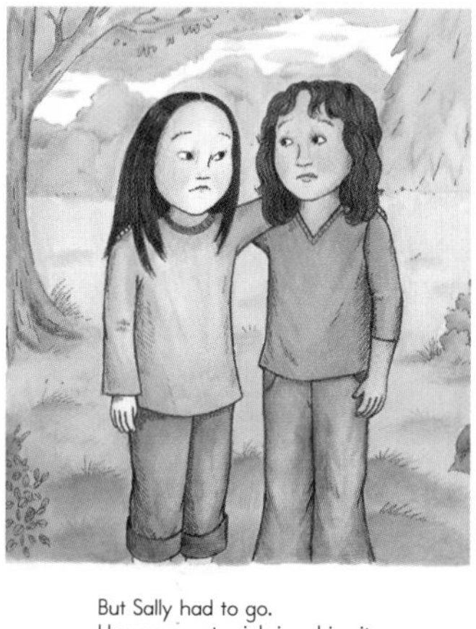

But Sally had to go.
Her mom got a job in a big city.

4

There was going to be a block party.
It was for Sally and her mom and dad.

5

Marcy was sad.
She was going to miss Sally.

6

Kids planned to have gifts for Sally.
Some kids shopped for gifts.
Some kids made gifts.

7

At first, Marcy did not have a gift.
She could not shop for a gift.
Marcy had just ten pennies.

8

What could Marcy make for Sally?
Marcy had to think.
What did Sally like?

9

Marcy looked at Sally.
It helped Marcy think.

10

Sally liked music.
She could sing.
Sally could dance.

11

Marcy looked at Sally some more.
Sally could skate fast.
She could skate in circles.

12

And Sally liked trucks!
She liked cement trucks.
Sally liked big vans.

13

Sally also liked the circus.
Here, Sally was at the circus and smiling.

14

These ideas helped Marcy plan a gift.
Then, Marcy made a gift.

15

Sally opened a fancy box.
Sally liked her gift. She hugged Marcy.

16

✦ As students answer the following questions, make sure they focus on the words in the story rather than getting the answers by listening or from the pictures. Have students answer by pointing to and reading aloud the answers in the text:

- **Who is Marcy's best pal?** *Sally*
- **What does Sally's mom get?** *a job in a big city*
- **How much money does Marcy have?** *ten pennies*
- **What does Marcy give to Sally?** *a fancy box*

Building Fluency

Have students build fluency by rereading ***Core Decodable*** 74 twice with a partner. The first time through, one partner should read the odd-numbered pages and the other partner the even-numbered pages. The second time through, they should switch pages. For additional practice with the sound/spellings students learned this week, have students reread one or more of the following: ***Core Decodable*** 71, 72, or 73 or ***Practice Decodable*** 59, 60, or 61. Have students record their readings on their Personal Title sheets, noting the title of each book they read, the date, and any difficult words they encounter.

Core Decodable 74

Marcy and Sally

High-Frequency Words Introduced in Core Decodable 74

going
here

Previously Introduced High-Frequency Words

a	down	in	see	well
after	every	is	she	went
all	for	it	six	were
am	get	its	some	what
an	girl	jump	take	when
and	go	just	that	will
as	got	like	the	with
ask	green	little	them	yes
at	had	look	then	you
be	has	make	there	
big	have	of	they	
boy	he	on	this	
but	help	or	to	
call	her	out	two	
can	him	over	up	
could	his	red	walk	
did	I	ride	was	
do	if	said	we	

Sound/Spelling Correspondences in Core Decodables

1. Pre-decodable
2. Pre-decodable
3. Pre-decodable
4. Pre-decodable
5. Pre-decodable
6. /s/ spelled *s*, /m/ spelled *m*, /a/ spelled *a*
7. /t/ spelled *t*, *tt*
8. Review
9. /d/ spelled *d*
10. /n/ spelled *n*
11. /i/ spelled *i*
12. /h/ spelled *h_*
13. Review
14. /p/ spelled *p*
15. /l/ spelled *l*, *ll*
16. /o/ spelled *o*
17. /b/ spelled *b*
18. Review
19. /k/ spelled *c*
20. /aw/ spelled *al*
21. /k/ spelled *k*, ■*ck*
22. /r/ spelled *r*
23. /f/ spelled *f*, *ff*
24. /s/ spelled *ss*
25. Review
26. /g/ spelled *g*
27. /j/ spelled *j*, ■*dge*
28. /u/ spelled *u*
29. /z/ spelled *z*, *zz*
30. /z/ spelled *_s*
31. Review
32. /ks/ spelled ■*x*
33. /e/ spelled *e*
34. -ed ending: /ed/, /d/
35. -ed ending: /t/
36. /e/ spelled *_ea_*
37. Review
38. /sh/ spelled *sh*
39. /th/ spelled *th*
40. /ch/ spelled *ch*, ■*tch*
41. /or/ spelled *or*, *ore*
42. Review
43. /ar/ spelled *ar*
44. /m/ spelled *_mb*
45. /w/ spelled *w_*
46. /hw/ spelled *wh_*
47. /er/ spelled *er*, *ir*
48. /er/ spelled *ur*
49. Review
50. Schwa
51. Review schwa
52. /ng/ spelled ■*ng*
53. /nk/ spelled ■*nk*
54. /kw/ spelled *qu_*
55. Review
56. /y/ spelled *y_*
57. /v/ spelled *v*
58. Syllable -le
59. /ā/ spelled *a* and *a_e*
60. Review
61. /ī/ spelled *i* and *i_e*
62. /s/ spelled *ce*, *ci_*
63. /j/ spelled *ge*, *gi_*
64. Review
65. /ō/ spelled *o* and *o_e*
66. /ū/ spelled *u* and *u_e*
67. Review
68. /ē/ spelled *e* and *e_e*
69. /ē/ spelled *ee* and *ea*
70. Review
71. /ē/ spelled *_y*, *_ie_*
72. /s/ spelled *cy*
73. Review /s/ spellings
74. Review

Decodable 74, inside back cover

Reading and Responding

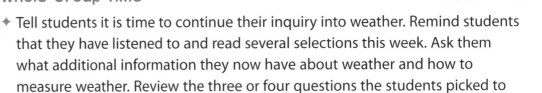

OBJECTIVES

Students will

- generate additional questions and conjectures about weather.
- use resources to confirm conjectures.
- revise conjectures as needed.
- learn and discuss concept vocabulary.

MATERIALS

- Writer's Notebooks
- ***What's the Weather? Big Book***

Inquiry Planner

Week 1

- Generate ideas and questions for the **Concept/Question Board.**
- Decide on a problem or question to research, and make a conjecture.

Week 2

- Collect information, and confirm or revise the conjectures and questions.

Week 3

- Prepare a presentation.

Teacher Tips

MATERIALS AND PREPARATION Before starting this lesson, arrange to have a large thermometer set up outside a window or in a place that students can easily see.

RESOURCES Have students identify types of resources they can use during this step of their Inquiry investigation, including magazines, appropriate Web sites, and newspapers.

DIGITAL RESEARCH Provide students with a list of specific Web sites that can be used to gather information and generate ideas for their Inquiry investigations.

Inquiry Process

Collect Information and Confirm or Revise Conjectures and Questions

Whole Group

Whole-Group Time

- Tell students it is time to continue their inquiry into weather. Remind students that they have listened to and read several selections this week. Ask them what additional information they now have about weather and how to measure weather. Review the three or four questions the students picked to investigate, in Lesson 5, Week 1.
- Ask students which questions have been answered in the selections "On the Same Day in March," "Clouds, Rain, Snow, and Ice," and "A Good Day for Kites." Discuss the selections with students. Discuss how this information helps them with their conjectures. Review the conjectures posted on the **Concept/Question Board** and ask students if they can confirm any of the conjectures. Ask students if they want to revise any conjectures. Ask students if the selections they read and listened to this week caused them to think of any additional questions. Record these questions and have the class select one or two to make conjectures on. Remind students that this step in their investigation includes identifying their research needs. To help with this process, students can use books, magazines, newspapers, and the Internet. They can also conduct interviews.
- Point to the Weather Chart. Discuss the current weather conditions, and record them on the chart. Encourage students to start adding more information to the chart. Use the model question *How is the weather in the morning different from the weather in the afternoon?* Remind students that they can investigate this question by using a thermometer in a place that will measure the temperature. Help students think of a good location to take an accurate temperature reading. Discuss why the thermometer should remain in the same place throughout the day. Tell students to take good notes in their notebooks as they observe the thermometer. Have students add these details to their weather observations with sentences or illustrations.

Small-Group Time

Small Group

- If students are working in groups, have them meet and talk about how to find answers to their questions. Encourage them to use information to confirm or revise their conjectures. If they revise their conjectures, have them use this sentence frame: Once I thought __________. Now I think _________. **Possible Answer** *Once I thought the weather was similar at the same time of the year. Now I think location affects weather.*
- Meet with groups, and talk with them about how they might do additional research and how they might present their findings. Suggestions include doing an experiment, putting together a book with illustrations, doing a skit of a weather forecast, using charts and graphs, or talking to the class using pictures and photographs.
- When students complete this phase of the Inquiry process, have them begin working on their presentations.

Concept Vocabulary

The second concept vocabulary word for the What's the Weather unit is *precipitation.* Write the word on an index card, and post it in your room. Read the word aloud and have students practice saying it. Have students tell whether they recognize this as an unfamiliar word. Explain that *precipitation* is "the falling of water in the form of rain, sleet, hail, or snow." Have students use the word in a sentence. Make sure students are able to relate this new vocabulary to prior knowledge. Remind them to refer to this word throughout the unit. Add the concept vocabulary word to the What's the Weather? Word Bank.

Concept/Question Board

Have students use the Board as a tool. It may contain information to help their investigations. Encourage your students to continue to research the questions they are investigating. Remind them to list multiple conjectures for their questions.

Teacher Tips

MULTIPLE CONJECTURES By this time in the year, you may want to encourage your students to make multiple conjectures about one class question and to work in small groups to investigate those conjectures. Provide only as much structure and guidance as your students need.

ORGANIZATIONAL FEATURES When students read nonfiction, tell them to locate specific information using the organizational features in the text. Some examples of these features are tables of contents, headings, captions, bold print, key words, and indices.

SEMANTIC MAP Work with students to continue building the semantic map for the unit. Have students tell you where to add the concept vocabulary word on the map.

Day 5

Language Arts

OBJECTIVES

Students will
- edit, publish, and share their news stories.
- form the letters *v* and *w* correctly.
- control the size and spacing of letters.
- increase fluency and speed while writing.
- review that the names of days and months begin with capital letters.
- use a comma between a date and a year.

MATERIALS
- Routines 15, 16
- ***Skills Practice 1,*** p. 194
- Writer's Notebooks
- Portfolios
- ***Lesson Assessment Book 1,*** pp. 61–64

Teacher Tips

PLAN AHEAD Set up an area in the classroom as an "anchor desk" where students can read their weather news stories as "reporters."

LANGUAGE Ask students whether they think a news story would use formal or informal language. Read aloud a few short articles, and have students tell whether the story sounded formal or informal. Encourage students to mix formal and appropriate informal language into their weather news stories.

Writing News Stories

ROUTINE 15

Editing and Publishing

Teach

- Tell students they should always review their work for mistakes before they turn it in. Explain that errors could give the reader incorrect information.
- **Teacher Modeling** Use your revised weather news story to model checking for errors. *Let's check our news story to make sure we have used capital letters and end marks where they are needed. Then we'll check all the words to make sure they are spelled correctly.*
- Remind students that the newspaper stories you have read this week include facts and descriptive details about the weather. Ask them to check whether they did the same in their writing. Remind them that using examples in their stories will help readers understand the information featured.

Guided Practice

- Work through the editing checklist on ***Skills Practice 1*** page 194 as a class. Remind students to make sure that any proper nouns, including names, days, and months as well as the pronoun *I* are capitalized.
- Encourage students to use a caret to add text or details as they make their edits.
- Tell students to review their work for mistakes one last time and make any corrections before copying their stories onto their final papers.

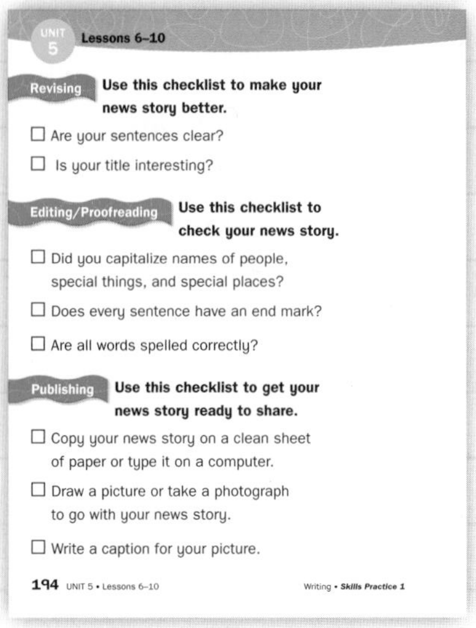

UNIT 5 Lessons 6–10

Revising **Use this checklist to make your news story better.**

- ☐ Are your sentences clear?
- ☐ Is your title interesting?

Editing/Proofreading **Use this checklist to check your news story.**

- ☐ Did you capitalize names of people, special things, and special places?
- ☐ Does every sentence have an end mark?
- ☐ Are all words spelled correctly?

Publishing **Use this checklist to get your news story ready to share.**

- ☐ Copy your news story on a clean sheet of paper or type it on a computer.
- ☐ Draw a picture or take a photograph to go with your news story.
- ☐ Write a caption for your picture.

194 UNIT 5 • Lessons 6–10 Writing • *Skills Practice 1*

Skills Practice 1, p. 194

Writing News Stories, cont.

- Encourage students to think of creative ways to publish their writing. They might add a headline and then type their stories to create a class newspaper. They might search online for pictures of weather events to attach to their story.

Apply

ROUTINE 16

- Have students complete the publishing checklist on page 194 of ***Skills Practice 1.*** Read through the instruction to make sure they understand each part.
- Invite volunteer "reporters" to sit at the "anchor desk" and share their news stories with the class. Encourage them to use details as they describe the weather.
- If you have access to a video recorder, consider taping students as they read their story during Workshop and then "broadcasting" the news to the class at the end of the Language Arts lesson.
- After each speaker, have volunteers tell what they liked about the story. Allow time for students to ask questions and offer helpful suggestions. Display students' writing around the classroom, or have them place it in their Portfolios.

Assessment

Use the Writing Rubrics found in the Level Appendix to evaluate students' news stories. You may use any of the rubrics for Genre, Writing Process, and Writing Traits.

Teacher Tips

TECHNOLOGY If your school owns computers with newsletter software, help students type their news stories during Workshop. Then combine all the stories into one newsletter to display in the reading area or on a bulletin board.

PRESENTING Before students read their news stories to the class, tell them to speak slowly and to pronounce all words correctly. Remind them that if they stand or sit up straight and use a loud, clear voice, everyone in the room will be able to hear and enjoy their stories.

Teacher Tips

PENMANSHIP Check and compare neatness during handwriting practice and during the final draft of writing exercises.

LETTER FORMATION As students form letters, observe their pencil grip and how much control they have as they make each stroke. If students struggle, model the correct pencil position again, and have them practice the form with you during Workshop.

Differentiating Instruction: English Learners

IF . . . students are native Spanish speakers, **THEN . . .** they may need extra help writing the letter *w*. The letter *w* does not appear in the Spanish alphabet or in Spanish words, although Spanish speakers use *w* occasionally for words borrowed from other languages.

Penmanship

Alphabet Practice: The Letters *v* and *w*

Guided Practice

Review how to form lowercase *v* and *w*, and then distribute handwriting paper. Have students write each letter twice within the lines as they say its name. Tell them to proofread their letters and circle their best *v* and *w*.

Apply

- To monitor students' handwriting fluency, write the following sentence on the board: *Steve will wash the van.* Read it to students, and tell them to copy the sentence onto their papers as quickly as they can without making any mistakes. After two or three minutes, have them proofread their sentence by circling any incorrect words and making them better by rewriting them above or next to the original words. Then have students underline their best *v* and *w*.
- Look for additional opportunities during writing activities and in other subject areas to provide handwriting practice and to encourage and praise students when they form the letters *v* and *w* correctly.

Grammar, Usage, and Mechanics

Capitalization: Days of the Week and Months of the Year
Punctuation: Commas between Date and Year

Guided Practice

- On the board, write the following sentence:

  Granddad was born on saturday, december 23 1958.

- Review the rule for capitalizing the names of days of the week and months of the year and the rule for using commas in dates. Ask students to make capitalization and punctuation corrections. *Granddad was born on Saturday, December 23, 1958.*

- Write the following sentences on the board. Have students circle the letters that should be capitalized and tell why. Then have them write each sentence correctly in their Writer's Notebooks. Then have them place commas in dates as necessary:
  - We went to Florida on the first wednesday in april. W *in* Wednesday *because it is a day of the week;* A *in* April *because it is a month*
  - Grandma was born on march 8 1941. M *in* March *because it is a month; a comma between* 8 *and* 1941 *because it is a date*
  - The library will have a story reading on every thursday in may. T *in* Thursday *because it is a day of the week;* M *in* May *because it is a month*

Apply

Tell students to search their portfolios for places they should capitalize a day of the week or month of the year. Have them select two sentences to edit or to add a date to, using correct capitalization and punctuation. Then have them share their favorite sentences with partners.

Teacher Tips

MECHANICS Tell students to remember the rules for capitalizing proper nouns and for using a comma in dates as they write in their What's the Weather? Notebooks and ***Skills Practice 1*** workbook. Tell them to work with partners to check each other's capitalization and punctuation as they work on their Inquiry investigations.

VOCABULARY Remind students that days of the week and months of the year are sight words they should memorize. Refer to the index cards posted on the wall if necessary.

Differentiating Instruction: English Learners

IF . . . students have difficulty reading dates, **THEN . . .** read aloud the date March 8, 1941, and some other random dates. Point out that Americans generally say *oh* for the zero in dates.

Monitor Progress: Formal Assessment

Use ***Lesson Assessment Book 1*** pages 61–64 to assess students' understanding of the skills taught in Lessons 6–10.

Lessons 11–15 Overview

Lesson Planner

Preparing to Read

MATERIALS
- ✦Routines 1–11
- ✦***Sound/Spelling Cards*** 19, 27–29
- ✦***Skills Practice 1,*** pp. 205–206, 209–212, 215–218
- ✦***Decodables*** 75–78

Day 1

Daily Warm-Ups, p. T254
Introduce the Sound/Spelling
/ā/ Spelled *ai_* and *_ay*, p. T255
✓ **Phonemic Awareness** Listening for /ā/, p. T255
✓ **Phonics**
- Blending, pp. T256–T257
- Developing Oral Language, p. T257
- Guided Practice, p. T258
- Dictation, p. T259

✓ **Fluency/Reading a Decodable**
Decodable 75, pp. T260–T261

Day 2

Daily Warm-Ups, p. T274
✓ **Phonics**
- Review /ā/ Spelled *ai_* and *_ay*, p. T275
- Guided Practice, p. T277
- Dictation: Word Building Game, p. T277

Reading and Responding

MATERIALS
- ✦***First Reader,*** pp. 16–35
- ✦Routines 12, 13
- ✦***Home Connection,*** pp. 39–40
- ✦***Transparencies*** 14, 20, 42
- ✦***What's the Weather? Big Book***
- ✦Writer's Notebooks

Day 1

Build Background, p. T262
Preview and Prepare, p. T263
✓ **Building Vocabulary,** p. T264
Reading the Selection, p. T265
Reading Recommendations, p. T265
First Reader, pp. 16–21
Comprehension Strategies, pp. T266, T268
Comprehension Skills, pp. T267, T269
Reading with a Writer's Eye, p. T269
Discussing the Selection, p. T270
✓ **Vocabulary Review,** p. T271
Print and Book Awareness, p. T271

Day 2

Build Background, p. T278
Preview and Prepare, p. T279
✓ **Building Vocabulary,** p. T280
Reading the Selection, p. T281
First Reader, pp. 22–27
✓ **Comprehension,** pp. T282–T285
Reading with a Writer's Eye, pp. T283, T285
Discussing the Selection, p. T286
✓ **Vocabulary Review,** p. T287
Print and Book Awareness, p. T287
Fine Art, p. T288
Science Connection, p. T289

Language Arts

MATERIALS
- ✦***Transparencies*** 40–44, 43a, 44a
- ✦***Language Arts Big Book,*** pp. 48–51, 138, 162
- ✦***Skills Practice 1,*** pp. 207–208, 213–214
- ✦***Alphabet Letter Cards***
- ✦***Sound/Spelling Cards***
- ✦***Lesson Assessment Book 1,*** pp. 65–70
- ✦Routines 14–16
- ✦Writer's Notebooks
- ✦Portfolios

Day 1

Writing Instructions Prewriting, p. T272
Penmanship Alphabet Practice: The Letters *k* and *z*, p. T273

Day 2

Writing Instructions Prewriting, p. T290
✓ **Penmanship** Alphabet Practice: The Letters *k* and *z*, p. T292
Grammar, Usage, and Mechanics Plural Nouns, p. T293

Monitor Progress

✓ = **Formal Assessment**

Day 1

- ✓ **Phonemic Awareness, p. T255**
- ✓ **Dictation, p. T258**
- ✓ **Decoding, pp. T260, T269**
- ✓ **Vocabulary, p. T264**

Day 2

- ✓ **Dictation, p. T277**
- ✓ **Decoding, p. T279**
- ✓ **Vocabulary, p. T280**
- ✓ **Sequence, p. T285**
- ✓ **Penmanship, p. T292**

Day 3

Daily Warm-Ups, p. T294

Introduce the Sound/Spelling

/ī/ spelled *_igh*, *_y*, and *_ie*, p. T295

Phonemic Awareness Listening for /ī/, p. T295

Phonics

- Blending, pp. T296–T297
- Developing Oral Language, p. T297
- Guided Practice, p. T298
- Dictation, p. T299

Fluency/Reading a Decodable

- ***Decodable*** 76, pp. T300–T301
- ***Decodable*** 77, pp. T302–T303

Build Background, p. T304
Preview and Prepare, p. T305
Building Vocabulary, p. T306
Reading the Selection, p. T307
First Reader, pp. 28–35
Comprehension Strategies, pp. T308, T310
Comprehension Skills, pp. T309, T311
Reading with a Writer's Eye, pp. T309, T311
Discussing the Selection, p. T312
Vocabulary Review, p. T313
Print and Book Awareness, p. T313

Writing Instructions Drafting, p. T314
Grammar, Usage, and Mechanics Plural Nouns, pp. T316–T317

Blending, p. T296
Dictation, p. T298
Decoding, p. T306
Writing, p. T315
Grammar, Usage, and Mechanics, p. T317

Day 4

Daily Warm-Ups, pp. T318–T319

Phonics

- Review /ī/ Spelled *_igh*, *_y*, and *_ie*, p. T320
- Blending, pp. T320–T321
- Guided Practice, p. T322
- Dictation: Word Building Game, p. T32

Inquiry Process Prepare a Presentation, pp. T324–T325
Concept/Question Board, p. T325

Writing Instructions Revising, p. T326
Listening/Speaking/Viewing Speaking: Clear Speech, p. T327

Dictation, pp. T322, T323
Inquiry, p. T325
Listening/Speaking/Viewing, p. T327

Day 5 Review

Daily Warm-Ups, pp. T328–T329

Phonics

- Review: General Blending, p. T330
- Developing Oral Language, p. T331
- Guided Practice, p. T331
- Dictation, p. T331

Fluency/Reading a Decodable

Decodable 78, pp. T332–T333

Theme Wrap-Up and Review, p. T340
Unit Review, p. T341

Writing Instructions Editing and Publishing, p. T334
Penmanship Review Letters *k* and *z*, p. T336
Grammar, Usage, and Mechanics Plural Nouns, p. T337

Phonics, p. T331
Lesson Assessment Book 1, pp. 65–70

Lessons 11-15 Overview

Student Resources

First Reader

Focus Questions What is the weather like in a desert?
What animals and plants live in a desert?
Deserts
"What is a desert?" asked Miss Cozy.
"The desert is hot," said Jack.
"The desert has lots of sand," said Tony.
"You are both right," said Miss Cozy. "The desert can be hot, and the desert can have lots of sand."
17

First Reader, pp. 16–17

Focus Questions What clothes do you wear outside when it is cold?
How do animals stay warm in the snow?
Snow Is Good!
Sally put on her winter jacket and ran outside. "The snow is growing deep," she said. "When will it stop?"
22
"Snow is like rain falling from the clouds," said Mom. "Only snowflakes are frozen drops of water. The snow will stop when the air is dry and the clouds are not so full of water."
23

First Reader, pp. 22–23

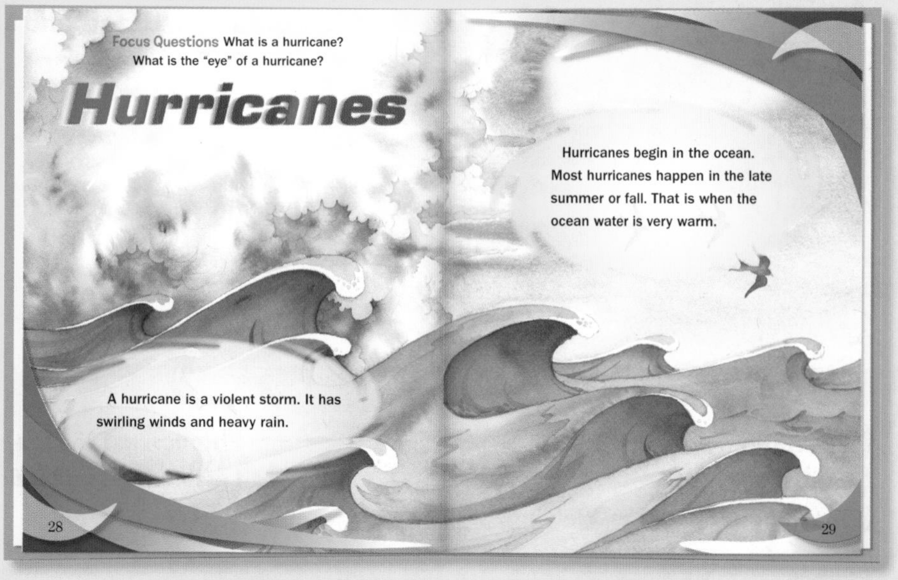

Focus Questions What is a hurricane?
What is the "eye" of a hurricane?
Hurricanes
A hurricane is a violent storm. It has swirling winds and heavy rain.
28
Hurricanes begin in the ocean. Most hurricanes happen in the late summer or fall. That is when the ocean water is very warm.
29

First Reader, pp. 28–29

Decodables 75–78

Curriculum Connections

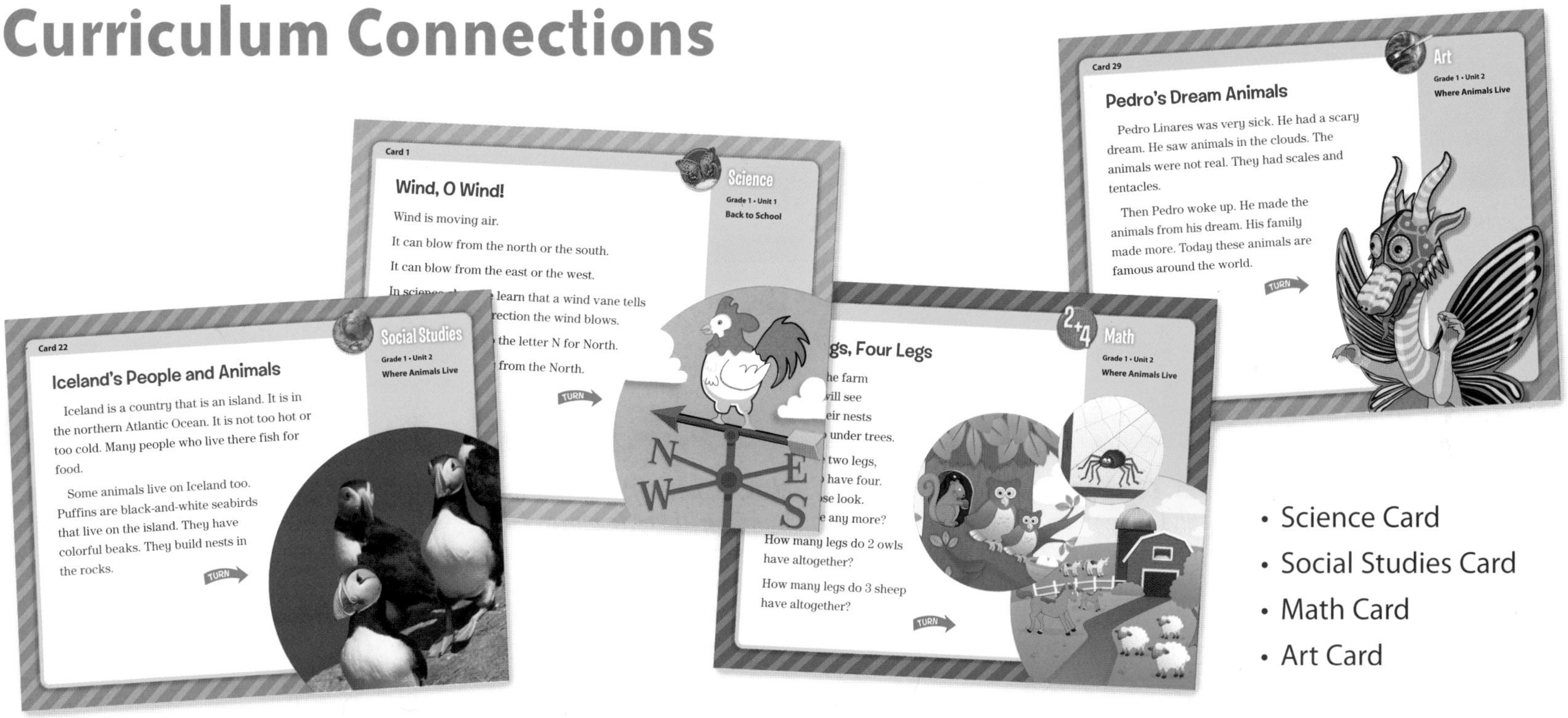
Card 1
Wind, O Wind!
Science
Grade 1 • Unit 1
Back to School
Wind is moving air.
It can blow from the north or the south.
It can blow from the east or the west.
TURN
N
E
W
S
Card 22
Iceland's People and Animals
Social Studies
Grade 1 • Unit 2
Where Animals Live
Iceland is a country that is an island. It is in the northern Atlantic Ocean. It is not too hot or too cold. Many people who live there fish for food.
Some animals live on Iceland too. Puffins are black-and-white seabirds that live on the island. They have colorful beaks. They build nests in the rocks.
TURN
Math
Grade 1 • Unit 2
Where Animals Live
How many legs do 2 owls have altogether?
How many legs do 3 sheep have altogether?
TURN
Card 29
Pedro's Dream Animals
Art
Grade 1 • Unit 2
Where Animals Live
Pedro Linares was very sick. He had a scary dream. He saw animals in the clouds. The animals were not real. They had scales and tentacles.
Then Pedro woke up. He made the animals from his dream. His family made more. Today these animals are famous around the world.
TURN

- Science Card
- Social Studies Card
- Math Card
- Art Card

Additional Skills Practice

Approaching Level

Reteach 1

- /ā/ Spelled *ai_, _ay,* pp. 153–154
- Plural Nouns, pp. 155–156
- /ī/ Spelled *_igh, _y, _ie,* pp. 157–158
- Phonics Review, pp. 159–160

On Level

Skills Practice 1

- /ā/ Spelled *ai_, _ay,* | pp. 205–206, 209–210
- Writing Instructions, pp. 207–208
- /ī/ Spelled *_igh, _y, _ie,* pp. 211–212, 215–216
- Plural Nouns, pp. 213–214
- Phonics Review, pp. 217–218

English Learner

English Learner Support Activities

Unit 5, Lessons 11–15

Above Level

Challenge Activities 1

- /ā/ Spelled *ai_, _ay,* p. 77
- Plural Nouns, p. 78
- /ī/ Spelled *_igh, _y, _ie,* p. 79
- Phonics Review, p. 80

Lessons 11-15 Overview

Differentiating Instruction for Workshop

AYP

Day 1

	Approaching Level	On Level	English Learner	Above Level
Preparing to Read				
	Phonics: Preteach the blending words to students.	**Phonics:** Have students extend the sentences in the blending lines.	**Phonics:** See ***English Learner Support Guide*** Unit 5 Lesson 11.	**Phonics:** Have students write sentences for three of the words on the blending lines.
Reading and Responding				
	Vocabulary: Use the ***SRA Imagine It! Photo Library CD*** pictures, objects, stick drawings, and pantomime to help them understand the vocabulary words.	**Vocabulary:** Pair students, and have them use the word to tell each other stories about the weather.	**Vocabulary:** Use the ***SRA Imagine It! Photo Library CD*** pictures, objects, stick drawings, and pantomime to help them understand the vocabulary words. **Comprehension:** Read "Deserts" with students before the class reads it. Use an illustration from the story to demonstrate the skill Main Idea and Details using the linguistic patterns *The main idea is ___; One detail about the main idea is ___.* See ***English Learner Support Guide*** Unit 5 Lesson 11.	**Vocabulary:** Pair students, and have them play an ***eSkills*** vocabulary game.
Language Arts				
	Writing: Help students decide on an idea for their instructions.	**Writing:** Have students write additional ideas for their instructions in their Writer's Notebooks.	**Writing:** Have students express their ideas in pictures, and help them add captions. See ***English Learner Support Guide*** Unit 5 Lesson 11.	**Writing:** Have students write additional ideas for their instructions in their Writer's Notebooks.

Day 2

	Approaching Level	On Level	English Learner	Above Level
Preparing to Read				
	Phonics: Have students complete ***Reteach 1*** pages 153–154 to practice /ā/ spelled *ai_* and *_ay.*	**Phonics:** Have students make a list of rhyming words with /ā/.	**Phonics:** See ***English Learner Support Guide*** Unit 5 Lesson 12.	**Phonics:** Have students complete ***Challenge Activities 1*** page 77 for a challenge with /ā/ spelled *ai_* and *_ay.*
Reading and Responding				
	Vocabulary: Help students draw and label pictures to show the meaning of the vocabulary word. **Comprehension:** Have students retell "Snow Is Good!" as you prompt them with questions such as *What happens first? What happens next? How does the story end?*	**Vocabulary:** Have students write a sentence for the vocabulary word. **Comprehension:** Have students write the events from the previous day in the appropriate sequence.	**Vocabulary:** Have students use the vocabulary words in oral sentences. **Comprehension:** Read "Snow Is Good!" with students before the class reads it. See ***English Learner Support Guide*** Unit 5 Lesson 12.	**Vocabulary:** Have students use the vocabulary words to retell "Snow Is Good!" **Comprehension:** Have students sequence the events of a vacation.
Language Arts				
	Penmanship: Give them paper copies of ***Transparency*** 41 to practice tracing models of the letters *k* and *z.*	**Penmanship:**: Have students find and copy words with *k* or *z* from the ***First Reader.***	**Writing:** See ***English Learner Support Guide*** Unit 5 Lesson 12. **Grammar, Usage, and Mechanics:** See ***English Learner Support Guide*** Unit 5 Lesson 12.	**Penmanship:** Have students look for and copy words that contain *k* or *z* in the Glossary, a classroom dictionary, or an encyclopedia.

Lessons **11-15** Overview

Differentiating Instruction
for Workshop

Day 3

	Approaching Level	On Level	English Learner	Above Level
Preparing to Read	**Phonics:** Review the words and sentences in the blending lines with students. **Dictation:** Review the dictation words and sentences with students.	**Phonics:** Have students make a list of words with /ī/ spelled *_igh*, *_y*, and *_ie*. **Dictation:** Have students dictate words from their lists to other students.	**Phonics:** See ***English Learner Support Guide*** Unit 5 Lesson 13.	**Phonics:** Have students make up rhymes using words that contain /ī/ spelled *_igh*, *_y*, and *_ie* and share their rhymes with others. **Dictation:** Have students choose dictation words different from the lesson and practice spelling them with partners.
Reading and Responding	**Fluency:** Read a short section of "Hurricanes" to students, and then have them read it.	**Fluency:** Have students reread one of the ***First Reader*** stories with partners to build fluency.	**Vocabulary:** See ***English Learner Support Guide*** Unit 5 Lesson 13. **Comprehension:** Discuss language related to the skill cause and effect, such as *because, since, therefore, as a result,* and *so*. See ***English Learner Support Guide*** Unit 5 Lesson 13.	**Fluency:** Have students reread one of the ***First Reader*** stories with partners to build fluency.
Language Arts	**Writing:** Write a list of action verbs on the board for students to choose from. Review time and order words, and then model how to use them in writing. **Grammar, Usage, and Mechanics:** Have students complete ***Reteach 1*** pages 155–156 for practice with plurals.	**Writing:** Have partners exchange drafts and point out the action verbs and time and order words in each other's work. **Grammar, Usage, and Mechanics:** Pair students, and have them play a game in the ***Workshop Kit.***	**Writing:** See ***English Learner Support Guide*** Unit 5 Lesson 13. **Grammar, Usage, and Mechanics:** See ***English Learner Support Guide*** Unit 5 Lesson 13.	**Writing:** Have students search for and copy action verbs and time and order words in the ***Little Big Books.*** **Grammar, Usage, and Mechanics:** Have students complete ***Challenge Activities 1*** page 78 for a challenge with plurals.

Day 4

	Approaching Level	On Level	English Learner	Above Level
Preparing to Read				
	Phonics: Have students complete ***Reteach 1*** pages 157–158 to practice /ī/ spelled *_igh, _y,* and *_ie.*	**Phonics:** Have students build words using words with /ī/ spelled *_igh, _y,* and *_ie,* such as *slight, tight; cried, dried; sly, tie.*	**Phonics:** See ***English Learner Support Guide*** Unit 5 Lesson 14.	**Phonics:** Have students complete ***Challenge Activities 1*** page 79 for a challenge with the /ī/ sound spelled *_igh, _y,* and *_ie.*
Reading and Responding				
	Inquiry: Help students decide on a method of presentation and how they will each contribute.	**Inquiry:** Have students practice their presentations and ask for feedback from others.	**Inquiry:** Have students practice their presentations, and ask for feedback from others.	**Inquiry:** Have students practice their presentations and ask for feedback from others.
Language Arts				
	Writing: Have students begin the illustrations for their writing. **Listening/Speaking/ Viewing:** Repeat the lesson on clear speech and model correct speaking skills for students.	**Writing:** Have students begin the illustrations for their writing. **Listening/Speaking/ Viewing:** Have small groups visit a nearby classroom to deliver today's weather forecast.	**Writing:** See ***English Learner Support Guide*** Unit 5 Lesson 14. **Listening/Speaking/ Viewing:** Help students practice their forecasts before they present them.	**Writing:** Have students begin the illustrations for their writing. **Listening/Speaking/ Viewing:** Have small groups of reporters work on a brief School News Update to share with the class.

Lessons 11-15 Overview

Differentiating Instruction
for Workshop

AYP

Day 5

	Approaching Level	On Level	English Learner	Above Level
Preparing to Read				
	Phonics: Have students complete ***Reteach 1*** pages 159–160.	**Phonics:** Have students play an ***eSkills*** phonics game.		**Phonics:** Have students complete ***Challenge Activities 1*** page 80.
Reading and Responding				
	Fluency: Have students reread one of the ***First Reader*** stories with you to build fluency.	**Fluency:** Have students reread one of the ***First Reader*** stories to build fluency.	**Fluency:** Have students read one of the ***First Reader*** stories along with the ***Listening Library CD*** to build fluency.	**Fluency:** Have students reread one of the ***First Reader*** stories to build fluency.
Language Arts				
	Penmanship: Have students practice writing the letters *k* and *z*.	**Penmanship:** Have students write a sentence using words with *k* and *z*.	**Writing:** Review the checklist on ***Skills Practice 1*** page 208, and provide models if necessary. See ***English Learner Support Guide*** Unit 5 Lesson 15. **Penmanship:** Have students practice writing the letters *k* and *z*. **Grammar, Usage, and Mechanics:** See ***English Learner Support Guide*** Unit 5 Lesson 15.	**Penmanship:** Have students write a sentence using words with *k* and *z*.

Resources for
Differentiating Instruction RtI

English Learner

English Learner Support Guide, Unit 5, Lessons 11–15

English Learner Support Activities Unit 5, Lessons 11–15

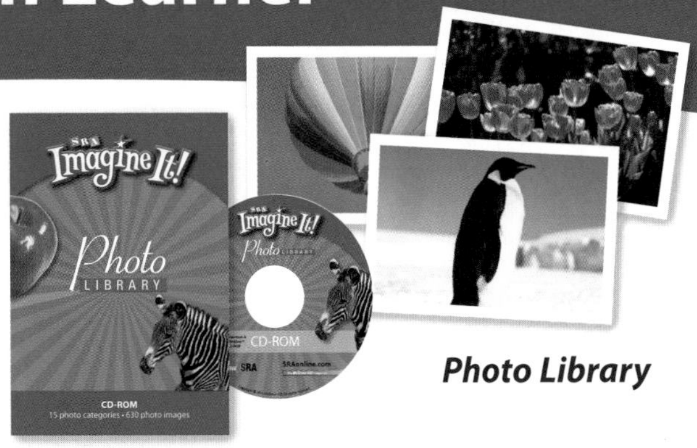

Photo Library

English Learner Realia Kit

Approaching Level

Intervention

Intervention Guide, Unit 5, Lessons 11–15

Intervention Workbook, Unit 5, Lessons 11–15

Workshop Kits

Technology

- ***eBig Books***
- ***eSkills & eGames***
- ***eDecodables***
- ***eAssess***

Listening Library CD Unit 5

Lessons 11-15 Overview

Lesson Assessment

Monitor Progress to Differentiate Instruction

Use these summative assessments along with your informal observations to assess student mastery.

UNIT 5 What's the Weather? • Lessons 11–15

Name ______________ Date ______ Score ______

Letters and Sounds

Teacher: I will say a word. I want you to fill in the bubble under the answer that shows how to spell that word.

Teacher: The word is *fly.* Fill in the bubble under the word *fly.*

1.	fly ●	fla ○	flo ○

Teacher: The word is *she.* Fill in the bubble under the word *she.*

2.	sha ○	she ●	shu ○

Teacher: The word is *pony.* Fill in the bubble under the word *pony.*

3.	poni ○	pona ○	pony ●

Teacher: The word is *clay.* Fill in the bubble under the word *clay.*

4.	clay ●	clee ○	claj ○

Teacher: The word is *light.* Fill in the bubble under the word *light.*

5.	lute ○	leet ○	light ●

Lesson Assessment Book 1 • What's the Weather? UNIT 5 • Lessons 11–15 65

Lesson Assessment Book 1, p.65

UNIT 5 What's the Weather? • Lessons 11–15 *(continued)*

Name ______________ Date ______ Score ______

High-Frequency Words

Teacher: Listen carefully to what I say. Fill in the bubble under the answer you think is correct.

Teacher: Fill in the bubble under the word *day . . . day.*

1.	dey ○	day ●	dai ○

Teacher: Fill in the bubble under the word *way . . . way.*

2.	way ●	wey ○	wah ○

Teacher: Fill in the bubble under the word *sleep . . . sleep.*

3.	slepe ○	sleap ○	sleep ●

Teacher: Fill in the bubble under the word *don't . . . don't.*

4.	dun't ○	don't ●	dor't ○

Teacher: Fill in the bubble under the word *my . . . my.*

5.	my ●	mi ○	mu ○

66 UNIT 5 • Lessons 11–15 What's the Weather? • Lesson Assessment Book 1

Lesson Assessment Book 1, p.66

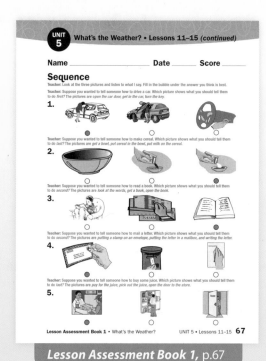

UNIT 5 What's the Weather? • Lessons 11–15 *(continued)*

Name ______________ Date ______ Score ______

Sequence

Teacher: Look at the three pictures and listen to what I say. Fill in the bubble under the answer you think is best.

Teacher: Suppose you wanted to tell someone how to drive a car. Which picture shows what you should tell them to do *first?* The pictures are *open the car door, get in the car, turn the key.*

1.

Teacher: Suppose you wanted to tell someone how to make cereal. Which picture shows what you should tell them to do *last?* The pictures are *get a bowl, put cereal in the bowl, put milk on the cereal.*

2.

Teacher: Suppose you wanted to tell someone how to read a book. Which picture shows what you should tell them to do *second?* The pictures are *look at the words, get a book, open the book.*

3.

Teacher: Suppose you wanted to tell someone how to mail a letter. Which picture shows what you should tell them to do *second?* The pictures are *putting a stamp on an envelope, putting the letter in a mailbox, and writing the letter.*

4.

Teacher: Suppose you wanted to tell someone how to buy some juice. Which picture shows what you should tell them to do *last?* The pictures are *pay for the juice, pick out the juice, open the door to the store.*

5.

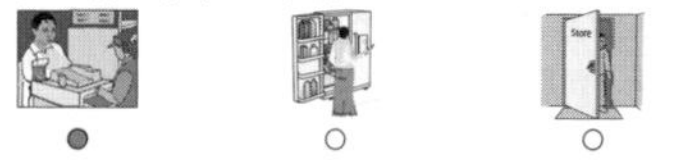

Lesson Assessment Book 1 • What's the Weather? UNIT 5 • Lessons 11–15 67

Lesson Assessment Book 1, p.67

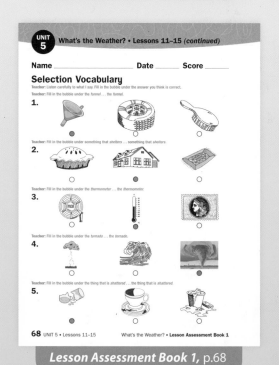

UNIT 5 What's the Weather? • Lessons 11–15 *(continued)*

Name ______________ Date ______ Score ______

Selection Vocabulary

Teacher: Listen carefully to what I say. Fill in the bubble under the answer you think is correct.

Teacher: Fill in the bubble under the *funnel . . .* the *funnel.*

1.

Teacher: Fill in the bubble under something that *shelters . . .* something that *shelters.*

2.

Teacher: Fill in the bubble under the *thermometer . . .* the *thermometer.*

3.

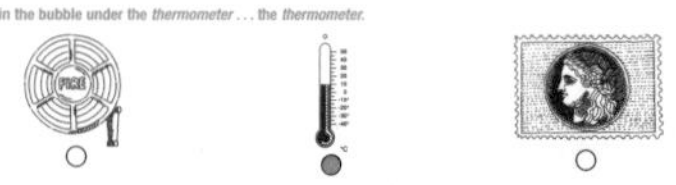

Teacher: Fill in the bubble under the *tornado . . .* the *tornado.*

4.

Teacher: Fill in the bubble under the thing that is *shattered . . .* the thing that is *shattered.*

5.

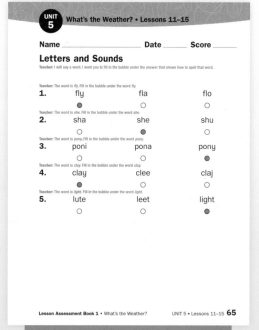

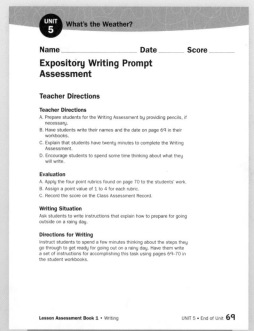

68 UNIT 5 • Lessons 11–15 What's the Weather? • Lesson Assessment Book 1

Lesson Assessment Book 1, p.68

UNIT 5 What's the Weather?

Name ______________ Date ______ Score ______

Expository Writing Prompt Assessment

Teacher Directions

Teacher Directions

A. Prepare students for the Writing Assessment by providing pencils, if necessary.
B. Have students write their names and the date on page 69 in their workbooks.
C. Explain that students have twenty minutes to complete the Writing Assessment.
D. Encourage students to spend some time thinking about what they will write.

Evaluation

A. Apply the four point rubrics found on page 70 to the students' work.
B. Assign a point value of 1 to 4 for each rubric.
C. Record the score on the Class Assessment Record.

Writing Situation

Ask students to write instructions that explain how to prepare for going outside on a rainy day.

Directions for Writing

Instruct students to spend a few minutes thinking about the steps they go through to get ready for going out on a rainy day. Have them write a set of instructions for accomplishing this task using pages 69–70 in the student workbooks.

Lesson Assessment Book 1 • Writing UNIT 5 • End of Unit 69

Lesson Assessment Book 1, p.69

UNIT 5 Four Point Rubrics for Expository Writing

Conventions	1 Point	2 Points	3 Points	4 Points
Mechanics: Capitalization	Inconsistently uses capitals at beginnings of sentences, seldom for proper nouns.	Consistently uses capitals at beginning of sentences and for some proper nouns.	Capitalizes sentences; may overcapitalize or undercapitalize other words.	Uses capitalization correctly at beginning of sentences and with proper nouns.
Genre				
Expository	Composition consists of statements loosely related to a topic, with no evident order or organization. Extraneous material may be present.	Statements are not only related to a topic but have an evident purpose.	Main points and supportive details can be identified but they are not clearly marked.	Composition is clearly organized around main points with supportive facts or assertions.
Writing Traits				
Ideas	Superficial and/or minimal content is included.	The reader can understand the main ideas, though these may be overly broad. Supporting detail is limited, overly general, or off topic.	The writing is clear and focused. The reader can easily understand the main ideas. Support is present, although it may be limited or rather general.	The writing is exceptionally clear, focused, and interesting. Main ideas stand out and are enhanced through strong support and rich details.

70 UNIT 5 Four Point Rubrics for Expository Writing • Lesson Assessment Book 1

Lesson Assessment Book 1, p.70

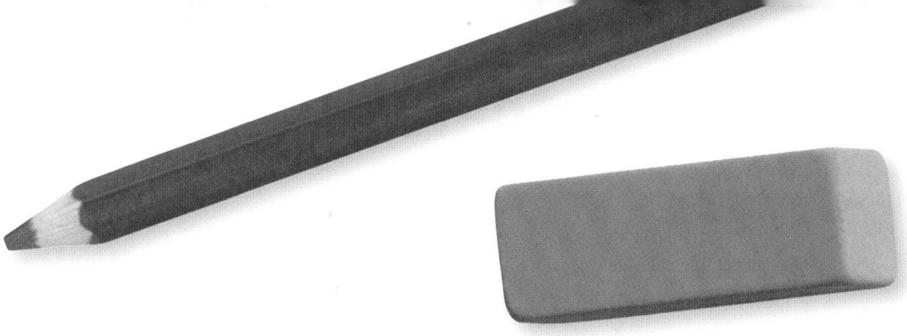

Formal Assessment

Lesson Assessment Book 1

Comprehension Observation Log

Student ______ Date ______

Unit ______ Lesson ______ Selection Title ______

General Comprehension
Concepts discussed: ______

Behavior Within a Group
Articulates, expresses ideas: ______

Joins discussions: ______

Collaborates (such as *works well with other students, works alone*): ______

Role in Group
Role (such as *leader, summarizer, questioner, critic, observer, non-participant*): ______

Flexibility (changes roles when necessary): ______

Use of Reading Strategies
Uses strategies when needed (either those taught or student's choice of strategy)/Describes strategies used: ______

Changes strategies when appropriate: ______

Changes Since Last Observation

92 Comprehension Observation Log • **Lesson Assessment Book 1**

Lesson Assessment Book 1, p. 92

The Comprehension Observation Log, found in the ***Lesson Assessment Annotated Teacher's Edition,*** is a vehicle for recording anecdotal information about individual student performance on an ongoing basis. Information such as students' strengths and weaknesses can be recorded at any time the occasion warrants. It is recommended that you maintain a folder for each student where you can store the logs for purposes of comparison and analysis as the school year progresses. You will gradually build up a comprehensive file that reveals which students are progressing smoothly and which students need additional help.

Preparing to Read

OBJECTIVES

Students will

- blend, spell, and read words that contain /ā/ spelled *ai_* and *_ay*.
- identify compound words.
- build fluency by reading ***Decodable*** 75.

MATERIALS

- Routines 1–4, 5–7, 9
- ***Sound/Spelling Card*** 27
- ***Skills Practice 1,*** pp. 205–206
- ***Decodable*** 75, *A Gray, Rainy Day*

Teacher Tip

WORD CHART Have students add more words that have /ā/ spelled *ai_* and *_ay* to the /ā/ word chart.

Daily Warm-Ups

Copy the Morning Message on the board or on chart paper. Have students answer the question. Read the message aloud, and discuss it with students. **Possible Answer** *The weather in a desert is hot and dry.*

MORNING MESSAGE
Good morning! Today we will read about deserts. What do you think the weather is like in a desert?

Daily Language Review

To review capitalization, write the following sentence on the board, or generate a similar one with students, and have them make corrections: did bill tell you he is from canada? *Did Bill tell you he is from Canada?*

Sound/Spelling Review Game

Name a ***Sound/Spelling Card,*** such as Card 18—Robot, and have students say the sound and spellings that the card represents. Call on a student to say and spell a word that contains the sound/spelling. Continue with two or three other cards, such as Card 16—Popcorn and Card 17—Quacking Ducks or use cards that have given the class difficulty. **Possible Answers** *rake; rack; rock; race*

Introduce the Sound/Spelling

ROUTINE 1

/ā/ Spelled *ai_* and *_ay*

- Point to ***Sound/Spelling Card*** 27—Long A, and use Routine 1, introducing sounds and spellings, to have students review the *a* and *a_e* spellings for this card. Tell students they will learn two new spellings for /ā/. Point to the *ai_* spelling. Ask what the blank after the spelling means. *The blank shows that this spelling may appear at the beginning or in the middle of a word or syllable but not at the end of a word or syllable.*
- Point to the *_ay* spelling, and explain that this is another /ā/ spelling. Explain that the blank in this spelling for /ā/ means it comes at the end of a word or syllable.

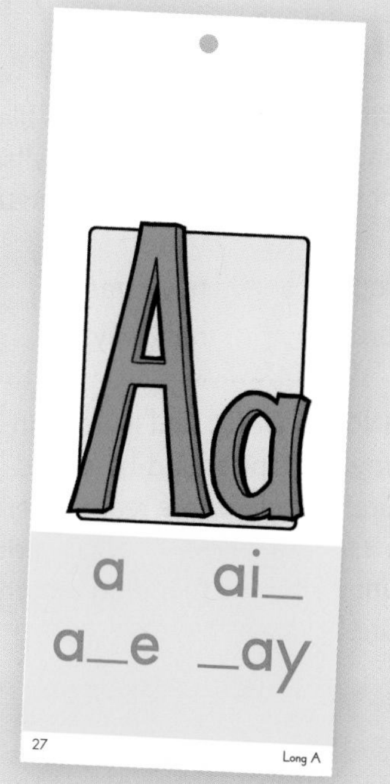

Sound/Spelling Card 27

Phonemic Awareness

Listening for /ā/

Read aloud the following words, and have students signal thumbs-up and say the sound if they hear /ā/.

stay	land	**mail**	fan
snake	sand	**waste**	hand
band	**May**	**taste**	hard

Monitor Progress to Differentiate Instruction

Formal Assessment

PHONEMIC AWARENESS Note how quickly students are identifying words with /ā/.

APPROACHING LEVEL

IF . . . students need additional practice with the *ai_* and *_ay* spellings for /ā/, **THEN . . .** preteach blending words during Workshop.

ON LEVEL

IF . . . students are on level, **THEN . . .** use ***eSkills*** for practice with /ā/ spelled *ai_* and *_ay*.

ABOVE LEVEL

IF . . . students are ready for a challenge, **THEN . . .** make two lists of three words that contain the target sounds, for students to dictate to each other.

Teacher Tips

SYLLABICATION To help students blend the words and build fluency, use the syllabication below of the multisyllable words on the word lines.

rain • drop	hay • stack
paint • brush	rail • way

BLENDING For words on Lines 1 and 2, refer to Routine 2 for the sound-by-sound blending procedure. If students are ready, refer to Routine 3 for the whole-word procedure. Use Routine 4 for the blending sentences procedure.

Phonics

ROUTINE 2 ROUTINE 3 ROUTINE 4 ROUTINE 10 ROUTINE 11

Blending

Use Routine 2, sound-by-sound blending, Routine 3, whole-word blending and Routine 4, blending sentences, to have students blend the words and sentences. Use Routine 10, closed syllables, and Routine 11, open syllables, to have students blend the multisyllable words.

Line 1	say	stay	pay	play
Line 2	mail	nail	snail	rain
Line 3	pail	pale	sail	sale
Line 4	raindrop	haystack	paintbrush	railway

Sentence 1 Jay checks <u>the</u> mail <u>every</u> <u>day</u>.

Sentence 2 May <u>can</u> tell <u>us</u> <u>the</u> <u>way</u> <u>to</u> <u>the</u> railway.

Line 1 **/ā/ spelled _*ay***

After blending, have students identify the letter that turns *say* into *stay*. Have students use each word in a sentence to show its meaning. Do the same for *pay* and *play*. Remind students that changing just one letter changes the meaning as well as the spelling of a word.

Line 2 **/ā/ spelled *ai_***

Remember to write *ai_* as a unit for students to blend. The word *rain* is also in the selection "Deserts." Tell students that rain is water that falls from the clouds. Use the word in a sentence, such as *The flowers got water from the rain.*

Line 3 **/ā/ spelled *ai_* and *a_e***

Have students notice that these pairs of words are homophones. Ask them what homophones are. *words that sound the same but have different spellings and meanings* Remind students to check the meaning of a homophone to make sure they are using the correct spelling.

Line 4 **/ā/ spelled *ai_* and _*ay***

Have students identify the two words that make up each compound word. *rain, drop; hay, stack; paint, brush; rail, way* Have students use the meanings of the individual words to predict the meanings of the compound words.

Sentences 1–2

Write the words *day* and *way* on the board. Read the words, repeat them, and have students read them. Then spell *day* and *way* together. Foster student engagement by having volunteers use the words in sentences. Write each word on an index card, and add the cards to the High-Frequency Word Bank.

Developing Oral Language

To review the words, say sentences with missing words, and have students point to, read, and erase the words that complete the sentences.

- At the beach, we use a ______ to carry sand. *pail*
- A big ______ splattered on our windshield. *raindrop*
- The shoe store is having a ______. *sale*
- On Grandpa's farm, we played in a tall ______. *haystack*

Monitor Progress

to Differentiate Instruction

Formal Assessment

DICTATION As students spell words, notice who uses the ***Sound/Spelling Cards*** and spells the words correctly. Note students who are asking for help with the spellings.

APPROACHING LEVEL

IF . . . students need additional practice with phonics and dictation,	**THEN . . .** review the words during Workshop.

ON LEVEL

IF . . . students are on level with phonics and dictation,	**THEN . . .** pair them, and have them play a game from ***eSkills.***

ABOVE LEVEL

IF . . . students need a challenge with phonics and dictation,	**THEN . . .** have them use one of the activities in the ***Workshop Kit.***

Guided Practice

Have students use ***Skills Practice 1*** pages 205–206 for practice with /ā/ spelled *ai_* and *_ay* and for dictation. Review the sound/spellings at the top of page 205. Have students write the words and sentences at the bottom of the page. Have students write the word next to its opposite on the lines on page 206. Students can use the bottom of the page for dictation.

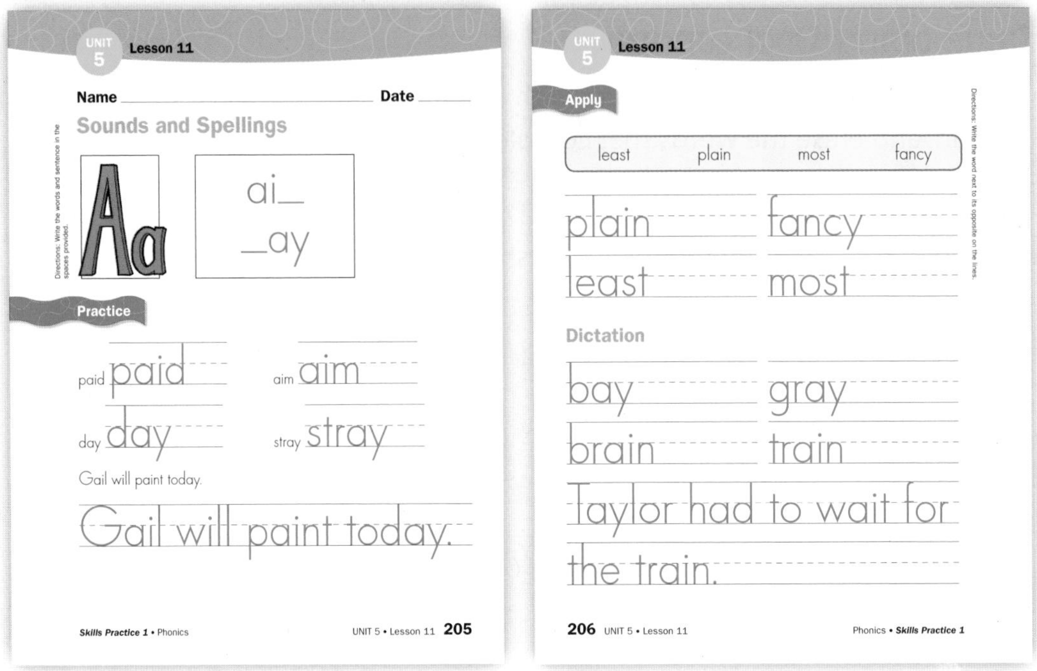
UNIT 5 Lesson 11

Name ____ Date ____

Sounds and Spellings

Directions: Write the words and sentence in the spaces provided.

Aa ai_ _ay

Practice

paid paid aim aim

day day stray stray

Gail will paint today.

Gail will paint today.

Skills Practice 1 • Phonics UNIT 5 • Lesson 11 205

UNIT 5 Lesson 11

Apply

Directions: Write the word next to its opposite on the lines.

least plain most fancy

plain fancy

least most

Dictation

bay gray

brain train

Taylor had to wait for the train.

206 UNIT 5 • Lesson 11 Phonics • Skills Practice 1

Skills Practice 1, pp. 205–206

Dictation

ROUTINE 5 ROUTINE 6 ROUTINE 7

Use Routine 5, sounds-in-sequence dictation, Routine 6, whole-word dictation, and Routine 7, sentence dictation, with the following:

Line 1	bay	gray
Line 2	brain	train
Sentence	Taylor had to wait for the train.	

Teacher Tip

HIGH-FREQUENCY WORDS The words *had* and *for* are decodable high-frequency words. Encourage students to write them without sounding them out. If they have difficulty, tell them they can spell the words sound by sound.

Differentiating Instruction: English Learners

IF . . . students have difficulty recording unknown dictated words, **THEN . . .** write each word on the board and read its correct pronunciation.

Fluency/Reading a Decodable Book

ROUTINE 9

Core Decodable 75: A Gray, Rainy Day

Phonics Focus: /ā/ Spelled *ai_*, *_ay*

High-Frequency Words

Review the high-frequency words *day* and *way* that students learned in Blending. Point to them in the High-Frequency Word Bank, or write them on the board, spell the words, and have students say the words. Have a volunteer use the words in sentences. Review other high-frequency words by pointing to them in the High-Frequency Word Bank and having students read them.

Reading the Decodable

- Follow Routine 9, reading a ***Decodable,*** as you read the story with students.
- Have students read the title, browse the story, and discuss what they think the story will be about.
- The first time through, have students read a page silently. Then have one student read it aloud. Repeat this procedure for each page.
- Reread the story at least twice, calling on various students to read. Then have the entire class do a choral reading of the story.

Responding

- After reading, be sure to talk about the story and answer any questions students have. Ask students to identify any difficult words in the book.

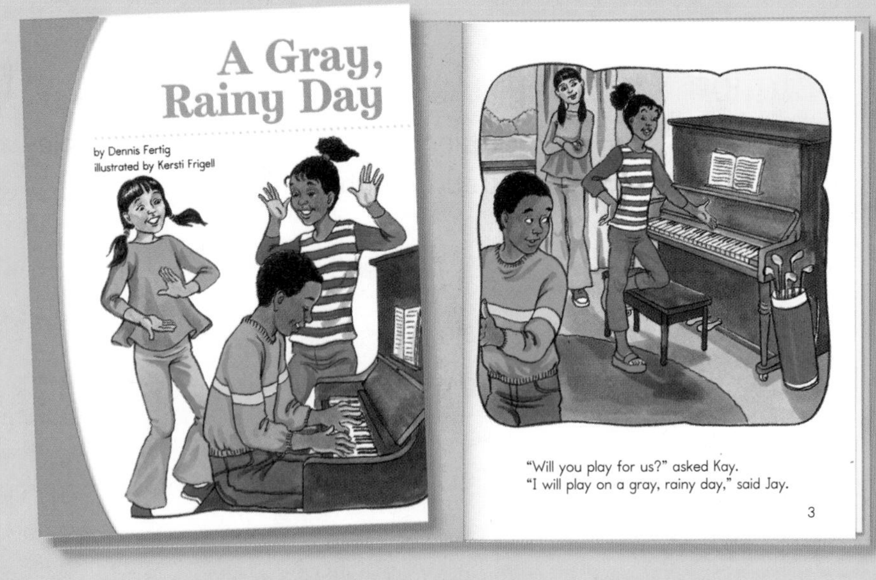

illustrated by Kersti Frigell
"Will you play for us?" asked Kay.

Kay liked to hear Jay play.
Kay had a way to make Jay play.
4
Kay made a gray painting.
Then Kay fixed the hose to spray.
5

Teacher Tip

SOUND/SPELLING CARDS Remind students to refer to the ***Sound/Spelling Cards*** if they are unsure of a sound/spelling.

Monitor Progress to Differentiate Instruction

Formal Assessment

DECODING Observe students as they read ***Decodable*** 75. Note any students who are having trouble with the /ā/ sound spelled *ai_* and *_ay*.

APPROACHING LEVEL	**IF . . .** students are having difficulty,	**THEN . . .** during Workshop, review ***Sound/Spelling Card*** 27—Long A and any other ***Sound/Spelling Cards*** students need to review. Then have students look through ***Decodable*** 75 to find words with the /ā/ sound spelled *ai_* and *_ay*.
ON LEVEL	**IF . . .** students are on level,	**THEN . . .** have them quiz one another during Workshop using the ***High-Frequency Flash Cards.***
ABOVE LEVEL	**IF . . .** students are ready for a challenge,	**THEN . . .** encourage them to browse and read classroom library books.

Kay set up the gray painting.
The hose sprayed.
6
Kay went back to find Jay.
"It is gray and rainy!" said Kay.
7

"I will play," said Jay.
"I like to play when it is rainy and gray."

- Have students retell the story.
- As students answer the following questions, make sure they focus on the words in the story rather than getting the answers by listening or from the pictures. Have students answer by pointing to and reading aloud the answers in the text:
  - **When will Jay play?** *on a gray, rainy day*
  - **What does Kay make?** *a gray painting*
  - **What does Kay fix?** *the hose to spray*

Building Fluency

Have students build fluency by rereading ***Core Decodable*** 75 twice with a partner. The first time through, one partner should read the odd-numbered pages and the other partner the even-numbered pages. The second time through, they should switch pages. For additional practice with the /ā/ sound spelled *ai_* and *_ay,* have students read ***Practice Decodable*** 62, *Jay Stays on the Job.* Have students record their readings on their Personal Title sheets, noting the title of each book, the date, and any difficult words they encountered.

Core Decodable 75

The Gray, Rainy Day

High-Frequency Words Introduced in Core Decodable 75

day
way

Previously Introduced High-Frequency Words

a	down	I	ride	was
after	every	if	said	we
all	for	in	see	well
am	get	is	she	went
an	girl	it	six	were
and	go	its	some	what
as	going	jump	take	when
ask	got	just	that	will
at	green	like	the	with
be	had	little	them	yes
big	has	look	then	you
boy	have	make	there	
but	he	of	they	
call	help	on	this	
can	her	or	to	
could	here	out	two	
did	him	over	up	
do	his	red	walk	

Sound/Spelling Correspondences in Core Decodables

1. Pre-decodable
2. Pre-decodable
3. Pre-decodable
4. Pre-decodable
5. Pre-decodable
6. /s/ spelled *s*, /m/ spelled *m*, /a/ spelled *a*
7. /t/ spelled *t, tt*
8. Review
9. /d/ spelled *d*
10. /n/ spelled *n*
11. /i/ spelled *i*
12. /h/ spelled *h_*
13. Review
14. /p/ spelled *p*
15. /l/ spelled *l, ll*
16. /o/ spelled *o*
17. /b/ spelled *b*
18. Review
19. /k/ spelled *c*
20. /aw/ spelled *al*
21. /k/ spelled *k, ■ck*
22. /r/ spelled *r*
23. /f/ spelled *f, ff*
24. /s/ spelled *ss*
25. Review
26. /g/ spelled *g*
27. /j/ spelled *j, ■dge*
28. /u/ spelled *u*
29. /z/ spelled *z, zz*
30. /z/ spelled *_s*
31. Review
32. /ks/ spelled *■x*
33. /e/ spelled *e*
34. -ed ending: /ed/, /d/
35. -ed ending: /t/
36. /e/ spelled *_ea_*
37. Review
38. /sh/ spelled *sh*
39. /th/ spelled *th*
40. /ch/ spelled *ch, ■tch*
41. /or/ spelled *or, ore*
42. Review
43. /ar/ spelled *ar*
44. /m/ spelled *_mb*
45. /w/ spelled *w_*
46. /hw/ spelled *wh_*
47. /er/ spelled *er, ir*
48. /er/ spelled *ur*
49. Review
50. Schwa
51. Review schwa
52. /ng/ spelled *■ng*
53. /nk/ spelled *■nk*
54. /kw/ spelled *qu_*
55. Review
56. /y/ spelled *y_*
57. /v/ spelled *v*
58. Syllable -le
59. /ā/ spelled *a* and *a_e*
60. Review
61. /ī/ spelled *i* and *i_e*
62. /s/ spelled *ce, ci_*
63. /j/ spelled *ge, gi_*
64. Review
65. /ō/ spelled *o* and *o_e*
66. /ū/ spelled *u* and *u_e*
67. Review
68. /ē/ spelled *e* and *e_e*
69. /ē/ spelled *ee* and *ea*
70. Review
71. /ē/ spelled *_y, _ie_*
72. /s/ spelled *cy*
73. Review /s/ spellings
74. Review
75. /ā/ spelled *ai_, _ay*

Decodable 75, inside back cover

Reading and Responding

OBJECTIVES

Students will
- activate prior knowledge about deserts.
- understand and use a table of contents.
- set and check purposes for reading.
- preview vocabulary words.
- use the comprehension strategies Asking Questions, Making Connections, and Clarifying.
- use the comprehension skill Main Idea and Details.
- review the use of quotation marks.

MATERIALS
- ***First Reader,*** pp. 16–21
- Routines 12, 13
- Writer's Notebooks
- ***Home Connection,*** pp. 39–40
- ***Transparency*** 20

Teacher Tips

ACTIVATE PRIOR KNOWLEDGE Use this discussion to become aware of any misconceptions or misunderstandings students may have about deserts. For example, some students may think all deserts are hot all the time. Be alert for information in the selection that can help students rethink their ideas and replace them with more accurate ones.

MATERIALS You may want to have pictures available of several different types of rodents as well as pictures of water holes. This visual support will help students as they read this story.

Differentiating Instruction **English Learner**

IF . . . students would benefit from reading the selection before the rest of the class reads it, **THEN . . .** have them read the selection in Workshop.

Build Background

Activate Prior Knowledge

- Remind students that they have heard or read many selections already this year. Help students recall the selections that talked about or had pictures of deserts. **Possible Answers** *"Day and Night in the Desert," "Back to School," "Finding Shelter," "On the Same Day in March"*
- Ask students the following to activate their prior knowledge about deserts:
  - *Have you ever been to a desert? If so, what was it like?* **Possible Answers** *very dry; very hot; sandy*
  - *What kinds of plants do you think might grow in a desert?* **Possible Answers** *plants that do not need lots of water; plants that like a lot of sunshine*
  - *What kinds of animals do you think might live in a desert?* **Possible Answers** *snakes; bugs; lizards; camels*
  - *What do you think would be the hardest thing about living in a desert?* **Possible Answers** *finding water and food; keeping cool*

Preview and Prepare

ROUTINE 12

Browse

- Follow Routine 12, reading the selection, to prepare students for the selection. Begin by displaying the cover of the ***First Reader.*** Point to and read aloud the title.
- Have students locate and turn to the Table of Contents, and point to the title of the selection, "Deserts." Have students read the title along with you as you point to it. Point to the page number 16, and have a volunteer read it and tell what the number means. Turn to page 16.
- Demonstrate how to browse the selection by commenting on illustrations and predicting how they might relate to the text. On page 17, for example, you might say *On this page, I see an animal. I'm not sure what it is, but it's in a desert. As I read, I'll probably find out more about how animals are able to live in deserts.*
- Have students browse the first few pages to look for clues to what the selection is about and for difficult and unfamiliar words. Two terms that students might have difficulty with are *rodents* and *water holes.* Tell students that rodents are small animals with hair that eat seeds and stems from plants. For water holes, tell students that animals need water to live. When water is available in a very dry place, it can bring a lot of visitors.

Set Purposes

- Have students think about the information gained while browsing. Ask students to use this information to tell what the purposes for reading this selection might be. Write the purposes on the board. Some suggestions are the following:
  - To find out about the weather in deserts
  - To find out how plants and animals live in a desert
- After reading the selection, have students return to these purposes.

Fluency

As students read "Deserts," have them practice reading the dialogue with expression and intonation. Remind them to pause at end punctuation marks.

- Students will learn that this selection is realistic fiction. Dialogue is included in the text. Have students adjust their reading rate to correspond with the way each character's words might be said.
- Have students apply letter-sound knowledge to decode phonetically regular words quickly and accurately as they read this selection.

Teacher Tips

GLOSSARY The words *cactus* and *water holes* appear in the Glossary. As students browse and identify interesting words or phrases, you may want to use the opportunity to have students practice glossary use. Have students locate and turn to the Glossary, find each word, and read each entry.

HIGH-FREQUENCY WORDS As students browse, you may want to have them look for the high-frequency words they know. The following are some of the high-frequency words that appear in the selection: *what, is, a, the, said, has, of, you, can, be, and, have, but, all, do, at, big, get.*

BIG Idea

What is weather?
Before reading the selection, reread the Big Idea question. Tell students to keep this question in mind as they listen to the selection.

From Your Teacher Home Connection

Give each student a copy of ***Home Connection*** page 39. This same information is also available in Spanish on ***Home Connection*** page 40. After students have listened to each selection, encourage them to discuss it with their families and complete the activity provided.

Selection Vocabulary

storing putting away for use in the future (page 19)

Teacher Tips

SEMANTIC MAP Have students continue building upon the semantic map. Encourage them to add selection vocabulary words and words they have learned throughout the unit.

DIGITAL TOOLS Have students look for definitions of selection vocabulary or difficult words from the text using an online dictionary.

Building Vocabulary

ROUTINE 13

- Use Routine 13, selection vocabulary, to introduce the vocabulary word to students. Write the word on the board or on a transparency. Have students review the word by having them pantomime storing something such as books in a desk or on a shelf.
- You will introduce one expanding vocabulary word to students as the selection is reread. The word is identified in a box where it appears in the selection. When you come to the word in the selection, read to students the word, the definition, and the sample sentence. Understanding this word will help students better comprehend the selection.

Monitor Progress to Differentiate Instruction

Formal Assessment

Notice how well students understand the words and their meanings.

APPROACHING LEVEL	
IF . . . students would benefit from additional work with recent vocabulary words,	**THEN . . .** use the ***SRA Imagine It! Photo Library CD,*** objects, stick drawings, and pantomime to help them understand the words.
ON LEVEL	
IF . . . students are on level,	**THEN . . .** pair them, and have them use the words to tell each other stories about weather.
ABOVE LEVEL	
IF . . . students are ready for a challenge,	**THEN . . .** pair them, and have them play one of the games in ***eSkills.***

Reading the Selection

Genre Realistic Fiction

Tell students that "Deserts" is an example of realistic fiction. It has characters that seem real and things that did not happen but *could* happen in real life. Then briefly review the elements of realistic fiction:

- It has people or animals that seem real.
- It has events and places that seem real.
- It is about things that did not happen but *could* happen in real life.

Comprehension Strategies

As students read "Deserts," model and prompt the use of the following comprehension strategies:

- Asking Questions
- Making Connections
- Clarifying

Comprehension Skills

As students reread "Deserts," apply the comprehension skill Main Idea and Details.

Reading with a Writer's Eye

As students reread "Deserts," you will discuss how the author uses dialogue to make the selection interesting and to help readers better understand what they are reading.

Focus Question

Read and discuss the Focus Question on page 16. Encourage students to think about the Focus Question as they read "Deserts."

Reading Recommendations

ROUTINE 12

Day 1 **ORALLY** Students will read the entire selection twice today. Follow Routine 12, reading the selection. The first time, model and prompt the use of the comprehension strategies. The second time, focus on the comprehension skills and Reading with a Writer's Eye.

Differentiating Instruction **English Learner**

IF . . . English learners are having difficulty with clarifying, **THEN . . .** refer to the ***English Learner Support Guide*** Unit 5 Lesson 11.

Teacher Tips

1st READ

THEME CONNECTIONS Remind students that as they read, they should think about how the selection relates to the theme What's the Weather? and about how it might help them generate ideas for Inquiry.

READING THE SELECTION If students are struggling with the ***First Reader*** stories, have them echo read "Deserts" with you for the first reading. Focus on reading the dialogue with expression and intonation. During the second reading, have students read the story orally.

2nd READ

PARTNER READING LIST Have students add information about this selection to their Partner Reading Lists. Remind them to write the title of the selection, the author's name, and the date they read it. If they also read the selection in a group, have them write the names of the group members.

2nd READ

UNFAMILIAR WORDS Remind students to look for unfamiliar words such as *inches* as they read. Tell them to use the text and illustrations to try to understand the word.

EFFECTIVE COMMUNICATION Remind students to speak clearly and use describing words when they make connections and share their personal experiences.

Phonics

Words in the selection containing sound/spellings from recent phonics lessons appear in boxes like this throughout the selection. At the end of the first reading, students should be prompted to identify the sound/spellings of these words.

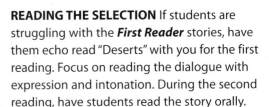

Day 1 Reading and Responding

Focus Questions What is the weather like in a desert?
What animals and plants live in a desert?

Deserts

"What is a desert?" asked Miss Cozy.

"The desert is hot," said Jack.

"The desert has lots of sand," said Tony. 1

16

"You are both right," said Miss Cozy. "The desert can be hot, and the desert can have lots of sand." 2

17

First Reader, pp. 16–17

Teacher Tips

GLOSSARY The word *cactus* on page 19 can be found in the Glossary.

CLARIFYING Be sure students understand the selection. Tell them to reread and ask clarifying questions when they do not understand ideas in the text.

SELF-CORRECT As students read, have them self-correct when subsequent reading indicates an earlier misreading.

Phonics

/ā/ spelled *ai_*: rain (page 18)

1st READ

Comprehension Strategies

❶ **Making Connections** Teacher Prompt: *Has anyone been to a desert? What was it like?* **Possible Student Response** *I've been to the Mojave Desert in California. It was hot and sandy.*

❷ **Clarifying** Teacher Modeling: *Miss Cozy says deserts* can *be hot, and they* can *have a lot of sand. That sounds as if some deserts aren't hot and sandy. Let's read on.*

❸ **Clarifying** Teacher Modeling: *Now I know that some deserts are cold and rocky. But* all *deserts are dry.*

❹ **Asking Questions** Teacher Modeling: *Plants and animals need water to live. How do they survive with so little water?*

❺ **Answering Questions** Teacher Modeling: *Some desert plants such as cacti hold lots of water. When it rains, they store water for use during the time when it isn't raining.*

"Some deserts are cold and rocky. Some deserts even have mountains. But all deserts are dry," said Miss Cozy. "Most deserts have less than ten inches of rain a year." ④

③

18

"Do deserts have plants?" asked Jack.

"The desert has plants," said Miss Cozy. "Desert plants are good at storing water. A big cactus holds lots of water." ⑤

19

First Reader, pp. 18–19

2nd READ

Comprehension Skills

Main Idea and Details

- Briefly review with students that a main idea is the most important idea and that details are pieces of information that explain or give details about the main idea. Reread pages of the selection with students, and ask what the main idea is and which details support this idea. *All deserts are dry. Most deserts have less than ten inches of rain per year.*
- Using ***Transparency*** 20, have students tell you where to record their responses.

2nd READ

Reading with a Writer's Eye

Dialogue

Remind students that "Deserts" is realistic fiction. When authors write realistic fiction, they try to make their characters seem like real people by having them talk the way real people do. Remind them that the name for this "talk written down" is *dialogue.*

Expanding Vocabulary

cactus a desert plant that has a thick stem covered with thorns (page 19)

Be careful of the thorns when you water a *cactus.*

Differentiating Instruction English Learners

IF . . . students are not accustomed to seeing quotation marks in dialogue, **THEN . . .** make sure they understand that in English, quotation marks are used to set off a speaker's exact words. In Spanish, for example, dashes are used to set off a speaker's exact words.

"Do deserts have animals?" asked Tony.

"Lots of animals live in the desert. Some live near water holes. Many desert rodents get their water from the seeds or stems they eat. Camels can go weeks without drinking water. They get their water from green plants too," said Miss Cozy. 6

20

"It must be hard to live in the desert," said Jack.

"Not really," said Miss Cozy. "The plants and animals that make the desert their home do just fine!" 7

21

First Reader, pp. 20–21

Teacher Tips

ASKING QUESTIONS Remind students to ask themselves questions throughout their reading and to keep coming back to those questions to make sure they have been answered. Tell students to think of questions on the **Concept/Question Board** as well. Information from the selection could help answer those questions.

FACT OR FICTION Although this selection is realistic fiction, it also contains some facts. This presents an excellent opportunity for students to differentiate fact from fiction. During the second reading, have students note which elements of the story are fact and which elements are fiction.

1st READ

Comprehension Strategies

6 Answering Questions Teacher Modeling: *Deserts have animals too. How do animals survive in the desert with so little water? Some of the animals survive in the desert by eating the plants that hold water. But deserts also have water holes, and some animals survive by living near the water holes.*

7 Making Connections Teacher Modeling: *The text says plants and animals that live in the desert do just fine. I suppose they are used to the weather conditions in the desert, just like we're used to our environment.*

Comprehension Check

How are deserts alike? **Possible Answers** *They are dry. They have very little precipitation each year.*

How are deserts different from each other? **Possible Answers** *Some are hot and dry, and some are cold and rocky. Some have mountains.*

Comprehension Skills

2nd READ

Main Idea and Details

- ✦ Reread pages 20 and 21 of the selection with students, and ask the following questions:
  - On page 20, what is the main idea? *Animals can live in the desert.*
  - What details support that main idea? *Animals can live near water holes. They can eat plants that store water.*
- ✦ As students identify the main ideas and details, have them tell you where to record the information on ***Transparency*** 20.

Reading with a Writer's Eye

2nd READ

Dialogue

- ✦ Remind students that "talk written down" is called dialogue.
- ✦ On page 16, have students find and point to the opening and closing quotation marks of Miss Cozy's dialogue. Ask what these marks are called. Then ask what they are used for. *to show the exact words a character says* Have them identify Miss Cozy's words. Do the same for Miss Cozy's dialogue on pages 17, 18, and 19.
- ✦ On page 20, have students find and point to the opening and closing quotation marks of Tony's dialogue. Have them identify Tony's exact words. Do the same for Miss Cozy's dialogue on page 21.
- ✦ Explain to students that the author uses a special kind of dialogue called question and answer. Ask students why an author might decide to use question-and-answer dialogue. **Possible Answers** *That is what students and teachers do in school.*

Differentiating Instruction — English Learners

IF . . . students have difficulty grasping main idea and details, **THEN . . .** use one of the story illustrations to demonstrate the concept as you teach the linguistic patterns *The main idea is _____. One detail about the main idea is _____.*

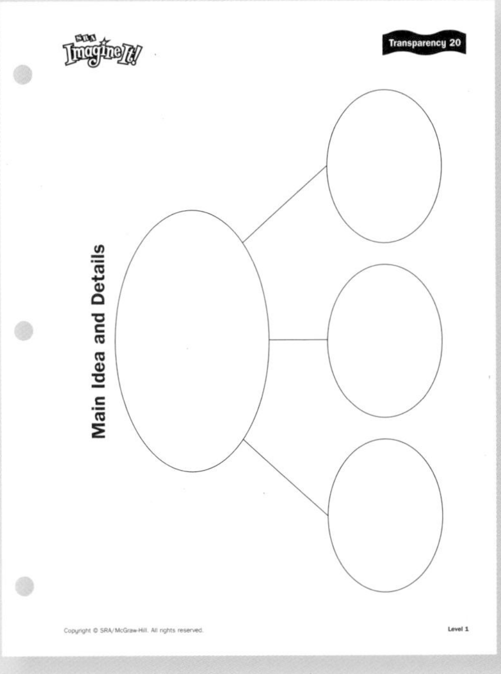

Transparency 20

Technology

LISTENING LIBRARY Encourage students to listen to "Deserts" on the ***Listening Library CD*** during Workshop for a model of fluent reading.

Audio CD

Monitor Progress to Differentiate Instruction — Formal Assessment

DECODING As students read, notice how they are decoding words containing sound/spellings they have learned.

APPROACHING LEVEL	**IF . . .** students are having difficulty decoding previously learned sound/spellings,	**THEN . . .** review problem sound/spellings with them during Workshop.
ON LEVEL	**IF . . .** students are able to decode most previously learned sound/spellings,	**THEN . . .** remind them to use the ***Sound/Spelling Cards*** to help them.
ABOVE LEVEL	**IF . . .** students are able to decode all the words in the story,	**THEN . . .** have them practice reading the story for fluency during Workshop.

Writer's Notebook

Have students use the illustrations and information in "Deserts" to draw pictures of a desert scene, including animals and plants. Help them each write a sentence to describe what is in the picture. Remind students to begin each sentence with a capital letter and end with a punctuation mark.

Concept/Question Board

Have students use the Internet to find photographs of different deserts around the world that they can download, label, and post on the **Concept/Question Board.** In particular, help them look for photographs of the Sahara, the Gobi, and the Mojave deserts. You might also help them find pictures of the Arctic and Antarctic. Explain that these areas are also deserts, even though they are cold. Have them think about investigating why these places are deserts.

BIG Idea

What is weather?

After reading the story, read the Big Idea question. Discuss with students how the story helps answer this question.

Differentiating Instruction **English Learners**

IF . . . students have difficulty participating in the discussion, **THEN . . .** ask questions that can be answered with a nod, a *yes* or *no*, or a short phrase. Examples: *Are all deserts alike?* no *What is one kind of desert?* hot and sandy

Discussing the Selection

- Before discussing the selection, have students retell the story. Remind them to use effective communication when they retell the facts of the selection. Have them use appropriate volume and describing words, and remind them to speak clearly.
- As the class discusses the selection, tell students to participate courteously in the discussion. Tell students they should listen attentively and take turns.
- Ask students the following to check their comprehension of "Deserts":
  - *What different kinds of deserts are there? Some are hot and sandy, some are cold and rocky, and some have mountains.*
  - *How are deserts alike? They are very dry; they receive less than ten inches of precipitation each year.*
  - *Why is it not hard for desert plants and animals to survive? It's their home, and they know how to stay alive in their environment.*
- Tell students that even though this story is realistic fiction they have learned facts about deserts. Have students compare the details about deserts from this selection with the details from previously read selections. Have them tell how they know the facts in this story are right.
- Have students return to the Focus Questions on page 16 of the story. Select a student to read the questions aloud, and have students answer and discuss the questions. Encourage students to return to the text when answering their questions.
- Talk about comprehension strategies used as students read the selection. Have students think about how they used strategies to help them better understand the selection.
  - *How did you make connections with information in the text?* **Possible Answer** *I thought about a movie I saw that had a desert in it.*
  - *How did you clarify words or confusing passages?* **Possible Answer** *I clarified things that confused me by rereading the text.*
  - *How did you use information in the text to answer questions?* **Possible Answer** *I looked for the answers in the text. If I didn't find the answers, I asked my teacher.*

Purposes for Reading

Review the purposes set for reading "Deserts." Have students tell whether they met their purposes for reading. Have them identify information from the text that talks about the purposes:

- To find out about the weather in deserts
- To find out how plants and animals live in a desert

Vocabulary Review

- To review the selection vocabulary word, write the word on the board, or display the transparency you made. Ask students the following:

  What kinds of things do you keep? What do you use for storing these things?
  Possible Answer *I keep coins. I use a bank for storing coins.*

- Have students think of things that can be used for storing. Write three or four of their choices on the board. Then have them list items in each of these categories that can be stored using that item. For example, a refrigerator can be used for storing. Food and drink can be stored in a refrigerator.

Print and Book Awareness

Print and Book Awareness

Punctuation: Review Quotation Marks

- Remind students that when characters in a selection say something, the words they say are put between quotation marks.
- Have volunteers say sentences about deserts for you to write on the board. For each sentence, add the appropriate comma, and write the word *said* and the student's name as follows:

  All deserts are dry, said Abby.

  Ask students to tell you where to put the opening and closing quotation marks. If necessary, remind them that the words *said Abby* are not part of what was said—they identify who said it.
- Have students look through "Deserts" for examples of dialogue. Call on volunteers to read only the words said by a character and then to tell who said the words.
- Conclude by having each student write a sentence about the selection and place quotation marks at the beginning and the end of the sentence. Help them add commas, the word *said*, and their names to complete the sentences.

Selection Vocabulary

storing (page 19)

Teacher Tips

WORD BANK Have students add the selection vocabulary word and any expanding vocabulary words to the What's the Weather? Word Bank.

UNIT VOCABULARY This story has one selection vocabulary word. You may want to take this opportunity to review vocabulary from earlier in the unit that students find difficult.

HIGH-FREQUENCY WORDS To help students review the high-frequency words they have learned, say some of the words aloud, and have students point to each one in the selection. Remind them to look at the High-Frequency Word Bank for help.

Phonics

Have students practice identifying sound/spellings from recent lessons. Turn to a page in the selection, and say a sound/spelling that appears on that page. Then have students point to the word with that sound/spelling. Remind them to look at ***Sound/Spelling Cards*** for help.

OBJECTIVES

Students will
- learn about writing instructions.
- organize ideas, audience, and purpose for writing instructions.
- form the letters *k* and *z* correctly.
- control the size and spacing of letters.

MATERIALS
- ***Transparencies*** 40, 41
- ***Language Arts Big Book,*** pp. 48–51
- Writer's Notebooks
- ***Skills Practice 1,*** p. 207
- ***Alphabet Letter Cards***

Writing Instructions

Prewriting

Teach

- Use ***Transparency*** 40 to introduce writing instructions to explain a process. Explain that instructions involve steps that a reader must follow in a certain order. If readers are to understand and follow instructions, the writer must include all the steps in a process and put the steps in the correct order.
- Refer to ***Language Arts Big Book*** pages 48–51 if more information on explaining a process is necessary.
- **Teacher Modeling** Show students how to brainstorm ideas for writing a set of instructions. *I've learned so much about weather, I think I'll write instructions to tell people how to get ready for some kind of bad weather. Bad weather can be thunderstorms, fog, strong winds, and blizzards. I'll write instructions for how to get ready for ____ weather. I'll be telling about things people should do, so I'll need to use action words or verbs. Some good action words I might use are* put, stay, keep, go, *and* close. *I'll think of more words as I write.*

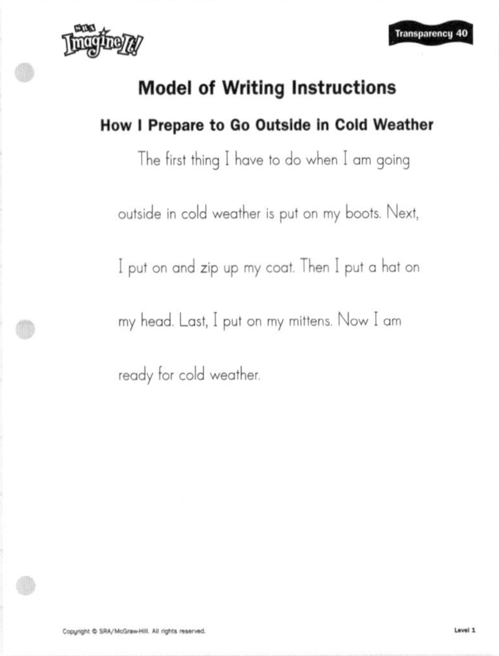

Imagine It! Transparency 40

Model of Writing Instructions

How I Prepare to Go Outside in Cold Weather

The first thing I have to do when I am going outside in cold weather is put on my boots. Next, I put on and zip up my coat. Then I put a hat on my head. Last, I put on my mittens. Now I am ready for cold weather.

 Level 1

Transparency 40

Teacher Tips

DISCUSSION Some students may have had a negative or traumatic experience with "bad weather." Keep this in mind as you begin class discussions on this topic, and watch for students who become upset or withdrawn.

ORGANIZATION It is okay if students develop ideas for instructions that do not require a sequential order. Help these students organize their ideas in a different way, such as alphabetically or in order of importance.

Differentiating Instruction: English Learners

IF . . . students are unable to generate written instructions, **THEN . . .** encourage them to express their ideas in pictures, and help them add captions.

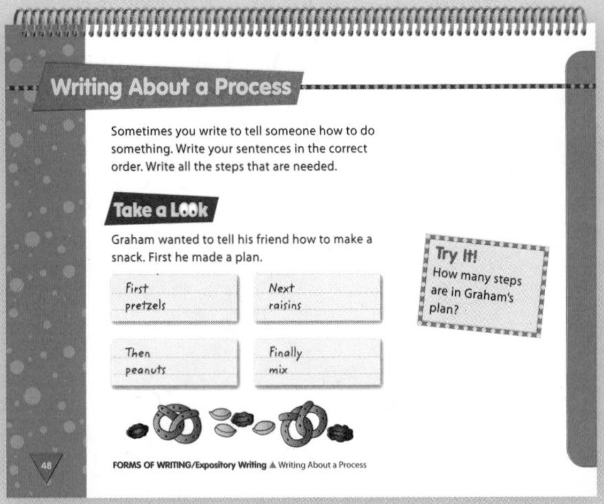

Writing About a Process

Sometimes you write to tell someone how to do something. Write your sentences in the correct order. Write all the steps that are needed.

Take a Look

Graham wanted to tell his friend how to make a snack. First he made a plan.

First pretzels | Next raisins | Then peanuts | Finally mix

Try It! How many steps are in Graham's plan?

48 FORMS OF WRITING/Expository Writing ▲ Writing About a Process

Language Arts Big Book, p. 48

Writing Instructions, cont.

Guided Practice

- Talk with students about different kinds of storms they have read about or experienced. Discuss ways people might prepare for each one.
- Write students' ideas on chart paper, and then help them organize the ideas into a step-by-step process. Have them help you add action words to the steps. Keep the chart for use in later lessons.

Apply

- Have students write ideas for their instructions in the writing ideas section of their Writer's Notebooks. Encourage them to draw pictures to help explain their ideas.
- Help them complete the audience and purpose sections of ***Skills Practice 1*** page 207.

Assessment

You will use the Writing Rubrics found in the Level Appendix to evaluate students' instructions. You may use any of the rubrics for Genre, Writing Process, and Writing Traits. Share with students what you will be looking for when assessing their instructions.

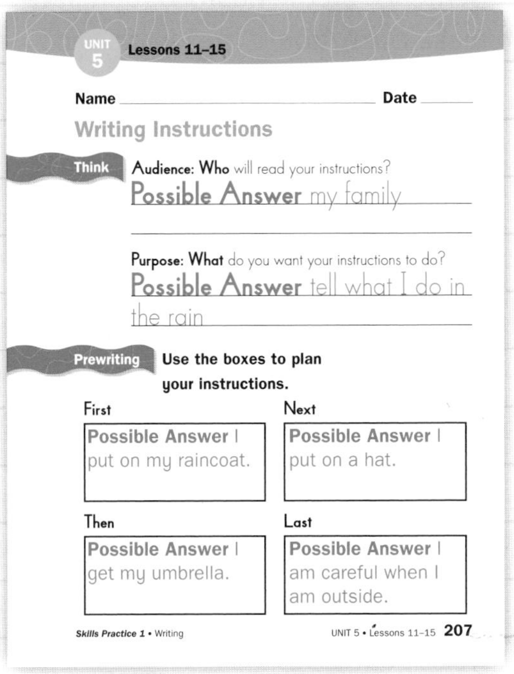

UNIT 5 Lessons 11–15

Name ______ Date ______

Writing Instructions

Think — Audience: Who will read your instructions?
Possible Answer my family

Purpose: What do you want your instructions to do?
Possible Answer tell what I do in the rain

Prewriting — Use the boxes to plan your instructions.

First	Next
Possible Answer I put on my raincoat.	Possible Answer I put on a hat.
Then	**Last**
Possible Answer I get my umbrella.	Possible Answer I am careful when I am outside.

Skills Practice 1 • Writing — UNIT 5 • Lessons 11–15 207

Skills Practice 1, p. 207

Penmanship

Alphabet Practice: The Letters *k* and *z*

Teach

Model how to form lowercase *k* and *z* by writing the letters on ***Transparency*** 41. Describe each stroke of the handwriting models as you trace them. Point out similarities in how these two letters are written. *Both letters have straight lines.*

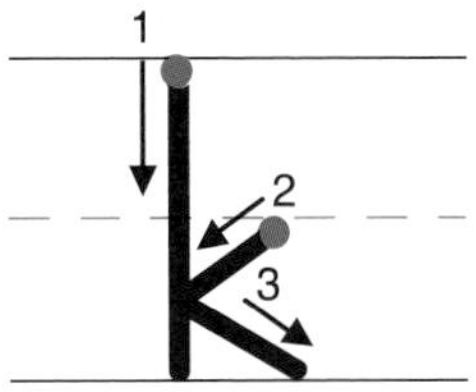

Starting point, straight down, starting point, slanting down left, touching the line, slanting down right: small *k*.

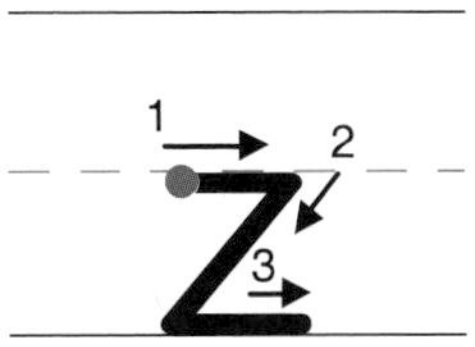

Starting point, straight across, slanting down left, straight across: small *z*.

Guided Practice

Help students use their index fingers to trace the letters *k* and *z* on the ***Alphabet Letter Cards*** as they say each letter name.

Apply

For letter-formation practice, provide students with handwriting paper. Have them write the letters *k* and *z* four times within the lines as they say the letter names. Have students proofread their line by circling any incorrect letters and making them better by rewriting them. Then have them underline their best *k* and *z*.

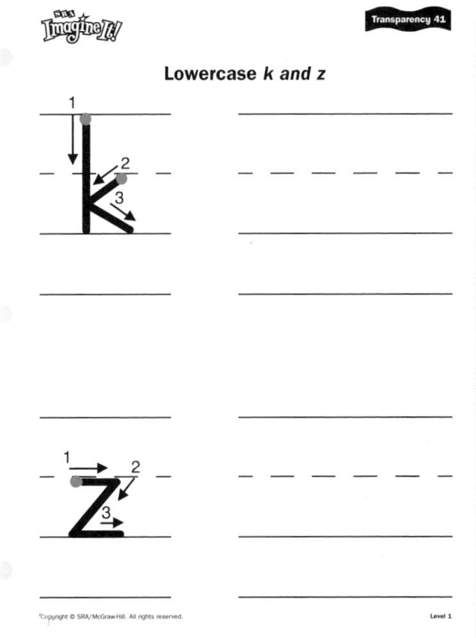

Transparency 41

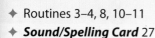

OBJECTIVES

Students will

- blend, spell, and read words that contain /ā/ spelled *ai_* and *_ay*.
- build fluency.

MATERIALS

- Routines 3–4, 8, 10–11
- ***Sound/Spelling Card*** 27
- ***Skills Practice 1,*** pp. 209–210

Teacher Tip

SOUND/SPELLING CARD REVIEW You may want to spend a few minutes each day reviewing the sounds and spellings students have learned.

Daily Warm-Ups

Copy the Morning Message on the board or on chart paper. Have students answer the questions. Read the message aloud, and discuss it with students **Possible Answer** *A deep snow sometimes feels like a cold, thick blanket.*

MORNING MESSAGE

Good morning! The story we will read today is about snow. Have you ever seen a deep snow? What might a deep snow feel like?

Daily Language Review

To review capitalization, write the following sentence on the board, or generate a similar one with students, and have them make corrections: "the weather in tampa, florida, is very hot," said carlos. *"The weather in Tampa, Florida, is very hot," said Carlos.*

Find a Word Game

Write the following words on the board. Say a long-vowel spelling. Then have a student come to the board, find and read a word with the sound/spelling, and underline the spelling for the sound.

flavor /ā/	equal /ē/	glee /ē/	achieve /ē/
pretty /ē/	compete /ē/	plain /ā/	payment /ā/
eat /ē/	grade /ā/		

Phonics

ROUTINE 3 ROUTINE 4 ROUTINE 10 ROUTINE 11

Review: /ā/ Spelled *ai_* and *_ay*

Blending

✦ Point to ***Sound/Spelling Card*** 27—Long A to review the *ai_* and *_ay* spellings for /ā/.

✦ Use Routine 3, whole-word blending, and Routine 4, blending sentences, to have students blend the words and sentences. Use Routine 10, closed syllables, and Routine 11, open syllables, to have students blend the multisyllable words.

Line 1	clay	claim	brave	able
Line 2	stale	rain	drain	grain
Line 3	blaze	ray	tray	drape
Line 4	Spain	Sunday	May	Thursday

Sentence 1 Dale will paint on a gray, rainy day.

Sentence 2 We play the game daily.

Line 1 **/ā/ spelled *_ay, ai_, a_e,* and *a***

Have students identify the spelling for /ā/ in each word. *clay, claim, brave, able*
When blending *able*, write *le* as a unit.

Line 2 **/ā/ spelled *a_e* and *ai_***

Remember to write each *a_e* and *ai_* as a unit for students to sound and blend.

Sound/Spelling Card 27

Teacher Tips

FIND A WORD On the board, write a long-vowel spelling such as *a_e, i_e,* or *e_e*. Write a consonant in the blank, and have students blend and read the word. Next change the consonant, and have students blend and read the word. Then add a consonant to the beginning or ending of the word, and repeat the procedure.

SYLLABICATION To help students blend the words and build fluency, use the syllabication below of the multisyllable words on the word lines.

a • ble Sun • day Thurs • day

Differentiating Instruction **English Learners**

IF . . . students are unable to identify the words that answer the questions, **THEN . . .** for oral practice and vocabulary building, ask them to repeat the words their classmates say.

Line 3 **/ā/ spelled *a_e* and *_ay***

If necessary, explain that *drape* means "to hang a piece of fabric over something." Demonstrate by draping a coat or scarf over a chair.

Line 4 **/ā/ spelled *ai_* and *_ay***

Ask students why all the words on the line begin with capital letters. *Special places and dates start with capital letters.*

Sentences 1–2

Review the high-frequency words before writing the sentences. Have students reread the sentences to promote fluency.

Developing Oral Language

To review the words, call on a student to underline the word that answers each question below and then use the word in a sentence.

- Which word is the first day of the week? *Sunday*
- Which word describes a hero? *brave*
- Which word means almost the same as *fire?* *blaze*
- Which word names a country? *Spain*
- Which word is the fifth day of the week? *Thursday*

Guided Practice

Have students use ***Skills Practice 1*** pages 209–210 to review /ā/ spelled *ai_* and *_ay*. Have students choose and write the correct word to complete each sentence on page 209. Have students write the word that correctly names each pictured item on page 210.

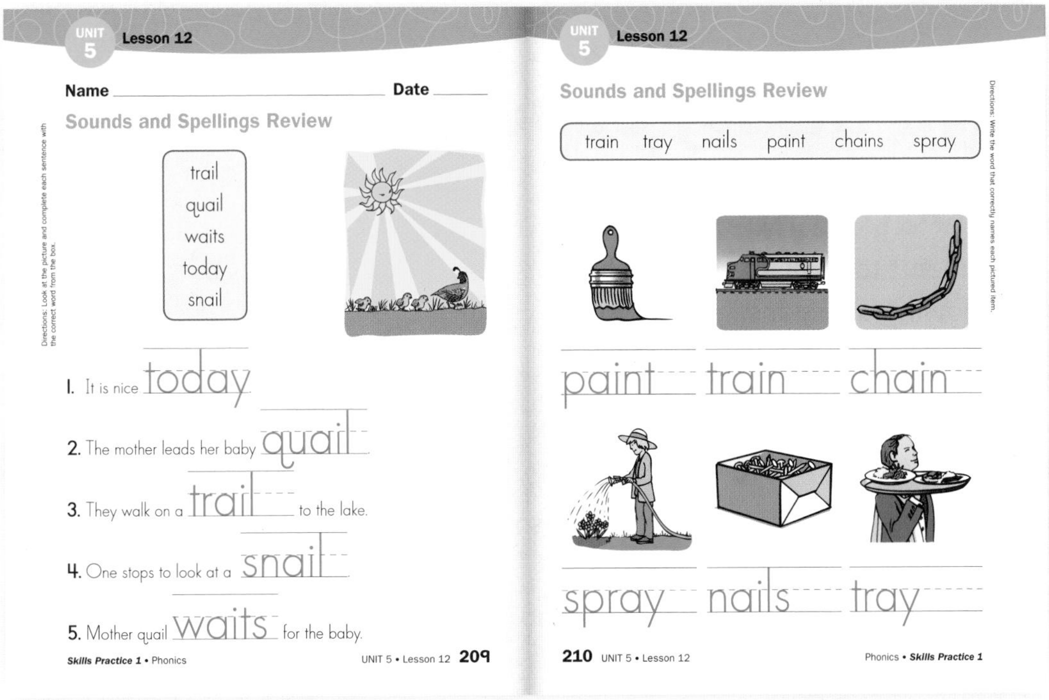

UNIT 5 Lesson 12

Name ______ Date ______

Sounds and Spellings Review

Directions: Look at the picture and complete each sentence with the correct word from the box.

trail
quail
waits
today
snail

1. It is nice today
2. The mother leads her baby quail
3. They walk on a trail to the lake.
4. One stops to look at a snail
5. Mother quail waits for the baby.

Skills Practice 1 • Phonics UNIT 5 • Lesson 12 209

UNIT 5 Lesson 12

Sounds and Spellings Review

Directions: Write the word that correctly names each pictured item.

train tray nails paint chains spray

paint train chain

spray nails tray

210 UNIT 5 • Lesson 12 Phonics • *Skills Practice 1*

Skills Practice 1, pp. 209–210

Dictation: Word Building Game

ROUTINE 8

Use Routine 8, word building, to have students spell words in the Word Building game. Have students use pencil and paper for the following words:

bay
hay
hail
tail
trail
rail
sail
say

Teacher Tip

WORD BUILDING GAME Be sure to have students proofread and correct their spelling before you dictate the next word.

Monitor Progress

to Differentiate Instruction
Formal Assessment

DICTATION As students spell words, notice who uses the ***Sound/Spelling Cards*** and spells the words correctly. Note students who are asking for help with the spellings.

APPROACHING LEVEL

IF . . . students need additional practice with phonics and dictation, **THEN . . .** have them complete ***Reteach 1*** pages 153–154.

ON LEVEL

IF . . . students are on level with phonics and dictation, **THEN . . .** pair them, and have them play a game from ***eSkills.***

ABOVE LEVEL

IF . . . students need a challenge with phonics and dictation, **THEN . . .** have them complete ***Challenge Activities 1*** page 77.

Day 2 **Reading and Responding**

OBJECTIVES

Students will
- set and check purposes for reading.
- learn vocabulary words.
- use the comprehension strategies Making Connections, Clarifying, and Summarizing.
- use the comprehension skill Sequence.
- talk about and appreciate fine art.
- make a rain gauge.

MATERIALS
- ***First Reader,*** pp. 22–27
- Routines 12, 13
- ***What's the Weather? Big Book,*** p. 60
- Writer's Notebooks
- ***Transparency*** 42

Teacher Tips

ACTIVATE PRIOR KNOWLEDGE Before reading the selection, you might want students to review pages 14–17 of "When a Storm Comes Up."

BACKGROUND INFORMATION To help students who may not be familiar with the rodents mentioned in the story, you may want to display pictures of groundhogs and squirrels.

MATERIALS For the Science Connection experiment, you will need a largemouth glass or plastic jar, an indelible marker, a ruler, and a plastic funnel.

Differentiating Instruction **English Learner**

IF . . . students would benefit from reading the selection before the rest of the class reads it, **THEN . . .** have them read the selection in Workshop.

Build Background

Activate Prior Knowledge

Ask students to recall the other selections they have read in this unit to answer the following questions:

- What is snow? *small drops of frozen water that fall from the sky*
- What causes it to snow? **Possible Answer** *When it's cold, the drops of water in clouds freeze and fall to the ground.*
- Have you ever played in the snow? If so, what did you do? **Possible Answers** *built snowmen or snow forts; had snowball fights; made snow angels*
- Have you ever seen wild animals in the snow? If so, what kinds of animals were they? **Possible Answers** *squirrels; rabbits; birds*

Preview and Prepare

ROUTINE 12

Browse

- Follow Routine 12, reading the selection, to prepare students to read the selection. Begin by displaying the cover of the ***First Reader.*** Point to and read aloud the title.
- Have students locate and turn to the Table of Contents, and point to the title of the selection, "Snow Is Good!" Have students read the title along with you as you point to each word. Point to the page number 22, and have a volunteer read it and tell what the number means. Turn to page 22.
- Demonstrate how to browse the selection by commenting on the title and the illustrations and predicting how they might relate to the text. On page 23, for example, you might say: *On this page, I see a girl and her mom. Mom is pointing to the clouds, and it is snowing. I imagine she is telling her daughter what snow is. I'll check that when we read this page.*
- Have students browse the first few pages to look for clues to what the selection is about and for difficult and unfamiliar words. Students may select the word *stated.* If so, tell them that *stated* means "said." When someone states something, he or she says something.

Set Purposes

- Have students think about the information they gained while browsing. Ask students to use this information to tell what the purposes for reading this selection might be. Write the purposes on the board. Some suggestions include the following:
  - To learn more about snow
  - To learn how plants and animals live when it is snowing
- After students read the selection, have them return to these purposes.

Fluency

- As students read "Snow Is Good!" have them practice reading with appropriate rate. Remind students to pause at end punctuation marks.
- Students will learn that this selection is realistic fiction. Dialogue is included in the text. Have students adjust their reading rate to correspond with the way each character's words might be said.
- Have students apply letter-sound knowledge to decode phonetically regular words quickly and accurately as they read this selection.

Teacher Tip

HIGH-FREQUENCY WORDS Use the High-Frequency Word Bank to review previously taught high-frequency words that appear in this selection, including *on, her, and, the, is, said, she, when, will, it, like, of, make, a, we, for, walk.*

BIG Idea

What is weather?

Before reading the selection, reread the Big Idea question. Tell students to keep this question in mind as they listen to the selection.

Monitor Progress

to Differentiate Instruction
Formal Assessment

DECODING As students read, notice how well students are decoding words containing sound/spellings they have learned.

APPROACHING LEVEL

IF . . . students are having difficulty decoding previously learned sound/spellings,	**THEN . . .** review problem sound/spellings with them during Workshop.

ON LEVEL

IF . . . students are able to decode most previously learned sound/spellings,	**THEN . . .** remind them to use the ***Sound/Spelling Cards*** to help them.

ABOVE LEVEL

IF . . . students are able to decode all the words in the story,	**THEN . . .** have them practice reading the story for fluency during Workshop.

Selection Vocabulary

shivered past tense of **shiver:** to shake, usually from the cold (page 27)

Teacher Tip

SEMANTIC MAP Have students continue building onto the semantic map. Encourage them to add selection vocabulary words and words that they have learned throughout the unit.

Concept/Question Board

Have students create multiple illustrations that represent what it means to feel cold. Tell students to write a sentence about their picture before they post it. Encourage students to use their imagination with this assignment. Students can refer to the different items that are posted on the **Concept/ Question Board** for ideas.

Technology

eSkills Students can get practice with vocabulary using ***eSkills*** online or on CD-ROM.

Building Vocabulary

ROUTINE 13

- Use Routine 13, selection vocabulary, to introduce the vocabulary word to students. Write the word on the board or on a transparency.

  To demonstrate the meaning of *shivered*, wrap your arms around yourself and shake slightly as you say *Brrrr*. Ask volunteers to use the word *shivered* to describe what you did. Then have them demonstrate shivering.

- You will introduce two expanding vocabulary words to students as the selection is reread. These words are identified in boxes where they appear in the selection. As you come to each word in the selection, read to students the word, the definition, and the sample sentence. Understanding these words will help students better comprehend the selection.

Monitor Progress to Differentiate Instruction

Formal Assessment

VOCABULARY During the Building Vocabulary activities, note how well students seem to understand the vocabulary.

APPROACHING LEVEL

IF . . . students would benefit from additional work with unit vocabulary, **THEN . . .** help them draw and label pictures to show the meaning of each word.

ON LEVEL

IF . . . students are comfortable with most vocabulary words and their meanings, **THEN . . .** pair them, and have them play one of the games in the ***Workshop Kit.***

ABOVE LEVEL

IF . . . students need a challenge, **THEN . . .** have them use the vocabulary words to retell a selection.

Reading the Selection

Genre Realistic Fiction

Tell students that "Snow Is Good!" is an example of realistic fiction. Briefly review the elements of realistic fiction.

- It has people or animals that seem real.
- It has events and places that seem real.
- It is about things that did not happen but *could* happen in real life.

Comprehension Strategies

1st READ

As students read "Snow Is Good!" model and prompt the use of the following comprehension strategies:

- Making Connections
- Clarifying
- Summarizing

Comprehension Skills

2nd READ

As students reread "Snow Is Good!" apply the comprehension skill Sequence.

Reading with a Writer's Eye

2nd READ

As students reread "Snow Is Good!" discuss how the author uses setting.

Focus Questions

Read and discuss the Focus Questions on page 22. Encourage students to think about the Focus Questions as they read "Snow Is Good!"

Reading Recommendations

ROUTINE 12

Day 2 Students will read the entire story twice today. Follow Routine 12, reading the selection. The first time, model and prompt the use of the comprehension strategies. The second time, focus on the comprehension skills and Reading with a Writer's Eye.

Teacher Tips

PARTNER READING LIST Have students add information about this selection to their Partner Reading Lists. Remind them to write the title of the selection and the date they read it. If they also read the selection in a group, have them write the names of the group members.

THEME CONNECTIONS Remind students that as they read, they should think about how the selection relates to the theme What's the Weather? and about how it might help them generate ideas for Inquiry.

READING THE SELECTION If students are struggling with the ***First Reader*** stories, have students echo reading "Snow Is Good!" with you for the first reading. Focus on reading at an appropriate rate. During the second reading, have students read the story orally.

FACT OR FICTION Although this selection is realistic fiction, it also contains some facts. This presents an excellent opportunity for students to differentiate fact from fiction. During the second reading, have students note which elements of the story are fact and which elements are fiction.

Phonics

Words in the selection that contain sound/spellings from recent phonics lessons appear in boxes like this throughout the selection. At the end of the first reading, students should be prompted to identify the sound/spellings of these words.

Technology

LISTENING LIBRARY Encourage students to listen to "Snow Is Good!" on the ***Listening Library CD*** during Workshop for a model of fluent reading.

Audio CD

Reading and Responding

Focus Questions What clothes do you wear outside when it is cold?
How do animals stay warm in the snow?

Snow Is Good!

Sally put on her winter jacket and ran outside. "The snow is growing deep," she said. "When will it stop?" ①

22

"Snow is like rain falling from the clouds," said Mom. "Only snowflakes are frozen drops of water. The snow will stop when the air is dry and the clouds are not so full of water." ②

23

First Reader, pp. 22–23

Phonics

/ā/ spelled *ai_*: rain (page 23); afraid (page 25)
/ē/ spelled *ee:* deep (page 22); freeze (pages 24, 25)
/ō/ spelled *o_e:* frozen (page 23)

Differentiating Instruction **English Learner**

IF . . . English learners are having difficulty with sequence, **THEN . . .** refer to the ***English Learner Support Guide*** Unit 5 Lesson 12.

1st READ

Comprehension Strategies

① **Making Connections** Teacher Prompt: *Have you ever bundled up in a coat and hat to run outside?* **Possible Student Response** *Once it snowed very hard. We were allowed outside if we dressed warmly. I could hardly walk because I had so many clothes on!*

② **Clarifying** Teacher Modeling: *I am confused about why it stops snowing. I need to reread this to clarify. I know that snow is frozen drops of water that fall from clouds. But I didn't know that snow stops when the air dries out and the clouds aren't so full of water.*

③ **Clarifying** Teacher Modeling: *I thought all snow was just snow, but all snow is not the same. The text says that some snow is dry and fluffy, and some is wet.*

④ **Summarizing** Teacher Modeling*: I'm going to summarize to make sure I understand what I've read so far. Sally goes outside in the snow. The snow is deep. Her mom explains when the snow will stop falling. Then her mom talks about kinds of snow.*

"It is cold," Sally said. "Let's make a snowman before we freeze!"

"Wet snow is good for making snowmen," said Mom. "Dry, fluffy snow is good for taking a walk or going for a sled ride. Whee!" 3

24

"What about all the plants and animals?" asked Sally. "I am afraid they will freeze. When we are cold, we go inside to get warm." 4

25

First Reader, pp. 24–25

Comprehension Skills

2nd READ

Sequence

✦ Review sequence and that it can help readers understand how events are related. Reread pages 22–24 with students. Then, using ***Transparency*** 42, have students tell you where to record their responses to the questions below.

- What happens first? *Sally puts on her coat and goes out into the snow.*
- What happens next? *They talk about when the snow will stop.*
- What happens after that? *Mom and Sally build a snowman.*

Reading with a Writer's Eye

2nd READ

Setting

Review the meaning of and how the author uses the setting to tell us about the topic. Ask students what the setting of this story is. *outside, in the snow*

Expanding Vocabulary

deep far down (page 22)
The water in the ocean is *deep.*
fluffy soft and light (page 24)
The kitten has *fluffy* fur.

Teacher Tips

CLARIFYING Be sure students understand the selection. Tell them to reread and ask clarifying questions when they do not understand ideas in the text.

SELF-CORRECT As students read, make sure they practice self-correction when they make a mistake in their reading.

"Snow is good for animals," said Mom. "It is like a blanket. Groundhogs sleep under the ground all winter.

"A snow blanket keeps the wind and cold from them. Squirrels have heavy fur. Snow in the trees helps keep the wind and cold from their nests. 5

26

"Snow is good for plants too," stated Mom. "A snow blanket keeps the wind and cold away from plants.

"Are you ready to go inside?" Mom asked.

"I'm ready for a real blanket!" shivered Sally. 6

27

First Reader, pp. 26–27

Phonics

/ē/ spelled _*y:* heavy (page 26); ready, Sally (page 27)

/ē/ spelled *ee:* sleep, trees, keep (page 26); keeps (pages 26, 27)

/ā/ spelled *a_e:* stated (page 27)

/ā/ spelled _*ay:* away (page 27)

/ī/ spelled *i_e:* inside (page 27)

/ē/ spelled *ea:* real (page 27)

1st READ

Comprehension Strategies

5 **Clarifying** Teacher Modeling: *Mom says snow is good for animals, but I'm not sure I understand why. I'll reread this page to see if I can clarify that idea. Oh, now I see. Snow is good for animals because it helps keep them warm in winter, like a blanket. It keeps out the cold and wind.*

6 **Making Connections** Teacher Prompt: *I know just how Sally must feel. After playing in the snow, I'd get cold and start to shiver. Have you ever shivered in the cold?* **Possible Student Response** *I shivered in the cold when Dad and I waited to get into a football game. It felt tingly, but Dad gave me a blanket to keep me warm.*

Comprehension Check

How is snow like rain? **Possible Answer** *Both start out as water in clouds. But when it's cold, the water freezes and becomes snow.*

Comprehension Skills

2nd READ

Sequence

- Remind students that retelling events in the correct order can help readers understand why events happen the way they do. Reread pages 26 and 27 with students. After reading, ask students the following:
  - *What happens first?* *Sally and Mom talk about how snow can be a blanket for animals.*
  - *What happens next?* *Sally and Mom talk about how snow can be a blanket for plants.*
  - *Then what happens?* *Sally wants her own blanket.*
- Then, using ***Transparency*** 42, have students tell you where to record their responses to the questions.

Differentiating Instruction **English Learners**

IF . . . students have difficulty identifying and discussing sequence, **THEN . . .** introduce order words such as *first, second, third, then, next, finally, before,* and *after*. Because many languages share the English number system, use of numerals *(1, 2, 3)* can help students learn ordinal number words *(first, second, third)* and other order words. List numerals *1* through *5* on the board. Explain that *1* is the *first* number; *2* is the *second,* or *next,* number; *3* comes *after 2* but *before 4; 5* is the *last* number; and so on.

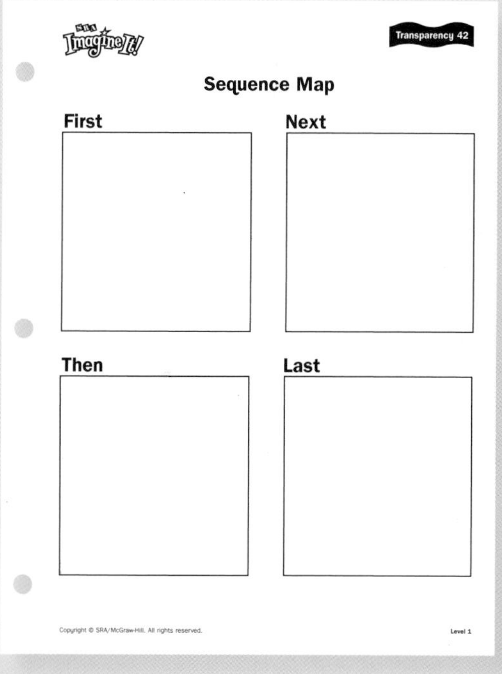

Transparency 42

Reading with a Writer's Eye

2nd READ

Setting

- Explain that the author of this selection wanted to tell readers about snow but in a way that would be interesting. The author made up a selection about a girl and her mother and had them play in the snow as the mother explained important things about snow.
- Remind students that "Snow Is Good" is realistic fiction. Explain that although it contains facts, the characters and the setting are not real.
- Ask students to think of another setting they might use to tell a story about snow. Prompt them by suggesting places such as a weather station, a science classroom, or the Arctic.

Monitor Progress to Differentiate Instruction — Formal Assessment

WORD STRUCTURE As you prompt students to apply the comprehension skill Sequence, note the accuracy and independence of student responses.

APPROACHING LEVEL	**IF . . .** students have difficulty with Sequence,	**THEN . . .** during Workshop, have them retell the selection as you prompt them with questions such as *What happens first? What happens next? Then what happens? How does the selection end?*
ON LEVEL	**IF . . .** students are comfortable applying Sequence,	**THEN . . .** have them write the events from the previous day in the appropriate sequence.
ABOVE LEVEL	**IF . . .** students need a challenge with Sequence,	**THEN . . .** have them sequence the events of a vacation or a previously read selection.

Writer's Notebook

Have students use the text and illustrations in "Snow Is Good!" to help them draw pictures that show an idea from the selection, such as how snow covers plants to keep them warm or how squirrels might look in a nest covered with snow. Help them write a sentence to describe what they have drawn. Encourage them to use action words in their sentences.

Concept/Question Board

Have students think of new questions they might have about snow after reading this selection. Tell students to post these questions and their drawings of "Snow Is Good!" on the **Concept/Question Board.** Remind them to check the Board to see whether they can answer any questions after reading this selection.

Differentiating Instruction English Learners

IF . . . students need help contributing to the **Concept/Question Board, THEN . . .** allow them to post words, questions, answers, and materials in their native languages. Help them also include vocabulary or short phrases in English with their postings.

BIG Idea

What is weather?

After reading the story, read the Big Idea question. Discuss with students how the story helps answer this question.

Discussing the Selection

✦ Before discussing the selection, have students retell the story. Remind them to use effective communication when they retell the facts of the selection. Have them use appropriate volume and describing words, and remind them to speak clearly.

✦ As the class discusses the selection, tell students to participate courteously in the discussion. Tell students they should listen attentively and take turns.

✦ Ask students the following:

- *How is snow good for plants? Snow covers plants like a blanket and keeps out the wind and cold.*
- *What do animals such as groundhogs do to survive during the winter? They sleep underground. The snow on the ground above them keeps out the wind and cold.*
- *How is snow good for animals such as squirrels? Snow covers their nests in trees and keeps out the wind and cold.*

✦ Students have listened to and read selections about snow and cold weather. Have them discuss the details from the previous selections that help them know the information in this story is true.

✦ Have students return to the Focus Questions on page 22 of the story. Select a student to read the questions aloud, and have students answer and discuss the questions. Encourage students to return to the text when answering their questions.

✦ Talk about comprehension strategies used as students read the selection. Have students think about how they used strategies to help them better understand the selection.

- *How did you make connections with information in the text?* **Possible Answer** *I remembered making snow people with my older brother.*
- *How did you clarify words or confusing passages?* **Possible Answer** *I clarified things that confused me by looking at the words I already know to figure out the ideas I didn't know.*
- *How did summarizing help you understand the story?* **Possible Answer** *Summarizing helped me remember information from the beginning of the story.*

Purposes for Reading

Review the purposes set for reading "Snow Is Good!" Have students tell whether they met their purposes for reading. Have them identify information from the text that talks about the purposes.

- To learn more about snow
- To learn how plants and animals survive when it is snowing

Vocabulary Review

Have students to role-play the word *shivered* in their seats. Then have them complete the sentence starters below to help them review the meaning of the word *shivered*. Encourage students to extend their sentences by asking them *who, what, why, when,* and *where* questions.

I shivered because ________.

Print and Book Awareness

Print and Book Awareness

Review: Sentences/Sentence Boundaries

- Have students recall what they know about sentences. If necessary, remind them that a sentence starts with a capital letter and ends with some kind of punctuation mark. Review briefly the different kinds of sentences—sentences that tell, sentences that ask questions, and sentences that show strong feelings. Then have students name the punctuation mark that goes at the end of each kind of sentence. *Periods go at the ends of sentences that tell. Question marks go at the ends of sentences that ask questions. Exclamation points go at the ends of sentences that show strong feelings.*
- Have students look at the first sentence on page 22 of "Snow Is Good!" Have them identify the first and last word in the sentence and the punctuation mark. Ask what kind of sentence it is. *a sentence that tells* On the same page, have them find a sentence that asks a question, and repeat the procedure. *"When will it stop?"* For this sentence, have students notice and name the quotation marks at the opening and closing of the sentence. Ask what these marks tell readers. *the exact words someone says* Then point out that the question mark is inside the quotation marks.
- Have students look through the selection for sentences that show strong feeling. *These sentences are found on page 24.* For each sentence they find, point out that the exclamation point is placed inside the quotation marks.

Differentiating Instruction English Learners

IF . . . students have difficulty participating in the discussion, **THEN . . .** ask questions that can be answered with a nod, a yes or no, or a short phrase. Examples: *Is snow good for plants? yes Where do animals such as groundhogs sleep during the winter? underground*

IF . . . students would benefit from added exposure to the vocabulary and themes of the unit, **THEN . . .** encourage them to copy the information from the **Concept/Question Board** into a notebook.

Teacher Tips

WORD BANK Have students add the selection vocabulary word and any expanding vocabulary words to the What's the Weather? Word Bank.

HIGH-FREQUENCY WORDS To help students review the high-frequency words they have learned, say some of the words aloud, and have students point to each one in the selection. Remind them to look at the High-Frequency Word Bank for help.

Selection Vocabulary

shivered (page 27)

Phonics

Have students practice identifying sound/spellings from recent lessons. Turn to a page in the selection, and say a sound/spelling that appears on that page. Then have students point to the word with that sound/spelling. Remind them to look at ***Sound/Spelling Cards*** for help.

Teacher Tip

WORD BANK Encourage students to use words from the What's the Weather? Word Bank when discussing the fine art in this unit.

Fine Art

What's the Weather?, p. 60

- Display ***What's the Weather? Big Book*** page 60. Tell students that previously you discussed each piece of fine art and how it related to weather. Tell students that since they have discussed those pieces of fine art, they have learned more about weather. They have read additional selections and conducted weather-related experiments and research in the Science Connections and Inquiry activities. Suggest that after gaining all this new knowledge, they might have a different opinion or more ideas about the pieces of art.
- Have students look at each piece of art again. Have them share any new thoughts or ideas they have about each piece.
- Review with students the artist's name and where the art was created.
- Have students compare and contrast the fine art pieces in terms of setting, medium, and the weather involved in the scene.

Science Connection

Make a Rain Gauge

Invite students to add amounts of rain to their daily weather observations and the inquiry section of their Writer's Notebooks by making and setting up a rain gauge.

- Help students use a ruler and an indelible marker to measure and mark three inches on the side of the container.
- Have students place the funnel on the top of the jar.
- Help students decide on the best place to put the jar to collect rain or snow. Arrange to set up the gauge in that place.
- Tell students to check the gauge several times over the course of the lesson. Have them record the readings in their What's the Weather? Notebooks.

Teacher Tip

LITERATURE Have students select age- and ability-appropriate fiction and nonfiction materials to read, based on interest and teacher recommendations, to begin a core base of knowledge about the unit theme.

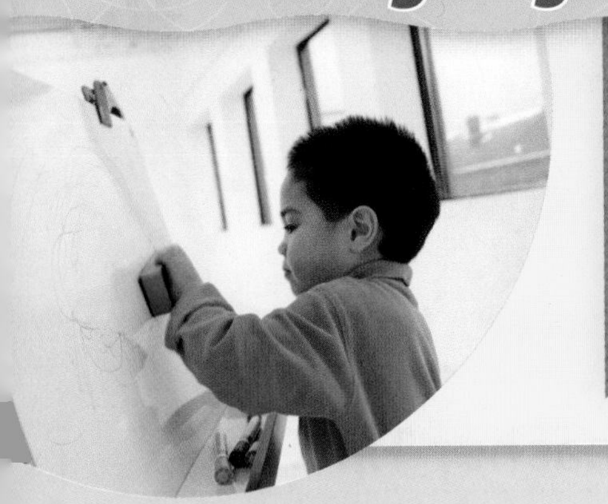

OBJECTIVES

Students will

- ✦ use a sequence map to organize ideas for instructions.
- ✦ understand time and order words.
- ✦ form the letters *k* and *z* correctly.
- ✦ form plural nouns by changing *y* to *i* and adding *es*.

MATERIALS

- ✦ Routine 15
- ✦ ***Language Arts Big Book,*** p. 138
- ✦ ***Transparencies*** 41, 42,
- ✦ ***Skills Practice 1,*** p. 207
- ✦ Portfolios

Traits of Good Writing

Organization Writers use a sequence map to help organize and sort ideas into sequential order.

Concept/Question Board

Remind students to check the **Concept/ Question Board** and the What's the Weather? Word Bank for words and information to use in planning their instructions.

Writing Instructions

ROUTINE 15

Prewriting

Teach—Using a Sequence Map

- ✦ Ask students to explain the purpose of instructions. **Possible Answers** *to tell someone how to do something; to explain how to respond to a situation* Remind them that most instructions involve steps a reader must follow in a certain order.
- ✦ Briefly review the time and order words *first, next, then,* and *last.* Refer to ***Language Arts Big Book*** page 138. Explain that words such as these are important in writing instructions because they show the order of steps that readers should follow to do something. Ask students what might happen if the steps were put in the wrong order. *Readers would do something incorrectly.*
- ✦ Tell students that writers sometimes use a sequence map to help organize their ideas. Explain that this type of graphic organizer allows a writer to sort ideas into a sequential order, or the order that they should happen.
- ✦ Ask students to suggest types of writing that could be organized with a sequence map. **Possible Answers** *directions from one place to another, recipes, summaries, reports, explaining how to do something*
- ✦ Briefly describe how students would fill out a sequence map before beginning to model this week's example.

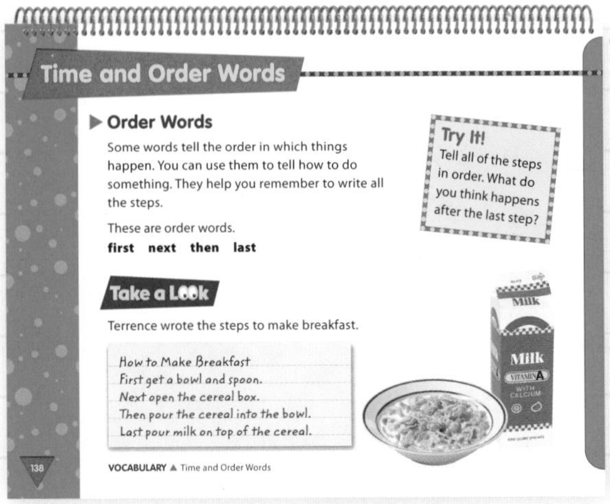
Time and Order Words

▶ Order Words

Some words tell the order in which things happen. You can use them to tell how to do something. They help you remember to write all the steps.

These are order words.

first next then last

Try It!
Tell all of the steps in order. What do you think happens after the last step?

Take a Look

Terrence wrote the steps to make breakfast.

How to Make Breakfast
First get a bowl and spoon.
Next open the cereal box.
Then pour the cereal into the bowl.
Last pour milk on top of the cereal.

138

VOCABULARY ▲ Time and Order Words

Language Arts Big Book, p. 138

Writing Instructions, cont.

Guided Practice

Teacher Modeling Use ***Transparency*** 42 to model how to organize ideas for writing instructions. *I want to write instructions to tell people how to get ready for ________ weather. I'll need to organize my ideas into the best order.* Uses the ideas and action words you thought of in Lesson 11. As you write on the transparency, use the time and order words *first, next, then*, and *last*. Point out that you are putting one idea in each box. Draw a picture in one of the boxes to show students how pictures can be used to support an idea.

Apply

- ✦ Have students complete the audience and purpose information on ***Skills Practice 1*** page 207 for the topic they have selected.
- ✦ Tell them to use their writing ideas from Lesson 11 to fill in the sequence map on page 207 to plan their writing. Tell them to use time and order words to help them organize their ideas into steps.
- ✦ Circulate to help with any reading or decodability issues. Review how a sequence map relates to the order of ideas if necessary.

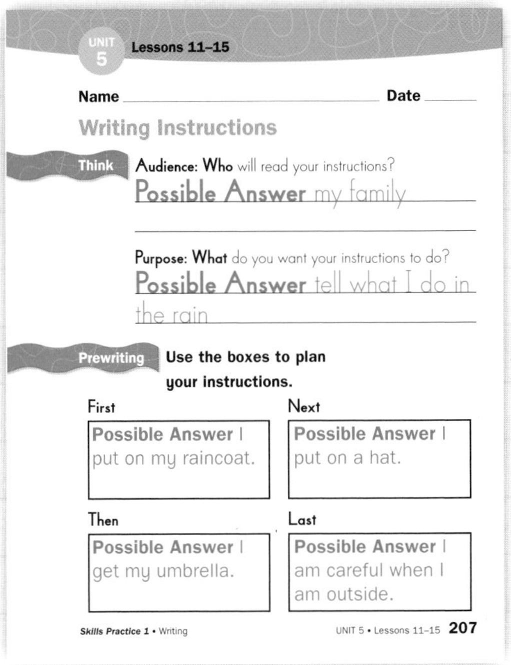

UNIT 5 Lessons 11–15

Name ________________ Date ______

Writing Instructions

Think Audience: Who will read your instructions?
Possible Answer my family

Purpose: What do you want your instructions to do?
Possible Answer tell what I do in the rain

Prewriting Use the boxes to plan your instructions.

First	Next
Possible Answer I put on my raincoat.	Possible Answer I put on a hat.
Then	**Last**
Possible Answer I get my umbrella.	Possible Answer I am careful when I am outside.

Skills Practice 1 • Writing UNIT 5 • Lessons 11–15 207

Skills Practice 1, p. 207

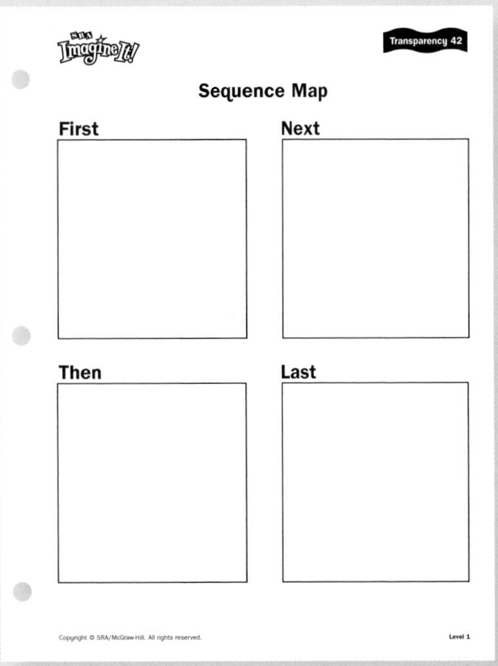

Transparency 42

Sequence Map

First	Next
Then	**Last**

Copyright © SRA/McGraw-Hill. All rights reserved. Level 1

Transparency 42

Differentiating Instruction — English Learners

IF . . . students need extra help with writing instructions, **THEN . . .** see ***English Learner Support Guide*** Unit 5 Lessons 11–15 to help them understand how to organize their ideas.

Technology

eSkills contains writing activities that students can use to practice organizing ideas and information.

Teacher Tips

PENMANSHIP AND VOCABULARY Look for opportunities for students to practice handwriting, using vocabulary words from the reading selection. This reinforces handwriting and vocabulary development in the same activity.

PENMANSHIP Students may need extra practice forming the letters *k* and *z*. Use a model that shows the strokes in different colors.

Differentiating Instruction English Learners

IF . . . students are native speakers of Spanish or of one of many Asian languages including Vietnamese, Khmer, and Hmong,
THEN . . . the /z/ sound does not appear in their natives languages. They may need extra help pronouncing the sound and associating it with the letter *z*. Have students practice saying word pairs that contrast the known /s/ sound with the unknown /z/ sound. *(sip/zip, bus/buzz, hiss/his)*

Penmanship

Alphabet Practice: The Letters *k* and *z*

Teach

- Review how to form lowercase *k* and *z* by writing the letters on the board as you describe the process. See the Level Appendix for penmanship models.
- If students need additional modeling of the strokes for lowercase *k* and *z*, review the letter models on ***Transparency*** 41 *with them during Workshop. Ask students how these two letters are similar.* *Both have straight lines.*

Guided Practice

- Have students follow your model to write each letter twice within the lines as they say its name. Tell them to underline their best *k* and *z*.

Apply

- Write the following words on the board: *freeze, kind, zip, bank*. Read the words, and have students write them on handwriting paper to practice letter formation.
- Have students proofread their line by circling any incorrect words and making them better by rewriting them above or next to the original words. Then have them underline their best words.
- Look for additional opportunities during writing activities and in other subject areas to provide handwriting practice and to encourage and praise students when they form the letters *k* and *z* correctly.

Monitor Progress to Differentiate Instruction — Formal Assessment

PENMANSHIP Check students' handwriting to make sure the letters *k* and *z* are formed correctly and have the proper spacing.

APPROACHING LEVEL	**IF . . .** students need additional practice forming the letters *k* and *z*,	**THEN . . .** give them paper copies of ***Transparency*** 41 to practice tracing the models during Workshop.
	IF . . . students have difficulty with letter formation,	**THEN . . .** see ***Intervention Guide*** Unit 5, Lesson 12, or have them use the ***Alphabet Letter Cards*** to trace the model for *k* and *z*. Then have students practice writing each of the letters twice.
ON LEVEL	**IF . . .** students form the letters *k* and *z* correctly,	**THEN . . .** give them a list of words to copy from the ***First Reader*** that contain the letters *k* or *z*.
ABOVE LEVEL	**IF . . .** students are ready for a challenge,	**THEN . . .** have them look for and copy words that contain *k* and *z* in a classroom dictionary or an encyclopedia.

Grammar, Usage, and Mechanics

Plural Nouns: Change *y* to *i* and Add *es*

Teach

- Ask students to suggest some words that name *who, what,* or *where* for you to write on the board. **Possible Answers** *brother, cousin, train, storm, school, house* Remind them that these words are nouns, or words that describe a person, place, or thing. Ask them how to form the plural of most nouns. *by adding s* Have students copy a few of their suggested words from the board and change them to plural.

- Next write the following words on the board: *sky, baby, city, pony*. Point out that each of these words ends in *y*. Then have students say the letter before the *y* in each word. *k, b, t, n* Remind them that these letters are consonants.

- Explain that if a noun ends with a consonant followed by *y*, the plural of the noun is formed by changing *y* to *i* and then adding *es*. Beside each word on the board, write the plural form: *skies, babies, cities, ponies.*

- Tell students that one way to remember how to form plurals is to learn this rhyme:

  For more than one,
  no need to guess.
  Change *y* to *i,* and add *es.*

Have them recite the rhyme with you several times.

Guided Practice

Write the following words on the board, and have students tell you how to spell the plural form of each one.

bunny *bunnies* puppy *puppies* lady *ladies* party *parties*

Apply

Tell students to search their Portfolios for nouns that end with a consonant followed by a *y*. Have them select a few sentences to edit and rewrite to change the noun from singular to plural. If necessary, tell them to recite the "more than one" rhyme as they work to help them remember the rule. Then have them share their favorite sentences with partners.

Differentiating Instruction — English Learners

IF . . . students need extra help with plural nouns, **THEN . . .** see ***English Learner Support Guide*** Unit 5 Lesson 12 to help them understand forming a plural by changing y to *i,* and add *es*.

Teacher Tip

WRITING LINK Tell students to think about the rules for singular and plural nouns as they work on their instructions throughout the week.

Preparing to Read

OBJECTIVES

Students will

- blend, spell, and read words that contain /ī/ spelled *_igh, _y,* and *_ie.*
- identify compound words.
- build fluency by reading ***Decodables*** 76 and 77.

MATERIALS

- Routines 1–7, 9–11
- ***Sound/Spelling Card*** 29
- ***Skills Practice 1,*** pp. 211–212
- ***Decodables*** 76, *The Opossum at Night,* and 77, *Why, Bly?*

Teacher Tip

WORD CHART Have students add more words that have /ī/ spelled *_igh, _y,* and *_ie* to the /ī/ word chart.

Daily Warm-Ups

Copy the Morning Message on the board or on chart paper. Have students answer the question. Read the message aloud, and discuss it with students. **Possible Answer** *Hurricanes are fierce.*

MORNING MESSAGE

Good morning! Today we will read a story that will tell us more about hurricanes. Hurricanes are big storms. What other word can you use to tell about hurricanes?

Daily Language Review

To review how to form plurals of nouns that end with a consonant and *y,* write the following sentence on the board, or generate a similar one with students, and have students tell you how to correct the mistake: Put the berrys on the blue plate. *Put the berries on the blue plate.*

Quick Change Game

Tell students they will change one word to another by changing spellings. Write the word *train* on the board, and have students tell you what new word to write:

- *train* without the *t rain*
- change the *n* to *l rail*
- change the *r* to *n nail*
- add *s* before *n snail*
- take away the *n sail*
- change the *s* to *p pail*
- change the *l* to *d paid*

Introduce the Sound/Spelling

ROUTINE 1

/ī/ Spelled _igh, _y, and _ie

- Point to ***Sound/Spelling Card*** 29—Long I to review the *i* and *i_e* spellings for /ī/.
- Point to the *_igh* spelling, and tell students this is another way to spell the /ī/ sound. Write *_igh* on the board. Sweep your hand under the *igh* spelling, and have students say /ī/.
- Point to the *_y* and *_ie* spellings on the card, and say that these are two more spellings for /ī/. Discuss what the blanks before the spellings mean. Explain that the blank before the *y* and *ie* indicates that these spellings are usually found at the end of a word or syllable.

Sound/Spelling Card 29

Phonemic Awareness

Listening for /ī/

Read aloud the following words, and have students signal thumbs-up and say the sound if they hear /ī/.

slight	slow	**tight**	tease	**ties**
pry	**iris**	lie	**item**	friend
title	**fries**	froze	**iron**	**size**

Teacher Tip

CONSONANTS AND VOWELS Point out that *y* is the only letter that can be a vowel or consonant depending upon its placement in a word. Compare the placement of *y* on the Yak card and the Long I card. Review what the black and red colors on the cards mean. *The* y *is black on the Yak card, so it is a consonant. The* y *is red on the Long I card, so it is a vowel.*

Differentiating Instruction English Learners

IF . . . students are native Spanish speakers or they speak certain other languages,
THEN . . . they may associate the letter *i* and the /ī/ sound with the letter *e,* because in their native languages *i* represents a sound similar to English /ē/. These students will need extra practice associating *i* with its English name and the /ī/ sound.

Teacher Tips

BLENDING For words on Lines 1 and 2, refer to Routine 2 for the sound-by-sound blending procedure. If students are ready, refer to Routine 3 for the whole-word procedure for the remaining words on the lines. Use Routine 4 for the blending sentences procedure.

SYLLABICATION To help students blend the words and build fluency, use the syllabication below of the multisyllable words on the word lines.

fright • en	fright • en • ing	light • ning
light • ly	tight • rope	fire • fly
night • time	high • way	

Monitor Progress

to Differentiate Instruction
Formal Assessment

BLENDING To discover whether any student needs extra help with blending, call on two or three students to read each word. During Workshop, provide additional practice for students who need help by pairing them with students who have mastered the blending activity.

APPROACHING LEVEL

IF . . . students have difficulty with the *_igh, _y,* and *_ie* spellings for /ī/, **THEN . . .** have them use ***eSkills*** during Workshop.

ON LEVEL

IF . . . students are on level, **THEN . . .** encourage them to add words that contain the spellings to the word chart.

ABOVE LEVEL

IF . . . students are ready for a challenge, **THEN . . .** encourage them to make up rhymes using words that contain the spellings and to share them with other students.

Phonics

ROUTINE 2 ROUTINE 3 ROUTINE 4 ROUTINE 10 ROUTINE 11

Blending

Use Routine 2, sound-by-sound blending, Routine 3, whole-word blending, and Routine 4, blending sentences, to have students blend the words and sentences. Use Routine 10, closed syllables, and Routine 11, open syllables, to have students blend the multisyllable words.

Line 1	might	tight	light	fright
Line 2	frighten	frightening	lightning	lightly
Line 3	dry	dried	fry	fries
Line 4	tightrope	firefly	nighttime	highway

Sentence 1: The light in my home shines brightly.

Sentence 2: Ty said, "I don't want to sleep too late."

Line 1 **/ī/ spelled _*igh***

Remember to write *igh* as a unit when writing the words.

Line 2 **/ī/ spelled _*igh***

Point out that the words on this line contain words from Line 1. Have students look for a small word, or root word, in each one. *fright, light* The words *frightening* and *lightning* are also in the selection "Hurricanes." Explain the meaning of each word, and have students use them in a sentence.

Line 3 **/ī/ spelled _*y* and *ie***

Have students identify the /ī/ spelling in each word. Point out that the *y* was changed to *i* before the endings *-ed* and *-es* were added.

Line 4 **/ī/ spelled _*igh* and *i_e***

Have students notice that these words are compound words. Have students find and blend the two smaller words and then blend them to read the longer word.

Sentences 1–2

Write the words *my, don't, sleep,* and *too* on the board. Read the words, repeat them, and have students read them. Then spell the words together. Have volunteers use the words in sentences. Write each word on an index card, and add the cards to the High-Frequency Word Bank.

Circle the quotation marks in Sentence 2. Explain that quotation marks go around a speaker's exact words. They help readers understand who is talking. Underline the words the speaker said, and circle the name of the speaker.

Developing Oral Language

To review the words, have students point to and read the following:

- two one-syllable words that begin with the /dr/ blend *dry, dried*
- a two-syllable word that contains the /ō/ sound *tightrope*
- a word that ends with the /ē/ sound *lightly*
- a two-syllable word that contains the /ā/ sound *highway*
- two one-syllable words that rhyme with *sky dry, fry*

Monitor Progress

to Differentiate Instruction
Formal Assessment

DICTATION As students spell words, notice who uses the ***Sound/Spelling Cards*** and spells the words correctly. Note students who are asking for help with the spellings.

APPROACHING LEVEL

IF . . . students need additional practice with phonics and dictation,	**THEN . . .** review the words during Workshop.

ON LEVEL

IF . . . students are on level with phonics and dictation,	**THEN . . .** pair them, and have them play a game from ***eSkills.***

ABOVE LEVEL

IF . . . students need a challenge with phonics and dictation,	**THEN . . .** have them use one of the activities in the ***Workshop Kit.***

Guided Practice

Help students complete ***Skills Practice 1*** pages 211–212 for practice with the /ī/ sound spelled *_igh*, *_y*, and *_ie* and for dictation. Review the sound/spellings at the top of page 211. Have students write the words and sentences at the bottom of the page. Have students choose and write the correct sentence at the top of page 212. Students can use the bottom of the page for dictation.

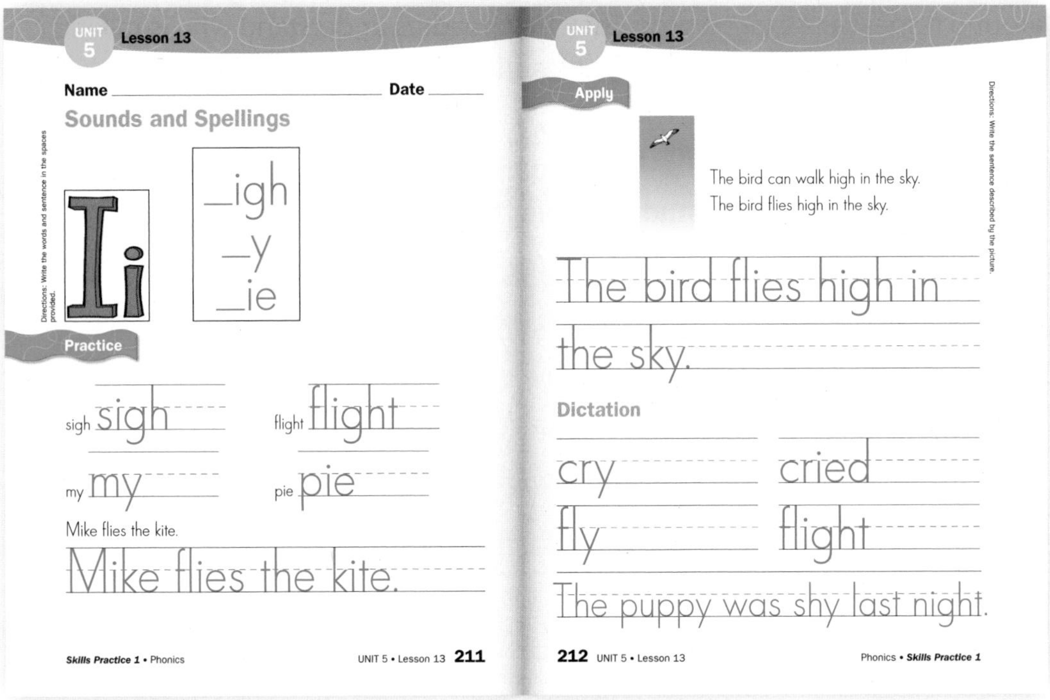
UNIT 5 Lesson 13

Name ______ Date ______

Sounds and Spellings

Ii _igh _y _ie

Directions: Write the words and sentence in the spaces provided.

Practice

sigh sigh flight flight

my my pie pie

Mike flies the kite.

Mike flies the kite.

Skills Practice 1 • Phonics UNIT 5 • Lesson 13 211

UNIT 5 Lesson 13

Apply

Directions: Write the sentence described by the picture.

The bird can walk high in the sky.
The bird flies high in the sky.

The bird flies high in the sky.

Dictation

cry cried

fly flight

The puppy was shy last night.

212 UNIT 5 • Lesson 13 Phonics • *Skills Practice 1*

Skills Practice 1, pp. 211–212

Dictation

ROUTINE 5 ROUTINE 6 ROUTINE 7

- Use Routine 5, sounds-in-sequence dictation, Routine 6, whole-word dictation, and Routine 7, sentence dictation, with the following:

Line 1	cry	cried
Line 2	fly	flight
Sentence	The puppy was shy last night.	

- Help students proofread the words after completing each line. Call attention to the *-ed* spelling at the end of *cried*. Remind students to circle any words or parts of words that could be better and to write the entire word correctly above or beside the original word.

Teacher Tips

HIGH-FREQUENCY WORDS The word *was* is a decodable high-frequency word. Encourage students to write it without sounding it out. If they have difficulty, tell them they can spell the word sound by sound.

SOUND/SPELLING CARDS Remind students to refer to the ***Sound/Spelling Cards.*** Encourage students to ask which /i/ spelling to use.

Fluency/Reading a Decodable Book

ROUTINE 9

Core Decodable 76: *The Opossum at Night*

Phonics Focus: /ī/ Spelled _*igh*

High-Frequency Words

Review the high-frequency word *sleep* that students learned in Blending by writing it on the board, spelling the word, and having students say the word. Have a volunteer use the word in a sentence. Review other high-frequency words by pointing to them in the High-Frequency Word Bank and having students read them.

Reading the Decodable

- ✦ Follow Routine 9, reading a ***Decodable,*** as you read the story with students.
- ✦ Have students read the title, browse the story, and discuss what they think the story will be about.
- ✦ The first time through, have students read a page silently. Then have one student read it aloud. Repeat this procedure for each page.
- ✦ Reread the story at least twice, calling on various students to read. Then have the entire class do a choral reading of the story.

Responding

- ✦ After reading, be sure to talk about the story and answer any questions students have. Ask students to identify any difficult words in the book.
- ✦ Have students retell the story.

The Opossum at Night
by Anne O'Brien
illustrated by
Deborah Colvin Borgo
Opossums do not like the light.
Daytime is bright.
An opossum sees better at night.
3

When it is night, an opossum wakes.
She hunts for insects to feed her babies.
4
A dog frightens the opossum.
The opossum freezes. She stays still and plays dead.
5

Night is over. It begins to get light.

6

The opossum returns to her tree.
Her babies wait for her.

7

It is time for sleep.
The opossum stays with her babies.
They might play later at night.

8

Teacher Tip

SOUND/SPELLING CARDS Remind students to refer to the ***Sound/Spelling Cards*** if they are unsure of a sound/spelling.

✦ As students answer the following questions, make sure they focus on the words in the story rather than getting the answers by listening or from the pictures. Have students answer by pointing to and reading aloud the answers in the text:

- **What don't opossums like?** *light*
- **What do opossums hunt for?** *insects*
- **When night is over, where does the opossum go?** *back to her tree*

Building Fluency

Have students build fluency by rereading ***Core Decodable*** 76 twice with a partner. The first time through, one partner should read the odd-numbered pages and the other partner the even-numbered pages. The second time through, they should switch pages. For additional practice with /ī/ spelled *_igh*, have students read ***Practice Decodable*** 63, *City Lights at Night.* Have students record their readings on their Personal Title sheets, noting the titles of the books, the date, and any difficult words they encountered.

Core Decodable 76

The Opossum at Night

High-Frequency Word Introduced in Core Decodable 76

sleep

Previously Introduced High-Frequency Words

a	do	his	red	walk
after	down	I	ride	was
all	every	if	said	way
am	for	in	see	we
an	get	is	she	well
and	girl	it	six	went
as	go	its	some	were
ask	going	jump	take	what
at	got	just	that	when
be	green	like	the	will
big	had	little	them	with
boy	has	look	then	yes
but	have	make	there	you
call	he	of	they	
can	help	on	this	
could	her	or	to	
day	here	out	two	
did	him	over	up	

Sound/Spelling Correspondences in Core Decodables

1. Pre-decodable
2. Pre-decodable
3. Pre-decodable
4. Pre-decodable
5. Pre-decodable
6. /s/ spelled *s*, /m/ spelled *m*, /a/ spelled *a*
7. /t/ spelled *t, tt*
8. Review
9. /d/ spelled *d*
10. /n/ spelled *n*
11. /i/ spelled *i*
12. /h/ spelled *h_*
13. Review
14. /p/ spelled *p*
15. /l/ spelled *l, ll*
16. /o/ spelled *o*
17. /b/ spelled *b*
18. Review
19. /k/ spelled *c*
20. /aw/ spelled *al*
21. /k/ spelled *k*, ■*ck*
22. /r/ spelled *r*
23. /f/ spelled *f, ff*
24. /s/ spelled *ss*
25. Review
26. /g/ spelled *g*
27. /j/ spelled *j*, ■*dge*
28. /u/ spelled *u*
29. /z/ spelled *z, zz*
30. /z/ spelled *_s*
31. Review
32. /ks/ spelled ■*x*
33. /e/ spelled *e*
34. -ed ending: /ed/, /d/
35. -ed ending: /t/
36. /e/ spelled *_ea_*
37. Review
38. /sh/ spelled *sh*
39. /th/ spelled *th*
40. /ch/ spelled *ch*, ■*tch*
41. /or/ spelled *or, ore*
42. Review
43. /ar/ spelled *ar*
44. /m/ spelled *_mb*
45. /w/ spelled *w_*
46. /hw/ spelled *wh_*
47. /er/ spelled *er, ir*
48. /er/ spelled *ur*
49. Review
50. Schwa
51. Review schwa
52. /ng/ spelled ■*ng*
53. /nk/ spelled ■*nk*
54. /kw/ spelled *qu_*
55. Review
56. /y/ spelled *y_*
57. /v/ spelled *v*
58. Syllable -le
59. /ā/ spelled *a* and *a_e*
60. Review
61. /ī/ spelled *i* and *i_e*
62. /s/ spelled *ce, ci_*
63. /j/ spelled *ge, gi_*
64. Review
65. /ō/ spelled *o* and *o_e*
66. /ū/ spelled *u* and *u_e*
67. Review
68. /ē/ spelled *e* and *e_e*
69. /ē/ spelled *ee* and *ea*
70. Review
71. /ē/ spelled *_y, _ie_*
72. /s/ spelled *cy*
73. Review /s/ spellings
74. Review
75. /ā/ spelled *ai_, _ay*
76. /ī/ spelled *_igh*

Decodable 76, inside back cover

Fluency/Reading a Decodable Book

ROUTINE 9

Core Decodable 77: Why, Bly?

Phonics Focus: /ī/ Spelled _ie and _y

High-Frequency Words

Review the high-frequency words *don't, my,* and *too* that students learned in Blending by writing them on the board, spelling the words, and having students say the words. Have a volunteer use the words in sentences. Ask students what kind of word *don't* is. *contraction* Then ask them what two words make *don't. do and not* Review other high-frequency words by pointing to them in the High-Frequency Word Bank and having students read them.

Reading the Decodable

- Follow Routine 9, reading a ***Decodable,*** as you read the story with students.
- Have students read the title, browse the story, and discuss what they think the story will be about.
- The first time through, have students read a page silently. Then have one student read it aloud. Repeat this procedure for each page.
- Reread the story at least twice, calling on various students to read. Then have the entire class do a choral reading of the story.

Responding

- After reading, be sure to talk about the story and answer any questions the students have. Ask students to identify any difficult words in the book.

by Dottie Raymer

Bly likes her head in dry sand.

"Why not lie in the sun?" asks Snake.
"I get too hot in the sun," Bly replies.
4
"Why not climb trees?" asks Chimp.
"I can't climb trees," Bly replies.
5

Teacher Tip

SOUND/SPELLING CARDS Remind students to refer to the ***Sound/Spelling Cards*** if they are unsure of a sound/spelling.

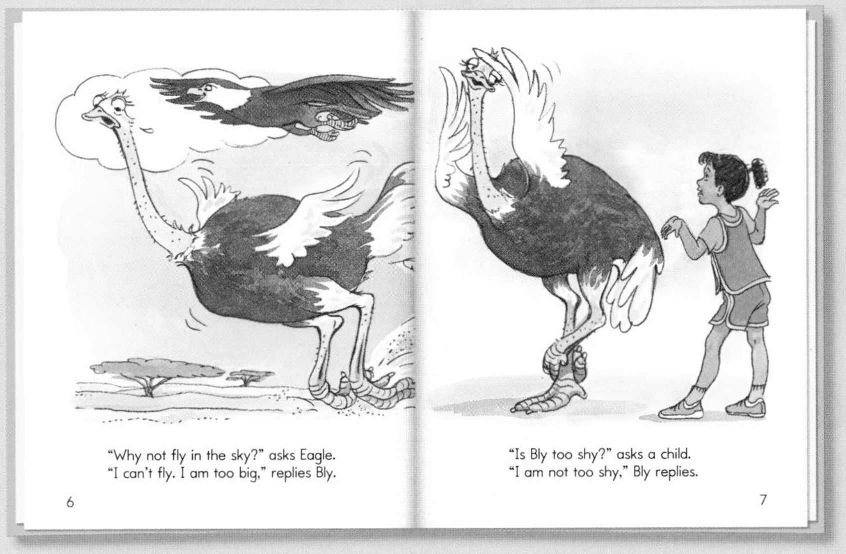

"Why not fly in the sky?" asks Eagle.
"I can't fly. I am too big," replies Bly.
6
"Is Bly too shy?" asks a child.
"I am not too shy," Bly replies.
7

"My head feels better in sand," explains Bly.
8

✦ Have students retell the story.

✦ As students answer the following questions, make sure they focus on the words in the story rather than getting the answers by listening or from the pictures. Have students answer by pointing to and reading aloud the answers in the text:

- **Where does Bly like her head?** *in the sand*
- **What can't Bly climb?** *trees*
- **Why can't Bly fly?** *She's too big.*

Building Fluency

Have students build fluency by rereading ***Core Decodable*** 77 twice with a partner. The first time through, one partner should read the odd-numbered pages and the other partner the even-numbered pages. The second time through, they should switch pages. For additional practice with /ī/ spelled *_ie* and *_y*, have students read ***Practice Decodable*** 64, *Trying Weather.* Have students record their readings on their Personal Title Sheets, noting the title of each book, the date, and any difficult words they encountered.

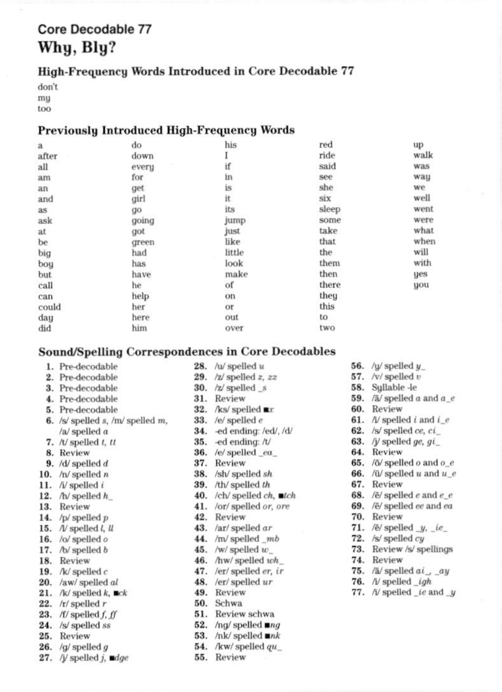

Core Decodable 77

Why, Bly?

High-Frequency Words Introduced in Core Decodable 77

don't
my
too

Previously Introduced High-Frequency Words

a	do	his	red	up
after	down	I	ride	walk
all	every	if	said	was
am	for	in	see	way
an	get	is	she	we
and	girl	it	six	well
as	go	its	sleep	went
ask	going	jump	some	were
at	got	just	take	what
be	green	like	that	when
big	had	little	the	will
boy	has	look	them	with
but	have	make	then	yes
call	he	of	there	you
can	help	on	they	
could	her	or	this	
day	here	out	to	
did	him	over	two	

Sound/Spelling Correspondences in Core Decodables

1. Pre-decodable
2. Pre-decodable
3. Pre-decodable
4. Pre-decodable
5. Pre-decodable
6. /s/ spelled *s,* /m/ spelled *m,* /a/ spelled *a*
7. /t/ spelled *t, tt*
8. Review
9. /d/ spelled *d*
10. /n/ spelled *n*
11. /i/ spelled *i*
12. /h/ spelled *h_*
13. Review
14. /p/ spelled *p*
15. /l/ spelled *l, ll*
16. /o/ spelled *o*
17. /b/ spelled *b*
18. Review
19. /k/ spelled *c*
20. /aw/ spelled *al*
21. /k/ spelled *k,* ■*ck*
22. /r/ spelled *r*
23. /f/ spelled *f, ff*
24. /s/ spelled *ss*
25. Review
26. /g/ spelled *g*
27. /j/ spelled *j,* ■*dge*
28. /u/ spelled *u*
29. /z/ spelled *z, zz*
30. /z/ spelled *_s*
31. Review
32. /ks/ spelled ■*x*
33. /e/ spelled *e*
34. -ed ending: /ed/, /d/
35. -ed ending: /t/
36. /e/ spelled *_ea_*
37. Review
38. /sh/ spelled *sh*
39. /th/ spelled *th*
40. /ch/ spelled *ch,* ■*tch*
41. /or/ spelled *or, ore*
42. Review
43. /ar/ spelled *ar*
44. /m/ spelled *_mb*
45. /w/ spelled *w_*
46. /hw/ spelled *wh_*
47. /er/ spelled *er, ir*
48. /er/ spelled *ur*
49. Review
50. Schwa
51. Review schwa
52. /ng/ spelled ■*ng*
53. /nk/ spelled ■*nk*
54. /kw/ spelled *qu_*
55. Review
56. /y/ spelled *y_*
57. /v/ spelled *v*
58. Syllable -le
59. /ā/ spelled *a* and *a_e*
60. Review
61. /ī/ spelled *i* and *i_e*
62. /s/ spelled *ce, ci_*
63. /j/ spelled *ge, gi_*
64. Review
65. /ō/ spelled *o* and *o_e*
66. /ū/ spelled *u* and *u_e*
67. Review
68. /ē/ spelled *e* and *e_e*
69. /ē/ spelled *ee* and *ea*
70. Review
71. /ē/ spelled *_y, _ie_*
72. /s/ spelled *cy*
73. Review /s/ spellings
74. Review
75. /ā/ spelled *ai_, _ay*
76. /ī/ spelled *_igh*
77. /ī/ spelled *_ie* and *_y*

Decodable 77, inside back cover

Day 3

Reading and Responding

OBJECTIVES

Students will

- activate prior knowledge about hurricanes.
- understand and use a Table of Contents.
- set and check purposes for reading.
- learn vocabulary words.
- use the comprehension strategies Making Connections, Clarifying, and Summarizing.
- use the comprehension skill Cause and Effect.
- understand paragraphs.

MATERIALS

- ***First Reader,*** pp. 28–35
- Routines 12, 13
- Writer's Notebooks
- ***Transparency*** 14

Teacher Tips

MAKE CONNECTIONS Before reading the selection, you may want to have students review pages 22–25 of "When a Storm Comes Up." Students will be better prepared to make connections to this previously read selection.

TALKING ABOUT STORMS Some students in your classroom may have experienced severe hurricanes. Before reading this selection, be aware that these students may find it upsetting to read or talk about hurricanes. Take time to talk privately with them and their families about their experiences and to look for ways to accommodate their specific needs.

MATERIALS For the vocabulary review activity, write the selection vocabulary words and additional vocabulary words on individual index cards.

Build Background

Activate Prior Knowledge

- Ask students to recall the main ideas from selections they have read or listened to in this unit to answer the following questions:
  - What is a hurricane? *one of the worst kinds of storms*
  - Where do hurricanes form? *over the ocean*
  - What happens when a hurricane moves over land? *It causes floods, washes away beaches, and blows down trees and houses.*
  - What does a weather service do when a hurricane might be forming? *It tracks where the hurricane might go and warns people to take shelter.*
  - What does the word *dangerous* mean? Dangerous *means that something is unsafe.*

Preview and Prepare

ROUTINE 12

Browse

- Follow Routine 12, reading the selection, to prepare students to read the story. Begin by displaying the cover of the ***First Reader.*** Point to and read aloud the title.
- Have students locate and turn to the Table of Contents, and point to the title of the selection, "Hurricanes." Have students read the title along with you as you point to it. Point to the page number 28, and have a volunteer read it and tell what the number means. Turn to page 28.
- Demonstrate how to browse the selection by commenting on the title and the illustrations and predicting how they might relate to the text. On page 29, for example, you might say: *I know hurricanes begin over the ocean, and this is a picture of the ocean, so I think this page will be about how hurricanes begin. I'll check that as we read.*
- Have students browse the first few pages to look for clues to what the selection is about and for difficult or unfamiliar words. Students might have difficulty with the word *violent*. Tell students that when the text says hurricanes can be violent, it means that hurricanes can be very dangerous.

Set Purposes

- Have students think about the information they gained while browsing. Ask students to use this information to tell what the purposes for reading this selection might be. Write the purpose on the board. Some suggestions are the following:
  - To learn more about hurricanes
  - To learn about the damage that hurricanes can do
- Discuss their purposes for reading the selection. Explain to students that they may need to adjust their reading rate based on their purposes. For example, when they are reading to gain more information, they may need to read the text more slowly in order to better understand the facts from the selection.
- After reading the selection, have students return to these purposes.

Fluency

- With the ***First Reader*** stories, students begin the transition to reading more challenging text. Have students adjust their reading rate based on this new challenging text.
- Have students apply letter-sound knowledge to decode phonetically regular words quickly and accurately as they read this selection.
- As students read "Hurricanes," have them focus on accuracy and expression. Remind students to pause at end punctuation marks.

Teacher Tips

GLOSSARY The words *swirling* (page 28), *tornado* (page 32), *floods* (page 33), *lightning* (page 33), and *shatter* (page 33) appear in the Glossary. As students browse and identify interesting words or phrases, you may want to use the opportunity to have students practice glossary use. Have students locate and turn to the Glossary, find each word, and read each entry.

HIGH-FREQUENCY WORDS As students browse, you may want to have them look for the high-frequency words they know. The following are some of the high-frequency words that appear in the selection: *a, is, it, has, and, in, the, or, that, when, big, to, over, two, have, of, do, go.*

BIG Idea

What is weather?

Before reading the selection, reread the Big Idea question. Tell students to keep this question in mind as they listen to the selection.

Differentiating Instruction — English Learners

IF . . . students need help with reading fluency, **THEN . . .** have them first listen as you read aloud a short section of text, and then have them read aloud the same text themselves.

Selection Vocabulary

tornado a storm with strong winds that move in a circle and heavy rain that forms over land (page 32)

shatter to break into pieces (page 33)

Teacher Tip

SEMANTIC MAP Have students continue building onto the semantic map. Encourage them add selection vocabulary words and words that they have learned throughout the unit.

Concept/Question Board

Have students search for information about tornadoes. This can include pictures or detailed articles that talk about different sightings of tornadoes. Provide different Web sites and books that students can use for their research. Post this information on the **Concept/Question Board.**

Building Vocabulary

ROUTINE 13

- Use Routine 13, selection vocabulary, to introduce the vocabulary words to students. Write the words on the board or on a transparency.
- To help students understand the meaning of *tornado,* have them look at the illustration on page 32 of their ***First Reader*** and at page 22 in their ***What's the Weather? Big Book.*** Have students explain what they see in the illustration.
- To help students understand the meaning of *shatter,* have them look at the illustration on page 33 of their ***First Reader.*** Have students explain what they see in the illustration.
  - Remind students that they have read about tornadoes before. Ask them to recall any additional information about tornadoes, using the word *tornado* as they talk. **Possible Answers** *A tornado is one of the worst storms. A tornado is funnel shaped. A tornado whirls.*
  - Demonstrate the meaning of *shatter* by pretending to drop a glass that breaks. React by putting your hands to your face and saying *I didn't mean to shatter the glass!*
- You will introduce four expanding vocabulary words to students as the selection is reread. These words are identified in boxes where they appear in the selection. As you come to each word in the selection, read to students the word, the definition, and the sample sentence. Understanding these words will help students better comprehend the selection.

Monitor Progress to Differentiate Instruction

Formal Assessment

DECODING As students read, notice how they are decoding words containing sound/spellings they have learned.

APPROACHING LEVEL	**IF . . .** students are having difficulty decoding previously learned sound/spellings,	**THEN . . .** review problem sound/spellings with students during Workshop.
ON LEVEL	**IF . . .** students are able to decode most previously learned sound/spellings,	**THEN . . .** remind them to use the ***Sound/Spelling Cards*** to help them.
ABOVE LEVEL	**IF . . .** students are able to decode all the words in the story,	**THEN . . .** have them practice reading the story for fluency during Workshop.

Reading the Selection

Genre Informational Writing

Tell students that "Hurricanes" is an example of informational writing. It was written to explain and provide information about hurricanes and the damage they can do.

Briefly review some of the elements of informational writing:

- It contains facts that can be checked in other sources.
- It is about real people, animals, places, or events.

Comprehension Strategies

As students read "Hurricanes," model and prompt the use of the following comprehension strategies:

- Making Connections
- Clarifying
- Summarizing

Comprehension Skills

As students reread "Hurricanes," apply the comprehension skill Cause and Effect.

Reading with a Writer's Eye

As students read "Hurricanes," discuss the author's purpose in writing the selection.

Focus Questions

Read and discuss the Focus Questions on page 28. Encourage students to think about the questions as they read "Hurricanes."

Reading Recommendations

ROUTINE 12

Day 3 Students will read the entire selection twice today. Follow Routine 12, reading the selection. The first time, model and prompt the use of the comprehension strategies. The second time, focus on the comprehension skills and the Reading with a Writer's Eye element.

Differentiating Instruction English Learner

IF . . . English learners are having difficulty with informational writing, **THEN . . .** refer to the ***English Learner Support Guide*** Unit 5 Lesson 13.

Teacher Tips

1st READ

PARTNER READING LIST Have students add information about this selection to their Partner Reading Lists. Remind them to write the title of the selection and the date they read it. If they also read the selection in a group, have them write the names of the group members.

THEME CONNECTIONS Remind students that as they read, they should think about how the selection relates to the theme What's the Weather? and about how it might help them generate ideas for Inquiry.

2nd READ

2nd READ

READING THE SELECTION If students are struggling with the ***First Reader*** stories, read "Hurricanes" to the class, focusing on reading at an appropriate rate and with expression. During the second reading, have students read the selection chorally.

EFFECTIVE COMMUNICATION Remind students to speak clearly and use describing words when they make connections and share their personal experiences.

Phonics

Words in the selection containing sound/spellings from recent phonics lessons appear in boxes like this throughout the selection. At the end of the first reading, students should be prompted to identify the sound/spellings of these words.

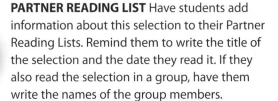

Reading and Responding

Focus Questions What is a hurricane? What is the "eye" of a hurricane?

Hurricanes

A hurricane is a violent storm. It has swirling winds and heavy rain. 1

Hurricanes begin in the ocean. Most hurricanes happen in the late summer or fall. That is when the ocean water is very warm. 2

28

29

First Reader, pp. 28–29

Teacher Tips

GLOSSARY The word *swirling* on page 28 can be found in the Glossary.

CLARIFYING Be sure students understand the selection. Tell them to reread and ask clarifying questions when they do not understand ideas in the text.

SELF-CORRECT As students read, have them self-correct when subsequent reading indicates an earlier misreading.

1st READ

Comprehension Strategies

1 Making Connections Teacher Modeling: *I've never been in a hurricane, but on television, I've seen the damage they can do.*

2 Clarifying Teacher Prompt: *Sometimes, the ocean is warm. How does that help form a hurricane? Let's think about our tornado experiment to figure out how a hurricane forms. Can someone summarize the experiment?* **Possible Student Response** *The tornado formed when cool, heavy water pressed down on warm air. The warm air pushed up and swirled through the cool water.*

3 Summarizing Teacher Modeling: *I'm going to summarize to make sure I understand this information. The swirling winds are pushed out of the eye, or middle, of a hurricane. The eye is quiet because it has almost no wind.*

Hurricanes are very big. During a hurricane, fast winds begin to gust in a huge circle over the ocean. A hurricane's winds may reach two hundred miles per hour! Some hurricanes have winds that are even faster.

The middle of the hurricane is called the "eye" of the hurricane. The swirling winds do not go into the eye. They are pushed out. It is very quiet in the eye of the hurricane. Almost no wind is there. 3

30

31

First Reader, pp. 30–31

Comprehension Skills

2nd READ

Cause and Effect

Display ***Transparency*** 14. Then remind students that a *cause* is why something happens, and an *effect* is what happens. Ask students to identify the causes and the effects on pages 29 and 31. *On page 29, the very warm ocean water is a cause; a hurricane is an effect of that cause. On page 31, the winds do not go into the eye; they are pushed out. No winds blow in the eye, so it is quiet.* Then have students tell you where on ***Transparency*** 14 to record each response.

Reading with a Writer's Eye

2nd READ

Author's Purpose

Remind students that "Hurricanes" is informational writing. Have them briefly review elements of informational writing.

Expanding Vocabulary

swirling going around and around in a circle (pages 28, 31)

The water was *swirling* down the drain.

late near the end (page 29)

I get tired *late* in the evening.

Differentiating Instruction: English Learners

IF . . . students have difficulty identifying and discussing causes and effects,

THEN . . . introduce or review vocabulary related to cause and effect, such as *because, since, therefore, as a result,* and *so.*

Reading and Responding

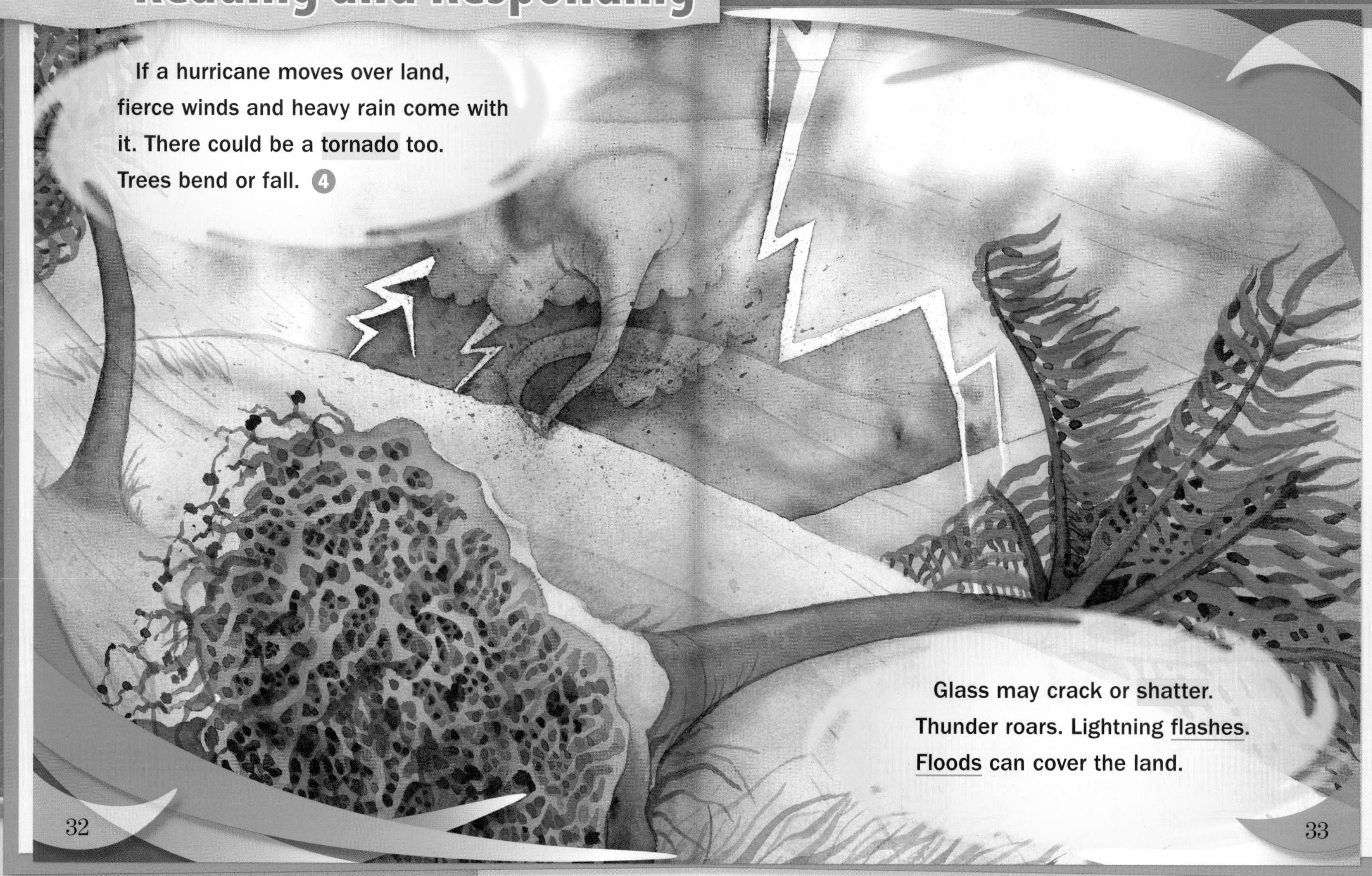

If a hurricane moves over land, fierce winds and heavy rain come with it. There could be a tornado too. Trees bend or fall. 4
Glass may crack or shatter. Thunder roars. Lightning flashes. Floods can cover the land.
32
33

First Reader, pp. 32–33

Phonics

/ī/ spelled *igh:* Lightning (page 33)

Vocabulary Tip

glossary The words *tornado* (page 32), *floods* (page 33), *lightning* (page 33), and *shatter* (page 33) can be found in the Glossary.

1st READ

Comprehension Strategies

4 **Clarifying** Teacher Modeling: *Hurricanes form over water, and tornadoes form over land, so how do hurricanes cause tornadoes? I'll reread to see if that helps clarify this idea. Now I see. A hurricane can cause tornadoes when it moves over land.*

5 **Summarizing** Teacher Prompt: *To make sure we remember this information about hurricanes, I'm going to summarize. Hurricanes are big violent storms. They form over the ocean. Who can help me finish the summary?* **Possible Student Responses** *The winds in a hurricane swirl. The eye of a hurricane has no winds. Hurricanes can cause tornadoes and can do a lot of damage.*

Comprehension Check

How can we stay safe if a hurricane comes? We can leave the area.

Hurricanes can be scary. Today we know when a hurricane will happen.
We know when to leave our homes and when to come back. It is important to be safe during a hurricane. 5
34
35

First Reader, pp. 34–35

Comprehension Skills

2nd READ

Cause and Effect

Remind students that a *cause* is why something happens, and an *effect* is what happens. Then have students identify the effects of a hurricane. *On pages 32 and 33, glass can shatter; trees can bend; floods can cover the land.*

Reading with a Writer's Eye

2nd READ

Author's Purpose

Tell students that "Hurricanes" has no characters or dialogue, and the information described is real. Then ask why they think the author used informational writing. **Possible Answer** *Hurricanes are scary, and the author wanted to make the writing sound serious so readers would pay attention to the facts.*

Vocabulary Tip

flashes a form of the verb **flash:** to be suddenly bright (page 33)

The *flashes* of color at the fireworks are fun to watch.

floods Plural of **flood:** a lot of water that flows over normally dry land (page 33)

The *floods* were caused by too much rain.

Writer's Notebook

Have students use the text and illustrations in "Hurricanes" to help them draw pictures that show an idea from the selection, such as the eye of a hurricane or the swirling air of a hurricane over water. Help them each write a sentence to describe what they have drawn. Encourage them to use action words in their sentences.

Concept/Question Board

Encourage students to think of any new questions they might have about hurricanes after reading this selection. Tell them to post these questions on the **Concept/Question Board.** Have them check to see whether they can use what they have learned from the selection to help them answer other questions on the Board.

Teacher Tip

AUTHOR'S PURPOSE Remind students that when they do their own writing, they should think about their purpose for writing and choose the kind of writing that will be best for their topic and audience.

BIG Idea

What is weather?

After reading the story, read the Big Idea question. Discuss with students how the story helps answer this question.

Discussing the Selection

✦ Before discussing the selection, have students retell the story. Remind them to use effective communication when they retell the facts of the selection. Have them use appropriate volume and describing words, and remind them to speak clearly.

✦ As the class discusses the selection, tell students to participate courteously in the discussion. Tell students they should listen attentively and take turns.

✦ Ask students the following to check their comprehension of "Hurricanes":

- *When and why do hurricanes form? In late summer or fall; cool air presses down on the warm air over the ocean, and the air starts to swirl and rise.*
- *How strong are the winds in a hurricane? The winds can be more than two hundred miles per hour, which is strong enough to shatter glass and make trees bend.*
- *What is the eye of a hurricane? the middle part, where there is no wind*

✦ Have students return to the Focus Questions on page 28 of the story. Select a student to read the questions aloud, and have students answer and discuss the questions. Encourage students to return to the text when answering their questions.

✦ Talk about comprehension strategies used as students read the selection. Have students think about how they used strategies to help them better understand the selection.

- *How did you make connections with information in the text?* **Possible Answer** *I remembered making snow people with my older brother.*
- *How did you clarify words or confusing passages?* **Possible Answer** *I clarified things that confused me by looking at the words I already know to figure out the ideas I didn't know.*
- *How did summarizing help you understand the story?* **Possible Answer** *Summarizing helped me remember information from the beginning of the story.*

✦ Previously, students were read "When a Storm Comes Up." Have them discuss the details from "When a Storm Comes Up" as well as any other weather-related selections and how these details help them know the information in "Hurricanes" is true.

Purposes for Reading

Review the purposes set for reading "Hurricanes." Have students tell whether they met their purposes for reading. Have them identify information from the text that talks about the purposes:

- To learn more about hurricanes
- To learn about the damage hurricanes can do

Vocabulary Review

Review the selection vocabulary words by calling a volunteer to the front of the room. Give him or her a card, and whisper the word on the card to the student. Have the student either role-play the meaning of the word or give clues for the class to guess its meaning. For example, for *tornado,* the student might turn around in a circle several times. For *shatter,* the student might pantomime throwing something at the window, following the model you used to introduce that word.

Print and Book Awareness

Print and Book Awareness

Introduce: Paragraphs

- Display ***Language Arts Big Book*** page 94. Read aloud the definition of a paragraph: *A paragraph is a group of sentences that go together. They tell about the same thing.* Explain that a paragraph can give more information about a topic than just one sentence.
- Use the example on the page to explain how sentences go together. Ask students what one thing the three sentences are about. *Coco the cat's day* Point out that although all the sentences tell about the cat, each sentence tells something new that he did during the day. The sentences go together. They make a paragraph about one thing—what Coco the cat did in one day.
- Display page 95. Read the final paragraph about Coco the cat's day. Point out the sentences the writer added to the beginning and the end of the paragraph. Explain that the first sentence tells what the paragraph will be about and that the last sentence states a conclusion. Have students note that the first line of the paragraph is slightly indented.
- Have students look at page 30 of "Hurricanes." Reread the page with them. Ask them what the paragraph is about. *how big and powerful hurricanes are* Help them see how each sentence in the paragraph adds information to show how big and powerful hurricanes are.
- Have students identify other paragraphs in the selection, noting what each one is about. For each paragraph, have them notice the indented first line.

Differentiating Instruction **English Learners**

IF . . . students have difficulty participating in the discussion, **THEN . . .** ask questions that can be answered with a nod, a yes or no, or a short phrase. Examples: *Is the eye of a hurricane in the middle?* *yes* *When do hurricanes form?* *in the fall*

Teacher Tips

HIGH-FREQUENCY WORDS To help students review the high-frequency words they have learned, say some of the words aloud, and have students point to each one in the selection. Remind them to look at the High-Frequency Word Bank for help.

WORD BANK Have students add the selection vocabulary words to the What's the Weather? Word Bank.

Selection Vocabulary

tornado (page 32)
shatter (page 33)

Phonics

Have students practice identifying sound/spellings from recent lessons. Turn to a page in the selection, and say a sound/spelling that appears on that page. Then have students point to the word with that sound/spelling. Remind them to look at ***Sound/Spelling Cards*** for help.

Day 3

Language Arts

OBJECTIVES

Students will

- use a sequence map to draft a set of instructions.
- understand and use action verbs and time and order words.
- practice forming plural nouns by changing *y* to *i* and adding *es.*

MATERIALS

- ***Routine*** 14
- ***Transparency*** 42
- ***Skills Practice 1,*** pp. 207, 213–214
- ***Sound/Spelling Cards***
- ***Language Arts Big Book,*** p. 162
- Writer's Notebooks

Teacher Tip

PEER EDITING Reinforce the use of time and order words by having students trade their instruction drafts with partners. Tell students to identify the time and order and action words their partners used. Then have the pairs talk about what other similar words they could add to their sentences.

Traits of Good Writing

Vocabulary Writers use action words to make their writing more exciting and interesting.

Writing Instructions

ROUTINE 14

Drafting

Teach—Using Action Verbs

- Tell students it is important to use action verbs when writing instructions. When telling someone how to do something, they should be careful to choose a verb that describes the action well so readers will know what to do. Remind them that every sentence needs to have nouns, a verb, and subject-verb agreement. If necessary, briefly model the correct sentence structure of a complete sentence.

- Before students begin to draft their instructions, remind them to think about what their purpose is for writing them. Remind them that during the Reading with a Writer's Eye activity, they learned that if an audience knows the author's purpose, they may better understand what they are reading.

Guided Practice

- Display ***Transparency*** 42, which contains the ideas you recorded for writing instructions. Review the map with students, and ask whether you should add any information.

- **Teacher Modeling** Next, model how to use the map to write sentences in the correct order. *I'll write a sentence for each idea on the map. I'll begin with the first step.* Write your sentences on the board or on chart paper. Be sure to use and point out any action verbs.

Writing Instructions, cont.

Apply

- Help students use their sequence map on ***Skills Practice 1*** page 207 to write sentences about the topic they have selected. Tell them to keep their audience and purpose in mind as they write. Encourage them to follow your model and turn each idea, phrase, or picture from their sequence map into a sentence or two in their instructions.
- Remind them to use time and order words and action words such as *put, stay,* and *go* in their sentences. They can use the ***Sound/Spelling Cards*** and the High Frequency Word Bank to check their spelling.
- Circulate among small groups of students, and spend a few minutes with each to review their writing and answer any questions.

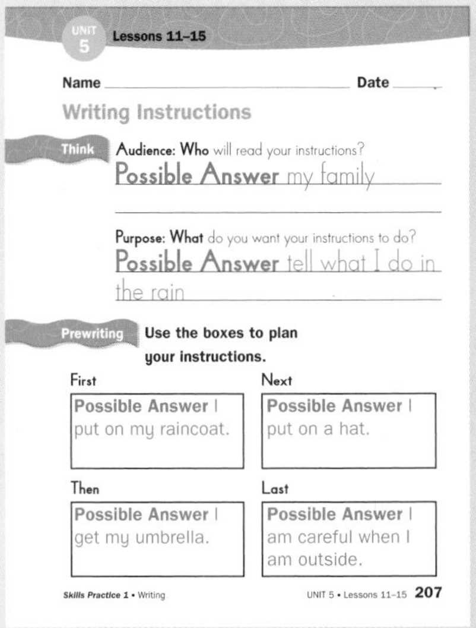
UNIT 5 Lessons 11–15

Name ______ Date ______

Writing Instructions

Think Audience: Who will read your instructions?
Possible Answer my family

Purpose: What do you want your instructions to do?
Possible Answer tell what I do in the rain

Prewriting Use the boxes to plan your instructions.

First	Next
Possible Answer I put on my raincoat.	Possible Answer I put on a hat.
Then	**Last**
Possible Answer I get my umbrella.	Possible Answer I am careful when I am outside.

Skills Practice 1 • Writing UNIT 5 • Lessons 11–15 207

Skills Practice 1, p. 207

Monitor Progress to Differentiate Instruction

Formal Assessment

WORD CHOICE Read students' drafts to see whether they have used action verbs and time and order words correctly in writing instructions.

APPROACHING LEVEL

IF . . .	THEN . . .
IF . . . students need additional practice with word choice,	**THEN . . .** write a list of action verbs on the board for students to choose from. Review time and order words during Workshop, and then model how to use them in the students' writing.

ON LEVEL

IF . . .	THEN . . .
IF . . . students understand how to use action verbs and time and order words,	**THEN . . .** have partners exchange drafts and point out the action verbs and time and order words in each other's work.

ABOVE LEVEL

IF . . .	THEN . . .
IF . . . students are ready for a challenge,	**THEN . . .** have them search for and copy action verbs and time and order words in the ***Little Big Books.***

Concept/Question Board

Tell students to check the **Concept/ Question Board** and the What's the Weather? Word Bank for words and information to use in writing their instructions.

Teacher Tip

GRAMMAR To help students memorize the rule, have them say the "more than one" rhyme:

"For more than one,
no need to guess.
Change *y* to *i* and add *es*."

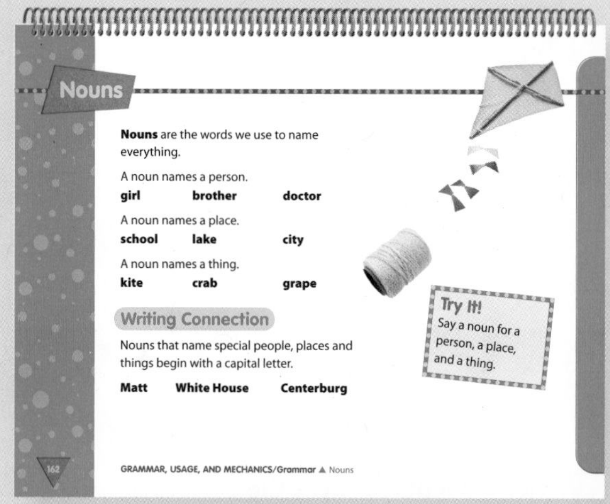

Language Arts Big Book, p. 162

Grammar, Usage, and Mechanics

Review Plural Nouns: Change *y* to *i* and Add *es*

Teach

- Use ***Language Arts Big Book*** page 162 to review singular and plural nouns and how to form the plural of most nouns. *by adding* s
- Next ask a volunteer how to form the plural of a noun that ends in a consonant followed by *y*. *change the* y *to* i *and add* es

Guided Practice

- Write the following words on the board, and ask students to tell you how to spell the plural form of each word:

try *tries*	storm *storms*	lily *lilies*
cloud *clouds*	buggy *buggies*	day *days*

- If students misspell *days,* have them notice that the letter before the *y* is a vowel. Remind them that the *y* changes to *i* after a consonant.
- Have students copy these words from the board and then work with partners to write their plural forms:

play *plays*   family *families*   sky *skies*

- Finally, write the sentences below on the board. Tell students to copy them into their Writer's Notebooks and edit each sentence by changing the nouns ending with *y* into their plural forms. Circulate to help students decode unfamiliar words.
  - My sister and I rode pony at the park. *ponies*
  - Aunt Bess has twin baby. *babies*
  - Dad gave us two puppy. *puppies*

Plural Nouns, cont.

Apply

- Have students work in small groups to complete ***Skills Practice 1*** pages 213–214. Complete the first few practice problems as a class, and then circulate and answer questions as students complete the pages. If necessary, review the instruction with students to help with any reading or decodability issues.
- If time permits, have students use some of the words ending in *y* from the Guided Practice section to compose new sentences in their Writer's Notebooks. Circulate to help with any reading as students practice using this grammar skill. Then tell them to share with partners their favorite sentence using a plural noun.

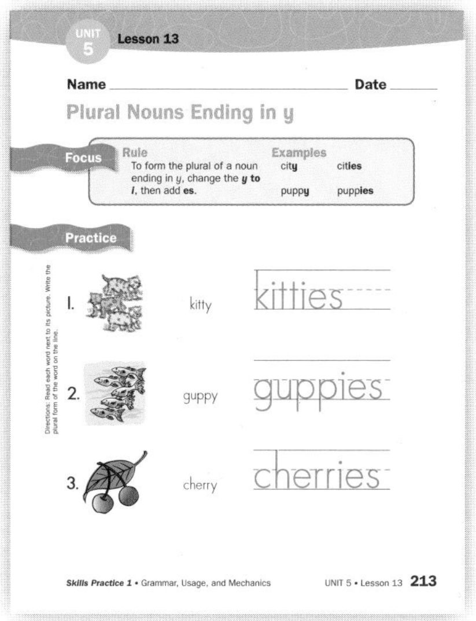
UNIT 5 Lesson 13

Name ______ Date ______

Plural Nouns Ending in y

Focus
Rule: To form the plural of a noun ending in y, change the y to i, then add es.
Examples: city — cities; puppy — puppies

Practice

1. kitty — kitties
2. guppy — guppies
3. cherry — cherries

Skills Practice 1 • Grammar, Usage, and Mechanics — UNIT 5 • Lesson 13 213

Skills Practice 1, p. 213

UNIT 5 Lesson 13

Apply

bunny puppy pony library

Across: 2. puppies 4. libraries

Down: 1. bunnies 3. ponies

214 UNIT 5 • Lesson 13 — Grammar, Usage, and Mechanics • Skills Practice 1

Skills Practice 1, p. 214

Monitor Progress
to Differentiate Instruction
Formal Assessment

PLURAL NOUNS As students practice spelling plural nouns, note which students memorize the "more than one" rhyme and respond quickly.

APPROACHING LEVEL

IF . . . students need additional practice with forming plural nouns,	**THEN . . .** have them complete ***Reteach 1*** pages 155–156.
IF . . . students have difficulty with the concept after working on the ***Reteach 1*** pages,	**THEN . . .** complete ***Intervention Guide*** Unit 5 Lesson 13, or play the Singular and Plural Nouns game from the ***Workshop Kit*** with them during Workshop.

ON LEVEL

IF . . . students understand the concept but need practice,	**THEN . . .** have them play the Singular and Plural Nouns grammar game from the ***Workshop Kit.***

ABOVE LEVEL

IF . . . students are ready for a challenge with plural nouns,	**THEN . . .** have them complete ***Challenge Activities 1*** page 78.

Differentiating Instruction: English Learners

IF . . . students have difficulty completing the ***Skills Practice 1*** pages independently,
THEN . . . pair them with proficient English speakers and have the partners complete the pages together.

OBJECTIVES

Students will

- blend, spell, and read words that contain /ī/ spelled *_igh*, *_y*, and *_ie.*

MATERIALS

- Routines 3–4, 8, 10–11
- ***Sound/Spelling Card*** 29
- ***Skills Practice 1,*** pp. 215–216

Daily Warm-Ups

Copy the Morning Message on the board or on chart paper. Have students answer the question. Read the message aloud, and discuss it with students. **Possible Answer** *I have learned that there are many different kinds of weather.*

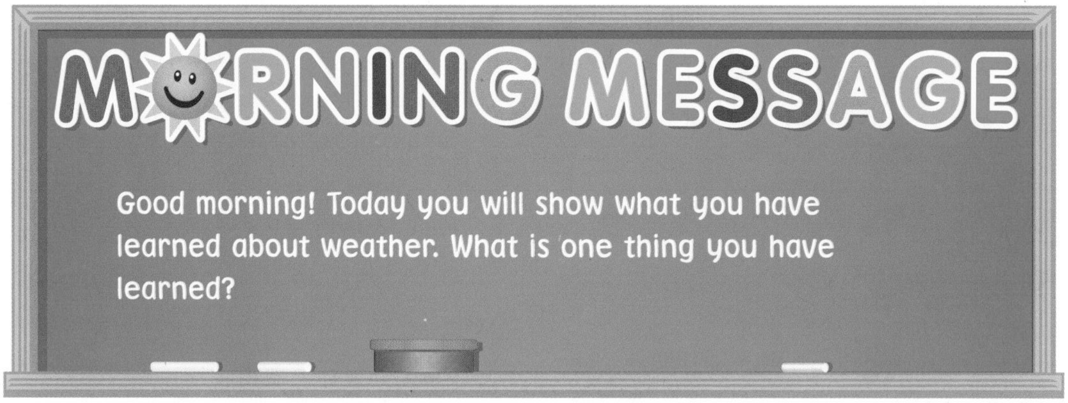
MORNING MESSAGE
Good morning! Today you will show what you have learned about weather. What is one thing you have learned?

Daily Language Review

To review how to form plurals of nouns that end with a consonant and *y,* write the following sentence on the board, or generate a similar one with students, and have students identify the noun and tell you how to write its plural form: When can we ride the two pony? *When can we ride the two ponies?*

Technology

eSkills provides Web-based practice with ***Imagine It!*** sounds and spellings. For more information about this program, visit **SRAonline.com.**

Riddle Me This Game

Have students explain the silent *e* rule in long-vowel spellings. *Silent* e *at the end of a word makes the vowel say its name.*

Refer to these ***Sound/Spelling Cards:*** Camera, Robot, Long A, and Timer. Ask students to say the sound for each card as you point to it. Then tell them to quickly determine the word the cards spell but not to say it aloud. Have them say the word together when you say *What's my word? crate*

- Have a volunteer point to the correct spelling of the /ā/ sound in the word *crate* as you write it on the board. Repeat this process with other words. After one or two examples, ask the riddle by naming the ***Sound/Spelling Cards*** without pointing to them.
- Use words such as the following:

Gopher, Long A, Timer *gate*

Camera, Long A, Camera *cake*

Robot, Long A, Timer *rate*

Robot, Long A, Camera *rake*

Popcorn, Long A, Jump *page*

Sausages, Timer, Long A, Jump *stage*

Teacher Tip

RIDDLE ME THIS This is a fun game to play at any time of the day. For example, play when you are waiting in line to go somewhere, on the bus during field trips, or in the lunchroom.

Sound/Spelling Card 29

Teacher Tips

RHYMES To help students remember the *_igh* spelling for /ī/, tell them that words with this spelling often rhyme with each other. Teach them the following rhyme: *The light at night is very bright.*

SYLLABICATION To help students blend the words and build fluency, use the syllabication below of the multisyllable words on the word lines.

wind • y	might • y	trick • y
re • plies	my • self	dry • ing
Wy • o • ming	Ju • ly	Ty • ler
Bry • an		

Phonics

ROUTINE 3 ROUTINE 4 ROUTINE 10 ROUTINE 11

Review: /ī/ Spelled *_igh*, *_y*, and *_ie*

Blending

Point to ***Sound/Spelling Card*** 29—Long I to review the /ī/ spellings *_igh*, *_y*, and *_ie*.

Use Routine 3, whole-word blending, and Routine 4, blending sentences, to have students blend the words and sentences. Use Routine 10, closed syllables, and Routine 11, open syllables, to have students blend the multisyllable words.

Line 1	why	by	windy	tricky
Line 2	high	sigh	bright	mighty
Line 3	flies	replies	myself	drying
Line 4	July	Wyoming	Tyler	Bryan

Sentence 1	We will try to see the bright lights.
Sentence 2	Mom might bake a pie for a snack.

Line 1 **/ī/ spelled *_y* and /ē/ spelled *_y***

Have students identify the sound that *y* spells in each line. *The words* why *and* my *have /ī/ spelled _y, and the words* windy *and* tricky *have /ē/ spelled _y.*

Line 2 **/ī/ spelled *_igh***

Remember to write the spelling *_igh* as a unit.

Line 3 **/ī/ spelled *_ie* and *_y***

Have students identify words in which the /ī/ sound comes at the end of a syllable. *myself, drying*

Line 4 **/ī/ spelled *_y***

Ask students why these words begin with capital letters. *They are proper nouns: July is the name of a month of the year; Wyoming is the name of a state; Tyler and Bryan are names of people.*

Sentences 1–2

Review the high-frequency words before writing the sentences. Have students reread the sentences to promote fluency.

Developing Oral Language

To review the words, use them in oral sentences. Ask students to find, read, and erase the word for each sentence.

- I painted the room all by ________. *myself*
- I haven't had any ________ to my questions. *replies*
- ____ is usually a hot month. *July*
- Threading a needle can be ________. *tricky*
- It is fun to fly a kite when it is ________. *windy*

Monitor Progress

to Differentiate Instruction

Formal Assessment

DICTATION As students spell words, notice who uses the ***Sound/Spelling Cards*** and spells the words correctly. Note students who are asking for help with the spellings.

APPROACHING LEVEL

IF . . . students need additional practice with dictation,	**THEN . . .** have them complete ***Reteach 1*** pages 157–158.

ON LEVEL

IF . . . students are on level with the words in the Word Building game,	**THEN . . .** make three lists of two words that contain the target spellings, such as *slight, tight; cried, dried; sly, tie.* Pair students, and tell them to take turns building words.

ABOVE LEVEL

IF . . . students need a challenge with building words,	**THEN . . .** use ***Challenge Activities 1*** page 79.

Guided Practice

Have students complete ***Skills Practice 1*** pages 215–216 to review /ī/ spelled *_igh*, *_y*, and *_ie*. Have students write the word that names each picture on page 215. Have students write the word that answers each riddle on page 216.

UNIT 5 Lesson 14

Name _______________ Date _______

Sounds and Spellings Review

Directions: Unscramble the letters and write the word that names the picture.

e p i — pie

r f y — fry

i h t g l — light

t g i f h r n e — frighten

r e d s i — dries

p s y — spy

Skills Practice 1 • Phonics UNIT 5 • Lesson 14 **215**

UNIT 5 Lesson 14

Sounds and Spellings Review

Directions: Read the riddles. Write the correct word from the box on the line. You will not use all the words.

fly sky lie bright night

I am dark.
I have stars.
You sleep at this time.
I am night

It is not nice to tell me.
I make others not believe you.
I am not the truth.
I am a lie

I am an insect.
I buzz here and there.
I have wings.
I am a fly

216 UNIT 5 • Lesson 14 Phonics • *Skills Practice 1*

Skills Practice 1, pp. 215–216

Dictation: Word Building Game

ROUTINE 8

✦ Use Routine 8, word building, to have students spell words in the Word Building game. Use the following words:

tie
pie
pry
fry
fly
flight
light
night

✦ Have students proofread and correct their spelling before you dictate the next word.

Differentiating Instruction **English Learner**

IF . . . students need extra help with phonics, **THEN . . .** see ***English Learner Support Guide*** Unit 5.

OBJECTIVES

Students will

- conclude weather investigations and make presentations.
- identify new questions to investigate.

MATERIALS

- ***What's the Weather? Big Book***

Inquiry Planner

Week 1

- Generate ideas and questions for the **Concept/Question Board.**
- Decide on a problem or question to research, and make a conjecture.

Week 2

- Collect information, and confirm or revise the conjectures and questions.

Week 3

- Prepare a presentation.

Differentiating Instruction English Learners

IF . . . students have difficulty participating in the discussion, **THEN . . .** ask questions that can be answered with a *yes* or *no,* or a short phrase. Examples: *Is it rainy today?* no *Yesterday, was it rainy or sunny?* sunny

IF . . . students are hesitant to participate in small groups, **THEN . . .** encourage English-speaking group members to invite English Learners to participate. You may want to assign one English speaker to be the partner of each English Learner and to help the English Learner participate.

Teacher Tip

CREATING PRESENTATIONS Photographs, illustrations from magazines, and students' artwork can be used in creating presentations. Most classes will require that the teacher scribe some or all of the presentation text for the students.

Inquiry Process

Prepare a Presentation

Whole-Group Time

Whole Group

- Point to the Weather Chart and tell students to use their Writer's Notebooks to review the weather conditions that were recorded during the unit. Encourage students to use the words from the What's the Weather? Word Bank as well as other words from the selections they have read to make the discussion more precise. As part of the discussion, have them answer the following questions:
  - What kind of weather have we had the most?
  - Which days were sunny, and which days were cloudy?
  - What were the highest and lowest temperature days?
  - Help students notice any patterns of weather that are revealed by their observations.
- Remind students that it is time for them to decide how to present their new understanding of weather. Remind students to ask any questions they have. Explain to students that they can continue to investigate any questions that have not been answered even though the unit is ending. Encourage students to continue to write weather-related observations in their notebooks.
- Review with student groups the presentation formats they will use. Monitor student discussions to make sure they understand what they will be doing. Answer questions, give suggestions if necessary, and ensure that all group members are involved in the project. Remind students to include their sources of information, including the names of authors, illustrators, and composers.
- Ensure that students have the materials they need for their presentations, for example:

  Doing an experiment Make sure that group members have supplies needed for experiments. Remind students to create a written summary of the experiment for you and the class. This summary should have detail of what each member of the group is doing in the experiment and the purpose of the experiment.

Putting together a book with illustrations Group members should have selected an idea for a book and the types of illustrations they will use. Provide markers, crayons, paper, and magazines for the students to use.

Skit Ensure that group members have the props and scripts needed for skits. Provide information on the type of graphs and charts students can use for a weather-forecasting skit.

Using illustrations and photographs Group members should have selected illustrations and photographs for their presentations. Students should write explanations to share about each illustration and photograph as part of the presentation.

- ✦ If possible, provide students access to certain Web sites on the Internet for additional presentation resources.
- ✦ Remind students to be good listeners while other students deliver their presentations. This includes listening attentively and, at the appropriate time, asking questions if they do not understand.
- ✦ Explain to students that as they deliver their presentations, it is important to face the audience. Tell them to speak clearly when it is their turn to speak.

Small-Group Time

Small Group

If students are working in groups, have them meet to prepare and rehearse their presentations.

Concept/Question Board

Tell students to continue posting information and questions on the What's the Weather? **Concept/Question Board** and to check the Board from time to time to see whether their questions have been answered.

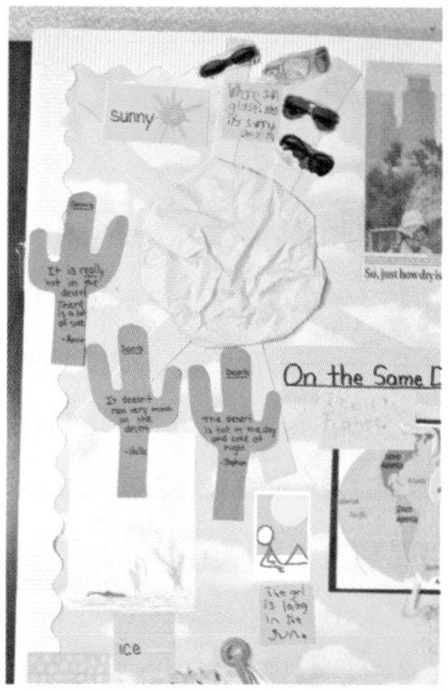

Monitor Progress

to Differentiate Instruction

Formal Assessment

PREPARING PRESENTATIONS Note how students are preparing their presentations.

APPROACHING LEVEL

IF . . . students are having difficulty agreeing on a method of presentation or roles for their presentations,	**THEN . . .** help them make decisions based on time available and the skills of individual students.

ON LEVEL

IF . . . students are progressing with their presentation development,	**THEN . . .** have them practice their presentations and ask for feedback from each other and other groups.

ABOVE LEVEL

IF . . . students need a challenge,	**THEN . . .** have them practice their presentations and ask for feedback from each other and other groups.

Teacher Tip

DIGITAL RESEARCH Provide students with a list of specific Web sites that can be used to gather information and generate ideas for their Inquiry investigations.

OBJECTIVES

Students will
- revise and rearrange instruction sentences.
- understand the importance of speaking clearly.
- practice speaking clearly by giving a weather forecast.

MATERIALS
- Routines 14, 15
- ***Transparencies*** 43, 43a
- ***Skills Practice 1,*** p. 208

Teacher Tip

PEER EDITING Reinforce the importance of sentence order by having students trade their instruction drafts with partners. Tell students to talk about whether they can follow their partners' instructions without confusion.

Traits of Good Writing

Sentence Fluency Writers will edit and rearrange sentences to make them easier for readers to understand.

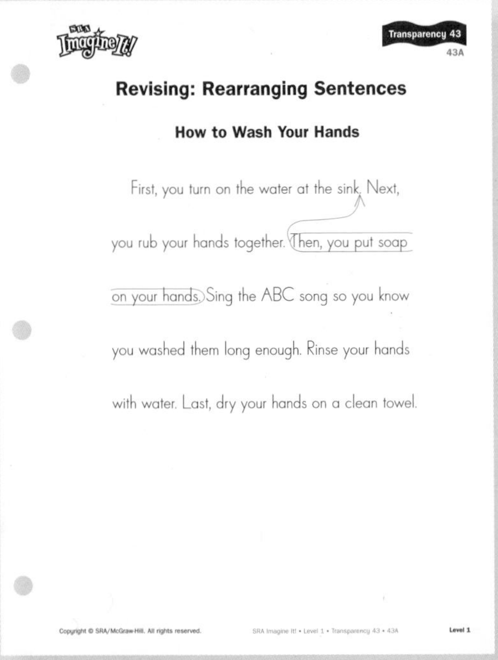
Imagine It! Transparency 43 43A

Revising: Rearranging Sentences

How to Wash Your Hands

First, you turn on the water at the sink. Next, you rub your hands together. Then, you put soap on your hands. Sing the ABC song so you know you washed them long enough. Rinse your hands with water. Last, dry your hands on a clean towel.

Copyright © SRA/McGraw-Hill. All rights reserved. SRA Imagine It! • Level 1 • Transparency 43 • 43A Level 1

Transparencies 43, 43a

Writing Instructions

Revising

ROUTINE 14

Teach—Rearranging Sentences

- Tell students that today they will revise their drafts and choose a title for their instructions. Explain that they can improve their instructions by rearranging any sentences that do not make sense.
- Model revising a draft by rearranging sentences and steps. Use ***Transparencies*** 43 and 43a to show students how to change the order of sentences. Read the original sentences to students, and then read the sentences in the revised order. Ask them why the rearranged sentences are more helpful to readers. *They give the order of steps in the correct sequence.*

Guided Practice

- **Teacher Modeling** Display the draft of your instructions from Lesson 13. Model how to choose and write a title: *Now I need to write a title for my instructions. My instructions tell what to do when the weather is ________ . So a good title is Get Ready for __________ .* Write the title above the sentences.

ROUTINE 15

Apply

Have students use your model and the checklist on ***Skills Practice 1*** page 208 to look for ways to revise and improve their writing. Make sure they understand each part of the checklist. Remind them to check the spelling of any plural nouns in their writing, especially those that end in *y*. Circulate, and help them rearrange sentences as needed. Then help them write titles for their instructions.

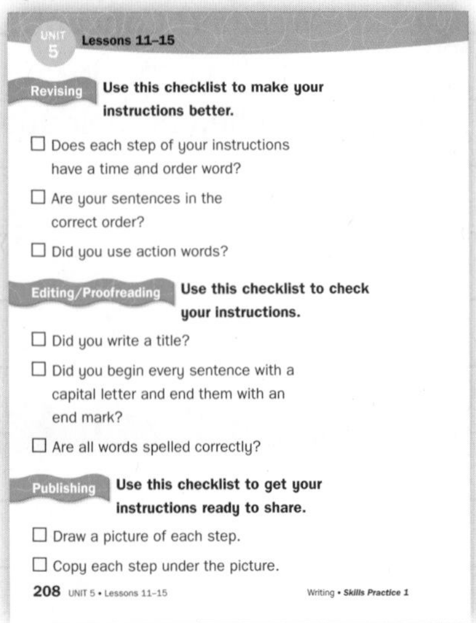
UNIT 5 Lessons 11–15

Revising Use this checklist to make your instructions better.
- ☐ Does each step of your instructions have a time and order word?
- ☐ Are your sentences in the correct order?
- ☐ Did you use action words?

Editing/Proofreading Use this checklist to check your instructions.
- ☐ Did you write a title?
- ☐ Did you begin every sentence with a capital letter and end them with an end mark?
- ☐ Are all words spelled correctly?

Publishing Use this checklist to get your instructions ready to share.
- ☐ Draw a picture of each step.
- ☐ Copy each step under the picture.

208 UNIT 5 • Lessons 11–15 Writing • Skills Practice 1

Skills Practice 1, p. 208

Listening/Speaking/Viewing

Speaking: Clear Speech

Teach

- Tell students that we must speak clearly so others can understand what we say. Explain that it is easier to understand someone who is speaking slowly and pronouncing all the words correctly than it is to understand someone who is speaking too fast or mumbling words while reading.
- Point out that people who give weather forecasts on radio and television are usually good speakers. They know that people who are listening or watching them are interested in the weather, so they speak clearly to make sure everyone can understand them.

Guided Practice

Teacher Modeling Remind students that a weather forecast predicts what the weather will be during the coming days. Model a weather forecast that is appropriate for your area. An example could be *The temperature will be cooler tonight. It will be 55 degrees by midnight. Tomorrow it will get much warmer. We expect to see temperatures of 70 degrees by noon. We'll have plenty of sunshine all day tomorrow. It looks as if it will stay warm and sunny for the rest of the week.*

Apply

In small groups, have students take turns giving a weather forecast. Tell them to speak clearly and to use the appropriate rate and volume. Encourage them to refer to the What's the Weather? Word Bank and the **Concept/Question Board** for words they might use in their forecasts. Remind listeners to be courteous by facing the speaker, making eye contact, and asking clarifying questions.

Teacher Tip

SPEAKING Tell students that they will be sharing their instructions during the next lesson. Explain that clear speech is important when giving instructions so that listeners will know what they should do.

Research in Action

Students who are inarticulate in trying to describe how they go about doing some mental task often come forth with clear statements . . . when asked to give advice to another student, particularly a younger one.

(Carl Bereiter and Marlene Scardamalia)

Differentiating Instruction: English Learners

IF . . . students have difficulty with pronunciation, **THEN . . .** give them an opportunity to practice their forecasts with you before they present to their groups.

Monitor Progress to Differentiate Instruction

Formal Assessment

SPEAKING Observe students to see who is able to speak clearly and use appropriate rate and volume.

APPROACHING LEVEL	**IF . . .** students have difficulty with this skill,	**THEN . . .** repeat the activity in Workshop and model the correct speaking skills again.
ON LEVEL	**IF . . .** students are comfortable with this skill,	**THEN . . .** have small groups visit a nearby classroom to deliver today's weather forecast.
ABOVE LEVEL	**IF . . .** students have mastered speaking clearly and need a challenge,	**THEN . . .** have small groups of "reporters" work on a brief School News Update to share with the entire class at the end of the day.

Preparing to Read

OBJECTIVES

Students will

- blend, spell, and read word with /ē/, /i/, and /ā/.
- build fluency by reading ***Decodable*** 78.

MATERIALS

- Routines 3–7, 9–11
- ***Sound/Spelling Cards*** 19, 27–28, 29
- ***Skills Practice 1,*** pp. 217–218
- ***Decodable*** 78, *Wait for Me*

Daily Warm-Ups

Copy the Morning Message on the board or on chart paper. Have students answer the questions. Read the message aloud, and discuss it with students. **Possible Answer** *I liked "On the Same Day in March" the best. I liked it because we learned about weather in different parts of the world.*

MORNING MESSAGE

Good morning! It is time for you to celebrate all the good work you have done. Think about what you have read. Which story or poem did you like best? Why did you like it?

Daily Language Review

To review how to form plurals of nouns that end with a consonant and *y*, write the following sentence on the board, or generate a similar one with students, and have students tell you how to correct the mistake: We read two story in class. *We read two stories in class.*

Consonant Riddle Game

Play the Consonant Riddle game with students. Ask them to say the word that answers each of the following:

What begins with /dr/ and rhymes with *hop?* *drop*

What begins with /sl/ and rhymes with *nice?* *slice*

What begins with /pl/ and rhymes with *fuss?* *plus*

What begins with /v/ and rhymes with *best?* *vest*

What begins with /r/ and rhymes with *light?* *right*

Teacher Tip

SYLLABICATION To help students blend the words and build fluency, use the syllabication below of the multisyllable words on the word lines.

de • ny	cheer • ing	par • ty
Sta • cy	pri • cy	de • cide
re • plied	yes • ter • day	

Phonics

ROUTINE 3 ROUTINE 4 ROUTINE 10 ROUTINE 11

Review: General Blending

Use Routine 3, whole-word blending, and Routine 4, blending sentences, to have students blend the words and sentences. Use Routine 10, closed syllables, and Routine 11, open syllables, to have students blend the multisyllable words.

Line 1	deny	Steve	cheering	each
Line 2	party	brief	Stacy	story
Line 3	sigh	sight	decide	replied
Line 4	gain	spray	plain	yesterday

Sentence 1 Pete came with me to eat french fries, hamburgers, and lime pie.

Sentence 2 Ray eats his meals in the high chair to the right of the table.

Line 1 **/ē/ spelled *e*, *e_e*, *ee*, and *ea_***

Have students identify the /ē/ spelling for each word. Help students notice the inflectional word ending *-ing* on the word *cheering.*

Line 2 **/ē/ spelled *_y* and *_ie_*, and /s/ spelled *cy***

Ask students why *Stacy* begins with a capital letter. *It is a proper noun;* Stacy *is the name of a person.*

Line 3 **/ī/ spelled *_igh*, *i_e*, and *_ie***

Have students identify the /ī/ spellings for each word.

Line 4 **/ā/ spelled *_ai* and *_ay***

Have students identify the /ā/ spellings for each word.

Sentences 1–2

Write the words *came, me,* and *right* on the board. Read the words, repeat them, and have students read them. Then spell the words together. Invite volunteers to use the words in sentences. Write each word on an index card, and add the cards to the High-Frequency Word Bank.

Developing Oral Language

To review the words, say sentences with missing words. Have students point to, read, and erase the word that will complete each sentence.

- We had cake at the ___________. *party*
- ___________ is a friend of mine. *Stacy, Steve*
- A ___________ is a deep breath. *sigh*
- I used the hose to ___________ water on the flowers. *spray*
- ___________ we went to the park. *Yesterday*

Guided Practice

Have students complete ***Skills Practice 1*** pages 217–218 to provide a review of the previously introduced sounds and spellings and for dictation.

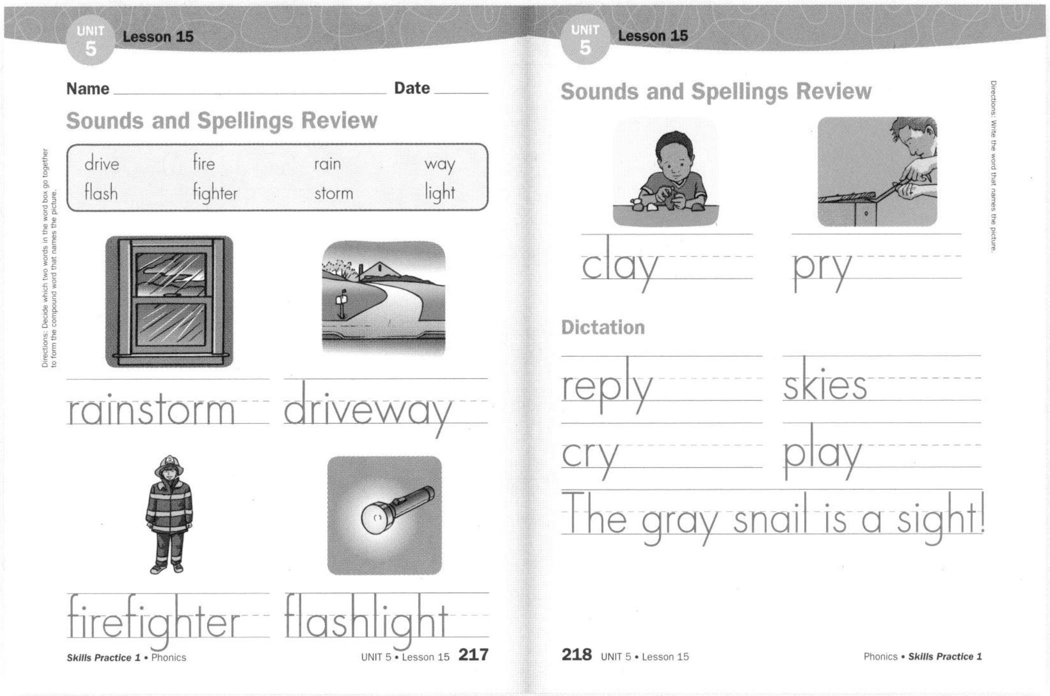

UNIT 5 Lesson 15

Name ____________ Date ______

Sounds and Spellings Review

drive	fire	rain	way
flash	fighter	storm	light

rainstorm driveway

firefighter flashlight

Skills Practice 1 • Phonics UNIT 5 • Lesson 15 217

UNIT 5 Lesson 15

Sounds and Spellings Review

clay pry

Dictation

reply skies

cry play

The gray snail is a sight!

218 UNIT 5 • Lesson 15 Phonics • *Skills Practice 1*

Skills Practice 1, pp. 217–218

ROUTINE 5 ROUTINE 6 ROUTINE 7

Dictation

Use Routine 5, sounds-in-sequence dictation, Routine 6, whole-word dictation, and Routine 7, sentence dictation, with the following:

Line 1	reply	skies
Line 2	cry	play
Sentence	The gray snail is a sight!	

Monitor Progress ✔ to Differentiate Instruction

Formal Assessment

DICTATION As students spell words, notice who uses the ***Sound/Spelling Cards*** and spells the words correctly. Note students who are asking for help with the spellings.

APPROACHING LEVEL

IF . . . students need additional practice with phonics and dictation, **THEN . . .** have them complete ***Reteach 1*** pages 159–160.

ON LEVEL

IF . . . students are on level with phonics and dictation, **THEN . . .** pair them, and have them play a game from ***eSkills.***

ABOVE LEVEL

IF . . . students need a challenge with phonics and dictation, **THEN . . .** have them complete ***Challenge Activities 1*** page 80.

Differentiating Instruction — English Learners

IF . . . students are unable to complete the sentences, **THEN . . .** for oral practice and vocabulary building, ask them first to repeat the words their classmates say and then to repeat each complete sentence.

Fluency/Reading a Decodable Book

ROUTINE 9

Core Decodable 78: *Wait for Me*

Phonics Focus: Review /ā/ Spelled *ai_*, *_ay*; /ī/ Spelled *_igh*, *_ie _y*

High-Frequency Words

Review the high-frequency words *came*, *me*, and *right* that students learned in Blending. Point to them in the High-Frequency Word Bank or write them on the board, spell the words, and have students say the words. Have volunteers use the words in sentences. Review other high-frequency words by pointing to them in the High-Frequency Word Bank and having students read them.

Reading the Decodable

- Follow Routine 9, reading a ***Decodable,*** as you read the story with students.
- Have students read the title, browse the story, and discuss what they think the story will be about.
- The first time through, have students read a page silently. Then have one student read it aloud. Repeat this procedure for each page.
- Reread the story at least twice, calling on various students to read. Then have the entire class do a choral reading of the story.

Responding

- After reading, be sure to talk about the story, and answer any questions the students have. Ask students to identify any difficult words in the book.
- Have students retell the story.

Teacher Tips

GRAMMAR Have students find words that begin with a capital letter and tell why they are capitalized. *Ray and Dad because they are names; each sentence begins with a capital letter.*

Wait for Me

by Sidney Allen illustrated by Diane Paterson

"Wait for me," called Ray.
But the kids were way ahead.

3

It was like this every day.
Ray kept trying.
But he could not keep up.

4

This time, the kids stopped on the corner.
But they came right back.

5

The kids passed Ray.
Ray turned his bike.
"Wait for me," he called.

6

Why was Ray always far back?
His bike still had training wheels.

7

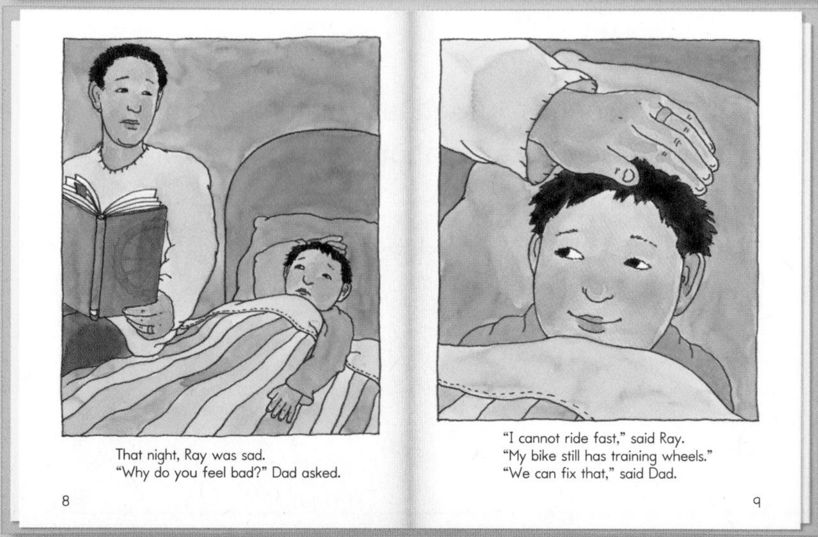
That night, Ray was sad.
"Why do you feel bad?" Dad asked.

8

"I cannot ride fast," said Ray.
"My bike still has training wheels."
"We can fix that," said Dad.

9

The next day, Dad called Ray.
"Go to the driveway," said Dad.

10

Ray spotted his bike in the bright sun.
It did not have training wheels!

11

Ray was glad.
But he was a little afraid.
He might need training wheels.

12

"Try riding this way," said Dad.
Dad held the bike as Ray pedaled.
Dad ran next to him.

13

Ray pedaled fast.
Dad let the bike go.
Could Ray tell?

14

Ray was riding alone.
"I am flying, Dad!" he yelled.

15

That day, the kids raced.
Ray stayed with them.
It was a tie!

16

✦ As students answer the following questions, make sure they focus on the words in the story rather than getting the answers by listening or from the pictures. Have students answer by pointing to and reading aloud the answers in the text:

- **Where do the kids stop?** *on the corner*
- **Why is Ray always far back?** *His bike still had training wheels.*
- **When Ray spots his bike in the sun, what does it not have?** *It does not have training wheels.*
- **Why is Ray a little afraid?** *He might need training wheels.*

Building Fluency

Have students build fluency by rereading ***Core Decodable*** 78 twice with a partner. The first time through, one partner should read the odd-numbered pages and the other partner the even-numbered pages. The second time through, they should switch pages. For additional practice with the sound/spellings students learned this week, have students reread one or more of the following: ***Core Decodable*** 75, 76, or 77 or ***Practice Decodable*** 62, 63, or 64. Have students record their readings on their Personal Title sheets, noting the title of each book they read, the date, and any difficult words they encounter.

Core Decodable 78

Wait for Me

High-Frequency Words Introduced in Core Decodable 78

came
me
right

Previously Introduced High-Frequency Words

a	do	him	out	to
after	don't	his	over	too
all	down	I	red	two
am	every	if	ride	up
an	for	in	said	walk
and	get	is	see	was
as	girl	it	she	way
ask	go	its	six	we
at	going	jump	sleep	well
be	got	just	some	went
big	green	like	take	were
boy	had	little	that	what
but	has	look	the	when
call	have	make	them	will
can	he	my	then	with
could	help	of	there	yes
day	her	on	they	you
did	here	or	this	

Sound/Spelling Correspondences in Core Decodables

1. Pre-decodable
2. Pre-decodable
3. Pre-decodable
4. Pre-decodable
5. Pre-decodable
6. /s/ spelled *s*, /m/ spelled *m*, /a/ spelled *a*
7. /t/ spelled *t*, *tt*
8. Review
9. /d/ spelled *d*
10. /n/ spelled *n*
11. /i/ spelled *i*
12. /h/ spelled *h_*
13. Review
14. /p/ spelled *p*
15. /l/ spelled *l*, *ll*
16. /o/ spelled *o*
17. /b/ spelled *b*
18. Review
19. /k/ spelled *c*
20. /aw/ spelled *al*
21. /k/ spelled *k*, ■*ck*
22. /r/ spelled *r*
23. /f/ spelled *f*, *ff*
24. /s/ spelled *ss*
25. Review
26. /g/ spelled *g*
27. /j/ spelled *j*, ■*dge*
28. /u/ spelled *u*
29. /z/ spelled *z*, *zz*
30. /z/ spelled *_s*
31. Review
32. /ks/ spelled ■*x*
33. /e/ spelled *e*
34. -ed ending: /ed/, /d/
35. -ed ending: /t/
36. /e/ spelled *_ea_*
37. Review
38. /sh/ spelled *sh*
39. /th/ spelled *th*
40. /ch/ spelled *ch*, ■*tch*
41. /or/ spelled *or*, *ore*
42. Review
43. /ar/ spelled *ar*
44. /m/ spelled *_mb*
45. /w/ spelled *w_*
46. /hw/ spelled *wh_*
47. /er/ spelled *er*, *ir*
48. /er/ spelled *ur*
49. Review
50. Schwa
51. Review schwa
52. /ng/ spelled ■*ng*
53. /nk/ spelled ■*nk*
54. /kw/ spelled *qu_*
55. Review
56. /y/ spelled *y_*
57. /v/ spelled *v*
58. Syllable -le
59. /ā/ spelled *a* and *a_e*
60. Review
61. /ī/ spelled *i* and *i_e*
62. /s/ spelled *ce*, *ci_*
63. /j/ spelled *ge*, *gi_*
64. Review
65. /ō/ spelled *o* and *o_e*
66. /ū/ spelled *u* and *u_e*
67. Review
68. /ē/ spelled *e* and *e_e*
69. /ē/ spelled *ee* and *ea*
70. Review
71. /ē/ spelled *_y*, *_ie_*
72. /s/ spelled *cy*
73. Review /s/ spellings
74. Review
75. /ā/ spelled *ai_*, *_ay*
76. /ī/ spelled *_igh*
77. /ī/ spelled *_ie* and *_y*
78. Review

Decodable 78, inside back cover

OBJECTIVES

Students will
- edit, publish, and share their instructions.
- form the letters *k* and *z* correctly.
- increase fluency and speed while writing.
- control the size and spacing of letters.
- form plural nouns by changing *y* to *i* and adding *es.*

MATERIALS
- Routines 15, 16
- ***Transparencies*** 44, 44a
- ***Skills Practice 1,*** p. 208
- Portfolios
- ***Lesson Assessment Book 1,*** pp. 65–70

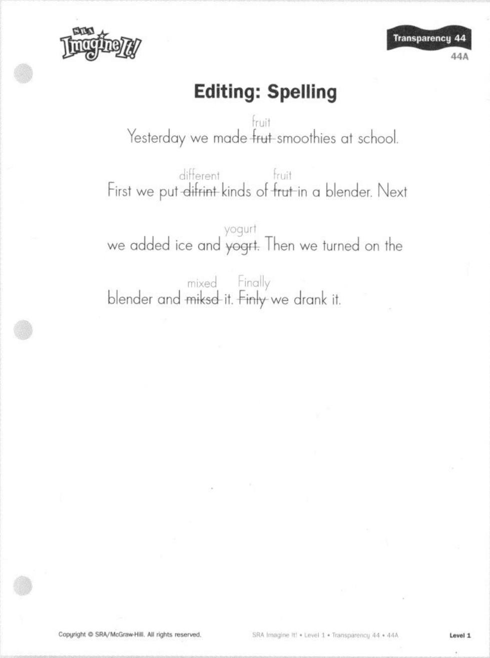

Imagine It! Transparency 44 44A

Editing: Spelling

Yesterday we made ~~frut~~ fruit smoothies at school.

First we put ~~difrint~~ different kinds of ~~frut~~ fruit in a blender. Next

we added ice and ~~yogrt~~ yogurt. Then we turned on the

blender and ~~miksd~~ mixed it. ~~Finly~~ Finally we drank it.

 SRA Imagine It! • Level 1 • Transparency 44 • 44A Level 1

Transparencies 44, 44a

Differentiating Instruction English Learners

IF . . . students have difficulty with the checklist in ***Skills Practice 1,*** **THEN . . .** go through it with them, pointing out the kind of error each item asks them to look for.

Writing Instructions

Editing and Publishing

Teach—Using Action Verbs

- Remind students to always look over their work for mistakes before they turn it in. If the steps to their instructions are out of order or unclear, the reader will not understand what he or she should do.
- **Teacher Modeling** Use your revised instructions from Lesson 14 to model how to check for sequence, punctuation, and capitalization errors. Then, use ***Transparencies*** 44 and 44a to model editing for spelling mistakes. *I'm going to check the instructions I've written to see whether I've misspelled any words.* Use proofreader's marks to correct grade-appropriate, high-frequency, and decodable words.

Guided Practice

ROUTINE 15

- Remind students to use action verbs and time and order words to make their writing interesting. Tell them to edit their drafts to make sure they have included each of these. Encourage them to use a caret as they make their edits.
- Have small groups work through the editing checklist on ***Skills Practice 1*** page 208 together. Remind them to make sure all plurals are formed correctly. Circulate, and offer help to each group as needed.

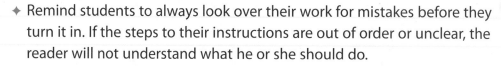

Writing Instructions, cont.

Apply

ROUTINE 16

- Tell students to look over their work for mistakes one last time and make any corrections before copying their instructions onto their final paper.
- Encourage students to think of creative ways to publish their writing. They might add a cover to create their own "instruction manual." They might find or draw pictures of the materials needed to complete their instructions and attach them to their papers.
- Have students complete the publishing checklist on ***Skills Practice 1*** page 208. Read through the instruction to make sure they understand each part.
- Allow students to share their instructions within their small groups. Encourage each group to give the speaker feedback on whether they could understand each step or if more information was needed. Remind students to also say something they liked about the writing.
- Display students' writing on a bulletin board, or have them place it in their Portfolios.

Assessment

Use the Writing Rubrics found in the Level Appendix to evaluate students' instructions. You may use any of the rubrics for Genre, Writing Process, and Writing Traits.

Teacher Tip

SPEAKING Remind students that they should speak clearly to make sure they are understood. Talking too softly, or too fast, or mumbling their words can make listening more difficult. Gently remind nervous speakers to take a deep breath and read slowly as they share so that the group can enjoy every word.

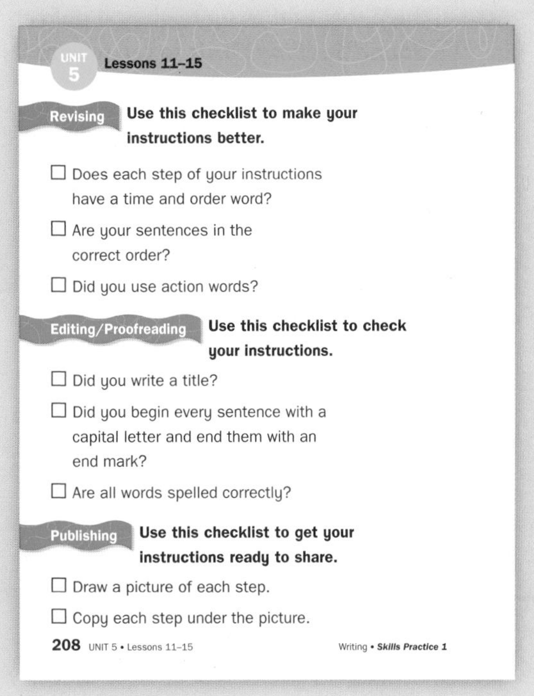
UNIT 5 Lessons 11–15

Revising Use this checklist to make your instructions better.

- ☐ Does each step of your instructions have a time and order word?
- ☐ Are your sentences in the correct order?
- ☐ Did you use action words?

Editing/Proofreading Use this checklist to check your instructions.

- ☐ Did you write a title?
- ☐ Did you begin every sentence with a capital letter and end them with an end mark?
- ☐ Are all words spelled correctly?

Publishing Use this checklist to get your instructions ready to share.

- ☐ Draw a picture of each step.
- ☐ Copy each step under the picture.

208 UNIT 5 • Lessons 11–15 Writing • *Skills Practice 1*

Skill Practice 1, p. 208

Technology

eSkills contains writing activities that students can use to practice combining sentences.

Penmanship

Alphabet Practice: The Letters *k* and *z*

Guided Practice

Review how to form lowercase *k* and *z,* and then distribute handwriting paper. Have students write each letter twice within the lines as they say its name. Tell them to proofread their letters and circle their best *k* and *z.*

Apply

- To monitor students' handwriting fluency, write the following sentence on the board: *Liz likes puzzles and kites.* Read it to students, and tell them to copy the sentence onto their papers as quickly as they can without making any mistakes. After two or three minutes, have them proofread their sentence by circling any incorrect words and making them better by rewriting them above or next to the original words. Then have students underline their best *k* and *z.*
- Look for additional opportunities during writing activities and in other subject areas to provide handwriting practice and to encourage and praise students when they form the letters correctly.

Teacher Tip

CAPITAL LETTERS Although students are reviewing the formation of lowercase letters, tell them that as they write, they should check the ***Sound/Spelling Cards*** to see how to form the capitals of *k* and *z.*

Differentiating Instruction: English Learners

IF . . . students have difficulty with handwriting, **THEN . . .** keep in mind that some students may be more familiar with other writing systems than they are with the Roman alphabet. Provide students with extra handwriting help as needed.

Grammar, Usage, and Mechanics

Review Plural Nouns: Change *y* to *i* and Add *es*

Guided Practice

Ask a volunteer how to form plurals of nouns that end with a consonant followed by *y*. *change y to* i *and add* es Have students recite the "more than one" rhyme:

For more than one,
no need to guess.
Change *y* to *i* and add *es*.

Apply

- Write the following words on the board, and have students work in groups to spell the plural forms on handwriting paper:

story *stories*	supply *supplies*
way *ways*	butterfly *butterflies*
sprinkle *sprinkles*	guppy *guppies*

- If students misspell *ways*, have them notice that the letter before *y* is a vowel. Remind them that the *y* changes to *i* after a consonant. If students misspell *sprinkles*, ask them to spell the word and notice that it does not end with *y*.
- Have students look through their Portfolios for places to add or change plural nouns especially ones that end with *y*.
- Have students edit and rewrite three sentences to feature plural nouns. Then have them share their favorite with partners.

Differentiating Instruction — English Learners

IF . . . students need extra help with plural nouns, **THEN . . .** see ***English Learner Support Guide*** Unit 5 Lesson 15 to help them understand creating a plural by changing *y* to *i* and adding *es*.

Monitor Progress — Formal Assessment

Use ***Lesson Assessment Book 1*** pages 65–70 to assess students' understanding of the skills taught in Lessons 11–15.

Unit 5

Benchmark Assessment

Day 9

Monitor Progress

Formal Assessment Options

You will need the following materials, along with your informal observations and ***Lesson Assessment*** results, to monitor student progress throughout the year.

Benchmark Assessment, pp. 32–42

Monitor student progess using ***SRA Imagine It!*** assessment tools.

Technology

- ***eAssess***
- ***eAssess CD-ROM***

At the end of Unit 6 you will administer Benchmark 4, which addresses the following skills:

- **Phonemic Awareness**
- **Phonics**
- **Vocabulary**
- **Comprehension**
- **Grammar, Usage, and Mechanics**
- **Spelling**

Results on ***Benchmark Assessment*** will serve as a performance indicator that shows how well students are prepared to take an end-of-the-year standardized test. ***Benchmark Assessment*** results also will allow you to intervene with those students who are at risk for failure.

Monitor Progress with Benchmark Assessment

Below are two sets of ***Benchmark Assessment*** cutoffs that can be used for predicting student performance—one for Benchmark Skills Assessments and the other for Oral Fluency Assessments. Each cutoff begins with a baseline score under Benchmark 1, which is given at the beginning of the year and ends with Benchmark 6, which is given at the end of the year. The cutoffs are determined by finding the amount of growth a student must make over the course of the year to ensure he or she will not be at risk for reading failure.

Benchmark Skills Assessment

The Benchmark Skills Assessment is a 100-point test, consisting of questions covering phonemic/phonological awareness; phonics; vocabulary; comprehension; grammar, usage, and mechanics; and spelling. The table below shows how many points out of 100 first-grade students should score on a particular Benchmark Skills Assessment over the course of the year. The highlighted score indicates where your students should be at the end of Unit 6.

Benchmark 1	Benchmark 2	Benchmark 3	Benchmark 4	Benchmark 5	Benchmark 6
10	25	40	55	67	85

Oral Fluency: Word Identification Assessment

The Oral Fluency Assessment is an individually administered assessment, consisting of a list of 100 high-frequency words. Students read aloud to the teacher as many words as they can in one minute. The table below shows how many words per minute first-grade students should read on a particular Oral Fluency Assessment over the course of the year. The highlighted score indicates where your students should be at the end of Unit 6.

Benchmark 1	Benchmark 2	Benchmark 3	Benchmark 4	Benchmark 5	Benchmark 6
10	16	22	28	34	40

Independent Tools to Monitor Progress

DIBELS and TPRI

Based on your DIBELS or TPRI scores, use the appropriate manipulatives from the ***Workshop Resource Book*** and ***Workshop Kit***.

Unit 5

Unit Celebration

Day 5

BIG Idea

What is weather?
Write the Big Idea question on the board. Ask students what they learned about weather. Ask which selections added something new to their understanding of the theme. Encourage students to share their thoughts about the overall unit.

Teacher Tip

UNIT VOCABULARY Take time during the Unit Celebration to review vocabulary from the unit that students find difficult.

Differentiating Instruction English Learners

IF . . . students would benefit from extra support during Small-Group Discussion, **THEN . . .** be sure to place them in groups with at least two proficient English speakers.

IF . . . students are beginning English Learners, **THEN . . .** pose self-evaluation questions they can answer with a *yes* or *no* or by choosing between two alternatives, such as *Was working on your Inquiry project easy or hard for you?*

Theme Wrap-Up and Review

Small Group

- Organize students into groups based on their favorite selection for the What's the Weather? unit. Within their groups, have students
  - summarize the selection.
  - tell why they liked the selection.
  - write a sentence about the selection in the response journal section of their Writer's Notebooks.
- Have each group share its ideas with the class.

Read Aloud

Share with students one of the following books about weather:

The Storm by Kathy Henderson

How's the Weather? by Melvin and Gilda Berger

Red Rubber Boot Day by Mary Lyn Ray, illustrated by Lauren Stringer

One Lucky Girl by George Ella Lyon

OH! by Kevin Henkes

Twister by Darleen Bailey Beard, illustrated by Nancy Carpenter

Snowballs by Lois Ehlert

Geoffrey Groundhog Predicts the Weather by Bruce Koscielniak

Share with Others

- If groups of students have conducted weather experiments, kept weather charts, or made other presentations of their work, arrange for them to present their experiments, charts, and presentations to the rest of the class, other classes, or to parents and families.
- Remind students that it is important to participate courteously in discussions, such as asking clarifying questions, taking turns, staying on topic, making eye contact, and facing the speaker.
- If groups have prepared books, make copies of the books for them to take home and share with family members. Place one copy of each book in the class library.

Unit Review

Evaluating the Unit

Whole Group

Use the Weather Chart to have students review the weather patterns they observed during the What's the Weather? unit. Have students share any additional weather-related information they recorded in their Writer's Notebooks.

- To monitor what students have learned from this unit, ask the Big Idea question "What is weather?" Have students use the information they have acquired during the unit to discuss and answer the question. Prompt students to share their new ideas.
- Have students select three or four words from the What's the Weather? Word Bank to keep posted in the classroom throughout the year. Have students identify the most interesting words and tell how each word was interesting or helpful. If students identify more than four words, have the class vote to decide which words will remain posted.

Teacher Tip

WHOLE-GROUP DISCUSSION It is important that each student has an opportunity to share thoughts and feelings about the unit.

Self-Evaluation

Ask students to evaluate their unit activity experiences.

- How did you feel about working on your Inquiry project?
- Which part of the project was hardest?
- Which part was easiest?
- What was the most interesting thing you learned about weather?
- What did you discover about the way you learn new things?
- How do you think you can learn more in later projects?

Concept/Question Board

After this unit, set up the **Concept/Question Board** for the next unit. Post the details from the What's the Weather? Board in a different location in the classroom. Remind students to continue to bring in photographs, news stories, brochures, and other materials to post on the Board throughout the year. Use the **Concept/Question Board** from time to time to talk about different kinds of weather and to relate the materials to weather changes in your region.

A

Australia
Kangaroos and koala bears live in **Australia**.

autumn
During **autumn**, some leaves change color and fall to the ground.

C

Canada
Canada is the country directly north of the United States.

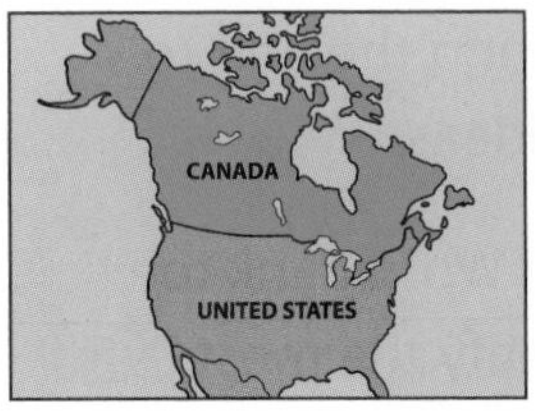

62

China
China is a large country in Asia.

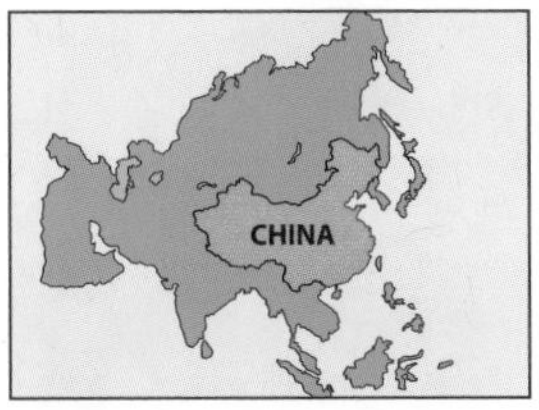

column
A tall **column** supports a building.

crouched
The baseball catcher **crouched** behind home plate.

63

What's the Weather Big Book, pp. 62–63

F

flashes
Bright **flashes** of lightning lit up the sky during the thunderstorm.

flock
A group of animals is sometimes called a **flock**.

fog
Dad had to drive slowly through the **fog** this morning.

64

G

government
In the United States, we choose people to run our **government**.

H

huddled
The football players **huddled** together before the next play of the game.

65

What's the Weather Big Book, pp. 64–65

K

kites
We like to fly **kites** in the park when it is windy.

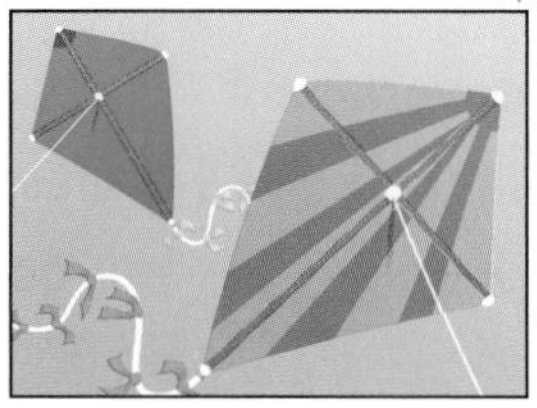

L

Louisiana
Louisiana is known for its special food and jazz music.

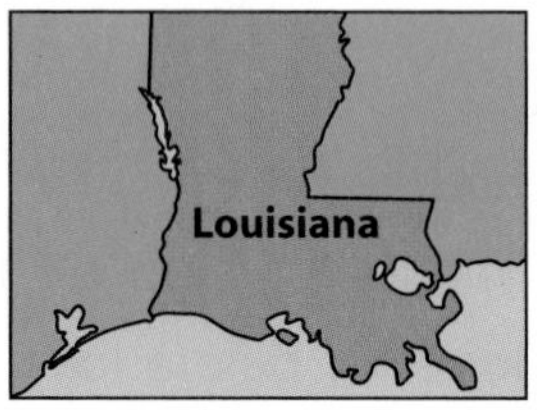

66

M

markets
Many farmers' **markets** sell fresh fruit, vegetables, and flowers.

P

patch
When the sun came out, our yard was left with just a **patch** of snow.

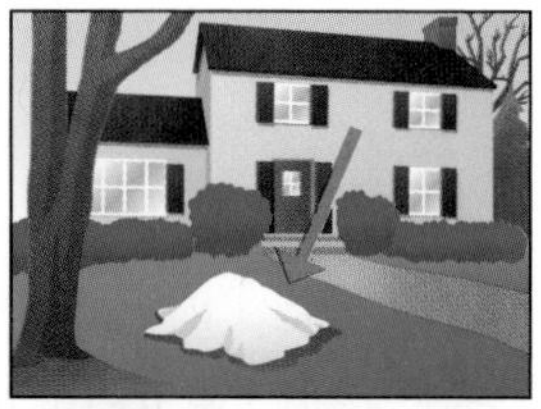

pearls
Mom likes to wear her **pearls** on special days.

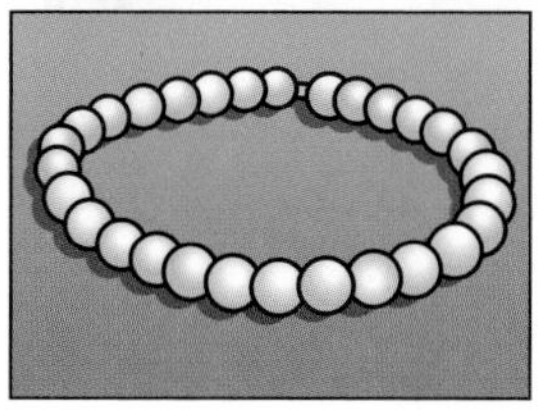

67

What's the Weather Big Book, pp. 66–67

pouring
A heavy rainstorm is sometimes called a **pouring** rain.

S

shore
My family went to the **shore** to look for shells in the sand.

sparkles
The North Star **sparkles** in the night sky.

sprinkle
A light rain is sometimes called a **sprinkle**.

68

swamp
Alligators, snakes, and birds live in a muddy **swamp** in Florida.

T

Texas Panhandle
Kyle lives in a small town in the **Texas Panhandle**.

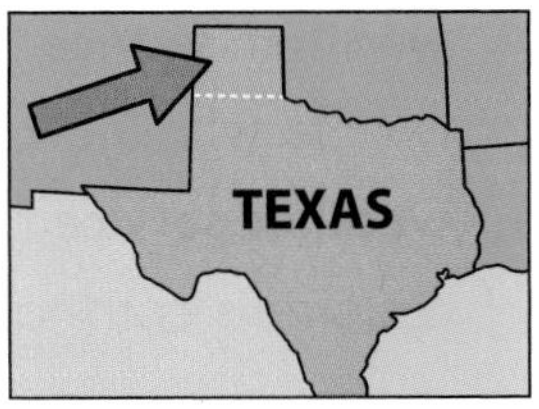

twister
Twister is another name for a tornado.

69

What's the Weather Big Book, pp. 68–69

W

weather
Katie looked at the sky to see what the **weather** was like.

weather service
People who work for the **weather service** can warn us if a storm is coming.

whirl
On a windy day, leaves **whirl** around the yard.

70

What's the Weather Big Book, p. 70

C

cactus
A **cactus** is a desert plant that can live a long time without water.

celebrate
Rosa had a party to **celebrate** her special day.

chopsticks
The Lee family uses **chopsticks** to eat their dinner.

cirrus
Cirrus clouds are thin clouds that form high in the sky.

68

F

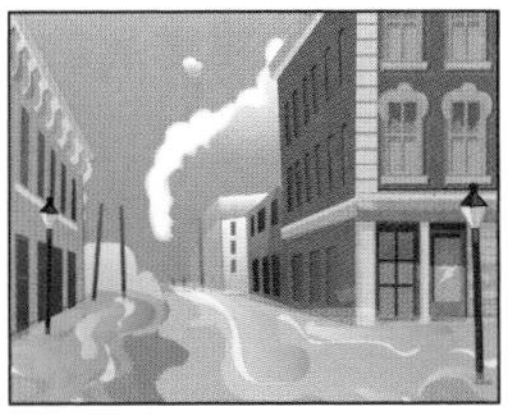

floods
After a heavy rainstorm, **floods** can cover the land with water.

H

house
A **house** is a building where people live.

L

lightning
Lightning can be a scary sight during a storm.

M

monkeys
The **monkeys** at the zoo sat in a tree.

69

First Reader, pp. 68–69

N

neighborhood
My family lives in a **neighborhood.**

P

pond
Many frogs and snakes were at the **pond.**

S

shatter
The window will **shatter** if a baseball is thrown at it.

subway
We took the **subway** downtown instead of driving a car.

swirling
The strong winds were **swirling** loudly today.

T

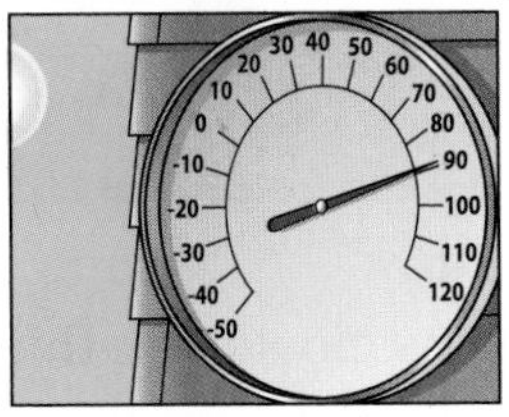

thermometer
On a hot summer day the **thermometer** may read 90 degrees Fahrenheit.

tornado
When there is a **tornado,** sirens sound in the town.

W

water holes
Animals gather at **water holes** to have a drink.

First Reader, pp. 70–71

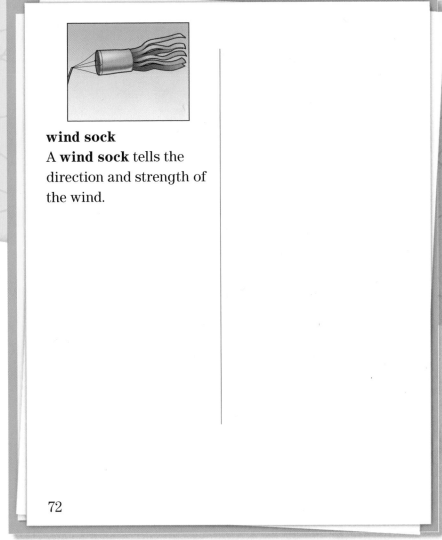

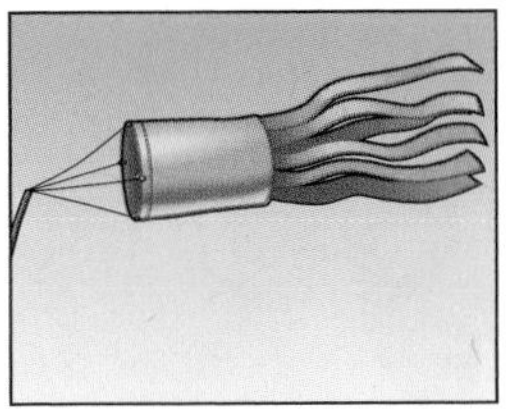

wind sock

A **wind sock** tells the direction and strength of the wind.

72

First Reader, p. 72

SRA Imagine It!

The Program Appendix includes a step-by-step explanation of procedures for research-based, effective practices in reading instruction that are repeatedly used throughout ***SRA Imagine It!*** These practices may also be used in other instructional materials.

Table of Contents

Phonological and Phonemic Awareness

Key to learning to read is the ability to identify different sounds and to connect those sounds to the letters of the alphabet. The basic purpose of providing structured practice in phonemic awareness is to help students hear and understand the sounds from which words are made. Before students can be expected to understand the sound/symbol correspondence that forms the base of written English, they need to have a strong working knowledge of the sound relationships that make up the spoken language. This understanding of spoken language lays the foundation for the transition to written language.

Phonological awareness is an umbrella term. It incorporates a range of oral language skills that involve the ability to notice, think about, and manipulate individual sounds in words. Phonological awareness involves working with sentences, words, rhyme, syllables, and sounds. The objective is for students to be able to manipulate words, word parts, and sounds without regard to meaning.

Phonological and phonemic awareness activities initially provide students with the opportunity to think about sentences and to break them into words and then to play with words and to break them into parts. It involves easy and fun activities that engage students in playing with and exploring the parts and sounds of language. The goal of these gamelike activities is to help students understand that speech is made of distinct, identifiable sounds. The playful nature of the activities makes them appealing and engaging, while giving students practice and support for learning about language. When students begin reading and writing, this experience with manipulating sounds will help them use what they know about sounds and letters to sound out and spell unfamiliar words when they read and write.

Developing phonological awareness engages students in activities that move from working with words and syllables — the larger units of language — to individual sounds (phonemes). Students progress by

- Identifying sentences
- Identifying words
- Working with rhymes
- Exploring compound words
- Listening for syllables
- Blending syllables
- Oral blending
- Deleting and substituting sounds
- Segmenting phonemes

As students progress through various phonemic awareness activities, they will become proficient at listening for and reproducing the sounds they hear. It is essential for their progression to phonics and reading that they are able to hear the sounds and the patterns used to make up recognizable words. The phonemic awareness activities support the phonics instruction. Initially students are not expected to read the words they are exploring and manipulating, so any consonant and vowel sounds may be used, even if students have not been formally taught the sounds and their spellings.

> *As students progress through various phonemic awareness activities, they will become proficient at listening for and reproducing the sounds they hear.*

After students have an awareness of phonemes, they can begin to connect sounds to letters and to engage in a variety of activities in which sounds and letters are substituted to make new words. Students begin to understand that if a sound changes, a letter must change, and a new word is created. As students move into phonics, research suggests that connecting sounds to spellings actually heightens their awareness of language. Phonological and phonemic awareness is both a prerequisite for and a consequence of learning to read.

Research suggests that the majority of instructional time should be focused on two critical phonemic awareness formats: phoneme or oral blending and phoneme segmentation. These are supported by discrimination and elision activities (deleting and substituting sounds) and general wordplay. Oral blending encourages students to combine sounds to make words and lays the foundation for decoding and reading. Segmentation, conversely, requires students to break words into discrete sounds and lays the foundation for spelling. Other activities support discrimination, or recognition, of particular sounds. Sometimes simple songs, rhymes, or games engage students in wordplay. In these, students manipulate words in a variety of ways. From these playful activities, students develop serious knowledge about their language.

Oral Blending

Purpose

In oral blending, students are led through a progression of activities designed to help them hear how sounds are put together to make words.

Until students develop an awareness of the component parts of words, they have no tools with which to decode words or to put letters together to form words. Oral blending helps students understand these component parts of words, from syllables down to single sounds, or phonemes. Oral blending is not to be confused with the formal blending of specific sounds whose spellings students will be taught through phonics instruction. Oral blending does not depend on the recognition of written words; it focuses instead on hearing the sounds.

Oral blending focuses on hearing sounds through a sequence that introduces the most easily distinguished word parts and then systematically moves to oral blending of individual sounds that contains all the challenges of phonic decoding (except letter recognition). This sequence provides support for the least-prepared student—one who comes to school with no concept of words or sounds within words. At the same time, the lively pace and playful nature of oral blending activities hold the interest of students who already have some familiarity with words and letters.

Oral blending prepares students for phonics instruction by developing an awareness of the separate sounds that make up speech. Oral blending activities then continue in concert with phonics instruction to reinforce and extend new learning. And because these activities involve simply listening to and reproducing sounds, oral blending need not be restricted to the sounds students have been or will be taught in phonics.

The tone of the activities should be playful and informal and should move quickly. Although these activities will provide information about student progress, they are not diagnostic tools. Do not expect mastery. Those students who have not caught on will be helped more by varied experiences than by more drilling on the same activity.

Procedure

The following is a description of the progression of oral blending activities.

Syllable Blending

Syllables are easier to distinguish than individual sounds (phonemes), so students can quickly experience success in forming meaningful words. Tell students that you are going to say some words in two parts. Tell them to listen carefully so they can discover what the words are. Read each word, pronouncing each part distinctly with a definite pause between syllables. The lists of words that follow are arranged in sequence from easy to harder. They cover different types of cues. Whenever they fit into the sequence, include multisyllable names of students in the class.

Model

Teacher: dino . . . saur. What's the word?
Students: dinosaur

Example Words

- First part of the word cues the whole word:
  vita . . . min
  vaca . . . tion
  hippopot . . . amus
  ambu . . . lance
- Two distinct words easily combined:
  butter. . . fly
  straw. . . berry
  surf . . . board
  basket . . . ball
- Two distinct words, but first word could cue the wrong ending:
  tooth . . . ache
  tooth . . . paste
  water . . . fall
  water . . . melon
- First part, consonant + vowel, not enough to guess whole word:
  re . . . member
  re . . . frigerator
  bi . . . cycle
  bi . . . ology
- Identifying clues in second part:
  light . . . ning
  sub . . . ject
  in . . . sect
- Last part, consonant + vowel sound, carries essential information:
  yester . . . day
  rain . . . bow
  noi . . . sy
  pota . . . to
- Changing the final part changes the word:
  start . . . ing
  start . . . er
  start. . . ed

Initial Consonant Sounds

Initial consonant blending prepares students for consonant replacement activities that will come later. Tell students that you will ask them to put some sounds together to make words. Pronounce each word part distinctly, and make a definite pause at the breaks indicated. When a letter is surrounded by slash marks, pronounce the letter's sound, not its name. When you see /s/, for example, you will say "ssss," not "ess." The words that follow are arranged from easy to harder. Whenever they fit into the sequence, include names of students in the class.

Model

Teacher: /t/ . . . iger. What's the word?
Students: tiger

Example Words

- Separated consonant blend, with rest of word giving strong cue to word identity:
  /b/. . . roccoli   */k/ . . . racker*
  /f/ . . . lashlight   */k/ . . . reature*
- Held consonant that is easy for students to hear, with rest of word giving strong cue:
  /s/ . . . innamon   */l/ . . . adybug*
  /s/ . . . eventeen   */n/ . . .* ewspaper
- Stop consonant that is harder for students to hear preceding vowel, with rest of word giving strong cue:
  /t/. . . adpole   */p/ . . . iggybank*
  /d/ . . . ragonfly   */b/ . . . arbecue*
- Single-syllable words and words in which the second part gives a weaker cue:
  /s/ . . . ing   */l/ . . . augh*   */v/ . . . ase*

Final Consonant Sounds

In this phase of oral blending, the last sound in the word is separated.

Model

Teacher: cabba . . . /j/. What's the word?
Students: cabbage

Example Words

- Words that are easily recognized even before the final consonant is pronounced:
  bubblegu . . . /m/   *Columbu . . . /s/*
  crocodi . . . /l/   *submari . . . /n/*
- Multisyllable words that need the final consonant for recognition:
  colle . . . /j/ (college)   *come . . . /t/ (comet)*
- Single-syllable words:
  sa . . . /d/   *gra . . . /s/ (grass)*   *snai . . . /l/*

Initial Consonant Sound Replacement

This level of oral blending further develops awareness of initial consonant sounds. The activity begins with a common word then quickly changes its initial consonant sound. Most of the words produced are nonsense words, which helps keep the focus on the sounds in the word. Note that the words are written on the board, but students are not expected to read them. The writing is to help students see that when the sounds change, the letters change, and vice versa.

Model

Teacher: [Writes word on board.] This word is *magazine*. What is it?
Students: magazine
Teacher: Now I'm going to change it. [Erases initial consonant.] Now it doesn't start with /m/; it's going to start with /b/. What's the new word?
Students: bagazine
Teacher: That's right . . . [Writes *b* where *m* had been.] It's *bagazine*. Now I'm going to change it again. . . .

Repeat with different consonant sounds. Then do the same with other words such as *remember, Saturday, tomorrow, lotion, and million.* Continue with single-syllable words such as *take, big, boot, cot, seat, look, tap, ride,* and *late*. There are two stages in using written letters:

- The replacement letter is not written until ***after*** the new "word" has been identified.

- Later, the replacement letter is written at ***the same time*** the change in the initial phoneme is announced. For example, erase *d* and write *m* while you say, "Now it doesn't start with /d/; it starts with /m/."

When the consonants used have already been introduced in phonics, you may wish to alter the procedure by writing the replacement letter and having students sound out the new word. Feel free to switch between the two procedures within a single exercise. If students are not responding orally to written spellings that have been introduced in phonics, do not force it. Proceed by saying the word before writing the letter, and wait until another time to move on to writing before pronouncing.

One-Syllable Words

Students now begin blending individual phonemes to form words. This important step can be continued well into the year. Continued repetitions of this activity will help students realize how they can use the sound/spellings they are learning to read and write real words.

At first, the blended words are presented in a story context that helps students identify the words. They soon recognize that they are actually decoding meaningful words. However, the context must not be so strong that students can guess the word without listening to the phonemic cues. Any vowel sounds and irregularly spelled words may be used because there is no writing involved.

Model

Teacher: When I looked out the window, I saw a /l/ /ī/ /t/. What did I see?
Students: A light.
Teacher: Yes, I saw a light. At first I thought it was the /m/ /ōō/ /n/. What did I think it was?
Students: The moon.
Teacher: But it didn't really look like the moon. Suddenly I thought, maybe it's a space /sh/ /i/ /p/. What did I think it might be?
Students: A spaceship!

When students are familiar with this phase of oral blending, they can move to blending one-syllable words without the story context.

Example Words

- CVC (consonant/vowel/consonant) words beginning with easily blended consonant sounds (/sh/, /h/, /r/, /v/, /s/, /n/, /z/, /f/, /l/, /m/):
  nip nap
- CVC words beginning with any consonant:
  ten bug lip
- Add CCVC words:
  flap step
- Add CVCC words:
  most band went
- Add CCVCC words:
  stamp grand scuffs

Final Consonant Sound Replacement

Final consonant sounds are typically more difficult for students to use than initial consonants.

- Begin with multisyllable words, and move to one-syllable words.
- As with initial consonants, first write the changed consonant after students have pronounced the new word.
- Then write the consonant as they pronounce it.
- For sound/spellings introduced in phonics instruction, write the new consonant spelling, and have students identify and pronounce it.

Model

Teacher: [Writes word on board.] This word is *teapot.* What is it?
Students: teapot
Teacher: Now I'm going to change it. [Erases final consonant.] Now it doesn't end with /t/; it ends with /p/. What's the word now?
Students: teapop
Teacher: That's right . . . [Writes *p* where *t* had been.] It's *teapop.* Now I'm going to change it again. . . .

Example Words

- Words that are easily recognized even before the final consonant is pronounced:
  picnic picnit picnis picnil picnid
  airplane airplate airplabe airplafe
- Multisyllable words that need the final consonant for recognition:
  muffin muffil muffim muffip muffit
  amaze amate amak amale amade
- Single-syllable words:
  neat nean neap neam neaj nead neaf
  broom broot brood broof broop broon

Initial Vowel Replacement

Up to now, oral blending has concentrated on consonant sounds because they are easier to hear than vowels. As you move to vowel play, remember that the focus is still on the sounds, not the spellings. Use any vowel sounds.

Model

Teacher: [Writes word on board.] This word is *elephant.* What is it?
Students: elephant
Teacher: Now I'm going to change it. [Erases initial vowel.] Now it doesn't start with /e/; it starts with /a/. What's the word now?
Students: alephant
Teacher: That's right . . . [Writes *a* where *e* had been.] It's *alephant.* Now I'm going to change it again. . . .

Example Words

- Multisyllable words:
  angry ingry oongry ungry engr
  ivy avy oovy evy ovy oivy
- One-syllable words:
  ink ank oonk unk onk oink
  add odd idd oudd edd udd

Segmentation

Purpose

Segmentation and oral blending complement each other: Oral blending puts sounds together to make words, while segmentation separates words into sounds. Oral blending will provide valuable support for decoding when students begin reading independently.

Procedure

Syllables

The earliest segmentation activities focus on syllables, which are easier to distinguish than individual sounds, or phonemes. Start with students' names, and then use other words. As with the oral blending activities, remember to move quickly through these activities. Do not hold the class back waiting for all students to catch on. Individual progress will vary, but drilling on one activity is less helpful than going on to others. Return to the same activity often. Frequent repetition is very beneficial and allows students additional opportunities to catch on.

- Say, for example, "Let's clap out Amanda's name. A-man-da."
- Have students clap and say the syllables along with you. Count the claps.
- Tell students that these word parts are called syllables. Don't try to explain; the idea will develop with practice. After you have provided the term, simply say, "How many syllables?" after students clap and count.
- Mix one-syllable and multisyllable words: *fantastic tambourine good imaginary stand afraid*

Oral blending will provide valuable support for decoding when students begin reading independently.

Comparative Lengths of Words

Unlike most phonemic awareness activities, this one involves writing on the board or on an overhead transparency. Remember, though, that students are not expected to read what is written. They are merely noticing that words that take longer to say generally look longer when written.

- Start with students' names. Choose two names, one short and one long, with the same first letter (for example, *Joe* and *Jonathan).*
- Write the two names on the board, one above the other, so that the difference is obvious.
- Tell students that one name is *Jonathan* and that one is *Joe.* Have them pronounce and clap each name. Then have them tell which written word they think says *Joe.*
- Move your finger under each name as students clap and say it syllable by syllable.
- Repeat with other pairs of names and words such as *tea/telephone, cat/caterpillar, and butterfly/bug.* Be sure not to give false clues. For example, sometimes write the longer word on top, sometimes the shorter one; sometimes ask for the shorter word, sometimes the longer; sometimes ask for the top word, sometimes the bottom; and sometimes point to a word and ask students to name it, and sometimes name the word and ask students to point to it.

Listen for Individual Sounds

Activities using a puppet help students listen for individual sounds in words. Use any puppet you have on hand. When you introduce the puppet, tell students that it likes to play word games. Each new activity begins with the teacher speaking to and for the puppet until students determine the pattern. Next, students either speak for the puppet or correct the puppet. To make sure all students are participating, alternate randomly between having the whole group or individuals respond. The activities focus on particular parts of words, according to the following sequence:

1. Repeating last part of word. Use words beginning with easy-to-hear consonants such as *f, l, m, n, r, s,* and *z.* The puppet repeats only the rime, the part of the syllable after the initial consonant.

Model

Teacher: farm
Puppet: arm
After the pattern is established, students respond for the puppet.
Teacher: rope
Students: ope

Example Words

Use words such as the following:
mine . . . ine soup . . . oup feet . . . eet

2. Restoring initial phonemes. Now students correct the puppet. Be sure to acknowledge the correction.

Model

Teacher: lake
Puppet: ake
Teacher: No, Illlake. You forgot the /l/.
Teacher: real
Puppet: eal
Teacher: What did the puppet leave off?
Students: /r/. It's supposed to be *real.*
Teacher: That's right. The word is *real.*

Example Words

Use words such as the following:
look . . . ook mouse . . . ouse sand . . . and

3. Segmenting initial consonants. The puppet pronounces only the initial consonant.

Model

Teacher: pay
Puppet: /p/

Example Words

Use words such as the following:
moon . . . /m/ nose . . . /n/ bell . . . /b/

4. Restoring final consonants. Students correct the puppet. Prompt if necessary: "What's the word? What did the puppet leave off?"

Model

Teacher: run
Puppet: ru
Students: It's run! You left off the /n/.
Teacher: That's right. The word is *run.*

Example Words

Use words such as the following:
meet . . . mee cool . . . coo boot . . . boo

5. Isolating final consonants. The puppet pronounces only the final consonant.

Model

Teacher: green
Puppet: /n/

Example Words

Use words such as the following:
glass . . . /s/ boom . . . /m/ mice . . . /s/

6. Segmenting initial consonant blends. The sounds in blends are emphasized.

Model

Teacher: clap
Puppet: lap
Next have students correct the puppet.
Teacher: stain
Puppet: tain
Students: It's stain! You left off the /s/.
Teacher: That's right. The word is *stain.*

Example Words

Use words such as the following:
blaze . . . laze draw. . . raw proud . . . roud

Discrimination

Purpose

Discrimination activities help students focus on particular sounds in words.

Listening for long-vowel sounds is the earliest discrimination activity. Vowel sounds are necessary for decoding, but young students do not hear them easily. This is evident in students' invented spellings, where vowels are often omitted. Early in the year, students listen for long-vowel sounds, which are more easily distinguished than short-vowel sounds:

- Explain to students that vowels are special because sometimes they say their names in words.
- Tell students which vowel sound to listen for.
- Have them repeat the sound when they hear it in a word. For example, if the target vowel sound is long *e,* students will say long *e* when you say *leaf,* but they should not respond when you say *loaf.*
- Initially students should listen for one long vowel sound at a time. Later they can listen for two vowel sounds. All Example Words, however, should contain one of the target vowels.

Procedure

Listening for short-vowel sounds

These discrimination activities should be done after the short vowels /a/ and /i/ have been introduced. Short vowels are very useful in reading. They are generally more regular in spelling than long vowels, and they appear in many short, simple words. However, their sounds are less easily distinguished than those of long vowels. Thus, the activities focus only on /a/ and /i/. All the words provided have one or the other of these sounds. Either have students repeat the sound of a specified vowel, or vary the activity as follows: Write an *a* on one side of the board and an *i* on the other. Ask students to point to the *a* when they hear a word with the /a/ sound and to point to the *i* when they hear a word with the /i/ sound. Use words such as the following:

bat mat sat sit spit
pit pat pan pin spin

Consonant sounds in multisyllable words

Discriminating these sounds helps students attend to consonant sounds in the middle of words.

- Say the word *rib,* and have students repeat it. Ask where they hear the /b/ in *rib.*
- Then say *ribbon,* and ask students where they hear the /b/ in *ribbon.*
- Tell students that you will say some words and that they will repeat each word.
- After they repeat each word, ask what consonant sound they hear in the middle of that word. Use words such as the following:
  famous message picky
  jogger flavor zipper

Phonemic Play

Purpose

Wordplay activities help students focus on and manipulate sounds, thus supporting the idea that words are made of specific sounds that can be taken apart, put together, or changed to make new words. Through wordplay, students gain important knowledge about language.

Procedure

Producing rhymes

Many phonemic play activities focus on producing rhymes. A familiar or easily learned rhyme or song is introduced, and students are encouraged to substitute words or sounds. An example is "Willaby Wallaby Woo," in which students change the rhyming words in the couplet "Willaby Wallaby Woo/ An elephant sat on you" so that the second line ends with a student's name and that the first line ends with a rhyme beginning with *W;* for example, "Willaby Wallaby Wissy/An elephant sat on Missy."

Generate alliterative words

Students can also say as many words as they can think of that begin with a given consonant sound. This is a valuable complement to discrimination activities in which the teacher produces the words and students identify them.

The Alphabetic Principle: How the Alphabet Works

The Alphabetic Principle

Purpose

A major emphasis in the kindergarten program is on letter recognition and attending to sounds. Students need to learn the alphabetic principle: that letters work together in a systematic way to connect spoken language to written words. This understanding is the foundation for reading. Students are not expected to master letter/sound correspondence at the beginning of kindergarten, nor are they expected to blend sounds into words themselves. They are expected to become an "expert" only on their Special Letters as they learn how the alphabet works. Through this introduction to the alphabetic principle, students will have the basic understanding required to work through the alphabet letter by letter, attaching sounds to each.

Key concepts of the alphabetic principle include the following:

- A limited number of letters combine in different ways to make many different words.
- Words are composed of sounds, and letters represent those sounds.
- Anything that can be pronounced can be spelled.
- Letters and sounds can be used to identify words.
- Meaning can be obtained by using letters and sounds to determine words.

Procedures for Kindergarten

The following steps can be used for introducing letters and sounds in kindergarten. These steps may be adapted for students at other grades if they do not understand the alphabetic principle. The tone of these activities should be informal, fun, and fast-paced. The purpose of these activities is to familiarize students with how the alphabet works by having them participate in group play with letters and sounds.

I Can Spell Anything

- Reinforce the idea that anything that can be pronounced can be spelled with the letters of the alphabet.
- Tell students that you can spell any word. Have them give you words to spell.
- Write the words on the board, naming each letter as you write it. This shows students that the words contain the letters displayed on the ***Alphabet Sound Wall Cards.***
- Have students help you spell the words again by pointing to letters as you say them.
- Encourage students to spell each word letter by letter.

The alphabetic principle is the understanding that speech sounds can be mapped onto print.

Letter Expert Groups

- Have ***Alphabet Letter Cards*** (Levels K and 1) available for the following set of letters: *b, d, f, h, l, m, n, p, s, t.* You will need two or three cards for each letter. (You will not need the ***Alphabet Sound Cards*** until later.)
- You will be the letter expert for the vowels.
- Organize the class into groups of two or three, and assign each group a letter. Give each student the appropriate ***Alphabet Letter Card.***
- Tell students that they are now in their Letter Expert groups and that they are going to become experts on their Special Letter's name, shape, and sound.

Making Words

- Begin each lesson with a rehearsal of each group's letter name.
- Demonstrate how letters work by writing a word in large letters on the board.
- Tell students the experts for each letter in the word should hold up their ***Alphabet Letter Cards*** and name the letter. One member of the group should stand in front of their letter on the board.
- Continue until all letters in the word are accounted for. Remember that you are responsible for the vowels.
- Demonstrate that you can make different words by changing a letter or by changing the letter order.

Identifying Sounds in Words

- Use the ***Alphabet Sound Cards*** to demonstrate that every letter has at least one sound.
- Give each student the ***Alphabet Sound Card*** for his or her Special Letter.
- Point out the pictures on the cards. Explain that each card has a picture of something that makes the letter's sound. The picture will help them remember the sound.
- Tell each group the sound for its letter. (Remember, you are the expert for the vowels.)
- Quickly have each group rehearse its letter's name and sound.
- Write a word on the board in large letters. Say the word first sound by sound, and then blend the word.
- For each letter/sound in the word, have one student from each Letter Expert group come forward, stand in front of the appropriate letter, and hold their cards. Although only one member of the group may come forward with the ***Alphabet Letter Card*** or ***Alphabet Sound Card,*** all students in a Special Letter group should say the name or sound of their letter when it occurs in words.
- Say the word again, pointing to the ***Alphabet Sound Cards.***
- Ask students who are not already standing to help you hold the vowel cards.
- Vary the activity by changing one letter sound and having an expert for that letter come forward.

- End the activity for each word by saying the sounds in the words one by one and then saying the entire word. Encourage students to participate.

Tips

- Remind students to use the picture on the ***Alphabet Sound Card*** for their Special Letter to help them remember the letter's sound. Students are expected to "master" only their own Special Letter and to share the information with their classmates. At this point in the year, they are not expected to blend and read the words by themselves. These are group activities in which you work with students to help them gain insight into the alphabet.
- Be sure to connect what students learn about the letters and words to the words they work with in ***Big Book*** selections.
- Occasionally, have students find their special letters in a ***Big Book*** selection. Play some of the letter replacement and rearrangement games with words encountered in the ***Big Books.***

Developing the Alphabetic Principle

Purpose

The alphabetic principle is the understanding that speech sounds can be mapped onto print. It is the association of sounds with letters and the understanding that speech can be turned into print and that print can be turned into speech sounds. Activities associated with the alphabetic principle help kindergarten students develop a more thorough understanding of how sounds "work" in words. In this group of activities, students are introduced to specific letter/sound correspondences, consonants, and short vowels. While students have previously been introduced to vowels and their special characteristics, students' understanding is extended by introducing students to the convention that a vowel has a short sound in addition to its long sound. With this information and a carefully structured set of activities, students can begin to explore and understand the alphabetic principle in a straightforward and thorough manner. Students not only listen for sounds in specified positions in words, they also link sounds to their corresponding letters. The activities in this group of lessons lay the groundwork for students to work their way through the entire alphabet as they learn letter-sound associations and to understand the purpose and the value of this learning.

Move students quickly through these activities. Do not wait for all students to master each letter/sound correspondence before going on. They will have more opportunities to achieve mastery. The goal of these activities is for students to obtain a basic understanding of the alphabetic principle.

Students need to learn the alphabetic principle: that letters work together in a systematic way to connect spoken language to written words. This understanding is the foundation for reading.

Procedures

Introducing Consonant Letters and Sounds

- Point to the ***Alphabet Sound Wall Card*** and ask students what they know about the card (the letter name, the capital and lowercase letter, and so on).
- Turn the card, and point to the picture. Name the picture, and point to and name the letter. Tell students the sound of the letter and how the picture helps them remember the sound. Repeat the sound several times.
- Tell students you will read them the short story or an alliterative sentence to help them remember the sound of the letter. Read the story several times, emphasizing the words with the target sound. Have students join in and say the sound.
- After introducing and reviewing a letter/sound correspondence, summarize the information on the ***Alphabet Sound Wall Card:*** the name of the card, the sound, and the letter.

Generating Words with the Target Sound

Brainstorm to create a list of words that begin with the target sound. Write the words on the board or on a chart. Include any of the students' names that begin with the target sound.

Listening for Initial Sounds

- Give each student an ***Alphabet Letter Card*** for the target sound.
- Point to the picture on the ***Alphabet Sound Wall Card,*** and have students give the sound.
- Tell students to listen for the first sound in each word you say. If it is target sound, they should hold up their cards. Establish a signal so that students know when to respond.
- Read the list of words, some beginning with the target sound and some beginning with other sounds.

Listening for Final Sounds

The procedure for listening for the final sound of a word is the same as that for listening for the initial sound. Students may need to be reminded throughout the activity to pay attention to the final sound.

Read a list of words, some ending with the target sound and some ending with other sounds. Avoid words that begin with the target sound.

Linking the Sound to the Letter

- **Word Pairs (initial sounds).** Write pairs of words on the board. One of each pair should begin with the target sound. Say the word beginning with the target sound, and ask students to identify it. Remind them to listen for the target sound at the beginning of the word, to think about which letter makes that sound, and to find the word that begins with that letter. For example,
  Target sound: /s/
  Word pair: *fit sit*
  Which word is *sit?*
- **Word Pairs (final sounds).** Follow the same procedure used for initial sounds, and direct students to think about the sound that they hear at the end of the word. Because it is often more difficult

for students to attend to the ending sound, you may need to lead them through several pairs of words. Remind students to listen for the target sound and to think about which letter makes that sound.

- **Writing Letters.** Using either of the handwriting systems outlined in this Program Appendix or the system in use at your school, have students practice writing uppercase and lowercase letters. Remind students about the letter sound, and have them repeat it.

Other activities that support the development of the alphabetic principle include the following:

Comparing Initial Consonant Sounds

This activity is exactly like Listening for Initial Sounds except that students must discriminate between two sounds. They are given ***Alphabet Letter Cards*** for both sounds and must hold up the appropriate card when they hear the sound.

Comparing Final Consonant Sounds

This activity is exactly like Listening for Final Sounds except that students must discriminate between two sounds. They are given ***Alphabet Letter Cards*** for both sounds and must hold up the appropriate card when they hear the sound.

Linking the Consonant Sound to the Letter

In this activity to help students link sounds and letters, students will make words either by adding initial consonants to selected word parts or by adding a different final consonant to a consonant-vowel-consonant combination.

- **I'm Thinking of Something That Starts with ___ Game.** Begin with the target sound, and add clues until students guess the word. If students give a word that does not begin with the target sound, emphasize the beginning sound, and ask if the word begins with the target sound.
- **Silly Sentences.** Make silly sentences with students that include many words with the target sound. Encourage students to participate by extending the sentences: Mary mopes. Mary mopes on Monday. Mary and Michael mope on Monday in Miami. For older students, have them make silly sentences using the sound at the beginning of their first name. Have them use the dictionary to find more words beginning with the target sound.

Introducing Short-Vowel Sounds

- Tell students that the vowels are printed in red to remind them that they are special letters. (They are not special because they are printed in red.) They are special because they have more than one sound, and every word in English must have a vowel sound.
- Point to the long *Aa* ***Alphabet Sound Wall Card,*** and remind students that this letter is called a vowel. Tell them vowels sometimes say their names in words (for example, say, *day, tray).* When the vowel says its name, the sound is long. Tell them this vowel sound is called long *a.*
- Have students repeat the sound.
- Tell students sometimes vowels say different sounds. Point to the picture of the lamb on the short *Aa* card, and tell students that *a* also makes the sound heard in the middle of *lamb.* This is the short *a.* Read the short vowel story to help students remember the short *a.*
- Have all students join in saying/ă/ /ă/ /ă/.

Listening for Short-Vowel Sounds Versus Long-Vowel Sounds

- Tell students that you will read words with long *a* and short *a.* Review the two sounds.
- Give students a signal to indicate when they hear the vowel sound. You may want one signal for short *a,* such as scrunching down, and another for long *a,* such as stretching up tall.
- Continue with lists of words such as *add, back, aid, tan, bake,* and *tame.*

Linking the Vowel Sound to the Letter

- **Writing Letters.** Have students practice writing the letter and review the sound of the letter.
- In this activity to help students link sounds and letters, students will make words either by adding initial consonants to selected word parts or by adding a different final consonant to a consonant-vowel-consonant combination. Change the beginning of the word or the word ending, but retain the vowel sound to make new words:

at	hat	mat	pat
ap	map	tap	sap
am	Sam	Pam	ham

Comparing Short-Vowel Sounds

This activity requires students to discriminate between short-vowel sounds in the middle of words. Review the vowel sounds.

- Say a word, and have students repeat it. Establish a signal to indicate whether they hear short *a* or short *o* in the middle of the word. For example, they can hold up the appropriate ***Alphabet Letter Card*** when they hear a sound. Sample words: *cap, cot, rat, rot, rack,* and *rock.*

Linking the Sound to the Letter

- In this activity, write a word on the board, and help students say it.
- Change the word by changing the vowel. Help students say the new word, for example, *map, mop; hot, hat; pot, pat.*
- For a variation of this activity, write the pairs of words, and simply have students say which word is the target word. For example, students see *tap* and *top.* Ask which word *top* is, directing students' attention to the vowel.

Introducing Long-Vowel Sounds

The introduction of short vowels and consonants helps students internalize the alphabetic principle—a sound can be mapped onto a letter. In English, however, some sounds are represented by more than one letter, for example, the /ē/ can be represented by the letter *e* as in *me* but also represented by e_e as in *Pete.* Toward the end of kindergarten, students will be introduced to long vowels and two common representations of those sounds. These include the single vowel such as *a* or *e* and the vowel consonant silent *e* (VCe). The introduction of the VCe pattern or unit gives students a wide range of common words to read by the end of kindergarten and sets a solid foundation for first grade.

- If necessary, remind students that vowels are written in red. Point to the long /ā/ card, and tell students that the sound of long /ā/ is /ā/.

- Have students say the sound with you.
- Tell students that long *a* can be written in more than one way; it can be written as a just like short *a* but it can also be written as *a_e.* When we see the blank, it is a clue that another sound and letter needs to be put on the blank or line to make a word.
- Write a_e, and have students give the sound: /ā/. Then write a *t* on the blank, say the sound, and blend the word: *ate.*
- The goal is to have students see the *a_e* or any of the other CVe patterns as a unit.
- While students have been blending and reading short-vowel words, long vowels create a shift in thinking: Combinations of letters can be used to represent a sound. Here are some easy tips when you are first working with the CVe patterns:
  - The CVe patterns are not written on the ***Alphabet Sound Cards.*** You may want to write the *a_e, e_e, i_e, o_e,* and *u_e* units on the respective long-vowel cards as a reminder for students. Do this as you introduce each long vowel unit. Use an erasable marker so you can reintroduce these special patterns each year.
  - Provide maximum support when first using the long-vowel units in blending.
  - Write the letter for the first sound, for example, /m/, and have students give the sound.
  - Write the unit for /ā/: *a_e.* Tell students this says /ā/. Be sure to write the whole unit.
  - Write the final letter ON the blank, for example, *k.* Give the sound for the *k,* and then blend the word.
  - Let students hear your voice during the blending, but gradually reduce it so they are doing more of the thinking.
  - Help students blend long vowel words as they are reading their ***Decodables.***

Tips

- Model and support the activities as necessary until students begin to catch on and can participate with confidence.
- To keep students focused on the various activities, have them tell you the task for each activity. For example, after telling students to listen for final sounds, ask students what they will be listening for.
- Actively involve students by giving them opportunities to tell what they know rather than supplying the information for them. *What is the letter name? What is the sound? What words begin with the sound?*
- Keeping students focused on the idea that they are learning about sounds and letters so they can read books themselves makes the lessons more relevant for students.

Introducing Sounds and Letters

Purpose

In ***SRA Imagine It!*** students learn to relate sounds to letters in kindergarten through the use of thirty-one ***Alphabet Sound Cards.*** In the upper grade levels, ***Sound/Spelling Cards*** (Levels 1–3) are used to relate sounds and spellings. The purpose of the ***Alphabet Sound Cards*** is to remind students of the sounds of the English language and their letter correspondences. These cards are a resource for students to use to remember sound-letter associations for both reading and writing.

Each card contains the capital and small letter and a picture that shows the sound being produced. For instance, the Sausage card introduces the /s/ sound and shows sausages sizzling in a pan. The sound the sausage make sizzling in the pan is /s/ /s/ /s/. The name of the picture on each card contains the target sound at the beginning of the word for the consonants and in the middle for most of the vowels. Vowel letters are printed in red, and consonants are printed in black. In addition, the picture associates a sound with an action. This action-sound association is introduced through a short, interactive story found in the ***Teacher's Edition,*** in which the pictured object or character "makes" the sound of the letter. Long vowels are represented by a tall—or "long"—picture of the letters themselves rather than by a picture for action-sound association. Short vowels have a green background, and long vowels have a yellow background.

Procedures

- Display Cards 1–26 with the picture sides to the wall. Initially post the first twenty-six cards in alphabetical order so that only the alphabet letters on the back show. The short-vowel cards may be posted as they are introduced later. As you introduce the sound of each letter, you will turn the card to show the picture and the letter on the other side. Because students will be referring to these cards for reading and writing, post them where all students can easily see them.
- Before turning a card, point to the letter. Ask students to tell what they know about the letter. For example, they are likely to know its name if the letter is one with which they have already worked. They might also note that there is an upper- and lowercase for the letter or that the letter is a consonant or a vowel.
- Turn the card, and point to the picture. Tell students the name of the picture (card), and explain that it will help them remember the sound the letter makes.
- Tell students the name and the sound of the letter.
- Read the story that goes with the card. Read it expressively, emphasizing the words with the target sound and the isolated sound when it occurs. Have students join in to produce the sound.

> *The purpose of the **Alphabet Sound Cards** is to remind students of the sounds of the English language and their letter correspondences.*

- Repeat the story a few times, encouraging all students to say the sound along with you.
- Repeat the name of the letter and the sound.
- Follow the story with the cards for the target sound. (These are listed within the lessons.)
- Name each picture, and have students listen for the target sound at the beginning of the word. Ask students to repeat the words and the sound.
- Listenig for the sound in different positions in words provides additional work with phonemic awareness. Give each student the letter card for the introduced sound and letter. Read the words from Listening for the Sound, and have students raise their letter card if they hear the target sound at the beginning of the word. For many letters, students will also listen for the sound at the ends of words as well.
- To link the sound and the letter, demonstrate how to form the uppercase and lowercase letters by writing on the board or on an overhead transparency. Have students practice forming the letter and saying the sound as they write.

Alphabet Sound Cards

The pictures and letters on the ***Alphabet Sound Wall Cards*** also appear on the small sets of individual ***Alphabet Sound Cards.*** The ***Teacher's Edition*** specifically suggests that you use the individual ***Alphabet Sound Cards*** for Workshop and small-group activities for review, reteaching, and practice sessions. Place sets of the cards in the appropriate Workshop area for students to use alone or with partners. Add each small card to the Activity Center after you have taught the lesson in which the corresponding individual ***Alphabet Sound Card*** is introduced. Here are some suggestions for activities using the individual ***Alphabet Sound Cards:***

1. **Saying sounds from pictures.** The leader flashes pictures as the others say the sound each picture represents.
2. **Saying sounds.** The leader flashes the letters on the cards as the others say the sound that the letters represent.
3. **Naming words from pictures.** The leader flashes pictures. The others say the sound and then say a word beginning with that sound.
4. **Writing letters from the pictures.** Working alone, a student looks at a picture and then writes the letter for the sound that picture represents.
5. **Making words using the pictures.** A student uses the pictures (Sausage, Pig, Timer for *sit*) or the letters to make words.

Tips

- Throughout the beginning lessons, help students remember that vowels are special by reminding them that vowels sometimes say their names in words. For example, tell them the picture of the *a* on the long *a* ***Alphabet Sound Card*** is long because the long *a* says its name. The short *a* ***Alphabet Sound Card*** pictures the lamb because the lamb makes the short *a* sound, and you can hear the sound in the word *lamb*.
- From the very beginning, encourage students to use the ***Alphabet Sound Cards*** as a resource to help them with their work.
- Mastery of letter recognition is the goal students should reach so that they will be prepared to link each letter with its associated sound. If students have not yet mastered the names of the letters, it is important to work with them individually in Workshop, or at other times during the day.
- Both the *Cc* and the *Kk* cards have the same picture—a camera. A camera makes the /k/ sound when it clicks, and the word *camera* begins with the /k/ sound. However, the word *camera* is not spelled with a *k*. Remember, the first sound of the word helps students remember the sound of the letter.
- The picture on the *Qq* card depicts quacking ducks. Make sure that students consistently call them quacking ducks, not ducks, and that they focus on the /kw/ sound.

Explicit, Systematic Phonics

The purpose of phonics instruction is to teach students the association between the sounds of the language and the written symbols—spellings—that have been chosen to represent those sounds.

As with all alphabetic languages, English has a limited number of symbols—twenty-six—that are combined and recombined to make the written language. These written symbols are a visual representation of the speech sounds we use to communicate. This is simply a code. The faster students learn the code and how it works, the faster the whole world of reading opens up to them.

Beginning at the kindergarten level, students are introduced to sounds and letters. Students learn that sounds can be mapped onto letters and that those sounds and letters can be blended to read words.

In Grade 1, students make the shift from mapping sounds onto letters to mapping sounds onto spellings. The introduction of both sounds and letters in kindergarten and the sounds and spellings in Grade 1 is done in a very systematic, sequential manner. This allows students to continually build on what they learned the day before. As each sound/symbol relationship is introduced, students learn about and practice with words containing the target sound and letter in kindergarten and sound/spelling in Grade1. This new knowledge is then reinforced through the use of engaging text specifically written for this purpose.

It can be very difficult for students to hear the individual sounds, or phonemes, that make up words. When phonics instruction is explicit—students are told the sounds associated with the different written symbols—there is no guesswork involved. They know that the sound /b/ is spelled *b*. Therefore, students in an ***SRA Imagine It!*** classroom spend time learning to discriminate individual speech sounds, and then they learn the spellings of those sounds. This systematic, explicit approach affords students the very best chance for early and continuing success.

Sound/Spelling Cards

(Grade 1 on) See The Alphabetic Principle for information on the introduction of sounds and letters in pre-kindergarten and kindergarten.

Purpose

The purpose of the ***Sound/Spelling Cards*** (Levels 1–3) is to remind students of the sounds of English and their spellings. The name of the picture on each card contains the target sound at the beginning of the name for consonants and in the middle for the short vowels. Long vowels are represented by elongated pictures of the vowel. The variant vowels such as /aw/ and /oi/ contain the vowel sound in the name as well. In addition, the picture associates a sound with an action. This association is introduced through an interactive story in which the pictured object or character "makes" the sound. This "action" cue is particularly helpful for students whose primary language is not English. In some cases, the name of the card and the initial sound may be similar to words in other languages. For example, the word for *lion* in Spanish is *león,* which begins with the same sound as the English word. This is not true for other languages. In Russian the word for *lion* is *лев* and in Japanese it is *raion.* The word for *zipper* in Spanish is *cremallera,* in Russian it is *застежка-молния* and in Japanese it is *jippa.* But all students can remember the action and sounds and use them as a resource for both reading and writing.

> *The faster students learn the code and how it works, the faster the whole world of reading opens up to them.*

Procedure

Posting the Cards

In Grade 1, initially post the first twenty-six cards with the picture to the wall so that only the alphabet letters on the backs show. As you introduce each card, you will turn it to show the picture and the spellings on the front of the card. Some Grade 1 teachers who have students who are familiar with the cards from kindergarten choose to place the first twenty-six cards (the alphabet) with the pictures facing the class. Because students are familiar with the cards and how to use them, this provides support for writing. Even these first-grade teachers, however, cover the spellings not introduced in kindergarten. In second- or third-grade classrooms in which students are reviewing what they learned the year before, place all the cards with the picture and the spellings facing forward so students can use these as a resource from the beginning of the school year. Make sure that the cards are positioned so that you can touch them with your hand or with a pointer when you refer to them and so that all students can see them easily. The cards should be placed where students can readily see and reference them throughout the day.

Special Devices

- Vowel spellings are printed in red to draw attention to them. It is the vowels and their different spellings that challenge us all. Consonants are printed in black. The blank line in a spelling indicates that a letter will take the place of the blank in a word. For example, the replacement of the blank with *t* in the spelling *a_e* makes the word *ate.* The blank lines may also indicate the position of a spelling in a word or a syllable. The blank in *h_*, for example, means that the sound /h/ spelled *h_* occurs at the beginning of a word or a syllable.
- The blanks in *_ie_* indicate that the *ie* spelling will not come at the beginning or the end of a word syllable as in *babies,* while the blank in *_oy* shows that the *oy* spelling comes at the end of a word or a syllable as in *toy.* Uses of blanks in specific spellings are discussed in the lessons. Please note now, however, that when you write a spelling of a sound on

the board or an overhead transparency, you should include the blanks.

- The color of the background behind the spellings also has a meaning. Consonants have a white background. The colors behind vowel spellings are pronunciation clues. Short-vowel spellings have a green background, which corresponds to the green box that appears before some consonant spellings. Thus, before *ck, tch,* or *x,* you will see a green box, which indicates that a short vowel always precedes that spelling. Long-vowel spellings have a yellow background; other vowel spellings such as *r*-controlled vowels, diphthongs, and variant vowels have a blue background. The color code reinforces the idea that vowels are special and have different pronunciations.

Introducing the Sound/Spelling Wall Cards

In first grade, each sound and spelling is introduced by using a see/hear/say/write sequence. In Grades 2 and 3 the same sequence is used in the review of the cards.

1. *See:* Students see the spelling or spellings on the ***Sound/Spelling Wall Card*** and the board or an overhead transparency.
2. *Hear:* Students hear the sound used in words and in isolation in the story. The sound is, of course, related to the picture (and the action) shown on the ***Sound/Spelling Wall Card.***
3. *Say:* Students say the sound.
4. *Write:* Students write the spelling(s) for the sound.

There are a number of important points to remember about this routine.

- Take down the ***Sound/Spelling Wall Card,*** tell the class the name of the card, the sound, and the spelling.
- Read the alliterative story so students hear the sound used in words as well as in isolation, and say the sound.
- After you present the sound and spelling, have several students go to the board to write the spelling. Have them say the sound as they write the spelling. After they have written the spelling of the sound, give them an opportunity to proofread their own work. Then give the other students the opportunity to help with proofreading by noting what is good about the spelling and then suggesting how to make it better.
- Difficulty in blending may be the result of not knowing the sounds or not being able to pronounce the sounds. Teach the sounds thoroughly during the introduction of the ***Sound/Spelling Wall Card*** and during initial sounding and blending. To help ensure success for all students, make certain that every student is able to see the board or screen.

Introducing the Sound /s/ spelled *s*

- Point to the back of ***Sound/Spelling Wall Card*** 18—Sausage, and have students tell you what they know about the card: it is a consonant and there is an upper and lowercase *s* on the card. Turn the card, and tell the class the name of the card: Sausage. Point to the sausage in the picture, and say the word *sausage,* emphasizing the initial consonant sound—*ssssssausage.* Note: teachers usually place a sticky note over the other spellings of /s/—the *ce, ci_,* and *cy*—in order to help students focus on the single spelling being introduced in the lesson.
- Point to the spelling *s*. Tell students that /s/ is spelled *s*.
- Read the alliterative story. In Grades 2 and 3, the stories for the card are printed in the Level Appendix of the ***Teacher's Edition.*** If your students in Grades 2 and 3 are familiar with the cards, have them tell you the name of the card, the sound, and the spelling and tell the story.
- If students had ***SRA Imagine It!*** before, you can ask them if they learned an action to help them remember the sound. If your students do not already have an action they associate with the cards, make some up with your students. They will have fun, and it will be another way for them to remember the sound/spelling relationships.
- Write *s* on the board or on an overhead transparency, and say the sound. Write the spelling again and ask students to say the sound with you as they write the spelling on slates, on paper, or with their index fingers in the air or in the palm of their hands. Repeat this activity several times.
- Have several students come to the board and write the upper- and lowercase spelling while the others continue to write them on slates or with their fingers. Be sure to encourage students to say the sound as they make the spelling. For students writing at the board, take time to have them proofread their work.
- Have students listen for words beginning with /s/, indicating by some signal, such as thumbs-up or thumbs-down, whether they hear the /s/ sound and saying /s/ when they hear it in a word. Repeat with the sound in various positions in words. Encourage students to tell you and the class words with /s/ at the beginning, as well as at the ends of words.
- Check students' learning by pointing to the card. Have students identify the sound, name the spelling, and discuss how the card can help them remember the sound.

Remember that saying the sound, listening to the alliterative story, and listening for the sound (discriminating it from other sounds) in different positions in words are all phonemic awareness activities that have been integrated into phonics.

Individual Sound/Spelling Cards

Use the individual ***Sound/Spelling Cards*** for review and for small-group reteaching and practice sessions. Students can use them alone or with partners. Here are some suggestions for activities using the individual ***Sound/Spelling Cards:***

1. **Saying sounds from pictures.** The leader flashes pictures as the others say the sound each picture represents.
2. **Saying sounds.** The leader flashes the spellings on the cards as the others say the sound that the spellings represent.
3. **Naming spellings from pictures.** The leader flashes pictures. The others name the card, say the sound, and then name as many spellings as they can.
4. **Writing spellings from the pictures.** Working alone, a student looks at a picture and then writes as many spellings for that ***Sound/Spelling Card*** as he or she can remember.
5. **Saying words from pictures.** The leader presents a series of individual cards, for example, Sausage, Lamb, Timer. The others tell the word by blending the sounds represented—*sat.*

Blending

Purpose

The purpose of blending is to teach students a strategy for figuring out unfamiliar words. Initially students will be blending sound by sound as they learn how to blend. After they understand the process, they will move to whole-word blending and develop the strategy they will use to read unfamiliar words. Ultimately students will sound and blend only those words that they cannot read. Eventually the blending process will become quick and comfortable for them.

Procedure

Learning the sounds and their spellings is only the first step in learning to read and write. The second step is learning to blend the sounds into words.

Blending Techniques

Blending lines are written on the board or an overhead transparency as students watch and participate. The lines and sentences should not be written out before class begins. It is through the sound-by-sound blending of the words and the sentences that students learn the blending process.

Sound-by-Sound Blending

- Write the spelling of the first sound in the word. Point to the spelling, and say the sound. For example, the word students will be blending is *sat.*
- Have students say the sound with you as you say the sound again. Write the spelling of the next sound. Point to the spelling, and say the sound. Have students say the sound with you as you say the sound again. After you have written the vowel spelling, blend through the vowel (unless the vowel is the first letter of the word), making the blending motion—a smooth sweeping of the hand beneath the sounds, linking them from left to right, for example, *sa.* As you make the blending motion, make sure that your hand is under the letter that corresponds to the sound you are saying at the moment.
- Write the spelling of the next sound—*t.* Point to the spelling, and have students, say the sound with you as you touch the spelling. If this is the last sound and spelling in the word, then have students blend and read the word—*sat.* If this is not the final sound and spelling, continue pointing to the spelling and asking for the sound. For example, in the word *sand,* you would blend through the vowel then ask for the sounds for the spellings *n* and *d* before blending the word. After pronouncing the final sound in the word, make the blending motion from left to right under the word as you blend the sounds. Then have students blend the word. Let them be the first to pronounce the word normally.
- Ask a student to read the word again naturally, as they would say or speak it. Then have a student use it in a sentence. Ask another student to extend the sentence, that is, make it more interesting by giving more information. Help the student by asking an appropriate question about the sentence, using, for example, *How? When? Where?* or *Why?* Continue blending the rest of the words in the blending line. At the end of each line, have students reread the words naturally.

Blending is the heart of phonics instruction and the key strategy students must learn to open the world of written language.

Whole-Word Blending

When students are comfortable with sound-by-sound blending, they are ready for whole-word blending.

- Write the whole word to be blended on the board or an overhead transparency.
- Ask students to blend the sounds as you point to each spelling.
- Then have students say the whole word.
- Ask students to use the word in a sentence and then to extend the sentence.
- After blending each line, have students read the words naturally, as they would say them.
- When all of the words have been blended, point to words randomly, and ask individuals to read them.

Blending Syllables

In reading the ***Student Readers,*** students will often encounter multisyllabic words. Some students are intimidated by long words, yet many multisyllabic words are easily read by reading and blending the syllables rather than the individual sounds. Beginning in first grade, students will learn about different syllable generalizations, open and closed syllables, consonant *-le*, and the like. Following a set of rules for syllables is difficult because so many of the rules have exceptions. Students need to remember that each syllable in a word contains one vowel sound. Early in the process, you will need to provide support.

- Have students identify the vowel sounds and spellings in the word.
- Have students blend the first syllable sound by sound if necessary or read the first syllable.
- Handle the remaining syllables the same way.
- Have students blend the syllables together to read the word.

Blending Sentences

Blending sentences is the logical extension of blending words. Blending sentences helps students develop fluency, which is critical to comprehension. Encourage students to reread sentences with phrasing and natural intonation.

Write the sentence on the board or on a transparency, underlining any high-frequency sight words—words that students cannot decode either because they are irregular or because they contain sounds or spellings that students have not yet learned or reviewed. High-frequency sight words are taught before blending. Write the word or words on the board or an overhead transparency, and introduce them before writing the sentence. Read the word, and have students repeat the word then spell the word. Use each word in a sentence. Point to the word or words, and have students read them again. These words should not be blended but read as whole words.

Tips

- The goal of blending in first grade is not to have students blend words sound by sound for the whole year. Sound-by-sound instruction should begin with maximum instructional support—with teachers and students blending together. As students understand the sound-by-sound blending routine, drop the verbal cues (sound, sound, blend, sound, blend), and simply point to the spellings after they are written, and have the class give the sounds.

- How do you know when to move from sound-by-sound to whole-word blending? When you are writing the final spelling and students are reading the word, it is time to move on to whole-word blending. This often occurs around Unit 3 in first grade.
- Keep in mind, however, that when you introduce more complex long-vowel and variant vowel spellings, you can always drop back to sound-by-sound blending for the first couple of blending lines in the lesson.
- Even though the entire class may be doing whole-word blending, sound-by-sound blending is an excellent preteaching tool for students needing extra help. After all the sounds and spellings have been introduced, students may be ready to move just to reading the words in the blending line. Have them read the words, stopping to blend only words they cannot read fluently and automatically.
- In Grades 2 and 3, teachers often begin the phonics review in the Getting Started lessons with sound-by-sound blending and then quickly move into whole-word blending. Again, the goal is to have students reading the words as quickly and automatically as possible. If the majority of the class can do this, then use whole-word blending. Use sound-by-sound blending to preteach the blending lines with students who need more support.

Building for Success

A primary cause of students' blending failure is their failure to understand how to use the ***Sound/Spelling Cards.*** Students need to practice sounds and spellings when the ***Sound/Spelling Cards*** are introduced and during initial blending. They also need to understand that if they are not sure of how to pronounce a spelling, they can check the cards. You may need to lead the group almost constantly. Soon, however, leaders in the group will take over. Watch to see whether any students are having trouble during the blending. Include them in small-group instruction sessions. At that time you may want to use the vowel-first procedure to reteach blending lines.

Extra Help

In working with small groups during Workshop, you may want to use some of the following suggestions to support students who need help with blending.

Vowel-First Blending

Vowel-first blending is an alternative to sound-by-sound and whole-word blending for students who need special help. Used in small-group sessions, this technique helps students who have difficulty with the other two types of blending focus on the most important part of each word—the vowels—and do only one thing at a time. These students are not expected to say a sound and blend it with another at virtually the same time. The steps to use in vowel-first blending follow:

1. Across the board or on an overhead transparency, write the vowel spelling in each of the words in the line. For a short vowel, the line may look like this:
   a a a
   For a long vowel, the line may look like this: *ee ea ea*
2. Point to the spelling as students say the sound for the spelling.
3. Begin blending around the vowels. In front of the first vowel spelling, add the spelling for the beginning sound of the word. Make the blending motion, and have students blend through the vowel, adding a blank to indicate that the word is still incomplete. Repeat this procedure for each partial word in the line until the line looks like this:
   ma__ sa__ pa__
   see__ mea__ ea__
4. Have students blend the partial word again as you make the blending motion, and then add the spelling for the ending sound.
5. Make the blending motion, and have students blend the completed word—for example, *mat* or *seed.*
6. Ask a student to repeat the word and to use it in a sentence. Then have another student extend the sentence.
7. Repeat steps 4, 5, and 6 for each word in the line, which might look like this:
   mat sad pan
   or
   seed meat team

Tips

- In the early lessons, blend with as much direction and dialogue as is necessary for success. Reduce your directions to a minimum as soon as possible. You have made good progress when you no longer have to say, "Sound—Sound—Blend," because students automatically sound and blend as you write.
- Blending is more than just reading words; it is an opportunity to build vocabulary and to develop oral language.

Always ask students to use less familiar words in sentences and then to extend the sentences. This sentence extension is a technique that can be applied to writing as well. Students will naturally extend sentences by adding phrases to the ends of the sentences. Encourage them to add phrases at the beginning or in the middle of the sentence as well.

- Use the vowel-first procedure in small-group preteaching or reteaching sessions with students who are having a lot of trouble with blending. Remember that you must adapt the blending lines in the lessons to the vowel-first method.
- The sight words in the sentences cannot be blended. Students must approach them as sight words to be memorized, If students are having problems reading sight words, tell them the words.
- Cue marks written over the vowels may help students.
  - Straight line cue for long vowels
    EXAMPLES: āpe, mē, fīne, sō, ūse
  - Curved line cue for short vowels
    EXAMPLES: căt, pĕt, wĭn, hŏt, tŭg
  - Tent cue for variations of *a* and *o*
    EXAMPLES: âll, ôff
  - Dot cue for schwa sound with multiple-syllable words
    EXAMPLES: salȧd, planėt, pencil, wagȯn

Dictation and Spelling

Purpose

The purpose of dictation is to teach students to segment words into individual sounds and to spell words by connecting sounds to spellings. In addition, learning dictation gives students a new strategy for reflecting on the sounds they hear in words to help them with their own writing.

As students learn about sounds and spellings, they begin to learn the standard spellings that will enable others to read their writing. As students learn to encode, they develop their visual memory for spelling patterns and words (spelling ability) and hence increase their writing fluency. Reinforcing the association between sounds and spellings and words through dictation gives students a spelling strategy that provides support and reassurance for writing independently. Reflecting on the sounds they hear in words will help students develop writing fluency as they apply the strategy to writing unfamiliar words.

A dictation activity is a learning experience; it is not a test. Students should be encouraged to ask for as much help as they need. The proofreading technique is an integral part of dictation. Students' errors lead to self-correction and, if need be, to reteaching. The dictation activities must not become a frustrating ordeal. Students should receive reinforcement and feedback.

There are two kinds of dictation: Sounds-in-Sequence Dictation and Whole-Word Dictation. The two types differ mainly in the amount of help they give students in spelling the words. The instructions vary for each type.

Procedure

Sounds-in-Sequence Dictation

Sounds-in-Sequence Dictation gives students the opportunity to spell words sound by sound, left to right, checking the spelling of each sound as they write. (Many students write words as they think they hear and say the words, not as the words are actually pronounced or written.)

- Pronounce the first word to be spelled. Use the word in a sentence, and say the word again (word/sentence/word). Have students say the word.
- Tell students to think about the sounds they hear in the word. Ask, "What's the first sound in the word?"
- Have students say the sound.
- Point to the ***Sound/Spelling Card,*** and direct students to check the card. Ask what the spelling is. Students should say the spelling and then write it.
- Proceed in this manner until the word is complete.
- **Proofread.** You can write the word on the board as a model, or have a student do it. Check the work by referring to the ***Sound/Spelling Cards.*** If a word is misspelled, have students circle the word and write it correctly, either above the word or next to it.

Whole-Word Dictation

Whole-Word Dictation gives students the opportunity to practice this spelling strategy with less help from the teacher.

- Pronounce the word, use the word in a sentence, and then repeat the word (word/sentence/word). Have students repeat the word. Tell students to think about the word and each sound in the word. Remind students to check the ***Sound/Spelling Cards*** for spellings and to write the word.
- **Proofread.** Write or have a volunteer write the word on the board as a model. Check the word by referring to the ***Sound/Spelling Cards.***

Sentence Dictation

Writing dictated sentences. Help students apply this spelling strategy to writing sentences. Dictation supports the development of fluent and independent writing. Dictation of a sentence will also help students apply conventions of written language, such as capitalization and punctuation.

- Say the complete sentence aloud.
- Dictate one word at a time, following the procedure for Sounds-in-Sequence Dictation.

Continue this procedure for the rest of the words in the sentence. Remind students to put a period at the end. Then proofread the sentence sound by sound or word by word. When sentences contain sight words, the sight words should be dictated as whole words, not sound by sound. Students should be encouraged to check the high-frequency sight words posted in the room if they are unsure how to spell them. As students learn to write more independently, the whole sentence can be dictated word by word.

Proofreading

Whenever students write, whether at the board or on paper, they should proofread their work. Proofreading is an important technique because it allows students to learn by self-correction, and it gives them an immediate second opportunity for success. It is the same skill students will use as they proofread their writing. Students should proofread by circling—not by erasing—each error. After they circle an error, they should write the correction beside the circle. This type of correction allows you and students to see the error as well as the correct form. Students also can see what needs to be changed and how they have made their own work better.

You may want to have students use a colored pencil to circle and write in the correction. This will make it easier for them to see the changes.

Procedure for Proofreading

- Write—or have a student write—the word or sentence on the board or on an overhead transparency.
- Have the other students tell what is good; for example, it is spelled correctly.
- Have students check their words and identify whether anything can be made better, the word needs to be spelled differently, or the handwriting needs to be improved.
- If there is a mistake, have the student circle it and write it correctly—make it better.
- Have the rest of the class proofread their own work.

The Word Building Game (Grades K and 1)

The major reason for developing writing alongside reading is that reading and writing are complementary communicative processes. Decoding requires that students blend the phonemes together into familiar cohesive words. Spelling requires that students segment familiar cohesive words into separate phonemes. Both help students develop an understanding of how the alphabetic principle works.

The Word Building game gives students a chance to exercise their segmentation abilities and to practice using the sounds and spellings they are learning. The game is a fast-paced activity in which students spell related sets of words with the teacher's guidance. (Each successive word in the list differs from the previous one by one sound.)

For the Word Building game, students use their ***Alphabet Letter Cards*** (Levels K and 1) to build the words. (As an alternative they can use pencil and paper.) You will be writing at the board.

Give students the appropriate ***Alphabet Letter Cards.*** For example, if the list for the Word Building game is *am, at,* and *mat,* they will need their *a, m,* and *t* ***Alphabet Letter Cards.***

- Say the first word, such as *am.* (Use it in a sentence if you wish.) Have students repeat the word. Say the word slowly sound by sound. Tell students to look at the ***Alphabet Sound Cards*** to find the letters that spell the sounds. Touch the first sound's card, in this case the Lamb card, and have students say the sound. Continue the process with the second sound. Write the word on the board while students use their ***Alphabet Letter Cards*** to spell it. Have students compare their words with your word, make changes as needed, and then blend and read the word with you.
- Students will then change the first word to make a different word. Say the next word in the list, (at). Segment the sounds of the word, and have students find the ***Alphabet Letter Cards*** that correspond. Write the new word *(at)* under the first word *(am)* on the board, and have students change their cards to spell the new word. Have them compare their words to yours and make changes as needed. Blend and read the word with students. Continue in a like manner through the word list.

Word Structure

Purpose

As students move into the upper grades, there is a shift from Phonics to Word Structure. Phonology is the study of the sounds that make up words. In the early grades, students learn to map sounds with spellings to read words. However, as students move into the upper grades and encounter more complex and longer words, the understanding of morphology and the morphological units that make up words is important for fluent reading, vocabulary development, and comprehension.

Morphology is the study of Word Structure. Word Structure activities support the development of fluency as students learn to identify and read meaningful chunks of words rather than individual spellings. Word Stucture also supports the development of vocabulary as students learn how inflectional endings change a word's tense, number, and so on and how affixes can be added to a base word to create or derive a new but related meaning.

Morphemes are the smallest units that have semantic meaning. Morphemes may be free or bound. A free morpheme can stand alone, such as the words *dog, man,* or *woman*. A bound morpheme, on the other hand, is a unit of meaning that must be combined with another morpheme to make a meaningful word. For example, in *rewrite* the prefix *re-* means to do again, and in dogs the *-s* changes the meaning to plural. Both *re-* and *-s* are bound morphemes because they must combine with other words to create new words.

Learning about word structure helps the reader at several levels. Being able to identify key-word parts not only helps with the pronunciation of longer, unfamiliar words but it also helps with meaning. In Word Structure, students learn how to deconstruct words—to identify the root of the word as well as the affixes. When affixes occur at the beginning of a word, they are called prefixes, and when they occur at the end of a word they are called suffixes. The prefix, root word, and suffix are all morphemes.

In the word *restatement,* there are three morphemes: the prefix *re-,* the root *state* and the suffix *-ment.*

prefix	*root*	*suffix*
re-	*state-*	*ment*

Suffixes, in particular, can impact the root word in different ways. Suffixes such as *-s* and *-ed* can change the tense of a verb; suffixes such as *-s* can change the number of a noun to make it a plural. Derviational morphemes, in contrast, can be added to words to create or derive another word, for example the addition of *-ness* to *sad* creates the new word *sadness,* or the addition of *-ly* changes *sad* to an adverb, *sadly.*

Word structure includes the study of the following:

- **Compound words** are made of two words that combine to form a new word. Compounds can be open or closed.
- **Root words** focus on learning about the basic element of words. Root words are the foundations upon which the meaning of a word is formed. A root may be a real word as in *audio,* meaning "sound," but it can also used with a suffix to become *audible,* changing the noun to an adjective. Although *audible* can have other elements, it does not need other elements to be complete. Most roots, however, do need other elements. Roots such as *duct, anthop,* and *cred* require affixes to form the words *deduct, anthropology,* and *incredible,* respectively. Knowledge of root words and affixes provides students with critical tools for understanding derived words.
- **Prefixes** include any morpheme that is attached to the beginning of a root or word and changes the meaning of that word. Prefixes do not change the form of the word, only the meaning. Common prefixes include: *con-, com-, ad-, de-, di-, dis-, per-, re-, sub-, hyper-, un-,* and so on as well as numbers *(bi-, tri-, uni-, mono-, octo-,* and so on.)
- **Suffixes** include any morpheme that is attached to the end of a word or root and that changes the meaning of that word. Suffixes often change the function of the word and often require a spelling change in the root as well. For example, the addition of *-ial* to *colony* changes a noun to an adjective

Common Latin Roots

Audi: auditory, auditorium, inaudible, audible, audition
Dict: dictate, predict, contradict, prediction
Ject: reject, inject, project, object, projection, objection
Port: transport, import, export, portable, support, report
Rupt: rupture, erupt, eruption, disrupt, interruption
Scrib/script: scribe, describe, manuscript, inscription, transcript, description, prescription
Spect: spectator, inspect, inspector, respect, spectacle, spectacular
Struct: structure, construct, instruct, destruction, reconstruction
Tract: tractor, traction, attract, subtraction, extract, retract, attractive
Vis: vision, visual, visit, supervisor, invisible, vista, visualize, visionary

Common Greek Roots

Auto: automatic, autograph, autobiography, automobile
Bio: biology, biography
Graph: graphite, geography, graphic, photograph, phonograph
Hydo: hydrogen, hydrant
Meter: speedometer, odometer, thermometer, metronome
Ology: geology, zoology, phonology
Photo: photography, photocopy, photosynthesis, photogenic
Scope: telescope, stethoscope, microscope, microscopic, periscope
Tele: telephone, television, telegraph
Therm: thermos, thermostat

Other examples of suffixes that change the word form include the following:

- Noun suffixes: *-age, -al, -ance, -ant, -ate, -ee, -ence, -ent, -er, -or, -ar, -ese, -ess, -hood, -ice, -isn, -ist, -ment, -ness, -sion, -tain, -tion, -ure*
- Suffixes that form adjectives: *-able, -al, -er, -est, -ette, -let, -ful, -fully, -ible, -ic, -ical, -ish, -ive, -less, -ous, -some, -worthy*
- Suffixes that form adverbs: *-ly, -wards, -ways, -wide, -wise*
- Suffixes that create verb forms: *-ate, -ed, -en, -ing, -ise, -ize, -yze*
- Inflectional endings are a special set of suffixes that change the number (singular to plural), case, or gender when added to nouns and change tense when added to verbs.

Teaching Word Structure

- ✦ *Have students read the words in a line.
- ✦ Tell students that words can be made of several individual parts.
- ✦ Examine the words in each line for meaningful parts, roots, and affixes.
- ✦ Identify the root or base word, and discuss the meaning.
- ✦ Underline and discuss the meaning of the prefix or suffix or both. If there is a prefix and a suffix, begin with the prefix. Tell students a prefix is a group of letters that is attached to the beginning of a base or root word. These letters have a specific meaning. For example, *un-* means "not" or "the opposite of," *non-* means "not," and *re-* means "again." A suffix is a group of letters that comes at the end of the base or root word and changes the meaning of the word. For example, *-er* changes a verb to a noun or the person doing the action as in *sing* and *singer,* or *-al* or *-ial* change nouns to adjectives as in *colony* and *colonial.*
- ✦ Reassemble the word, thinking about the meaning of the word parts.
- ✦ Say the word.
- ✦ Use the word in a sentence.

*Sometimes students are intimidated by longer words. Understanding syllable breaks helps when reading these longer words. The following chart includes information on syllable "generalizations." These may help your students when reading longer words during Word Structure activities and in the reading.

Word	Break into Syllables	Syllable Generalizations
Puppet	Pup-pet	Closed. If a word has two consonants in the middle, divide the word between the two consonants. The first syllable is closed, and the vowel pronunciation is short.
Music	Mu-sic	Open. If a word has a VCV pattern, break the syllables before the consonant, which makes the first syllable an open syllable and the first vowel long.
Closet	Clos-et	Some VCV patterns have the break after the consonant, which makes the first syllable a closed syllable and the vowel pronunciation short.
Hundred	Hun-dred	When there is a VCCV pattern, the break is usually between the consonants. The first syllable is closed, and the vowel pronunciation is short.
Coward	Cow-ard	When there are two diphthongs, the syllable break comes between them.
Chaos	Cha-os	When there is a VV pattern, the syllable break comes between the vowels, and the first vowel is usually long.
Handle	Hand-le	Consonant plus *-le.* If a word has an *-le* (or *-el*) at the end, it usually forms a separate syllable and is pronounced /ə/ /l/.
Excitement Reform	Ex-cite-ment Re-form	Prefixes and suffixes are separate syllables.
Entertain Hurdle	En-ter-tain Hur-dle	*R*-controlled vowels. In most syllables where the vowel is followed by an *r,* the vowel sound is *r*-controlled.
Complete	Com-plete	Final *e.* When there is a vowel, consonant, and then an *e* at the end, the vowel before the consonant is pronounced long, and the *e* is silent.

Developing Vocabulary

For students to develop a deeper understanding of words, they should have multiple experiences with them. There are any number of activities that students can do to help them use words and internalize their meanings. The following activities can be used with the whole class or in small groups during Workshop.

- ✦ Give a word, and ask the student to find it in the line and to give a definition.
- ✦ Give a word, and ask the student to add a prefix or a suffix and to tell the meaning of the new word and the new part of speech.
- ✦ If the word is a multiple-meaning word, have the student point to the word, and then have the student give one meaning and use it in a sentence. Then have a second student give another meaning and use it in a sentence. (Be sure that the words that are used are truly multiple-meaning words and not words that can be used as different parts of speech, for example, a verb and a noun that have the same basic meaning.)
- ✦ Give two words, and have the student point to them. Ask what is the difference between these two words. For example, *hot* and *cold* are antonyms. The same could be done for synonyms, homonyms,

and homophones. This gets students to use the vocabulary and do the thinking. Point to two words, and have students tell how they are alike and different. For example, *history, historical,* and *historian* all have the same roots. All three words have a common root, but *history* and *historian* are nouns, and *historical* is an adjective.

- Give students a word, and have them point to the word. If it is a singular noun, have them change it to a plural or vice versa. If it is a verb, have students change the tense, or if it is an adjective, change it into an adverb if appropriate. In all cases, be sure that students spell the new word.
- Give students a word, have them point to and read the word, and then give the part of speech.
- Give a student a word, and have him or her use the word in a sentence. Have the class decide if the sentence truly shows the meaning of the word. For example, if the word is *camouflage,* and the student says, "Animals use camouflage," have the class add to the sentence to show the meaning: "Animals use camouflage to protect themselves from predators."
- Give students a word with a base word, and ask them to point to the word and read it and then to tell the root of the word.
- Give students a word with a Greek or Latin root. Have them point to and read the word, and then have them identify the root word. Challenge students to think of other words that have the same root word.
- Give students a word with a prefix or suffix. Have a student point to and read the word and then identify the prefix or suffix and tell the meaning of the affix. Then, if appropriate, have the student or a different student replace the affix with a different one and tell the meaning of the new word.
- When appropriate, give students a word, and have them give a synonym or antonym. When appropriate, work on gradations of words. For example, if the word is *hot* then the opposite is *cold.* Gradations would be *hot, warm, tepid, cool, cold.* These kinds of activities expand vocabulary.
- Give two words that are connected in some way, for example, *colony* and *colonial.* Have students come to the board, point to the words, and read them. Then have them tell why or how the words are connected.
- Have students find other words that follow comparable patterns to those taught in the lesson. If *colony, colonial, colonist* is a line in Word Knowledge, many students could find related nouns and use them with affixes, *(history, historical, historian).* Challenge students to think more about words.

Tip

- Be sure students understand the limits of structural analysis. The *un-* in *unhappy* is a prefix, but the *un* in *under* and *uncle* is not.
- Help students realize that many words are related and that using their knowledge of a word can help them understand related words.
- Encourage students to use their knowledge of word structure during all reading to clarify unfamiliar words.

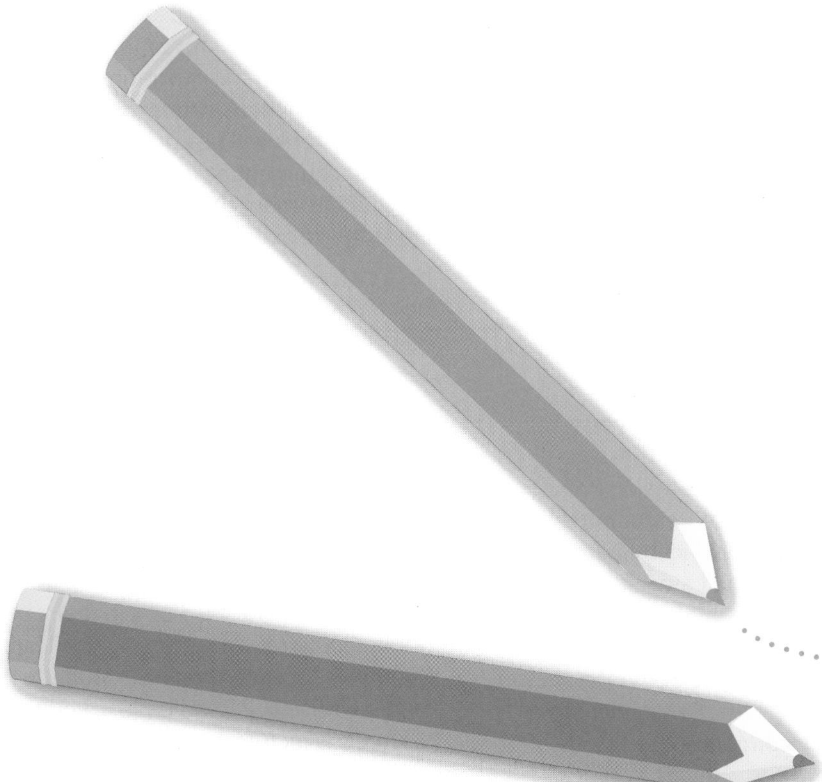

Fluency

Fluency is the ability to read or access words effortlessly with seemingly little attention to decoding. Fluent readers decode words not only automatically but accurately. In addition, fluent readers group words into meaningful units, utilize punctuation to guide their voices, and use expression appropriately to help them comprehend what they are reading. Fluent readers also adjust their reading rate as necessary.

To become proficient readers who fully understand what they read, the whole process of decoding must become automatic. Readers need to be so familiar with the sound/spellings, with common meaningful units like prefixes and suffixes and with the most common nondecodable sight words that they automatically process the spellings and word chunks. This enables them to read the word effortlessly and expend most of their energy on comprehending the meaning of the text. Automacity is a key component of fluency.

The concept of fluency is introduced in the early grades, even before students are reading. When reading aloud, teachers are modeling fluency and using expression and intonation to support meaning. In pre-kindergarten and kindergarten, emergent readers learn about concepts of print that support fluency: learning about spaces and ending punctuation, reading from left to right, and automatically recognizing high-frequency sight words. Students apply this knowledge to reading ***Pre-Decodables.*** These skills are then applied to reading ***Decodables.*** While fluency begins in first grade, many students will continue to need practice in building fluency in second and third grades. Initially students can use the ***SRA Imagine It! Decodable Stories*** in Grades 2 and 3, but fluency practice should include using materials from a variety of different sources, including selections from the ***Student Readers, Leveled Readers,*** and the ***Leveled Science*** and ***Social Studies Readers.*** At all grade levels using ***Pre-Decodables, Decodables, Readers,*** or any other materials, students need to appreciate that fluency is about meaning. Take time to ask questions after students have read, talk about new and interesting words, and discuss any problems students encountered.

Building Fluency: Reading Pre-Decodables (K–1)

Purpose

Pre-Decodables play an important role in students' early literacy development by providing them with meaningful "reading" experiences before they are actually reading on their own and by expanding their awareness of the forms and uses of print. By following along as you read aloud a ***Pre-Decodable,*** students learn about the left-to-right and top-to-bottom progression of print on a page, the clues that indicate the beginnings and endings of sentences, the connections between pictures and words, and important book conventions such as front and back covers, authors' and illustrators' names, title pages, and page numbers.

The ***Pre-Decodables*** provide students with opportunities to apply their growing knowledge of letter names, shapes, and sounds and to become familiar with individual words. In addition, students practice reading high-frequency sight words. The automatic recognition of these words, the identification of ending punctuation, and reading with expression support the development of foundational fluency skills.

Through retelling the story in a ***Pre-Decodable,*** predicting or wondering about what will happen, and asking and responding to questions about the book, students not only learn about the relationship between spoken and written language, they learn to think about what they have read.

About the Pre-Decodables

Each ***Pre-Decodable*** contains a story that engages students' interest as it provides them with opportunities to practice what they are learning in their lessons. These "pre-decodable" stories each contain several high-frequency words that most students already have in their spoken vocabularies and that are a basic part of all meaningful stories. Learning to identify high-frequency words quickly, accurately, and effortlessly is a critical part of students' development as fluent, independent readers. The inside back cover of each ***Pre-Decodable*** contains a list of high-frequency words.

How to Use the Pre-Decodables

- Before reading a ***Pre-Decodable,*** take time to familiarize students with any new high-frequency words in the book and to review previously introduced words. To reinforce the idea that it is important to know these words because they are used so often in print, always point out the words in context. For example, focus students' attention on the words in ***Big Book*** selections or on signs and posters around the classroom.
- Give each student a copy of the book. Tell students that you will read the book together. Hold up your book. Read the title. If the title has a rebus picture, point to it, and tell students what it is. Then point to the word beneath it, and explain that the picture represents that word. Point to and read the names of the author and illustrator, reminding students that an author writes a book, and an illustrator draws the pictures. Page through the book, pointing to and naming the rebus pictures. Have students say the name of each rebus. To avoid confusion, always tell them the exact word that a rebus represents. Do not encourage them to guess at its meaning.
- Allow students time to browse through the book on their own, commenting on what they see in the illustrations and making predictions about what they think the book will be about. Encourage them to comment on anything special they notice about the story, the illustrations, or the words in the book.
- Help students find page 3. Read the book aloud without stopping. As you read, move your hand beneath the words to show the progression of print. Pause at each rebus as you say the word it represents, pointing first to the rebus then to the word beneath it.
- Reread the book. This time, ask students to point to and read the high-frequency words.
- Tell students to follow along in their books as you read the story again. Read the title aloud, and then have students read it with you. Reread page 3. Point to each rebus picture, and ask a volunteer

to "read" it. Point to the word beneath the picture, and remind students that the picture shows what the word is. Continue through each page of the book, calling on volunteers to "read" and stopping as necessary to clarify and help students with words.

- After reading, answer any questions students might have about the book. Encourage them to discuss the illustrations and to explain what is happening in each one.

Building Fluency: Reading Decodables (K–3)

Purpose

The most urgent task of early reading instruction is to make written thoughts intelligible to students. This requires a balanced approach that includes systematic instruction in phonics as well as experiences with authentic literature. Thus, from the very beginning, ***SRA Imagine It!*** includes the reading of literature. At the beginning of first grade, when students are learning phonics and blending as a tool to access words, the teacher reads aloud. During this time students are working on using comprehension strategies and skills and discussing stories. As students learn the code and blend words, recognize critical sight words, and develop some level of fluency, they take more responsibility for the actual reading of the text.

This program has a systematic instruction in phonics that allows students to begin reading independently. This instruction is supported by ***SRA Imagine It! Decodables.***

About the Decodables

The ***SRA Imagine It! Decodables*** are designed to help students apply, review, and reinforce their expanding knowledge of sound/spelling correspondences. Each story supports instruction in new phonic elements and incorporates elements and words that have been learned earlier. There are eight-page and sixteen-page ***Decodables.*** Grade K has eight-page ***Decodables.*** In Grade 1, the eight-page books focus on the new element introduced in the lesson, while the sixteen-page books review and reinforce the elements that have been taught since the last sixteen-page book. They review sounds from several lessons and provide additional reading practice. Grades 2–3 have eight-page ***Decodable Stories*** in Getting Started, and sixteen-page stories in the first 4–5 units of the grade level. The primary purpose is to provide practice reading the words. It is important that students also attach meaning to what they are reading. Questions are often included in the ***Teacher's Edition*** to check both understanding and attention to words.

How to use Decodables

Preparing to Read

- Introduce and write on the board or cards any nondecodable high-frequency or story words introduced or reviewed in the story. Tell students how to pronounce any newly introduced high-frequency words. Then point to each new word, and have students spell and say it. Have them read any previously introduced sight word in the Word Bank list. All the ***SRA Imagine It! Decodables*** contain high-frequency words that may not be decodable. For example, the word *said* is a common high-frequency word that is not decodable. Including words such as *said* makes the language of the story flow smoothly and naturally. Students need to be able to recognize these words quickly and smoothly.
- Read the title. At the beginning of the year, you may need to read the title of the book to students, but as the year goes on, you should have a student read it whenever possible. The sixteen-page ***SRA Imagine It! Decodables*** contain two related chapters, each using the same sounds and spellings. In such cases, read the title of the ***Decodable,*** and then point out the two individual chapter titles. Have volunteers read the title of the chapter you are about to read.
- Browse the story. Have students look through the story, commenting on whatever they notice in the text or illustrations and telling what they think the story will tell them.

Reading the Story

After this browsing, students will read the story a page at a time. Again, these stories are designed to support the learning of sounds and spellings. The focus should not be on comprehension. Students should understand what they are reading, and they should feel free to discuss anything in the story that interests them. Any areas of confusion are discussed and clarified as they arise, as described below.

- Have students read a page to themselves. Then call on one student or groups of students to read the page aloud, or have the entire group read it aloud.
- If a student has difficulty with a word that can be blended, help her or him blend the word. Remind the student to check the ***Sound/Spelling Cards*** for help. If a word cannot be blended using the sound/spellings learned so far, pronounce the word for the student.
- If a student has trouble with a word or sentence, have the reader call on a classmate for help and then continue reading after the word or sentence has been clarified. After something on a page has been clarified or discussed, have a different student reread that page before moving on to the next page.
- Repeat this procedure for each page.
- Reread the story twice more, calling on various students to read or reading it in unison. These readings should go more quickly, with fewer stops for clarification.

Responding to the Story

After the story has been read aloud a couple of times, have students respond as follows:

- Ask students which difficult words they found in the story and how they figured them out. They may mention high-frequency words they did not recognize, words they had to blend, and words whose meanings they did not know.
- Have students tell about the story, retelling it in their own words, describing what they liked about it, or citing what they found interesting or surprising. Specific suggestions to use are listed in the ***Teacher's Edition.***
- Questions are provided in the ***Teacher's Edition.*** They are designed to focus students' attention on the words and not just the pictures. Ask students the questions, and have all students point to the answer in the story rather than having one student respond orally. Having students point to the answers is important. First, it ensures that all students are engaged in finding the answer, not just one. Second, by pointing to the answer, you know that students know the answer from reading and not

just from having heard it read. Third, locating information in a text is an important skill. Finally, by pointing to the answer, you can quickly monitor who is understanding the story and who may still need more support during Workshop.

- Have students reread the story with partners. Circulate among the pairs, listening to individual students read. This allows you to monitor students' reading and to identify any students who may need additional help during Workshop.

Building Fluency beyond Decodables (middle of grade 1 on)

For some students, fluency develops naturally, seemingly without instruction. Other students, however, can benefit from more explicit instruction. There are students who can decode and read words but lack the critical phrasing, intonation, and expression that support meaning. Teach the text characteristics that support fluency, model them for students, and then provide students regular opportunities to practice fluency. Instruction can focus on any or all of the following areas:

- Discuss and model ending punctuation and what this means in terms of expression and intonation. This should be modeled and then discussed with students. Begin with ending punctuation, and then move to internal punctuation such as commas and semicolons. During modeling,
    - pause longer at a period or other ending punctuation.
    - raise your voice at a question mark.
    - use expression when you come to an exclamation point.
    - pause at a commas or other internal punctuation such as semicolons.
    - when you come to quotation marks, think of the character and how he or she might say his or her words.
    - pause at an ellipsis.
    - pause at dashes.
- Discuss and model words written in a special way—typographical signals such as underlined words, boldfaced words, or those in all caps—need to be read with expression and changed in intonation for emphasis.
- Talk about reading rate. Oral reading should be done at a normal speaking rate. Students should not be reading so fast that someone listening could not hear the individual words and make sense of what is being read.
- Dicuss and model intonation. Let students hear how voices change with different ending punctuation, how voices change when reading dialogue, and how intonation changes with cues from the author. In dialogue, think of the difference between "screamed Jennifer" versus "pleaded Jessie."
- Work on phrase cue boundaries. A good way to teach this is by using an overhead of what students are reading. Mark natural phrase boundaries—for example, clauses, propositional phrases, subject phrases, verb phrases, and so on, with slashes. For example, *In the summertime,/Josh likes to play baseball/ at the park/down the street from his house.* Have students listen to you read the text, noticing how you paused at the markers. Then have students read the sentences naturally, using the markers as guides. Scaffold the instruction. In the beginning, mark the boundaries, and have students practice reading using the already marked passages. As students become comfortable, have them mark what they are reading with boundary markers. Gradually fade out the markers or slashes.

Fluency develops over time, and students should be given repeated opportunities to practice fluency with a variety of different texts. After students have read a text, take time to go back and discuss any new vocabulary or interesting words that students encountered while reading. Fluency is not an isolated activity; it is about supporting comprehension.

There are a number of techniques for practicing fluency: repeated readings, partner reading, tape-assisted reading, and Reader's Theater. All of these techniques can be done with a variety of different reading materials, including selections from the ***Student Readers,*** the ***Leveled Readers,*** and the ***Science*** and ***Social Studies Leveled Readers.***

- Repeated readings increase reading rate, accuracy, and comprehension by providing students with multiple exposures to words and spelling patterns. In addition, it helps students improve their ability to break sentences into meaningful phrases and to use intonation. It is effective with both older and younger students. Repeated readings involve the student reading segments of text of between 50 to 200 words, depending upon students' ability. Students should practice repeated readings with a variety of different text types. While repeated readings can be done with materials from ***SRA Imagine It!*** using segments from science and social studies texts helps students in the upper grades apply their reading knowledge across the curriculum. The goal is to have students read the text fluently and automatically at a per-minute rate commensurate with grade-level norms.
- Tape-assisted readings help build confidence and is an excellent support for second-language learners. Tape-assisted reading allows students to hear good models of reading and to develop their awareness of phrasing and prosody, or expressive reading. Tapes should provide students with experiences from a variety of text types. Tape selections should be read at approximately 80–100 words per minute by fluent readers with natural intonation, phrasing, and expression. Students read along with the text, aloud or subvocalizing. When the student is comfortable with the text, the student should practice reading the text independently and then read a portion of it to the teacher. The CDs in ***SRA Imagine It!*** can help students develop fluency with selections in their ***Student Readers.***
- Reader's Theater legitimizes practicing fluency because it involves reading a script. While students do not memorize the script the way actors do in a play, they must be able to read the script fluently so the audience—the rest of the class—can enjoy the play. Several students can work together on a single play or playlet. They will need to practice reading the script several times before presenting it to the class. Reader's Theater also provides students with a writing opportunity. They can use a selection from their ***Student Readers,*** write a playlet, and then practice it for Reader's Theater.
- Radio Reading, like Reader's Theater, connects reading aloud to real-life situation. Students, with copies of the text, read aloud in front of the class as if

they were a radio announcers or news broadcasters. Expository text works particularly well for this. Students can practice, and then once a week, several students can be the radio announcers. Students can also write weekly news reports and read them.

- Partner Reading involves students reading with a partner. They can take turns reading pages or the entire selection. While one student reads, the listening-partner should note misread words and then discusses them with the partner after the reading. If the pairs are reading for one-minute-fluency checks, the nonreading partner can be responsible for timing the reading. Selections should be read multiple times with the goal being that students achieve a higher fluency rate on successive readings.

Assessing Fluency

Fluency should be assessed periodically to determine students' growth and to monitor progess. Listening to students read regularly is key. Fluency assessment should include not just reading rate but decoding accuracy, prosody (phrasing and intonation), and expression. In addition, checks should be done using various text types.

Generally accepted procedures for assessment include the following:

- Use a passage of approximately 250 words at student's reading level. In the first half of first grade, use the appropriate ***Decodable*** in the Practice set. Have two copies—one for the student and one for you to mark.
- Have the student read the passage for one minute. Use a timer, if possible, so you do not have to keep watching a stopwatch or the minute hand on a clock. You can also tape-record the reading. The goal is to have students read the text aloud in a natural way, the way they would speak the words. This is not a race! Use the following scoring conventions. Mark any errors made by the reader.
- Draw a line through any misread word, and count it as an error.
- Circle any words the student omits or refuses to read, and count them as errors.
- Indicate with a caret any extra words the student inserts.
- Draw an arrow between words that student reverses, and count as one error.
- Put two check marks above a word that a student repeats, but do not count it as an error.
- Draw a box around the last word student reads in the one-minute time frame.

To calculate the student's accuracy rate, count the total number of words read in one minute. Subtract the number of errors from the total number of words read, and use that number to find the number of correct words read per minute.

For example, to calculate the rate:

Total words read – errors = words correct per minute
75 words read – 10 errors = 65 words per minute

For example, to calculate the accuracy:

Number of words ÷ the total number of words = percent of accuracy
145 (words correct) ÷ 156 (total number of words) = 93%

Curriculum-Based Norms in Oral Reading Fluency for Grades 2–5 (Medians)

		Fall		Winter		Spring		
Grade	Percentile	n[1]	WCPM[2]	n	WCPM	n	WCPM	SD[3] of raw scores
2	75	4	82	5	106	4	124	39
	50	6	53	8	78	6	94	
	25	4	23	5	46	4	65	
3	75	4	107	5	123	4	142	39
	50	6	79	8	93	6	114	
	25	4	65	5	70	4	87	
4	75	4	125	5	133	4	143	37
	50	6	99	8	112	6	118	
	25	4	72	5	89	4	92	
5	75	4	126	5	143	4	151	35
	50	6	105	8	118	6	128	
	25	4	77	5	93	4	100	

[1]n = number of median scores from percentile tables of ditricts (maximum possible = 8)

[2]WCPM = words correct per minute

[3]SD = the average standard deviation of scores from fall, winter, and spring for each grade level

SOURCE
From "Curriculum-Based Oral Reading Fluency Norms for Students in Grades 2 Through 5" (1992) by Jan E. Hasbrouck and Gerald Tindal. Teaching Exceptional Children, Vol. 24 (Spring).

In addition, watch for and note the following:

- Expression
- Ability of the reader to read words in natural syntactic clusters

Assessing accuracy, pace or rate, and expression provide information for instruction.

In addition to the qualitative information, some teachers like to use rubrics in their evaluation of fluency.

- **Level 1:** Reads basically word by word with limited phrasing, little expression. Reading is labored with difficulty in reading words automatically and fluently.
- **Level 2:** Reads in limited phrases of two words, but grouping of words is not natural. There is little or no appropriate expression or intonation.
- **Level 3:** Reads in phrases with most having appropriate breaks. Most of the reading has appropriate expression and intonation. There is limited comprehension.
- **Level 4:** Reads with appropriate phrasing, intonation, and expression and demonstrates understanding of the piece.

Interpreting Fluency Data

First compare the student's number of correct words per minute with accepted fluency norms.

Then examine the student's accuracy percentage. Reading accuracy should remain constant or gradually increase within and between grades until it stabilizes at 90 percent or higher. Compare the student's accuracy percentage after each assessment to ensure that his or her accuracy percentage is holding constant or improving.

Next examine the types of errors the student made, and consider what they mean for instruction.

- Inserting extra words suggest that the student understands what is being read but is reading perhaps impulsively or carelessly.
- Refusing to attempt to read words suggests that the student may be uncertain of his or her abilities, unwilling to take risks, or needs additional work with decoding at the sound/spelling or morpheme level. Look at the words the student does not read. Are they one-syllable words or multisyllable words?
- Misreading routine CVC and CVCe words suggest that the student may need more work with the sounds and spellings. In some cases, a student may be able to read words with common sounds and spellings but needs more work with long vowels, diphthongs, and diagraphs.
- Looking for patterns in errors is key.
- Using or not using intonation, expression, and phrasing but reading quickly and accurately suggests that students need to think about how words combine to make meaning and how our expression can support understanding.

Tips

- Use Workshop time for building fluency. Introduce different ways to practice fluency one at a time.
- Set up a listening area for Workshop that students can use for tape-assisted instruction.
- Make sure ***Pre-Decodables, Decodables,*** and ***Leveled Readers*** are available to students.
- Have simple timers available for students to check their fluency rate.
- Encourage students to chart their fluency growth. If students are doing repeated reading, have them chart the number of words read each day for several days so they can see their fluency improving.
- When students have developed some degree of fluency with a ***Pre-Decodable, Decodable,*** or ***Leveled Reader,*** send the materials home for additional practice.
- Use a range of materials to practice building fluency throughout the day. Remember, fluency practice can be as short as one minute several times a day.

Reading Aloud

Purpose

Adults read aloud a variety of materials to students. In this program there are ***Big Books,*** picture books, novels, and excerpts for reading aloud. Research has shown that students who are read to are more likely to develop the skills they need to read successfully on their own.

In kindergarten and Grade 1, there are **Big Books.** In every grade level of ***SRA Imagine It!*** there are opportunities for teachers to read aloud to students. At the beginning of each unit is a Read Aloud selection tied to the unit theme. This Read Aloud selection allows students the opportunity to think about the unit theme before reading selections on their own.

Reading aloud at any age serves multiple purposes. Reading aloud

- provokes students' curiosity about text.
- conveys an awareness that text has meaning.
- demonstrates the various reasons for reading text (to find out about the world, to learn useful new information and new skills, or simply for pleasure).
- exposes students to the "language of literature," which is more complex than the language they ordinarily use and hear.
- provides an opportunity to teach the problem-solving strategies that good readers employ. As students observe you interacting with the text, expressing your own enthusiasm, and modeling your thinking aloud, they perceive these as valid responses and begin to respond to text in similar ways.

Procedures

The following set of general procedures for reading aloud is designed to help you maximize the effectiveness of any Read Aloud session.

- **Read-Aloud sessions.** Set aside time each day to read aloud.
- **Introduce the story.** Tell students that you are going to read a story aloud to them. Tell its title, and briefly comment on the topic. To allow students to anticipate what will happen in the story, be careful not to summarize.
- **Activate prior knowledge.** Ask whether anyone has already heard the story. If so, ask them to see if this version is the same as the one they have heard. If not, activate prior knowledge by saying, "First, let's talk a little about ______." If the story is being read in two (or more) parts, before reading the second part, ask students to recall the first part.
- **Before reading.** Invite students to interrupt your reading if there are any words they do not understand or ideas they find puzzling or to ask questions. Throughout the reading, encourage them to do this.
- **Read the story expressively.** Occasionally react verbally to the story by showing surprise, asking questions, giving an opinion, expressing pleasure, or predicting events. Expressive reading not only supports comprehension but serves as a model for fluency. Think-aloud suggestions are outlined below.
- **Use Comprehension Strategies.** While reading aloud to students, model the use of comprehension strategies in a natural, authentic way. Remember to try to present a variety of ways to respond to text. These include visualizing, asking questions, predicting, making connections, clarifying, and summarizing.
- **Retell.** When you have finished reading the story, call on volunteers to retell it.
- **Discuss.** After reading, discuss with students their own reactions: how the story reminded them of things that have happened to them, what they thought of the story, and what they liked best about the story.
- **Reread.** You may wish to reread the selection on subsequent occasions, focusing the discussion on the unit theme.

Think-Aloud Responses

The following options for modeling thinking aloud will be useful for reading any story aloud. Choose responses that are most appropriate for the selection you are reading.

- React emotionally by showing joy, sadness, amusement, or surprise.
- Ask questions about ideas in the text. This should be done when there are points or ideas that you really do wonder about.
- Identify with characters by comparing them to yourself.
- Show empathy with or sympathy for characters.
- Relate the text to something you already know or something that has happened to you.
- Show interest in the text ideas.
- Question the meaning or clarity of the author's words and ideas.

Questions to Help Students Respond

At reasonable stopping points in reading, ask students general questions to get them to express their own ideas and to focus their attention on the text. These types of generic questions will help students discuss their reactions to the reading and demonstrate their comprehension.

- What do you already know about this?
- What seems really important here? Why do you think so?
- Was there anything that you did not understand? What?
- What did you like best about this?
- What did you not like about this?
- What new ideas did you learn from this?
- What does this make you wonder about?
- What surprised you in the story?

Vocabulary

Purpose

Strong vocabulary skills are correlated to achievement throughout school. The purpose of vocabulary instruction is to introduce students to new words (and ideas) and to teach students a range of strategies for learning, remembering, and incorporating unknown vocabulary words into their existing reading, writing, speaking, and listening vocabularies.

Words chosen for inclusion in ***SRA Imagine It!*** are based upon the vocabulary research of Andrew Biemiller, who has developed a comprehensive database of words students with large vocabularies know by the end of sixth grade. Biemiller's work identifies words that all students need to know and provides evidence that students from various backgrounds acquire these word meanings in roughly the same order. For practical purposes, this means that a child with an average-sized vocabulary of 6,000 root word meanings at the end of Grade 2 knows mainly the same word meanings as a grade 4 child who knows about 6,000 root word meanings. It appears that for students with small vocabularies, improving vocabulary mainly means moving them through the sequence faster. Because vocabulary knowledge is so critical to comprehension, vocabulary instruction is integrated throughout ***SRA Imagine It!***

Vocabulary is taught throughout every part of the lesson.

Part 1: Preparing to Read

- In Grades 2–6, Word Structure develops vocabulary and the understanding that words can be deconstructed and related through known elements to determine meaning. In addition, students are learning about Greek and Latin roots, antonyms, synonyms, and multiple-meaning words. The emphasis on root words and affixes, in particular, serves to expand students' knowledge of words and their vocabulary.
- In Grades K–1, students are using words they blend in sentences to develop vocabulary and oral language. Learning about inflectional endings also helps children see the relationship between root words and various forms of the root. Reviews of blending lines focus on using words based on teacher clues as well as finding synonyms and antonyms.

Part 2: Reading and Responding

- The selection vocabulary instruction in this part of the lesson focuses on teaching specific vocabulary necessary for understanding the literature selection more completely.
- In kindergarten and the first half of Grade 1, the teacher introduces the selection vocabulary orally before reading the selection. Suggestions are made throughout the reading to discuss new and interesting words as the class reads the ***Big Books.*** Work from Biemiller suggests that clarifying words in the context of reading is an effective technique for expanding student vocabulary. Suggestions for which words to stop and clarify are suggested throughout the lessons. Vocabulary review activities are found throughout the lesson.
- From the middle of Grade 1 on, critical word meanings needed to understand the story are pre-taught as students read the Vocabulary Warm-Up in the ***Student Reader.*** This provides an initial exposure to the selection vocabulary. This is followed by guided vocabulary practice in which students discuss the definitions of critical words; learn to apply critical skills such as context, structure and apposition; use the vocabulary words in a variety of activities, and then return to the Vocabulary Warm-Up to reread the sentences containing the vocabulary words and to discuss the words. The clarification of additional vocabulary words is highlighted throughout the reading of each selection. Vocabulary review activities are found throughout the lesson.
- Students write the word and their definitions in their Writer's Notebooks.
- Vocabulary words, along with any other words students find interesting, are posted on charts to remind students to use these words in discussion of their reading as well as in their writing.

Part 3: Language Arts

During writing, students are encouraged to use their new vocabulary in writing.

General Strategies

There is no question that having students read and reading to students are effective vocabulary instructional strategies. Most word learning occurs through exposure to words in listening and reading. Multiple exposures to words, particularly when students hear, see, say, and write words, is also effective. Wordplay, including meaning and dictionary games, helps develop a word consciousness as well.

Vocabulary Skills and Strategies

Word Relationships People effectively learn new words by relating them to words they already know. An understanding of different word relationships enables students to quickly and efficiently secure new vocabulary. The weekly vocabulary lessons are organized around these types of word groups. Word relationships include the following:

- **Antonyms** Words with opposite or nearly opposite meanings. *(hot/cold)*
- **Synonyms** Words with similar meanings. *(cup, mug, glass)*
- **Multiple Meanings** Words that have more than one meaning. *(run, dressing, bowl)*
- **Shades of Meaning** Words that express degrees of a concept or quality. *(like, love, worship)*
- **Levels of Specificity** Words that describe at different levels of precision. (living thing, plant, flower, daffodil)
- **Analogies** Pairs of words that have the same relationship. *(ball* is to *baseball* as *puck* is to *hockey)*
- **Compound Words** Words comprised of two or more words. *(daylight)*
- **Homographs** Words that are spelled the same but have different meanings and come from different root words. *(bear, count)*

- **Homophones** Words that sound the same but have different spellings and meanings. *(mane/main, to/two/too)*
- **Base-Word Families** Words that have the same base word. *(care, careless, careful, uncaring, carefree)*
- **Prefixes** An affix attached before a base word that changes the meaning of the word. *(misspell)*
- **Suffixes** An affix attached to the end of a base word that changes the meaning of the word and often the part of speech. *(careless)*
- **Concept Vocabulary** Words that help develop understanding of a concept. *(space, sun, Earth, satellite, planet, asteroid)*
- **Classification and Categorization** Sorting words by related meanings. *(colors, shapes, animals, foods)*

Contextual Word Lists Teaching vocabulary in context is another way to secure understanding of unknown words. Grouping words by subject area such as science, social studies, math, descriptive words, new words, and so on enables students to connect word meanings and to build vocabulary understanding.

- **Figurative Language** Idioms, metaphors, similes, personification, puns, and novel meanings need to be specifically taught, especially for English-language learners.
- **Derivational Word Lists** Presenting groups of words derived from particular languages or with specific roots or affixes is an effective way to reinforce meanings and spellings of foreign words and word parts.

Vocabulary Strategies for Unknown Words

Different strategies have been shown to be particularly effective for learning completely new words. These strategies are included in the ***Skills Practice*** activities.

Key Word This strategy involves providing or having students create a mnemonic clue for unknown vocabulary. For example, the word *mole* is defined in chemistry as a "gram molecule." By relating *mole* to *molecule,* students have a key to the meaning of the word.

Definitions Copying a definition from a dictionary is somewhat effective in learning new vocabulary. Combining this with using the word in writing and speaking adds to the effectiveness of this strategy. Requiring students to explain a word or to use it in a novel sentence helps ensure that the meaning is understood. It is not uncommon when students use words in sentences that the meaning of the vocabulary word is not clear. For example, a typical sentence a student might give for the word *camouflage* is "The octopus uses camouflage." The word *camouflage* is correctly used, but there is no real indication that the student knows the meaning of the word. Having students extend the sentence to explain why or how in the sentence helps: "The octopus uses camouflage to protect itself from predators." Or "The camouflage an octopus uses when it is in danger is to change it shape and color."

Context Clues Some words can be inferred from context and can be learned with repeated exposure to words in reading and listening. While using context can be useful, it is not the most effective way to learn new words. Also, as students move into content area reading, context becomes a less effective tool for determining the meaning of unfamiliar words.

- **Syntax** How a word is used in a sentence may provide some clue as to its meaning. This is particularly effective with homographs. "The lead pipe is a hazard to the community." Here lead is an adjective and is pronounced with a short e. In the sentence "He will lead the troops into battle," *lead* has a very different meaning, is a verb, and is pronounced with a long e.
- **Apposition** Sometimes the word is actually defined within the text. In an appositive, the definition of a word is often set off by commas for the reader.

Word Structure Examining the affixes and roots of a word often provides clues to its meaning. Knowing the meaning of at least part of the word can provide a clue as to its meaning. For example, *unenforceable* can be broken down into meaningful word parts. This is a particularly important tool in content area reading.

Developing Vocabulary

Purpose

Vocabulary is closely connected to comprehension. Considerable vocabulary growth occurs incidentally during reading. A clear connection exists between vocabulary development and the amount of reading a person does, and there are strong indications that vocabulary instruction is important and that understanding the meanings of key words helps with comprehension.

In ***SRA Imagine It!*** vocabulary is addressed before, during, and after reading. Before reading, the teacher presents vocabulary words from the selection. Students use skills such as context clues, apposition, and structural analysis to determine the meanings of the words. These selection vocabulary words are not only important to understanding the text but are also high-utility words that can be used in discussing and writing about the unit theme.

During reading, students monitor their understanding of words and text. When they do not understand something, they stop and clarify what they have read. Students will use these same skills—context clues, apposition, structural elements, and so on—to clarify the meanings of additional words encountered while reading. Determining the meanings of words while reading prepares students for the demands of independent reading both in and out of school.

After reading, students review the vocabulary words that they learned before reading the selection. They also review any interesting words that they identified and discussed during reading. Students record in their Writer's Notebooks both the selection vocabulary words and the interesting words they identified during their reading and are encouraged to use both sets of words in discussion and in writing.

Procedure

Before students read a selection, the teacher uses an overhead transparency to introduce the selection vocabulary to the class. The transparency contains two sentences for each selection vocabulary word. Students must use context clues, apposition, or word structure in the sentences to determine the meaning of the underlined vocabulary words. If students cannot determine the meaning of the word using one of these skills, they can consult the glossary or dictionary.

Below are suggestions for modeling the use of context clues, apposition, or word structure to determine the meaning of a word.

Modeling Using Context Clues

Have students read the sentences on the transparency. Explain to students that they will use context clues, or other words in the sentence, to determine the meaning of the underlined word. For example, if the word is *treacherous*, the sentences might include the following:

1. Mrs. Frisby must undertake a <u>treacherous</u> journey to bring her son some medicine.
2. We took a <u>treacherous</u> walk near a swamp filled with crocodiles.

Have students look for clues in the sentences that might help them understand the meaning of the underlined word. Point out that a good clue in the second sentence is "near a swamp filled with crocodiles." This clue should help them understand that *treacherous* probably has something to do with danger. Guide students until they can give a reasonable definition of *treacherous.* To consolidate understanding of the word, ask another student to use the definition in a sentence.

Modeling Using Apposition

Have students read the sentences on the transparency. Explain to students that they will use apposition to determine the meaning of the word. In apposition, the word is followed by the definition, which is set off by commas. For example, if the word is *abolitionist,* the sentences might include the following:

1. The conductor thought he was an abolitionist, a person who wanted to end slavery.
2. John Brown was a famous abolitionist, a person who wanted to end slavery.

It should be clear to students using apposition that the definition of the word *abolitionist* is "a person who wanted to end slavery."

Modeling Using Word Structure

Have students read the sentences on the transparency. Explain to students that they will use word structure, or parts of the selection vocabulary word, to determine the meaning. For example, if the word is *uncharted,* the sentences might include the following:

1. The strong wind blew Ivan's ship away into uncharted seas.
2. The explorers Lewis and Clark went into uncharted territory.

Have students look at the word *uncharted* and break it into parts: the prefix *un-*, chart, and the suffix *-ed.* Students should know that the suffix *un-* means "not" and that the suffix *-ed* usually indicates the past tense of a verb. However, you may need to remind students about the meanings of these affixes. Ask students for the meaning of the word *chart.* Students should know that a chart could be a map or a table. Guide them as they put together the definitions of the word parts: *un-* (not), *charted* (mapped or tabled). They should be able to come up with the definition "not mapped" or "unmapped" or even "unknown." Have them substitute their definition in the sentences to see if the definition makes sense. For instance, the first sentence would read, "The strong wind blew Ivan's ship away into unmapped (or unknown) seas." Confirm with students that the new sentence makes sense, and then repeat the same process for the second sentence.

Everything students learn about phonemic awareness, phonics, and decoding has one primary goal—to help them understand what they are reading. Without comprehension, there is no reading.

Take time to review words and their meanings. Help students connect new words to familiar words. Each unit in ***SRA Imagine It!*** revolves around a theme, and there are key words. In every lesson, there is a concept.

Semantic Mapping Having students create a semantic map of an unknown word after learning its definition helps them learn it. Have students write the new word and then list in a map or web all words they can think of that are related to it.

Semantic Feature Analysis A semantic feature analysis helps students compare and contrast similar types of words within a category to help secure unknown words. Have students chart, for example, the similarities and differences between various types of sports, including new vocabulary such as *lacrosse* and *cricket.*

Reading Comprehension

Purpose

The primary aim of reading is comprehension. Without comprehension, neither intellectual nor emotional responses to reading are possible—other than the response of frustration. Reading is about problem solving. Expert readers bring their critical faculties to bear on everything they read. They generally understand most of what they read, but just as importantly, they recognize when they do not understand, and they have at their command an assortment of strategies for monitoring and furthering their understanding.

The goal of comprehension strategy instruction is to turn responsibility for using strategies over to students as soon as possible. Research has shown that students' comprehension and learning problems are not a matter of mental capacity but rather their inability to use strategies to help them learn. Expert readers use a variety of strategies to help them make sense of the text and to get the most out of what they read. Trained to use a variety of comprehension strategies, students dramatically improve their learning performance. To do this, the teacher models strategy use and gradually incorporates various kinds of prompts and possible student think-alouds as examples of the types of thinking students might do as they read to comprehend what they are reading.

Setting Reading Goals

Even before they begin reading and using comprehension strategies, good readers set reading goals and expectations. Readers who have set their own goals and have definite expectations about the text they are about to read are more engaged in their reading and notice more in what they read. Having determined a purpose for reading, they are better able to evaluate a text and to determine whether it meets their needs. Even when the reading is assigned, the reader's engagement is enhanced when he or she has determined ahead of time what information might be gathered from the selection or how the selection might interest him or her.

Comprehension Strategies

Descriptions of strategies expert readers use to comprehend the text follow.

Good readers continually monitor their speed and ability to understand throughout reading.

Summarizing

Periodically it is important to summarize and check our understanding as we read. Sometimes readers reread to fill in gaps in their understanding. They use the strategy of summarizing to keep track of what they are reading and to focus their minds on important information. The process of putting the information in one's own words not only helps good readers remember what they have read but also prompts them to evaluate how well they understand the information. Sometimes the summary reveals that one's understanding is incomplete, in which case it might be appropriate to reread the previous section to fill in the gaps. The strategy of summarizing is particularly helpful when readers are reading long or complicated text. When to stop and summarize depends on the difficulty of the text as well as the type of text. Often in content area reading, it makes sense to stop and summarize the key ideas after each section. In narratives, the reader often stops to summarize after an episode has been read. Many of us will automatically summarize what has happened if we have put down a book and are about to continue reading it again. Students should think to themselves the following:

- Does this make sense? What is this selection about?
- What are the big ideas the writer is trying to get at?
- What can I delete from my summary? What is not important?
- Have I said the same thing more than once in my summary?
- How can I put what I just read into my own words?
- What is unclear? What is the meaning of the word or sentence? How can I determine this?

Clarifying

Monitoring understanding is key to reading. It allows readers to make sure they understand what they read. They note the characteristics of the text, such as whether it is difficult to read or whether some sections are more challenging or more important than others are. In addition, when readers become aware that they do not understand, they stop and take appropriate action, such as rereading, to understand the text better. As they read, good readers stay alert for problem signs such as loss of concentration, unfamiliar vocabulary, or lack of sufficient background knowledge to comprehend the text. This ability to self-monitor and identify aspects of the text that hinder comprehension is crucial to becoming a proficient reader. Clarifying may occur at the word, the sentence, the paragraph, or at the whole-text level. Students should think to themselves the following:

- What does not make sense? If it is a word, how can I figure it out? Do I use context, structure, or apposition, or do I need to ask someone or to look it up in the dictionary or glossary?
- What does not make sense? The paragraph is long and full of details. What can I do? I can take some notes, I can reread it more slowly; I can discuss it with someone.
- These sentences are endless. How can I deal with long, complicated sentences?
- What is the main idea of what I just read?
- Can I put what I just read into my own words?

Asking Questions

Asking questions allows the reader to constantly check his or her understanding and to follow the writer's train of thought. Good readers ask questions that may prepare them for what they will learn. If their questions are not answered in the text, they may try to find answers elsewhere and thus add even more to their store of knowledge. Certain kinds of questions occur naturally to a reader, such as to clear up confusion or to wonder why something in the text is as it is. Intentional readers take this somewhat informal questioning one step further by formulating questions with the specific intent of checking their understanding. They literally test themselves by thinking of questions a teacher might ask and then by determining answers to those questions. Students should think to themselves the following:

- ✦ Why is this the way it is? What else is there to know about this?
- ✦ What question can I ask to check if I have understood what I just read?
- ✦ How does this connect to the unit theme? What new information will I learn?
- ✦ What questions do I think the author will answer as I read this selection?
- ✦ Do I understand the author? What is not making sense?
- ✦ What is interfering with my understanding?

Predicting

Predicting what will happen in the story allows the reader to summarize what has been read so far, to identify clues and events in the text, and to use prior knowledge and personal experience to make inferences about what will happen next. When reading fiction, readers make predictions about what they are reading and then confirm or revise those predictions as they go. Predictions are not wild guesses. They are made based on information provided by the author as well as the reader's background knowledge. Students should think to themselves the following: What do I already know that will help me predict? What are the clues in the text that will help me predict?

- ✦ Why was my prediction confirmed?
- ✦ Why was my prediction not confirmed?
- ✦ What clues did I miss that would have helped me make a better prediction?

The responsibility for using strategies by students should begin as soon as they understand that reading is about problem solving and making sense of text and that these strategies will help them do both.

Making Connections

Making connections between the text and what is known from personal experience or previous reading deepens our understanding of text and expands our understanding. Comprehension is enhanced when we relate what is read to what is known. Students should think to themselves the following:

- ✦ What does this remind me of? What else have I read like this?
- ✦ What does this remind me of in my own life? In my own experiences?
- ✦ How does this connect with other selections I have read?
- ✦ How does this connect with what is going on in the world today?

Visualizing

Creating a mental image about the text involves not just the literal interpretation of the author's word but going beyond the literal to incorporating prior knowledge and experiences that deepen understanding. Readers form mental images as they read. They picture the setting, the characters, and the action in a story. Visualizing can also be helpful when reading expository text. Visualizing helps readers understand descriptions of complex activities or processes. When a complex process or an event is being described, the reader can follow the process or the event better by visualizing each step or episode. Sometimes an author or an editor helps the reader by providing illustrations, diagrams, or maps. If no visual aids have been provided, it may help the reader to create one. Creating mental images helps the reader create pictures that can be stored efficiently in his or her long-term memory. Students should think to themselves the following:

- ✦ What picture does the words create in my mind? How do the words suggest feelings, actions, and settings?
- ✦ Would a drawing help me understand the process?
- ✦ How does my mental picture extend beyond the words in the text?
- ✦ How did this picture help me understand what I am reading?

Adjusting Reading Speed

Some texts are easy to read; others are more challenging. How difficult a text is to read depends on both author and reader variables. Good readers understand that not all text is equal. Because of this, they continuously monitor what they are reading and adjust their reading speed accordingly. Efficient readers skim parts of the text that are not important or relevant to their reading goals, and they purposely slow down when they encounter difficulty in understanding the text. Students should think to themselves the following:

- ✦ When I reread does this make sense?
- ✦ This is a long and involved sentence. Rereading may help.

Procedures

Modeling and Thinking Aloud

One of the most effective ways to help students understand and use critical comprehension is to make strategic thinking public. Modeling these behaviors and encouraging students to think aloud as they attempt to address comprehension problems and to understand text can demonstrate for everyone in a class how these behaviors are put into practice. Suggestions for think-alouds are provided throughout the ***Teacher's Edition.***

The most effective models you can offer will be those that come from your own reading experiences. What kinds of questions did you ask yourself? What kinds of things surprised you the first time you read a story? What kinds of new information did you learn? What kinds of things were confusing until you reread or read further? Drawing on these questions and on your students' questions and comments as they read will make the strategic reading process more meaningful to students. Below are suggestions for modeling each of the comprehension strategies.

Before Reading

✦ **Modeling Setting Reading Goals.** To model setting reading goals, engage students in the following:

- **Activate prior knowledge.** As you approach a new text, consider aloud what you already know about the subject or what your experiences have been in reading similar material.
- **Browse the text.** To get an idea of what to expect from a text, look at the title and the illustrations. When students are reading fiction, they will browse the text to look for Clues, Problems and Wonderings. Possible clues will support comprehension— for example, genre, content, author, setting, and so on—potential problems might include things such as difficult words or dense paragraphs as well as unfamiliar concepts; and wonderings are the things students are curious to find out about from their reading— questions about the selection. Wonderings are students' purposes for reading. When students read nonfiction, they will use a KWL chart— this is what I know (K), this is what I want to find out (W), and this is what I have learned (L). Both these activities— Clues, Problems, and Wonderings and KWL engage students in thinking before reading the selection by having them activate their own background knowledge, identify potential problems, and set purposes for reading. Have students glance quickly at the selection, looking briefly at the illustrations and the print. Have them tell what they think they might be learning about as they read the selection. Early in the year, model the thinking involved with these activities and then begin to turn the responsibility for completing them over to students.

During Reading

Modeling— or thinking aloud— about how to use strategies to solve problems is a powerful tool for teaching comprehension. While think-aloud models are included in all lessons, relate your own thinking and experiences to the lesson and the think-alouds. Early in the process you will need to model thinking about how, when, and why to use the strategies. Encourage students to stop and use them as well; engage them in thinking!

✦ **Modeling Summarizing.** Just as the strategy of summarizing the plot and then predicting what will happen next can enhance a student's reading of fiction, so too can the same procedure be used to the student's advantage in reading nonfiction. In expository text, it is particularly logical to stop and summarize at the end of a chapter or section before going on to the next. One way to model the valuable exercise of making predictions and at the same time to expand knowledge is to summarize information learned from a piece of expository writing and then to predict what the next step or category will be. Appropriate times to stop and summarize include the following:

- When a narrative text has covered a long period of time or a number of events
- When many facts have been presented
- When an especially critical scene has occurred
- When a complex process has been described
- Any time there is the potential for confusion about what has happened or what has been presented in the text
- When returning to a selection

✦ **Modeling Clarifying.** A reader may need clarification at any point in the reading. Model this strategy by stopping at points that confuse you or that may confuse your students. Indicate that you are experiencing some confusion and need to stop and make sure you understand what is being read. Difficulty may arise from a challenging or unknown word or phrase. It may also stem from the manner in which the information is presented. Perhaps the author did not supply needed information. As you model this strategy, vary the reasons for stopping to clarify so that students understand that good readers do not simply skip over difficult or confusing material—they stop and determine what they do not understand.

✦ **Modeling Asking Questions.** Learning to ask productive questions is not an easy task. Students' earliest experiences with this strategy take the form of answering teacher-generated questions. However, students should be able to move fairly quickly to asking questions like those a teacher might ask. Questions that can be answered with a simple *yes* or *no* are not typically very useful for helping them remember and understand what they have read. Many students find it helpful to ask questions beginning with Who? What? When? Where? How? and Why? As students become more accustomed to asking and answering questions, they will naturally become more adept at phrasing their questions. As their question asking becomes more sophisticated, they progress from simple questions that can be answered with explicit information in the text to questions that require making inferences based on the text.

✦ **Modeling Predicting.** Predicting can be appropriate at the beginning of a selection—on the basis of the titles and the illustrations—or at any point while reading a selection. At first, your modeling will take the form of speculation about what might happen next, but tell students from the start what clues in the text or illustrations helped you predict to make it clear that predicting is not just guessing. When a student makes a prediction—especially a far-fetched one—ask on what in the selection or in his or her own experience the prediction is based. If the student can back up the prediction, let the prediction stand; otherwise, suggest that the student make another prediction on the basis of what he or she already knows. Often it is appropriate to summarize before making a prediction. This will help students consider what has come before as they make their predictions about what will happen next. When reading aloud, stop whenever a student's prediction has been confirmed or contradicted. Have students tell whether the prediction was correct. If students seem comfortable with the idea of making predictions but rarely do so on their own, encourage them to discuss how to find clues in the text that will help them.

- **Modeling Making Connections.** To model making connections, share with students any thoughts or memories that come to mind as you read the selection. Perhaps a character in a story reminds you of a childhood friend, allowing you to better identify with interactions between characters. Perhaps information in an article on Native American life in the Old West reminds you of an article that you have read on the importance of the bison to Native Americans. Sharing your connections will help students become aware of the dynamic nature of reading and show them another way of being intentional, active learners.
- **Modeling Visualizing.** Model visualizing by describing the mental images that occur to you as you read. A well-described scene is relatively easy to visualize, and if no one does so voluntarily, you may want to prompt students to express their own visualizations. If the author has not provided a description of a scene, but a picture of the scene would make the story more interesting or comprehensible, you might want to model visualizing as follows: "Let's see. The author says that the street was busy, and we know that this story is set during the colonial period. From what I already know about those times, there were no cars, and the roads were different from the roads of today. The street may have been paved with cobblestones. Horses would have been pulling carriages or wagons. I can almost hear the horses' hoofs going clip-clop over the stones." Remind students that different readers may picture the same scene quite differently, which is fine. Every reader responds to a story in her or his own way.
- **Modeling Adjusting Reading Speed.** Just as readers need to monitor for problems, they need to be aware that various texts can be approached in various ways. For example, if reading a story or novel for enjoyment, the reader will typically read at a relaxed speed that is neither so fast as to miss information nor as slow as they might read a textbook. If on the other hand, the reader is reading a textbook, he or she will probably decrease speed to assure understanding and make sure that all important information is read and understood. When modeling this strategy, be sure you indicate why you, as the reader, have chosen to slow down or speed up. Good readers continually monitor their speed and ability to understand throughout reading.

If your students have not previously engaged in the sort of strategic thinking aloud that is promoted throughout ***SRA Imagine It!,*** you will have to do all or most of the modeling at first, but encourage students to participate as soon as possible. Remember, however, the goal is for students to use these strategies independently as they read both in and out of school. In addition to the think-alouds for the teachers, there are also prompts to encourage students to do the thinking. The responsibility for using strategies by students should begin as soon as they understand that reading is about problem solving and making sense of text and that these strategies will help them do both.

Reading Aloud

At the beginning of the year, students should be encouraged to read selections aloud. This practice will help you and them understand some of the challenges posed by the text and how individual students approach these challenges.

Reading aloud helps students build fluency, which in turn will aid their comprehension. Students in Grades K–3 can use ***Decodables*** to build fluency, while students in Grades 4–6 can use the literature from the ***Student Readers. Leveled Readers*** are also available for Grades 1–6. Fluent second graders read between 82 and 124 words per minute with accuracy and understanding, depending on the time of the year (fall/spring). Fluent third graders can be expected to read between 107 and 142 words per minute; fourth (125/143); fifth (126/151); sixth (127/153).

Make sure that you set aside time to hear each student read during the first few days of class—the days devoted to Getting Started are perfect for this—so that you can determine students' abilities and needs. Workshop is also a good time to listen to any students who do not get to read aloud while the class is reading the selection together.

As the year progresses, students should continue reading aloud often, especially with particularly challenging text. Model your own use of strategies, not only to help students better understand how to use strategies but also to help them understand that actively using strategies is something that good, mature readers do constantly.

Most students are unaccustomed to thinking aloud. They will typically stand mute as they try to determine an unfamiliar word or to deal with a confusing passage. When this happens, students should be encouraged to identify specifically with what they are having difficulty. A student might identify a particular word, or he or she may note that the individual words are familiar but that the meaning of the passage is unclear.

Active Response

Not only are good readers active in their reading when they encounter problems, but they respond constantly to whatever they read. In this way they make the text their own. As students read they should be encouraged to

- make as many connections as they can between what they are reading and what they already know.
- visualize passages to help clarify their meanings or simply to picture appealing descriptions.
- ask questions about what they are reading. The questions that go through their minds during reading will help them examine, and thus better understand, the text. Doing so may also interest them in pursuing their own investigations. The questions may also provide a direction for students' research or exploration.
- summarize and make predictions as a check on how well they understand what they are reading.

Tips

- Remember that the goal of all reading is comprehension. If a story or article does not make sense, the reader needs to choose whatever strategies will help make sense of it. If one strategy does not work, the reader should try another.
- Always treat problems encountered in text as interesting learning opportunities rather than something to be avoided or dreaded.
- Encourage students to think aloud about text challenges.
- Encourage students to help each other build meaning from text. Rather than telling each other what a word is or what

a passage means, students should tell each other how they figured out the meanings of challenging words and passages.

- Assure students that these are not the only strategies that can be used while reading. Any strategy that they find helpful in understanding text is a good, useful strategy.
- Encourage students to freely share strategies they have devised on their own. You might want to write these on a large sheet of paper and tape them onto the board.
- An absence of questions does not necessarily indicate that students understand what they are reading. Be especially alert to students who never seem to ask questions. Be sure to spend tutorial time with these students occasionally, and encourage them to discuss specific selections in the context of difficulties they might have encountered and how they solved them as well as their thoughts about unit concepts.
- Observing students' responses to text will enable you to ascertain not only how well they understand a particular selection but also their facility in choosing and applying appropriate strategies. Use the strategy rubrics to evaluate students' understanding of and ability to use the different reading strategies. Take note of the following:
    - Whether the strategies a student uses are effective in the particular situation.
    - Whether the student chooses from a variety of appropriate strategies or uses the same few over and over.
    - Whether the student can explain to classmates which strategies to use in a particular situation and why.
    - Whether the student can identify alternative resources to pursue when the strategies she or he has tried are not effective.
    - Whether students' application of a given strategy is becoming more effective over a period of time.
- Encourage students to use the reading strategies throughout the day in all their reading activities.

Becoming familiar and comfortable with these self-monitoring techniques gives readers the confidence to tackle material that is progressively more difficult. A good, mature reader knows when understanding what he or she is reading is becoming a problem and can take steps to correct the situation. He or she has internalized the strategies, values them, and uses strategies automatically.

Comprehension Skills

Purpose

An important purpose of writing is to communicate thoughts from one person to another. The goal of instruction in reading comprehension skills is to make students aware of the logic behind the structure of a written piece. If the reader can discern the logic of the structure, he or she will be more able to understand the author's logic and to gain knowledge both of the facts and the intent of the selection. By keeping the organization of a piece in mind and considering the author's purpose for writing, the reader can go beyond the actual words on the page and make inferences or draw conclusions based on what was read. Strong, mature readers utilize these "between the lines" skills to get a complete picture of not only what the writer is saying but what the writer is trying to say.

Effective comprehension skills include the following:

Author's Point of View

Point of view involves identifying who is telling the story. If a character in the story is telling the story, that one character describes the action and tells what the other characters are like. This is first-person point of view. In such a story, one character will do the talking and use the pronouns *I, my,* and *me.* All other characters' thoughts, feelings, and emotions will be reported through this one character.

If the story is told in third-person point of view, someone outside the story who is aware of all of the characters' thoughts, feelings, and actions is relating them to the reader. All of the characters are referred to by their names or the pronouns *he/she, him/her,* and *it*.

If students stay aware of who is telling a story, they will know whether they are getting the full picture or the picture of events as seen through the eyes of only one character.

Sequence

The reader cannot make any decisions about relationships or events if he or she has no idea in which order the events take place. The reader needs to pay attention to how the writer is conveying the sequence. Is it simply stated that first this happened and then that happened? Does the writer present the end of the story first and then go back and let the reader know the sequence of events? Knowing what the sequence is and how it is presented helps the reader follow the writer's line of thought.

Fact and Opinion

Learning to distinguish fact from opinion is essential to critical reading and thinking. Students learn what factors need to be present for a statement to be provable. They also learn that an opinion, while not provable itself, should be based on fact. Readers use this knowledge to determine for themselves the validity of the ideas presented in their reading.

Main Idea and Details

An author always has something specific to say to his or her reader. The author may state this main idea in different ways, but the reader should always be able to tell what the writing is about.

To strengthen the main point or main idea of a piece, the author provides details to help the reader understand. For example, the author may use comparison and contrast to make a point, to provide examples, to provide facts, to give opinions, to give descriptions, to give reasons or causes, or to give definitions. The reader needs to know what kinds of details he or she is dealing with before making a judgment about the main idea.

Compare and Contrast

Using comparison and contrast is one of the most common and easiest ways a writer gets his or her reader to understand a subject. Comparing and contrasting unfamiliar thoughts, ideas, or things with familiar thoughts, ideas, and things gives the reader something within his or her own experience base to use in understanding.

Cause and Effect

What made this happen? Why did this character act the way he or she did? Knowing the causes of events helps the reader see the whole story. Using this information to identify the probable outcomes (effects) of events or actions will help the reader anticipate the story or article.

Classify and Categorize

The relationships of actions, events, characters, outcomes, and such in a selection should be clear enough for the reader to see the relationships. Putting like things or ideas together can help the reader understand the relationships set up by the writer.

Author's Purpose

Everything that is written is written for a purpose. That purpose may be to entertain, to persuade, or to inform. Knowing why a piece is written—what purpose the author had for writing the piece—gives the reader an idea of what to expect and perhaps some prior idea of what the author is going to say.

If a writer is writing to entertain, then the reader can generally just relax and let the writer carry him or her away. If, on the other hand, the purpose is to persuade, it will help the reader understand and keep perspective if he or she knows that the purpose is to persuade. The reader can be prepared for whatever argument the writer delivers.

Drawing Conclusions

Often, writers do not directly state everything—they take for granted their audience's ability to "read between the lines." Readers draw conclusions when they take from the text small pieces of information about a character or event and use this information to make a statement about that character or event.

Making Inferences

Readers make inferences about characters and events to understand the total picture in a story. When making inferences, readers use information from the text, along with personal experience or knowledge, to gain a deeper understanding of a story event and its implications.

Procedures

Read the Selection

First, have students read the selection using whatever skills they need to help them make sense of the selection. Then discuss the selection to assure that students did, indeed, understand what they read. Talk about any confusion they may have, and make any necessary clarifications.

Reread

Revisiting or rereading a selection allows the reader to note specific techniques that authors use to organize and present information in narratives and expository genres. When students have a basic understanding of the piece, have them reread the selection in whole or in part, concentrating on selected skills. Students learn to appreciate that writers use different structures, for example, cause and effect or compare/contrast, to organize their work and that recognizing these structures can help readers understand what they have read. It is these same structures that students will use in their own writing.

Limit this concentration on specific comprehension/writing skills to one or two that can be clearly identified in the piece. Trying to concentrate on too many things will just confuse students and make it harder for them to identify any of the organizational devices used by the writer. If a piece has many good examples of several different aspects, then go back to the piece several times over a span of days.

Write

Solidify the connection between how an author writes and how readers make sense of a selection by encouraging students to incorporate these organizational devices into their own writing. As they attempt to use these devices, they will get a clearer understanding of how to identify them when they are reading.

Remind students often that the purpose of any skill exercise is to give them tools to use when they are reading and writing. Unless students learn to apply the skills to their own reading—in every area of reading and study—then they are not gaining a full understanding of the purpose of the exercise.

Writing is a complicated process. A writer uses handwriting, spelling, vocabulary, grammar, usage, genre structures, and mechanics skills with ideas to create readable text. In addition, a writer must know how to generate content, or ideas, and understand genre structures to effectively present ideas in writing. Many students never progress beyond producing a written text that duplicates their everyday speech patterns. Mature writers, however, take composition beyond conversation. They understand the importance of audience and purpose for writing. They organize their thoughts, eliminating those that do not advance their main ideas, applying what they have learned in reading, and elaborating on those that do so that their readers can follow a logical progression of ideas in an essay or story. Mature writers also know and can use the conventions of grammar, usage, spelling, and mechanics. They proofread and edit for these conventions, so their readers are not distracted by errors.

Reading Big Books

Purpose

Many students come from homes where they are read to often, but a significant number of other students have not had this valuable experience. ***Big Books*** (Levels K and 1) offer all students crucial opportunities to confirm and expand their knowledge about print and reading, to develop vocabulary, and to enjoy literacy experiences. They are especially useful for shared reading experiences in the early grades.

The benefits of reading ***Big Books*** include engaging even nonreaders in

- unlocking the books' messages.
- developing print awareness.
- participating in good reading behaviors.
- observing what a good reader does: remarking on the illustrations and the title, asking questions about the content and what might happen, making predictions, and clarifying words and ideas.
- promoting the insights about print, for example, that a given word is spelled the same way every time it occurs as high-frequency words are identified.
- reinforcing the correspondence between spoken and written words and spelling patterns.
- enjoying the illustrations and connecting them to the text to help students learn to explore books for enjoyment and information.
- learning about different genre and the langauge of print.
- developing vocabulary and academic language.
- interpreting and responding to literature and expository text before they can read themselves.

Procedure for Reading Big Books

During the first reading of the ***Big Books,*** you will model reading behaviors and comprehension strategies similar to those that will later apply to their own reading. This focus on strategies encourages students to think about the ideas in the stories, to ask questions, and to learn new vocabulary. During the second reading, you will address print awareness and teach comprehension skills such as classifying and categorizing or sequencing, which help the reader organize information and focus on the specifics in the selection. In addition, you will teach skills such as making inferences and drawing conclusions, which help the reader focus on the deeper meaning of the text. At first, teachers should expect to do all of the reading but should not prevent students from trying to read on their own or from reading words they already know.

- **Activate Prior Knowledge.** Read the title of the selection and the author's and illustrator's names. At the beginning of each ***Big Book,*** read the title of the book and discuss what the whole book is about before going on to reading the first selection. Initiate a brief discussion of any prior knowledge students have that might help them understand the selection.

> **Big Books** *offer all students opportunities to confirm and expand their knowledge about print and reading.*

- **Browse the Selection.** Explain to the classs that browsing means to look through the pages of the story to get a general idea of what the story is about, to see what interests them, and to ask questions. Ask students to tell what they think the story might be about just from looking at the illustrations. This conversation should be brief so that students can move on to a prereading discussion of print awareness.
- **Develop Print Awareness.** The focus of browsing the ***Big Books*** is to develop awareness of print. Urge students to tell what words or letters they recognize rather than what they expect the selection to be about.

  To develop print awareness, have students look through the selection page by page and to comment on whatever they notice in the text. Some students may know some of the words, while others may recognize only specific letters or sounds. The key is to get students to look at the print separately from the illustrations even before they have heard the actual text content. This process isolates print awareness so that it is not influenced by content. It also gives you a clearer idea of what your students do or do not know about print.
- **Read Aloud.** Read the selection aloud expressively, using intonation and pauses at punctuation. Not only does this enable students to hear and enjoy the text as it is read through once, it serves as an early model for fluency. Good fluency and expression support comprehension. As you read, you will stop periodically to model behaviors and comprehension strategies that all students will need to develop to become successful readers—for example, asking questions; clarifying unfamiliar words, first by using the pictures and later by using context; or predicting what might happen next.
- **Reread.** Read the selection expressively again. During the second reading of the stories, you will focus on teaching comprehension skills. Also, to develop print awareness, point to each word as it is read, thus demonstrating that text proceeds from left to right and from top to bottom and helping advance the idea that words are individual spoken and written units. Invite students to

identify the rhyming words in a poem or to chime in on repetitive parts of text as you point to the words. Or students can read with you on this second reading, depending on the text. As students' knowledge of words and phonics grows, they can participate in decoding words and reading high-frequency sight words.

- **Discuss Print.** Return to print awareness by encouraging discussion of anything students noticed about the words. Young students should begin to realize that you are reading separate words that are separated by spaces. Later, students will begin to see that each word is made of a group of letters. Students should be encouraged to discuss anything related to the print. For example, you might ask students to point to a word or to count the number of words on a line. Or you might connect the words to the illustrations by pointing to a word and saying it and then asking students to find a picture of that word.
- **Responding.** Responding to a selection is a way of insuring comprehension. Invite students to tell about the story by asking them what they like about the poem or story or calling on a student to explain in his or her own words what the poem or story tells about. Call on others to add to the telling as needed. For nonfiction selections, this discussion might include asking students what they learned about the topic and what they thought was most interesting.

Tips for Using Big Books

- Make sure the entire group is able to see the book clearly while you are reading.
- If some students are able to read words, encourage them to do so during the rereading.
- Encourage students to use their knowledge of print.
- Encourage students' use of academic language as they talk about reading. Students should be comfortable using strategic reading words such as *predict* and *clarify* and book and prints words such as *author* and *illustrator.*
- Allow students to look at the ***Big Books*** whenever they wish.
- Provide small versions of the ***Big Books*** for students to browse through and to try to read at their leisure.
- The reader of the ***Big Book*** should try to be part of the collaborative group of learners rather than the leader.

Strategic Reading

Purpose

Reading is a complex process that requires students not only to decode automatically and correctly what they read but also to understand and respond to it. The purpose of this section is to help you identify various reading behaviors used by good readers and to encourage those behaviors in your students.

Reading Behaviors and Comprehension Strategies

There are four basic behaviors that good readers engage in during reading: Setting Reading Goals and Expectations, Responding to Text, Checking Understanding, and Monitoring and Clarifying Unfamiliar Words and Passages. Engaging in these behaviors involves the application of certain comprehension strategies. These strategies are initially modeled while reading the ***Big Books*** (Levels K and the first half of Level 1) and ***Student Readers*** (Levels 1–6). The goal of strategy instruction, however, is to ultimately turn over responsibility for using strategies to students so they set their own goals for reading, respond to text, and check their own understanding and solve problems while reading. Students need to take responsibility for doing the thinking and making sense of text.

Setting Reading Goals and Expectations

Good readers set reading goals and expectations before they begin reading. This behavior involves a variety of strategies that will help students prepare to read the text.

- **Activate prior knowledge.** When good readers approach a new text, they consider what they already know about the subject or what their experiences have been in reading similar material.
- **Browse the text.** To get an idea of what to expect from a text, good readers look at the title and the illustrations. They may look for potential problems, such as difficult words. When browsing a unit, have students glance quickly at each selection, looking briefly at the illustrations and the print. Have them tell what they think they might be learning about as they read the unit.
- **Decide what they expect from the text.** When reading for pleasure, good readers anticipate enjoying the story or the language. When reading to learn something, they ask themselves what they expect to find out.

Responding to Text

Good readers are active readers. They interact with text by using the following strategies:

- **Making connections.** Good readers make connections between what they read and what they already know. They pay attention to elements in the text that remind them of their own experiences. Readers make connections to personal experiences, to other stories they have read, and to world knowledge.
- **Visualizing, or picturing.** Good readers visualize what is happening in the text. They not only form mental images as they read but make inferences based on their own experiences. Visualizing goes beyond the words in text. They imagine the setting and the emotions it suggests, they picture the characters and their feelings, and they visualize the action in a story. When reading expository text, good readers picture the objects, processes, or events described. Visualizing helps readers understand descriptions of complex activities or processes.
- **Asking questions.** Good readers ask questions that may prepare them for what they will learn. If their questions are not answered in the text, they may try to find answers elsewhere and thus add even more to their store of knowledge.
- **Predicting.** Good readers predict what will happen next. When reading fiction, they make predictions about what they are reading and then confirm or revise those predictions as they go.
- **Thinking about how the text makes you feel.** Well-written fiction touches readers' emotions; it sparks ideas.

Checking Understanding

One of the most important behaviors good readers exhibit is the refusal to continue reading when something fails to make sense. Good readers continually assess their understanding of the text with strategies such as the following:

- **Interpreting.** As they read, good readers make inferences that help them understand and appreciate what they are reading.
- **Summarizing.** Good readers summarize to check their understanding as they read. Sometimes they reread to fill in gaps in their understanding.
- **Adjusting reading speed.** Good readers monitor their understanding of what they read. They slow down as they come to difficult words and passages. They speed up as they read easier passages.

Monitoring and Clarifying Unfamiliar Words and Passages

Monitoring understanding involves knowing when meaning is breaking down. The reader needs to stop and identify what the problem or source of confusion is. It might be an unfamiliar word, complex and hard-to-understand sentences or unfamiliar concepts that need clarifying. At the word level, the reader might

- apply decoding skills to sound out unknown words.
- apply context clues in text and illustrations to figure out the meanings of words.
- use structural elements to figure out the meaning of the word.
- ask someone the meaning of the word.
- reread the passage to make sure the passage makes sense.
- check a dictionary or the glossary to understand the meanings of words not clarified by clues or rereading.

Complex sentences may require the reader to look for the main idea in the sentence, to pull out clauses that may interfere with the main idea, or to ask for help. When faced with unfamiliar concepts, readers often ask for clarification from someone.

These cognitive activities engage the reader in thinking about text before, during, and after reading. Readers think about text before they read by activating background knowledge, anticipating content, setting purposes, and wondering about the text and what they will learn. During reading, the reader is constantly checking understanding—asking whether what is being read makes sense and constructing conclusions or summary statements. When the text is not making sense, the reader uses strategies to clarify words, ideas, and larger units of text or may reread more slowly for clarification. After reading, the reader reflects on what was read, connecting new information to prior knowledge, evaluating purposes, and connecting the relevance of the new information to the purpose.

Procedures

Modeling and Thinking Aloud

Modeling and encouraging students to think aloud as they attempt to understand text can demonstrate for everyone how reading behaviors are put into practice. Modeling and thinking aloud helps students learn how to process information and learn important content. It is more than asking students questions; it is letting students in on the thinking that help readers make sense of text, solve problems while reading, and use strategies differentially and intentionally. The most effective models will be those that come from your own reading. As you model the different strategies, let students know what strategy you are using and why you are using it.

Model comprehension strategies in a natural way, and choose questions and comments that fit the text you are reading. Present a variety of ways to respond to text.

- Pose questions that you really do wonder about.
- Identify with characters by comparing them with yourself.
- React emotionally by showing joy, sadness, amusement, or surprise.
- Show empathy with or sympathy for characters.
- Relate the text to something that has happened to you or to something you already know.
- Show interest in the text ideas.
- Question the meaning or clarity of the author's words and ideas.

Encourage Students' Responses and Use of Strategies

Most students will typically remain silent as they try to figure out an unfamiliar word or a confusing passage. Encourage students to identify specifically with what they are having difficulty. When the problem has been identified, ask students to suggest a strategy for dealing with the problem. Remind students to

- treat problems encountered in text as interesting learning opportunities.
- think aloud about text challenges.
- help each other build meaning. Rather than tell what a word is, students should tell how they figured out the meanings of challenging words and passages.
- consider reading a selection again with a partner after reading it once alone. Partner reading provides valuable practice in reading for fluency.
- make as many connections as they can between what they are reading and what they already know.
- visualize to clarify meanings or enjoy descriptions.
- ask questions about what they are reading.
- notice how the text makes them feel.

In addition, using open-ended questions such as the following, as well as your students' questions and comments, will make both the text and the strategic reading process more meaningful to students.

- What kinds of things did you wonder about?
- What kinds of things surprised you?
- What new information did you learn?
- What was confusing until you reread or read further?

Discussion

The more students are able to discuss what they are learning, to voice their confusions, and to compare perceptions of what they are learning, the deeper and more meaningful their learning becomes.

Purpose

Through discussions, students are exposed to points of view different from their own and learn how to express their thoughts and opinions coherently. Through discussion, students add to their own knowledge that of their classmates and learn to explain themselves coherently. They also begin to ask insightful questions that help them better understand what they have read and all that they are learning through their inquiry/research and explorations. The purpose of classroom discussion is to provide a framework for learning.

Procedure

Reflecting on the Selection

After students have finished reading a selection, provide an opportunity for them to engage in discussion about the selection. Students should

- check to see whether the questions they asked before reading as part of Clues, Problems and Wonderings and KWL (What I Know, What I Want to Know and What I Have Learned)have been answered. Encourage them to discuss whether any unanswered questions should still be answered. If unanswered questions are related to the theme, add those questions to the **Concept/ Question Board.**
- discuss any new questions that have arisen because of the reading. Encourage students to decide which of these questions should go on the **Concept/ Question Board.**
- share what they expected to learn from reading the selection and tell whether expectations were met.
- talk about whatever has come to mind while reading the selection. This discussion should be an informal sharing of impressions of, or opinions about, the selection; it should never take on the aspects of a question-and-answer session about the selection.
- give students ample opportunity to ask questions and to share their thoughts about the selection. Participate as an active member of the group, making your own observations about information in a selection or modeling your own appreciation of a story. Be especially aware of unusual and interesting insights suggested by students so that these insights can be recognized and discussed. To help students learn to keep the discussion student-centered, have each student choose the next speaker instead of handing the discussion back to you.

The purpose of classroom discussion is to provide a framework for learning.

Recording Ideas

As students finish discussions about their reactions to a selection, they should be encouraged to record their thoughts, feelings, reactions, and ideas about the selection or the subject of the selection in their Writer's Notebooks. This will not only help keep the selections fresh in students' minds; it will strengthen their writing abilities and help them learn how to write about their thoughts and feelings.

Students may find that the selection gave them ideas for their own writing, or it could have reminded them of some person or incident in their own lives. Perhaps the selection answered a question that has been on their minds or raised a question they had never thought before. Good, mature writers—especially professional writers—learn the value of recording such thoughts and impressions quickly before they fade. Students should be encouraged to do this also.

Handing Off

Handing off (Levels 1–6) is a method of turning over to students the primary responsibility for controlling discussion. Often, students who are taking responsibility for controlling a discussion tend to have all "turns" go through the teacher. The teacher is the one to whom attention is transferred when a speaker finishes, and the teacher is the one who is expected to call on the next speaker—the result being that the teacher remains the pivotal figure in the discussion.

Having students "hand off" the discussion to other students instead of the teacher encourages them to retain complete control of the discussion and to become more actively involved in the learning process. When a student finishes his or her comments, that student should choose (hand off the discussion to) the next speaker. In this way, students maintain a discussion without relying on the teacher to decide who speaks.

When handing off is in place, the teacher's main roles are to occasionally remind students to hand off, to help students when they get stuck, to encourage them to persevere on a specific point, and to get them back to a discussion, and to monitor the discussion to ensure that everyone gets a chance to contribute. The teacher may say, for example, "Remember, not just boys (or girls)." or "Try to choose someone who has not had a chance to talk yet." It is not unusual early in the process for students to roam from the topic and selection. To bring the discussion back to the topic and selection, be a participant, raise your hand, and ask a question or make a statement that refocuses students' thinking and discussion.

For handing off to work effectively, a seating arrangement that allows students to see one another is essential. It is hard to hold a discussion when students have their backs to each other. A circle or a semicircle is effective. In addition, all students need to have copies of the materials being discussed.

Actively encourage this handing-off process by letting students know that they, not you, are in control of the discussion.

If students want to remember thoughts about, or reactions to, a selection, suggest that they record these in the Writing Journal section of their Writer's Notebooks.

Encourage students to record the thoughts, feelings, or reactions that are elicited by any reading they do.

Exploring Concepts within the Selection

To provide an opportunity for collaborative learning and to focus on the concepts, you may want to have students form small groups and spend time discussing what they have learned about the concepts from this selection. Topics may include new information that they have acquired, new ideas that they have had, or new questions that the selection raised.

Students should always base their discussions on postings from the **Concept/Question Board** as well as on previous discussions of the concept. The small-group discussions should be ongoing throughout the unit; during this time, students should continue to compare and contrast any new information with their previous ideas, opinions, and impressions about the concepts. How does this selection help confirm their ideas? How does it contradict their thinking? How has it changed their outlook?

As students discuss the concepts in small groups, circulate around the room to make sure that each group stays focused upon the selection and the concepts. After students have had some time to discuss the information and the ideas in the selection, encourage each group to formulate some statements about the concept that apply to the selection.

Sharing Ideas about Concepts

Have a representative from each group report and explain the group's ideas to the rest of the class. Then have the class formulate one or more general statements related to the unit concepts and write these statements on the **Concept/Question Board.** As students progress through the unit, they will gain more and more confidence in suggesting additions to the **Concept/Question Board.**

- **Visual Aids** During this part of the discussion, you may find it helpful to use visual aids to help students as they build the connections to the unit concepts. Not all units or concepts will lend themselves to this type of treatment; however, aids such as time lines, charts, graphs, and pictographs may help students see how each new selection adds to their growing knowledge of the concepts.

Encourage students to ask questions about the concepts that the selection may have raised. Have students list on the **Concept/Question Board** those questions that cannot be answered immediately and that they want to explore further.

> *Through discussions, students are exposed to points of view different from their own and learn how to express their thoughts and opinions coherently.*

Exploring Concepts across Selections

As each new selection is read, encourage students to discuss its connection with the other selections and with the unit concepts. Also encourage students to think about selections that they have read from other units and how they relate to the concepts for this unit.

Ultimately, this ability to make connections between past knowledge and new knowledge allows any learner to gain insights into what is being studied. The goal of the work with concepts and the discussions is to help students to start thinking in terms of connections—how is this like what I have learned before? Does this information confirm, contradict, or add a completely different layer to that which I already know about this concept? How can the others in the class have such different ideas than I do when we just read the same selection? Why is so much written about this subject?

Learning to make connections and to delve deeper through self-generated questions and substantive discussions give students the tools they need to become effective, efficient, lifelong learners.

Tips

- Create an environment that facilitates discussion. Have students sit in circles or some other configuration so everyone can see each other.
- When students are discussing the selection, they should have their books with them, and students should feel free to refer to them throughout the discussion.
- Discussions offer a prime opportunity for you to introduce, or seed, new ideas about the concepts. New ideas can come from a variety of sources: Students may draw on their own experiences or on the books or videos they are studying; you may introduce new ideas into the discussion; or you may at times invite experts to speak to the class.
- If students do not mention an important idea that is necessary to the understanding of some larger issue, you may "drop" that idea into the conversation and, indeed, repeat it several times to make sure that it does get picked up. This seeding may be subtle ("I think that might be important here") or quite direct ("This is a big idea, one that we will definitely need to understand and one that we will return to regularly").
- To facilitate this process for each unit, you must be aware of the unit concepts and be able to recognize and reinforce them when they arise spontaneously in discussions. If central unit concepts do not arise naturally, then, and only then, will you seed these ideas by direct modeling. The more you turn over discussions to students, the more

involved they will become, and the more responsibility they will take for their own learning. Make it your goal to become a participant in, rather than the leader of, class discussions.

- Help students see that they are responsible for carrying on the discussion. After a question is asked, always wait instead of jumping in with a comment or an explanation. Although this wait time may be uncomfortable at first, students will come to understand that the discussion is their responsibility and that you will not jump in every time there is a hesitation.
- As the year progresses, students will become more and more adept at conducting and participating in meaningful discussions about what they have read. These discussions will greatly enhance students' understanding of the concepts that they are exploring.

Discussion Starters and Questions

The following examples of discussion starters can be modeled initially, but then the responsibility for using them should be turned over to students. The starters provide the opportunity for open-ended discussions by students.

- I didn't know that . . . .
- Does anyone know . . . .
- I figured out that . . . .
- I liked the part where . . . .
- I'm still confused about . . . .
- This made me think . . . .
- I agree with ______________ because . . . .
- I disagree with ______________ because . . . .
- The reason I think _________ is . . .
- I found _______ interesting because. . . .
- I learned . . .
- What I learned in this selection reminds me of what we read in _________ because . . .
- This author's writing reminds me of . . .
- I had problems understanding _______ because . . .
- I wonder why the author chose to . . .
- I still do not understand . . .
- I was surprised to find out . . .
- I like the way the author developed the character by . . .
- The author made the story really come alive by . . .

In addition to these open-ended discussion starters, students should be encouraged to ask open-ended questions. When students ask questions, other students should respond to the question before moving on to another idea or topic. One student asking a question often helps to clarify something for the whole class and places a value on asking questions as a critical part of learning.

- Why did the author . . .?
- What did the author mean when he or she wrote . . . ?
- Who can help me clarify . . . ?
- Who can help me figure out . . . ?
- How does this piece connect to the unit theme?
- What does this section mean?

Writing

Purpose

The writing program in ***SRA Imagine It!*** teaches students how to write skillfully. This is essential, as writing is a powerful tool that fosters learning, communication, creativity, and self-discovery. ***SRA Imagine It!*** writing teaches students how to use writing effectively for these purposes.

Writing is a complex process. It involves deftly juggling a variety of skills, strategies, and knowledge. Writers must make plans, consider the reader, draw ideas from memory, develop new ideas, organize thoughts, consider the conventions of the genre, translate ideas into words, craft sentences, evaluate decisions, make needed revisions, transcribe words into correctly spelled print, and monitor the writing process, among other things.

SRA Imagine It! writing is designed to ensure that students acquire the skills, knowledge, strategies, and dispositions they need to become skilled writers. This includes the following:

- Knowledge about the qualities of good writing, characteristics of different genres, intended audience, and writing topics. Skilled writers know how to obtain information about their topics, are familiar with basic features of different genres, and possess basic schemas or frameworks for accomplishing common writing tasks.
- The writing strategies involved in basic composing processes such as prewriting, drafting, monitoring, evaluating, revising, editing/proofreading, and publishing. Skilled writers flexibly employ these strategies to create text.
- Command of basic writing skills such as handwriting, spelling, sentence construction, grammar and usage. Skilled writers execute these basic writing skills with little conscious effort.
- Interest and motivation to write as well as perceptions of competence as a writer. Skilled writers possess an "I can do" attitude.

Procedures

With ***SRA Imagine It!*** writing, evidence-based practices are used to teach students to write skillfully. These evidence-based practices are drawn from research on the effectiveness of specific writing interventions that show that the quality of students' writing can be improved by

- explicitly teaching strategies for prewriting, revising, editing/proofreading, and publishing.
- modeling effective use of writing strategies.

*Children start school wanting to learn how to write and enjoying writing. The goal of **SRA Imagine It!** writing is for children to become lifelong writers—people who enjoy writing and use writing effectively at work as well as in their personal lives.*

- having students work together to prewrite, draft, revise, edit/proofread, and publish their compositions.
- using prewriting activities such as graphic organizers to gather information.
- involving students in inquiry activities designed to help them further develop their ideas for writing.
- making the goals for writing assignments clear and specific.
- teaching students how to construct more sophisticated sentences.
- providing students with the opportunity to read, evaluate, and emulate models of good writing.
- teaching students how to use word processing as a tool for composing.

The evidence-based practices in ***SRA Imagine It!*** are also based on the study of expert teachers who

- make sure their students are engaged, spending most of their writing time doing something that involves thoughtfulness, such as crafting a story or learning how to construct a complex sentence.
- teach basic writing skills, strategies, and knowledge balanced by ample opportunity to apply what is learned.
- involve students in writing for a variety of different purposes.
- create a writing classroom environment that is supportive, pleasant, and motivating.
- encourage students to accomplish as much as possible on their own (to act in a self-regulated fashion), but who are ready to offer support and instruction as needed.
- use reading to support writing development and vice versa.
- monitor students' growth in writing and encourage students to monitor their own growth.
- provide extra assistance to students who experience difficulty.
- are passionate about writing.

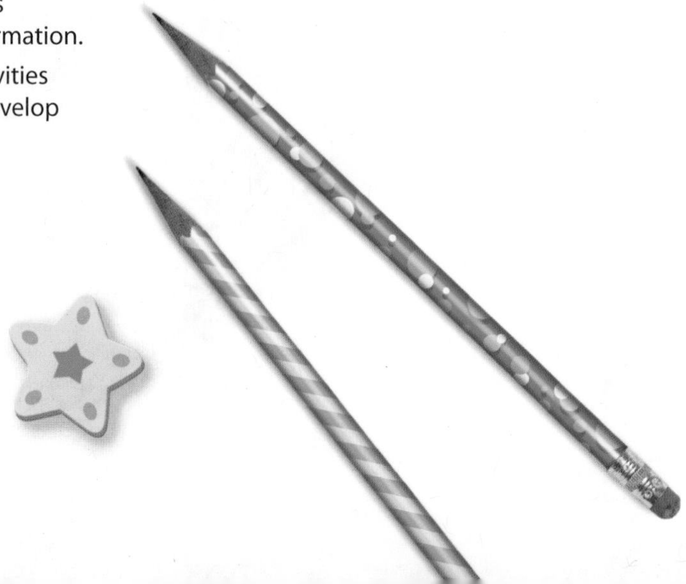

Knowledge about Writing

Purpose

Writing can be used to communicate, entertain, inform, reflect, persuade, and learn. To take full advantage of this flexible tool, students must acquire knowledge about the qualities of good writing and the various purposes and forms of writing. They must also carefully consider their audience and be knowledgeable about the topics they write about.

Procedures

Qualities of Good Writing

One way students learn about the qualities of good writing is by directly teaching them that good writing is characterized by the following seven traits:

- Clearly presented and fully developed ideas
- Writing that is easy to follow and logically organized
- Effective and precise word choice
- Varied use of sentence structure to promote fluency, rhythm, and natural speech patterns
- Writing that captures appropriate tone or mood to make the desired impact on the reader
- Correct spelling, usage, and grammar
- A written product that is legible, attractive, and accessible

For each writing assignment, teachers concentrate on one or more of these traits, teaching students strategies for enhancing the trait(s) in their writing. For example, students are taught to circle words that are vague in their writing and to replace them with more precise ones.

Another way that students learn about the qualities of good writing is through reading. The reading material in ***SRA Imagine It!*** provides concrete models that illustrate the characteristics of good writing, such as how authors

- present, develop, and organize ideas.
- use words to evoke specific images and feelings.
- manipulate sentences to speed up or slow down the flow of text.
- set and change the mood to match the action of the characters.
- use illustrations to reinforce and sharpen readers' understanding.

This knowledge is fostered in ***SRA Imagine It!*** through Reading with a Writer's Eye. Teachers and students discuss what the author of a reading selection did to achieve certain purposes. For example, after reading a mystery, the class discusses how the author planted a false lead to make the story more interesting and complex. Students are then encouraged to use the same technique in a mystery they write.

Different Purposes and Forms of Writing

Students learn the purpose and forms of a wide range of genres they need to master for success both in and out of school. This includes using writing to do the following:

- Communicate with others (personal letters, business letters, notes, cards, and e-mail)
- Create personal narratives (journal writing, autobiography, writing about a personal event, and so on)
- Entertain (stories, plays, poems, and so on)
- Learn (learning logs, reports, journal entries, summarizing, and biographies)
- Inform (writing lists, explaining how to do something, describing objects or places, describing events, news reports, reports, and biographies)
- Respond to literature (book evaluations, book reports, and book reviews)
- Persuade (advertisements, opinions about controversial topics)
- Demonstrate knowledge (for example, traditional classroom tests, high-stakes tests involving writing, high-stakes tests involving multiple-choice answers)

In ***SRA Imagine It!*** writing, students learn to write stories, poetry, plays, journal entries, summaries, book reviews, informative reports, descriptions, explanations, letters, critiques, and e-mail. They also use these various forms of writing to gather, think about, and report what they have learned when doing extended Inquiry projects.

One way they learn about the purposes and forms of these various genres is through the use of models of each type of writing. As students begin working on a new genre, the class analyzes an exemplary model of this type of writing to determine its characteristics and functions. They are encouraged to incorporate these features in their writing. In addition, what they write is frequently tied to what they read, so their reading material provides a model and source of information on the purpose and form of their writing.

Students are also asked to carefully consider the purpose for each of their compositions and include this determination as part of the planning process. As they plan, the form and purpose of their compositions is further emphasized through the use of graphic organizers, in which students typically generate and organize ideas for each of the basic elements included in the type of composition they are composing.

Knowledge of Writing Topics

To write well, students must have something to write about. Good writers typically know a lot about their topics or have strategies for acquiring such information. With ***SRA Imagine It!*** writing, students are taught effective strategies for gathering information to write about. This includes how to

- locate information in written and electronic sources.
- obtain information through interviews or surveys.
- summarize information in notes.
- reference informational sources.

Developing a Sense of Audience

While writing is often viewed as a solitary activity, it is typically meant to be read by others. Children and adults most often use writing to communicate, persuade, or inform others. Because the writer is usually not present when the composition is read, he or she must carefully consider the needs of the readers. ***SRA Imagine It!*** writing helps students develop a sense of audience by asking them to identify their audience when they write collaboratively or independently. Students are also encouraged to share what they write with their peers and others. The following are procedures for presenting and sharing:

- Before presenting, have the writer
  - decide what will be shared.
  - practice what will be shared.
- During presenting,
  - have the writer tell what is to be shared and why.

- have the writer read aloud his or her work or idea.
- remind students to listen carefully.

✦ After presenting,

- have students tell what they like.
- have students offer the writer helpful suggestions.
- take notes of students' comments to share with the writer.

Tips

✦ Have students keep a log of new information they have learned about the attributes of good writing.

✦ Develop wall charts that specify the purpose and attributes of specific writing genres.

✦ Ask students to evaluate their writing and the writing of others based on seven traits of good writing.

✦ Before students begin work on a writing assignment, hold a class discussion on the topic to share information, clarify misperceptions, and identify information students still need to locate.

Mastering the Writing Process

Purpose

To write skillfully, young writers must master the basic processes involved in writing. These processes include the strategic "know-how" involved in writing and include the following:

✦ **Prewriting:** Writers spend time thinking about and planning their topics. They consider their purposes, audience, and the focus of their topics. Writers make plans to guide the composing process, establishing goals for what to do and say. They gather possible ideas for their writing, drawing on memory and external sources such as books, interviews, articles, and the Internet. Writers make decisions about which information to include and how to organize it.

✦ **Drafting:** Writers draft or put their ideas into words, using the initial plans they developed as a guide. These plans are expanded, modified, and even reworked as writers create a first draft of their composition, often in a rough form.

✦ **Revising:** While some revising may occur during prewriting and drafting, writers revisit and revise their first drafts. They reread them to see whether the drafts say what the writers intended. Writers check to be sure the drafts make sense and that the meaning is clear for the audience. They consider whether their writing will have the desired impact on the audience. As they make changes in their text, they discover new things to say and new ways to present their ideas.

> *Writers need feedback throughout the writing process. Feedback is one of our most powerful tools for helping developing writers.*

✦ **Editing/Proofreading:** Writers edit/proofread their work. They recognize that spelling, grammar, and usage errors make it harder for others to understand and enjoy their published work. Writers know that readers are more likely to value their message when they correct these mistakes.

✦ **Publishing:** Writers share their writing by reading their entire work, or part of their work, to others. They publish their work in books, newspapers, magazines, anthologies, and so on.

Skilled writers move back and forth through these processes—from prewriting to drafting to revising and back—to create their final pieces.

Procedures

Much of what happens during writing is not visible. It occurs inside the writer's head. ***SRA Imagine It!*** writing makes the processes involved in writing concrete and visible in the following four ways:

✦ Establishing a predictable writing routine during which students are expected to prewrite, draft, revise, edit/proofread, and publish.

✦ Using graphic organizers and revising, editing/proofreading, and publishing checklists that help developing writers carry out basic writing processes.

✦ Teaching strategies for prewriting, drafting, revising, editing/proofreading, and publishing.

✦ Providing feedback throughout the writing process through writing conferences and students' presentation of their works in progress and completed compositions.

Establishing a Predictable Writing Routine

One way to make the basic writing processes more concrete is to create a predictable classroom writing routine, during which students plan, draft, revise, edit, and publish their work. This establishes that these processes are important and ensures that time is provided for each process. It also allows students to work with minimum teacher direction and at their own pace.

Tips

✦ Guide students through the steps of the writing routine. Model each step of prewriting, drafting, revising, editing/proofreading, and publishing.

✦ Make sure students learn that the processes of writing do not always occur in the same order but are recursive. For example, revising may occur at any stage of the composing process. You should not only model this by showing how this is done, but the predictable routine should vary at times to reflect this flexibility.

Using Graphic Organizers and Revising, Editing/Proofreading, and Publishing Checklists

Graphic organizers and revising, editing/proofreading, and publishing checklists provide students with assistance in carrying out the thinking activities involved in a writing assignment. They provide structure and information for how to carry out the process. The graphic oganizer typically includes a series of prompts that ask the student to think about the purpose for writing a particular piece and the intended audience. It also provides prompts designed to help the student generate and organize possible writing ideas. This frequently involves generating possible content for each part of the target composition. The revising, editing/proofreading, and publishing checklists direct students' attention to specific features or aspects of text that would be useful to consider while writing.

Tips

It is important to be sure that students understand how to use graphic organizers and revising, editing/proofreading, and publishing checklists. Be sure to

- explain the purpose of the graphic organizer or revising, editing/proofreading, and publishing checklist.
- describe how students are to use the graphic organizer or revising, editing/proofreading, and publishing checklist.
- model aloud how to carry out the basic activities on the graphic organizer or revising, editing/proofreading, and publishing checklist.
- make sure students understand each part of the graphic organizer or revising, editing/proofreading, and publishing checklist.

Teaching Strategies for Carrying Out Basic Writing Processes

A strategy involves a series of actions a writer undertakes to achieve a desired goal. In ***SRA Imagine It!*** students are taught strategies to help them carry out each of the basic writing processes—prewriting, drafting, revising, editing/proofreading, and publishing. Each strategy is also designed to enhance one or more of the seven traits of good writing. These include clearly presented and fully developed ideas; writing that is easy to follow and logically organized; effective and precise word choice; varied use of sentences to promote fluency, rhythm, and natural speech patterns; writing that captures appropriate tone or mood to make maximum impact on readers; correct spelling, usage, and grammar; and a written product that is legible, attractive, and accessible.

The goal is for students to be able to use the strategy independently and to make it part of their writing tool kit. The steps for teaching writing strategies are to

- describe the strategy.
- tell why the strategy is important.
- tell students when they should use the strategy.
- model how to use the strategy when writing, making your thoughts visible by saying aloud each thing you are doing and thinking.
- make sure students understand why the strategy is important, when to apply it, and how to use it.
- provide students with assistance in applying the strategy until they can do it on their own.
- remind students to use the strategy when they write.

Tips

- Ask students to evaluate their progress and how the strategy improved their writing.
- Be enthusiastic about learning the strategy.
- Establish the importance of effort in learning and using the strategy.
- Provide opportunities for students to see how the strategy improves their writing.
- Praise and reinforce students' use of the strategy.
- Foster students' ownership of the strategy.

Providing Feedback through Conferencing and Presentation

Writers need feedback throughout the writing process. They need reactions to ideas, drafts, and revisions. Feedback is one of our most powerful tools for helping developing writers. Writers want to know how their works-in-progress sound to someone else, whether their compositions make sense, whether they contain any incorrect or misleading information, and where and how to make changes.

Regular feedback encourages developing writers to solve problems and make meaningful changes throughout the writing process.

One way of providing feedback is through conferences. Teachers may initiate conferences, but students should also be encouraged to call conferences on an as-needed basis. Because conferences can be held at various times throughout the writing process, the focus will vary. Conferences held during the early stages of the writing process help students identify and refine a topic or identify research references. During the revision process, conferences help students learn to elaborate and reorganize their writing. During the final stages, students learn to edit and proofread stories before they are published. Conferences offer an excellent opportunity for the teacher and student to evaluate jointly the student's progress and set goals for future growth.

The basic procedures for writing conferences are as follows:

- Have the student read aloud his or her work.
- Review any feedback the student has received so far.
- Identify positive elements of the work.
- Use one or more of these strategies to help the student improve his or her work.
  - Have the student explain how he or she got his or her ideas.
  - Have the student think aloud about how he or she will address the feedback he or she has received.
  - Ask the student to help you understand any confusion you may have about his or her writing.
  - Have the student add, delete, or rearrange something in the work, and ask how it affects the entire piece.
  - Think aloud while you do a part of what the student was asked to do. Then ask the student to compare what you did to what he or she did.
  - Have the student prescribe as if to a younger student how to revise the work.
- Ask two or three questions to guide the student through revising (see below).
- Conclude the conference by having the student state his or her plan for continuing work on the piece of writing.

Tips

- Set aside a special area of the classroom for you to work with students or for students to work with each other.
- You don't have to meet with every student every day.
- Conferences should be brief; don't overwhelm students with too many comments or suggestions. Several short conferences are often more effective than one long one.
- If appropriate, suggest that students take notes to help them remember where changes are to be made.

- Don't take ownership of the students' work. Encourage students to identify what is good and what needs to be changed, and let the students make the changes.
- Focus on what is good about the students' work; discuss how to solve problems rather than telling students what to do.
- Peer conferencing should be encouraged during Workshop.
- As students engage in peer conferencing, note which students are participating, the types of questions they ask, and the comments they make. Use this information to help students become more effective in peer conferencing.
- You may need to structure peer conferences by asking students to first explain what they liked about the composition, and then teaching them how to give constructive feedback.

Having students present or share their work provides another opportunity for them to receive feedback about their writing. Student presentations can involve

- presenting an initial idea or plan for a writing assignment.
- sharing a first draft of a paper.
- presenting orally part or all of a final piece of writing.

Tips

- Everyone must listen carefully and provide constructive feedback. Focus on what is good about a piece and ways to make it better.
- The student author has ownership and can decide which suggestions to use. The author does not have to incorporate all suggestions from the audience.
- Have a chair designated as the "Author's Chair" from which the student author can read his or her work or share ideas. This lends importance to the activity.
- The student author should be encouraged to give a bit of background, including where he or she is in the process, why he or she chose a particular part, or what problem he or she is having. This helps orient the audience.
- Short pieces of writing can be read in their entirety. As students become more proficient and write longer papers, they should be encouraged to read just a part of their writing; for example, a part they need help with, a part that has been revised, or a part they particularly like.
- Take notes during the presentations, and encourage older students to do the same.
- Be sensitive to the attention span of the class and the feedback being given. Students have a tendency to repeat the same comments to each author.

Word Processing and Other Aspects of Electronic Composing

Using a word processor to compose a piece of writing makes many aspects of the writing process easier. Text can easily be changed, deleted, or moved during drafting or revising. Software such as spell-checkers or word prediction provides assistance with basic writing skills. Information for writing can be obtained on-line or through other electronic sources, such as encyclopedias. Students can use publishing software to develop a more polished and attractive final product by adding pictures to their composition, developing a cover, changing fonts, and so on. ***SRA Imagine It!*** supports the use of these technologies.

Teaching Basic Writing Skills

Purpose

Young writers need to learn many basic writing skills to the point that the skills can be executed with minimal effort so they do not interfere with other writing processes. Correct handwriting, spelling, and grammar should be mastered to the point that they require little attention on the part of the writer. While sentences cannot and should not be constructed without conscious attention and effort, developing writers need to become familiar with different sentence types, and they need to become proficient at building them.

Procedures

Sentence Construction

SRA Imagine It! teaches sentence construction skills through the use of sentence frames, sentence expansion, and sentence combining.

- **Sentence Frames** With sentence frames, students are given part of a sentence and asked to generate the rest of it. For example, students can be taught to write a simple sentence, with a single subject and predicate, by giving them a frame containing the subject (The dog ____________.) and asking them to complete the sentence by telling what happened (The dog ran.).
- **Sentence Expansion** With sentence expansion, students are given a kernel sentence and asked to expand it by adding additional words. For example, students can be taught to make sentences more colorful by adding descriptive words to a kernel sentence: *Rewrite* ***The cat and dog like the toy*** *so the sentence tells more about the cat and dog and the toy — The big dog and gray cat like the fuzzy little toy.*
- **Sentence combining** With sentence combining, students learn how to combine two or more kernel sentences into a more complex single sentence. For example, you can lead students to produce sentences with relative clauses by combining the following two sentences:

  John will win the race.

  John is very fast. (who)

  John who is very fast will win the race.

When teaching sentence construction skills, the following three steps should be followed:

- Describe the skill, establish why it is important, and model how to use it.
- Provide students with assistance until they can apply the skill correctly and independently.
- Ask students to apply the skill when they write.

Tips

- Use more than one method to teach a sentence construction skill.
- Ask students to monitor how often they use the sentence construction skill.
- Encourage students to set goals to use sentence construction skills in their writing.

Handwriting

Students need to develop both legible and fluent handwriting. An important aspect of meeting this goal is to teach them an efficient pattern for forming individual letters (both lowercase and uppercase letters). Effective teaching procedures include

- modeling how to form the letter.
- describing how the letter is similar to and different from other letters.
- using visual cues, such as numbered arrows, as a guide to letter formation.
- providing practice tracing, copying, and writing the letter from memory.
- keeping instructional sessions short, with frequent review and practice.
- asking students to identify or circle their best formed letter or letters.
- encouraging students to correct or rewrite poorly formed letters.
- monitoring students' practice to ensure that letters are formed correctly.
- reinforcing students' successful efforts and providing corrective feedback as needed.

In addition to learning how to write the letters of the alphabet correctly, students must be able to produce them quickly. Fluency generally develops as a consequence of writing frequently, but it can also be fostered by having students copy short passages several times, and trying to write them a little faster each time.

Tips

- Make sure that each student develops a comfortable and efficient pencil grip.
- Encourage students to sit in an upright position, leaning slightly forward, as they write.
- Show students how to place or position their papers when writing.
- Implement appropriate procedures for left-handed writers, such as how to properly place or position their papers when writing.
- Monitor students' handwriting, paying special attention to their instructional needs in letter formation, spacing, slant, alignment, size, and line quality.
- Encourage students to make all final drafts of their papers neat and legible.

Spelling

Purpose

To become good spellers, students must learn to spell correctly and easily the words they are most likely to use when writing. They need to be able to generate and check plausible spellings for words whose spellings are uncertain. They also need to learn to use external sources such as spell-checkers to ensure correct spelling during writing. In ***SRA Imagine It!*** students are taught how to spell words they frequently use when writing as well as spelling patterns that help them spell untaught words.

Tips

- Teach students an effective strategy for studying spelling words.
- Reinforce the correct spelling of taught words in students' writing.
- Have students build words from letters or letters and phonograms, for example, c - at.
- Teach strategies for determining and checking the spelling of unknown words.
- Model the use of correct spelling and how to correct spelling errors when you write in front of the class.
- Encourage students to correct misspelled words in all final drafts of their writing.
- Provide instruction and practice in proofreading.
- Encourage students to use spell-checkers, dictionaries, and so on to determine the correct spelling of unknown words.

Grammar and Usage

Traditional methods of teaching grammar and usage skills are not effective. With such instruction, students are initially provided with an abstract definition, such as an adjective is a word that describes a noun or pronoun. This is often followed by asking students to practice applying the skill correctly without actually generating any textual material longer than a word or a phrase. For example, students might be asked to complete the following sentence: The ____________ wagon rolled through the ____________ town. It is not surprising that many students do not understand the rules they are taught or how to use them in their writing, because such instruction is abstract and decontextualized.

To make grammar instruction effective, ***SRA Imagine It!*** applies the following five principles. To make these principles concrete, the program illustrates each as it would apply to the rule for capitalizing the first letter in a person's name.

- Grammar and usage skills need to be defined in a functional and concrete manner. The rule of capitalizing the first letter in a person's name can be introduced by writing a sentence with two or three familiar names on the board. With the students' help, identify each name in the sentence, and ask them what they notice about the first letter in each name—They are capital letters. Repeat this process with a second sentence, and then establish the "capitalization rule" with students' help.
- As soon as the skill is functionally described or defined, establish why it is important—Capitalizing the first letter in a person's name makes the name stand out and shows respect for the person named. This is an important rule for writing.
- Show students how to use the skill when writing. Generate a sentence using the names of students in the class, or have your students help you generate such a sentence. Write it on the board, capitalizing the first letter while simultaneously telling the class what you are doing.

- Provide students with guided practice in applying the skill when writing. Generate with the class another sentence that includes three of your students' names. Tell the class you will write the sentence on the board, but they will need to tell you when to capitalize a word. Next, have students work together in pairs to generate two sentence using names of their friends, capitalizing the first letter in each name. Provide support as needed. Finally, have each student generate one sentence of his or her own containing two names. Monitor to ensure that students capitalize the first letter in each name. Have them share their sentences with a peer.
- Ask students to apply the skill in their compositions. Have students look at one of the papers in their writing portfolio and correct any capitalization mistakes involving people's names. Remind students to capitalize people's names when writing and revising subsequent writing assignments.

Tips

- Ask students to correct other students' papers, focusing on specific grammar and usage rules and mistakes.
- Encourage students to read their papers aloud when revising. This will help them spot grammar and usage mistakes.

Fostering Motivation

Purpose

Children start school wanting to learn how to write and enjoying writing. Too quickly, however, many begin to view writing as a chore or something to be avoided. The goal of ***SRA Imagine It!*** writing is for children to become lifelong writers—people who enjoy writing and use writing effectively at work as well as in their personal lives.

Procedures

One way to foster an interest in writing is to have students write for real purposes and audiences. This includes having students identify why they are writing and what they hope to accomplish. Likewise, students need to share their writing with others. They are more likely to do their best writing when there is an audience. Students can share their plans, an initial draft, a portion of their composition, or the completed paper with you, their peers, or other children or adults.

Students are also likely to give their best effort when the writing environment is supportive and pleasant. This can be accomplished by the following:

- Establishing clear rules for student behavior during the writing period. Keep the rules simple and reasonable in number and consistently reinforce them. Students are not likely to enjoy writing, or learn well, if the classroom environment is chaotic.
- Creating a low-risk environment in which students feel comfortable taking risks with their writing. This means being accepting and encouraging of students' efforts and encouraging them to act in the same manner. For example, make it a rule in your class that when someone shares his or her writing, the first thing that you or other students do is say what you liked most about it.
- Supporting students as they begin to apply the knowledge, skills, or strategies you teach them. This can include reteaching, providing hints and reminders, giving useful feedback, and initially helping students apply what was taught.
- Having students help each other as they plan, draft, revise, edit/proofread, and publish their work. This is most effective when the process of working together is structured. For instance, students are more likely to give good advice for revising if they are asked to focus on specific aspects of the composition, such as identifying places where the writing is unclear or more detail is needed.
- Celebrating student success by displaying their work. This can be done by prominently displaying student work in the classroom or in other places in the school. Students can also be asked to publish their work in a class or school newspaper or to read their compositions aloud to younger children, in other classes, or at a special event.
- Fostering an "I can do" attitude among your students. Consistently emphasize that the key to good writing is effort and the use of what they have learned.
- Setting a positive mood during writing time. Be enthusiastic about writing and what your students write.

Tips

- Allow students to make their own decisions and to accomplish as much on their own as possible.
- Increase students' ownership of a writing topic by allowing them to develop unique interpretations of the topic.
- Encourage students to take ownership of their writing. This includes allowing them to arrange a suitable writing environment, construct a personal plan for accomplishing the writing task, to work at their own pace when possible, and to decide what feedback from you and their peers is most pertinent for revising their writing.
- Look for opportunities to give students positive feedback about their work. Let them know when they have done something well in their writing.
- Encourage students to monitor their progress. For example, have students select their best writing to keep in a writing portfolio, identifying why they selected each piece.
- Show your students that you are a writer too. Share your writing with them. Talk about the various ways you use writing each day.
- Connect writing to students' lives and the world in general. Have them document the types of writing they do outside school. Develop a wall chart on which the class can identify how they use writing away from school.
- Provide incentives for writing at home. For example, have parents document that their child writes for twenty minutes at home a set number of nights for a month. Provide a special party for these children, allowing each one to select a book to keep from an array of books donated by parents or a sponsoring business partner.

Spelling Strategies

Spelling

Many people find English difficult, because English sound/spelling patterns seem to have hundreds of exceptions. The key to becoming a good speller, however, is not just memorization. The key is recognizing and internalizing English spelling patterns. Some people do this naturally as they read and develop large vocabularies. They intuitively recognize spelling patterns and apply them appropriately. Others need explicit and direct teaching of vocabulary and spelling strategies and spelling patterns before they develop spelling consciousness.

Purpose

Spelling is a fundamental skill in written communication. Although a writer may have wonderful ideas, he or she may find it difficult to communicate those ideas without spelling skills. Learning to spell requires much exposure to text and writing. For many it requires a methodical presentation of English spelling patterns.

English Spelling Patterns

A basic understanding of English spelling patterns will help provide efficient and effective spelling instruction. Just as the goal of phonics instruction is to enable students to read fluently, the goal of spelling instruction is to enable students to write fluently so they can concentrate on ideas rather than spelling.

Sound Patterns Many words are spelled the way they sound. Most consonants and short vowels are very regular. When a student learns the sound/spelling relationships, he or she has the key to spelling many words.

Structural Patterns Structural patterns are employed when adding endings to words. Examples of structural patterns include doubling the final consonant, adding *-s* or *-es* to form plurals, and dropping the final *e* before adding *-ing, -ed, -er,* or *-est.* Often these structural patterns are very regular in their application. Many students have little trouble learning these patterns.

Meaning Patterns Many spelling patterns in English are morphological; in other words, the meaning relationship is maintained regardless of how a sound may change. Prefixes, suffixes, and root words that retain their spellings regardless of how they are pronounced are further examples of meaning patterns.

Foreign Language Patterns Many English words are derived from foreign words and retain those language patterns. For example, kindergarten (German), boulevard (French), and ballet (French from Italian) are foreign-language patterns at work in English.

Developmental Stages of Spelling

The most important finding in spelling research in the past thirty years is that students learn to spell in a predictable developmental sequence, much as they learn to read. It appears to take the average student three to six years to progress through the developmental stages and emerge as a fairly competent, mature speller.

Prephonemic The first stage is the prephonemic stage, characterized by random letters arranged either in continuous lines or in wordlike clusters. Only the writer can "read" it, and it may be "read" differently on different days.

Semiphonemic As emergent readers learn that letters stand for sounds, they use particular letters specifically to represent the initial consonant sound and sometimes a few other very salient sounds. This marks the discovery of phonemic awareness that letters represent speech sounds in writing.

Phonemic When students can represent most of the sounds they hear in words, they have entered the phonemic stage of spelling. They spell what they hear, using everything they know about letter sounds, letter names, and familiar words. Many remedial spellers never develop beyond this stage and spell a word the way it sounds whenever they encounter a word they cannot spell.

Transitional or Within-Word Pattern As they are exposed to more difficult words, students discover that not all words are spelled as they sound. They learn that they must include silent letters, spell past tenses with *-ed,* include a vowel even in unstressed syllables, and remember how words look. The transitional stage represents the transition from primarily phonemic strategies to rule-bound spelling.

Derivational The derivational stage occurs as transitional spellers accumulate a large spelling vocabulary and gain control over affixes, contractions, homophones, and other meaning patterns. They discover that related or derived forms of words share spelling features even if they do not sound the same. As spellers gain control over these subtle word features and spell most words correctly, they become conventional spellers.

Procedures

The spelling lessons are organized around different spelling patterns, beginning with phonetic spelling patterns and progressing to other types of spelling patterns in a logical sequence. Word lists including words from the literature selection focus on the particular patterns in each lesson. In general, the sound patterns occur in the first units at each grade, followed by structural patterns, meaning patterns, and foreign-language patterns in the upper grade levels.

- As you begin each new spelling lesson, have students identify the spelling pattern and how it is like and different from other patterns.
- Give the pretest to help students focus on the lesson pattern.
- Have students proofread their own pretests immediately after the test, crossing out any misspellings and writing the correct spelling.
- Have them diagnose whether the errors they made were in the lesson pattern or in another part of the word. Help students determine where they made errors and what type of pattern they should work on to correct them.
- As students work through the spelling pages from ***Skills Practice,*** encourage them to practice the different spelling strategies in the exercises.

Sound Pattern Strategies

Pronunciation Strategy As students encounter an unknown word, have them say the word carefully to hear each sound. Encourage them to check the ***Sound/Spelling Cards.*** Then have them spell each sound. (/s/ + /i/ + /t/: sit). This strategy builds directly on the Dication and Spelling introduced in kindergarten and taught in Levels 1–3.

Consonant Substitution Have students switch consonants. The vowel spelling usually remains the same. (bat, hat, rat, flat, splat) This is a natural extension of Phonemic Awareness activities begun in prekindergarten and kindergarten.

Vowel Substitution Have students switch vowels. The consonant spellings usually remain the same. (CVC: hit, hat, hut, hot; CVCV: mane, mine; CVVC: boat, beat, bait, beet) This is a natural extension of Phonemic Awareness activities begun in prekindergarten and kindergarten.

Rhyming Word Strategy Have students think of rhyming words and the rhymes that spell a particular sound. Often the sound will be spelled the same way in another word. (cub, tub, rub) This is a natural extension of Phonemic Awareness activities begun in prekindergarten and kindergarten.

Structural Pattern Strategies

Conventions Strategy Have students learn the rule and exceptions for adding endings to words (dropping *y*, dropping *e*, doubling the final consonant, and so on).

Proofreading Strategy Many spelling errors occur because of simple mistakes. Have students check their writing carefully and specifically for spelling.

Visualization Strategy Have students think about how a word looks. Sometimes words "look" wrong because a wrong spelling pattern has been written. Have them double-check the spelling of any word that looks wrong.

Meaning Pattern Strategies

Family Strategy When students are not sure of a spelling, have them think of how words from the same base word family are spelled. (critic, criticize, critical; sign, signal, signature; nation, national, nationality)

Meaning Strategy Have students determine a homophone's meaning to make sure they are using the right word. Knowing prefixes, suffixes, and base words will also help.

Compound Word Strategy Tell students to break apart a compound and to spell each word. Compounds may not follow convention rules for adding endings. (homework, nonetheless)

Foreign-Language Strategy Have students think of foreign-language spellings that are different from English spelling patterns. (ballet, boulevard, sauerkraut)

Dictionary Strategy Ask students to look up the word in a dictionary to make sure their spelling is correct. If they do not know how to spell a word, have them try a few different spellings and look them up to see which one is correct. (fotograph, photograph) Have students use the ***Sound/Spelling Cards*** to help them look up words. This develops a spelling consciousness.

Use the post test to determine understanding of the lesson spelling pattern and to identify any other spelling pattern problems. Encourage student understanding of spelling patterns and use of spelling strategies in all their writing to help transfer spelling skills to writing.

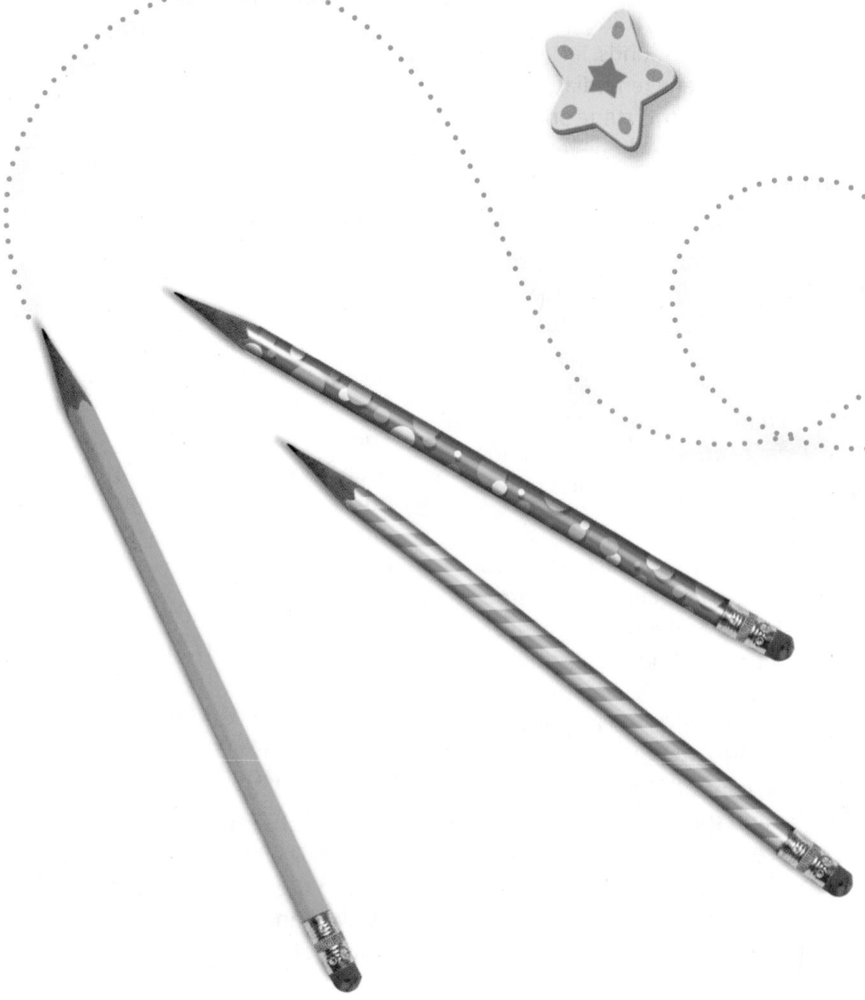

Grammar, Usage, and Mechanics

Purpose

The Study of English Conventions

Over the years the study of grammar, usage, and mechanics has gone in and out of favor. In the past century much research has been done to demonstrate the effectiveness of traditional types of instruction in the conventions of English. Experience and research have shown that learning grammatical terms and completing grammar exercises have little effect on the student's practical application of these skills in the context of speaking or writing. These skills, in and of themselves, do not play a significant role in the way students use language to generate and express their ideas—for example, during the prewriting and drafting phases of the writing process. In fact, emphasis on correct conventions has been shown to have a damaging effect when it is the sole focus of writing instruction. If students are evaluated only on the proper use of spelling, grammar, and punctuation, they tend to write fewer and less complex sentences.

Knowledge of English conventions is, however, vitally important in the editing and proofreading phases of the writing process. A paper riddled with mistakes in grammar, usage, or mechanics is quickly discounted. Many immature writers never revise or edit. They finish the last sentence and turn their papers in to the teacher. Mature writers employ their knowledge of English language conventions in the editing phase to refine and polish their ideas.

The study of grammar, usage, and mechanics is important for two reasons.

1. Educated people need to know and understand the structure of their language, which in large part defines their culture.
2. Knowledge of grammar gives teachers and students a common vocabulary for talking about language and makes discussions of writing tasks more efficient and clearer.

Procedure

The key issue in learning grammar, usage, and mechanics is how to do it. On the one hand, teaching these skills in isolation from writing has been shown to be ineffective and even detrimental if too much emphasis is placed on them. On the other hand, not teaching these skills and having students write without concern for conventions is equally ineffective. The answer is to teach the skills in a context that allows students to directly apply them to a reading or writing activity. Students should be taught proper use of punctuation or subject/verb agreement at the same time they are taught to proofread for those conventions. As they learn to apply their knowledge of conventions during the final stages of the writing process, they will begin to see that correcting errors is an editorial rather than a composition skill.

A paper riddled with mistakes in grammar, usage, or mechanics is quickly discounted.

History of English

A basic understanding of the history and structure of the English language helps students understand the rich but complex resource they have for writing.

Old English

The English language began about A.D. 450 when the Angles, Jutes, and Saxons--three tribes that lived in northern Europe--invaded the British Isles. Much of their language included words that had to do with farming (*sheep, dirt, tree, earth*). Many of their words are the most frequently used words in the English language today. Because of Latin influences, English became the first of the European languages to be written.

Middle English

In 1066 William the Conqueror invaded England and brought Norman French with him. Slowly Old English and Norman French came together, and Middle English began to appear. Today forty percent of Modern English comes from French. With the introduction of the printing press, English became more widespread.

Modern English

With the Renaissance and its rediscovery of classical Greek and Latin, many new words were created from Greek and Latin word elements. This continued intensively during the Early Modern English period. This rich language was used in the writings of Shakespeare and his contemporaries and profoundly influenced the nature and vocabulary of English. With dictionaries and spelling books, the English language became more standardized, although it continues to be influenced by other languages and new words and trends. These influences continue to make English a living, dynamic language.

Punctuation

Early writing had no punctuation or even spaces between words. English punctuation had its beginning in ancient Greece and Rome. Early punctuation reflected speaking rather than reading. By the end of the eighteenth century, after the invention of printing, most of the rules for punctuation were established, although they were not the same in all languages.

The Structure of English

Grammar is the sound, structure, and meaning system of language. People who speak the same language are able to communicate because they intuitively know the grammar system of that language, the rules to make meaning. All languages have grammar, and yet each language has its own grammar.

Traditional grammar study usually involves two areas:

- **Parts of speech** (nouns, verbs, adjectives, adverbs, pronouns, prepositions, conjunctions) are typically considered the content of grammar. The parts of speech involve the form of English words.
- **Sentence structure** (subjects, predicates, objects, clauses, phrases) is also included in grammar study. Sentence structure involves the function of English.

Mechanics involves the conventions of punctuation and capitalization. Punctuation helps readers understand writers' messages. Proper punctuation involves marking off sentences according to grammatical structure. In speech students can produce sentences as easily and unconsciously as they can walk, but in writing they must think about what is and what is not a sentence.

In English there are about fourteen punctuation marks (period, comma, quotation mark, question mark, exclamation point, colon, semicolon, apostrophe, hyphen, ellipsis, parenthesis, bracket, dash, and underscore). Most immature writers use only three: period, comma, and question mark. The experienced writer or poet with the command of punctuation adds both flexibility and meaning to his or her sentences through his or her use of punctuation.

Usage is the way in which we speak in a given community. Language varies over time, across national and geographical boundaries, by gender, across age groups, and by socioeconomic status. When the variation occurs within a given language, the different versions of the same language are called dialects. Every language has a prestige dialect associated with education and financial success. In the United States, this dialect is known as Standard English and is the language of school and business.

Usage involves the word choices people make when speaking certain dialects. Word choices that are perfectly acceptable in conversation among friends may be unacceptable in writing. Usage is often the most obvious indicator of the difference between conversation and composition. Errors in word usage can make a writer seem ignorant and thus jeopardize his or her credibility, no matter how valid or important his or her overall message might be. Usage depends on a student's cultural and linguistic heritage. If the dialect students have learned is not the formal language of school settings or if it is not English, students must master another dialect or language in order to write Standard English.

The Grammar, Usage, and Mechanics lessons in ***SRA Imagine It!*** are structured to focus on skills presented in a logical sequence. A skill is introduced on the first day of the lesson with appropriate models and then practiced in reading and writing on subsequent days to ensure that skills are not taught in isolation. Encourage students to use the focused English language convention presented in each lesson as they complete each Writing Process Strategies activity. Also encourage them to reread their writing, checking for proper use of the conventions taught. With practice, students should be able to apply their knowledge of conventions to any writing they do.

Tips

- Some of the errors students make in writing are the result simply of not carefully reading their final drafts. Many errors occur because the writer's train of thought was interrupted and a sentence is not complete or a word is skipped. These may look like huge errors that a simple rereading can remedy. Most often the writer can correct these types of errors on his or her own. A major emphasis of any English composition program should be to teach the editing and proofreading phases of the writing process so students can eliminate these types of errors themselves. This involves a shift in perception—from thinking of grammar as a set of discrete skills that involve mastery of individual rules to understanding grammar as it applies to the act of communicating in writing.
- As students learn English language conventions, they should be expected to incorporate them into their written work.
- Sometimes, students write sentences that raise grammatically complex problems that require a deep understanding of English grammar. Use the Sentence Lifting strategies outlined in the Proofreading part of the Appendix to identify and discuss these more sophisticated types of errors that can include the following:
- **Faulty Parallelism.** Parts of a sentence parallel in meaning are not parallel in structure.
- **Nonsequiturs.** A statement does not follow logically from something said previously.
- **Dangling Modifiers.** A phrase or clause does not logically modify the word next to it.
- **Awkwardness.** Sentences are not written simply.
- **Wordiness.** Thoughts are not written in as few words as possible. Precise words are not used.

Listening/Speaking/Viewing

Some people are naturally good listeners, and others have no trouble speaking in front of groups. Many people, however, need explicit instruction on how to tune in for important details and how to organize and make an oral presentation. While some people naturally critique what they read, hear, and see, many others need specific guidance to develop skills for analyzing what they encounter in images and the media. The abilities to listen appropriately and to speak in conversations and in groups, as well as to critically evaluate the information with which they are presented, are fundamental skills that will serve students throughout their lives.

Purpose

In addition to reading and writing, listening, speaking, and viewing complete the language arts picture. Through the development of these language arts skills, students gain flexibility in communicating orally, visually, and in writing. When speaking and listening skills are neglected, many students have difficulty speaking in front of groups, organizing a speech, or distinguishing important information they hear. A top anxiety for many adults is speaking in front of groups. Much of this anxiety would not exist if listening, speaking, and viewing skills were taught from the early years.

The Listening/Speaking/Viewing instruction focuses on the literature selection or the Writing Process Strategies to provide context, to reinforce other elements of the lesson, and to integrate the other language arts. Many of the listening, speaking, and viewing skills are very similar to reading or writing skills. For example, listening for details is the same type of skill as reading for details. Preparing an oral report employs many of the same skills as preparing a written report. Learning to use these skills effectively gives students flexibility in how they approach a task. Furthermore, listening and speaking are naturally integrated into all aspects of learning as students listen and respond to each other during discussions, writing, and Inquiry.

Procedure

Listening, speaking, and viewing skills are presented with increasing sophistication throughout every grade level of ***SRA Imagine It!*** in the Language Arts part of each lesson. Every unit includes at least one lesson on each of the following skills so that students encounter the skills again and again throughout a grade level:

- **Listening.** Listening skills include comprehending what one hears and listening for different purposes, such as to identify sequence or details, to summarize or draw conclusions, or to follow directions.
- **Speaking.** Speaking skills include speaking formally and conversationally, using appropriate volume, giving oral presentations, and using effective grammar. Speaking skills also include using descriptive words, figurative language, and formal and informal language.
- **Viewing.** Viewing skills include comprehending main ideas and messages in images, mass media, and other multimedia.
- **Interaction.** Interaction instruction focuses on a combination of listening and speaking skills. These include asking and responding to questions; nonverbal cues such as eye contact, facial expression, and posture; and contributing to and interacting in group settings.
- **Presenting Information.** The last Listening/Speaking/Viewing lesson in every unit usually focuses on presentation skills. These include sharing ideas, relating experiences or stories, organizing information, and preparing for speeches. These lessons often parallel the Writing Process Strategies instruction so that students can prepare their information in written or oral form. These skills are an integral part of the Inquiry process as students share their ideas, questions, conjectures, and findings.

Tips

- Identify the parallels among the language arts skills: providing written and oral directions, telling or writing a narrative, and so on. Encourage students to see that they have choices for communicating. Discuss the similarities and differences between different forms of communication, and determine whether one is preferable in a given situation.
- Ensure that all students have opportunities to speak in small groups and whole-class situations.
- Provide and teach students to allow appropriate wait time before someone answers a question.
- Encourage students (when they are able) to take notes to help them remember what they heard so they can better respond.
- Remind students to use visuals when appropriate in their presentations to support their presentations and to help keep the listeners' attention.
- Set up simple class rules to show respect for the listener and speaker. These rules should be used during Inquiry or handing off or any time of the day and should foster respect for the speaker and listeners.
  - Students should speak in a voice loud and clear enough for everyone in the class to hear.
  - Students should raise their hands and not interrupt.
  - If someone asks a question, then the person who responds should address the question before going on to another idea or topic.
  - The speaker should look at the audience, and the audience should look at the speaker.

Inquiry

Even in elementary school, students can produce works of genuine research—research that seeks answers to real questions or solutions to real problems.

Inquiry—research, investigation, and exploration—forms the heart of the ***SRA Imagine It!*** program. To encourage students to understand how reading and writing are tools for learning that can enhance their lives and help them become mature, educated adults, they are asked in each unit to use the content they are learning in the unit as the basis for further inquiry, exploration, and research. The unit information is simply the base for their investigations.

There are two types of units in the ***SRA Imagine It!*** program—units based on universal topics of interest such as friendship, perseverance, and courage and content units that provide students a very solid base of information upon which they can begin their own inquiry and research. Units delving into science-related areas such as camouflage, energy, and ecology or into social studies units that address American history, geography, or money invite students to become true researchers by exploring personal areas of interest driven by problems or questions raised by students. Based upon common areas of interest, students conduct Inquiry in small collaborative groups and then present their findings to their classmates. In this way, students recognize the importance of sharing knowledge and gain much more knowledge of the unit theme than they would have simply by reading the selections in the unit.

The selections in the units are organized so that each selection will add more information or a different perspective to students' growing bodies of knowledge.

Inquiry through Reflective Activities

Purpose

The units in ***SRA Imagine It!*** that deal with universal topics tend to be explored through reflective activities. These units—such as Courage, Friendship, and Risks and Consequences—are organized to help students expand—perhaps even change—their perspectives of familiar concepts. As they explore and discuss the concepts that emerge from reading selections related to each unit topic, students are involved in activities that extend their experiences and offer opportunities for reflection. Such activities include writing, drama, art, interviews, debates, and panel discussions. Students will choose the activities and presentation format best suited to explore or investigate their research questions. Throughout each unit, students may be involved in a single ongoing investigative activity, or they may participate in a number of different activities. They may choose to produce a final written project or a multimedia presentation. They will share with the rest of the class the new knowledge that they have gained from their investigations. Workshop provides an ideal time for students to work individually or in collaborative groups on their investigation and/or projects.

The Inquiry activities will be those of students' own choosing, thereby allowing them to explore the unit concepts more fully. They are free, of course, to make other choices or to devise activities of their own.

Procedure

Choosing an Area to Investigate

Students may work on activities alone, in pairs, or in small groups. They have the option of writing about or using other methods for presenting their findings to the entire group. Students should decide what concept-related question or problem they wish to explore. Generally, it is better for students to generate wonderings, questions, or problems after they have engaged in some discussion at the beginning of each unit. This should be done, however, before they have had a chance to consult source materials. The goal is to have students ask questions that will drive their inquiry. This approach is more likely to bring forth ideas that students actually wonder about or wish to understand. Students may also look at the questions posted on the **Concept/Question Board** or introduce fresh ideas inspired by material they have just finished reading.

Inquiry pairs or groups are developed based upon common areas of interest or common questions that appear on the **Concept/Question Board.** Students who share a common interest for inquiry should work together to develop a common question to explore. Some of students may need your assistance in deciding upon, or narrowing down, a question or a problem so that it can be explored more easily. A good way to model this process for students is to make webs for a few of your own ideas on the board and to narrow down these ideas to a workable question or problem.

Organizing the Group

After a question or a problem has been chosen, students may choose an activity that will help them investigate that problem or question. For example, if students in Grade 3 are exploring the question "What are the common characteristics that define friendship?" they may want to develop and conduct a survey of classmates, friends, and so on. To develop the survey, group participants may want to do some additional reading about friendship, explore resources on the Internet, and so on to have a sense of the kinds of questions to include in the survey. Students' next responsibility is to decide who is going to investigate which facet of the question or the problem (when they are conducting a literature search, for example) or who is going to perform which activity related to the particular reflective activity (when they are writing and performing an original playlet or puppet show, for example). Lastly, students need to decide how, or if, they want to present their findings. For instance, after conducting a literature search, some students may want to read and discuss passages from a book with a plot or theme that relates to a unit concept. Other students may prefer performing and discussing scenes from the book.

Deciding How to Investigate

The following suggestions may help you and your students choose ways in which to pursue their investigations. For units on universal topics that are more literary in nature, students may want to do one of the following activities to pursue answers to their questions.

- Conduct a literature search to pursue a question or a problem. Discussion or writing may follow.

- Write and produce an original playlet or puppet show based on situations related to the concepts.
- Play a role-playing game to work out a problem related to the concepts.
- Stage a panel discussion with audience participation on a question or problem.
- Hold a debate on an issue related to the concept.
- Write an advice column dealing with problems related to the concepts.
- Write a personal-experience story related to the concepts.
- Invite experts to class. Formulate questions to ask.
- Conduct an interview with someone on a subject related to the concepts.
- Produce and carry out a survey on an issue or question related to the concept.
- Produce a picture or photo-essay about the concept.

You may want to post this list in the classroom so that groups have access to it as they decide what they want to investigate and how they want to proceed. Encourage students to explore other possibilities as well and to add these ideas to the list.

EXAMPLE: In the Heritage unit in Grade 5 of ***SRA Imagine It!,*** students read "In Two Worlds: A Yup'ik Eskimo Family." This selection is about how three generations of Eskimos living in Alaska near the Arctic strive to adopt the best of modern ways without abandoning their traditional values. During the class discussion, some students may note that Alice and Billy Rivers want their students to learn both the new and the old ways of living. As the discussion continues, many students may conclude from the story that the older generations hope that future generations will continue to value their roots and their cultural traditions. Students then relate this story to their own heritage. Some students may share information about their customs or traditions.

Students choose some reflective activities that will help them learn more about family heritage and that will answer some of their questions about the unit concepts. These questions may relate to the value of maintaining traditional customs and values versus. adopting contemporary ones. Other students may ask exploring questions related to how to maintain traditional values in the face of contemporary changes. Some students may be interested in interviewing family members or close family friends about their cultural traditions and heritages or interviewing students in their class about their cultural heritage and then looking for commonalities and differences. These students review what they know about interviewing. They should proceed by performing the following:

- Researching examples of interviews to see what they might look like and how to build in space to write answers
- Preparing a list of questions to ask
- Preparing a list of subjects to interview, deciding how to record the interview (by audiotape, videotape, or taking notes)
- Contacting in advance the person(s) they want to interview
- Deciding whether to photograph the person and, if so, getting permission to do so in advance—collecting the equipment necessary for conducting the interview
- After they conduct the interviews, students decide how they wish to present the information that they have collected.

EXAMPLE: Another group of students in the same fifth-grade class may be more interested in planning a photo-essay about one family or about a neighborhood with many families belonging to a particular culture. These students may decide to reexamine "In Two Worlds" in terms of how the text and the photographs complement each other and what information is conveyed in each photograph. They may also decide to examine some photo-essays listed in the unit bibliography. These students will need to make some advance preparations as well. They should proceed by performing the following:

- Determining which neighborhood and which family or families to photograph
- Contacting in advance the persons to be interviewed and photographed
- Touring the neighborhood in advance of the photo shoot
- Making a list of questions to ask the family or families about their heritage or about their neighborhood
- Thinking about what information to include in their essay so that they can determine what photographs to take
- Collecting the equipment necessary for conducting interviews and photographing subjects

After students collect the information and take photographs, they may write and organize the photo-essay and present it to the class. The teacher should remind students of the phases of the writing process and encourage them to plan, draft, revise, and proofread their work until they are completely satisfied with it.

Not all questions on the **Concept/ Question Board** will be explored in depth. Throughout the unit, students can continue discussing family heritage and raising and posting new questions. The teacher should remind them that as they read further, they may think of additional ways to explore the unit concepts. Students should sign or initial their questions or ideas so that they can identify classmates with similar interests and exchange ideas with them. The teacher should encourage students to feel free to write an answer or a note on someone else's question or to consult the Board for ideas for their own explorations. From time to time, the teacher should post his or her own questions on the **Concept/Question Board.**

Tips

- The ***Leveled Readers*** contain books related to the unit concepts. Remind students that these are good sources of information and that they should consult them regularly—especially when they are investigating concept-related ideas and questions.
- Some students work better within a specified time frame. Whenever they are beginning a new activity, discuss with students a reasonable period of time within which they will be expected to complete their investigations. Post the completion date somewhere in the classroom so that students can refer to it and pace themselves accordingly. At first, you may have to help them determine a suitable deadline, but eventually they should be able to make this judgment on their own.
- Some teachers like to do the Inquiry for the first unit with a common question decided upon by the whole class. Then students break into small groups and work on different ways to explore the question. One group may do a literature search while another might conduct a survey. The end results in students sharing new knowledge that addresses the common research question.

Inquiry through Research

Purpose

Students come to school with a wealth of fascinating questions. Educators need to capitalize on this excitement for learning and natural curiosity. A classroom in which the teacher is the only person who asks the questions and defines the assignments, only correct answers are accepted, and students are not allowed to make errors and consider alternative possibilities to questions can quickly deaden this natural curiosity and enthusiasm. The purpose of the inquiry and research aspect of this program is to capitalize on students' questions and natural curiosity by using a framework or structure based upon the scientific method. This structure helps students ask questions and preserve the open-ended character of real research, which can lead to unexpected findings and to questions that were not originally considered.

The conventional approach to school research papers can be found, with minor variations, in countless textbooks and instructional resources. This approach consists of a series of steps such as the following: Select a topic or choose a topic from a list suggested by the teacher, narrow the topic to something of interest, collect materials, take notes, outline, and write. By following these steps, a student may produce a presentable paper, but the procedure does not constitute research in a meaningful sense. Indeed, this restrictive approach gives students a distorted notion of what research is about. We see students in universities and even in graduate schools still following this procedure when they do library research papers or literature reviews; we see their dismay when their professors regard such work as mere cutting and pasting and ask them where their original contribution is.

Elementary school students can produce works of genuine research—research that seeks answers to real questions or solutions to real problems—when they are provided the opportunity, taught how to ask good questions and develop conjectures, and work collaboratively to find information or data that will support or refute their conjecture. Being able to collect, analyze, and evaluate information are critical twenty-first century skills. In the adult world, as knowledgeable consumers, productive members of a sophisticated workforce, and lifelong learners, students will be expected to constantly identify problems, raise questions, analyze new information, and make informed decisions on the basis of this information. Preparing students for the analytic demands of adult life and teaching them how to find answers to their questions are goals of education.

Procedure

To make the research productive, the following important principles are embodied in this approach:

1. Research is focused on problems, not topics.
2. Questions and wonderings are the foundation for inquiry and research.
3. Conjectures—opinions based on less than complete evidence or proof—are derived from questions and guide the research; the research does not simply produce conjectures.
4. New information and data are gathered to test and revise conjectures.
5. Discussion, ongoing feedback, and constructive criticism are important in all phases of the research but especially in the revising of problems and conjectures.
6. The cycle of true research is essentially endless, although presentations of findings are made from time to time; new findings give rise to new problems and conjectures and thus to new cycles of research.

Following a Process

While working with the science and social studies units, students are encouraged to use this framework to keep their research activities focused and on track. Within this framework, there is flexibility. Students may begin with a question, develop a conjecture, and begin collecting information only to find that they need to redefine their conjecture. Like the writing process, there is a recursive nature to this framework. Students may go through these steps many times before they come to the end of their research. Certainly for adult researchers, this cycle of question, conjecture, research, and reevaluation can go on for years and, in some cases, lifetimes.

This cycle uses the following process:

1. Decide on a problem or question to research. Students should identify a question or problem that they truly wonder about or wish to understand and then form research groups with other students who have the same interests.
   - My problem or question is ________.
2. Formulate an idea or conjecture about the research problem. Students should think about and discuss with classmates possible answers to their research problems or questions and meet with their research groups to discuss and record their ideas or conjectures.
   - My idea/conjecture/theory about this question or problem is ________.
3. Identify needs and make plans. Students should identify knowledge needs related to their conjectures and meet with their research groups to determine which resources to consult and to make individual job assignments. Students should also meet periodically with the teacher, other classmates, and research groups to present preliminary findings and to make revisions to their problems and conjectures on the basis of these findings.
   - I need to find out ________.
   - To do this, I will need these resources: ________
   - My role in the group is ________.
   - This is what I have learned so far: ________
   - This is what happened when we presented our findings ________
4. Reevaluate the problem or question based on what we have learned so far and the feedback we have received.
   - My revised problem or question is ________.
5. Revise the idea or conjecture.
   - My new conjecture about this problem is ________.
6. Identify new needs and make new plans.
   - Based on what I found out, I still need to know ________.
   - To do this, I will need these resources: ________
   - This is what I have learned: ________
   - This is what happened when we presented our new findings: ________

Procedure for Choosing a Problem to Research

1. Discuss with students the nature of the unit. Explain to students that the unit they are reading is a research unit and that they will produce and publish in some way the results of their

explorations. They are free to decide what problems or questions they wish to explore, with whom they want to work, and how they want to present their finished products. They may publish a piece of writing, produce a poster, write and perform a play, or use any other means to present the results of their investigations and research. They may work with partners or in small groups.

2. Discuss with students the schedule you have planned for their investigations: how long the project is expected to take, how much time will be available for research, when the first presentation will be due. This schedule will partly determine the nature of the problems that students should be encouraged to work on and the depth of the inquiry students will be encouraged to pursue.
3. Have students talk about things they wonder about that are related to the unit subject. For example, in the Grade 3 unit Money, students might wonder where money in the money machine comes from or how prices are determined. Conduct a free-floating discussion of questions about the unit subject.
4. Brainstorm possible questions for students to think about. It is essential that students' own ideas and questions be the starting point of all inquiry. Helpful hint: For the first research unit, you might wish to generate a list of your own ideas, having students add to this list and having them choose from it.
5. Using their wonderings, model for students the difference between a research topic and a research problem or question by providing several examples. For example, have them consider the difference between the topic California and the problem Why do so many people move to California? Explain to them that if they choose to research the topic California, everything they look up under the subject heading or index entry California will be related in some way to their topic. Therefore, it will be quite difficult to choose which information to record. This excess of information also creates problems in organizing their research. Clearly, then, this topic is too broad and general. Choosing a specific question or problem, one that particularly interests them, helps them narrow their exploration and advance their understanding. Some possible ideas for questions can be found in the unit introduction. Ideas can also be generated as you and your students create a web of their questions or problems related to the unit concept. For example, questions related to the subject California might include the following: Why do so many people move to California? How have the different groups of people living in California affected the state?
6. A good research problem or question not only requires students to consult a variety of sources but is engaging and adds to the groups' knowledge of the concepts. Furthermore, good problems generate more questions. Help students understand that the question Why do so many people move to California? is an easy one to research. Many sources will contribute to an answer to the question, and all information located can be easily evaluated in terms of usefulness in answering the question. Helpful hint: Students' initial responses may indeed be topics instead of problems or questions. If so, the following questions might be helpful: What aspect of the topic really interests you? Can you turn that idea into a question?
7. Remember that this initial problem or question serves only as a guide for research. As students begin collecting information and collaborating with classmates, their ideas will change, and they can revise their research problem or question. Frequently, students do not sufficiently revise their problems until after they have had time to consider their conjectures and to collect information.
8. As students begin formulating their research problems, have them elaborate on their reasons for wanting to research their stated problems. They should go beyond simple expressions of interest or liking and indicate what is puzzling, important, or potentially informative, and so forth about the problems they have chosen.
9. At this stage, students' ideas will be of a very vague and limited sort. The important thing is to start them thinking about what really interests them and what value it has to them and the class.
10. Have students present their proposed problems or questions, along with reasons for their choices, and have an open discussion of how promising proposed problems are. As students present their proposed problems, ask them what new things they think they will be learning from their investigations and how that will add to the group's growing knowledge of the concepts. This constant emphasis on group knowledge building will help set a clear purpose for students' research.
11. Form research groups. To make it easier for students to form groups, they may record their problems on the board or on self-sticking notes. Final groups should be constituted in the way you find best for your class—by self-selection, by assignment on the basis of common interests, or by some combination of methods. Students can then meet during Workshop to agree on a precise statement of their research problem, the nature of their expected research contributions, and lists of related questions that may help later in assigning individual roles. They should also record any scheduling information that can be added to the planning calendar.

Using Technology

Students and teachers can access the Web site **www.SRAonline.com** to find information about the themes in their grade level.

What does Inquiry look like in the classroom?

Inquiry is a new concept for many students and is performed over an extended period of time. The following series of vignettes are an example of what Inquiry might look like in a third-grade classroom that is studying the third-grade unit Money.

Lesson 1

Developing questions

For the unit on money, Ms. Hernandes introduced the theme through "A New Coat for Anna" and now is focusing on having her students generate some questions. To maximize the number of resources available to her students to do their inquiry, she talked with the librarian at her local library as well as local high school teachers who are knowledgeable in the area. Both were able to provide resources for the class.

Ms. Hernandes began with a discussion of money. She had prepared some basic questions to get the class started.

- Why do you think it is important to have a system of money like ours?
- What is money?
- Why do you think we have both paper money and coins?
- How have you learned about money?
- How would your life change if suddenly there were no money in the world?
- When people are using credit cards to pay for something, are they paying with real money?
- When someone writes a check, are they paying with real money?
- What is the difference between credit cards and checks and cash, or actual money?
- Why do you think people use credit cards and checks instead of cash?

The teacher felt that using open-ended questions like these would help get her students talking about what they know about money as well as give her an opportunity to informally assess students' background knowledge.

Students were able to provide some basic information such as the following:

- Money is used to buy things.
- There was not always money in the world.
- Some people used things such as animals instead of money.
- Sometimes people traded things to get something they wanted.
- Coins are made of metal.
- Some things cost more than other things.
- Sometimes you need to determine ways to get things when you do not have money.

But there were some basic misunderstanding that arose during the conversation, such as the following:

- All countries use dollars and cents.
- Everything costs the same no matter where you live.
- Money is made of paper.
- You can use credit cards whenever you want.

By discussing money in such general terms, students were able to share basic information.

To move students to the next level—asking questions—Ms. Hernandes began by thinking aloud about things related to the unit that interested her.

"I really am curious about how money is made. And another thing I've wondered about is how the government knows how much money to print." Ms. Hernandes encouraged her students to share some of their wonderings or things they are curious about. Some student wonderings included the following:

- What kind of money do people in other countries use?
- Does everyone make the same amount of money?
- What would happen if there were only credit cards and no money?
- How much money do people make?
- Does ripped money get thrown away?
- How come we cannot make our own money?

Lesson 2:

Forming groups based on shared interest

Developing good research questions

Ms. Hernandes and her class have been reading about money for the past week. Many students read different trade books during Workshop to learn more about money. Every day at the end of Workshop, they shared some of their new questions. Some students even started bringing in articles from newspapers and magazines and posting them on the **Concept/Question Board.**

By now there are a number of questions on the **Concept/Question Board** and Ms. Hernandes wants to work with the class to generate more questions, questions that will help students connect what they are learning in school to the real world. She began by modeling or thinking aloud and sharing some of her own thoughts: "I know that at the checkout stand in stores, you can buy plastic cards that have a dollar amount printed on them. I wonder how might this change our whole idea about money. Maybe instead of getting cash from the automatic money machines, we'll get a coded card."

The focus is on asking questions. She recognized that students' questions needed to be refined to lead to functional conjectures. The class discussed what makes a good question.

- Question or wonderings should be things that students are truly curious about.
- Questions should be generated without consulting an encyclopedia or reference source.
- Good questions cannot be answered with a simple *yes* or *no.*
- Questions should help students deepen their understanding of the unit theme rather than focus on a character or incident in a specific story.
- A good research question often begins with *how.*

Ms. Hernandes and the class talked about their questions and how to refine them. For example, one question the class raised earlier was "Does money change?" The class decided to change the question to "How does money change over time?"

- What possible changes might we see in the future?
- Given the changes in technology today, how might our use of money change over time?

Based on the selections the class has read, students generated the following questions to add to their existing ones on the **Concept/Question Board:**

- I wonder when and how the government decided to change coins and bills.
- I wonder if the government can ever run out of money.
- What happens when people make fake money?
- How do people choose the metals they use to make coins?
- How can money be made so people cannot copy it or make counterfeits?
- What do other countries use for money?
- Where do you save money?

To help move students toward developing some good questions for inquiry, the class reviewed all the questions and grouped them together. They discussed these groups of questions and decided to think of a good representative question. The class worked over the next couple of days to think of a question they were all interested in.

Lesson 3

Forming Conjectures

Identifying Needs and Making Plans

A goal of Inquiry is to have students move from asking questions to forming conjectures. Ms. Hernandes explained to the class that they were now going to take their question and develop a conjecture. Developing a conjecture simply means thinking of what they think the best answer is, given what they know now and have read so far.

Ms. Hernandes modeled this by using one of the questions students raised in the earlier lesson. The question was "How do people choose the metals to make coins?" Ms. Hernandes thought aloud about possible answers to this question: "I think that people choose a strong metal that will last a long time but that is not too heavy for people to carry."

Then Ms. Hernandes wrote the question the class thought of last week. They discussed the question and talked about what possible answers they might find. The question the class decided to focus on was "How is money made so that people cannot copy it?"

The class conjecture was "Special paper and really detailed pictures are used so no one can copy it." However, Ms. Hernandes realized that there could be other conjectures for the same question. She arranged the class into small groups and had them think about other possible conjectures. Some additional conjectures included the following:

- Every dollar has a different number that is recorded in a computer.
- Special ink is used so colors cannot be duplicated.
- When you hold up a bill to the light, you can see a special band in it that maybe only a special government machine can make.

At the end of the lesson, Ms. Hernandes created a chart with the question and all the conjectures students developed.

During the week, Ms. Hernandes continued working with the class on Inquiry. To help the group get started on identifying needs and materials related to their conjecture, Ms. Hernandes asked the following questions:

- What information will we need to help us decide if our conjecture is accurate?
- Where can we find this information?
- Who can help us find information related to our conjecture?
- What people in our school might be able to help us?
- What family members might know something about this?
- What words could we plug in on the Internet to help us get more information?

During the rest of this week, students started collecting different resources and reading various books during Workshop. Students were encouraged to take notes and to share with their groups each day.

Lesson 5

Revising Plans as Necessary

Collecting Data and Information

Now that students have started collecting material, they need to identify individual job assignments so they are not duplicating efforts. At the beginning of this week, Ms. Hernandes took time to have students meet in their groups. During this time she met with the small groups to track their progress, discuss any problems, and help them focus their research efforts.

The group working with the conjecture "Every dollar has a different number that is recorded in a computer" was having trouble finding information to support or refute their conjecture. They had looked in books but did not really find anything. As they talked with the teacher, someone mentioned the term *mint.* As they discussed what happened in the mint, someone suggested that they write the mint with their question to see if they could get some help. This simple activity led students to the Internet to find out the address of the mint and then spent the rest of that period composing a letter.

At the end of Inquiry that day, Ms. Hernandes made time for each group to present a summary of what it had done. If the group had any unsolved problems, it shared them with the class to get possible suggestions on how to solve the problem. When the group who wrote to the mint shared its problem and solution, several other groups realized that this would be a good resource for them to use as well.

Lesson 6

Continuing Working and Planning Final Presentation

At this point students are beginning to conclude their investigations. Several of the groups realized as they collected information that they really needed to change or revise their conjectures. Ms. Hernandes asked in what ways their ideas have changed—what do they know now that they did not know before? For example, the group had the conjecture that special ink was used so colors cannot be duplicated revised its conjecture by broadening it. After doing some research, their new conjecture was that there are many different things that the government does in addition to using special ink to protect money from being copied.

As groups presented their conjectures and progress, Ms. Hernandes modeled constructive comments such as the following: "Your points are clearly made." "Your charts and graphs help us understand each of your points." "Each one of you presented different pieces of information that all connect to your conjecture." "How was your conjecture supported?" After the lesson, Ms. Hernandes took time to reflect and realized that it was very hard for her students to give constructive feedback. She knew that this is an area they would need to work on. She would have to continue modeling but also thought about having groups exchange conjectures and provide feedback in writing to each other. This might reduce anxiety as well as give students time to reflect on the questions and conjectures and to develop some thoughtful feedback.

During this week, Ms. Hernandes took time to discuss possible ways that students could present their findings. The class brainstormed other ideas including the following:

- Writing a series of articles on their information for a magazine
- Creating a poster with diagrams of a process
- A panel discussion
- A computer presentation

Students returned to their groups to decide how they wanted to present their findings.

Final Presentation

Students have been busy working on completing their investigations and developing their presentations. While the class decided on a single research question at the beginning of the unit, different groups developed their own conjectures. Because their conjectures guided their research, each group will be presenting different information. Ms. Hernandes has created a simple web with the class's research question in the center and circles around the question. After groups present their work, the class will discuss what information was found to address the research question. As presentations are made, students will also be encouraged to make connections not only to the question but to each others findings.

Throughout the unit, Ms. Hernandes recognized that students need more work on asking questions of each other and providing constructive feedback. She plans on modeling questions and comments as groups complete their presentations. Some examples include the following:

- How does what you presented support or refute your conjecture?
- Would you clarify . . .
- It would be helpful if . . .
- Have you thought about . . .
- Your visuals really helped me better understand your ideas.
- That was a great idea. Where can we find more information on it so we can learn more about it?
- What other questions did you think of as you were researching your conjecture?

Overall, Ms. Hernandes felt that this first attempt at Inquiry with the entire class focusing on a single question but generating multiple conjectures made Inquiry manageable for students and herself. Ms. Hernandes is now thinking about how to plan the next Inquiry unit so there are multiple questions as well as multiple conjectures. From the final presentations, she has really begun to appreciate how Inquiry incorporates all the reading and writing skills she has been teaching and how it takes students to the next level of learning—delving deeper into ideas that personally interest them, taking time and responsibility to learn about something, working collaboratively, and sharing new ideas and information.

Tips

- Inquiry takes time to develop. You may want to do the first unit as an entire class.
- Provide time throughout the unit for students to work on Inquiry. Use Workshop as well as computer and library time to support Inquiry.
- If students are careful about the problems or questions they choose to research, they should have few problems in following through with the research. If the problem is too broad or too narrow, they will have problems.
- Have students take sufficient time in assessing their needs—both knowledge needs and physical needs in relation to their research. Careful preplanning can help the research progress smoothly with great results.
- Encourage students to reevaluate their needs often so they are not wasting time finding things they already have or ignoring needs that they have not noticed.
- Interim presentations of material are every bit as important, if not more so, than final presentations. It is during interim presentations that students have the opportunity to rethink and reevaluate their work and change direction or to decide to carry on with their planned research.
- Connect Inquiry to learning in the content areas. Have students apply their Inquiry skills to learning science, social studies, and the arts.

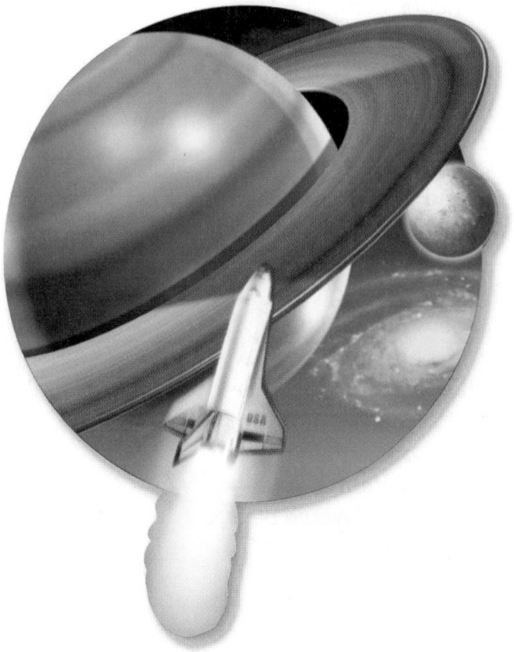

Assessment

Assessment can be your most effective teaching tool if it is used with the purpose of informing instruction and highlighting areas that need special attention.

Purpose

The assessment components of ***SRA Imagine It!*** are designed to help you make informed instructional decisions, make adequate yearly progress, and help ensure you meet the needs of all your students. The variety of assessments is intended to be used continuously and formatively. That is, students should be assessed regularly as a follow-up to instructional activities, and the results of the assessment should be used to inform subsequent instruction.

You can use assessment as a tool to monitor students' progress, to diagnose students' strengths and weaknesses, to prescribe forms of intervention as necessary, and to measure student outcomes. Both formal and informal assessment can be used, though formal assessment will be your main assessment tool. Formal assessment of student learning consists of performance assessment (both reading and writing), objective tests (multiple choice, short answer, and essay), progress assessment (through students' everyday oral and written work), and assessment rubrics (used for writing, inquiry, and comprehension strategies). Informal assessment can be done by observing or listening to students as they work and jotting down notes either in the Comprehension Observation Log or in a notebook.

Procedure

Formal Assessment

Formal assessment is addressed in ***SRA Imagine It!*** in the form of ***Benchmark Assessments*** and ***Lesson Assessments.*** Both will help you use the results to differentiate instruction, especially for students needing some type of intervention to ensure they will not be at risk for reading failure.

Benchmark Assessments

The ***Benchmark Assessments*** are a form of general outcome measurement that offer an overall framework for assessment and serve as a predictor of how well students will perform at the end of the school year. Each ***Benchmark Assessment*** has material that students will learn over the course of the school year, and each ***Benchmark Assessment*** is of equivalent difficulty. Students are not expected to score high on the initial screening benchmark; instead, students are expected to show growth as they move on to each subsequent benchmark. Only at the end of the year are students expected to have mastered the materials on these assessments.

> *Observing students as they go about their regular classwork can be an effective way to learn you students' strengths and areas of need.*

One ***Benchmark Assessment*** will be administered at the beginning of the year for screening. This can serve as a baseline score against which you can measure students' progress throughout the year. Subsequent benchmarks will also be given at regular intervals—at the end of every other unit in grades K–1, for a total of six assessments, and at the end of each unit for students in grades 2–6, for a total of seven assessments. Since the tests are of equivalent difficulty and contain the same types of items, students' higher scores will reflect their increasing mastery of the curriculum over the course of the year. Use the data from the ***Benchmark Assessments*** to identify students who are at risk for reading failure, to identify strengths and weaknesses of students, and to gauge student progress toward high-stakes tests.

Depending upon the grade level, tested benchmark skills include the following:

- letter recognition,
- phonemic/phonological awareness,
- phonics,
- high-frequency word recognition,
- vocabulary,
- spelling,
- grammar, usage, and mechanics,
- comprehension.
- oral fluency, and
- maze fluency.

In addition, a writing assessment is given in the initial screening, at midyear, and also again at the end of the year for students in grades 3–6. This assessment is the type of on-demand writing performance students will encounter in high-stakes tests. Each writing assessment is of equal difficulty, and student outcomes should reflect an increased mastery of writing convention and genre expectations.

Lesson Assessments

The ***Lesson Assessments*** cover the most important skills featured in the lesson of a given unit—skills that are closely related to reading success and are typically in state and national standards. These assessments will help you determine how well students are grasping the skills and concepts as they are taught and will help inform you about any additional instruction they might need.

The ***Lesson Assessments*** are easily administered and scored. They feature the same language used in the instructional components of ***SRA Imagine It!*** and correspond to its sequence of instruction. The format of these weekly assessments range from multiple choice questions to short answer to an extended writing response. Depending upon the grade level, skills assessed include the following:

- letter and number recognition
- phonological and phonemic awareness
- phonics
- print and book awareness
- high frequency words

- selection vocabulary
- spelling
- grammar, usage, and mechanics skills
- comprehension skills
- oral fluency
- writing

The ***Lesson Assessments*** are offered in several formats so that students can demonstrate their knowledge of content in a number of developmentally appropriate ways. Wherever possible, the assessments are designed to be administered to the whole class or small groups of students. In some cases, however, individually administered assessments are included, such as the oral fluency assessments, as well as critical pre-literacy skills such as phoneme blending or segmentation as well as letter and number recognition.

The ***Lesson Assessments*** will allow you to monitor students' progress as they are assessed on the specific skills taught in a given lesson. The results will provide instructionally relevant information that you can use to differentiate instruction for students who may need additional learning opportunities.

Progress Assessment

Written Practice

Students work on several different skills throughout the day. Each of these assignments can provide you with valuable information about your students' progress. One very helpful resource that students will work in daily is the ***Skills Practice Book*** (Levels K–6). The ***Skills Practice Books*** includes lessons that act as practice and reinforcement for the skills lessons taught before and during the reading of the lesson as well as in conjunction with the Language Arts lesson. These skill pages give you a clear picture of students' understanding of the skills taught. Use them as a daily assessment of student progress in the particular skills taught through the program.

Also included in the ***Skills Practice Books*** are lessons that help students with their Inquiry activities. Students can record what they know about the concepts and what they learn, they can keep a record of their research, and they can practice study and research skills that will help them in all of their schooling. You will be able to monitor their growing ability to make connections, find resources, and enhance their knowledge base as they find the answers to the research questions they have posed.

Dictation

In grades 1–3, students use dictation to practice the sound/spelling associations they are learning and/or reviewing. Collect the dictation papers and look through them to see how the students are doing with writing and with proofreading their words. Record notes on the papers and keep them in the student portfolios.

Portfolios

Portfolios are more than just a collection bin or gathering place for student projects and records. They add balance to an assessment program by providing unique benefits to teachers, students, and families.

- ✦ Portfolios help build self-confidence and increase self-esteem as students come to appreciate the value of their work. More importantly, portfolios allow students to reflect on what they know and what they need to learn. At the end of the school year, each student will be able to go through their portfolios and write about their progress.
- ✦ Portfolios provide the teacher with an authentic record of what students can do. Just as important, portfolios give students a concrete example of their own progress and development. Thus, portfolios become a valuable source of information for making instructional decisions.
- ✦ Portfolios allow families to judge student performance directly. Portfolios are an ideal starting point for discussions about a student's achievements and future goals during teacher/family conferences.

You will find that there are many opportunities to add to students' portfolios.

Fluency

- ✦ During partner reading, during Workshop, or at other times of the day, invite students, one at a time, to sit with you and read a story from an appropriate ***Decodable*** (grades 1–3), ***Leveled Readers*** (grades 1–6), ***Leveled Readers for Science*** or ***Social Studies*** (grades 1–6), or the ***Student Reader.***
- ✦ As each student reads to you, follow along and make note of any recurring problems the student has while reading. Note students' ability to decode unknown words as well as any attempt—successful or not—to use strategies to clarify or otherwise make sense of what they are reading. From time to time, check students' fluency by timing their reading and noting how well they are able to sustain the oral reading without faltering.
- ✦ If a student has trouble reading a particular ***Decodable*** or ***Leveled Reader,*** encourage the student to read the story a few times on her or his own before reading it aloud to you. If the ***Decodable*** has two stories, use the alternate story to reassess the student a day or two later.
- ✦ If after practicing with a particular Decodable Book or Leveled Reader and reading it on his or her own a few times, a student is still experiencing difficulty, try the following:
  - Drop back two ***Decodables***. (Continue to drop back until the student is able to read a story with no trouble.) If the student can read that book without problems, move up one book. The same is true for ***Leveled Readers.***
  - Continue the process until the student is able to read the current ***Decodable*** or ***Leveled Readers.***

Assessment Rubrics

In addition to the formal assessment opportunities available in ***Benchmark Assessments, Lesson Assessments,*** and progress assessment, ***SRA Imagine It!*** provides rubrics for you to evaluate students' performance in comprehension, Inquiry, and writing. Rubrics provide criteria for different levels of performance. Rubrics established before an assignment is given are extremely helpful in evaluating the assignment. When students know what the rubrics for a particular assignment are, they can focus their energies on the key issues. Rubrics can be found in the Level Appendix.

Informal Assessment

Observation

Informal assessment is a part of the everyday classroom routine. Observing students as they go about their regular classwork can be an effective way to learn your students' strengths and areas of need. The more students become accustomed to you jotting down informal notes about their work, the more it will become just another part of classroom life that they accept and take little note of. This gives you the opportunity to assess their progress constantly without the interference and possible drawback of formal testing situations.

One tool that will help you make

informal assessment of student progress a part of your everyday classroom routine is the Comprehension Observation Log. You can record information quickly on this observation sheet and even extend your observations over several days, until you have had a chance to observe each student's performance in a particular area.

- Enter students' names in the Comprehension Observation Log, found in the ***Lesson Assessment Books.***
- Before each day's lesson begins, decide which students you will observe.
- Keep the Comprehension Observation Log available so that you can easily record your observations.
- Decide what aspect of the students' learning you wish to monitor.
- During each lesson, observe this aspect in the performances of several students.
- When observing students, do not pull them aside; rather, observe students as part of the regular lesson, either with the whole class or in small groups.
- Record your observations.
- It may take four to five days to make sure you have observed and recorded the performance of each student. If you need more information about performance in a particular area for some of your students, you may want to observe them more than once.

Responding to Assessment Results

The point of assessment is to monitor progress in order to inform instruction, diagnose students' strengths and weaknesses, and differentiate instruction for students who need extra practice in certain skills or an extra challenge. ***SRA Imagine It!*** offers you opportunity to diagnose areas that may cause problems for students, differentiate instruction according to their abilities, monitor their progress on an ongoing basis, and measure student outcomes through ***Lesson Assessments*** or ***Benchmark Assessments,*** in addition to high-stakes state assessments. ***SRA Imagine It!*** also provides several ways to differentiate instruction based on the results of the various assessments. These include the following:

- Reteach lessons are available for students who are approaching level and appear to grasp a given concept but need more instruction and practice to solidify their learning. All skills taught in the ***Skills Practice Books*** are available in a ***Reteach*** format.
- Intervention lessons provide options for you to use with students who need more intensive support and who are struggling to understand the on-level material. In addition to the support for the weekly lesson, controlled vocabulary lessons and specific skills lessons can help bring students up to grade level.
- ***English Learner Support*** lessons are available for students who are having difficulty with the concepts because they lack the necessary English language background. These resources will provide English Learners with the vocabulary, phonics, comprehension, grammar, and writing support they need to access the ***SRA Imagine It!*** lessons.
- ***Challenge Activities*** provide continued stimulation for those students who are doing well and working above grade level. All skills covered in the ***Skills Practice Books*** are also available in ***Challenge Activities.***
- ***Workshop Resource Book*** activities give students alternative activities to strengthen or extend their skills in areas such as letter recognition, phonics, vocabulary, comprehension, fluency, word structure, and grammar.
- ***Leveled Readers*** provide students at all different levels of instruction—Approaching Level, On Level, Above Level, and English Learners—with additional opportunities to practice fluency, vocabulary, and comprehension skills. Besides the general ***Leveled Readers, Leveled Readers for Science*** and ***Leveled Readers for Social Studies*** provide students cross-curricular opportunities.

These materials, along with formal and informal assessments, help ensure that assessment and instruction work together to meet every student's needs.

Workshop

Every teacher and every student needs time during the day to organize, to take stock of work that is done, to make plans for work that needs doing, and to finish up incomplete projects. In addition, teachers need time for differentiating instruction, for holding conferences with students, and for doing fluency checks.

Purpose

Workshop is the period of time each day in which students work independently or collaboratively to practice and review material taught in the lessons.

A variety of activities may occur during this time. Students may work on a specific daily assignment, complete an ongoing project, work on unit inquiry activities, focus on writing, or choose from a wide range of possibilities. With lots of guidance and encouragement, students gradually learn to make decisions about their use of time and materials and to collaborate with their peers.

A goal of Workshop is to get students to work independently and productively. This is essential because Workshop is also the time during which the teacher can work with individuals or groups of students to reinforce learning, to provide extra help for those having difficulties, to extend learning, or to assess the progress of the class or of individuals.

Procedure

Initially for many students you will need to structure Workshop carefully. Eventually students will automatically go to the appropriate areas, take up ongoing projects, and get the materials they will need. Workshop will evolve slowly from a very structured period to a time when students make choices and move freely from one activity to the next.

Setting up Workshop guidelines is key. By the time students have completed the first few weeks of school, they should feel confident during Workshop. If not, continue to structure the time and limit options. For young students, early periods of Workshop may run no more than five to eight minutes. The time can gradually increase to fifteen minutes or longer as students gain independence. Older students may be able to work longer and independently from the very beginning of the school year.

Introducing Workshop

Introduce Workshop to students by telling them that every day there will be a time when they are expected to work on activities on their own or in small groups. For younger students explain that in the beginning there may be just a couple of activities but that gradually new ones will be introduced and that students can choose what they want to do. With older students and for those who have experienced Workshop in early grades, you may want to introduce the concept of Workshop and discuss the range of Workshop options from working on fluency to completing their writing to

Workshop is the period of time each day in which students work independently or collaboratively to practice and review material taught in the lessons.

Establish and discuss rules for Workshop with students. Keep them simple and straightforward. You may want to write the finalized rules on the board or on a poster. You may want to review these rules each day at the beginning of Workshop for the first few lessons or so. You may also wish to revisit and revise the rules from time to time. Suggested rules include the following:

- Share.
- Use a quiet voice.
- Take only the materials you need.
- Return materials.
- Always be working.
- When the teacher is working with small groups, do not interrupt.

Early in the process, review rules routinely, and discuss how Workshop is going. Is the class quiet enough for everyone to work on his or her own? Are there any rules that need changing? What problems are students having with materials?

For young students in the beginning you will assign the Workshop activities to help them learn to work on their own. Point out the shelf or area of the classroom where Workshop materials are stored. Tell students that when they finish working with the materials for one activity, they will choose something else from the Workshop shelf. New activity materials will be added to the shelf from time to time. Make sure students know that they may always look at books during Workshop.

Tell older students that they will have an opportunity each day to work on their unit explorations, their writing, and other projects. Students will be working independently and collaboratively during this time.

Guidelines

- ✦ Make sure each student knows what he or she needs to do during Workshop.
- ✦ Demonstrate for the entire group any activity or game assigned for Workshop, for example, teaching students a new game, introducing new materials or projects, or explaining different areas.
- ✦ For young students, it is essential to introduce and demonstrate different activities and games before students do them on their own. With games, you may want to have several students play while the others watch. Make sure that all students know exactly what is expected of them.
- ✦ In the beginning, plan to circulate among students, providing encouragement and help as necessary.
- ✦ When students are engaged in appropriate activities and can work independently, meet with those students who need your particular attention. This may include individual students or small groups.
- ✦ Let students know that they need to ask questions and to clarify assignments during Workshop introduction so that you are free to work with small groups.
- ✦ Be sure that students know what they are to do when they have finished an activity and where to put their finished work.

Setting Up Your Classroom for Workshop

Carefully setting up your classroom to accommodate various Workshop activities will help assure that the Workshop period progresses smoothly and effectively. While setting up your classroom, keep the primary Workshop activities in mind. During Workshop, students will be doing independent and collaborative activities. In kindergarten and first grade, these activities may include letter recognition and phonemic awareness activities and writing or illustrating stories or projects. In addition, they will be working on individual or small-group projects.

Many classrooms have areas that students visit on a regular or rotating basis. Unlike traditional centers, all students do not rotate through all the areas each day.

The following are suggestions for space and materials for use during Workshop:

1. Reading Area supplied with books and magazines. The materials in the Reading Area should be dynamic—changing with students' abilities and reflecting unit themes they are reading. You may wish to add books to your classroom library.
2. Writing Area stocked with various types and sizes of lined and unlined paper, pencils, erasers, markers, crayons, small slates, and chalk. The area should also have various ***Letter Cards,*** other handwriting models, and worksheets for those students who want to practice letter formation or handwriting. Students should know that this is where they come for writing supplies. In addition to the supplies described above, the Writing Area can also have supplies to encourage students to create and write on their own:
   - Magazines and catalogs to cut up for pictures; stickers, paint, glue, glitter, and so on to decorate books and book covers; precut and stapled blank books for students to write in (Some can be plain and some cut in special shapes.)
   - Cardboard, tag board, construction paper, and so on for making book covers (Provide some samples.)
   - Tape, scissors, yarn, hole punches for binding books
   - Picture dictionaries, dictionaries, thesaurus, word lists, and other materials that may encourage independence
3. Listening Area supplied with tape recorder, CD player, optional headphones, and tapes of stories, poems, and songs for students to listen to and react to. You might also want to provide blank tapes and encourage students to retell and record their favorite stories or to make up and tell stories for their classmates to listen to on tape. You may also want to make available the Listening Library CDs that are available with the program.
4. Phonics Activities supplied with ***Alphabet Flash Cards,*** individual ***Alphabet Sound Card*** sets (Kindergarten), individual ***Sound/Spelling Cards*** and ***High-Frequency Flash Cards*** (Grades K, 1, 2, and 3), and other materials that enhance what students are learning. Other commonly used classroom materials that enhance reading can be included, for example, plastic letters, puzzles, and games.
5. Fluency Area supplied with ***Pre-Decodables and Decodables, Leveled Readers, Leveled Science Readers*** and ***Leveled Social Studies Readers,*** and other resources for practicing fluency. Some teachers have folders for each student with materials to practice during the week. In addition, some Fluency areas have times and tape recorders as well.

Because students will be working on their inquiry/investigations during Workshop, make sure there are adequate supplies to help them with their research. These might include dictionaries, encyclopedias, magazines, newspapers, and computers—preferably with Internet capability.

Students thrive in an environment that provides structure, repetition, and routine. Within a sound structure, students will gain confidence and independence. This setting allows you to differentiate instruction to provide opportunities for flexibility and individual choice. This will allow students to develop their strengths, abilities, and talents to the fullest.

Suggestions for English Learners

Workshop affords students who are English Learners a wealth of opportunities for gaining proficiency in English. It also encourages them to share their backgrounds with peers. Since you will be working with all students individually and in small groups regardless of their reading ability, students who need special help with language will not feel self-conscious about working with you.

In addition, working in small groups made of students with the same interests rather than the same abilities will provide them with the opportunity to learn about language from their peers during the regular course of Workshop activities.

Some suggestions for meeting the special needs of students with diverse backgrounds are as follows:

- Preread a selection with English Learners to help them identify words and ideas they wish to talk about. This will prepare them for discussions with the whole group.
- Preteach vocabulary and develop selection concepts that may be a challenge for students.
- Negotiate the meaning of selections by asking questions, checking for comprehension, and speaking with English Learners as much as possible.
- Draw English Learners into small-group discussions to give them a sense that their ideas are valid and worth attention.
- Pair English Learners with native English speakers to share their experiences and to provide new knowledge to other students.
- Have English Learners draw or dictate to you or another student a description of a new idea they may have during Workshop activities.

Reading Roundtable

When Workshop is underway and students are working independently, introduce Reading Roundtable. Adult readers discuss their reading, give opinions on it, and recommend books to each other. Reading Roundtable, an activity students may choose to participate in during Workshop, provides the same opportunity for students in the classroom. Sessions can be small or large. During Reading Roundtable, students share the reading they do on their own. They can discuss a book they have all read, or one person can review a book for the others and answer questions from the group.

During Reading Roundtable, students can discuss and review a variety of books:

- Full-length versions of Student Reader selections.
- Books that students learn about when discussing authors and illustrators
- Books related to the investigations of unit concepts that can be shared with others who might want to read them

- Interesting articles from magazines, newspapers, and other sources

When a student reviews a book others have not read, he or she can use some of the sentence starters to tell about the book. These may include "This book is about . . . ," "I chose this book because . . . ," "What I really like/don't like about this book is . . ., " and so on.

- When several students read the same book and discuss it during Reading Roundtable, they can use discussion starters.

Encouraging Reading

- Read aloud to your students regularly. You can read from your classroom library or full-length versions of Student Reader selections.
- Provide a time each day for students to read silently. This time can be as short as 10–15 minutes but should be strictly observed. You should stop what you are doing and read. Students should be allowed to choose their own reading materials during this time and record their reactions in the response journal section of their Writer's Notebooks.
- Establish a classroom library and reading center with books from the school or local library, or ask for donations of books from students, parents, and community members.
- Take your students to the school library or to the public library.

Workshop Management Tips

Use the following Workshop management tips to ensure that Workshop runs smoothly.

Note that these suggestions for a weekly unit/lesson may not exactly correspond to a particular unit/lesson in a given grade level but will give you a sense of how Workshop should progress. All of the time suggestions depend upon the needs of the class and their readiness to work independently.

Kindergarten through Grade 1

Unit 1, Week 1 Introduce Workshop as whole-class workshop. Explain Workshop and its rules. Give the class an activity to do, for example, putting letters in alphabetical order (Grade 1) or copying their names (kindergarten). Tell the class that they will be doing Workshop today. As they do their activity, you will walk around, observing students and noting how well Workshop is going. The class is working quietly and independently. Workshop may last only a few minutes in kindergarten and about ten minutes in first grade.

Unit 1, Weeks 2 and 3 Depending upon your class, you can move to whole-group Workshop with two activities. Give half the class one activity and the other half the other. Explain to the class that for the next few Workshop sessions, there will be two different activities but that the class is supposed to work quietly and independently. Switch activities for the next day, and repeat this format for the next few days or so. Introduce the concept of "debriefing." Take a few minutes at the end, have several students share what they did or learned during Workshop. You may want to have students tell what they like about Workshop and if any changes need to be made.

Unit 2, Week 1 on Begin introducing Workshop Areas, explaining the materials and how they can be used. Explain to students that the materials in these areas will be changing regularly so students will be able to practice and use their new reading and writing skills. Workshop activities should change routinely and reflect the changing nature of the curriculum. Often, during the early weeks of Workshop, teachers assign students to different activities and, as students become ready, turn over to students the responsibility for choosing activities.

Unit 3 Add new activities for students. Encourage them to do a couple of Workshop activities each day, perhaps working on their writing in progress and fluency practice (reading a Pre-Decodable or Decodable). Other options might include on-line phonemic awareness and phonics activities, phonics activities such as word sorts, using blended words in written sentences, practicing high-frequency sight words, and so on.

Unit 4 By this time, students should be making choices and working independently. Each Workshop session may be fifteen minutes long with the teacher working with small groups. Take time to review Workshop activities to be sure they are being used and that students are learning from the activities. If activities become stale, vary them, or change them altogether.

Grades 2–6

Unit 1, Lesson 1 Introduce Workshop to students. Make sure they know where materials are located. Post the rules on the board or other prominent place in the classroom. Keep Workshop time short (less than thirty minutes) and very directed during the first few weeks until students can work independently.

Unit 1, Lesson 2 Discuss using small groups for pre-/reteaching purposes and how you will indicate who will be in the groups. Start by forming one small group randomly and having other students do something specific such as a writing assignment. When you have finished with the small group, send them to do independent work. Call another small group of students to work with you. Continue this each day until students are accustomed to forming groups and working independently.

Unit 1, Lesson 3 Reading Roundtable is a student-formed and student-run book discussion. Encourage students participating in Reading Roundtable to choose a book that they all will read and discuss. Several different Reading Roundtable groups may form on the basis of the books students choose.

Unit 1, Lesson 4 For the first few weeks of the school year, make sure each student has a plan for using Workshop time.

Unit 1, Lesson 5 Allow time for presentation and discussion of research activities. Use an entire Workshop day, and have all groups present their findings, or split the presentations over several days, depending on the small-group needs of your class.

Unit 1, Lesson 6 Review how students have used Workshop during this unit. Have they used their time well? Do they have the materials they need? Discuss suggestions for improving their use of this time. Take a few minutes at the beginning of each Workshop to make sure students know what they will be doing.

Unit 2, Lesson 1 Form small extra-practice groups with the more advanced students from time to time, as they also need special attention.

Unit 2, Lesson 2 To keep the entire class informed about the independent research being done, every other day or so invite a research group to explain what it is doing, how the research is going, and any problems they are encountering.

Unit 2, Lesson 3 Discuss the use of Workshop time for doing Inquiry and research projects, and share eInquiry with different research activities.

Unit 2, Lesson 4 Make sure small extra-practice groups are formed based on your observations of students' work on the different daily lessons. Small groups should be fluid and based on demonstrated need rather than become static and unchanging.

Unit 2, Lesson 5 One purpose of Workshop is to help students learn independence and responsibility. Assign students to monitor Workshop materials. They should alert you whenever materials are running low or missing, and they can be responsible for checking on return dates of library books and making sure the books are either returned or renewed.

Unit 2, Lesson 6 Students sometimes have difficulty starting discussions in Reading Roundtable. Try some of these discussion starters with students, and print them on a poster paper for student use.

I didn't know that . . . *I liked the part where . . .*
Does anyone know . . . *I'm still confused by . . .*
I figured out that . . . *This made me think . . .*
I agree/disagree with because . . .

Unit 3, Lesson 1 By this time students should be accustomed to the routines, rules, expectations, and usage of Workshop time and be moving smoothly from small teacher-led groups to independent work. Monitor small groups occasionally to see that they are on task and making progress on their activities.

Unit 3, Lesson 2 Make a practice of reading aloud to students. All students enjoy being read to, no matter their age or grade. Encourage them to discuss the shared reading in Reading Roundtable groups and to bring books and read them aloud to their classmates.

Unit 3, Lesson 3 Encourage cooperation and collaboration by providing students with opportunities to engage in small groups.

Unit 3, Lesson 4 Spend a few minutes each day circulating around the room and monitoring what students are doing independently or in small groups. Students can then share with you on a timely basis any questions or problems they are having.

Unit 3, Lesson 5 Take note of various small groups. Make sure that quieter students are able to participate in the discussions. Often the stronger, more confident students dominate such discussions. Encourage them to give all participants an opportunity to share their ideas.

Unit 3, Lesson 6 If students are not productive during Workshop, keep them in the small group you are working with until they can successfully benefit from independent work. Discuss strategies they could use to become more independent.

Unit 4, Lesson 1 Individual students can monitor Workshop materials and alert you when materials or supplies are running low or missing and can check that library books are either returned or renewed.

Unit 4, Lesson 2 From time to time, join a Reading Roundtable group, and take part in their discussion. Make sure students lead the discussion.

Unit 4, Lesson 3 Encourage responsibility and independence by reminding students to show respect for each other and the materials provided.

Unit 4, Lesson 4 Be sure students discuss during Reading Roundtable what they like or dislike about a book, why they wanted to read it, and how the book either lived up to their expectations or disappointed them. Discussions should not be about basic comprehension but should help students think more deeply about the ideas presented in the book.

Unit 4, Lesson 5 Make sure students continue to use the activities provided for use with this unit at www.sraonline.com.

Unit 4, Lesson 6 If students are not productive in Workshop, keep them in the small group you are working with until they can successfully benefit from independent work. Discuss strategies they could use to become more independent.

Unit 5, Lesson 1 Students often make great tutors for other students. They are uniquely qualified to understand problems that others might be having. Encourage students to pair up during Workshop to help each other with their daily lessons.

Unit 5, Lesson 2 Form small extra-practice groups with the more advanced students from time to time, as they also need special attention.

Unit 5, Lesson 3 To keep the entire class informed about the independent research being done, every other day or so, invite a research/investigation group to explain what it is doing, how the research is going, and any problems they are encountering.

Unit 5, Lesson 4 Most of the authors of the student anthology selections are well known and have written many, many pieces of fine literature. Encourage students who enjoy the anthology selections to find other books by the same author. Encourage them to think about and discuss what about that particular author's work attracts them.

Unit 5, Lesson 5 Share your impressions of books from your classroom library or other readings during Reading Roundtable. Note which students initiate sharing and which are reluctant to share.

Unit 5, Lesson 6 Review with students the time they have used in Workshop. Have they used their time well? Do they have the materials they need? Discuss suggestions for improving the use of this time.

Unit 6, Lesson 1 Spend a few minutes each day circulating around the room and monitoring what students are doing independently or in small groups. Students can share with you on a timely basis any questions or problems they are having.

Unit 6, Lesson 2 Students should be accustomed to the routines, rules, expectations, and usage of Workshop time and be moving smoothly from small teacher-led groups to independent work. Make sure to monitor small groups occasionally to see that they are on task and making progress with their activities.

Unit 6, Lesson 3 Make sure students continue to use the activities provided for use with this unit at www.sraonline.com.

Unit 6, Lesson 4 Allot time for presentation and discussion of research activities. You may want to use a whole Workshop day and have all groups present their findings or split the presentations over several days, depending on the urgency of the small-group instruction your class needs.

Unit 6, Lesson 5 Students often make great tutors for other students. The fact that they, too, are just learning the materials makes them uniquely qualified to understand problems that others might be having. Encourage students to pair up during Workshop to help each other on their daily lessons.

Unit 6, Lesson 6 If the reading selection is an excerpt from a longer piece, encourage students to read the book from which the excerpt is taken and to discuss how the excerpt fits into the larger work.

Scope and Sequence

Reading

	K	1	2	3	4	5	6
Print/Book Awareness (Recognize and understand the conventions of print and books)							
Capitalization	X	X					
Constancy of Words		X					
Differentiate between Letter and Word	X						
Differentiate between Word and Sentence	X						
End Punctuation	X	X					
Follow Left-to-Right, Top-to-Bottom	X	X					
Letter Recognition and Formation	X	X					
Page Numbering	X	X					
Parts of a Book	X	X					
Picture/Text Relationship	X	X					
Punctuation	X	X					
Quotation Marks	X	X					
Relationship Between Spoken and Printed Language	X	X					
Sentence Recognition	X	X					
Spacing Between Sentences	X	X					
Spacing Between Words	X	X					
Table of Contents	X	X					
Text Features		X					
Text Relationships		X					
Word Length	X	X					
Word Boundaries		X					
Write Left-to-Right, Top-to-Bottom	X	X					
Phonemic Awareness (Recognize Discrete Sounds in Words)							
Oral Blending: Words/Word Parts	X	X					
Oral Blending: Onset and Rime	X	X					
Oral Blending: Syllables	X	X					
Oral (Phoneme) Blending: Initial Sounds	X	X					
Oral (Phoneme) Blending: Final Sounds	X	X					
Oral Blending: Initial Vowels		X					
Oral Blending: Vowel Replacement		X					
Rhyming	X	X					
Phoneme Matching: Initial Sounds	X	X					
Phoneme Matching: Final Sounds	X	X					
Phoneme Matching: Medial Sounds	X	X					
Phoneme Manipulation: Initial Sounds	X	X					
Phoneme Manipulation: Final Sounds	X	X					
Phoneme Manipulation: Medial Sounds	X	X					
Segmentation: Final Consonants	X	X					
Segmentation: Initial Consonants/Blends		X					
Segmentation: Words/Word Parts	X	X					
Segmentation: Syllables	X	X					
Segmentation: Identifying the Number and Order of Sounds in Words	X	X					

Reading (continued)

	K	1	2	3	4	5	6
How the Alphabet Works							
Letter Knowledge (Alphabetic Knowledge)	X	X					
Letter Order (Alphabetic Order)	X	X					
Letter Sounds	X	X					
Sounds in Words	X	X					
Phonics (Associate Sounds and Spellings to Read Words)							
Blending Sounds into Words	X	X	X	X			
Consonant Clusters		X	X	X			
Consonant Digraphs		X	X	X			
Phonograms		X	X	X			
Silent Consonants			X	X			
Syllables		X	X	X			
Vowel Diphthongs		X	X	X			
Vowels: l-controlled				X			
Vowels: Long Sounds and Spellings	X	X	X	X			
Vowels: r-controlled		X	X	X			
Vowels: Short Sounds and Spellings	X	X	X	X			
Comprehension Strategies							
Adjusting Reading Speed			X	X	X	X	X
Asking Questions/Answering Questions	X	X	X	X	X	X	X
Clarifying	X	X	X	X	X	X	X
Making Connections	X	X	X	X	X	X	X
Predicting/Confirming Predictions	X	X	X	X	X	X	X
Summarizing		X	X	X	X	X	X
Visualizing	X	X	X	X	X	X	X
Comprehension Skills							
Author's Point of View			X	X	X	X	X
Author's Purpose			X	X	X	X	X
Cause and Effect	X	X	X	X	X	X	X
Classify and Categorize	X	X	X	X	X	X	X
Compare and Contrast	X	X	X	X	X	X	X
Drawing Conclusions	X	X	X	X	X	X	X
Fact and Opinion			X	X	X	X	X
Main Idea and Detail	X	X	X	X	X	X	X
Making Inferences		X	X	X	X	X	X
Reality/Fantasy	X	X	X	X			
Sequence	X	X	X	X	X	X	X
Vocabulary							
Apposition		X	X	X	X	X	X
Concept Words		X	X	X	X	X	X
Context Clues		X	X	X	X	X	X
Expanding Vocabulary		X	X	X	X	X	X
High-Frequency Words	X	X	X	X			
Idioms				X	X	X	X
Multiple-Meaning Words		X	X	X	X	X	X
Selection Vocabulary	X	X	X	X	X	X	X
Time and Order Words (Creating Sequence)	X	X	X	X	X	X	X
Utility Words (Colors, Classroom Objects, etc.)	X	X					

Reading (continued)

	K	1	2	3	4	5	6
Reading with a Writer's Eye							
Author's Purpose	X		X	X	X	X	
Alliteration			X				X
Captions and Headings			X	X		X	X
Characterization	X	X	X	X	X	X	X
Choosing Good Examples				X	X		
Description		X	X	X	X	X	X
Diagrams							X
Dialect						X	
Dialogue		X	X	X	X	X	X
Effective Beginnings					X	X	
Effective Endings					X		
Event Sequence	X	X	X	X		X	
Expository Writing Techniques					X	X	
Fable Characteristics					X		
Figurative Language		X	X	X	X	X	X
Flashback							X
Genre Knowledge	X		X	X	X	X	X
Idiom						X	X
Irony					X		
Language Use	X		X	X	X	X	X
Mood and Tone		X	X	X			X
Onomatopoeia			X	X	X		X
Personification			X	X		X	X
Persuasive Techniques					X	X	
Plot (Problem/Solution)	X	X	X	X	X	X	X
Point of View					X	X	
Punctuation					X	X	
Quoting Sources					X		
Rhyme	X		X			X	X
Sensory Details		X		X		X	
Sentence Variety						X	
Setting	X	X	X	X	X	X	X
Sidebars							X
Similes and Metaphors				X			X
Stage Directions					X		
Style							X
Suspense and Surprise				X		X	
Text Structure	X		X	X	X	X	X
Theme	X		X	X	X	X	X
Transitions					X		X
Using Comparisons		X	X	X		X	
Voice					X	X	X
Word Choice				X			X
Word Structure							
Antonyms			X	X	X	X	X
Comparatives/Superlatives			X	X	X	X	
Compound Words	X	X	X	X	X	X	X
Contractions			X	X	X	X	
Connotation and Denotation							X
Content/Concept Words							X

Reading (continued)

	K	1	2	3	4	5	6
Foreign Words and Phrases						X	X
Gerunds							X
Greek and Latin Roots				X	X	X	X
Homographs			X	X	X	X	X
Homonyms/Homophones			X	X	X	X	X
Inflectional Endings			X	X	X	X	X
Irregular Plurals			X	X	X	X	
Multiple-Meaning Words					X	X	X
Multisyllabic Words			X	X	X	X	
Plurals			X	X	X	X	
Position Words	X	X					
Prefixes			X	X	X	X	X
Root or Base Words			X	X	X	X	X
Shades of Meaning/Levels of Specificity						X	X
Suffixes			X	X	X	X	X
Synonyms			X	X	X	X	X
Word Families			X	X	X	X	X
Word Origins					X	X	X

Inquiry and Study Skills

	K	1	2	3	4	5	6
Study Skills							
Comparing Information across Sources		X		X		X	
Charts, Graphs, and Diagrams/Visual Aids	X	X	X	X	X	X	X
Collaborative Inquiry	X	X	X	X	X	X	X
Communicating Research Progress Results		X	X	X	X	X	X
Compile Notes			X		X	X	X
Conducting an Interview		X	X	X	X	X	X
Finding Needed Information	X	X	X	X	X	X	X
Follow Directions	X		X	X	X		X
Formulate Questions for Inquiry and Research	X	X	X	X	X	X	X
Give Reports	X		X	X	X	X	X
Make Outlines			X	X	X	X	X
Making Conjectures	X	X	X	X	X	X	X
Maps	X	X	X	X	X	X	
Note Taking		X	X	X	X	X	X
Parts of a Book	X	X	X	X	X		
Planning Inquiry		X	X	X	X	X	X
Recognizing Information Needs		X	X	X	X	X	X
Revising Questions and Conjectures	X	X	X	X	X	X	X
Summarize and Organize Information		X	X	X	X	X	X
Time Lines			X	X	X	X	
Use Appropriate Resources (Media Sources, Reference Books, Experts, Internet)		X	X	X	X	X	X
Using a Dictionary/Glossary		X	X	X	X		
Using a Media Center/Library		X	X	X	X		
Using a Thesaurus			X	X	X	X	
Using an Encyclopedia		X	X	X	X		
Using Newspapers and Magazines		X	X		X		X
Using Technology	X	X	X	X	X	X	X

Language Arts

Writing/Composition

	K	1	2	3	4	5	6
Approaches							
Collaborative Writing	X	X	X	X	X	X	X
Individual Writing	X	X	X	X	X	X	X
Writing Process							
Brainstorming/Prewriting	X	X	X	X	X	X	X
Drafting	X	X	X	X	X	X	X
Revising	X	X	X	X	X	X	X
Editing	X	X	X	X	X	X	X
Proofreading	X	X	X	X	X	X	X
Publishing	X	X	X	X	X	X	X
Writing Genres							
Action Tale			X				
Autobiography/Biography	X	X	X	X	X	X	X
Book Review		X	X	X		X	
Business Letter			X	X		X	X
Describe a Process		X	X	X	X	X	X
Descriptive Writing	X	X	X	X	X	X	X
Expository/Informational Text	X	X	X	X	X	X	X
Fantasy		X	X	X			
Folklore (Folktales, Fairy Tales, Tall Tales, Legends, Myths)		X	X	X	X	X	
Friendly Letter	X	X	X	X	X	X	X
Historical Fiction					X		X
Invitation		X		X		X	
Journal Writing			X	X	X		
Magazine Article						X	X
Making a List	X	X	X	X	X	X	X
Mystery				X			
Narrative	X	X	X	X	X	X	X
News Story		X	X	X			
Personal Writing	X	X	X	X	X	X	X
Persuasive Writing	X	X	X	X	X	X	X
Play/Dramatization			X	X	X	X	X
Poetry	X	X	X	X	X	X	X
Realistic Fiction		X	X	X	X	X	X
Summary		X	X	X	X	X	X
Timed Writing		X	X	X	X	X	X
Writing Traits							
Audience		X	X	X	X	X	X
Conventions	X	X	X	X	X	X	X
Elaboration		X	X	X	X	X	X
Focus		X	X	X	X	X	X
Ideas/Content	X	X	X	X	X	X	X
Organization		X	X	X	X	X	X
Presentation	X	X	X	X	X	X	X
Purpose		X	X	X	X	X	X
Sentence Fluency	X	X	X	X	X	X	X
Sentence Variety		X			X	X	X
Vocabulary		X	X	X	X	X	X
Voice	X	X	X	X	X	X	X
Word Choice	X	X	X	X	X	X	X

Language Arts

Writing/Composition (continued)

Writing Strategies	K	1	2	3	4	5	6
Action and Describing Words	X	X	X	X			
Adding Details	X	X	X	X	X	X	X
Addressing Audience Needs		X	X	X	X	X	X
Brainstorming	X	X	X	X	X	X	X
Categorizing Ideas							X
Cause and Effect					X	X	X
Character Sketch					X	X	
Choosing a Topic	X	X	X	X	X	X	X
Compare and Contrast			X			X	X
Conveying a General Mood				X	X	X	
Creating Suspense				X			X
Creating Vivid Images		X		X	X	X	
Dialogue	X	X	X	X	X	X	X
Effective Beginnings					X	X	X
Elements of a Letter		X	X	X	X	X	X
Elements of Persuasion			X	X	X	X	
Eliminating Irrelevant Information		X	X	X	X	X	X
Eliminating Wordiness			X	X	X	X	X
Evaluate Personal Growth as a Writer			X	X	X	X	
Explanatory Paragraphs		X					
Figurative Language			X	X	X	X	X
Formality of Language		X	X	X	X	X	
Format		X			X	X	X
Generate Additional Ideas		X	X	X	X		
Highlight a Memorable Event		X			X		
Identifying Best Feature of Something Written			X	X			
Illustrations and Drawings	X	X	X	X			
Information from Multiple Sources				X	X	X	X
Main Idea and Details					X	X	
Making Connections							X
Organizing a Multi-Paragraph Composition					X	X	X
Planning		X			X	X	X
Plot Structure—Beginning, Middle, Climax, and End		X		X	X	X	X
Point of View						X	X
Presenting Facts and Examples Objectively				X	X	X	X
Proofreading	X	X	X	X	X	X	X
Purpose		X	X	X	X	X	X
Realism					X	X	X
Referencing a Source					X	X	
Revising	X	X	X	X	X	X	X
Rhythm and Rhyme		X	X			X	
Sensory Details				X	X	X	X
Sentence Combining			X	X	X	X	X
Sequence	X	X	X	X		X	
Setting		X	X	X	X	X	X
Story Elements		X	X	X	X	X	
Style							X
Summary			X	X	X	X	X
Taking Notes		X	X	X	X	X	X

Language Arts
Writing/Composition (continued)

	K	1	2	3	4	5	6
Timed Writing		X	X	X	X	X	X
Timeline			X	X		X	
Transition Words/Devices			X	X	X	X	X
Using a Checklist		X	X	X	X	X	
Using a Graphic Organizer		X	X	X	X	X	X
Using a Model as a Guide to Writing			X	X		X	
Using Outlines to Organize Information				X	X	X	X
Using Multimedia Sources			X	X	X	X	X
Vary Sentence Beginnings			X	X	X	X	
Vary Sentence Length		X	X			X	
Vary Sentence Types	X	X	X	X	X	X	
Voice				X		X	
Voicing an Opinion		X				X	X
Word Choice		X	X	X	X	X	X
Working Collaboratively						X	X
Writing Coherent Paragraphs		X	X	X	X	X	X

Language Arts
Grammar

	K	1	2	3	4	5	6
Parts of Speech							
Adjectives (Describing Words)	X	X	X	X	X	X	X
Adverbs			X	X	X	X	X
Conjunctions			X	X	X	X	X
Nouns	X	X	X	X	X	X	X
Prepositions				X	X	X	X
Pronouns	X	X	X	X	X	X	X
Verbs	X	X	X	X	X	X	X
Sentences							
Complete and Incomplete Sentences		X	X	X	X	X	X
Fragments			X	X	X	X	X
Independent and Dependent Clauses							X
Parts (Subjects and Predicates)			X	X	X	X	X
Run-on Sentences							X
Sentence Combining			X	X	X	X	X
Structure (Simple, Compound, Complex, Compound-Complex)			X	X	X	X	X
Subject/Verb Agreement		X	X	X	X	X	X
Types (Declarative, Interrogative, Exclamatory, Imperative)	X	X	X	X	X	X	X
Usage							
Adjectives		X	X	X	X	X	X
Adverbs			X	X	X	X	X
Antonyms		X	X				
Articles			X	X		X	X
Contractions			X	X			
Nouns		X	X	X	X	X	X
Pronouns		X	X	X	X	X	X
Regular and Irregular Plurals					X	X	X
Synonyms		X	X				
Verb Tenses		X	X	X	X	X	X
Verbs (Action, Helping, Linking, Regular/Irregular)		X	X	X	X	X	X

Language Arts
Grammar (continued)

	K	1	2	3	4	5	6
Mechanics							
Capitalization (Sentence, Proper Nouns, Titles, Direct Address, Pronoun "I")	X	X	X	X	X	X	X
Punctuation (End Punctuation, Comma Use, Quotation Marks, Apostrophe, Colon, Semicolon, Hyphen, Parentheses)	X	X	X	X	X	X	X
Spelling							
Antonyms					X	X	X
Base or Root Words					X	X	
Comparatives/Superlatives				X	X	X	X
Compound Words				X	X	X	
Connotation and Denotation							X
Content/Concept Words							X
Contractions				X	X		X
Foreign Words and Phrases							X
Gerunds							X
Greek and Latin Roots				X	X	X	X
Homographs				X	X	X	X
Homonyms/Homophones				X	X	X	X
Inflectional Endings		X		X	X	X	X
Irregular Plurals		X		X	X	X	
Irregular Verbs						X	
Long Vowel Patterns		X	X	X	X		
Multiple-Meaning Words						X	X
Multisyllabic Words		X	X	X	X		X
Phonograms		X					
Prefixes				X	X	X	X
r-Controlled Vowel Spellings		X	X				
Shades of Meaning							X
Short Vowel Spellings		X	X	X	X		
Silent Letters			X	X	X		
Sound/Letter Relationships	X	X	X				
Special Spellings Patterns/Rules		X	X	X	X	X	
Special Vowel Spellings		X	X	X			
Suffixes		X		X	X	X	X
Synonyms						X	X
Word Families		X		X		X	X

Listening/Speaking/Viewing

	K	1	2	3	4	5	6
Listening							
Analyze/Evaluate Intent and Content of Speaker's Message		X	X	X		X	X
Ask Questions		X	X	X	X	X	X
Determine Purposes for Listening		X	X	X	X	X	X
Drawing Conclusions and Making Inferences						X	
Follow Directions	X	X		X	X	X	X
Learn about Different Cultures through Discussion				X	X		
Listen for Poetic Language (Rhythm/Rhyme)	X	X			X		X
Listening for Details			X	X	X		
Listening for Information				X	X		
Participate in Group Discussions	X	X	X	X	X	X	X
Recalling What Was Heard				X			
Recognizing Fact and Opinion				X			
Respond to Speaker	X	X	X	X	X	X	X
Use Nonverbal Communication Techniques		X		X	X	X	X
Speaking							
Answer Questions	X	X	X	X	X	X	X
Asking Questions		X		X	X		
Describe Ideas and Feelings	X	X	X				X
Effective Word Choice/Voice			X	X	X	X	
Engaging the Audience					X	X	
Give Directions		X			X	X	X
Learn About Different Cultures through Discussion		X		X			X
Listen and Respond		X		X	X		
Making Announcements and Introductions		X					
Organizing Presentations				X	X	X	X
Paraphrasing			X	X			
Participate in Group Discussion	X	X	X	X	X	X	X
Present Oral Reports		X	X	X	X	X	X
Purposes of Speech			X				
Read Fluently with Expression, Phrasing, and Intonation		X	X	X	X	X	X
Read Orally	X	X	X	X	X	X	X
Share Information		X	X	X	X	X	X
Small Group Discussion			X	X	X	X	X
Speak Clearly at Appropriate Volume		X	X	X	X	X	X
Speaking Strategies				X	X		
Staying on Topic		X					
Summarize/Retell Stories	X	X	X	X	X	X	X
Understand Formal and Informal Language		X		X	X	X	X
Use Appropriate Language for Audience		X		X	X	X	X
Use Nonverbal Communication Techniques		X	X	X	X	X	X

Listening/Speaking/Viewing (continued)

	K	1	2	3	4	5	6
Viewing							
Analyze Purposes and Techniques of the Media			X	X	X	X	X
Appreciate/Interpret Artist's Techniques		X					
Compare Visual and Written Material on the Same Subject		X					X
Culture in Media		X			X	X	
Describe Pictures			X				
Gather Information from Visual Images		X	X	X	X	X	X
Interpreting Media				X	X		
Language Development							X
Literary Devices				X			X
Relating to Content				X	X		
Understanding Gestures				X	X		
Using Multimedia				X	X	X	
View Critically		X		X	X	X	X
Penmanship							
Cursive Letters			X	X			
Manuscript Letters	X	X					
Numbers	X	X					

Unit Themes

	Level K	Level 1	Level 2
Unit 1	Off to School	Back to School	Kindness
Unit 2	Patterns	Where Animals Live	Let's Explore
Unit 3	Finding Friends	I Am Responsible!	Around the Town
Unit 4	By the Sea	Our Neighborhood at Work	Look Again
Unit 5	Stick to It	What's the Weather?	Courage
Unit 6	My Shadow	North, South, East, West	America's People
Unit 7	Teamwork	I Think I Can	
Unit 8	Ready, Set, Grow!	Away We Grow!	
Unit 9	Red, White, and Blue	Home, Sweet Home	
Unit 10	Windy Days	I Am Brave	

Level 3	Level 4	Level 5	Level 6
Friendship	Risks and Consequences	Heritage	Taking a Stand
Animals and Their Habitats	Nature's Delicate Balance	Energy at Work	Ancient Civilizations
Money	A Changing America	Making a New Nation	Ecology
Earth, Moon, and Sun	Science Fair	Our Corner of the Universe	Great Expectations
Communities across Time	America on the Move	Going West	Earth in Action
Storytelling	Dollars and Sense	Call of Duty	Art and Impact

Glossary of Reading Terms

This glossary includes linguistic, grammatical, comprehension, and literary terms that may be helpful in understanding reading instruction.

acronym a word formed from the initial letter of words in a phrase, **scuba (self-contained underwater breathing apparatus)**.

acrostic a kind of puzzle in which lines of a poem are arranged so that words or phrases are formed when certain letters from each line are used in a sequence.

adjective a word or group of words that modifies or describes a noun.

adventure story a narrative that features the unknown or unexpected with elements of excitement, danger, and risk.

adverb a word or group of words that modifies a verb, adjective, or other adverb. An adverb answers questions such as **how, when, where,** and **how much.**

affective domain the psychological field of emotional activities such as interests, attitudes, opinions, appreciations, values, and emotional sets

affix a word part, either a prefix or a suffix, that changes the meaning or function of a word root or stem.

affricate a speech sound that starts as a stop but ends as a fricative, the /ch/ in **catch.**

agreement the correspondence of syntactically related words; subjects and predicates are in agreement when both are singular or plural.

alliteration the repetition of the initial sounds in neighboring words or stressed syllables.

alphabet the complete set of letters representing speech sounds used in writing a language. In English there are twenty-six letters.

alphabet book a book for helping young children learn the alphabet by pairing letters with pictures whose sounds they represent.

alphabetic principle the association between sounds and the letters that represent them in alphabetic writing systems.

alveolar a consonant speech sound made when the tongue and the ridge of the upper and lower jaw stop to constrict the air flow, as /t/.

anagram a word or phrase whose letters form other words or phrases when rearranged, for example, **add** and **dad.**

analogy a likeness or similarity.

analytic phonics also deductive phonics, a whole-to-part approach to phonics in which a student is taught a number of sight words and then phonetic generalizations that can be applied to other words.

antonym a word that is opposite in meaning to another word.

appositive a word that restates or modifies a preceding noun, for example, **my daughter, Charlotte.** Appositives are also definitions of words usually usually set off by commas.

aspirate an unvoiced speech sound produced by a puff of air, as /h/ in **heart.**

aspirated stop a stop consonant sound released with a puff of air, as /k/, /p/, and /t/.

auditory discrimination the ability to hear phonetic likenesses and differences in phonemes and words.

author's purpose the motive or reason for which an author writes; includes to entertain, inform, persuade, and explain how.

automaticity fluent processing of information, requiring little effort or attention.

auxiliary verb a verb that precedes another verb to express time, mood, or voice; includes verbs such as **has, is,** and **will.**

ballad a narrative poem, composed of short verses to be sung or recited, usually containing elements of drama and often tragic in tone.

base word a word to which affixes may be added to create related words.

blank verse unrhymed verse, especially unrhymed iambic pentameter.

blend the joining of the sounds of two or more letters with little change in those sounds, for example, /spr/ in **spring;** also **consonant blend** or **consonant cluster.**

blending combining the sounds represented by letters or spellings to sound out or pronounce a word; contrast with **oral blending.**

breve the symbol placed above a vowel to indicate that it is a short vowel.

browse to skim through or look over in search of something of interest.

canon in literature, the body of major works that a culture considers important at a given time.

case a grammatical category that indicates the syntactic/semantic role of a noun phrase in a sentence.

cause-effect relationship a stated or implied association between an outcome and the conditions that brought it about; also the comprehension skill associated with recognizing this type of relationship as an organizing principle in text.

chapter book a book long enough to be divided into chapters, but not long or complex enough to be considered a novel.

characterization the way in which an author presents a character in a story, including describing words, actions, thoughts, and impressions of that character.

choral reading oral group reading to develop oral fluency by modeling.

cinquain a stanza of five lines, specifically one that has successive lines of two, four, six, eight, and two syllables.

cipher a system for writing in code.

clarifying a comprehension strategy in which the reader rereads text, uses a dictionary, uses decoding skills, or uses context clues to comprehend something that is unclear.

clause a group of words with a subject and a predicate used to form a part of or a whole sentence, a dependent clause modifies an independent clause, which can stand alone as a complete sentence.

collaborative learning learning by working together in small groups.

command a sentence that asks for action and usually ends with a period.

common noun in contrast to **proper noun,** a noun that denotes a class rather than a unique or specific thing such as **girl** versus **Susan.**

comprehension the understanding of what is written or said.

comprehension skill a skill that aids in understanding text, including identifying **author's purpose**, **comprehending cause-and-effect relationships, comparing and contrasting** items and events, **drawing conclusions,** distinguishing **fact from opinion,** identifying **main ideas,** making **inferences,** distinguishing **reality from fantasy,** and understanding **sequence.**

comprehension strategy a sequence of steps for monitoring and understanding text, includes asking questions, clarifying, making connections, predicting, summarizing, and visualizing.

conjugation the complete set of all possible inflected forms of a verb.

conjunction a part of speech used to connect words, phrases, clauses, or sentences, including the words **and, but,** and **or.**

consonant a speech sound, and the alphabet letter that represents that sound, made by partial or complete closure of part of the vocal tract, which obstructs air flow and causes audible friction.

context clue information from the immediate and surrounding text that helps identify a word.

contraction a short version of a written or spoken expression in which letters are omitted, for example, **can't.**

convention an accepted practice in spoken or written language, usually referring to spelling, mechanics, or grammar rules.

cooperative learning a classroom organization that allows students to work together to achieve their individual goals. Related term is **collaboration.**

creative writing prose and poetic forms of writing that express the writer's thoughts and feelings imaginatively.

cueing system any of the various sources of information that help identify an unrecognizable word in reading, including phonetic, semantic, and syntactical information.

cumulative tale a story, such as "The Gingerbread Man," in which details are repeated until the climax.

dangling modifier usually a participle that because of its placement in a sentence modifies the wrong object.

decodable text text materials controlled to include a majority of words whose sound/spelling relationships are known by the reader.

decode to analyze spoken or graphic symbols for meaning.

diacritical mark a mark, such as a breve or macron, added to a letter or graphic character to indicate a specific pronunciation.

dialect a regional variety of a particular language with phonological, grammatical, and lexical patterns that distinguishes it from other varieties.

dialogue a piece of writing written as conversation, usually punctuated by quotation marks.

digraph two letters that represent one speech sound, for example, /sh/ or /ch/.

diphthong a vowel sound produced when the tongue glides from one vowel sound toward another in the same syllable, for example, /oi/ or /ou/.

direct object the person or thing that receives the action of a verb in a sentence, for example, the word **cake** in this sentence: **Madeline baked a cake.**

drafting the process of writing ideas in rough form to record them.

drama a story in the form of a play, written to be performed.

edit in the writing process, to revise or correct a manuscript. Often this is part of the final step in the process with a focus on correcting grammar, spelling, and mechanics rather than content, structure, and organization.

emergent literacy the development of the association of meaning and print that continues until a child reaches the stage of conventional reading and writing.

emergent reading a child's early interaction with books and print before the ability to decode text.

encode to change a message into symbols, for example, to change speech into writing.

epic a long narrative poem, usually about a hero.

exclamatory sentence a sentence that shows strong emotion and ends with an exclamation point.

expository writing or **exposition** a composition in writing that explains an event or process.

fable a short tale that teaches a moral.

fantasy a highly imaginative story about characters, places, and events that cannot exist.

fiction imaginative narrative designed to entertain rather than to explain, persuade, or describe.

figure of speech the expressive, nonliteral use of language usually through metaphor, simile, or personification.

fluency freedom from word-identification problems that hinder comprehension in reading. Fluency involves rate, accuracy, and expression.

folktale a narrative form of genre such as an epic, myth, or fable that is well-known through repeated storytellings.

foreshadowing giving clues to upcoming events in a story.

free verse verse with irregular metrical pattern.

freewriting writing that is not limited in form, style, content, or purpose; designed to encourage students to write.

genre a classification of literary works, including tragedy, comedy, novel, essay, short story, mystery, realistic fiction, and poetry.

grammar the study of the classes of words, their inflections, and their functions and relations in sentences; includes phonological, morphological, syntactic, and semantic descriptions of a language.

grapheme a written or printed representation of a phoneme, such as **c** for /k/.

guided reading reading instruction in which the teacher provides the structure and purpose for reading and responding to the material read.

handing off a method of turning over to students the primary responsibility for controlling discussion.

indirect object in a sentence, the person or thing to or for whom an action is done, for example, the word **dog** in this sentence: **Madeline gave the dog a treat.**

inference a conclusion based on facts, data, or evidence.

infinitive the base form of a verb, usually with the infinitive marker, for example, **to go.**

inflectional ending an ending that expresses a plural or possessive form of a noun, the tense of a verb, or the comparative or superlative form of an adjective or adverb.

interrogative word a word that marks a clause or sentence as a question, including **interrogative pronouns who, what, which, where.**

intervention a strategy or program designed to supplement or substitute instruction, especially for those students who fall behind.

invented spelling the result of an attempt to spell a word based on using the sounds in the letter names to determine the sound the letter names. Gradually sounds are connected to letters, which leads to conventional spelling..

irony a figure of speech in which the literal meaning of the words is the opposite of their intended meaning.

journal a written record of daily events or responses.

juvenile book a book written for children or adolescents.

legend a traditional tale handed down from generation to generation.

leitmotif a repeated expression, event, or idea used to unify a work of art such as writing.

letter one of a set of graphic symbols that forms an alphabet and is used alone or in combination to represent a phoneme, also **grapheme.**

linguistics the study of the nature and structure of language and communication.

literary elements the elements of a story such as **setting, plot,** and **characterization** that create the structure of a narrative.

macron a diacritical mark placed above a vowel to indicate a long vowel sound.

main idea the central thought or chief topic of a passage.

making connections a reading strategy used to connect information being read to one's own experiences to other reading materials or to one's knowledge of the world. Making connections fosters engagement, while reading helps the reader make sense of the text and connect information.

mechanics the conventions of capitalization and punctuation.

metacognition awareness and knowledge of one's mental processes or thinking about what one is thinking about.

metaphor a figure of speech in which a comparison is implied but not stated; for example, **She is a jewel.**

miscue a deviation from text during oral reading in an attempt to make sense of the text.

modeling an instructional technique in which the teacher makes public the thinking needed to use critical reading and writing behaviors.

mood the literary element that conveys the emotional atmosphere of a story.

morpheme a meaningful linguistic unit that cannot be divided into smaller units, for example, **word**; **a bound morpheme** is a morpheme that cannot stand alone as an independent word, for example, the prefix **re-**; a **free morpheme** can stand alone, for example, **dog.**

myth a story designed to explain the mysteries of life.

narrative writing or **narration** a composition in writing that tells a story or gives an account of an event.

nonfiction prose designed to explain, argue, or describe rather than to entertain with a factual emphasis; includes biography and autobiography.

noun a part of speech that denotes persons, places, things, qualities, or acts.

novel an extended fictional prose narration.

onomatopoeia the use of a word whose sound suggests its meaning, for example, **purr.**

oral blending the ability to fuse discrete phonemes into recognizable words; oral blending puts sounds together to make a word, **see also segmentation.**

orthography correct or standardized spelling according to established usage in a language.

oxymoron a figure of speech in which contrasting or contradictory words are brought together for emphasis.

paragraph a subdivision of a written composition that consists of one or more sentences, deals with one point, or gives the words of one speaker, usually beginning with an indented line.

participle a verb form used as an adjective, for example, **the skating party.**

personification a figure of speech in which animals, ideas, or things take on human characteristics.

persuasive writing a composition intended to persuade the reader to adopt the writer's point of view.

phoneme the smallest sound unit of speech, for example, the /k/ in **book.**

phonemic awareness the ability to recognize that spoken words are made of discrete sounds and that those sounds can be manipulated.

phonetic spelling the respelling of entry words in a dictionary according to a pronunciation key.

phonetics the study of speech sounds.

phonics a way of teaching reading that addresses sound/symbol relationships, especially in beginning instruction.

phonogram a letter or symbol that represents a phonetic sound.

phonological awareness the ability to attend to the sound structure of language; includes sentence, word, syllable rhyme and phonological awareness.

plot the literary element that provides the structure of the action of a story, which may include rising action, climax, and falling action leading to a resolution or denouement.

plural a grammatical form of a word that refers to more than one in number; an irregular plural is one that does not follow normal patterns for inflectional endings.

poetic license the liberty taken by writers to ignore conventions.

poetry a metrical form of composition in which language is chosen and arranged to create a powerful response through meaning, sound, or rhythm.

possessive showing ownership either through the use of an adjective, an adjectival pronoun, or the possessive form of a noun.

predicate the part of the sentence that expresses something about the subject and includes the verb phrase; a **complete predicate** includes the principal verb in a sentence and all its modifiers or subordinate parts.

predicting a comprehension strategy in which the reader attempts to anticpate what will happen, using clues from the text and prior knowledge, and then confirms predictions as the text is read.

prefix an affix attached before a base word that changes the meaning of the word.

preposition a part of speech in the class of function words such as **of, on,** and **at** that precede noun phrases to create prepositional phrases.

prewriting the planning stage of the writing process in which the writer formulates ideas, gathers information, and considers ways to organize them.

print awareness in emergent literacy, a child's growing recognition of conventions and characteristics of written language, including reading from left to right and from top to bottom in English and that words are separated by spaces.

pronoun a part of speech used as a substitute for a noun or noun phrase.

proofreading the act of reading with the intent to correct, clarify, or improve text.

pseudonym an assumed name used by an author; a pen name or nom de plume.

publishing the process of preparing written material for presentation.

punctuation graphic marks such as comma, period, quotation marks, and brackets used to clarify meaning and to give speech characteristics to written language.

question an interrogative sentence that asks a question and ends with a question mark.

realistic fiction a story that attempts to portray characters and events as they actually are.

rebus a picture or symbol that suggests a word or syllable.

revise in the writing process, to change or correct a manuscript to make its message more clear.

rhyme identical or very similar recurring final sounds in words, often at the ends of lines of poetry.

rime a vowel and any following consonants of a syllable.

segmentation the ability to break words into individual sounds; **see also oral blending.**

semantic mapping a graphic display of a group of words that are meaningfully related to support vocabulary instruction.

semantics the study of meaning in language, including the meanings of words, phrases, sentences, and texts.

sentence a grammatical unit that expresses a statement, question, or command; a **simple sentence** is a sentence with one subject and one predicate; a **compound sentence** is a sentence with two or more independent clauses usually separated by a comma and conjunction, but no dependent clause; a **complex sentence** is a sentence with one independent and one or more dependent clauses.

sentence combining a teaching technique in which complex sentence chunks and paragraphs are built from basic sentences.

sentence lifting the process of using sentences from children's writing to illustrate what is wrong or right to develop children's editing and proofreading skills.

sequence the order of elements or events.

setting the literary element that includes the time, place, and physical and psychological background in which a story takes place.

sight word a word that is taught to be read as a whole word, usually words that are phonetically irregular.

simile a figure of speech in which a comparison of two things that are unlike is directly stated, usually with the words **like** or **as**; for example, **She is like a jewel.**

spelling the process of representing language by means of a writing system.

statement a sentence that tells something and ends with a period.

study skills a general term for the techniques and strategies that help readers comprehend text with the intent to remember; includes following directions, organizing, locating, and using graphic aids.

style the characteristics of a work that reflect the author's particular way of writing.

subject the main topic of a sentence to which a predicate refers, including the principal noun; a **complete subject** includes the principal noun in a sentence and all its modifiers.

suffix an affix attached at the end of a base word that changes the meaning of the word.

summarizing a comprehension strategy in which the reader constructs a brief statement that contains the essential ideas of a passage.

syllable a minimal unit of sequential speech sounds comprised of a vowel sound or a vowel-sound combination.

symbolism the use of one thing to represent something else to represent an idea in a concrete way.

synonym a word that means the same as another word.

syntax the grammatical pattern or structure of word order in sentences, clauses, and phrases.

tense the way in which verbs indicate past, present, and future time of action.

text structure the various patterns of ideas that are built into the organization of a written work.

theme a major idea or proposition that provides an organizing concept through which, by study, students gain depth of understanding.

topic sentence a sentence intended to express the main idea of a paragraph or passage.

tragedy a literary work, often a play, in which the main character suffers conflicts and which presents a serious theme and has an unfortunate ending.

usage the way in which a native language or dialect is used by the members of the community.

verb a word that expresses an action or state that occurs in a predicate of a sentence; an irregular verb is a verb that does not follow normal patterns of inflectional endings that reflect past, present, or future verb tense.

visualizing a comprehension strategy in which the reader constructs a mental picture of a character, setting, or process.

vowel a voiced speech sound and the alphabet letter that represents that sound, made without stoppage or friction of the air flow as it passes through the vocal tract.

vowel digraph a spelling pattern in which two or more letters represent a single vowel sound.

word calling proficiency in decoding with little or no attention to word meaning.

writing also **composition** the process or result of organizing ideas in writing to form a clear message; includes persuasive, expository, narrative, and descriptive forms.

writing process the many aspects of the complex act of producing a piece of writing, including prewriting, drafting, revising, proofreading, and publishing.

Alphabet Song

Purpose

To teach the names of the letters in their proper order

About the Song

There are several versions of the "Alphabet Song." Students might never have heard the version used in this program, and they might insist that the version they already know is the "correct" one. You can explain that this is the classroom version and the one you prefer. Have them listen as you play or sing it.

In some versions, the alphabet letters are sung faster and with different pauses. The last two lines of the song also might differ. In this version, all letters except *W* are sung slowly. The first rhyme of the song is sacrificed, but each letter is pronounced distinctly and the song is more instructive for students than the traditional version.

Instruction

After listening to this version of the song two or three times, most of the students should be able to join in and sing along. The best way to teach this version of the "Alphabet Song" (especially if students already know the more traditional version) is to teach it in steps: the first phrase, *A* to *G;* then the second phrase, *H* through *N;* then the next two phrases, *O* through *T;* then two more phrases, *U* through *Z;* and finally the last two rhyming phrases.

If the ***Sound/Spelling Cards*** are on the wall, help students make the connection between the names for the letters and their written symbols by touching each letter as you and the students sing the song. You or the students can then lead the song, touching each letter on the chart as it is sung. (Using lowercase letters on the chart will help students learn to recognize these.)

a b c d e f g
h i j k l m n
o p q
r s t
u v w
x y z

Alphabet Rap

In addition to the traditional "Alphabet Song," students might enjoy singing this "Alphabet Rap." You might want to point to the letters on the ***Sound/Spelling Cards*** as you recite their names, or copy the words onto a chart.

This ***A B C***
is just for me,
And ***D E F***
is next you see,
G H I J
comes after that,
K L M N
I've got down pat.
O P Q R
S T U V
are all that's left,
'cept ***W***
X Y and ***Z.***

Sing Your Way to ____________ Game

The Sing Your Way to ______ Game provides students with a way of finding the name of any letter they might have forgotten. You can use the ***Lion Puppet*** to help introduce this activity. Use the ***Lion Puppet*** at your discretion for later lessons.

- Have the ***Lion Puppet*** point to the letter of the alphabet for the lesson you are teaching. Do not have the puppet name the letter. Ask students to sing the "Alphabet Song" with you until you reach this letter, and then have them stop. When the class stops, have the ***Lion Puppet*** ask, "What is the letter?"
- Have the ***Lion Puppet*** point to other letters that have already been introduced. Ask students to sing the "Alphabet Song" with you to the letter indicated and then to stop. Then have the puppet ask for the letter name.
- Point to the letter of the alphabet for the lesson you are teaching, but do not name it. Ask a student to sing his or her way to the letter and then to stop. Students should sing the "Alphabet Song," pointing to each letter and stopping as he or she comes to the letter you have indicated.
- Ask other students to sing their way to other letters that have already been introduced. Remind them that they can sing their way to any letter of the alphabet by stopping when they reach the name of that letter.

Apples and Bananas

Purpose

To help students listen for and repeat the long-vowel sounds

About the Song

"Apples and Bananas" is a vowel-replacement song. It requires students to consciously control vowel sounds in words while leaving the consonants unchanged.

Instruction

The song "Apples and Bananas" is a repeated couplet, as you see in the first verse. In the second verse, some vowels are replaced with long *a:*

I like to ate, ate, ate

ayples and baynaynays.

I like to ate, ate, ate

ayples and baynaynays.

In the next verse, the same vowels are replaced with long *e:*

I like to eat, eat, eat

eeples and beeneenees.

I like to eat, eat, eat

eeples and beeneenees.

Continue in the same way with the remaining verses, replacing the vowel each time with long *i*, long *o*, and finally, long *u*.

If you sing slowly, it will be easy for students to make these vowel replacements. As you start to sing the new verse yourself, students will most likely join right in. You may find that it is helpful to announce the new verse; for example, "And now /ō/!"

Later, you may want to let volunteers lead the class. Write the letters *a, e, i, o,* and *u* on the board, and let the leader touch any letter at random to tell students how to sing the next verse.

Did You Ever?

Purpose

To provide an opportunity for students to have fun with rhyming words and to make up rhyming verses of their own

Instruction

Write the words for the song on the board, or provide a song sheet for each student. Explain that the lines enclosed within quotation marks can change with each verse they sing. Then list those two-line changes on the board, or include them on the song sheet.

After learning the song, students may enjoy making up additional verses. They probably should not do so the first time they sing the song.

In further verses, the lines within quotation marks change. Some suggested variations follow:

"Did you ever see a goose
Riding a moose?"

"Did you ever see a cat
Wearing a hat?"

"Did you ever see a duck
Driving a truck?"

"Did you ever see a bear
Curling her hair?"

When students are familiar with the song and the rhyme pattern of the changing lines, suggest that they make up their own rhyming lines. You might first generate a list of animals that have not yet appeared in the verses. Students may suggest pig, bird, snake, and so on. Then ask students to think of words that rhyme with the animal's name, such as *pig* and *wig*. Finally, they can make up a verse, such as "Did you ever see a pig/Wearing a wig?"

Scrambled Sentences

Purpose

To provide practice constructing sentences

Materials

- index cards
- business-sized envelopes

Preparing Materials

Using sentences that students have blended in recent lessons, write each word of each sentence on a separate index card. Include the capital letter on the first word and the period on the last word. Place the words for one sentence in an envelope. Prepare several envelopes in this way. You may want to write the complete sentence on the inside of the envelope flap for students to use to check their work.

How to Play the Game

A student arranges the words in an envelope to make a sensible sentence. This game can be an individual activity, or small groups of students can do the activity as a game, if they wish, competing to see who can unscramble his or her sentence the fastest. Have players write the sentence they make and then read the sentence to their classmates.

Variations

The following are variations of the Scrambled Sentences game.

- Use sentences from selections students have read, such as ones from the ***Decodables, First Reader, Leveled Readers,*** or ***Student Readers.***
- Students may work in groups or alone to create their own scrambled sentences. Provide index cards on which they can write words, and envelopes in which they can place the cards. Remind them to use capital letters and periods in their sentences and to write the complete sentence on the inside flap of each envelope.

Spelling Activities

Purpose
To reinforce phonics skills through spelling

Picture Spelling Game
Materials

- index cards or other small blank cards
- magazines, stickers, and other picture sources
- glue or paste
- marking pens

Preparing Materials
On one side of each index card, print an appropriate spelling word. On the other side of the card, draw or paste a picture as a clue to the word. Make as many cards as you feel are appropriate. Add to the set of cards as students learn new words.

How to Play the Game
The Picture Spelling game can be played alone or with a partner. The picture-word cards are stacked in a pile or spread out with the pictures facing up. One player chooses a picture card, prints the word that names the picture on a blank sheet of paper, and then checks the spelling by turning the card over. If the game is played with a partner, one player can show a picture to a partner and have him or her spell the word aloud.

Spelling Challenge
How to Play the Game

Divide the class into teams of three or four students each. Explain that you will write a spelling of a sound on the board. Give the teams one minute to think of words that contain that spelling. When the time is up, call on each team in turn to say and to spell its words. Write the words on the board as each is spelled, and award a point for each correct spelling. The team with the most points wins the game. (Remind the teams to whisper as they brainstorm words so that the other teams won't hear their words.)

Compound Word Puzzles
Materials

- posterboard or heavy construction paper
- scissors
- marking pen
- a large envelope

Preparing Materials
From poster board or heavy construction paper, cut 2-by-6-inch strips. Print a compound word on each strip, leaving some space between the two parts of each word. You might begin with the words listed below and then add or replace the compound word cards as the year goes by. Cut each strip in half between the word parts, using a different curved or zigzag line for each strip (see illustration). Store all of the puzzle pieces in an envelope.

nearby	**nighttime**	**cornbread**
seaweed	**playground**	**hairbrush**
firefly	**notebook**	**haircut**
bathtub	**mailbox**	**footprint**

How to Play the Game
A student spills the puzzle pieces onto a work area, turns them faceup, and reads each card. When the student thinks that two words can form a compound word, he or she tries to fit the puzzle pieces together. If the two pieces fit together exactly, a correct compound word is formed.

Yoo-oo Owls

Materials

- construction paper
- marking pens

Preparing Materials

This can be an individual or a whole-class activity. For individual work, prepare a blackline master for each student. For a whole-class activity, prepare a bulletin board display. On a bulletin board or on a blackline master, draw the outlines of two large trees. On the trunk of one tree, draw an owl for /o͞o/. Explain to students that the owl hoots by saying /o͞o/, /o͞o/, /o͞o/. On the trunk of the other tree, draw a big red letter *U*, like the one on the ***Sound/Spelling Card*** for /ū/ (see illustration).

How to Play the Game

Ask students to make leaves for each tree. For the blackline master, have students draw leaves on each tree and print an /o͞o/ word or a /ū/ word, as appropriate, on each leaf. For the bulletin board display, you might want to have a supply of leaf shapes cut from construction paper. Have students print an /o͞o/ word or a /ū/ word on each leaf and then place it on the appropriate tree on the bulletin board.

Puzzle Word Game

Materials

Alphabet Letter Cards

How to Play the Game

The Puzzle Word game may be an individual, a partner, or a group activity. Choose a word from a ***Big Book, First Reader,*** or ***Student Reader*** selection that students have read or listened to recently—for example, *trembling* from "My Brother Is Afraid of Just about Everything." (The word must be one with no double letters, because students will be using their ***Alphabet Letter Cards*** to unscramble the word.) On the board, write the letters of the word *trembling* in mixed-up order—for example *b e g i l m n r t*. Have students take out their ***Alphabet Letter Cards*** for those nine letters and place them on the work area in front of them. They should use those nine ***Alphabet Letter Cards,*** moving them around to spell as many words as they can. The words may be of varying lengths, and the letters may be reused to spell different words. However, the letters may not be used more than once in a single word. For example, students may spell the words *big, rig, bin, grin*, and *trim*, but not the word *meet*. Remind students that they can refer to the ***Sound/Spelling Cards*** to help them spell words. Have them write down each new word they spell. Tell students that all of the letters will make a special word from the selection "My Brother Is Afraid of Just about Everything." They may look through the story if they wish.

At the end of the time limit you set, which can be as long as all day or as short as ten minutes, have students share their lists of words.

Introduction to Sound/Spellings

Lesson	Letters and Sound/Spelling(s)	High-Frequency Words Introduced	Core Decodables	Practice Decodables
Getting Started				
Day 1	*Aa, Bb*			
Day 2	*Cc, Dd*			
Day 3	*Ee, Ff, Gg*	see, the	***Pre-Decodable*** 1 *See!*	***Pre-Decodable*** 1 *See the Backpack*
Day 4	*Hh, Ii, Jj*			
Day 5	*Kk, Ll, Mm*	is, up	***Pre-Decodable*** 2 *Up*	***Pre-Decodable*** 2 *The Flag*
Day 6	*Nn, Oo, Pp*			
Day 7	*Qq, Rr, Ss*	have, I	***Pre-Decodable*** 3 *I Have*	***Pre-Decodable*** 3 *Up! Up! Up!*
Day 8	*Tt, Uu, Vv*			
Day 9	*Ww, Xx, Yy, Zz*	a, there	***Pre-Decodable*** 4 *There Is*	***Pre-Decodable*** 4 *Up the Hill*
Day 10	*Review Aa–Zz*			
Unit 1				
Lesson 1	/s/ spelled *s*			
Lesson 2	/m/ spelled *m*	can, on	***Pre-Decodable*** 5 *I Can See*	***Pre-Decodable*** 5 *See the Bike*
Lesson 3	/a/ spelled *a*	am	***Decodable*** 6 *Sam, Sam, Sam*	***Decodable*** 6 *Sam on the Hill*
Lesson 4	/t/ spelled *t, tt*	and	***Decodable*** 7 *Matt and Sam*	***Decodable*** 7 *Matt?*
Lesson 5	Review		***Decodable*** 8 *On a Mat*	***Decodable*** 8 *A Mat*
Lesson 6	/d/ spelled *d*		***Decodable*** 9 *Dad Sat*	***Decodable*** 9 *Tad*
Lesson 7	/n/ spelled *n*		***Decodable*** 10 *Ants*	***Decodable*** 10 *A Sad Ant*
Lesson 8	/i/ spelled *i*	did, in, it	***Decodable*** 11 *Sit*	***Decodable*** 11 *Sis and Sid*
Lesson 9	/h/ spelled *h_*	had, him, said	***Decodable*** 12 *A Hint*	***Decodable*** 12 *A Mitt*
Lesson 10	Review		***Decodable*** 13 *Mints*	
Lesson 11	/p/ spelled *p*		***Decodable*** 14 *Pat's Map*	***Decodable*** 13 *Pam and Hap*
Lesson 12	/l/ spelled *l, ll*		***Decodable*** 15 *Lin and Hal*	***Decodable*** 14 *A Plant*
Lesson 13	/o/ spelled *o*	has	***Decodable*** 16 *A Spot*	***Decodable*** 15 *Tom and Pop*
Lesson 14	/b/ spelled *b*	at	***Decodable*** 17 *Bob at Bat*	***Decodable*** 16 *Bob's Bib*
Lesson 15	Review		***Decodable*** 18 *Bill*	

Lesson	Sound/Spelling(s)	High-Frequency Words Introduced	Core Decodables	Practice Decodables
Unit 2				
Lesson 1	/k/ spelled *c* /aw/ spelled *al, all*	call	***Decodable*** 19 *Nat's Cap* ***Decodable*** 20 *At the Mall*	***Decodable*** 17 *A Cab Man* ***Decodable*** 18 *Tall Dot*
Lesson 2	/k/ spelled *k,* ■*ck*		***Decodable*** 21 *Picnic*	***Decodable*** 19 *Kip Can Spin*
Lesson 3	/r/ spelled *r*		***Decodable*** 22 *Rick and Rob*	***Decodable*** 20 *A Rabbit Ran*
Lesson 4	/f/ spelled *f, ff* /s/ spelled *ss*	look was, what	***Decodable*** 23 *Bobcat* ***Decodable*** 24 *Pat's Class Trip*	***Decodable*** 21 *Traffic* ***Decodable*** 22 *A Blimp Can Pass*
Lesson 5	Review		***Decodable*** 25 *Fran and Kip*	
Lesson 6	/g/ spelled *g*	big, got	***Decodable*** 26 *Rag Bits*	***Decodable*** 23 *A Big Rig*
Lesson 7	/j/ spelled *j,* ■*dge*	to	***Decodable*** 27 *Jack's Job*	***Decodable*** 24 *Jill*
Lesson 8	/u/ spelled *u*		***Decodable*** 28 *Plum Pond*	***Decodable*** 25 *Ron on the Run*
Lesson 9	/z/ spelled *z, zz* /z/ spelled *_s*	ask, of as, he	***Decodable*** 29 *Buzz and Zip* ***Decodable*** 30 *Hills of Fuzz*	***Decodable*** 26 *Zap! Zap!* ***Decodable*** 27 *A Bobcat and a Rabbit*
Lesson 10	Review	his, just	***Decodable*** 31 *Rock and Jazz*	
Lesson 11	/ks/ spelled ■*x*		***Decodable*** 32 *Max and Sam*	***Decodable*** 28 *A Fox and His Box*
Lesson 12	/e/ spelled *e*	down, if, its, red	***Decodable*** 33 *A Red Fox*	***Decodable*** 29 *Blend In*
Lesson 13	*-ed* ending: /ed/, /d/ *-ed* ending: /t/	help	***Decodable*** 34 *The Glass* ***Decodable*** 35 *Best Mom*	***Decodable*** 30 *Spilled Milk* ***Decodable*** 31 *Fred and Jen Jumped*
Lesson 14	/e/ spelled *_ea_*	then	***Decodable*** 36 *Ted's List*	***Decodable*** 32 *Bread and Milk*
Lesson 15	Review	six	***Decodable*** 37 *Fix a Truck*	
Unit 3				
Lesson 1	/sh/ spelled *sh*	get	***Decodable*** 38 *Trish's Ship*	***Decodable*** 33 *A Flash*
Lesson 2	/th/ spelled *th*	that, this	***Decodable*** 39 *Beth Gets a Snack*	***Decodable*** 34 *Thick Fog*
Lesson 3	/ch/ spelled *ch,* ■*tch*		***Decodable*** 40 *Mitch on a Ranch*	***Decodable*** 35 *Chet*
Lesson 4	/or/ spelled *or, ore*	for, out	***Decodable*** 41 *At a Port*	***Decodable*** 36 *Chores or Sports*
Lesson 5	Review	jump	***Decodable*** 42 *Sports Camp*	
Lesson 6	/ar/ spelled *ar*	little	***Decodable*** 43 *In a Jar*	***Decodable*** 37 *Clark's Horn*
Lesson 7	/m/ spelled *_mb*		***Decodable*** 44 *A Lamb on a Limb*	***Decodable*** 38 *A Numb Thumb*
Lesson 8	/w/ spelled *w_* /hw/ spelled *wh_*	went, will when	***Decodable*** 45 *Wes Gets Wet* ***Decodable*** 46 *The Whiz*	***Decodable*** 39 *Wes Wags* ***Decodable*** 40 *Whip the Cat*
Lesson 9	/er/ spelled *er, ir* /er/ spelled *ur*	girl, her with	***Decodable*** 47 *Bird Shirts* ***Decodable*** 48 *A Blur with Fur*	***Decodable*** 41 *Bert's Shirt* ***Decodable*** 42 *Curt the Surfer*
Lesson 10	Review		***Decodable*** 49 *Burns Farm*	
Lesson 11	Schwa	an, they	***Decodable*** 50 *The Children Get a Rabbit*	***Decodable*** 43 *Animal in the Closet*
Lesson 12	Review schwa		***Decodable*** 51 *Pump and Pedal*	***Decodable*** 44 *Animal Prints*
Lesson 13	/ng/ spelled ■*ng* /nk/ spelled ■*nk*	but, do	***Decodable*** 52 *Big Bing* ***Decodable*** 53 *In the Tank*	***Decodable*** 45 *Ding Dong* ***Decodable*** 46 *Frank's Banks*
Lesson 14	/kw/ spelled *qu_*	she	***Decodable*** 54 *Quick Quin*	***Decodable*** 47 *It Will Not Quit*
Lesson 15	Review		***Decodable*** 55 *King Frank*	

Introduction to Sound/Spellings, continued

Lesson	Sound/Spelling(s)	High-Frequency Words Introduced	Core Decodables	Practice Decodables
Unit 4				
Lesson 1	/y/ spelled *y_* /v/ spelled *v*	yes all, were	**Decodable** 56 *Beth's Yak* **Decodable** 57 *Seven Pals*	**Decodable** 48 *Adopt a Yak* **Decodable** 49 *What's Next?*
Lesson 2	Syllable *-le*		**Decodable** 58 *Twinkle, Twinkle*	**Decodable** 50 *Purple*
Lesson 3	/ā/ spelled *a, a_e*		**Decodable** 59 *April's Bake Shop*	**Decodable** 51 *Late*
Lesson 4	Review /ā/ spelled *a, a_e*			
Lesson 5	Review		**Decodable** 60 *Tab*	
Lesson 6	/ī/ spelled *i, i_e*	ride, walk, we, well	**Decodable** 61 *A Mess*	**Decodable** 52 *Nine Little Flags*
Lesson 7	Review /ī/ spelled *i, i_e*			
Lesson 8	/s/ spelled *ce, ci_*	make, you	**Decodable** 62 *Grace and Vince*	**Decodable** 53 *At the Fitness Center*
Lesson 9	/j/ spelled *ge, gi_*	go, like	**Decodable** 63 *Ginger and Gem*	**Decodable** 54 *A Change*
Lesson 10	Review	after	**Decodable** 64 *Riding in Gem Park*	
Lesson 11	/ō/ spelled *o, o_e*	over	**Decodable** 65 *Frozen*	**Decodable** 55 *Smoke*
Lesson 12	Review /ō/ spelled *o, o_e*			
Lesson 13	/ū/ spelled *u, u_e*	them	**Decodable** 66 *Muse the Mule*	**Decodable** 56 *A Little Help*
Lesson 14	Review /ū/ spelled *u, u_e*			
Lesson 15	Review		**Decodable** 67 *A Better Mule*	
Unit 5				
Lesson 1	/ē/ spelled *e, e_e*	or	**Decodable** 68 *A Zebra*	**Decodable** 57 *Picnic Weather*
Lesson 2	Review /ē/ spelled *e, e_e*			
Lesson 3	/ē/ spelled *ee, ea*	two	**Decodable** 69 *Summer Heat*	**Decodable** 58 *East or West*
Lesson 4	Review /ē/ spelled *ee, ea*			
Lesson 5	Review	be, green, take	**Decodable** 70 *Green River*	
Lesson 6	/ē/ spelled *_y, _ie_*	every	**Decodable** 71 *A Party for Puppies*	**Decodable** 59 *Hot or Cold*
Lesson 7	Review /ē/ spelled *_y, _ie_*			
Lesson 8	/s/ spelled *cy*	could	**Decodable** 72 *A Fancy Jacket*	**Decodable** 60 *Tracy, Stacy, Marcy, and Tommy*
Lesson 9	Review /s/ spellings	boy, some	**Decodable** 73 *Skating*	**Decodable** 61 *Salt on Ice*
Lesson 10	Review	going, here	**Decodable** 74 *Marcy and Sally*	
Lesson 11	/ā/ spelled *ai_, _ay*	day, way	**Decodable** 75 *The Gray, Rainy Day*	**Decodable** 62 *Jay Stays on the Job*
Lesson 12	Review /ā/ spelled *ai_, _ay*			
Lesson 13	/ī/ spelled *_igh* /ī/ spelled *_ie, _y*	sleep don't, my, too	**Decodable** 76 *The Opossum at Night* **Decodable** 77 *Why, Bly?*	**Decodable** 63 *City Lights at Night* **Decodable** 64 *Trying Weather*
Lesson 14	Review /ī/ spelled *_igh, _ie, _y*			
Lesson 15	Review	came, me, right	**Decodable** 78 *Wait for Me*	

Lesson	Sound/Spelling(s)	High-Frequency Words Introduced	Core Decodables	Practice Decodables
Unit 6				
Lesson 1	/ō/ spelled *oa_, _ow*	no, their	***Decodable*** 79 *Crow and Goat*	***Decodable*** 65 *To the North Pole*
Lesson 2	Review /ō/ spelled *oa_, _ow*			
Lesson 3	/ū/ spelled *_ew, _ue*		***Decodable*** 80 *Rescue That Cat!*	***Decodable*** 66 *Eva to the Rescue*
Lesson 4	Review /ū/ spelled *_ew, _ue*			
Lesson 5	Review	away	***Decodable*** 81 *Eat at Joan's*	
Lesson 6	/o͞o/ spelled *oo*	saw	***Decodable*** 82 *A Cool Balloon*	***Decodable*** 67 *Jayce Helps*
Lesson 7	Review /o͞o/ spelled *oo*			
Lesson 8	/o͞o/ spelled *_ue, u*	blue, one	***Decodable*** 83 *A True Bird*	***Decodable*** 68 *Sue, Rudy, and the Truth*
Lesson 9	Review /o͞o/ spelled *oo, _ue,* and *u*			
Lesson 10	Review		***Decodable*** 84 *Ants: The True Story*	
Lesson 11	/o͞o/ spelled *_ew, u_e*	very	***Decodable*** 85 *A New Tune*	***Decodable*** 69 *June Flew*
Lesson 12	Review /o͞o/ spellings			
Lesson 13	/oo/ spelled *oo*	good, now	***Decodable*** 86 *A Good Ride*	***Decodable*** 70 *The Best Cook*
Lesson 14	Review /oo/ spelled *oo*			
Lesson 15	Review		***Decodable*** 87 *Mom's Book*	
Unit 7				
Lesson 1	/ow/ spelled *ow*	are, brown, how	***Decodable*** 88 *A Clown in Town*	***Decodable*** 71 *Maggy's Flower*
Lesson 2	/ow/ spelled *ou_*	about, around, long	***Decodable*** 89 *Max the Grouch*	***Decodable*** 72 *Lost and Found*
Lesson 3	Review /ow/ spelled *ow, ou_*			
Lesson 4	/n/ spelled *kn_*	know, want	***Decodable*** 90 *King Knox and His Knight*	***Decodable*** 73 *I Kept Trying*
Lesson 5	Review	by	***Decodable*** 91 *Foul Ball!*	
Lesson 6	/aw/ spelled *au_, aw*		***Decodable*** 92 *Paul's Sauce*	***Decodable*** 74 *Crows, Owls, and Hawks*
Lesson 7	Review /aw/ spelled *au_, aw*			
Lesson 8	/aw/ spelled *augh, ough*	into	***Decodable*** 93 *Mr. Daw Thought*	***Decodable*** 75 *Blossom Fishes*
Lesson 9	Review /aw/ spellings			
Lesson 10	Review	before, yellow	***Decodable*** 94 *At Dawn*	
Lesson 11	/oi/ spelled *oi, _oy*		***Decodable*** 95 *Roy and Royal*	***Decodable*** 76 *A Choice*
Lesson 12	Review /oi/ spelled *oi, _oy*			
Lesson 13	/r/ spelled *wr_*		***Decodable*** 96 *Little Wren's Surprise*	***Decodable*** 77 *Write Right*
Lesson 14	/f/ spelled *ph*		***Decodable*** 97 *The Phantom Frog*	***Decodable*** 78 *A Photo for Fred*
Lesson 15	Review	old	***Decodable*** 98 *A Hike*	
Lesson 16	/er/ spelled *ear*	any, from, water	***Decodable*** 99 *Earnest's Search*	***Decodable*** 79 *Digging to Learn*
Lesson 17	/ē/ spelled *ey*		***Decodable*** 100 *Dudley the Donkey*	***Decodable*** 80 *What?*
Lesson 18	Review /ē/ spelled *ey*			
Lesson 19	Review			
Lesson 20	Review	come	***Decodable*** 101 *Casey and Earl*	

Introduction to Sound/Spellings, continued

Lesson	Sound/Spelling(s)	High-Frequency Words Introduced	Core Decodables	Practice Decodables
Unit 8				
Lessons 1–5	Review /ā/ and /a/		***Decodable*** 102 *Garden in the Sky*	
Lessons 6–10	Review /ī/ and /i/	five, would	***Decodable*** 103 *Picking Flowers*	
Lessons 11–15	Review /ō/ and /o/		***Decodable*** 104 *A Farm Visit*	
Lessons 16–20	Review /ū/ and /u/		***Decodable*** 105 *Mr. Plant Expert*	
Lessons 21–25	Long-Vowel Review	pretty, your	***Decodable*** 106 *Weeds or Flowers*	
Unit 9				
Lessons 1–5	Review /ē/ and /e/	four, put	***Decodable*** 107 *A Family House*	
Lessons 6–10	Review Consonant Blends	where	***Decodable*** 108 *Gramps's Pals*	
Lessons 11–15	Review Consonant Digraphs		***Decodable*** 109 *Houses*	
Lessons 16–20	Review *R*-Controlled Vowels		***Decodable*** 110 *A Summer Home*	
Lessons 21–25	General Review		***Decodable*** 111 *The Every Kid Club*	
Unit 10				
Lessons 1–5	Review /oo/ and /o͞o/		***Decodable*** 112 *Brave Tony*	
Lessons 6–10	Review Diphthongs		***Decodable*** 113 *Camping Out*	
Lessons 11–15	Review Word Endings		***Decodable*** 114 *Andy Lee*	
Lessons 16–20	General Review		***Decodable*** 115 *How the Rabbit Caught the Tiger*	

High-Frequency Word List

High-Frequency Words Introduced in Kindergarten

a	down	it	there
all	for	little	they
am	girl	look	to
and	go	of	up
as	had	on	was
at	have	out	we
be	he	said	were
boy	her	see	what
but	him	she	when
can	his	some	with
could	I	that	you
did	in	the	
do	is	then	

High-Frequency Words Introduced in Grade 1

about	five	long	their
after	four	make	them
an	from	me	this
any	get	my	too
are	going	no	two
around	good	now	very
ask	got	old	walk
away	green	one	want
before	has	or	water
big	help	over	way
blue	here	pretty	well
brown	how	put	went
by	if	red	where
call	into	ride	will
came	its	right	would
come	jump	saw	yellow
day	just	six	yes
don't	know	sleep	your
every	like	take	

Sound/Spelling Card Stories

Card 1: /a/ Lamb

I'm Pam the Lamb, I am.
This is how I tell my Mommy where
I am: /a/ /a/ /a/ /a/ /a/.

I'm Pam the Lamb, I am.
This is how I tell my Daddy where
I am: /a/ /a/ /a/ /a/ /a/.

I'm Pam the Lamb, I am.
That young ram is my brother Sam.
This is how I tell my brother where
I am: /a/ /a/ /a/ /a/ /a/.

I'm Pam the Lamb; I'm happy where
I am.

Can you help me tell my family where
I am?
(Have the children respond.) /a/ /a/ /a/ /a/ /a/

Card 2: /b/ Ball

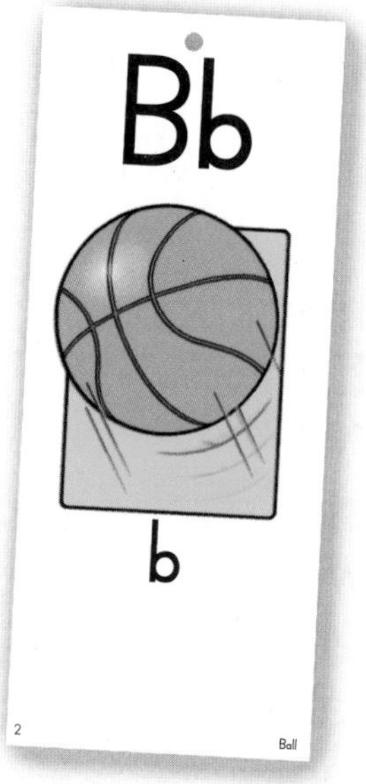

Bobby loved to bounce his basketball.
He bounced it all day long.
This is the sound the ball made:
/b/ /b/ /b/ /b/ /b/.

One day, while Bobby was bouncing
his basketball,
Bonnie came by on her bike.

Bonnie said, "Hi, Bobby. I have a little
bitty ball.
May I bounce my ball with you?"

Bobby said, "Sure!" and Bonnie
bounced her little bitty ball.
What sound do you think Bonnie's ball
made?
(Encourage a very soft reply.) /b/ /b/ /b/ /b/ /b/

Soon Betsy came by. "Hi, Bobby. Hi, Bonnie," she said.
"I have a great big beach ball. May I bounce my ball with you?"

Bobby and Bonnie said, "Sure!" and Betsy bounced her
big beach ball.
What sound do you think the beach ball made?
(Encourage a louder, slower reply.) /b/ /b/ /b/ /b/ /b/

(Designate three groups, one for each ball sound.)

Now when Bobby, Bonnie, and Betsy bounce their balls
together, this is the sound you hear:
(Have all three groups make their sounds in a chorus.)
/b/ /b/ /b/ /b/ /b/

Card 3: /k/ Camera

Carlos has a new camera. When he
takes pictures, his camera makes a
clicking sound like this:
/k/ /k/ /k/ /k/ /k/.

In the garden, Carlos takes pictures of
caterpillars crawling on cabbage:
/k/ /k/ /k/ /k/ /k/.

At the zoo, Carlos takes pictures of a
camel, a duck, and a kangaroo:
/k/ /k/ /k/.

In the park, Carlos takes pictures of his
cousin flying a kite: /k/ /k/ /k/ /k/ /k/.
In his room, Carlos takes pictures of his
cute kitten, Cozy: /k/ /k/ /k/ /k/ /k/.

Can you help Carlos take pictures with his camera?
(Have the children join in.) /k/ /k/ /k/ /k/ /k/ /k/ /k/

Card 4: /d/ Dinosaur

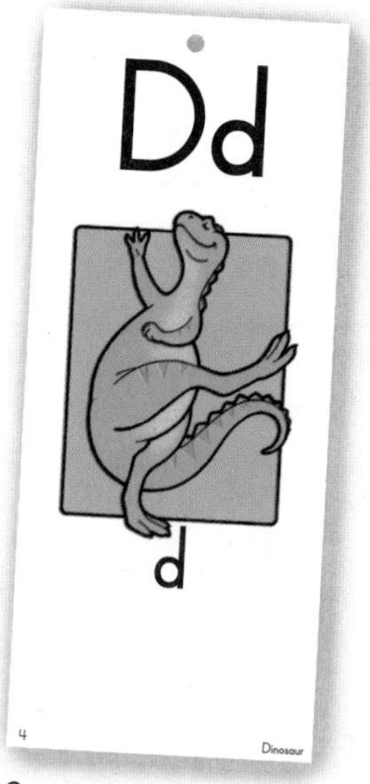

Dinah the Dinosaur loves to dance.
She dances whenever she gets the chance.
Whenever that dinosaur dips and whirls,
this is the sound of her dancing twirls:
/d/ /d/ /d/ /d/ /d/ /d/!

Dinah the Dinosaur dances all day.
From dawn to dark, she dances away.
And when Dinah dances, her dinosaur feet
make a thundering, thudding, extremely
loud beat:
(loudly, with an exaggerated rhythm)
/d/ /d/ /d/ /d/ /d/ /d/!

Now if you were a dinosaur just like Dinah,
you would certainly dance just as finely as she.
And if you were a Dino, and you had a chance,
what sound would your feet make when you did a dance?
(Have the children join in.) /d/ /d/ /d/ /d/ /d/ /d/

Card 5: /e/ Hen

Jem's pet hen likes to peck, peck, peck.
She pecks at a speck on the new red deck.
This is how her pecking sounds:
/e/ /e/ /e/ /e/ /e/.

Jem's pet hen pecks at corn in her pen.
She pecks ten kernels, then pecks again.
This is how her pecking sounds:
/e/ /e/ /e/ /e/ /e/.

Jem's hen pecks at a cracked egg shell.
She's helping a chick get out, alive and well.
This is how her pecking sounds:
/e/ /e/ /e/ /e/ /e/.

Can you help Jem's hen peck?
(Have children say:) /e/ /e/ /e/ /e/ /e/.

Card 6: /f/ Fan

/f/ /f/ /f/ /f/ /f/—What's that funny sound?
It's Franny the Fan going round and round,
and this is the sound that old fan makes:
/f/ /f/ /f/ /f/ /f/.

When it gets too hot, you see,
Franny cools the family: /f/ /f/ /f/ /f/ /f/ /f/.
She fans Father's face
and Foxy's fur
and Felicity's feet.
Hear the Fan whir: /f/ /f/ /f/ /f/ /f/ /f/.

Can you make Franny the Fan go fast?
(Have the children say quickly:)
/f/ /f/ /f/ /f/ /f/.
Faster? /f/ /f/ /f/ /f/ /f/
Fastest? /f/ /f/ /f/ /f/ /f/

Card 7: /g/ Gopher

Gary's a gopher.
He loves to gulp down food.
/g/ /g/ /g/ /g/ /g/, gulps the gopher.

Gary the Gopher gulps down grass
because it tastes so good.
/g/ /g/ /g/ /g/ /g/, gulps the gopher.

Gary the Gopher gulps down grapes—
gobs and gobs of grapes.
/g/ /g/ /g/ /g/ /g/, gulps the gopher.

Gary the Gopher gobbles green beans
and says once more,
/g/ /g/ /g/ /g/ /g/. He's such a hungry gopher!

Gary the Gopher gobbles in the garden
until everything is gone.

What sound does Gary the Gopher make?
(Ask the children to join in.) /g/ /g/ /g/ /g/ /g/

Card 8: /h/ Hound

Harry the Hound dog hurries around.
Can you hear Harry's hurrying hound-
dog sound?
This is the sound Harry's breathing
makes when he hurries:
/h/ /h/ /h/ /h/ /h/ /h/!

When Harry the Hound dog sees a
hare hop by,
he tears down the hill, and his four
feet fly.
Hurry, Harry, hurry! /h/ /h/ /h/ /h/ /h/ /h/!

How Harry the Hound dog loves to hunt
and chase!
He hurls himself from place to place.
Hurry, Harry, hurry! /h/ /h/ /h/ /h/ /h/ /h/!

When Harry the Hound dog sees a big skunk roam,
he howls for help and heads for home.

What sound does Harry make when he hurries?
(Have the children answer.) /h/ /h/ /h/ /h/ /h/ /h/

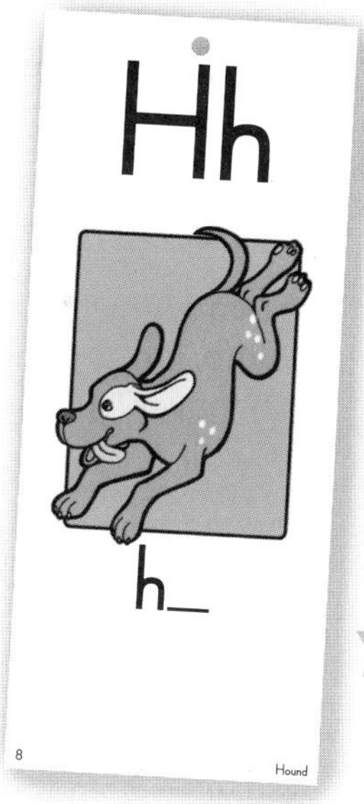

Card 9: /i/ Pig

This is Pickles the Pig.
If you tickle Pickles, she gets the giggles.
This is the sound of her giggling:
/i/ /i/ /i/ /i/ /i/.

Tickle Pickles the Pig under her chin.
Listen! She's giggling: /i/ /i/ /i/ /i/ /i/.
Wiggle a finger in Pickles' ribs.
Listen! She's giggling: /i/ /i/ /i/ /i/ /i/.

Give Pickles the Pig a wink,
and what do you think? First comes a grin.
Then listen!
She's giggling again: /i/ /i/ /i/ /i/ /i/.

Quick! Tickle Pickles the Pig. What will
she say?
(Have the children join in.) /i/ /i/ /i/ /i/ /i/

Card 10: /j/ Jump

When Jenny jumps her jump rope,
it sounds like this: /j/ /j/ /j/ /j/ /j/.
When Jackson jumps his jump rope,
it sounds like this: /j/ /j/ /j/ /j/ /j/.

The judges generally agree
that Jenny jumps most rapidly:
(quickly) /j/ /j/ /j/ /j/ /j/.

When Jenny jumps, she jumps to this jingle:
"Jump, jump, jump so quick.
Whenever I jump, I like to kick."
/j/ /j/ /j/ /j/ /j/

The judges generally agree
that Jackson jumps most quietly:
(quietly) /j/ /j/ /j/ /j/ /j/.

When Jackson jumps, he jumps to this jingle:
"Jump, jump, nice and quiet.
See what happens when you try it." /j/ /j/ /j/ /j/ /j/

(to the children) Jump rope like Jenny.
(quickly) /j/ /j/ /j/ /j/ /j/
(to the children) Jump rope like Jackson.
(quietly) /j/ /j/ /j/ /j/ /j/

Card 11: /k/ Camera

Carlos has a new camera. When he
takes pictures,
His camera makes a clicking sound like this:
/k/ /k/ /k/ /k/ /k/.

In the garden, Carlos takes pictures of
caterpillars crawling on cabbage:
/k/ /k/ /k/ /k/ /k/.

At the zoo, Carlos takes pictures of a camel,
a duck, and a kangaroo:
/k/ /k/ /k/.

In the park, Carlos takes pictures of his
cousin flying a kite: /k/ /k/ /k/ /k/ /k/
In his room, Carlos takes pictures of his
cute kitten, Cozy. /k/ /k/ /k/ /k/ /k/

Can you help Carlos take pictures with his camera?
(Have the children join in.) /k/ /k/ /k/ /k/ /k/ /k/ /k/

Card 12: /l/ Lion

Look! It's Leon the Lion.
Leon loves to lap water from lakes,
and this is the sound the lapping lion
makes: /l/ /l/ /l/ /l/ /l/.

Let's join Leon. Quick!
Take a little lick: /l/ /l/ /l/ /l/ /l/.

Are you a thirsty lass or lad?
Then lap until you don't feel bad:
/l/ /l/ /l/ /l/ /l/.

What sound do you make when you lap
like Leon the Lion?
(Have the children say:) /l/ /l/ /l/ /l/ /l/.

Card 13: /m/ Monkey

For Muzzy the Monkey, bananas
are yummy.
She munches so many, they fill up
her tummy.
When she eats, she says:
/m/ /m/ /m/ /m/ /m/!

Bananas for breakfast, bananas
for lunch.
Mash them up, mush them up,
munch, munch, munch, munch!
What does Muzzy the Monkey say?
(Have the children say:) /m/ /m/ /m/ /m/ /m/.

Bananas at bedtime? I have a hunch
Muzzy will mash them up, mush them up,
munch, munch, munch, munch!
Then what will Muzzy the Monkey say?
(Have the children say:) /m/ /m/ /m/ /m/ /m/.

Card 14: /n/ Nest

Nine feet up in a neighbor's tree
is a noisy, noisy nest.
I cannot see what's in there,
but it's a noisy pest!
/n/ /n/ /n/ /n/

What is in that noisy nest?
A nervous night owl crying?
A nosy nuthatch chatting?
A nightingale that's sighing?
/n/ /n/ /n/ /n/

I think it's time we take a look,
but please, do not start yapping.
Now I see what's in that nest!
A snoring bluebird napping!
/n/ /n/ /n/ /n/

Card 15: /o/ Fox

Bob the Fox did not feel well at all.
He jogged to the doctor's office.
"Say /o/ Mr. Fox! /o/ /o/ /o/."

"My head is hot, and my throat hurts a lot,"
said the fox.
"Say /o/, Mr. Fox!
"/o/ /o/ /o/ /o/."

"Yes, you've got a rotten cold," said
the doctor.
"Say /o/, Mr. Fox!
"/o/ /o/ /o/."

"Find a spot to sit in the sun," said the doctor.
"Say /o/, Mr. Fox!
"/o/ /o/ /o/."

He sat on a rock in the sun.
Soon he felt much better.
(with a satisfied sigh) "/o/," said Mr. Fox.
/o/ /o/ /o/

Card 16: /p/ Popcorn

Ping and Pong liked to pop corn. As
it cooked, it made this sound:
/p/ /p/ /p/ /p/ /p/ /p/ /p/.

One day Ping poured a whole package of
popcorn into the pot. It made this sound:
/p/ /p/ /p/ /p/ /p/ /p/ /p/.

The popcorn popped and popped. Ping filled
two pots, and still the popcorn popped:
/p/ /p/ /p/ /p/ /p/ /p/ /p/.

Pong filled three pails with popcorn, and still
it kept popping: /p/ /p/ /p/ /p/ /p/ /p/ /p/.

"Call all your pals," said their pop. "We'll have a party."
And the popcorn kept popping.

(Have the children say the /p/ sound very fast.)

Card 17: /kw/ Quacking ducks

Quincy the Duck couldn't quite quack like all the other quacking ducks.
Oh, he could say /kw/ /kw/ /kw/ /kw/, but it never seemed just right.

When Quincy tried to quack quietly,
(softly) /kw/ /kw/ /kw/ /kw/
his quack came out loudly.
(loudly) /kw/ /kw/ /kw/ /kw/!

When he tried to quack slowly,
(slowly) /kw/ . . . /kw/ . . . /kw/ . . . /kw/
his quack came out quickly.
(quickly) /kw/ /kw/ /kw/ /kw/!
Quincy just couldn't quack right!

One day Quincy was practicing quacks.
His friend Quip quacked along with him.
"Repeat after me," said Quip.
(quietly) /kw/ /kw/ /kw/ /kw/
But Quincy quacked back,
(in normal voice) /kw/ /kw/ /kw/ /kw/ /kw/!

Quincy still couldn't quack quite right.
But Quincy kept quacking. He said, "I won't quit until I quack like the best quackers around."
Can you show Quincy how quacking ducks quack?
(Have the children join in.)
/kw/ /kw/ /kw/ /kw/ /kw/ /kw/ /kw/ /kw/

Card 18: /r/ Robot

Little Rosie Robot just runs and runs and runs.
She races round and round to get her chores all done.
Here's how Rosie sounds when she's working:
/r/ /r/ /r/ /r/ /r/!

Rosie can rake around your roses.
Here comes that running robot!
/r/ /r/ /r/ /r/ /r/!

Rosie can repair your wrecked radio.
Here comes that racing robot!
(softly) /r/ /r/ /r/ /r/ /r/

Rosie can mend your round red rug.
Here comes that roaring robot!
(loudly) /r/ /r/ /r/ /r/ /r/!

Rosie rarely does anything wrong.
But there are two things that Rosie can't do: rest and relax.
Here comes that roaring robot!

What does she say?

(Have the children call out the answer:)
/r/ /r/ /r/ /r/ /r/.

Card 19: /s/ Sausages

Sue and Sammy had a nice place in the city.
On Saturday, Sue and Sammy decided to have sausages for supper.
Sammy put seven sausages in a skillet. /s/ /s/ /s/ /s/ /s/ /s/ /s/

Soon the smell of sausages filled the air.
/s/ /s/ /s/ /s/ /s/, sizzled the sausages.

"Pull up a seat, Sue," said Sammy.
"The sausages are almost ready to serve."
/s/ /s/ /s/ /s/ /s/, sizzled the sausages.

Sue and Sammy ate the delicious sausages.
Soon they wanted more, so Sam put six more sausages in the frying pan.
/s/ /s/ /s/ /s/ /s/ /s/, sizzled the sausages.

If you were cooking sausages with Sammy and Sue,
what sound would the sausages make as they sizzled?
(Have the children join in:) /s/ /s/ /s/ /s/ /s/ /s/

Card 20: /t/ Timer

When Tom Tuttle cooks, he uses his timer.
Tom Tuttle's timer ticks like this:
/t/ /t/ /t/ /t/ /t/ /t/ /t/

Tonight Tom Tuttle wants tomatoes on toast.
Tom turns on the oven.
Tom puts tomatoes on toast in the oven.
Tom sets the timer.
The timer will Ding! when Tom's toast and tomatoes are done.
Until the timer dings, it ticks: /t/ /t/ /t/ /t/ /t/ /t/ /t/.

Tomatoes on toast takes ten minutes.
/t/ /t/ /t/ /t/ /t/ /t/ /t/
Tom can hardly wait. /t/ /t/ /t/ /t/ /t/ /t/ /t/
He taps out the time: /t/ /t/ /t/ /t/ /t/ /t/ /t/.

What is the sound of Tom Tuttle's ticking timer?
(Have the children join in.) /t/ /t/ /t/ /t/ /t/ /t/ /t/
Ding! Time for dinner, Tom Tuttle!

Card 21: /u/ Tug

Tubby the Tugboat can huff and puff
and push and pull to move big stuff.
/u/ /u/ /u/ /u/ /u/ /u/ /u/
That's the sound of Tubby the Tug.

If a boat is stuck and will not budge,
Tubby the Tugboat can give it a nudge.
/u/ /u/ /u/ /u/ /u/ /u/ /u/
It's Tubby the Trusty Tug.

If a ship is caught in mud and muck,
Tubby the Tugboat can get it unstuck.
/u/ /u/ /u/ /u/ /u/ /u/ /u/
It's Tubby the Trusty Tug.

Can you help Tubby push and pull?
(Have the children join in.)
/u/ /u/ /u/ /u/ /u/ /u/ /u/

Card 22: /v/ Vacuum

Vinny the Vacuum is cleaning again.
Before visitors visit, he always begins.
This is the sound of his very loud voice:
/v/ /v/ /v/ /v/ /v/!
If only that Vinny could clean without noise!

Vinny sucks up the crumbs baby Vicki dropped.
/v/ /v/ /v/ /v/ /v/!
He visits nearly everywhere except the tabletop.
/v/ /v/ /v/ /v/ /v/!
Three vine leaves, two vitamins, part of a vase—
all vanish when Vinny goes over the place!
/v/ /v/ /v/ /v/ /v/

As Vinny vacuums the velvety rug
a van full of visitors starts to drive up.
But Vinny's not done with the very last room!
Will you help Vinny the Vacuum vacuum?
(Ask groups of children to say /v/ in a round to make the continuous sound of a vacuum cleaner.)

Card 23: /w/ Washer

Willie the Washer washed white
clothes all week.
When he washed, he went:
/w/ /w/ /w/ /w/ /w/ /w/ /w/.

All winter, Willie worked well.
/w/ /w/ /w/ /w/ /w/ /w/ /w/
But last Wednesday, Willie was weak.
(softly) /w/ /w/ /w/ /w/ /w/ /w/ /w/
This week, he got worse.
(slower and slower) /w/. . . /w/. . . /w/. . .
Poor Willie was worn out.
(slowly) /w/

Then a worker came and fixed Willie's wires.
Willie felt wonderful.
(more loudly) /w/ /w/ /w/ /w/ /w/ /w/ /w/!
Now Willie can wash and wash wildly!
(quickly) /w/ /w/ /w/ /w/ /w/ /w/ /w/!

How does Willie the Washer sound now when he washes?
(Have the children join in.) /w/ /w/ /w/ /w/ /w/ /w/ /w/
Can you wash just like Willie?
(Children together:) /w/ /w/ /w/ /w/ /w/ /w/ /w/.

Card 24: /ks/ Exit

Rex is called the Exiting X;
he runs to guard the door.
To get past Rex, make the sound of X:
/ks/ /ks/ /ks/ /ks/.
That is what Rex expects!

The ox knows the sound of X,
so she says /ks/ /ks/ /ks/ /ks/
and gets past Rex.

The fox knows the sound of X,
so he says /ks/ /ks/ /ks/ /ks/
and gets past Rex.

Can you say /ks/ /ks/ /ks/ /ks/
and get past Rex the Exiting X?
(Have the children respond:) /ks/ /ks/ /ks/ /ks/!
Did we get past Rex?
(Have the children say:) Yes!

Card 25: /y/ Yaks

Yolanda and Yoshiko are yaks.
They don't yell.
They don't yelp.
They don't yodel.
They don't yawn.
These young yaks just yak.
Yakety-yak, yakety-yak!
Can you hear the sound they make?
/y/ /y/ /y/ /y/ /y/ /y/ /y/

Yolanda and Yoshiko yak in the yard.
/y/ /y/ /y/ /y/ /y/ /y/ /y/
They yak on their yellow yacht.
/y/ /y/ /y/ /y/ /y/ /y/ /y/
They yak in the yam patch.
/y/ /y/ /y/ /y/ /y/ /y/ /y/
These yaks yak all year!
/y/ /y/ /y/ /y/ /y/ /y/ /y/

Do you think these yaks like to yak?
(Have the children answer:) Yes!
(Ask the children to yak like Yolanda and Yoshiko.)

Card 26: /z/ Zipper

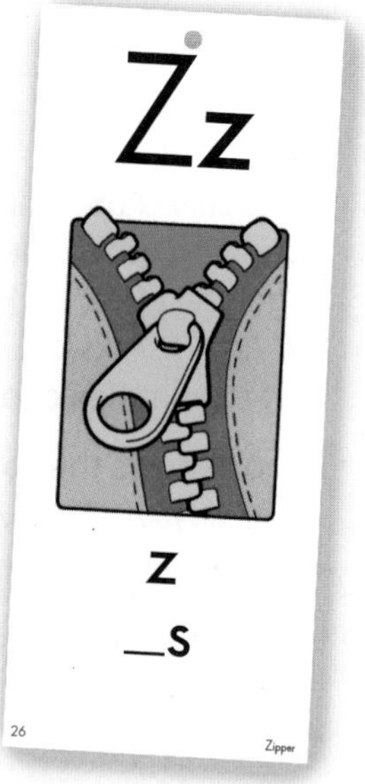

Zack's jacket has a big long zipper.
The zipper zips like this: /z/ /z/ /z/ /z/.

When little Zack goes out to play,
he zips the zipper up this way:
/z/ /z/ /z/ /z/.
Later, when he comes back in,
Zack zips the zipper down again.
/z/ /z/ /z/ /z/

Can you help Zack zip his jacket zipper?
(Have the children join in.) /z/ /z/ /z/ /z/

Card 32: /sh/ Shell

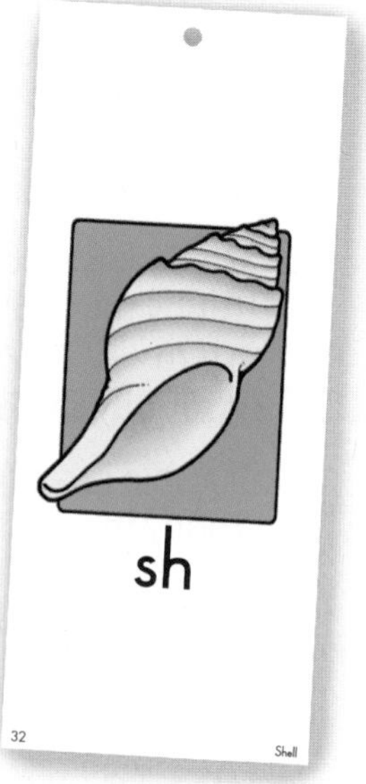

Sheila and Sharon went to the seashore.
They saw lots of shells.
Sheila rushed from shell to shell.
Sharon held a shell to Sheila's ear.

"Do you hear anything?" asked Sharon.
"Yes, it sounds like the ocean crashing on
the shore," shouted Sheila,
"/sh/ /sh/ /sh/ /sh/ /sh/."

"Let's try different-shaped shells," said Sharon.
She found a big shell. It made a loud
/sh/ /sh/ /sh/ /sh/.
Sheila found a small shell.
It made a soft /sh/ /sh/ /sh/ /sh/.
They found a thin shell.
It made a high /sh/ /sh/ /sh/ /sh/.
They found a fat shell. It made a deep /sh/ /sh/ /sh/ /sh/.

Sheila and Sharon listened to lots of shells. But no matter what the size and shape, what do you think Sheila and Sharon heard in every shell?
(Have the children join in.) /sh/ /sh/ /sh/ /sh/

Card 33: /th/ Thimble

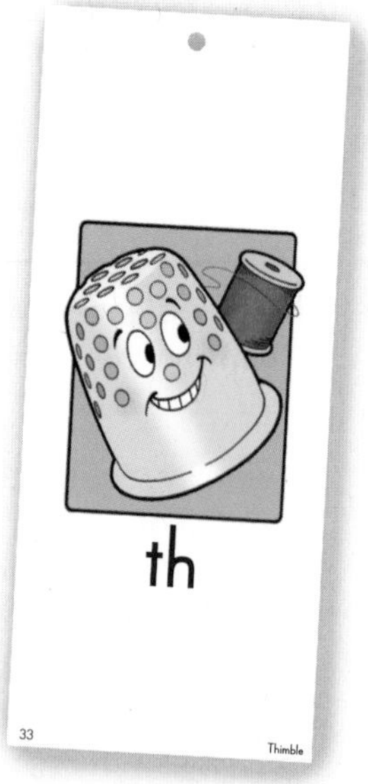

Theodore Thimble is a thinker.
Theodore thinks and thinks and thinks.
And when he thinks, he rubs his head.
/th/ /th/ /th/ /th/ /th/ /th/ /th/ /th/ /th/

Theodore thinks of thumbs—
thin thumbs,
thick thumbs,
all different kinds of thumbs.
/th/ /th/ /th/ /th/ /th/ /th/ /th/ /th/ /th/

Theodore thinks of thread—
red thread,
blue thread,
all different-colored thread.
/th/ /th/ /th/ /th/ /th/ /th/ /th/ /th/ /th/

Thread and thumb,
thumb and thread.
These are the thoughts
in Theodore's head.
/th/ /th/ /th/ /th/ /th/ /th/ /th/ /th/ /th/

Card 34: /ch/ Chipmunk

Chipper the chipmunk is cheerful and chubby.
He chats and he chatters all day:
/ch/ /ch/ /ch/ /ch/ /ch/ /ch/
He sits on a chimney.
Can you hear him chat?
He chats and he chatters this way:
/ch/ /ch/ /ch/ /ch/ /ch/ /ch/.

Chipper stuffs cherries into his cheek.
Then he chatters /ch/ /ch/ /ch/ /ch/ /ch/ /ch/.
Chipper likes chestnuts and acorns to eat.
Then he chatters /ch/ /ch/ /ch/ /ch/ /ch/ /ch/.

Can you children chatter like Chipper?
(Have the children answer.)
/ch/ /ch/ /ch/ /ch/ /ch/ /ch/

Now chat with the chipmunk child beside you.
(Ask partners to have chipmunk conversations.)
/ch/ /ch/ /ch/ /ch/ /ch/ /ch/

Card 35: /hw/ Whales

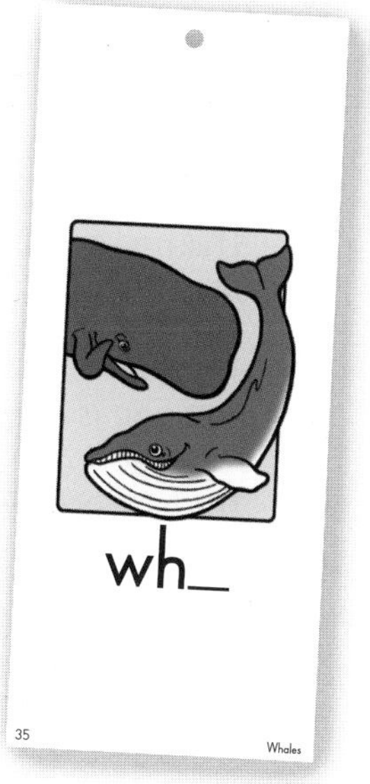

Look! It's Whitney the Whispering Whale!
Listen to her whisper: /hw/ /hw/ /hw/ /hw/ /hw/.

When Whitney meets with other whales,
she entertains them, telling tales.
She whispers: /hw/ /hw/ /hw/ /hw/ /hw/.
She's Whitney the Whispering Whale.

What ocean wonders does Whitney relate?
Does she whisper of whirlpools or whales
that are great?
We're only people, so we'll never guess.
She's Whitney the Whispering Whale!
/hw/ /hw/ /hw/.

Whatever Whitney whispers must be fun.
The other whales whistle when she's done.
They whoop and whack the white-capped waves.
They love Whitney the Whispering Whale! /hw/ /hw/ /hw/

If you were Whitney, what sounds would you whisper
to your whale friends as they gathered to listen?
(Have the children whisper:) /hw/ /hw/ /hw/ /hw/ /hw/

Card 36: /ng/ Gong

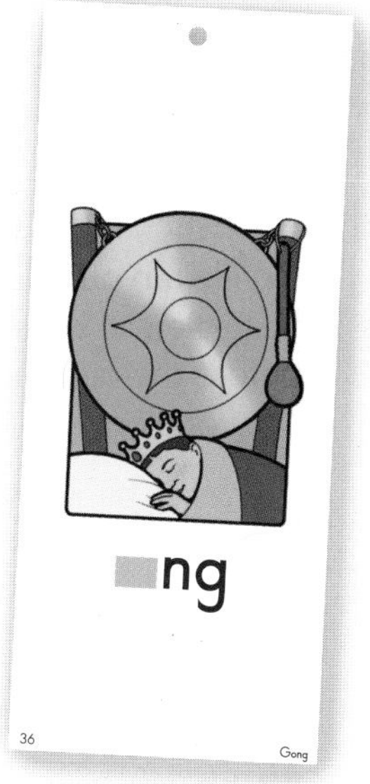

The young king has slept much
too long.
Let's go and awaken the king with
a gong.

A pinging gong? It makes a quiet song:
(softly) /ng/ /ng/ /ng/ /ng/ /ng/.

That gong is wrong.
(softly) /ng/ /ng/ /ng/ /ng/
We need a louder gong!

A dinging gong? It makes this song:
(a bit louder) /ng/ /ng/ /ng/ /ng/ /ng/ /ng/.

That, too, is wrong.
(as before) /ng/ /ng/ /ng/ /ng/
We need an even louder gong!

A clanging gong?
It makes this song:
(loudly) /ng/ /ng/ /ng/ /ng/ /ng/!

That's just the thing! /ng/ /ng/ /ng/ /ng/ /ng/!
That's the gong we needed all along!

Now, which gong should we bring to awaken the King?
(Have children make the /ng/ *sound loud enough to wake
the king.)* /ng/ /ng/ /ng/ /ng/ /ng/!

Card 37: /nk/ Skunk

Sammy the Skunk
finds his skates in the trunk.
He thinks he'll go skating today.
Once at the rink,
poor Sammy does think
his pink nose feels funny some way.
/nk/ /nk/ /nk/

Home from the rink
he gets hot soup to drink.
Sammy hopes his cold slinks away.
/nk/ /nk/ /nk/ /nk/

Then the poor skunk
spends the night in his bunk.
Sammy's sneezes and honks do stay.
/nk/ /nk/ /nk/ /nk/ /nk/

Now the sun winks,
the skunk's eyes start to blink.
Sammy gets up and feels okay!
Sammy the Skunk finds his skates in the trunk.
He thinks he'll go skating today.

Can you make the sound Sammy the Skunk makes when he
has a cold?

(Have the students join in.) /nk/ /nk/ /nk/ /nk/ /nk/

Card 38: /or/ Storк

Orville McCormick was quite a stork.
He liked to eat pork while holding a fork.
He also ate corn while blowing a horn:
/or/ /or/ /or/ /or/ /or/ /or/ /or/ /or/

Orville ran out of corn and needed more pork.
So he flew to the store and tore through the door
before the rain came and started to pour.
/or/ /or/ /or/ /or/ /or/ /or/ /or/

He was so happy now with his pork and his corn
that all he could say was "/or/ /or/ /or/ /or/!"

Card 39: /ar/ Armadillo

Arthur Armadillo likes to whistle,
hum, and sing.
But when he gets a head cold,
his voice won't do a thing.

To sing and still sound charming—
and not sound so alarming—
Arthur has thought up the thing
of very often gargling.

Then Arthur Armadillo sounds like this:
/ar/ /ar/ /ar/ /ar/ /ar/.
Arthur gargles in the park.
/ar/ /ar/ /ar/ /ar/ /ar/
He gargles in the dark.
/ar/ /ar/ /ar/ /ar/ /ar/
He gargles on the farm.
/ar/ /ar/ /ar/ /ar/ /ar/
He gargles in the barn.
/ar/ /ar/ /ar/ ar/ /ar/
Arthur is great at gargling!
/ar/ /ar/ /ar/ /ar/ /ar/

What does Arthur Armadillo's gargling sound like?
(Have the children respond.) /ar/ /ar/ /ar/ /ar/ /ar/

Card 40: /er/ Bird

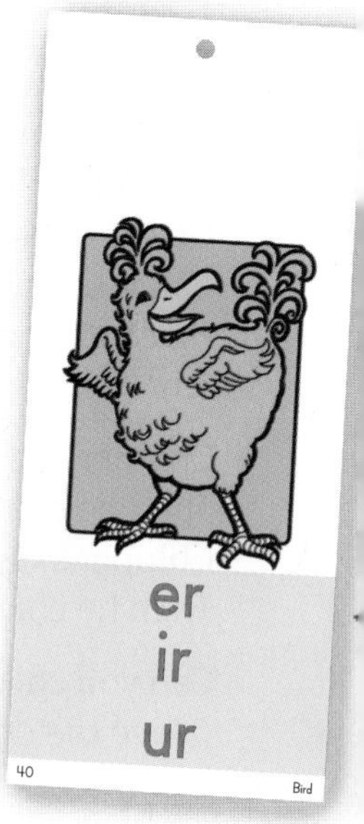

Bertie the Bird is the oddest bird
that anyone has ever heard.
He doesn't caw like a crow or a gull,
or tweet like a robin or a wren.
Instead, he makes a chirping sound—
over and over again!
/er/ /er/ /er/ /er/ /er/ /er/!

Bert can't fly, since his wings are too short.
He arranges his feathers in curls.
He admits, "I've short wings and I don't really sing,
but I still am an interesting bird!"
/er/ /er/ /er/ /er/ /er/ /er/

Can you chirp like Bertie the Bird?
(Have children say:) /er/ /er/ /er/ /er/ /er/ /er/!

Card 41: /o͞o/ Goo

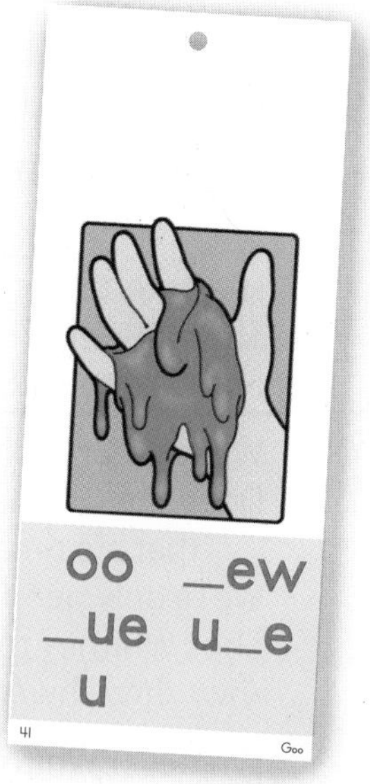

What can be making that sound?
Could it be a new flute playing a tune?
No. It's goo!
/o͞o/ /o͞o/ /o͞o/ /o͞o/

The goo is oozing all over my hand.
/o͞o/ /o͞o/ /o͞o/ /o͞o/
The goo is oozing on my boots.
/o͞o/ /o͞o/ /o͞o/ /o͞o/

The goo is oozing off the roof.
The goo is oozing everywhere!
/o͞o/ /o͞o/ /o͞o/ /o͞o/
The goo is as sticky as glue.
It is as thick as stew.
/o͞o/ /o͞o/ /o͞o/ /o͞o/

Soon the goo will fill the school!
/o͞o/ /o͞o/ /o͞o/ /o͞o/
Soon the goo will reach the moon!
/o͞o/ /o͞o/ /o͞o/ /o͞o/

What sound does the oozing goo make?
(Have the children join in.) /o͞o/ /o͞o/ /o͞o/ /o͞o/

Card 42: /o͝o/ Foot

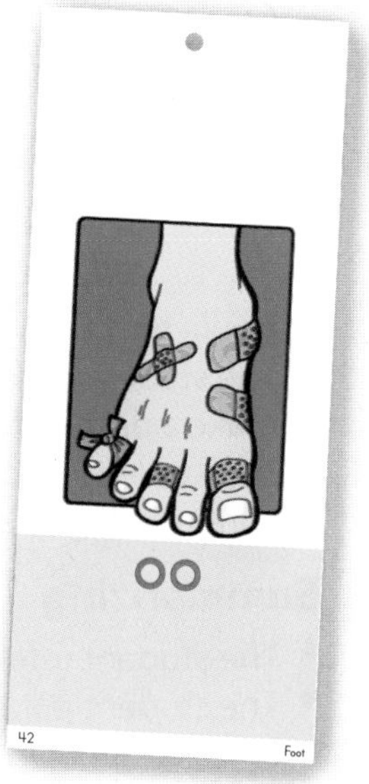

Mr. Hood took off his shoes and socks
and went out walking in the wood.
He kicked a rock and hurt his foot.
/o͝o/ /o͝o/ /o͝o/ /o͝o/

"Look, look!" said Mr. Hood. "There's a
babbling, bubbling brook. I'll walk
in the brook, so I won't hurt my foot."

So he stepped in the water, and guess what?
/o͝o/ /o͝o/ /o͝o/ /o͝o/
Mr. Hood stepped on a hook!
/o͝o/ /o͝o/ /o͝o/ /o͝o/
Mr. Hood stood. He shook his foot.
/o͝o/ /o͝o/ /o͝o/ /o͝o/

"This isn't good," said Mr. Hood.
"I think I'll go home and read a book.
At least that won't hurt my foot."
(Have the children join in.) /o͝o/ /o͝o/ /o͝o/ /o͝o/

Card 43: /ow/ Cow

Wow! Can you see poor Brownie
the Cow?
She got stung by a bee, and look at
her now!
She jumps up and down with an
/ow/ /ow/ /ow/ /ow/.

Poor Brownie found that a big
buzzing sound
meant bees all around—in the air,
on the ground.
Just one little bee gave Brownie a sting.
Now you can hear poor Brownie sing:
/ow/ /ow/ /ow/ /ow/.

Now if you were a cow and a bee found you,
you'd probably jump and shout out too!
(Have the children join in.) /ow/ /ow/ /ow/ /ow/

Card 44: /aw/ Hawk

Hazel the Hawk never cooks her food;
instead, she eats it raw.
And when she thinks of dinnertime
she caws: /aw/ /aw/ /aw/ /aw/.

Hazel the Hawk likes rabbits and mice
and catches them with her claws.
In August, she flies high above the fields
and spies them below, in the straw.
Sometimes she even snatches a snake!
And when she's caught one, she caws:
/aw/ /aw/ /aw/ /aw/.

If you were a hawk thinking of dinnertime,
what do you think you'd say?
(Have the children answer.) /aw/ /aw/ /aw/ /aw/

Card 45: /oi/ Coil

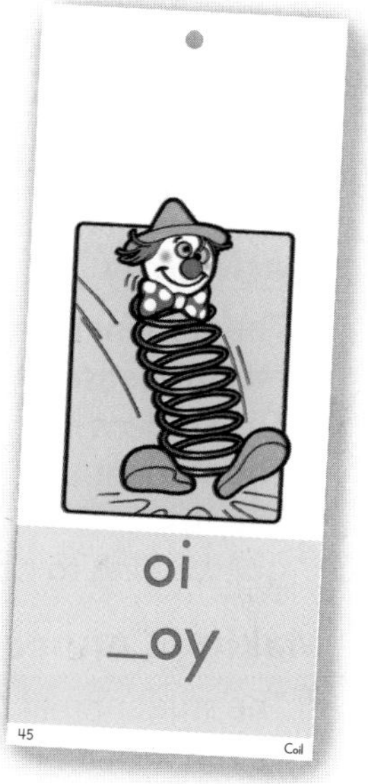

Boing! Boing! Boing! Boing!
Roy the Coil is a bouncing toy,
and this is the sound of his bounce:
/oi/ /oi/ /oi/ /oi/ /oi/.

Doing! Doing! Doing! Doing!
Roy the Coil just dances for joy.
This is the sound of his dance:
/oi/ /oi/ /oi/ /oi/ /oi/.

Ke-boing! Ke-boing!
Roy the Coil springs over a boy.
What springing sound does he make?
(Have the children join in.)
/oi/ /oi/ /oi/ /oi/ /oi/

Rubrics

Comprehension Strategy Rubrics

The following rubrics can be used to gauge students' growing knowledge of the comprehension strategies and how adept they are becoming in their use. Use the rubrics as a guide because students will probably develop strategies of their own. The important thing to consider is whether students are becoming strategic, active readers—do they employ these and other strategies, or do they continue to simply plow through text, unaware of any problems they might be having? The rubrics indicate the types of behaviors strategic readers use and will help you identify the growing facility your students can gain in dealing with text of all sorts.

Asking Questions

- The student stops to ask questions—any question.
- The student asks questions directly related to the text.
- The student asks *who, what, why, when, where,* or *how* questions as opposed to *yes* or *no* questions.
- The student asks questions that help clarify information in the text.

Clarifying

- The student recognizes when a word or idea is not making sense.
- The student uses decoding skills to read unfamiliar words.
- The student uses structural elements in words to read them.
- The student uses structural elements, context, and questioning to clarify the meanings of unfamiliar words.

Making Connections

- The student makes connections between prior knowledge and information in the text.
- The student makes connections between or relates personal experiences to what is read in the text (text-to-self connections).
- The student makes connections across or relates information from different selections (text-to-text connections).
- The student makes connections or relates information between what is happening in the text to what is happening in the world today (text-to-world connections).

Predicting

- The student stops to make a prediction about the text.
- The student identifies the clues in the text used to make a prediction.
- The student uses clues in the text and prior knowledge to make a prediction.
- The student recognizes when a prediction is or is not confirmed by the text.

Summarizing

- The student retells information from the story.
- The student paraphrases or puts the main ideas and details in his or her own words.
- The student gives a summary that includes only the important or main ideas.
- The student recognizes when the same ideas are included more than once in a summary and deletes them.

Visualizing

- The student recognizes appropriate places in the text to stop and visualize.
- The student visualizes literal ideas or scenes described by the author.
- The student makes inferences while visualizing to show understanding of characters' feelings, mood, and setting. The visualizations go beyond the author's literal words.
- The student uses visualizing differently depending on the type of text (for example, characters, setting, and actions in narratives or a process description in nonfiction).

Inquiry Rubrics

Throughout each unit, students engage in Inquiry activities based on the unit concepts. They will present the findings of their research to the class. In this way they exhibit the wealth of knowledge and understanding they have gained about that particular concept. In addition to gaining knowledge about the concepts, students will be honing their research skills. With each unit, they will progress with their research in the same manner that professional researchers do. With each new unit of study, students should also become more sophisticated in their ability to formulate questions, make conjectures about those questions, recognize their own information needs, conduct research to find that information, reevaluate their questions and conjectures as new information is added to their knowledge base, and communicate their findings effectively. In addition, they will become more adept at working as a team and being aware of the progress being made as individuals and as a group. The Inquiry Rubrics will help you to assess the students' progress as researchers and as members of collaborative teams. ***SRA Imagine It!*** provides four-point rubrics for each step in the Inquiry process. This enables teachers to clearly distinguish among different levels of performance.

1 Point score indicates that a student is performing below basic level.
2 Point score indicates that a student's abilities are emerging.
3 Point score indicates that a student's work is adequate and achieving expectations.
4 Point score indicates that a student is exceeding expectations.

Generating Ideas and Questions

1 With much teacher assistance, identifies something he or she wonders about or articulates an idea, though the idea may not be on topic.
2 With teacher assistance, identifies something that he or she wonders about or articulates an idea, using some relevant background knowledge and vocabulary.
3 With little teacher assistance, contributes information through discussion to develop research questions about the topic.
4 Independently identifies things he or she wonders about in relation to a topic and contributes research questions and ideas.

Identifying a Question to Investigate

1 With much teacher assistance, narrows two to three ideas to a broad question to research.
2 With teacher assistance, identifies one question to investigate though it may be broad in scope.
3 With little teacher assistance, narrows varying ideas to a researchable question.
4 Independently chooses a question he or she wonders about and would like to research.

Making a Conjecture

1 Makes a conjecture based on personal opinions or well-known facts.
2 Makes a conjecture based on somewhat relevant background knowledge.
3 Makes a conjecture based on relevant background knowledge and begins to address the research question.
4 Makes a conjecture based on relevant background knowledge and addresses the research question.

Identifying Information Needs

1 With much teacher assistance, identifies information needs.
2 With teacher assistance, identifies information needs.
3 With some teacher assistance, identifies information needs.
4 With little or no teacher assistance, identifies information needs.

Collecting Information

1 With much teacher guidance, recognizes information that is relevant to the research question.
2 With teacher guidance, collects information that is somewhat relevant to the research question.
3 With some teacher guidance, collects information that is relevant to the research question.
4 With little or no teacher guidance, seeks and finds information from sources to find information relevant to the research question.

Confirming and Revising Conjectures

1 Even with much teacher guidance, minimally participates in confirming or revising a conjecture.
2 With teacher guidance, recognizes whether information confirms a conjecture or requires the revision of the conjecture.
3 With some teacher guidance, recognizes whether new information confirms a conjecture or causes the conjecture to be revised.
4 With little teacher guidance, or independently, revises or confirms a conjecture based on new knowledge and information.

Sharing Knowledge and Preparing Presentations

1 Can represent or explain a key fact or idea in words and pictures to the teacher.
2 Shares some new ideas and information with the teacher.
3 With teacher support, is willing to risk sharing new ideas and information with a small group of peers.
4 With little or no teacher support, shares new ideas and information in an organized fashion.

Overall Research

1 With much teacher guidance, shows a limited understanding that research has led to new knowledge being gained about the research question.
2 With teacher guidance, shows some understanding that research efforts have led to new knowledge being gained about the research question.
3 Understands that research efforts have led to new knowledge related to the research question.
4 Understands that ideas change and develop and explains how.

Participation in Collaborative Inquiry

1 With much teacher prompting, works collaboratively with peers throughout the Inquiry process.
2 With some teacher prompting, works collaboratively with peers throughout the Inquiry process.
3 With little teacher prompting, works collaboratively with peers to share questions, ideas, and information sources.
4 With no teacher prompting, works collaboratively with peers sharing questions, conjectures, information sources.

Writing Rubrics

Rubrics are particularly effective for writing assignments, which do not have simple right or wrong answers. Different sets of rubrics cover various elements of the writing, including genre, writing process, and writing traits. They are intended to help teachers provide criteria and feedback to students.

SRA Imagine It! provides four-point rubrics for writing in each of four areas. This enables teachers to clearly distinguish among different levels of performance.

1 Point score indicates that a student is performing below basic level.
2 Points score indicates that a student's abilities are emerging.
3 Points score indicates that a student's work is adequate and achieving expectations.
4 Points score indicates that a student is exceeding expectations.

Narrative Writing Genres

Genre	1 Point	2 Points	3 Points	4 Points
Narrative: Character	Describes characters in increasing detail in original stories, including physical and mental qualities, such as strong or kind.	Describes the internal mental world of story characters by explicitly describing thoughts, feelings, and desires.	Creates lifelike characters whose actions and speech reflect unique qualities, which are integral to the plot.	Creates complex characters, identifying psychological traits that are represented throughout the narrative.
Narrative: Plot	Plot includes problem, failed attempts, subproblems, and resolution. Evidence of coherence and cohesion, but may depend on formulaic structure. Subject and theme are clear and maintained.	Plot is elaborated with descriptive details and elements that add excitement or color. Narrative structure is clear. Subject and theme are clear and developed throughout.	Plot is well developed with subplots and complications integrated into the resolution.	Includes more complicated plot lines with varied time lines, flashbacks, or dual story lines.
Narrative: Setting	Creates settings that simply include descriptions of time, character, and place.	Describes settings in ways that contribute to the mood, suspense, humor, or excitement of the story.	Identifies how settings influence story problems and their resolutions or contribute to other story elements, such as character and plot.	Creates settings that include metaphoric or symbolic elements that help develop story elements.
Narrative: Theme	No theme is apparent	Superficial theme is included but not integrated.	A theme is expressed but not well developed.	The narrative fully develops a theme that expresses an underlying message beyond the narrative plot.
Biography/ Autobiography	The events included are sketchy and do not clearly describe the life of the subject. The time line of events is not clear.	The writing describes a few events in the life of the subject but leaves unexplained gaps. Several events in the life of the subject are described out of chronological order.	The writer describes many important events in the subject's life, perhaps including family, education, early influences, and accomplishments. A few gaps remain. Most events are described chronologically.	The writer describes the most important events in the subject's life (such as family, education, early influences, accomplishments) and summarizes the rest. All events are described chronologically.
Play	Play does not list and describe characters or describe all scenes. Sketchy, confusing dialogue and stage directions do not result in lifelike characters. The role of several characters is unclear. Most stage directions are missing or confused with dialogue.	Play does not begin with a list and description of characters and does not describe all scenes. Dialogue and stage directions are vague and do not create unique characters. The role of some characters in the plot is unclear. Many stage directions are missing or confused with the dialogue.	Play either does not begin with a list and description of characters or does not describe all scenes. The actions and speech of some characters may be inconsistent. Some of their traits are overly exaggerated. One or two characters may be superfluous to the plot. Some stage directions are confused with the dialogue.	Play begins with a list and description of its characters. Script describes the time and place of each scene or setting. Dialogue and stage directions create unique, believable characters with consistent actions and speech. All characters are important to the plot. Stage directions are set off from the dialogue with italics, parentheses, and/or brackets.

Expository Writing Genres

Genre	1 Point	2 Points	3 Points	4 Points
Expository Structure	Main points and supportive details can be identified, but they are not clearly marked.	Composition is clearly organized around main points with supportive facts or assertions.	Presents adequate, appropriate evidence to make a point or support a position. Positions are compared and contrasted while developing the main points. Main points and supportive details can be identified, but they are not clearly marked.	Traces and constructs a line of argument, identifying part-to-whole relations. Main points are supported with logical and appropriate evidence.
Book Review (Fiction Book)	Information about the title, author, and illustrator is missing. Only a sketchy description of characters, setting, and plot is included. The reviewer's opinion about the book is vague or missing.	Characters are named but not described; the setting and summary are unclear. The author's main point is not mentioned. The reviewer offers an opinion about the book without supporting it.	The review describes the main characters and setting and includes plot summary, but parts may be unclear. The reviewer may not explain the author's main point. The reviewer does not strongly support an opinion about the book.	The review includes the book's title, author, and illustrator. It describes the main characters and setting and summarizes the plot. The writer explains the author's main point. The reviewer also gives an opinion about the book and supports it with examples from the story.
Compare and Contrast Essay	Subjects being compared are not clear. The writer doesn't make connections between the subjects. The essay lacks a summary.	The writer does not clearly explain how the subjects are similar and different. The essay has few clue words (such as *also, like, but, although)* and lacks a summary.	The writer describes some things the subjects have in common and some ways they are each unique. The writer uses some clue words (such as *also, like, but, although)*. The summary might not be strong.	The writer describes what the subjects have in common using clue words such as also, like, and too. The writer also describes how each subject is unique using clue words such as *but, however,* and *although.* The essay concludes with a summary of the main points.
Explaining a Process	The process being described is not clear. The steps are sketchy, incomplete, and/or out of order.	Several steps are missing, described incorrectly, or placed out of order.	The introduction names the process but a step may be missing, described incorrectly, or placed out of order. An explanation is included.	The introduction names the process, lists materials (if applicable), and defines the terms. Every step in the process is described accurately and in the correct order.
Informative Report	The report has no introduction or clear topic. It offers a group of loosely related facts or a series of poorly written steps. No graphic or conclusion is included.	The report has no clear introduction, but its topic is identifiable. However, it includes many facts that are unrelated to the topic, or it describes things in a disorganized way. No graphic or conclusion is included.	The report has an introduction and offers facts about the topic. Some facts may be irrelevant, or some ideas may be vague or out of order. A chart, diagram, or map is included. The report is fairly well organized but doesn't have a strong conclusion.	The report begins with an introduction and offers relevant facts about the topic or describes the topic appropriately. A chart, diagram, map, or other graphic is well integrated. The report is organized using cause/effect, comparison/contrast, or another pattern. It ends with a strong conclusion.
News Story	The topic of the story is vague. It lacks a headline and/or byline. The lead paragraph provides little accurate information.	The story describes a recent event and includes a headline and/or byline. The lead paragraph answers two or three of the five *Ws* (*who, what, where, when,* and *why*) and how but includes many inaccuracies. Information is collected mainly by observation.	The story describes a recent event and includes a headline and byline. The lead paragraph answers four of the five *Ws* and *how* but may have slight inaccuracies. Information is collected mainly through research or observation.	The story describes a recent event or development and includes a headline and byline. The lead paragraph accurately answers the five Ws and how. Information and quotations are collected through interviews, research, or observation.
Summary	Sentences and phrases are taken from the original document with little attempt to identify main ideas.	The summary includes some of the main ideas, a few important details, and a number of minor details. Much of the wording is from the original document.	The summary includes most main ideas and important details. Some minor details are also included. Some wording is from the original document. The writer may change the meaning of the original document slightly.	The summary includes only the main ideas and most important details, organized by key points. The writer uses his or her own words without changing the meaning of the original document.

Persuasive Writing Genres

Genre	1 Point	2 Points	3 Points	4 Points
Persuasive	Position is absent or confusing. Insufficient writing to show that criteria are met.	Position is vague or lacks clarity. Unrelated ideas or multiple positions are included.	An opening statement identifies position. Writing may develop few or more points than delineated in opening. Focus may be too broad.	Sets scope and purpose of paper in introduction. Maintains position throughout. Supports arguments. Includes effective closing.
Persuasive Letter	The writer's viewpoint is not clear and/or not supported with facts, reasons, and examples.	The letter begins with the writer's viewpoint but includes few facts, reasons, or examples to support that viewpoint.	The letter is likely to influence some readers to think, feel, or act in a certain way. The letter begins with the writer's viewpoint and includes some facts, reasons, and examples to support that viewpoint.	The letter is likely to influence most readers to think, feel, or act in a certain way. The letter begins with the writer's viewpoint and includes concrete facts, logical reasoning, and specific examples to support that viewpoint.

The Writing Process

The Writing Process	1 Point	2 Points	3 Points	4 Points
Getting Ideas	Shows little awareness that own ideas are the material of writing.	Consciously calls on own experience and knowledge for ideas in writing.	Is aware that writing requires thinking about content and ideas.	Evaluates and alters ideas as writing proceeds.
Prewriting—Organizing Writing	Makes little or no attempt to develop a plan for writing.	Uses a given model to plan.	Elaborates on the model for planning.	Develops own plan based on the model.
Drafting	Writes without attention to plan or is unable to write.	Writes a minimal amount with some attention to plan.	Uses plan to draft.	Elaborates on plan to draft.
Revising	Quickly finishes writing assignments and doesn't seek feedback.	Pays attention as teacher provides feedback about written work.	Welcomes feedback and advice from teacher or other students.	Actively seeks feedback from teacher or other students.
Editing	Demonstrates no attention to correcting grammar, usage, mechanics, or spelling errors.	Some errors in English language conventions are corrected, but many are not corrected.	Corrects many errors in English language conventions.	Corrects most errors in English language conventions. Uses resources or seeks assistance to address uncertainties.
Presentation/ Publishing	Presents revised and edited draft as final.	Recopies final draft with no extra presentation.	Includes adequate presentation efforts with illustration, format, and style.	Impressive presentation of written work with attention to format, style, illustration, and clarity.
Self-Management	Does not have a plan for writing. Does not use graphic organizers or checklists when writing.	Employs an unclear plan for writing. Sometimes uses graphic organizers to plan writing or checklists to revise/proofread writing.	Employs a plan for writing. Often uses graphic organizers to plan writing or checklists to revise/proofread writing.	Employs a clear plan for writing. Uses graphic organizers to plan writing and checklists to revise/ proofread writing.
Time Management	Puts writing task off until the last minute and seldom finishes work on time.	Allows some, but often not enough, time for writing task.	Allows time for writing, but not enough for revising or proofreading.	Listens to advice about time requirements and plans accordingly.

Writing Traits

Writing Traits	1 Point	2 Points	3 Points	4 Points
Audience	Displays little or no sense of audience.	Displays some sense of audience.	Writes with audience in mind throughout.	Displays a strong sense of audience. Engages audience.
Citing Sources	Does not understand the difference between one's own work and the work of others. Clearly copies work of others.	Uses others' work as a model.	Writes own words and refrains from copying the work of others.	Takes pride in own words and acknowledges ideas of others.
Conventions Overall	Demonstrates little evidence of standard writing conventions.	Demonstrates limited but inconsistent control of standard writing conventions.	Demonstrates emerging, consistent use of standard writing conventions such as capitalization and end punctuation.	Demonstrates consistent use and awareness of standard writing conventions.
Conventions: Capitalization	Inconsistently uses capital letters.	Inconsistently uses capitals at beginning of sentences and for some proper nouns.	Capitalizes sentences; may overcapitalize other words.	Uses capitalization correctly at beginning of sentences and for proper nouns.
Conventions: Grammar and Usage	Demonstrates minimal awareness of standard usage.	Demonstrates some awareness of standard usage.	Demonstrates emerging awareness of standard usage and subject/verb agreement.	Includes standard usage and demonstrates understanding of subject/verb agreement in writing.
Conventions: Punctuation	Makes little use of punctuation.	Uses period correctly for end punctuation.	Uses most end punctuation correctly.	Uses end punctuation and some commas correctly.
Conventions: Sentence Structure	Writes words or labels, but not sentences.	Writes very simple sentences.	Uses sentences to express ideas in writing.	Uses simple or compound sentences to express ideas.
Conventions: Spelling	Mainly uses invented spelling.	Uses sound spellings as a primary strategy, though many words are misspelled.	Uses mostly correct sound/spellings and structural patterns.	Uses correct sound/spelling and structural patterns.
Elaboration (Supporting Details and Examples that Develop the Main Idea)	Little or no elaboration or detail.	Minimal detail.	Includes sufficient detail to develop or support ideas.	Elaborates on ideas with supporting details.

Writing Traits

Writing Traits	1 Point	2 Points	3 Points	4 Points
Focus	No focus is present. Main idea cannot be inferred.	Topic/position/direction is unclear and must be inferred.	Topic/position is stated and direction/purpose is previewed and maintained. Mainly stays on topic.	Topic/position is clearly stated, previewed, and maintained. Topics and details are tied together.
Ideas/Content	Superficial and/or minimal content is included.	Main ideas are understandable, although they may be overly broad or simplistic. Supporting detail is limited.	Main ideas are easily understandable. Support is present, although it may be limited or rather general.	Main ideas stand out and are developed by strong support and rich details.
Organization	Organization is not apparent.	An attempt has been made to organize the writing, though the writing may be a list of facts or ideas.	Organization is clear and coherent. Beginning or conclusion is included.	Organization develops the central idea. The order and structure move the reader through the text easily. Beginning grabs attention. Conclusion adds impact. Uses paragraphs appropriately.
Sentence Fluency	The writing is difficult to follow.	The writing tends to be choppy rather than fluid.	At times the writing flows, but connections between phrases or sentences may not always be present.	The writing has an effective flow and rhythm with connections between phrases and sentences. Sentence patterns are somewhat varied.
Voice	The writing provides little sense of voice.	The voice is either inappropriately personal or inappropriately impersonal.	A voice is present, though in places, the writing is less expressive, engaging, or sincere.	The writer has chosen a voice appropriate for the topic, purpose, and audience.
Word Choice	The writing shows an extremely limited vocabulary and frequent misuse of words.	Language is ordinary, filled with familiar words and phrases. Exhibits minimal word usage. Words and expressions are clear, but usually more general than specific.	Words effectively convey the intended message. Exhibits adequate word usage. Contains some interesting words. Includes some vivid descriptive language.	Words convey the intended message in an interesting, precise, and natural way appropriate to the audience and purpose. Exhibits exceptional word usage and frequently contains interesting words.

Penmanship

SRA Imagine It! develops handwriting skills through weekly Penmanship lessons. The instruction for these lessons appears in the Sounds and Letters part of the lesson in Level K, and in the Language Arts part of the lesson in Levels 1–3. The purpose of these lessons is to develop important handwriting skills that are necessary for producing legible, properly spaced documents.

The overhead projector, in addition to the board, can be a very effective device for teaching penmanship. Students can move their pencils at the same time you form letters on the transparency. It also helps to recite the descriptions or chants that go with each letter.

Penmanship in Levels K and 1

Beginning in kindergarten, the Penmanship lessons expand on the sound/letter instruction by introducing letters that students study in Sounds and Letters. Students learn that those letters are made of four basic lines: curved lines, horizontal lines, vertical lines, and slanted lines.

Next, students learn letter and number formation. Students practice letter formation by writing the letter being studied and then words that contain that particular letter. This instruction continues in Level 1 and is tied to the letter formation instruction in Phonics.

Manuscript Handwriting Models

The lessons present ball-and-stick models of manuscript handwriting, while the Appendix offers an alternative method with continuous stroke models.

Cursive Handwriting Models

Penmanship is developed and practiced through Level 3, with cursive instruction beginning in the first unit of Level 2. Students are taught that most cursive letters are comprised of four strokes: undercurve, downcurve, overcurve, and slanted lines. These lessons teach students the essentials of cursive handwriting, such as proper slant; loop; joining; and spacing between letters, words, and sentences. As in the earlier levels, students practice letter formation by writing the letters and then words that contain that particular letter.

The writing exercises progress with each level. Students begin writing words in kindergarten and graduate to writing sentences by the end of Level 1. Level 2 eases students into cursive by having them practice letters, words, and sentences. By Level 3, students are writing complete paragraphs in cursive.

Hand and Paper Positioning

The **hand and paper positioning** models are for your reference and enhance the written instruction of positioning lessons. The diagrams give you a visual aid so you may better understand and demonstrate an effective technique of positioning.

A right-handed student should hold the pencil loosely about one inch above the point, between the thumb and middle finger. A left-handed student should hold the pencil the same way, but up to one half inch farther away from the point. The index fingers of both writers should rest lightly on the top of the pencil. The wrist should be level and slightly raised from the desk.

Left-handed writers   Right-handed Writers

For both kinds of writers, the paper should lie straight in front of the student with the edges parallel to the edges of the desk. A left-handed writer may find it easier to slant the paper slightly to the right and parallel to the left forearm. A right-handed writer's writing hand should be kept well below the writing. The left hand should hold down the paper.

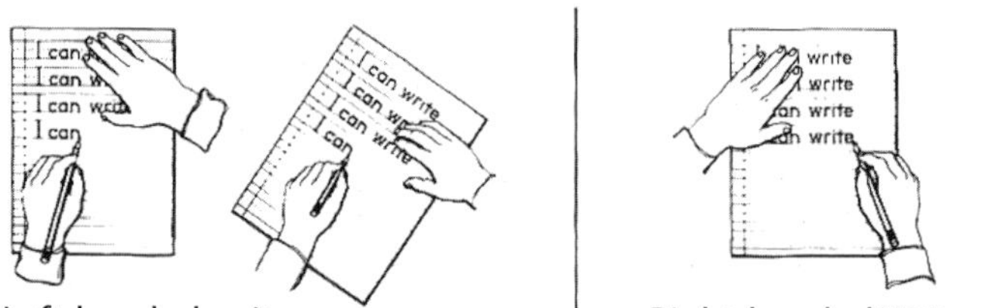

Left-handed writers   Right-handed Writers

Ball and Stick Handwriting Models

The **ball-and-stick** models of manuscript handwriting provide you with a systematic method for teaching students to form uppercase and lowercase letters of the alphabet. The dots on the letters indicate starting points for students. The numbered arrows show students in which order and direction the line they are drawing should go to form the particular letter. You may use the chants to describe the letter step by step as students model the formation on the board. Students may also recite the chants in unison as they practice the formation, whether they are writing the letter or tracing it on the board.

Ball-and-Stick Handwriting Models

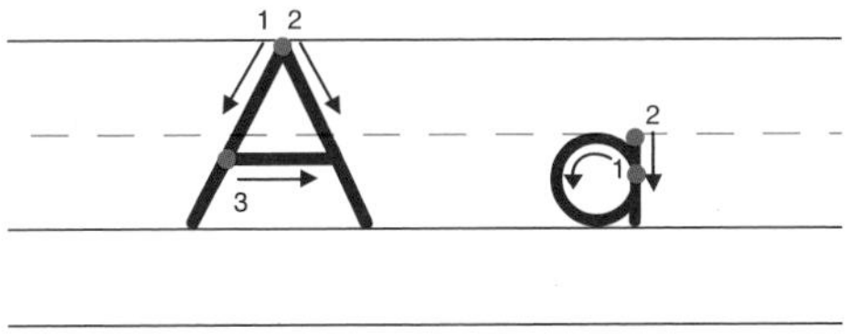

A Starting point, slanting down left
Starting point, slanting down right
Starting point, across the middle: capital *A*

a Starting point, around left all the way
Starting point, straight down, touching the circle: small *a*

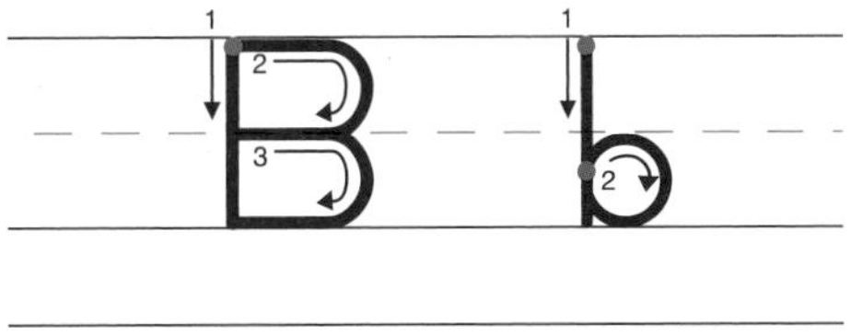

B Starting point, straight down
Starting point, around right and in at the middle, around right and in at the bottom: capital *B*

b Starting point, straight down, back up, around right all the way: small *b*

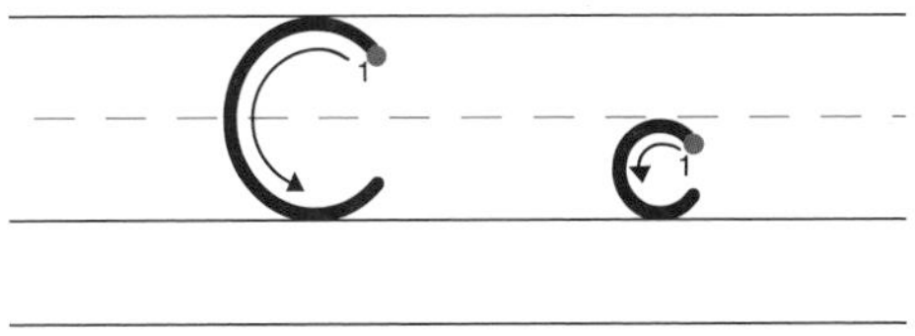

C Starting point, around left to stopping place: capital *C*

c Starting point, around left to stopping place: small *c*

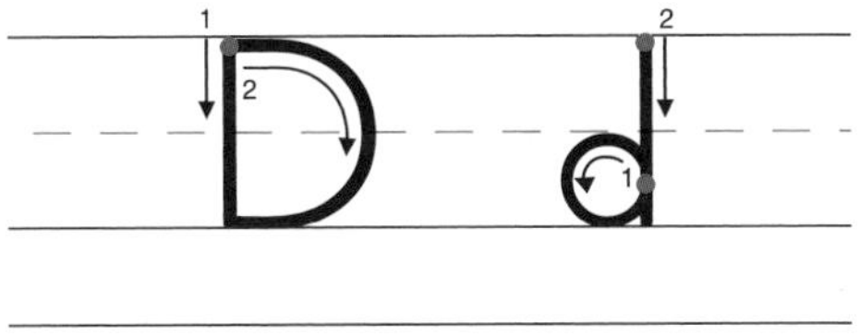

D Starting point, straight down
Starting point, around right and in at the bottom: capital *D*

d Starting point, around left all the way
Starting point, straight down, touching the circle: small *d*

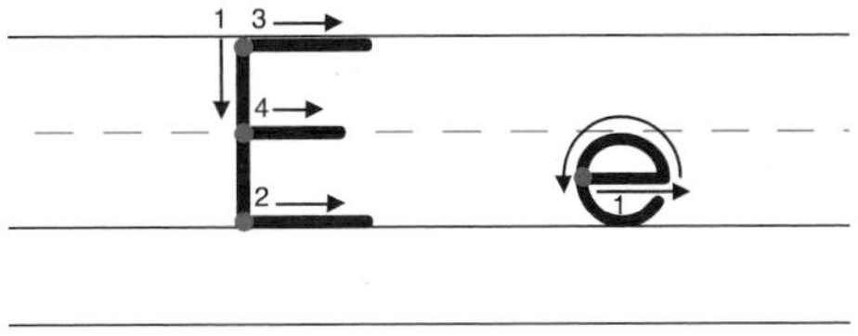

E Starting point, straight down
Starting point, straight out
Starting point, straight out
Starting point, straight out: capital *E*

e Starting point, straight out, up and around to the left, curving down and around to the right: small *e*

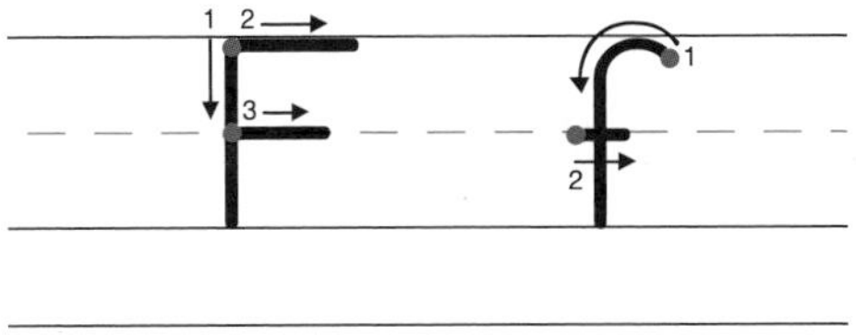

F Starting point, straight down
Starting point, straight out
Starting point, straight out: capital *F*

f Starting point, around left and straight down
Starting point, straight across: small *f*

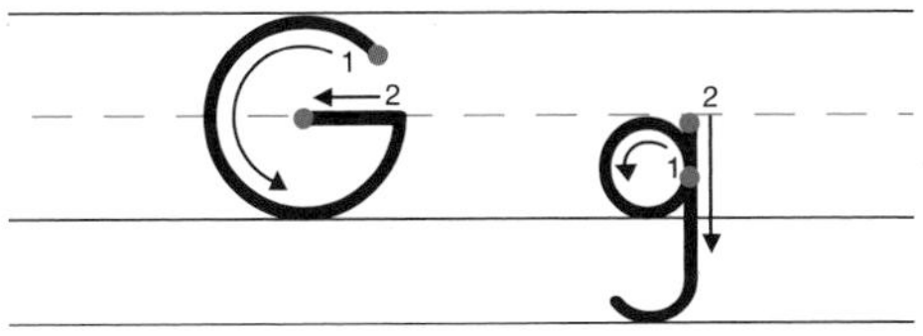

G Starting point, around left, curving up and around
Straight in: capital *G*

g Starting point, around left all the way
Starting point, straight down, touching the circle, around left to stopping place: small *g*

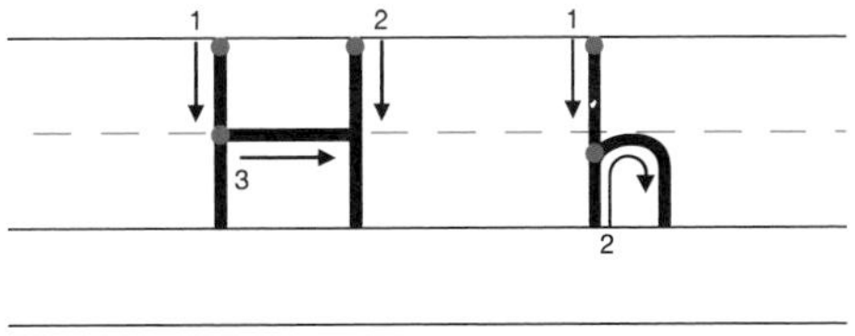

H Starting point, straight down
Starting point, straight down
Starting point, across the middle: capital *H*

h Starting point, straight down, back up, around right, and straight down: small *h*

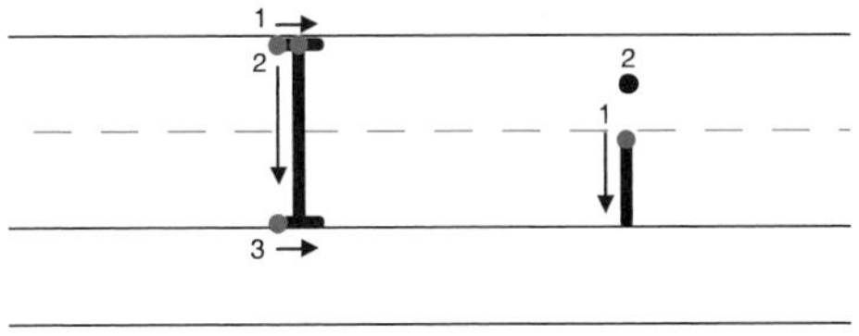

I Starting point, across
Starting point, straight down
Starting point, across: capital *I*

i Starting point, straight down
Dot exactly above: small *i*

Ball-and-Stick Handwriting Models

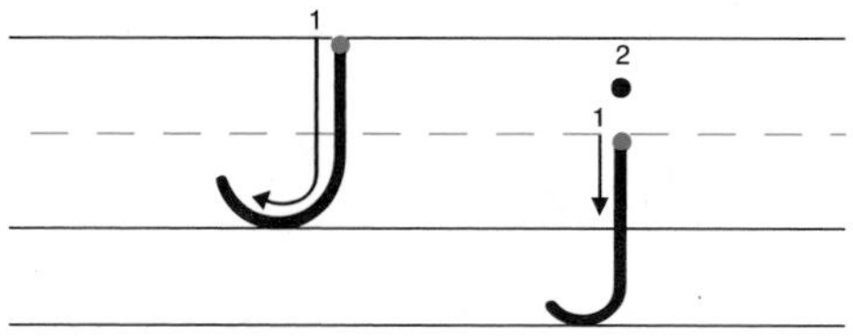

J Starting point, straight down, around left to stopping place: capital *J*

j Starting point, straight down, around left to stopping place Dot exactly above: small *j*

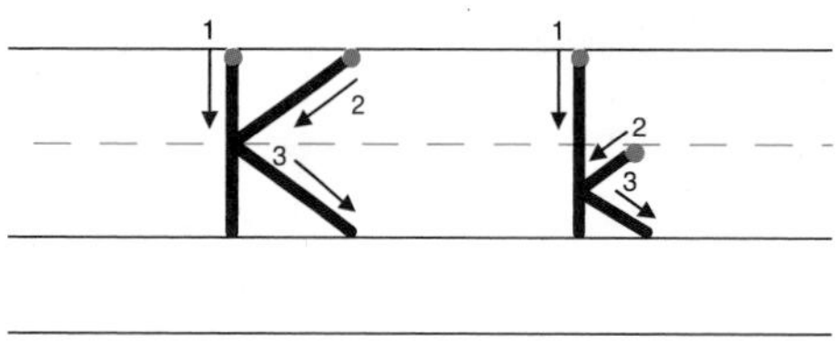

K Starting point, straight down Starting point, slanting down left, touching the line, slanting down right: capital *K*

k Starting point, straight down Starting point, slanting down left, touching the line, slanting down right: small *k*

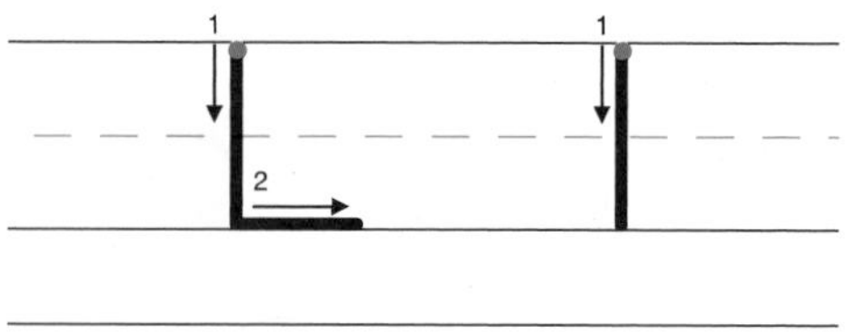

L Starting point, straight down, straight out: capital *L*

l Starting point, straight down: small *l*

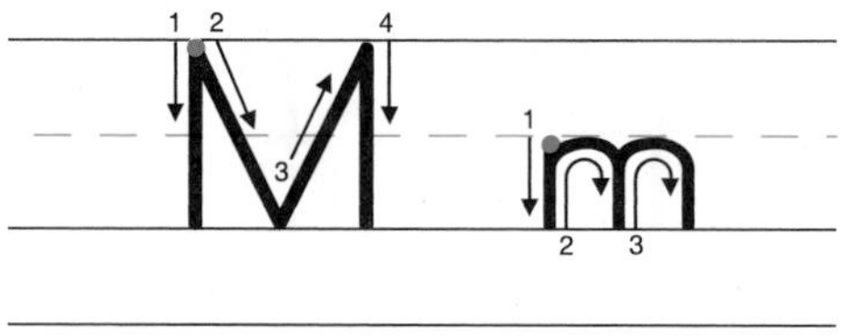

M Starting point, straight down Starting point, slanting down right to the point, slanting back up to the right, straight down: capital *M*

m Starting point, straight down, back up, around right, straight down, back up, around right, straight down: small *m*

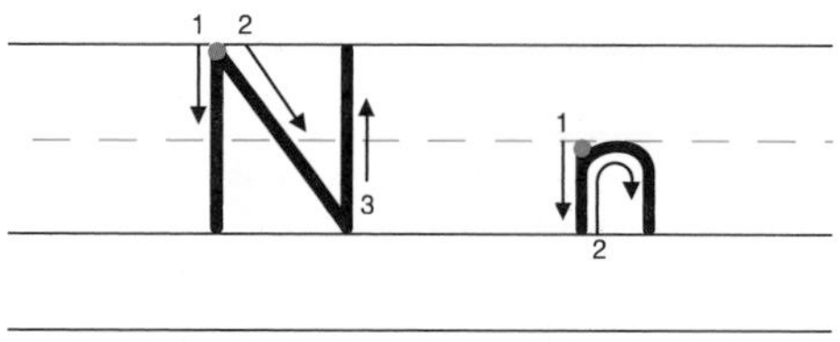

N Starting point, straight down Starting point, slanting down right, straight back up: capital *N*

n Starting point, straight down, back up, around right, straight down: small *n*

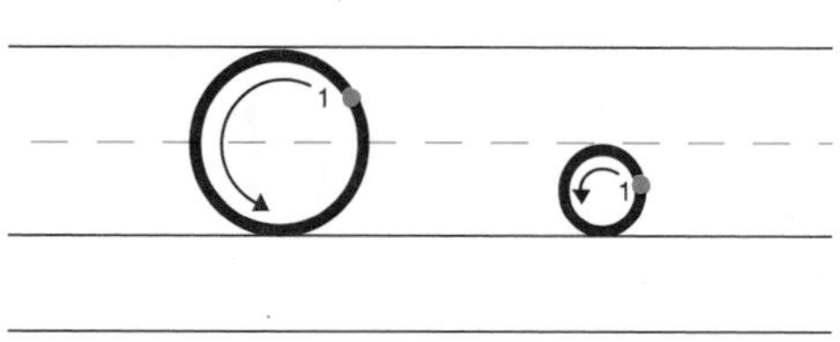

O Starting point, around left all the way: capital *O*

o Starting point, around left all the way: small *o*

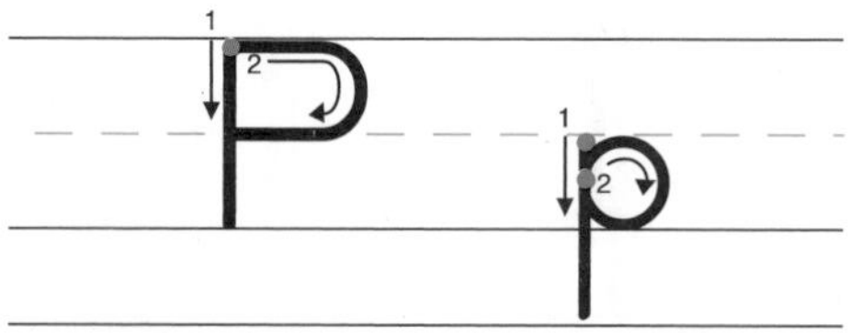

P Starting point, straight down Starting point, around right and in at the middle: capital *P*

p Starting point, straight down Starting point, around right all the way, touching the line: small *p*

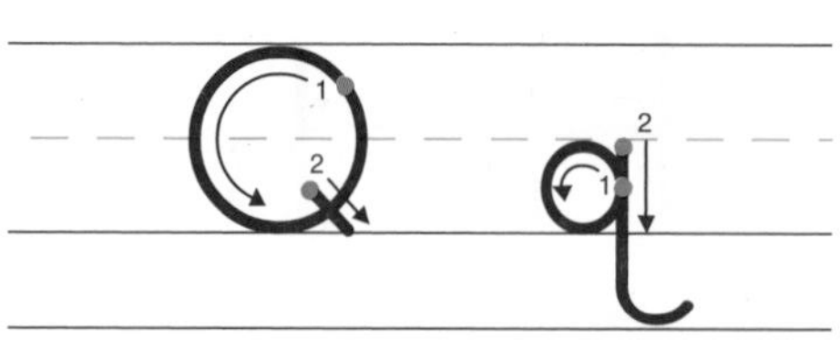

Q Starting point, around left all the way Starting point, slanting down right: capital *Q*

q Starting point, around left all the way Starting point, straight down, touching the circle, curving up right to stopping place: small *q*

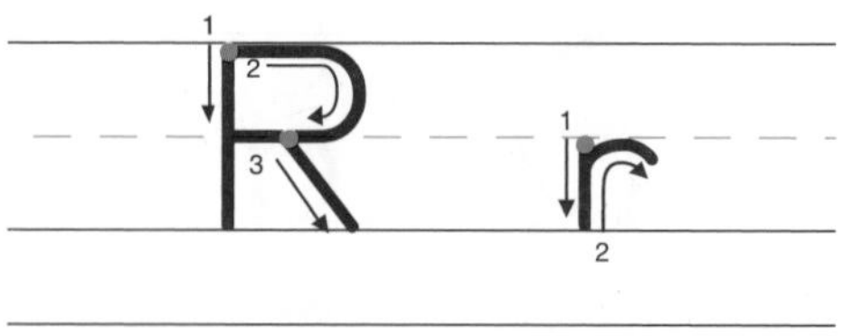

R Starting point, straight down Starting point, around right and in at the middle, touching the line, slanting down right: capital *R*

r Starting point, straight down, back up, curving around right to stopping place: small *r*

Ball-and-Stick Handwriting Models

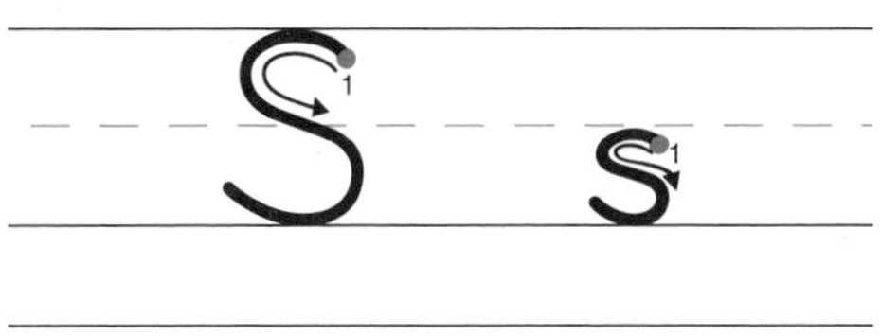

S Starting point, around left, curving right and down around right, curving left and up: capital *S*

s Starting point, around left, curving right and down around right, curving left and up to stopping place: small *s*

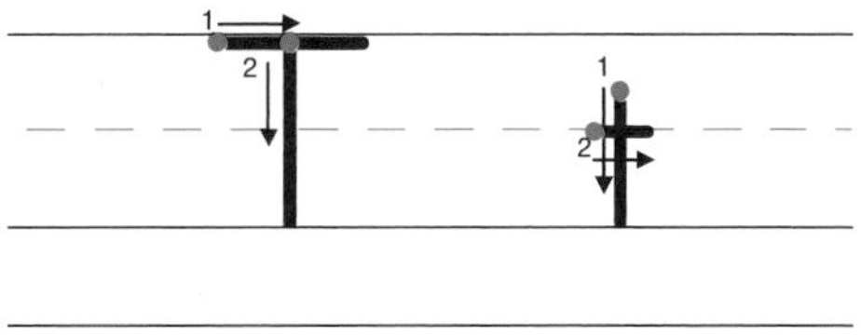

T Starting point, straight across
Starting point, straight down: capital *T*

t Starting point, straight down
Starting point, across short: small *t*

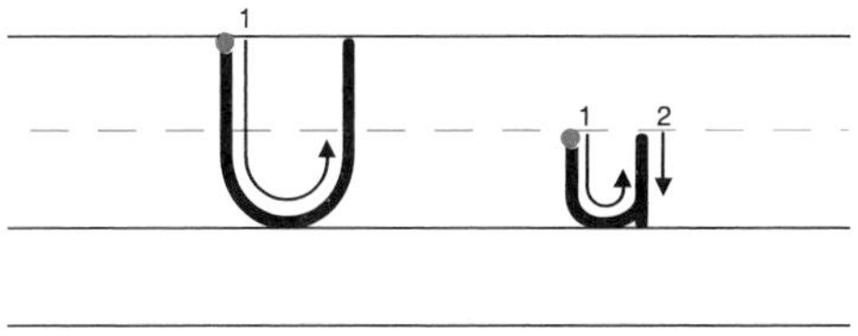

U Starting point, straight down, curving around right and up, straight up: capital *U*

u Starting point, straight down, curving around right and up, straight up, straight back down: small *u*

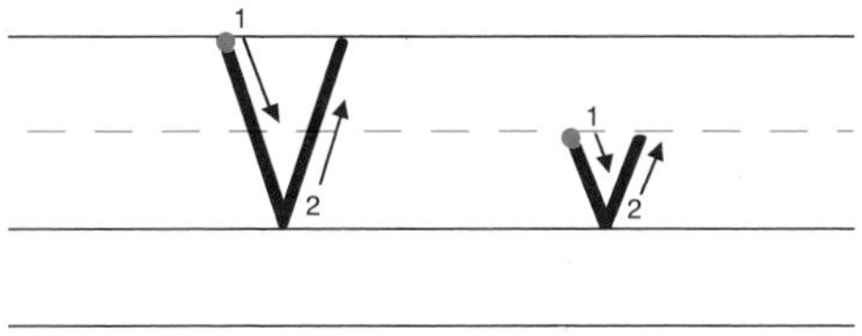

V Starting point, slanting down right, slanting up right: capital *V*

v Starting point, slanting down right, slanting up right: small *v*

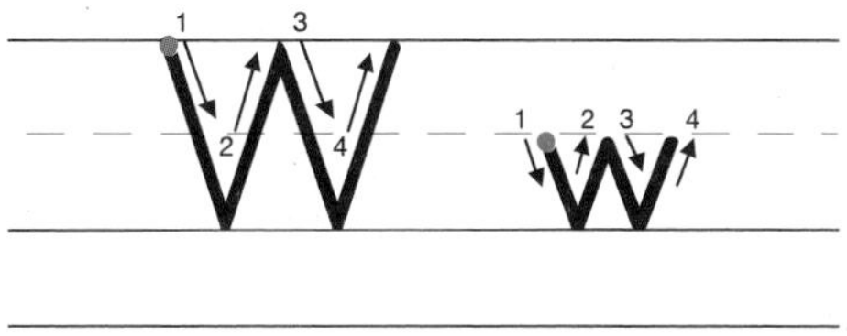

W Starting point, slanting down right, slanting up right, slanting down right, slanting up right: capital *W*

w Starting point, slanting down right, slanting up right, slanting down right, slanting up right: small *w*

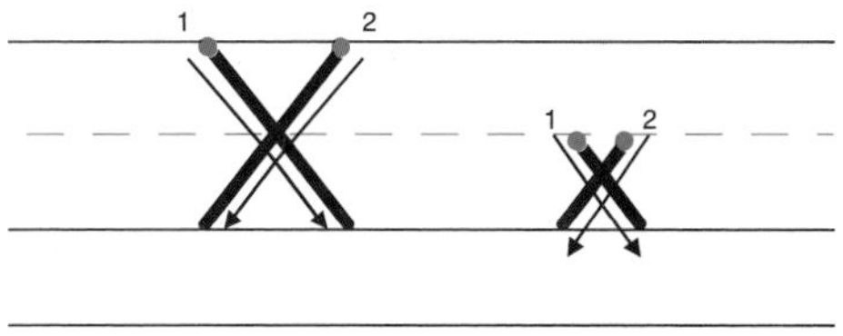

X Starting point, slanting down right
Starting point, slanting down left: capital *X*

x Starting point, slanting down right
Starting point, slanting down left: small *x*

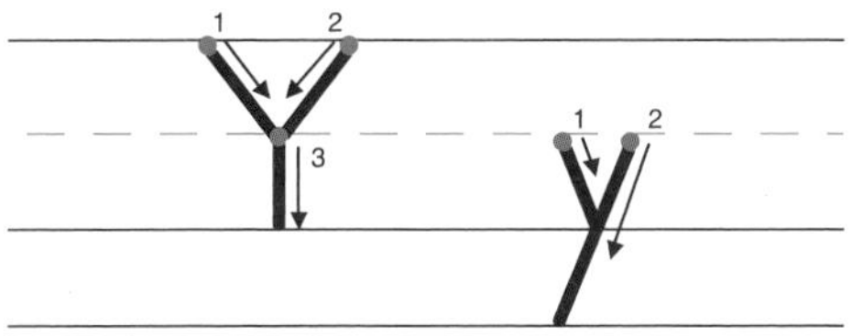

Y Starting point, slanting down right, stop
Starting point, slanting down left, stop
Starting point, straight down: capital *Y*

y Starting point, slanting down right
Starting point, slanting down left, connecting the lines: small *y*

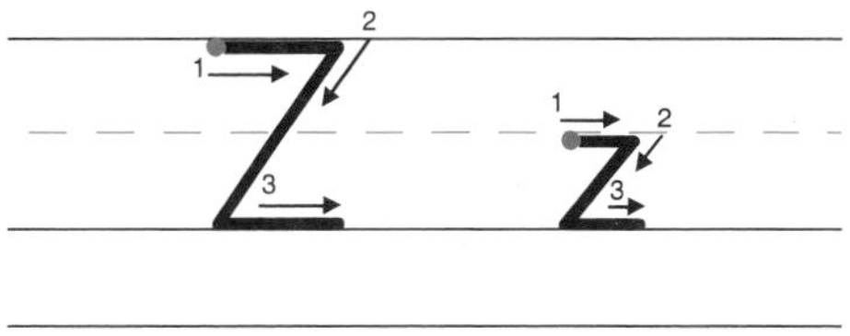

Z Starting point, straight across, slanting down left, straight across: capital *Z*

z Starting point, straight across, slanting down left, straight across: small *z*

Continuous Stroke Handwriting Models

Continuous stroke models of manuscript handwriting provide you with an alternative to the ball-and-stick method. The purpose of these models is geared toward teaching students to write letters without lifting their pencils.

Aa Bb Cc Dd Ee

Ff Gg Hh Ii Jj

Kk Ll Mm Nn Oo

Pp Qq Rr Ss Tt

Uu Vv Ww Xx

Yy Zz

Numbers and Punctuation Marks

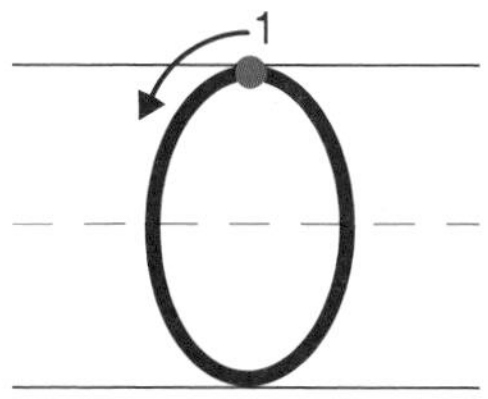

0 Starting point, curving left all the way around to starting point: *0*

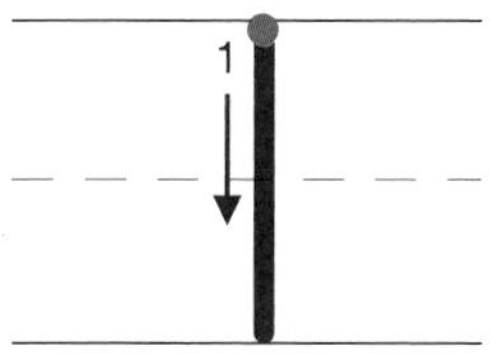

1 Starting point, straight down: *1*

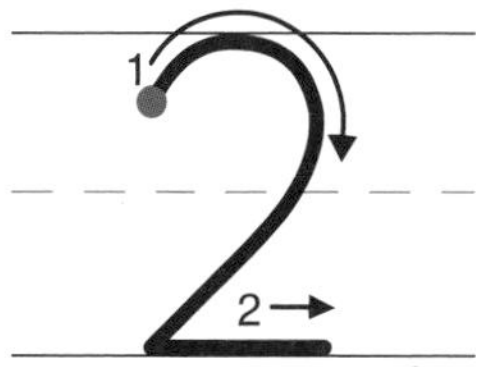

2 Starting point, around right, slanting left and straight across right: *2*

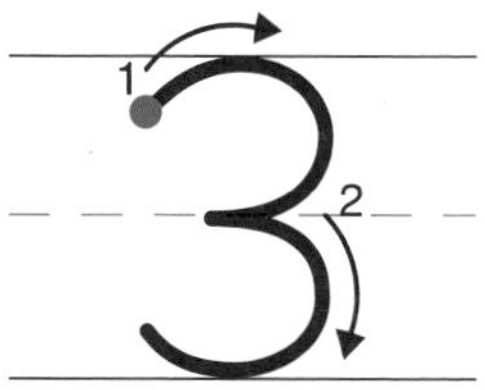

3 Starting point, around right, in at the middle, around right: *3*

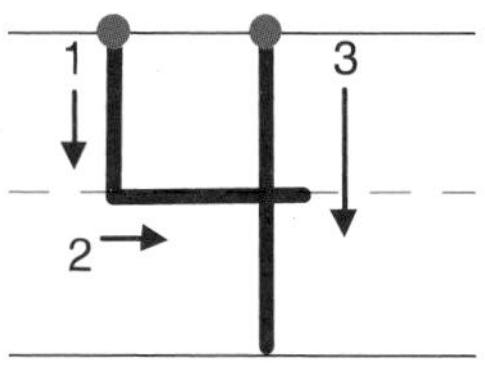

4 Starting point, straight down
Straight across right
Starting point, straight down, crossing line: *4*

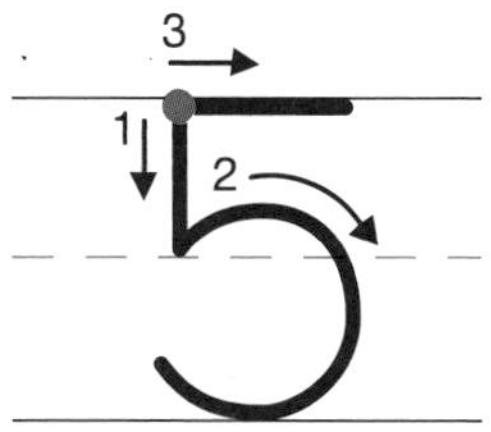

5 Starting point, straight down, curving around right and up
Starting point, straight across right: *5*

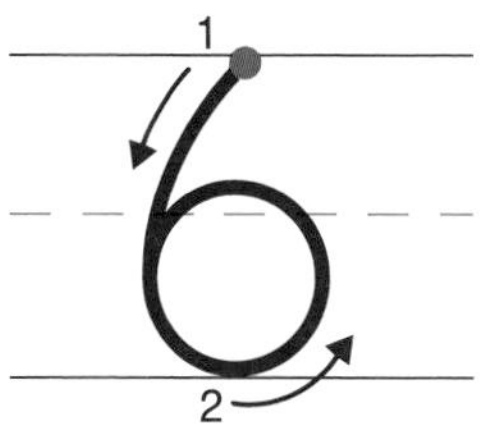

6 Starting point, slanting left, around the bottom curving up, around right and into the curve: 6

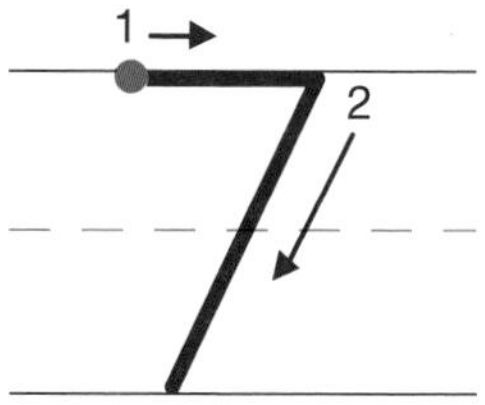

7 Starting point, straight across right, slanting down left: *7*

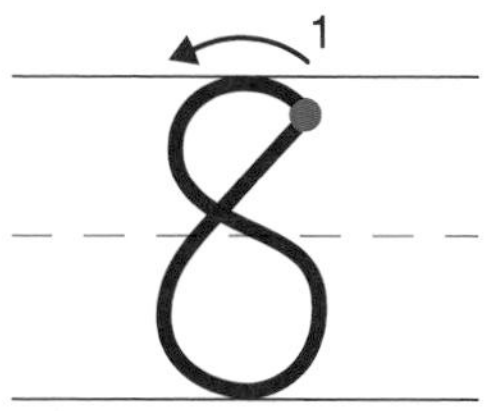

8 Starting point, curving left, curving down and around right, slanting up right to starting point: *8*

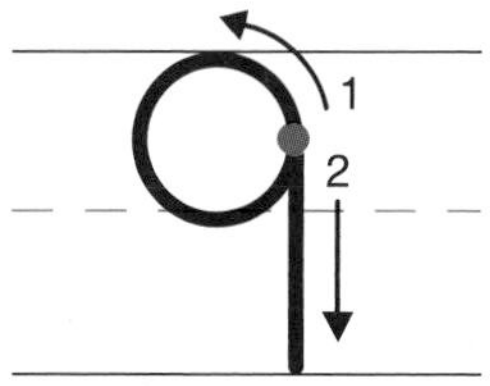

9 Starting point, curving around left all the way, straight down: *9*

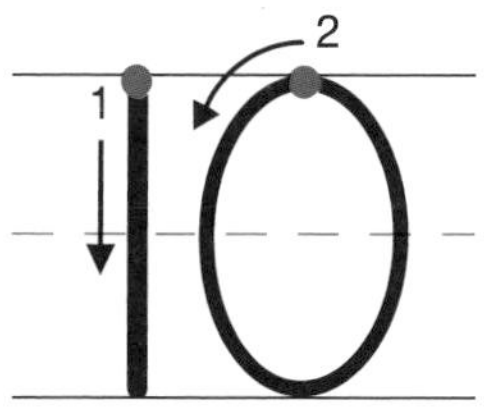

10 Starting point, straight down
Starting point, curving left all the way around to starting point: *10*

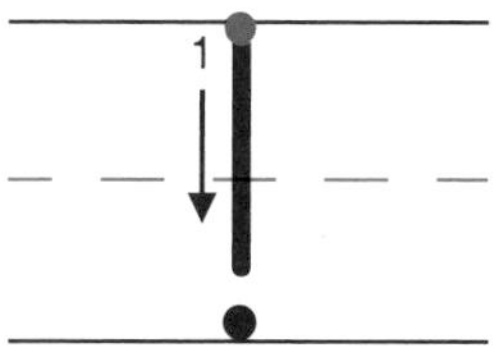

! Starting point, straight down
Dot exactly below: *!*

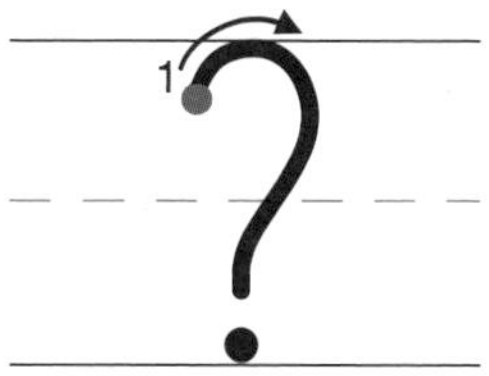

? Starting point, curving around right, straight down
Dot exactly below: *?*

A

B

D

E

F

G

H

I

Illustrators

K

L

M

N

O

P

T

U

V

W

Notes

Use this page to record lessons or elements that work well or need to be adjusted for future reference.

Lessons that work well.

Lessons that need adjustments.

Notes

Use this page to record lessons or elements that work well or need to be adjusted for future reference.

Lessons that work well.

Lessons that need adjustments.

Notes

Use this page to record lessons or elements that work well or need to be adjusted for future reference.

Lessons that work well.

Lessons that need adjustments.

Notes

Use this page to record lessons or elements that work well or need to be adjusted for future reference.

Lessons that work well.

Lessons that need adjustments.

Notes

Use this page to record lessons or elements that work well or need to be adjusted for future reference.

Lessons that work well.

Lessons that need adjustments.

Notes

Use this page to record lessons or elements that work well or need to be adjusted for future reference.

Lessons that work well.

Lessons that need adjustments.

Notes

Use this page to record lessons or elements that work well or need to be adjusted for future reference.

Lessons that work well.

Lessons that need adjustments.

Notes

Use this page to record lessons or elements that work well or need to be adjusted for future reference.

Lessons that work well.

Lessons that need adjustments.

Notes

Use this page to record lessons or elements that work well or need to be adjusted for future reference.

Lessons that work well.

Lessons that need adjustments.

Notes

Use this page to record lessons or elements that work well or need to be adjusted for future reference.

Lessons that work well.

Lessons that need adjustments.

Notes

Use this page to record lessons or elements that work well or need to be adjusted for future reference.

Lessons that work well.

Lessons that need adjustments.